COVENTRY
Medieval Art, Architecture and Archaeology in the City and its Vicinity

General Editor Sarah Brown

COVENTRY
Medieval Art, Architecture and Archaeology in the City and its Vicinity

Edited by
Linda Monckton and Richard K. Morris

The British Archaeological Association
Conference Transactions XXXIII

The publication of this volume has been assisted by a generous grant of £1,000 from the Nini Isabel Stewart Trust

Cover illustration: Bayley Lane, Coventry, with St Michael's church (left) and St Mary's Hall (centre)
Valentine's Series postcard, c. *1900*

ISBN Hardback 978 1 906540 63 0
Paperback 978 1 906540 62 3

Maney Publishing

PUBLISHED FOR THE BRITISH ARCHAEOLOGICAL ASSOCIATION BY MANEY PUBLISHING
JOSEPH'S WELL, HANOVER WALK, LEEDS LS3 1AB, UK
PRINTED AND BOUND BY CHARLESWORTH PRESS, WAKEFIELD, UK

Contents

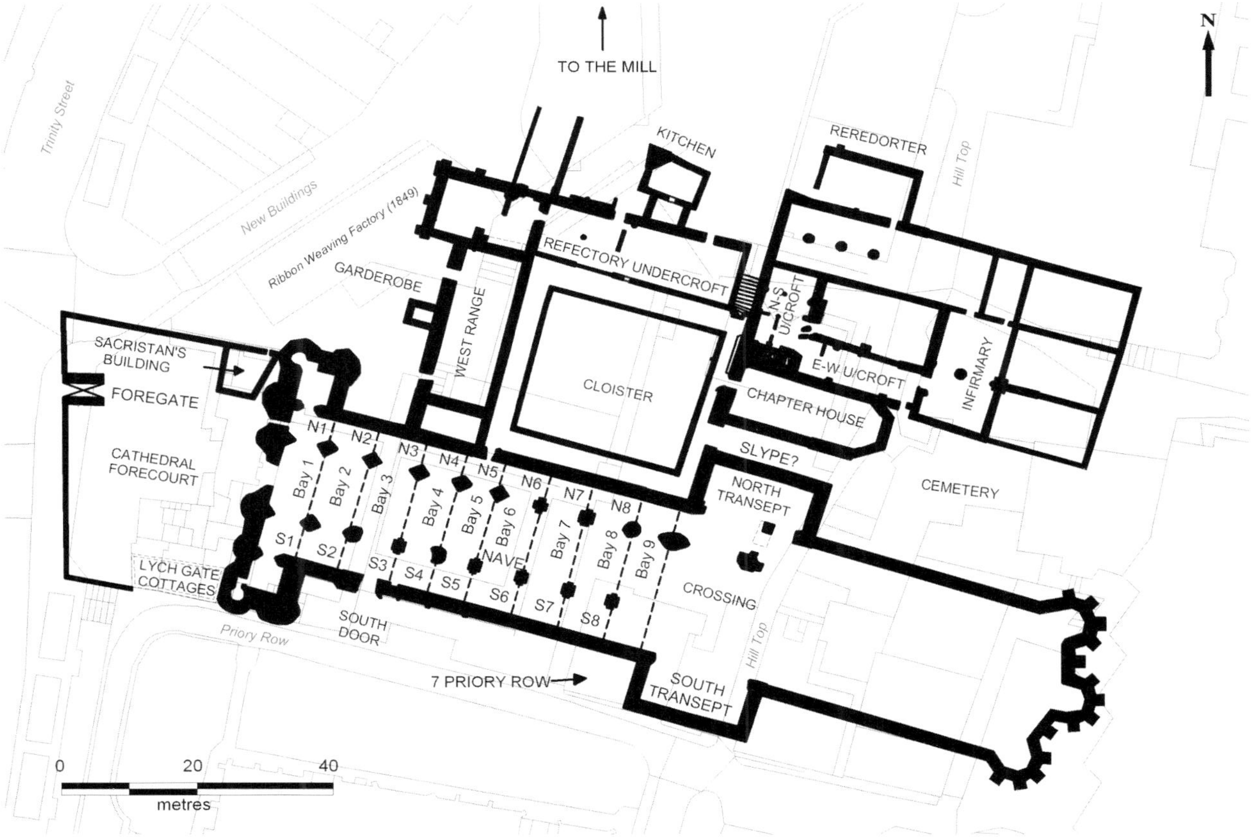

Plan A. Cathedral Priory of St Mary, Coventry, in the late middle ages; plan reconstructed from archaeological and documentary evidence, superimposed on the current street map. The nave piers are numbered from the west end; N1 = pier 1 of the north arcade, etc.

Drawing, George Demidowicz and Anna Wilson, Conservation and Archaeology, Coventry City Council

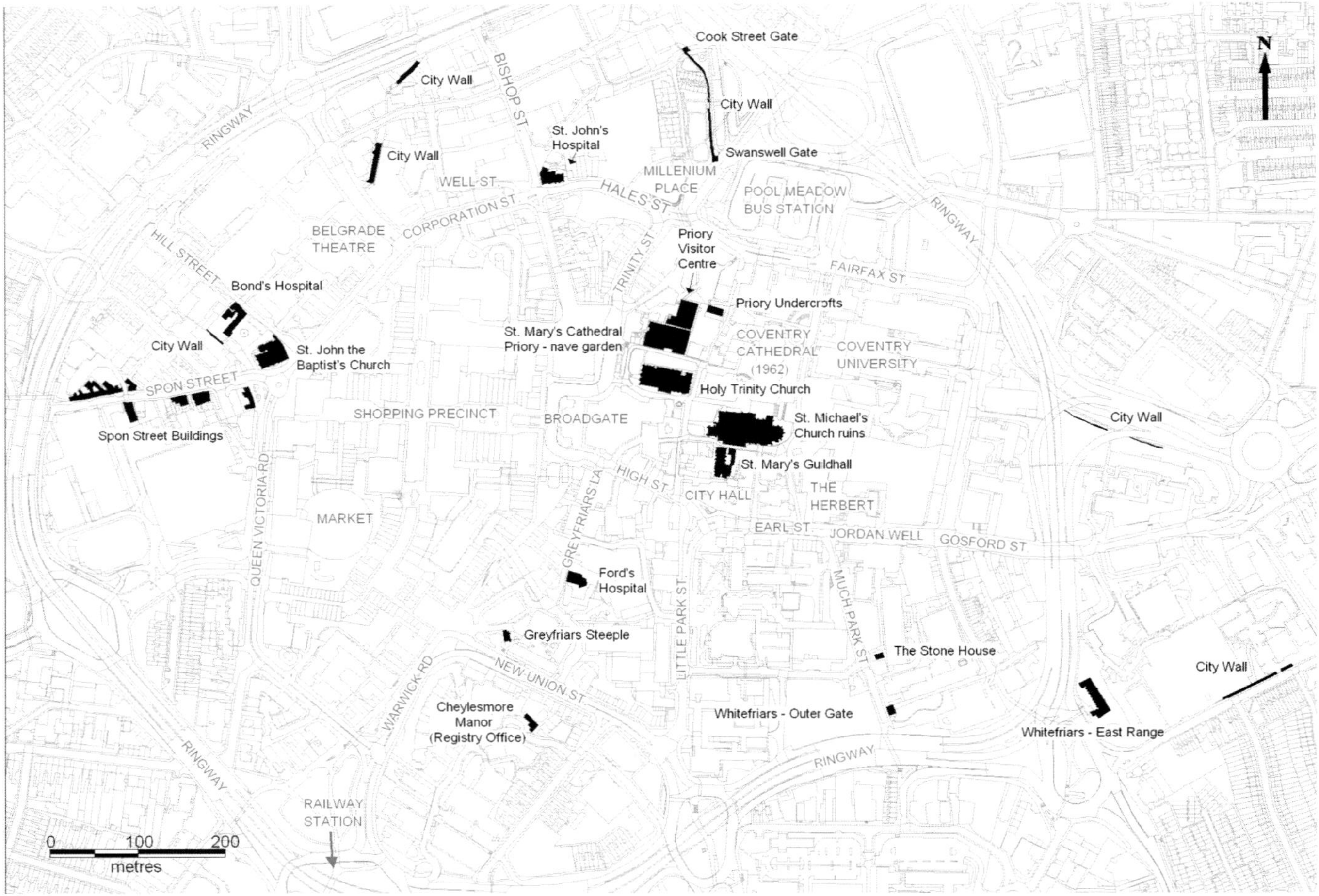

PLAN B. Main surviving sites and buildings of medieval Coventry, on the modern street plan

Drawing, George Demidowicz and Anna Wilson, Conservation and Archaeology, Coventry City Council

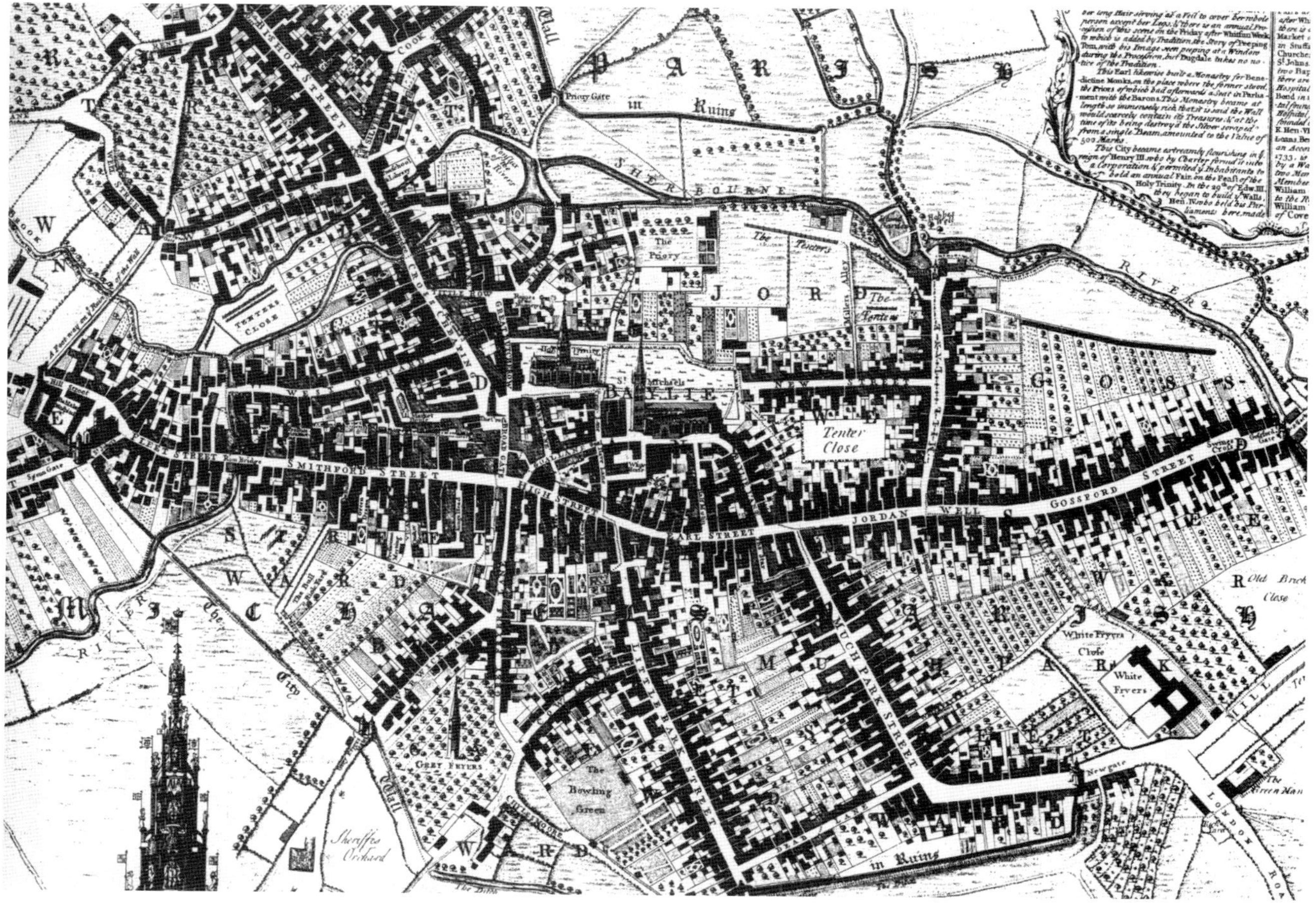

PLAN C. Samuel Bradford's map of Coventry, 1748–49, showing the survival of the medieval street pattern, published by Thomas Jeffreys, London, 1750

Courtesy of the Herbert Art Gallery and Museum

Preface

THE ASSOCIATION's annual conference in 2007 was held in Coventry between 21 and 25 July, attended by 109 members and guests, including three student scholars. The conference was accommodated at Priory Hall, Coventry University, in the heart of the medieval city. The conference programme mixed lectures, site visits and receptions to create a convivial atmosphere for scholarly exchange. Twenty-one papers were read at the University's Goldstein Lecture Theatre, of which eighteen are published here. In addition, following the conference George Demidowicz was invited to contribute a nineteenth paper on the development of St Mary's Guildhall, expanding his presentation at the site visit.

On Saturday evening, the delegates visited the Herbert Art Gallery and Museum for a reception, where they were welcomed by Roger Vaughan, Arts and Heritage Officer for Coventry City Council. On Sunday afternoon, the conference visited the ruins of St Michael's church, guided by Linda Monckton, Holy Trinity church, where John Burbidge gave an address on the Doom painting, and the Priory site, where the guides were George Demidowicz, Iain Soden, Richard Plant and Richard K. Morris. Some delegates also had the opportunity to see the medieval glass in the Chapel of Industry, Coventry Cathedral, with Heather Gilderdale Scott. The evening was spent at the site of Combe Abbey, with a presentation by Warwick Rodwell, followed by dinner at the Coombe Abbey Hotel.

Monday afternoon was occupied by a busy walkabout in the city centre, taking in the Whitefriars, the remains of Cheylesmore Manor, the Greyfriars steeple, St John the Baptist's church and the Bablake college buildings, the former St John's Hospital (the 'Old Grammar School') and the Cook Street and Swanswell Gates. Our guides at the Whitefriars were Charmian and Paul Woodfield and George Demidowicz, whilst Chris Kirby and Paul Thompson allowed us privileged access into the archaeological stores there. Iain Soden talked briefly at Cheylesmore Manor and the Greyfriars, and at St John the Baptist's the conference was welcomed by the rector, the Revd Paul Such. Charles Tracy gave a talk at St John's Hospital on the choir stalls moved there from the Whitefriars after the Dissolution, and Jeremy Ashbee was our guide for the two city gates. In the evening, delegates were honoured with a reception and dinner at St Mary's Guildhall, where they were welcomed by the Lord Mayor of Coventry, Councillor Dave Batten, and where their guide to the building was George Demidowicz.

On Tuesday afternoon, the conference moved away from the city centre to visit the Charterhouse, where our guides were Julian Luxford, Mellie Naydenova-Slade, Iain Soden and Richard K. Morris, and then to Kenilworth for the Abbey site, St Nicholas' church and the Castle. Our guides at the Abbey 'barn' and gatehouse were members of the Kenilworth History and Archaeology Society, including Irene Potter, Harry Sunley, Norman Stevens, Geoff Hilton and Brian Jackson; Jenny Alexander also talked about the barn, and Duncan Givans about the west door of St Nicholas' church. Brian Dix addressed the conference about the archaeology of the Elizabethan garden on the evening visit to Kenilworth Castle, and tours of the castle were guided by David Robinson, John Goodall and Richard K. Morris; afterwards the Association was honoured by an English Heritage reception, addressed by Loraine Knowles (Head of Visitor Operations West, English Heritage), followed by a buffet supper in the Stable. The conference concluded on Wednesday morning with a visit to the former collegiate church of St Mary at Astley, north of the city, where Charles Tracy gave an address on the canons' stalls, and closing speeches and presentations were made. The President, Nicola Coldstream, was in attendance throughout, introducing proceedings and offering eloquent thanks to our various hosts, as well as herself hosting the reception and dinner at the Coombe Abbey Hotel.

The Association would like to record its gratitude to all those who helped open doors and assisted in the smooth running of the conference. In particular, it is immensely indebted to George Demidowicz (Head of Conservation and Archaeology, Coventry City Council) for his enthusiastic support and assistance for the convenors in the preparation, running and publication of the conference. Also, in addition to those already mentioned, the Association would like to thank the following: Dr John Gledhill and Natasha Gittins at Coventry University; Anna Wilson and Mark Singlehurst of Coventry City Council; Michael Hinman at Coventry Archives; Mark Twissell and George Wilkinson at St Mary's Guildhall; Jo Hibbard at Coventry Cathedral; Lynn Jones at Holy Trinity church and the volunteers who provided Sunday tea; the volunteers who provided Monday tea at St John the Baptist's church; Bethany Ryan at the Coombe Abbey Hotel; Irene Cooke and Jim Edwards of City College, Coventry, at the Charterhouse; Jennifer Higgins and volunteers at St Nicholas' church, Kenilworth, for Tuesday tea; Simon Thurley (Chief Executive of English Heritage) and Steve Bax at Kenilworth Castle, and Emery's Catering for the evening buffet; and Jeanette Sutton at St Mary's church, Astley, and the volunteers for Wednesday morning coffee. I am also grateful to my fellow convenor, Linda Monckton, to Karen Lundgren (Conference Organiser) and Kate Heard (Conference Secretary) for their parts in making the conference such a successful and enjoyable event.

Richard K. Morris
Joint-Convenor

List of Abbrevations

Antiq. J.	*Antiquaries Journal*
Archaeol. J.	*Archaeological Journal*
BAA Trans.	*British Archaeological Association Conference Transactions*
Bassett, *Anglo-Saxon Coventry*	S. Bassett, *Anglo-Saxon Coventry and its Churches*, Dugdale Society (2001)
B/E	N. Pevsner *et al.*, *The Buildings of England* (Harmondsworth various dates). From 2002, New Haven and London, various dates, and the series retitled *Pevsner Architectural Guides*
B/E *Warwickshire*	N. Pevsner and A. Wedgwood, *Warwickshire* B/E (1966; reprinted 1974, 1981, 1986, 1990, 1996]
CA	Coventry Archives, including the History Centre
Cal. Papal Reg.	*Calendar of Entries in the Papal Registers relating to Great Britain and Ireland: Papal Letters*, various volumes
CBA *WM Archaeology*	Council for British Archaeology, *West Midlands Archaeology*
Chatwin, 'Cathedral Glass'	P. B. Chatwin, 'Medieval stained glass from the Cathedral, Coventry', *TBAS*, 66 (1950), 1–5
Chatwin, 'Early Coventry'	P. B. Chatwin, 'Early Coventry', *TBAS*, 53 (1928), 132–44
Coss, *Early Records*	P. R. Coss (ed.), *The Early Records of Medieval Coventry* (London 1986)
Demidowicz ed. *First Cathedral*	G. Demidowicz (ed.), *Coventry's First Cathedral: the Cathedral and Priory of St Mary* (Stamford 1994)
Dugdale, *Warwickshire* (1656)	Sir W. Dugdale, *The Antiquities of Warwickshire* (1656)
Dugdale, *Warwickshire* (1730)	Sir W. Dugdale, *The Antiquities of Warwickshire* (rev. edn, London 1730)
EETS	Early English Text Society
Gill and Morris, 'Apocalypse'	M. Gill and R. K. Morris, 'A wall painting of the Apocalypse in Coventry rediscovered', *Burlington Magazine* (August 2001), 467–73.
Goddard, *Coventry 1043–1355*	R. Goddard, *Lordship and Medieval Urbanisation: Coventry, 1043–1355* (Woodbridge 2004)
Harris ed., *Dr Troughton's Sketches*	*A Selection from the Pencil Drawings of Dr Nathaniel Troughton, with descriptive notes by Mary Dormer Harris* (Coventry and London, n.d., *c.* 1910)
Harris ed., *Guild Register*	*Register of the Guild of the Holy Trinity, St Mary, St John the Baptist and St Katherine of Coventry*, ed. M. D. Harris, Dugdale Society Publications (Oxford 1939)

Hobley, 'Cathedral Excavations'	B. Hobley *et al.*, 'Excavations at the Cathedral and Benedictine Priory of St. Mary, Coventry', *TBWAS*, 84 (1971), 45–139
JBAA	*Journal of the British Archaeological Association*
Lancaster, *St Mary's Hall*	J. Lancaster, *St Mary's Hall, Coventry: a Guide to the Building* (Coventry 1981)
Lancaster, 'Thornton'	J. Lancaster, 'John Thornton of Coventry, glazier', *TBAS*, 74 (1956), 56–9
Leet Book	M. Dormer Harris (ed.), *The Coventry Leet Book 1420–1555*, EETS, o.s., 134, 135 (London 1907–1913)
Lobel, *Historic Towns*	M. D. Lobel (ed.), *The Atlas of Historic Towns II: Coventry* (London 1975)
Morris, 'Cathedral Church'	R. K. Morris, 'The lost Cathedral Priory Church of St. Mary, Coventry', in Demidowicz ed. *First Cathedral*, 16–66
Morris, 'St Mary's Hall'	R. K. Morris, 'St Mary's Hall and the medieval architecture of Coventry', *Ancient Monuments Society Transactions* 32 (1988), 8–27
Poole, *Antiquities*	B. Poole, *Coventry: its History and Antiquities* (Coventry 1870)
PRO	Public Record Office
RCHME	Royal Commission on the Historical Monuments of England
Rylatt and Mason, *Cathedral Priory*	M. Rylatt and P. Mason, *The Archaeology of the Medieval Cathedral and Priory of St Mary, Coventry* (Coventry 2003)
Sharp, *Papers*	T. Sharp, *Illustrative Papers on the History and Antiquities of the City of Coventry*, ed. W. G. Fretton (Coventry 1871)
Soden, *Charterhouse*	I. Soden *et al.*, *Excavations at St Anne's Charterhouse, Coventry, 1968–87* (Coventry 1995)
Soden, *Hidden History*	I. Soden, *Coventry: the Hidden History* (Stroud 2005)
TBAS	*Transactions of the Birmingham Archaeological Society*
TBWAS	*Transactions of the Birmingham and Warwickshire Archaeological Society*
Templeman ed., *Guild Records*	*Records of the Guild of the Holy Trinity, St Mary, St John the Baptist and St Katherine of Coventry*, ed. G. Templeman, Dugdale Society Publications (Oxford 1944)
Troughton	CA, Dr N. Troughton's Collection of Drawings, *c*. 1850–68, 10 vols; e.g. Troughton III/6 = Troughton vol. 3, drawing no. 6
VCH *Warwickshire*	Victoria County History, *Warwickshire*
WCRO	Warwickshire County Record Office

Woodfield, *Whitefriars*	C. Woodfield *et al.*, *The Church of Our Lady of Mount Carmel and some conventual buildings at the Whitefriars, Coventry*, BAR British Series 389 (Oxford 2005).
Woodhouse, *Coventry Churches*	F. Woodhouse, *The Churches of Coventry*, Bell's Guides (London 1909)

Editors' Introduction

COVENTRY is rarely perceived by the public as a great medieval city. For many, the iconic period of Coventry's history begins in 1940, when incendiary devices were dropped on the city during a series of night-time raids. The recording of the aftermath and the subsequent construction of Britain's first pedestrian precinct, a monument to Modernist optimism and associated concepts of urban life, are now well known. Even better known, however, is the building that made Sir Basil Spence a household name, the new cathedral church of St Michael. However catastrophic the impact of World War II was on Coventry, historians will be aware of the complexities of the city's history. For example, the fundamental decision to transform the centre of the city had been taken in the 1930s, when surviving medieval streets around the former market area were demolished in the redevelopment based on the new Trinity Street. Early photographs show a city that retained its medieval street plan intact and a significant number of medieval buildings. The reconstruction of the city in 1950s and 1960s sealed the fate of the majority of the domestic buildings that survived and divorced many of the remaining institutional buildings from their historical context. It is perhaps largely for this reason that 'medieval' Coventry is not seen as an entity that can be easily understood by the passer-by.

Coventry was England's fourth wealthiest city in the later middle ages, hosting a number of parliaments in the 15th century and acting as an economic centre for the midlands, trading with towns in the east such as Boston and in the west such as Bristol. The rehabilitation of Coventry's medieval past has been addressed, in part, by a series of important excavations since the 1970s. Iain Soden's paper places them in the context of the evolution of archaeological enquiry in the city, and explains their significance for our understanding of Coventry's history and topography. Chris Patrick's paper continues the story since 2004, charting a series of major developer-funded archaeological investigations in the historic city centre, as well as highlighting the potential both of new work and of the synthesis and dissemination of past investigations.

The history of Coventry is inextricably linked with the area of land aptly termed 'Hill Top'. Here stand the city's most significant surviving church buildings, and here stood its most important lost building, the Cathedral Priory of St Mary. The first real attempt to give this building the serious consideration it deserves was in *Coventry's First Cathedral* (1994), edited by George Demidowicz. Subsequently, the Phoenix Initiative project (1999–2003) has transformed our understanding of the church and its precinct. The architectural fabric and fragments discovered during the excavations (some of which are displayed in the new Priory Visitor Centre) are evaluated in the papers by Richard Plant and Richard K. Morris — both proposing new assessments of some of the buildings from the 12th to the 15th centuries. St Mary's was the only cathedral church completely demolished at the Reformation, together with its monastic complex. The development of the site from the Dissolution to the present day is described in a paper by George Demidowicz, using a wide range of documentary and cartographic sources to redefine the geographical extent of the pre-Dissolution precinct, and to show how socially distinct areas of housing emerged in the upper and lower areas; the latter characterised by industrial use continued from the medieval water mill and dye house.

For a long time the cathedral priory was considered the earliest church institution in the city, a theory enhanced by the reputation of its founders, Leofric and Godiva. However, Steve Bassett has convincingly argued in print elsewhere that the 1043 foundation of St Mary's Priory does not represent the first ecclesiastical building in Coventry, but rather the moment when the existing Anglo-Saxon minster underwent Benedictine reform. The requirement of the Benedictines to be physically separate from the parochial part of the church was catered for by the use of the existing minster church and chapels; these took on parochial functions but may not have had full parochial status at this stage. It seems that four chapels existed on the hill-top site by 1043: Holy Trinity, St Michael's, St Mary's and Holy Cross.[1] The cruciform plan of Holy Trinity and its prominent location on the highest point of the hill lends weight to the suggestion that this was the original minster church, surrounded by a number of smaller buildings acting as dependent chapels.[2]

By the mid-11th century, it is likely that Holy Trinity served the inhabitants of land owned by the newly founded and endowed Benedictine priory, and the chapel of St Michael served the same function for those living on land owned by the priory's founders, Leofric and Godiva. This division of lordship, created on the foundation of the priory and resulting in a 'prior's half' and an 'earl's half', influenced the nature of commercial and physical development within the medieval city and led to a series of lesser and greater disputes between the two lordships. The issue of division or unity within the town was the subject of much debate amongst historians in the 1970s and 1980s,[3] and Richard Goddard, following their lead, has shown that the prior's half was exhibiting significant urban characteristics by the late 11th century, part of a conscious development of a centre for trade by the new priory.[4] Despite a history of episcopal conflict in the 12th century, the priory continued to show an astute approach to land acquisition and commercialisation, and the prior's half developed characteristics not yet shared by the earl's half. The character of the earl's half and the prior's half, therefore, differed substantially in the late 11th and early 12th centuries.

Most of the buildings that survive in Coventry date, however, from the 14th and 15th centuries, reflecting the building boom that occurred in these years, not just in and around Hill Top, but impacting on every religious institution in the city (a status granted to Coventry in 1345). The link between commercial vitality and this explosion of activity, the result not just of the political shifts of the mid-century but also of the presence of disposal income and pious acts of the merchant class, is set out in Richard Goddard's paper in this volume. The reflection of the wealth and economic vibrancy of the late 14th century is seen nowhere more clearly than through the rise to power of the mercantile elite. During what might be considered Coventry's 'golden age' in the second half of the 14th century, St Michael's parish church became the main focus for the pious acts of the merchants and guilds, and underwent a series of architectural transformations, resulting in complete reconstruction. Linda Monckton's paper reassesses the history of this spectacular building, which is generally less than appreciated in modern literature on the architectural history of the late middle ages, largely on account of the destruction of its interior during the 1940s.

The foundation of the various Coventry guilds and their later amalgamation was given formal expression with the construction of St Mary's Guildhall. It occupied a site of symbolic importance which had once been inside the castle bailey and stood directly opposite the south porch of St Michael's. The story of how the land for the hall was acquired is recounted in detail for the first time in George Demidowicz's second paper in this volume, together with a new interpretation of the development of the Guildhall buildings. A material survival from the city's medieval guilds is the 15th-century seal matrix of the fraternity of the Shearmen and Fullers of the Guild of the Nativity of our Lord in Coventry, and is the subject of John Cherry's paper. He considers the issue of where it was made, setting out the potential relationships between Coventry and London craftsmen with regard to the high quality of the metalwork circulating in Coventry in the 15th century.

The recent discovery of painted architectural fragments from the lost chapter-house of the priory, previously published by Gill and Morris,[5] directed the attention of art historians to the city with renewed interest. The fragments, from a painted Apocalypse cycle, warranted more than favourable comparison with the only known surviving scheme of similar type, that in the chapter-house of Westminster Abbey. The discovery provided striking evidence that patrons in Coventry were seeking out superior artists and craftsmen in the 14th century. That patrons in Coventry and its hinterland commissioned works of high quality is exemplified in the papers by Richard Marks and Miriam Gill: the former dealing with the authorship of the Decorated stained glass at Stanford on Avon (Northants.), and the latter focusing on the recently conserved painting of the Doom in Holy Trinity church. Heather Gilderdale Scott's paper on the famous master glazier, John Thornton of Coventry, takes the story into the 15th century. She shows that his success was based not only on his outstanding talent as a glass painter, but moreso on his ability as a business man, managing a large, complex workshop. He was an archetypal example of the successful entrepreneurial class in later medieval Coventry. Andrew Rudebeck also presented a paper at the conference on the attribution to Thornton of some of the window glass in St Mary's Guildhall, which has since been published elsewhere.[6]

Perhaps the greatest expression of the need for a collective and city-based identity was through the decision to build the city wall in stone (called locally the 'town wall'), a project begun in 1355 or 1356, when the mayor, Richard of Stoke, laid the foundation stone of the New Gate, at the southern end of Much Park Street.[7] The town wall, and its associated gates, was an essential element in the display of the city's corporate identity, not primarily a measure for civic defence. Before 1355, a grand statement of this kind would have been difficult to achieve, with a fluid power balance between the various individuals and institutions, and at least in the southern part of the city, considerable expansion of the built-up area which a new wall should enclose and protect.[8] It was probably no coincidence that the famous 'Tripartite Indenture' was sealed in 1355 by the prior, the mayor and the dowager queen Isabella, which laid the ground for a period of ascendancy for the city authorities and made possible the creation of the wall. A licence to crenellate was issued in 1363, but the campaign was protracted. Its subsequent history shows that internal conflicts had gone underground rather than gone away completely: the wall was built in fits and starts, opposed in some quarters and given lukewarm financial support in others.

Important new religious institutions — the Whitefriars and the Charterhouse — were founded around the same time as the inception of the town wall. The east range at the Whitefriars is a highly significant survival, retained through its conversion into a private house after the Dissolution. The church site was excavated in the 1960s in advance of constructing the inner ring road, which sweeps unsympathetically past the standing fabric and over the foundations of the nave. The important publication of the excavations, edited by Charmian Woodfield, appeared shortly before the conference.[9] The friary, constructed just within the city boundary, was founded by John Pulteney, a merchant and sometime mayor of London in the 1340s, adding weight to the arguments about strong links between the capital and Coventry at this date. By contrast, the Carthusian priory of St Anne, founded outside the city walls in the 1380s, was in essence a royal foundation. The history of its construction and institutional life is explored in Julian Luxford's paper. Inside the surviving western range are the remains of a monumental crucifixion scene, painted on what was the southern wall of the monastic refectory. The history and iconography of this remarkable painting are the subject of the paper by Mellie Naydenova-Slade.

The remaining papers deal with significant and previously understudied buildings beyond the city. Warwick Rodwell's paper on Combe Abbey describes the history and development of this important Cistercian monastery, founded with a large estate outside Coventry in 1150, and its conversion to a grand country house after the Dissolution. In contrast, John Goodall's paper on Guy's Cliffe, the hermitage of the Beauchamps outside Warwick, focuses on a small building, the result of a local family's devotional practice and association with pious myth. Another modest construction, the so-called 'Barn' in the outer court of the former Kenilworth Abbey, is examined in the paper by Jenny Alexander and Harry Sunley. Though originally a high-status building, their close scrutiny of the fabric revealed that at some stage it served as a tracing house and workshop for stonemasons. At the conference, another paper was read by Charles Tracy on the 14th-century canons' stalls at the former collegiate church at Astley, north of Coventry, and which he has since published elsewhere.[10]

A recurring theme in some of the architectural papers on later medieval Coventry is the acknowledgement of the significance of buildings in the vicinity resulting from the patronage of the earls of Warwick and the earls and dukes of Lancaster. These works, at Warwick and Kenilworth, are key monuments in the development of Perpendicular architecture in the region. Common perceptions on the nature of Perpendicular tend to apply the principles of its architectural form, such as unity, to the study of the period as a whole, lending it the qualities of an unchanging style with a 'national' character. However, it cannot be understood fully without an appreciation of the regional variations and 'hotspots' that influenced its formation and later character. John Goodall's second paper, on the College of St Mary in the Newarke at Leicester (founded by Henry of Lancaster), addresses this issue, revealing the potential of this lost building in the development of Perpendicular in the region, along with Kenilworth Castle and St Mary's, Warwick. Kenilworth Castle in the 14th century is the subject of Richard K. Morris' second paper, which considers the works of John of Gaunt's predecessors at the castle and lays out the evidence for reconsidering whether some features of Gaunt's new palace there should be attributed to them instead. This final paper is in the spirit of the volume as a whole, in which little known sites and objects are brought to prominence, and traditional interpretations reassessed, from the art and architecture of one of England's great medieval cities. How unfortunate it is that, as we go to press almost four years after the conference, the future for archaeology and historic buildings in the city and its vicinity is so threatened as cuts in local government funding begin to take their toll.

Linda Monckton and *Richard K. Morris*

NOTES

1. Bassett, *Anglo-Saxon Coventry*, 1–33.
2. J. Blair, 'Introduction: from Minster to Parish Church', in *Minsters and Parish Churches: the local church in transition 950–1200*, ed. J. Blair (Oxford 1988), 14. Blair refers to 'the frequency with which ex-minsters are

perpetuated as grand 12th-century churches, either cruciform or in some other way imposing'. The phenomenon is also explored in M. Thurlby, 'Minor Cruciform Churches in Norman England and Wales', in *Anglo-Norman Studies XXIV*, ed. J. Gillingham (Woodbridge 2002), 239–76.

3. For example, R. H. C. Davis, *The Early History of Coventry*, Dugdale Society Occasional Papers 24 (Oxford 1976); A. and E. Gooder, 'Coventry before 1355: Unity or Division?', *Midland History* 6 (1981), 1–38; T. John ed., *Medieval Coventry — a City Divided?*, Coventry & Warwickshire Pamphlets 11 (Coventry 1981); Coss, *Early Records*.

4. Goddard, *Coventry*, 22–33.

5. Gill and Morris, 'Apocalypse'.

6. A. Rudebeck, 'John Thornton and the stained glass of St Mary's Hall, Coventry', *Journal of Stained Glass* XXI (2007), 14–34.

7. Jeremy Ashbee gave a paper at the conference on Coventry's town wall and gates, and, though he decided subsequently not to offer it for publication, the information in this editorial is indebted to his presentation.

8. See most recently N. W. Alcock, 'Queen Isabella's new suburb in Coventry in 1348', *Midland History* XXXIII/2 (Autumn 2008), 240–8.

9. Woodfield, *Whitefriars*.

10. C. Tracy, 'The 14th-Century Canons' Stalls in the Collegiate Church of St Mary, Astley, Warwickshire', *JBAA* 162 (2009), 88–124. Duncan Givans also gave a paper on 'Investment in parochial fabric in Warwickshire *c.* 1050–1250', with case studies from such churches as Berkswell, Corley and Stoneleigh; we regret that the author was unable to prepare it in time to appear in this volume.

Three master-plans of Coventry appear on pp. vii–ix: the Cathedral Priory, medieval sites in the city, and Bradford's 1750 city map. These are referenced in the text of the papers as 'Prelim., Plan A', 'Prelim., Plan B', and 'Prelim., Plan C' respectively.

The colour plates are located after p. xx. They are repeated in the printed edition as black-and-white Figures. In such instances, the reference in the text reads, for example, '(Fig. 1 and Col. Pl. IA *in print edn*)'.

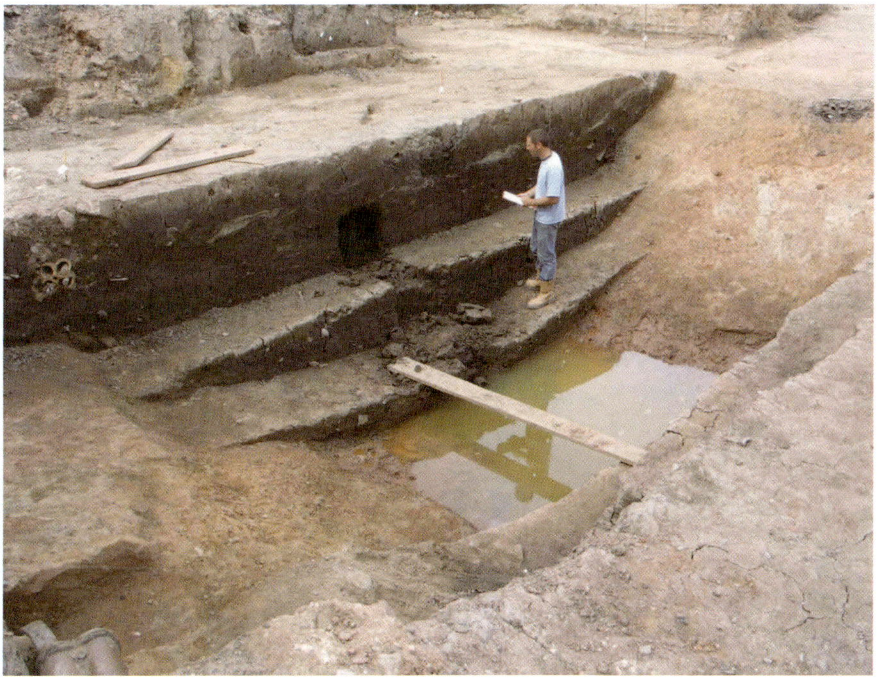

PLATE IA (Patrick, Figure 5). Recording a section across the Coventry town ditch during the Hill Street excavation (2005)

Photo, author

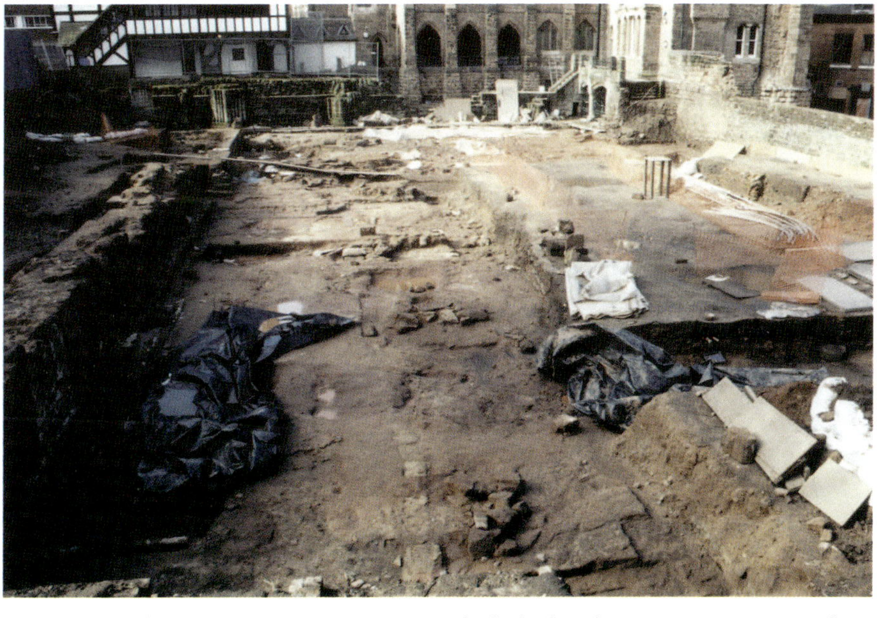

PLATE IB (Plant, Figure 1). Coventry, Cathedral Church: nave site as excavated, looking west along the south arcade pier foundations

Photo, March 2000, R. K. Morris

COLOUR PLATE II

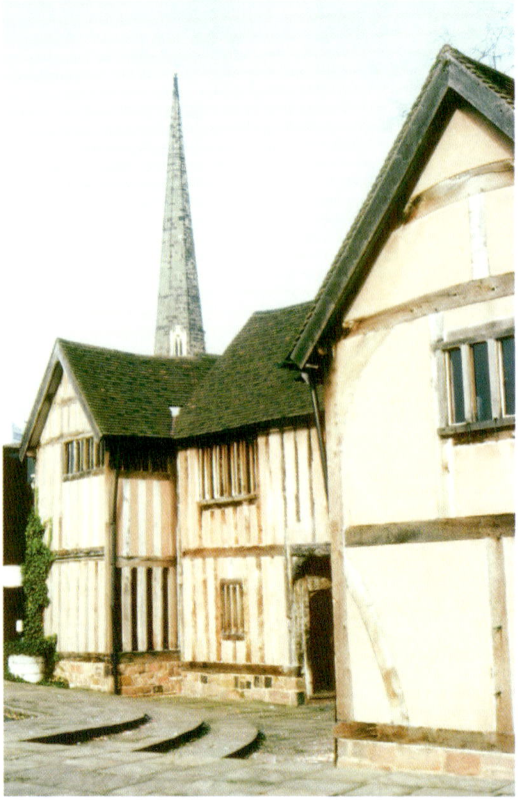

PLATE IIA (Soden, Figure 9). Former Cheylesmore Manor, north range, now the City Register Office: courtyard elevation, with the spire of the Greyfriars behind

Photo, R. K. Morris, 1982

PLATE IIB (Soden, Figure 6). St Mary's Cathedral Priory: the 14th-century tiled floor of the refectory, as excavated in 2000; scale 1m

Photo, author

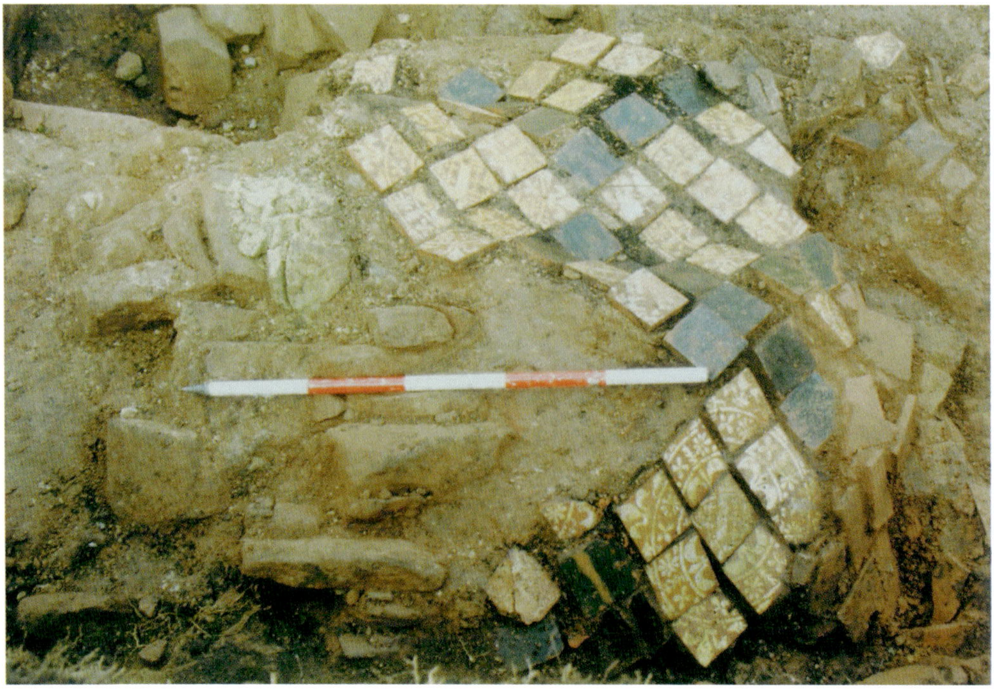

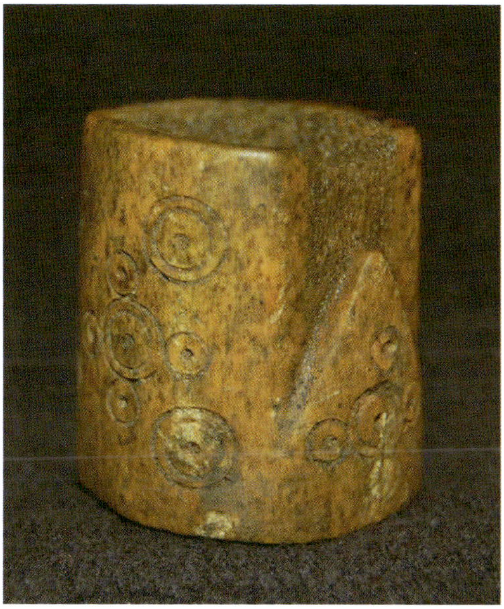

PLATE IIIA (Patrick, Figure 1). Chess piece from the Bayley Lane excavation (2006), possibly 12th-century; Herbert Art Gallery, Coventry

Photo, P. Thompson

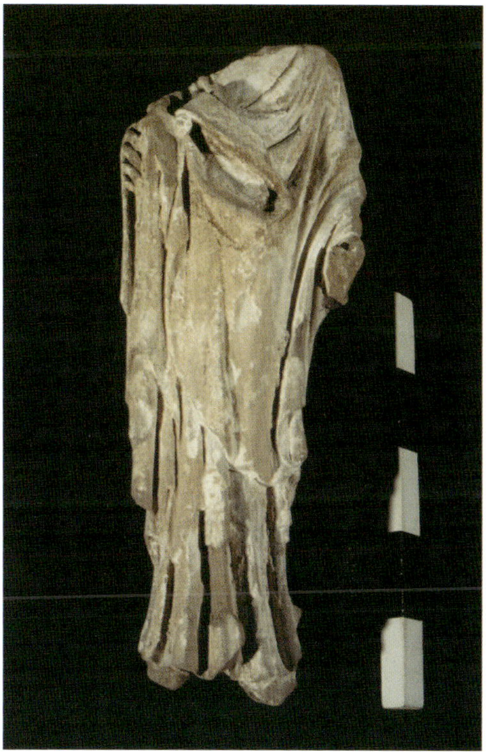

PLATE IIIB (Morris, 'Priory', Figure 18a). Coventry Priory: statuette T919, from the chapter-house(?), front (scale 25cm)

Photo, author

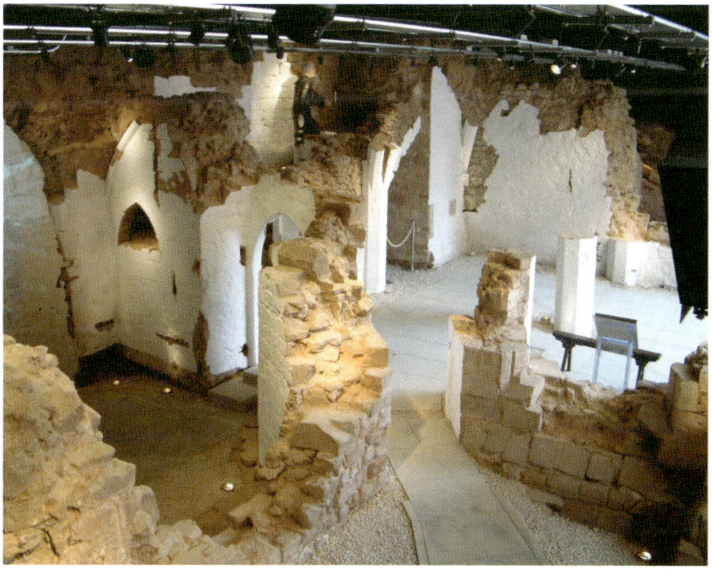

PLATE IIIC (Demidowicz, 'Priory', Figure 25). The priory undercrofts today, interior looking south-west; the east–west undercroft is in the left foreground, the north–south undercroft with its pier to the right

Photo, author

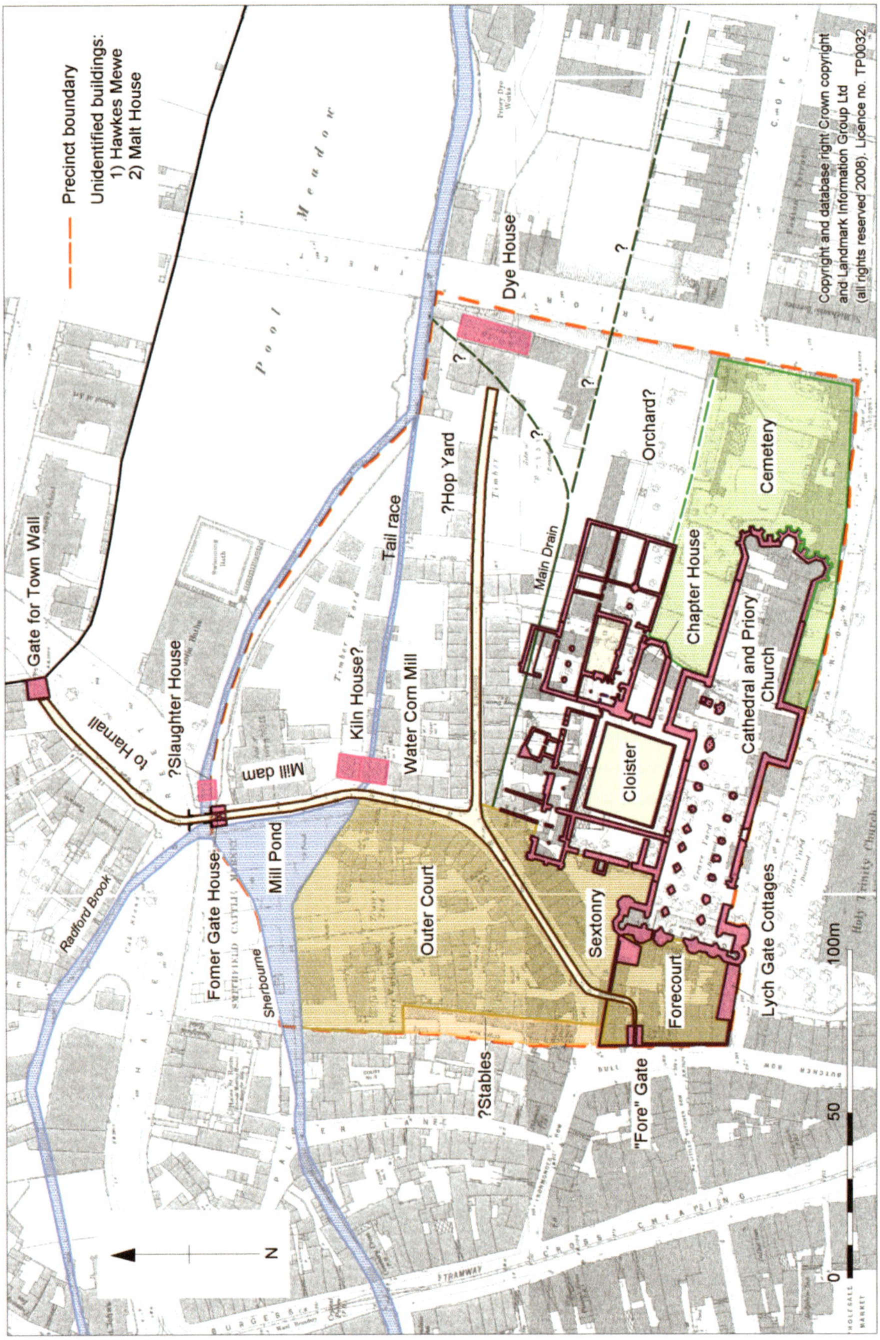

PLATE IV (Demidowicz, 'Priory', Figure 1). The priory precinct *c.* 1540, laid over Ordnance Survey map 1:500, 1st edition 1886
Drawing, author and Historic Environment Record, Coventry City Council

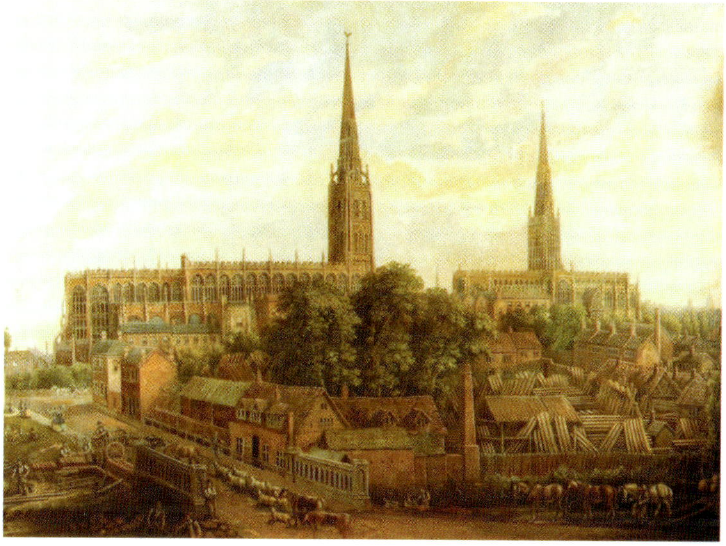

Plate Va (Demidowicz, 'Priory', Figure 8). View of St Michael's, Holy Trinity and the former priory precinct (foreground) from the north-east. David Gee, 1861, oil painting

Courtesy of The Herbert Art Gallery and Museum, Coventry

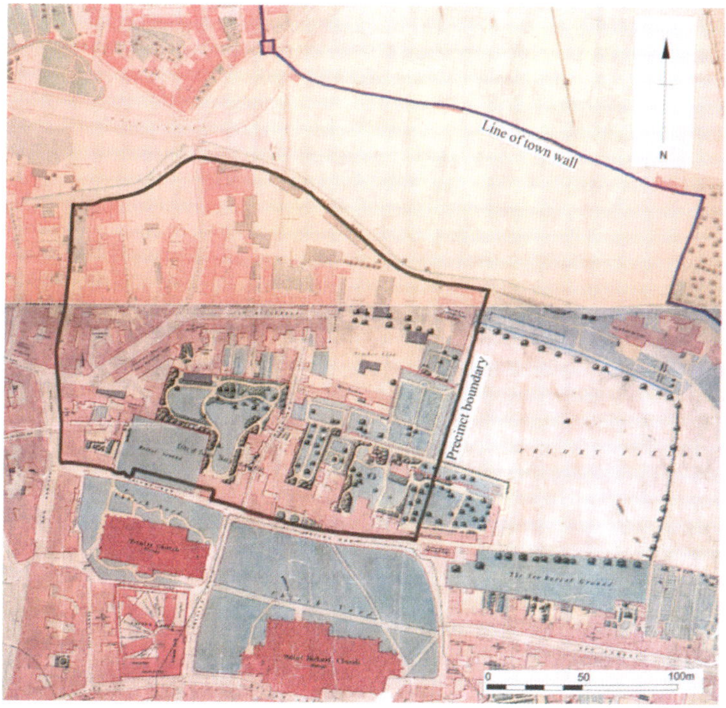

Plate Vb (Demidowicz, 'Priory', Figure 11). Board of Health Map, Coventry 1850: detail, overlain with the priory precinct boundary

Photo, courtesy of Coventry History Centre

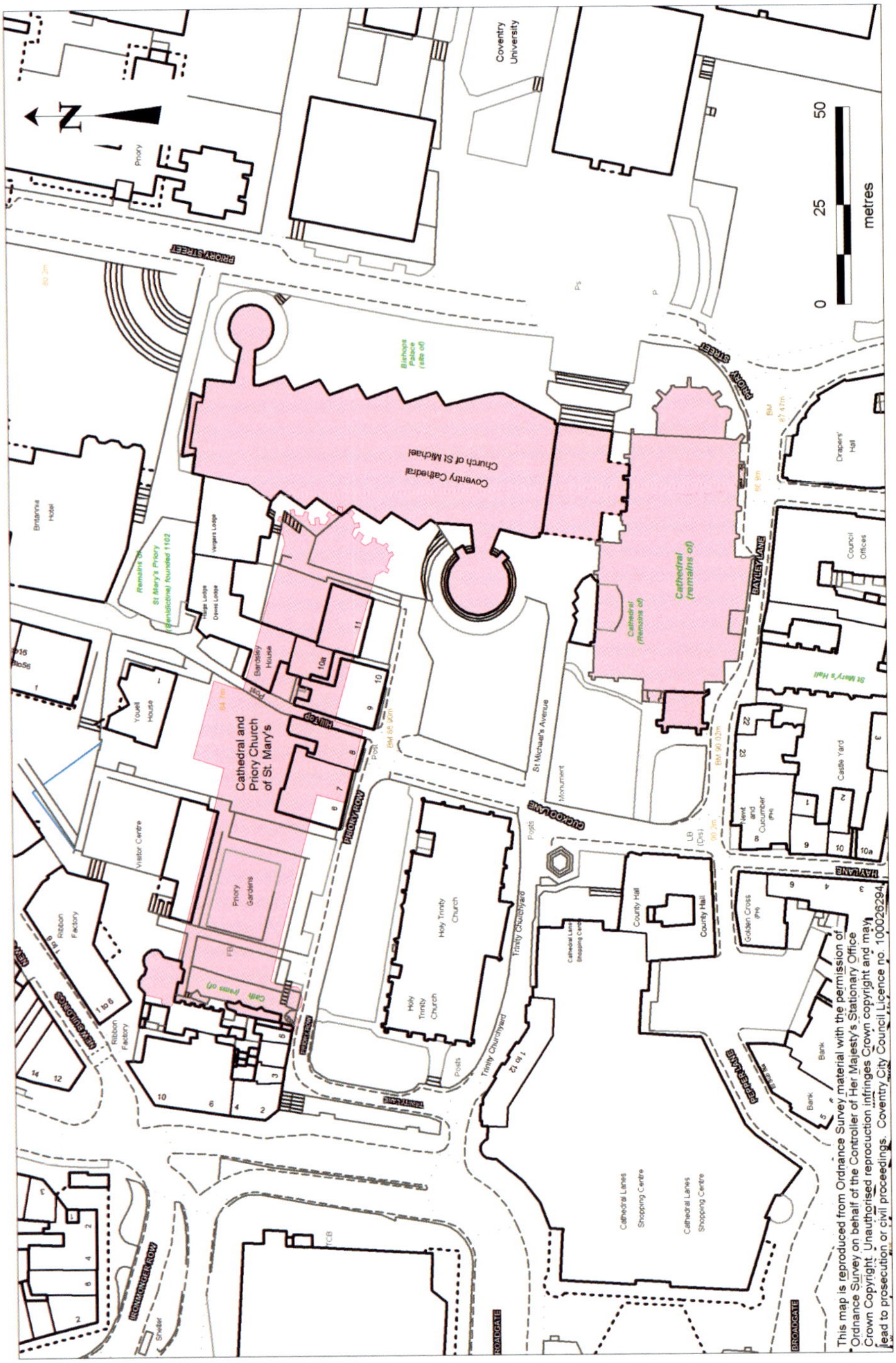

PLATE VI (Demidowicz, 'Priory', Figure 22). Plan of the three cathedral sites, Coventry
Drawing, author

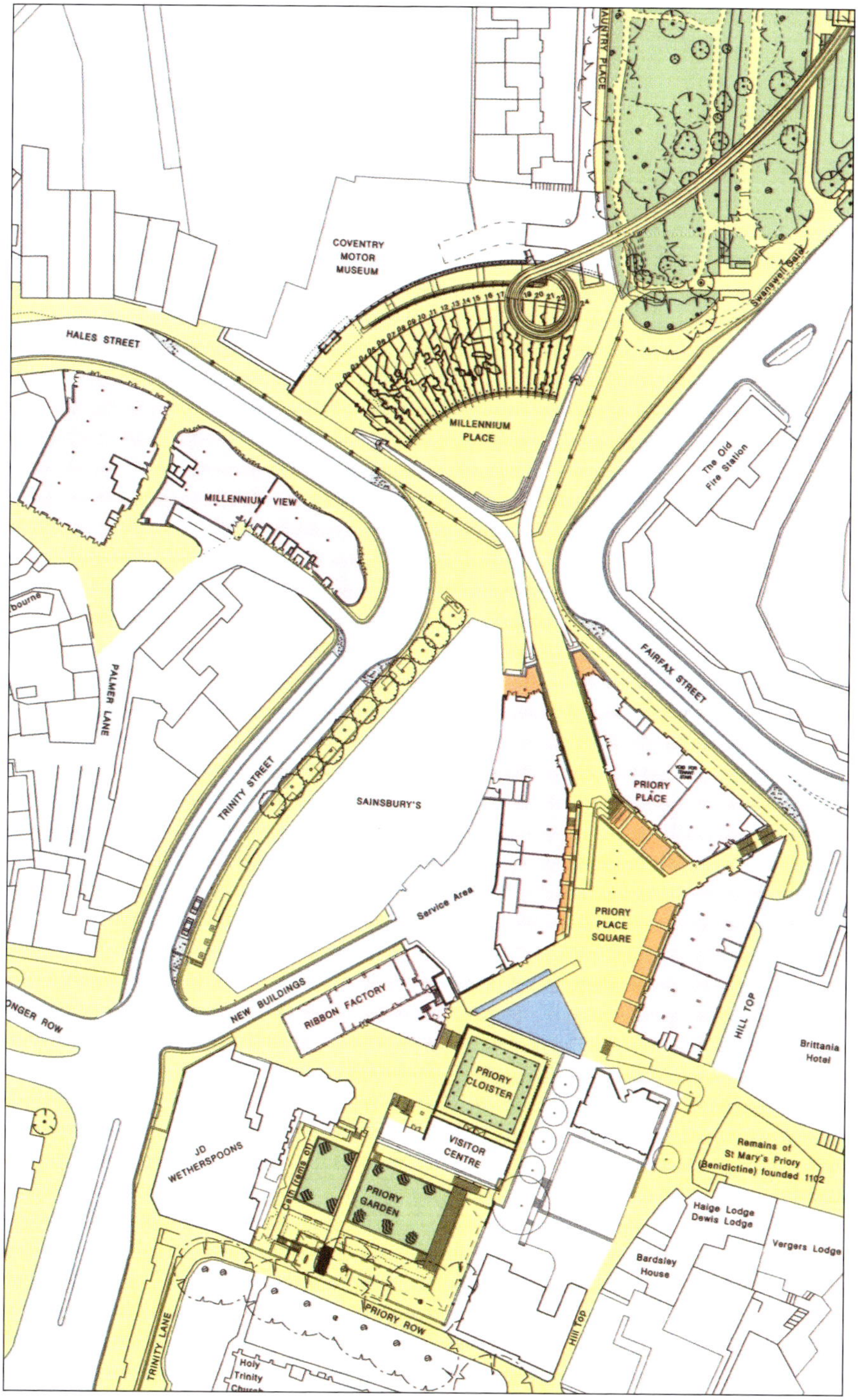

Plate VII (Demidowicz, 'Priory', Figure 24). Plan of the Phoenix Initiative project (*c.* 2000)

Drawing, Coventry City Council

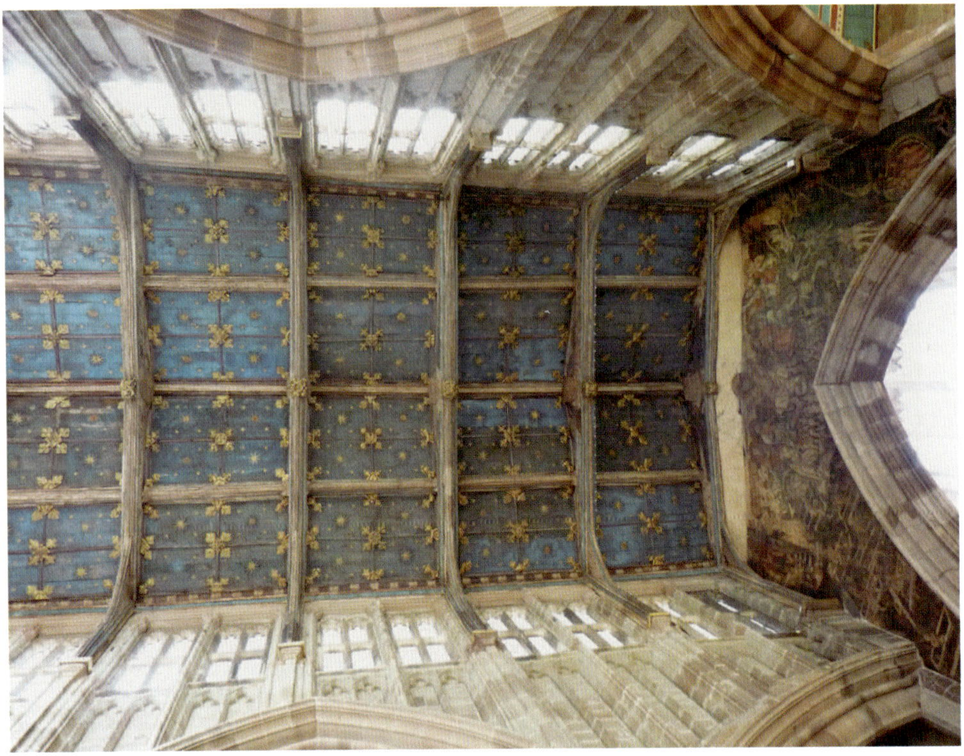

Plate VIIIa (Monckton, Figure 21). Coventry, Holy Trinity: nave clerestory
Photo, author

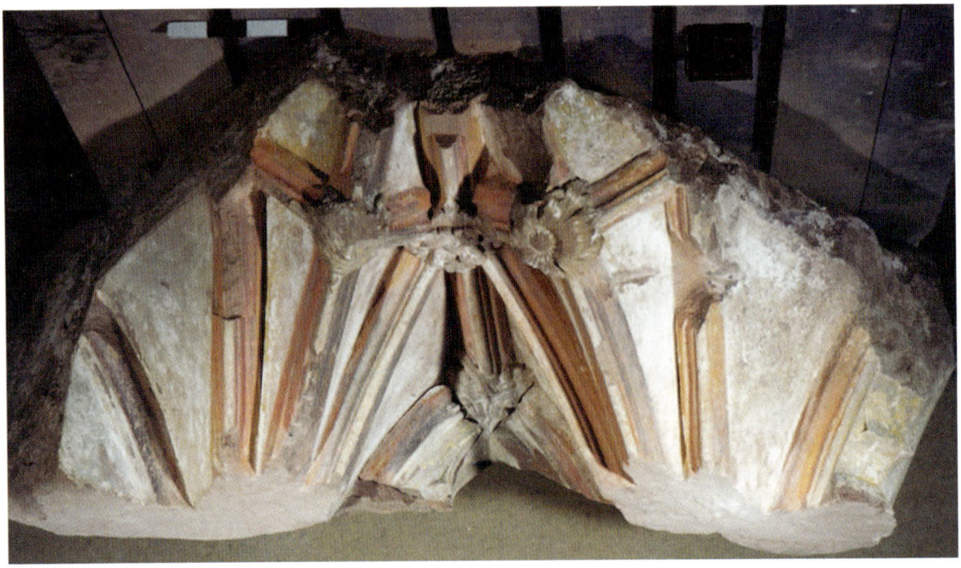

Plate VIIIb (Morris, 'Priory', Figure 22). Coventry Priory: refectory pulpit, piece T640/1, underside, miniature vault with original polychromy (scale 25cm)
Photo, author

COLOUR PLATE IX

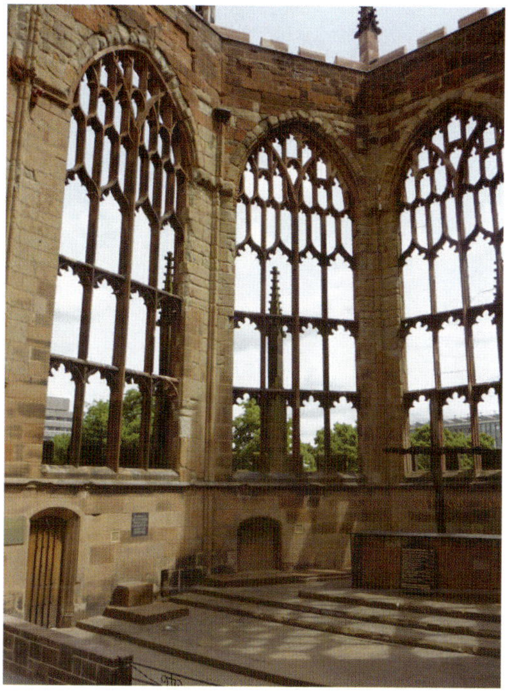

Plate IXa (Monckton, Figure 13). Coventry, St Michael's: windows of the eastern apse

Photo, author

Plate IXb (Demidowicz, 'Hall', Figure 11). Coventry, St Mary's Hall: interior of the hall looking north to the tapestry

Courtesy of Coventry City Council, St Mary's Guildhall

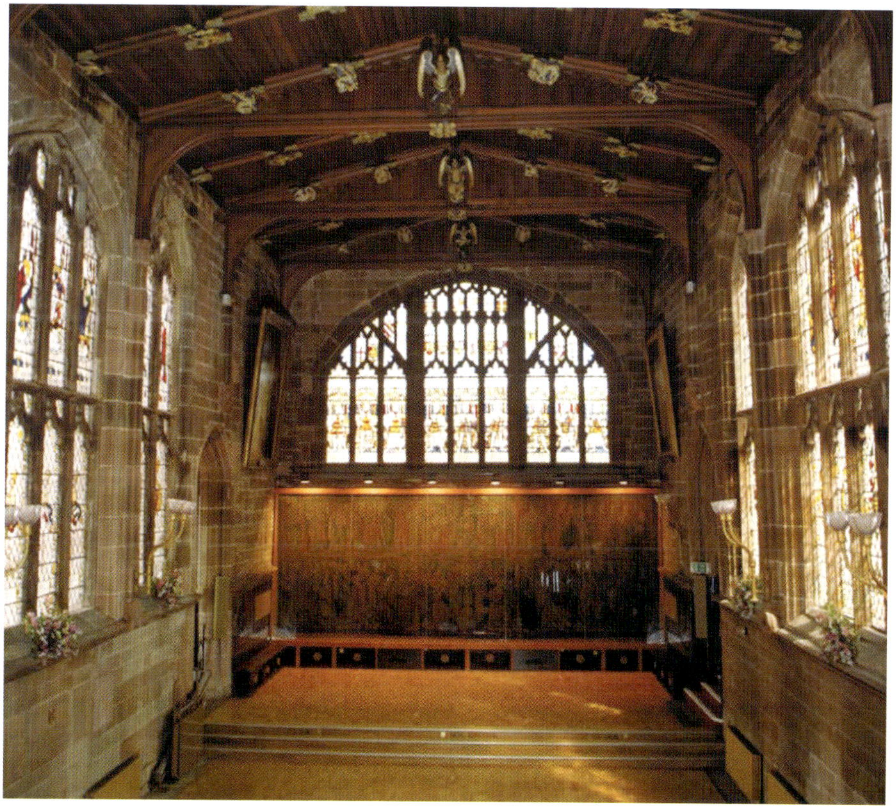

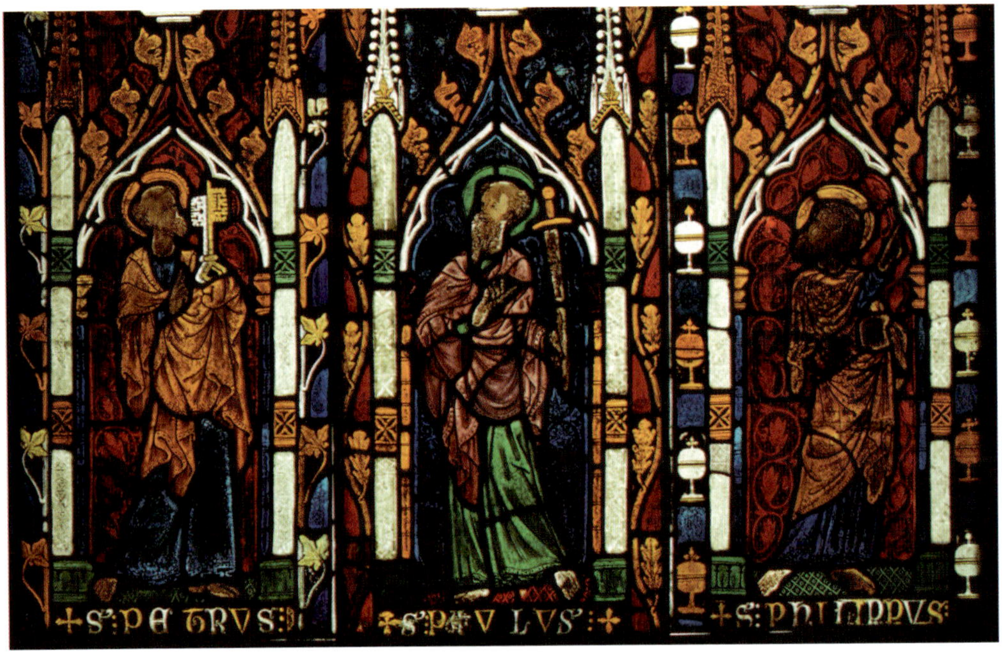

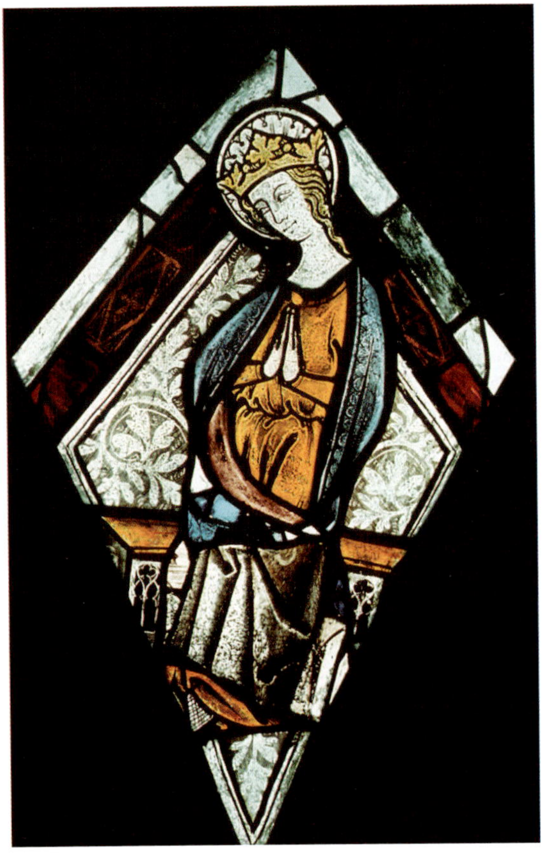

PLATE XA (Marks, Figure 2). Stanford on Avon: SS Peter, Paul and Philip in the chancel glazing, *c.* 1324–40
Photo, author

PLATE XB (Marks, Figure 5). Stanford on Avon: The Virgin from the Coronation of the Virgin, now in a chancel window, *c.* 1341–52
Photo, author

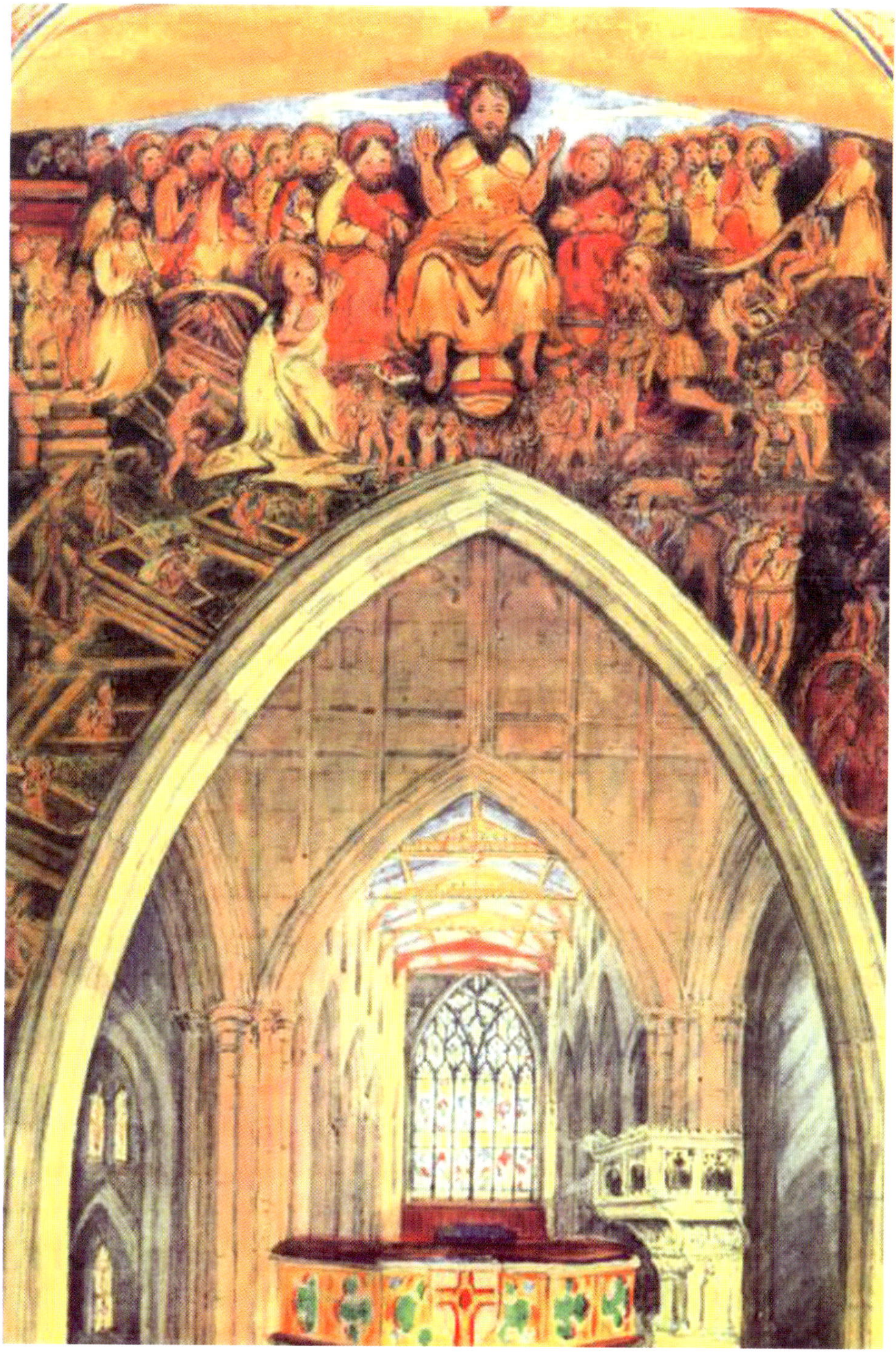

PLATE XI (Gill, Figure 1). Holy Trinity church, Coventry: water-colour painting of the Doom, Nathaniel Troughton, after 1855 (Troughton VIII/21)

Photo, History of Art Department, University of Warwick

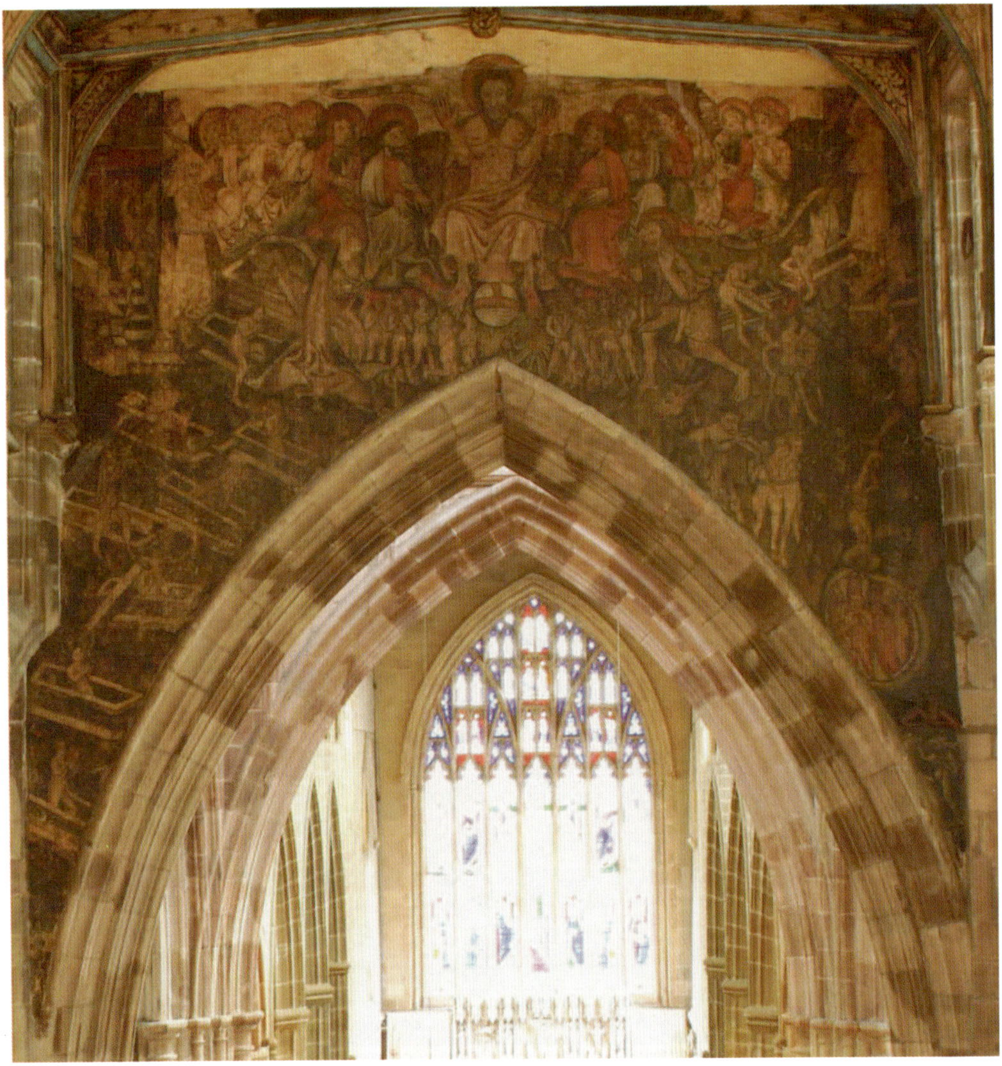

PLATE XII (Gill, Figure 2). Holy Trinity: the Doom painting after recent cleaning and conservation

Photo 2004, J. Burbidge

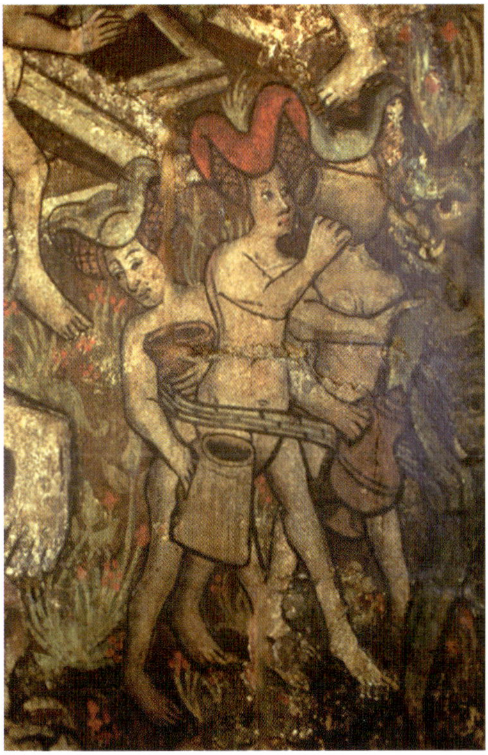

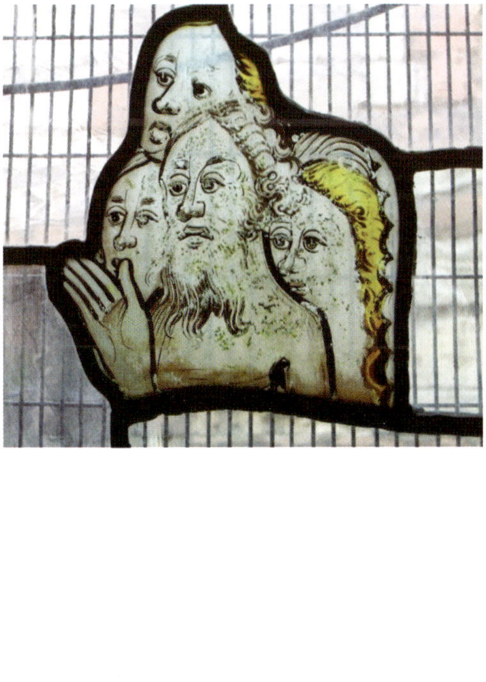

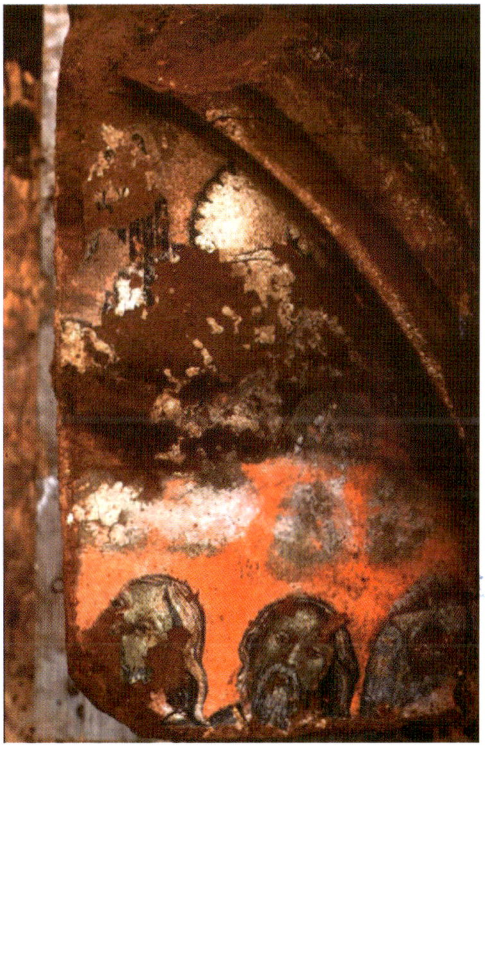

PLATE XIIIA (*top left*) (Gill, Figure 4).
Holy Trinity: the Doom, three alewives led by a demon
Photo, J. Burbidge

PLATE XIIIB (*bottom left*) (Gill, Figure 5).
Coventry Cathedral: Haigh Memorial Chapel, reset glass from St Michael's church, souls rising from the grave, detail
Photo, R. K. Morris

PLATE XIIIC (*bottom right*) (Gill, Figure 10).
Coventry Priory, chapter-house: piece T698/5, detail showing figures looking up
Photo, R. K. Morris

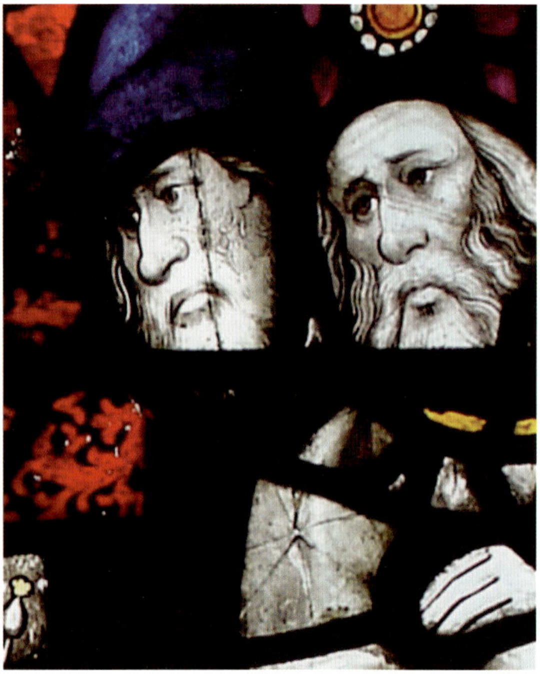

Plate XIVa (Scott, Figure 1a). York Minster: the Great East window (I), for which Thornton was contracted 1405–08; detail

Photo, The York Glaziers Trust, reproduced by kind permission of the Dean and Chapter of York

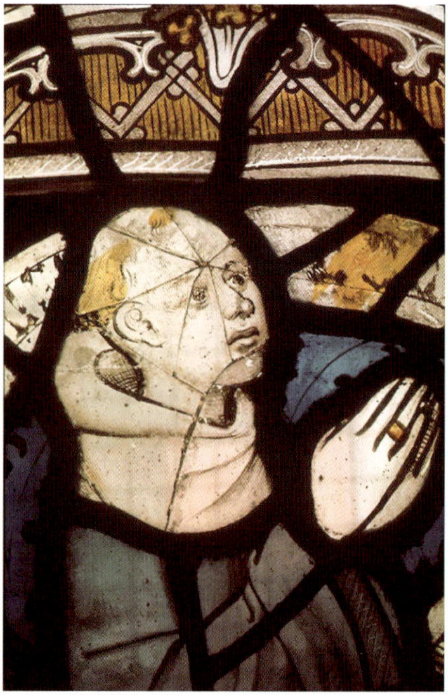

Plate XIVb (Scott, Figure 1b). York, All Saints: North Street (window nIV), early 15th century; detail

Photo, author

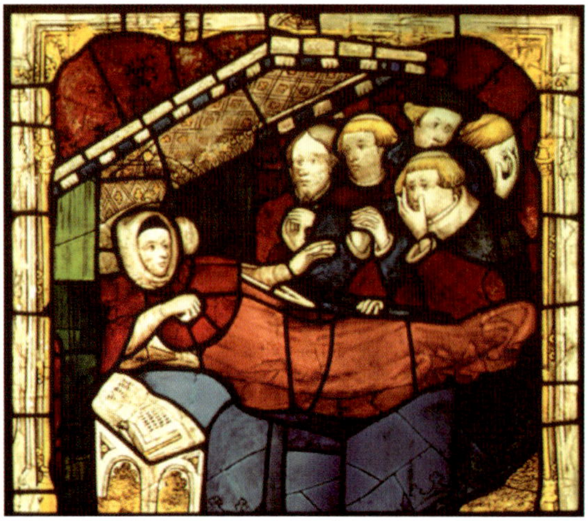

Plate XIVc (Scott, Figure 2a). York Minster: St William window (nVII), St William retires from the feast, *c.* 1415

Photo, The York Glaziers Trust, reproduced by kind permission of the Dean and Chapter of York

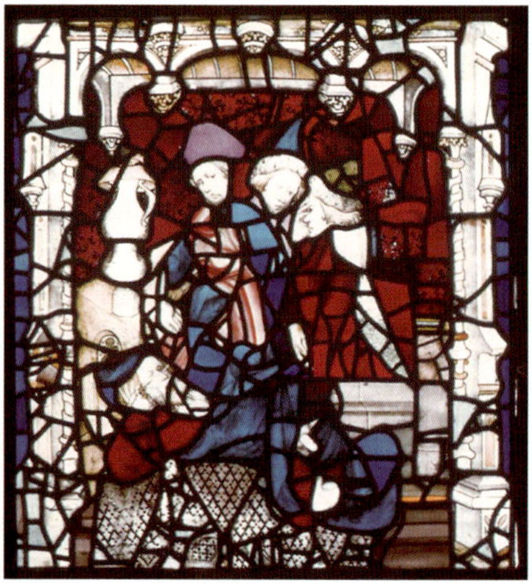

Plate XIVd (Scott, Figure 2b). York Minster: the Great East window (I), the Shame of Noah, 1405–08

Photo, The York Glaziers Trust, reproduced by kind permission of the Dean and Chapter of York

COLOUR PLATE XV

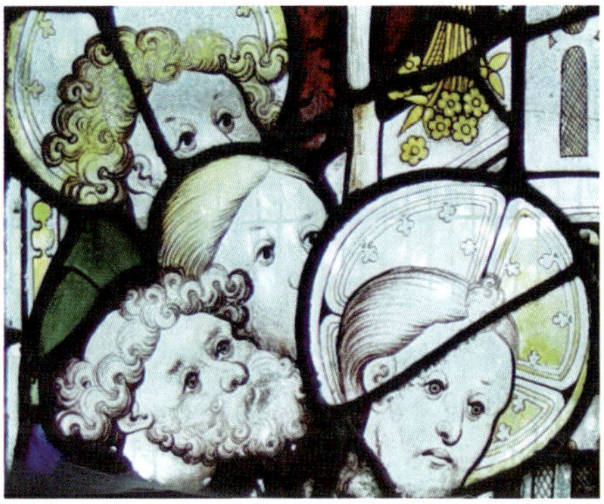

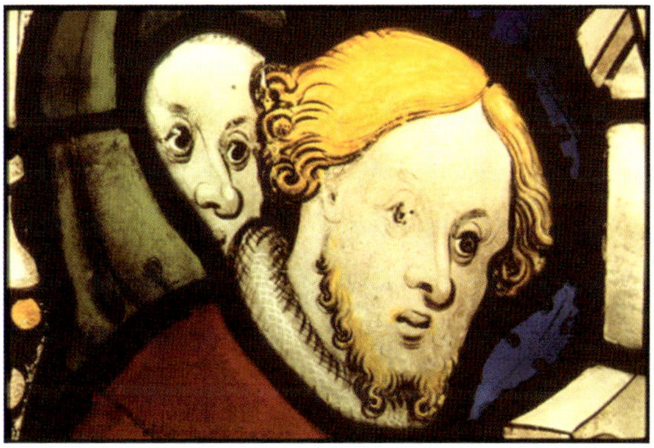

A B

Plate XVa (Scott, Figure 3a). Great Malvern Priory: the Great East window (I), detail

Photo, John Jones

Plate XVb (Scott, Figure 3b). York Minster: the St William window (nVII), detail

Photo, The York Glaziers Trust, reproduced by kind permission of the Dean and Chapter of York

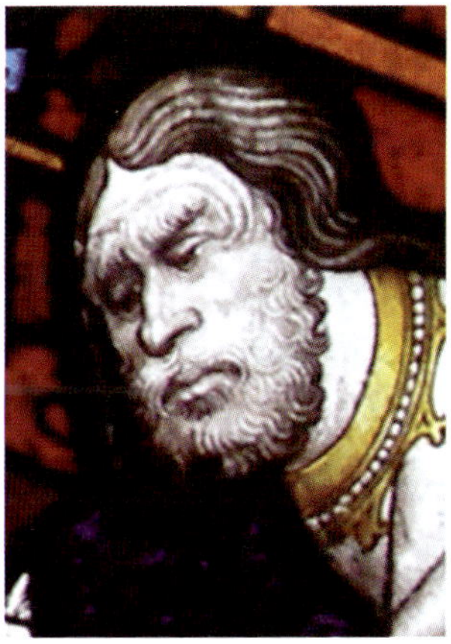

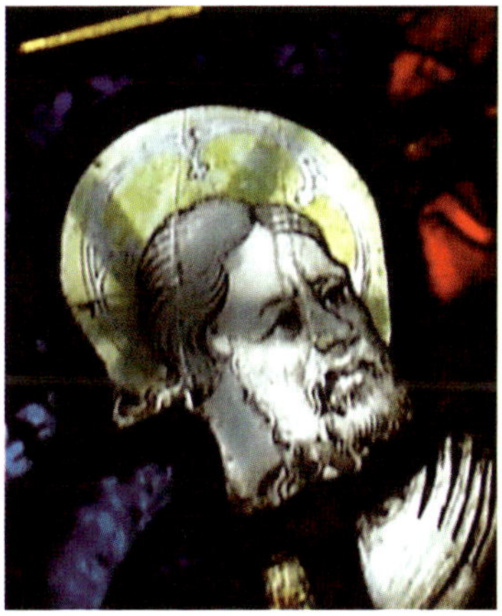

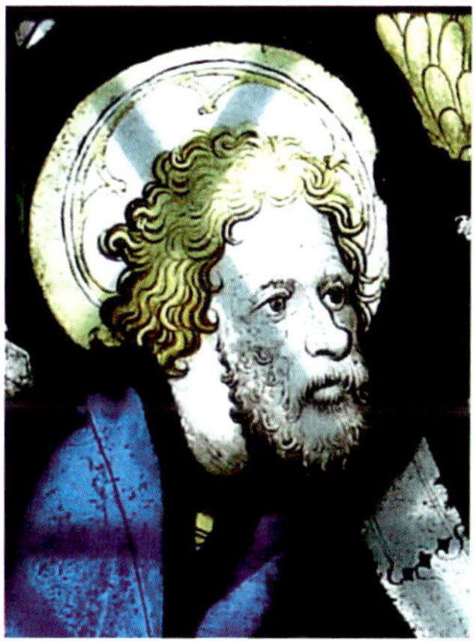

C D E

Plate XVc, d, e (Scott, Figures 5a, b, c). York Minster: the Great East window (I), faces of St John from scenes from the Apocalypse, highlighting the variations within the window's painting

Photos, The York Glaziers Trust, reproduced by kind permission of the Dean and Chapter of York

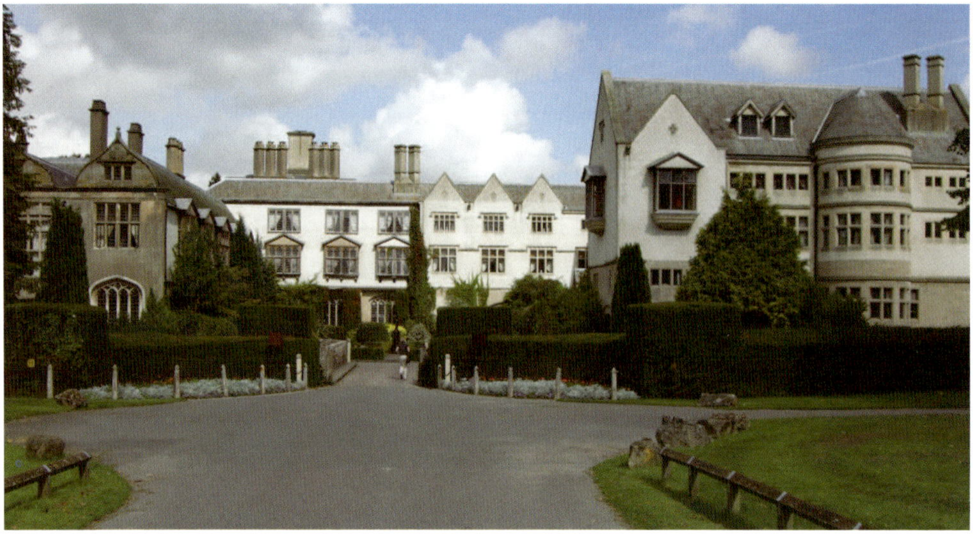

Plate XVIa (Rodwell, Figure 1). Combe Abbey from the south, after the recent hotel conversion. The bridge over the moat is in the foreground; the superstructures of the east range (right foreground) and of the gabled section of the north range are new

Photo, 2010, R. K. Morris

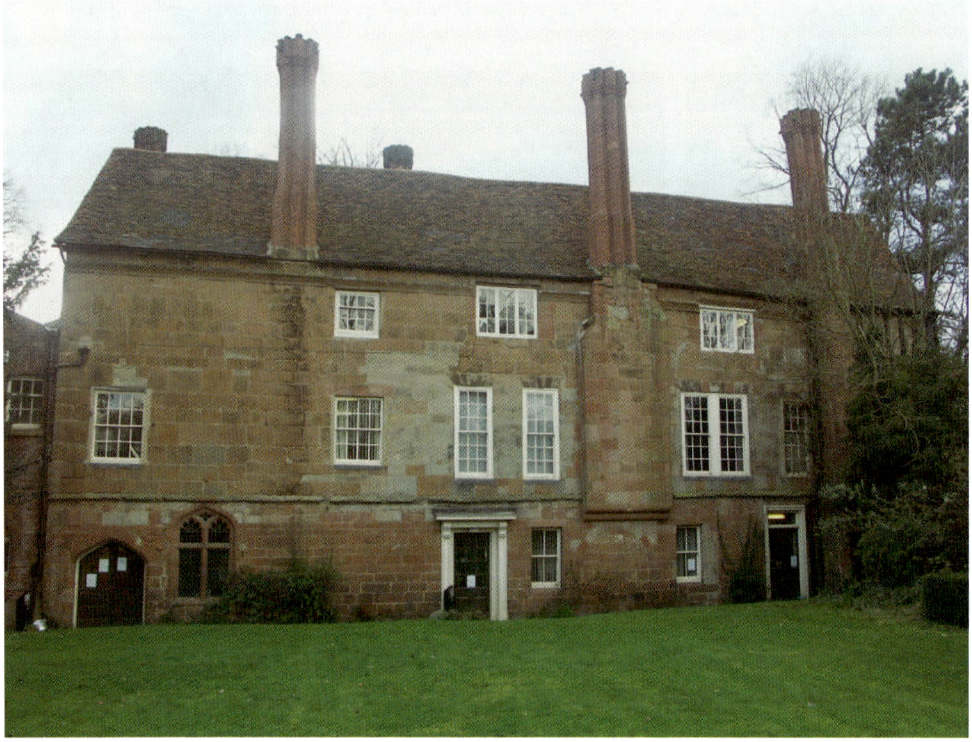

Plate XVIb (Luxford, Figure 5). Coventry Charterhouse: surviving block from the east

Photo, author

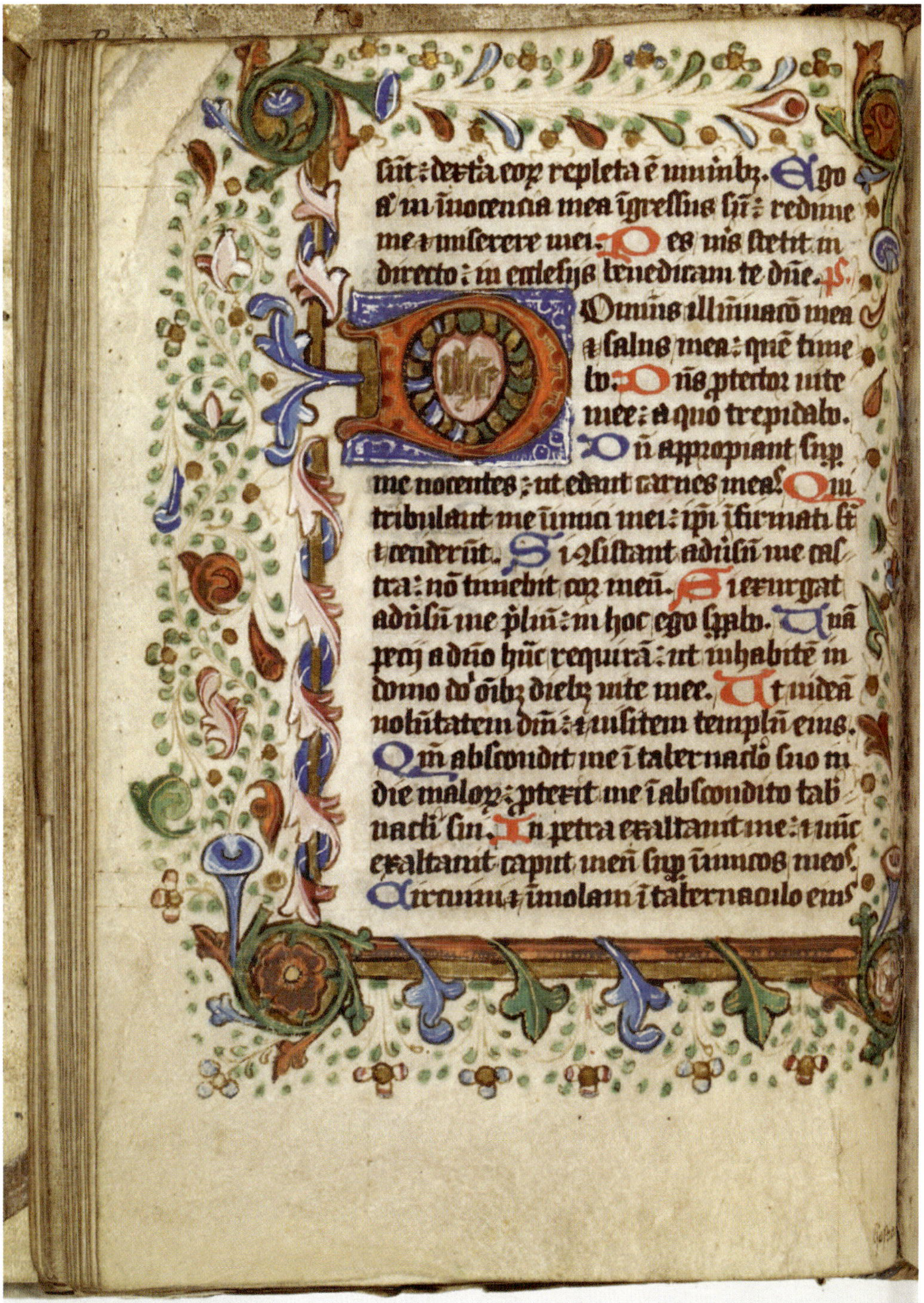

PLATE XVII (Luxford, Figure 18). Cambridge, Peterhouse MS 276, fol. 32v, probably second quarter of the 15th century

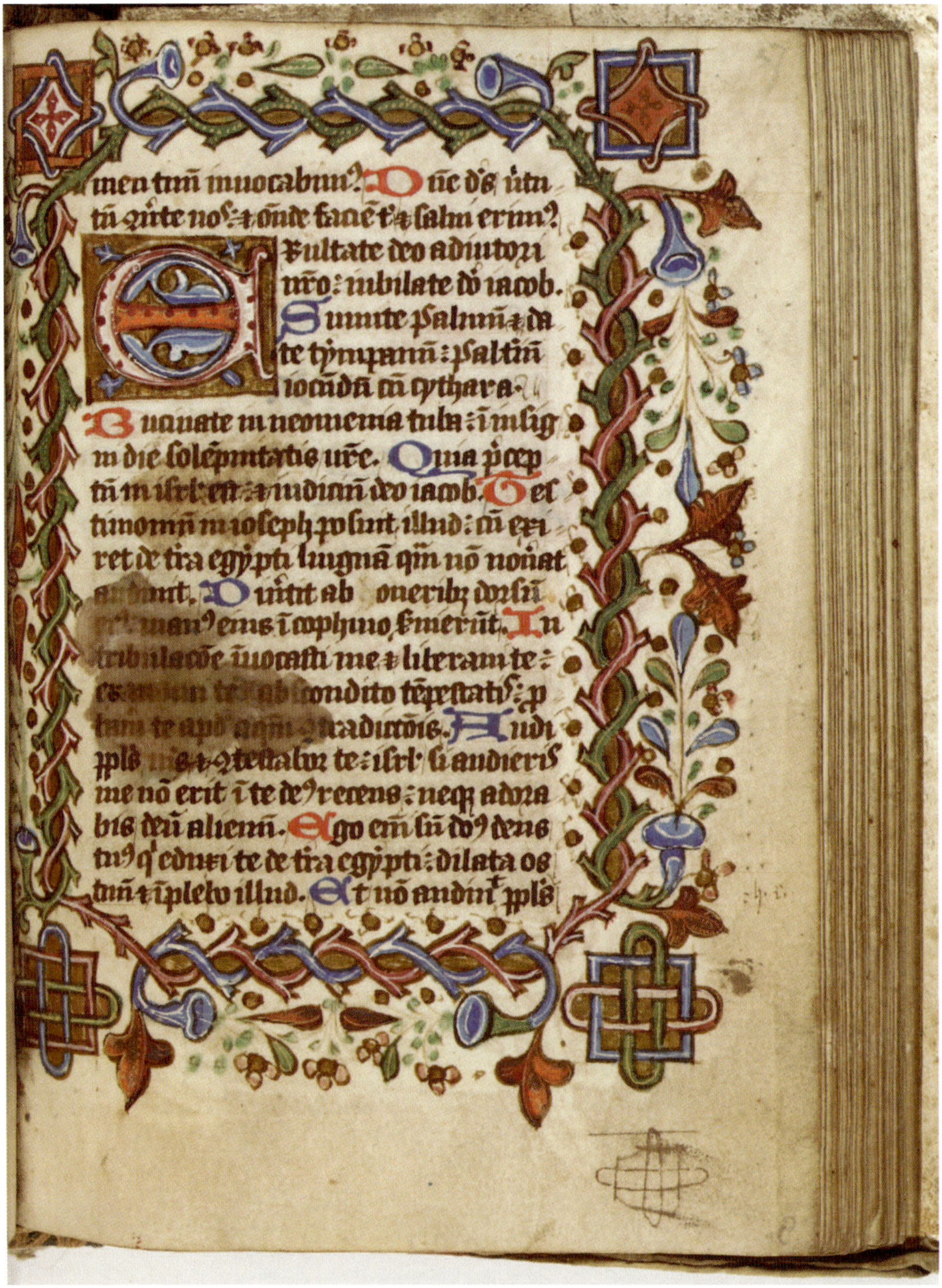

PLATE XVIII (Luxford, Figure 20). Cambridge, Peterhouse MS 276, fol. 73r, probably second quarter of the 15th century

COLOUR PLATE XIX

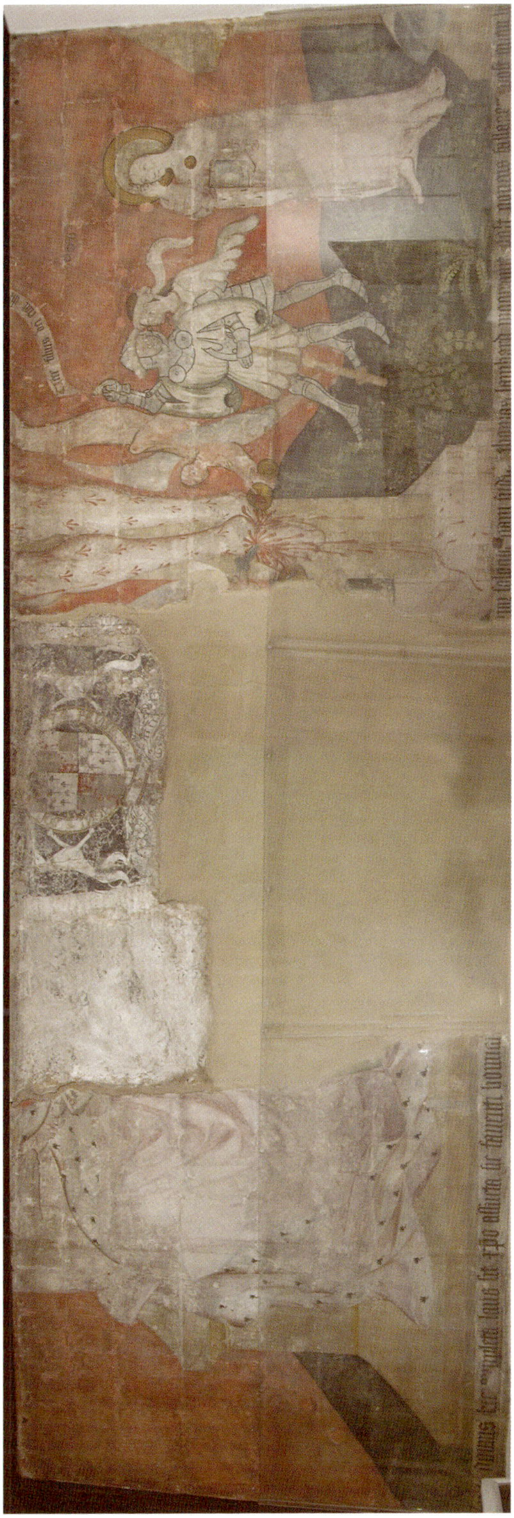

PLATE XIX (Naydenova-Slade, Figure 2). Coventry, St Anne's Charterhouse: 15th-century mural
Photo, author

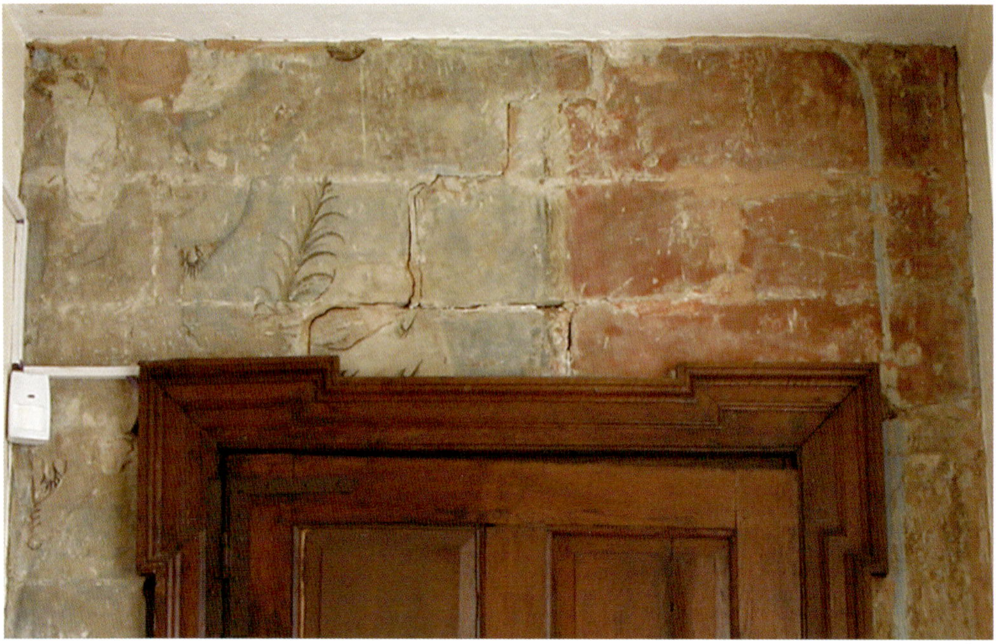

Plate XXa (Naydenova-Slade, Figure 4). Coventry, St Anne's Charterhouse: 15th-century mural, fragments in passage, detail

Photo, author

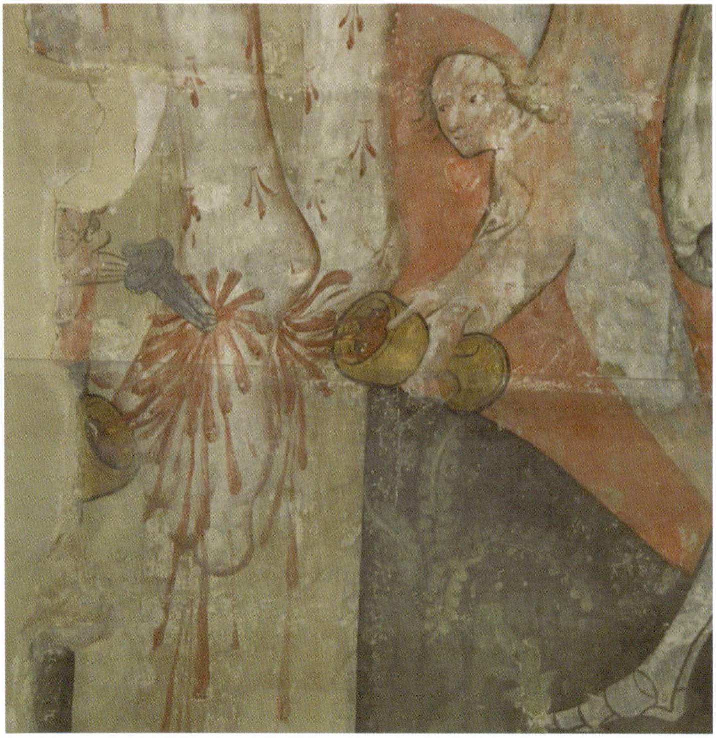

Plate XXb (Naydenova-Slade, Figure 5). Coventry, St Anne's Charterhouse: 15th-century mural, detail: angels gathering blood

Photo, author

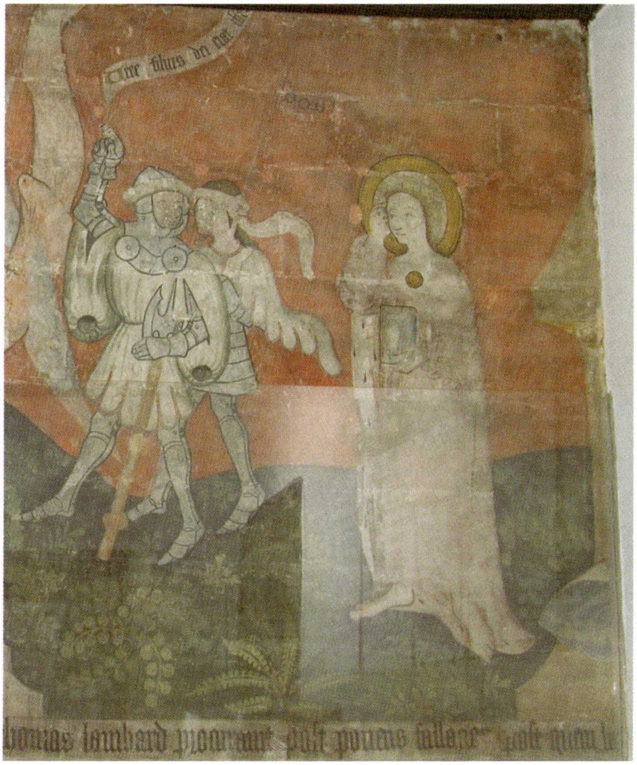

PLATE XXIA (Naydenova-Slade, Figure 6). Coventry, St Anne's Charterhouse: 15th-century mural, detail: the centurion and his standard bearer (left), St John the Evangelist (right)
Photo, author

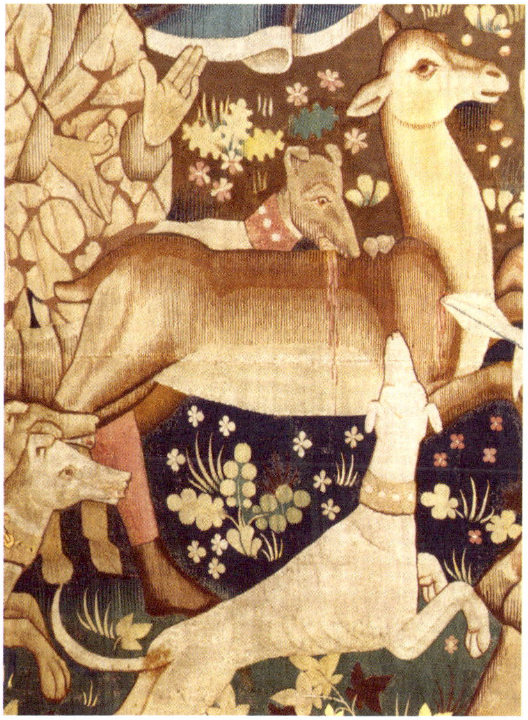

PLATE XXIB (Naydenova-Slade, Figure 12). Devonshire Hunting Tapestries, Deer Hunt, foliage detail
Photo, ©V&A Images/Victoria and Albert Museum, London

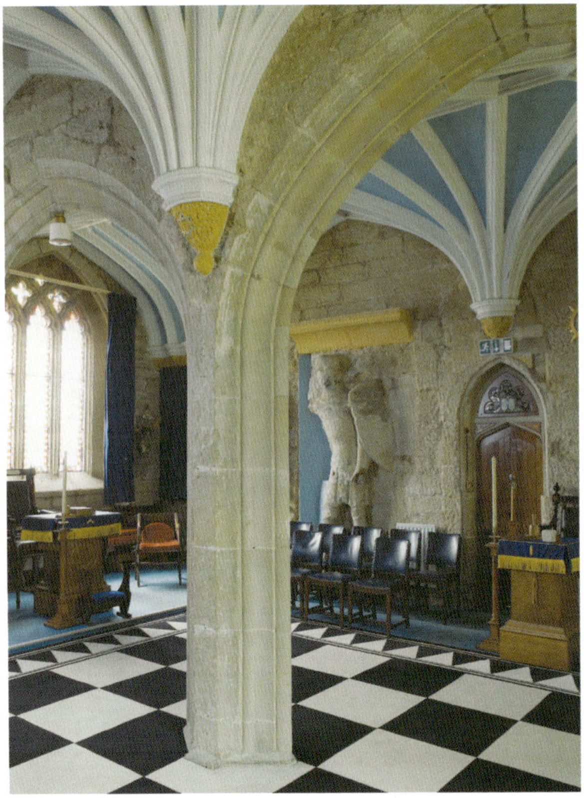

Plate XXIIa (Goodall, 'Guy's Cliffe', Figure 2). Guy's Cliffe: chapel interior

Photo, Paul Barker/Country Life

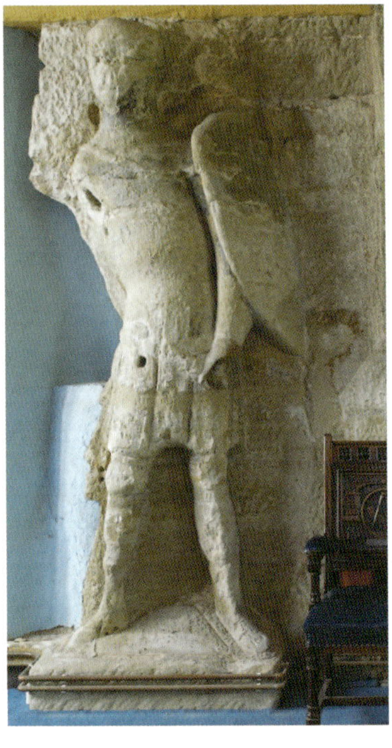

Plate XXIIb (Goodall, 'Guy's Cliffe', Figure 3). Guy's Cliffe: chapel, statue of Guy of Warwick, 1340s

Photo, Paul Barker/Country Life

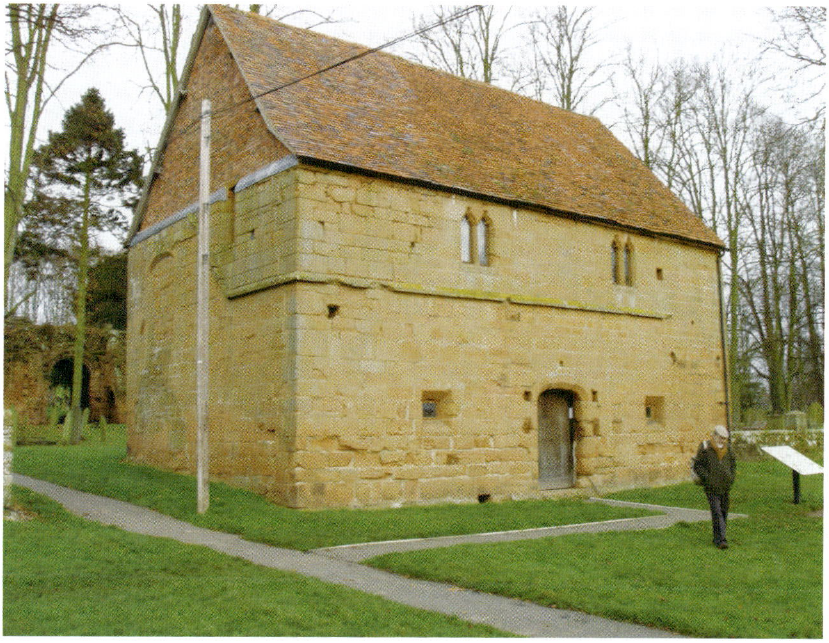

Plate XXIIIa (Alexander and Sunley, Figure 1). Kenilworth Abbey: the Barn, from the south-west, with Harry Sunley

Photo, J. S. Alexander

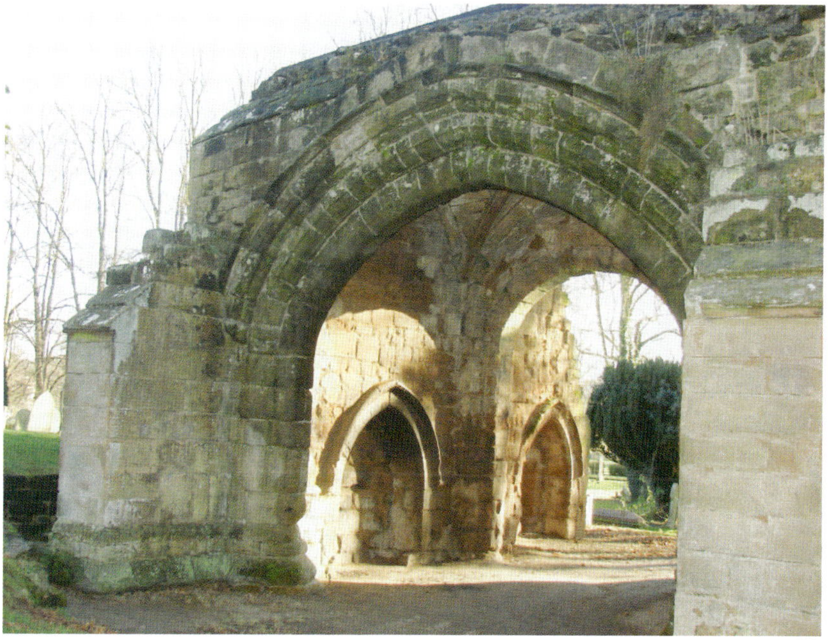

Plate XXIIIb (Alexander and Sunley, Figure 10). Kenilworth Abbey: the gatehouse, from the north

Photo, J. S. Alexander

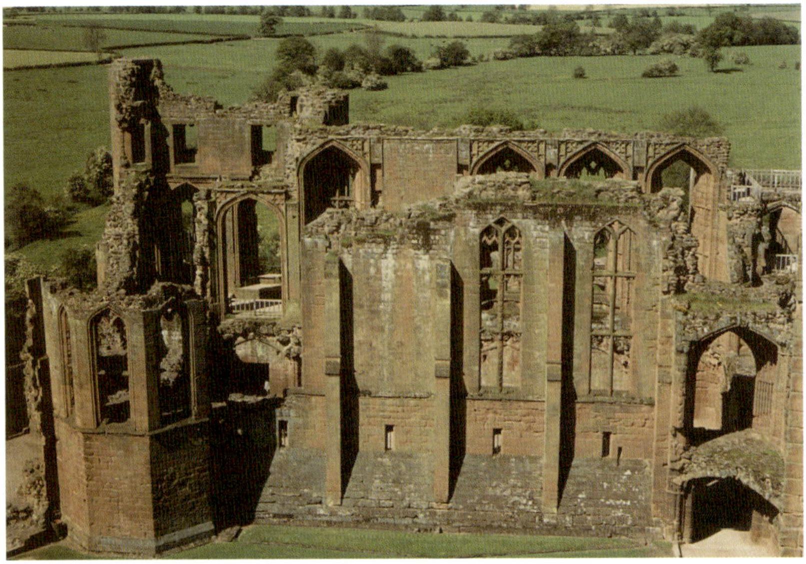

PLATE XXIVA (Morris, 'Kenilworth', Figure 1). Kenilworth Castle: the great hall, viewed from the great tower

Photo, 1985, author

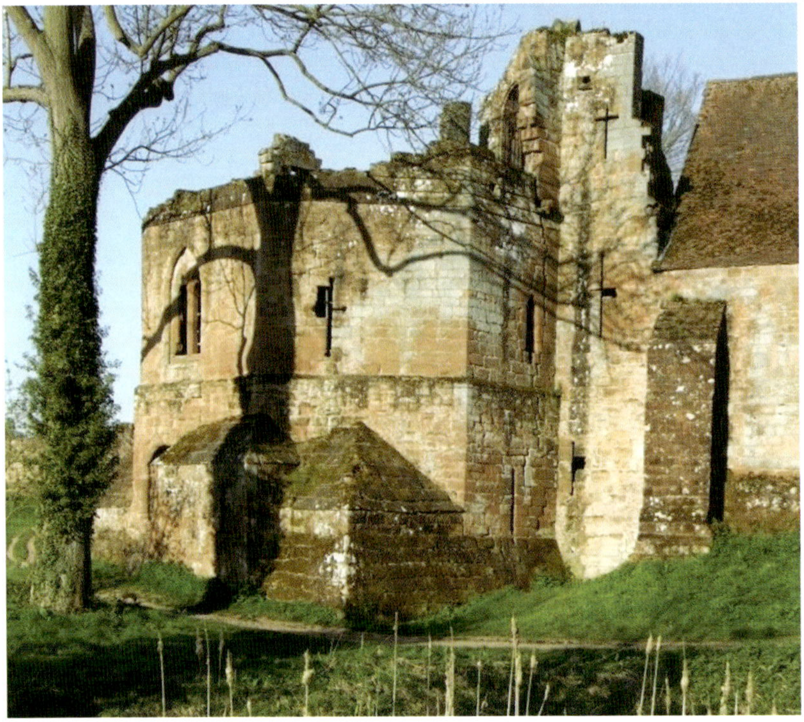

PLATE XXIVB (Morris, 'Kenilworth', Figure 7). Kenilworth Castle: Water Tower, from the north-east

Photo, author

An Introduction to the Archaeology of Medieval Coventry

IAIN SODEN

This paper summarises the history of archaeological enquiry in Coventry together with the individuals who have been prominent in fieldwork. It charts the landmark excavations which have characterised fieldwork in the city, beginning with antiquarian investigations as early as 1815, but concentrating on modern research of the 1970s, 1980s and 1990s, in order to provide a backdrop for the most recent enquiry. It introduces the principal sites towards which research continues to be directed, some of which will feature later in this volume.

ARCHAEOLOGICAL ENQUIRY IN THE CITY

IT was a fitting culmination to many decades of dedicated archaeological work that the British Archaeological Association brought its annual conference to Coventry in 2007. Since Coventry's widespread destruction in the Second World War and some questionable planning decisions since the 1950s, the city has been much maligned when compared with more picturesque midland neighbours. Comparison, however, usually overlooks the variety of archaeological research and enquiry which the city has supported since the 19th century.

It is modern Coventry's blessing but historic Coventry's curse that the results of its post-war redevelopment actually reflect the city's economic success in the last fifty years. While above ground the city's historic character has to be summed up by a few desperately isolated buildings and lashings of imagination, below ground is a different matter. A wealth of excavated information is available from which to paint a rich and varied picture of its medieval past. This is complemented by documentary and artefactual archives, curated by the City Archives and the Herbert Art Gallery and Museum, and which in 2008 have been combined under one roof in the new purpose-built History Centre. However, such resources were not always available for archaeologists, who have often laboured against the odds in a city which has embraced change with a will.

THE ANTIQUARIAN YEARS (1815–1957)

COVENTRY was the place where the great 17th-century historian Sir William Dugdale was schooled, and even today his work remains a starting point for archaeological enquiry[1]. Then, during the 19th and 20th centuries, the city benefited from the attentions of a series of antiquarians who could revel in the old medieval fabric which still stood all around them. Their names are unheard by some, half-forgotten by others: Mr Percy, Thomas Sharpe (whose tomb-chest rests just outside Coventry University, where the 2007 conference was held), Benjamin Poole, Frederick Humberstone, Alderman William Andrews, William Wyley and John Shelton.

As early as 1815 Mr Percy was conducting excavations in the village of Stoke,[2] now one of Coventry's suburbs, but it was not really until the work of John Shelton, William Wyley and experts from outside Coventry such as Philip Chatwin that a kernel of systematic fieldwork began to be applied to the disappearing medieval fabric. The first set-piece excavation since 1815 was conducted at the former Opera House site on Hales Street in the 1920s. At about the same time Wyley was excavating at the Charterhouse where he lived,[3] whilst Mr Shelton's distinctive self-appointed, city-wide watching brief on redevelopments lasted from 1926 until his death in 1957.[4] Most bomb-sites and redevelopments in that period would have gone unwatched but for his efforts. His archive formed the core for the archaeological collections of the (then new) Herbert Art Gallery and Museum, which would have been much greater had it not been that his own private museum was bombed in 1940 and a substantial portion of the city's other artefactual collections were also lost in the Blitz. The city's documentary archive was once also much larger, but was denuded by a catastrophic fire in Birmingham Reference Library in the late 19th century.

A NEW BEGINNING (1957–73)

EVEN as Mr Shelton's day passed, the national Society for Medieval Archaeology was being formed (1957). It soon drew attention to the gap left by Mr Shelton's death, as the pace of redevelopment of the city outstripped the will to preserve, conserve or record the old. However, the city had refounded the Herbert Art Gallery and Museum on a new site in Jordan Well in 1955 and soon afterwards it appointed its first City Archaeologist, Charmian Woodfield. She began a life-long study of Coventry's Carmelite Friary, Whitefriars, as well as conducting the first serious research on the town wall and ditch. At this time a core of enthusiasts with a shared interest both in archaeology generally and in Coventry in particular founded the Coventry and District Archaeological Society (CADAS) in 1960. Its membership remains a potent force today.

Mrs Woodfield was succeeded by Brian Hobley in 1965, whose extensive evaluation work at St Mary's Cathedral and Benedictine Priory vied briefly for the public's attention with his seminal research on the Lunt Roman Fort at nearby Baginton.[5] Elsewhere in the city, archaeology went largely unrecorded as redevelopment outstripped the best efforts of archaeologists.

The course of events began to change with the excavations at Much Park Street in 1970–74, led by Bill Foard (Fig. 1).[6] Numerous plots became vacant for excavation as medieval houses were dismantled piece by piece and moved to Spon Street for re-erection as part of architect Freddie Charles' bold and sometimes controversial conservation scheme (Fig. 2). Just as the buildings were painstakingly dismantled piece by piece for re-erection, so an opportunity was provided for meticulous excavation of their footprints to trace the archaeological development of their plots from the 12th century onwards. These salvaged buildings now in Spon Street are among the last of a wealth of medieval timber-framed structures captured so emotively in the paintings, washes and drawings of a number of 18th- and 19th-century local artists, such as Nathaniel Troughton.[7]

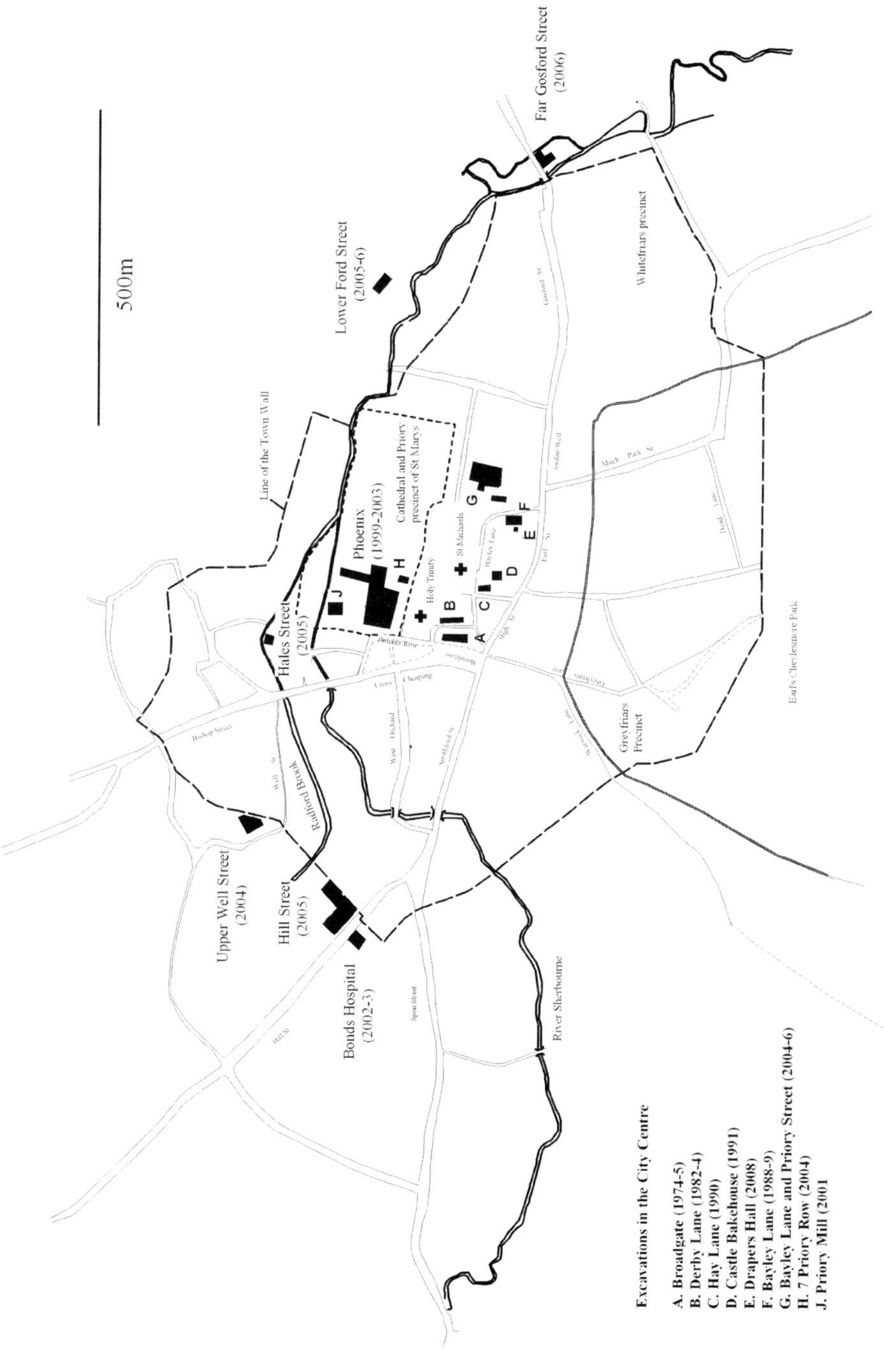

Fig. 1. Medieval Coventry, showing the locations of recent archaeological excavations
Drawing, C. Patrick and author

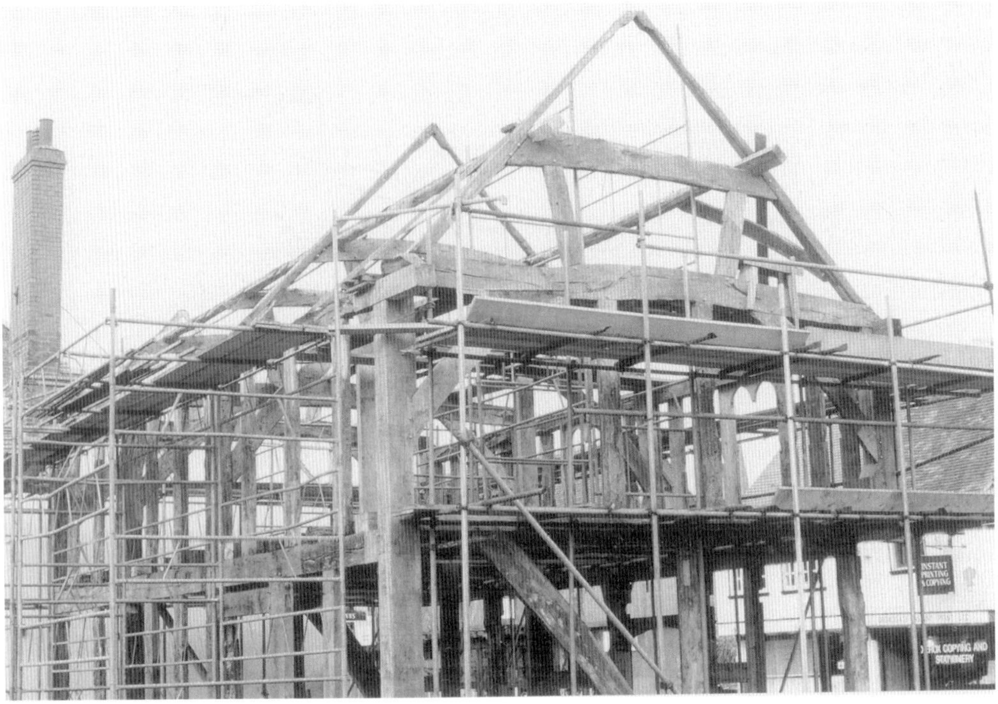

FIG. 2. Timber-framed house from 122/3 Much Park Street being re-erected in Spon Street, January 1982
Photo, R. K. Morris

GROWTH: PEOPLE AND OPPORTUNITIES (1973–2000)

IN 1973 Brian Hobley was succeeded as City Archaeologist by his erstwhile assistant, Margaret Rylatt. She steered the museum's archaeology section through twenty-seven years of sometimes turbulent times, being awarded an MBE on her retirement. Her period in charge saw numerous flagship excavations, such as Broadgate (1974–75), Cox Street (1976–78), Charterhouse (1981 and 1984–87), Derby Lane (1982, 1984), Bayley Lane (1988–89), The Cheylesmore (1991), the Castle Bakehouse (1991) and Cheylesmore Manor (1992) (Fig. 1). Not everything was conventional excavation, however. In 1989 she led a team in the rediscovery of an intact charnel house of 1528–1660 beneath Holy Trinity church, while in 1990 she was pioneering the application of ground-probing radar when considering major excavations in the ruins of St Michael's in search of blocked-up vaults.

In 1977 Margaret published a far-reaching report, in which she set out the sites and priorities which archaeological enquiry in Coventry sought to address through the planning process.[8] It is testimony to her foresight that one of the most recent large-scale excavations, at what is now Belgrade Plaza (Fig. 1), was dug in 2005–07, a full twenty-eight years after she had identified its potential. Coventry's singular place in archaeological research in the west midlands was cemented in 2003 with a stand-alone chapter in a regional framework and agenda.[9]

A second great change during Margaret's tenure was the growth of public archaeology in the mid-1980s, moving out of the periphery of the academic world and into the public imagination. With government funding through the Manpower Services Commission, the interested public, often without any academic background, was able to participate at all levels with training provided on the job. The amount of fieldwork being done in Coventry grew enormously, producing the excavations at Charterhouse, Bayley Lane and a variety of city centre sites. In 1990, the government's new Planning Policy Guidance (PPG16) placed responsibilities for conducting archaeological fieldwork into the planning legislation and archaeology grew once more on the back of a building boom. Margaret now oversaw the difficult change to museum-based fieldwork funded from private monies.

After her retirement, reorganisation in the museum meant that the provision for archaeology changed drastically in 2002. Advice on planning issues, together with the embryonic Historic Environment Record (Coventry's portion of the obsolete West Midlands Sites and Monuments Record) was moved to the city's Planning Department under George Demidowicz, now Head of Archaeology and Conservation, and the post of Planning Archaeologist was created. A separate museum provision with its own curatorial archaeologist remained autonomous. As a result the city ceased to offer fieldwork services, but archaeology emerged with a stronger remit at the heart of planning decisions and with a stand-alone museum ready to face its own new challenges. Today fieldwork is carried out by competing contracting organisations. Archaeologists at Birmingham Archaeology, University of Leicester, Northamptonshire Archaeology and Warwick Museum, amongst others, all bring their own wider experience of urban excavation to bear on the city's archaeological resource in the 21st century.

UNDERSTANDING THE CITY'S ARCHAEOLOGY FROM EXCAVATIONS SINCE 1973

Beginnings

DISCUSSION of the origins of medieval Coventry have been largely dominated by historians who, working largely before the introduction of systematic large-scale excavations, relied upon the authenticity and plausibility of late Saxon accounts. The traditional beginnings of Coventry around a nunnery dedicated to St Osburg have received a disproportionate amount of research, especially given that such a pre-Conquest settlement was soon so utterly smothered by a hugely successful medieval town. The best recent historical assessment of the city's origins is that of Bassett who actively visited contemporary excavations as part of his enquiry and sought out the results of specialist research.[10] Otherwise the results of previous research into these pre-Conquest origins were well summed up by the late Mike Stokes:

> What can be said of this archaeological evidence? All the artefacts of pre-1066 date have been recovered from the discretely-bounded north-west quadrant of the city centre, bounded by the Broadgate/Trinity Street axis in the east, Smithford Way to the south and the River Sherbourne to north and west [Fig. 1]. There are no finds of pre-12th century date from within or even near the later circuit of the castle defences in the High Street area and very few from areas south and east of it, those being confined to residual sherds of pottery from agrarian contexts.[11]

Excavations at St Mary's Cathedral and Benedictine Priory (1999–2003) have continued to bear out his summary and lend weight to Bassett's understanding. Now, the addition of scientific dating to early burials around the fragments of a pre-Conquest stone church beneath the later St Mary's Cathedral attests a Christian presence at the heart of Coventry since *c.* 875.[12]

The post-Conquest town, by contrast, is far better known, although perhaps not better understood. Familiarity with previous fieldwork is no certain guide to the outcomes of future work. The buried medieval remains continue to confound the best-informed predictions in their wealth and variety since areas once covered only by John Shelton now respond to a range of scientific methods not available until the 1970s or later. In places such as Bayley Lane (1988) and Hay Lane (1990), or at St Mary's Cathedral and Priory (1999–2002), the sequence of buried deposits approaches 5m in depth. Study of samples of both seeds and pollens, as at Priory Mill (2001) and Hales Street (2004), is providing a valuable benchmark for the city's medieval riparian environment, the former course of the River Sherbourne being now lost from view in culverts of the 1930s. So, too, are the wetter parts of the city's defensive ditch in the 14th, 15th and 16th centuries, such as at Hill Street to Upper Well Street (Belgrade Plaza, 2005, see Patrick, Fig. 5). Future, positive recognition of the castle ditches should provide similar comparative material for the 12th to 13th century. All are waterlogged and rich, anaerobic environments for the preservation of organic materials.

The Anglo Norman town of the 12th and early 13th centuries was perhaps slow to grow at first. Contemporary elements have been excavated in what is presumed above to be the old, pre-Conquest core, principally the Benedictine Cathedral Priory and the castle.[13] Beyond this tight core of occupation and immediate seigneurial or monastic influence, areas which were later characterised by busy streets, were still the edge of a rural hinterland, where the remains of 12th- and 13th-century ridge-and-furrow cultivation have been excavated.[14]

Cathedral Priory

ST MARY'S Cathedral and Benedictine Priory was the largest and at one time the richest monastic house in Warwickshire. Its temporal influence on Coventry was phenomenal, becoming the largest landowner in the medieval city. The wealth lavished on its buildings resulted in a magnificent cathedral church, begun *c.* 1102 as a Romanesque leviathan and completed in Early English style in the first half of the 13th century.[15] The Phoenix Initiative excavations there (1999–2003), carried out by a partnership of Northamptonshire Archaeology with Coventry's Herbert Art Gallery and Museum, uncovered a rich vein of surviving buildings. These had survived largely due to the awkward terrace of the hillside, preserving the medieval cut-and-fill, always difficult ground which had continued to defy destruction by new development.[16]

The growth of the early cathedral seems to have been inhibited by political events through the 12th century. The Anarchy between Stephen and Matilda saw the incomplete cathedral apparently briefly turned into a siege-castle in 1144. A defensible ditch aligned beneath the later west cloister range and under the site of pier N2 of the Early English north nave arcade, then turning eastwards up the nave, may belong to this ill-conceived act of war (Prelim., Plan A).[17] Resumption was again brought to a halt by the depradations of Bishop Hugh Nonant who ejected the monks in the 1190s and carried out unspecified acts of destruction upon the early conventual buildings.

The excavated nave and aisles comprised a vast space, broken only by the likely locations of tomb-chests and chantry-chapels (Fig. 3). The site of a chapel adjacent to

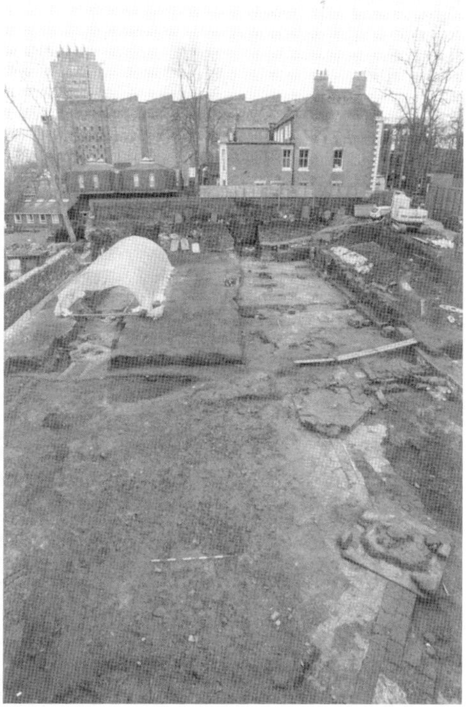

FIG. 3. St Mary's Cathedral Priory: nave under excavation in 2000, looking east. The foundations of south arcade piers S1 and S2 are in the right foreground; scale 2m

Photo, author

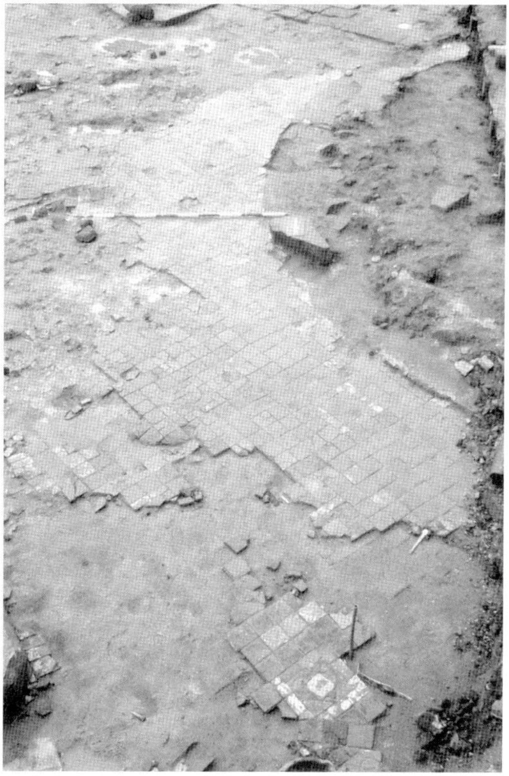

FIG. 4. St Mary's Cathedral Priory: the tiled floor at the west end of the nave

Photo, author, 2000

the south door is attributed to Copston's Chantry, founded in 1299 (Fig. 4).[18] Elements of an early stone-flagged floor were present, as were fragments of large, unwieldy 13th-century ceramic floor tiles. However, most of the nave was dominated by wide open spaces of late 14th-century locally made ceramic tiles. Laid in bands and zones, they were very heavily worn and had lost their once gaudy stamp-impressions long before the cathedral priory was dissolved (Fig. 4). The floor was punctuated by regular lines of tile patches slumping into intra-mural graves, since the nave continued to offer a place of spiritual humility in death, in that the grave was walked over. The choice of cathedral location might generally reflect the continued standing of the family though, in comparison with the Charterhouse, no work has yet been done on early wills to trace the benefactors who sought burial here. A total of ten named family or individual chantries are currently the only guides.[19]

Excavation suggests there were no major structural alterations to the nave and aisles after the 13th century, except for replacement of the original Romanesque south door by a new south porch further west, perhaps before 1299.[20] The new porch involved introducing a flight of stone stairs into the south aisle, of which vestiges remained,

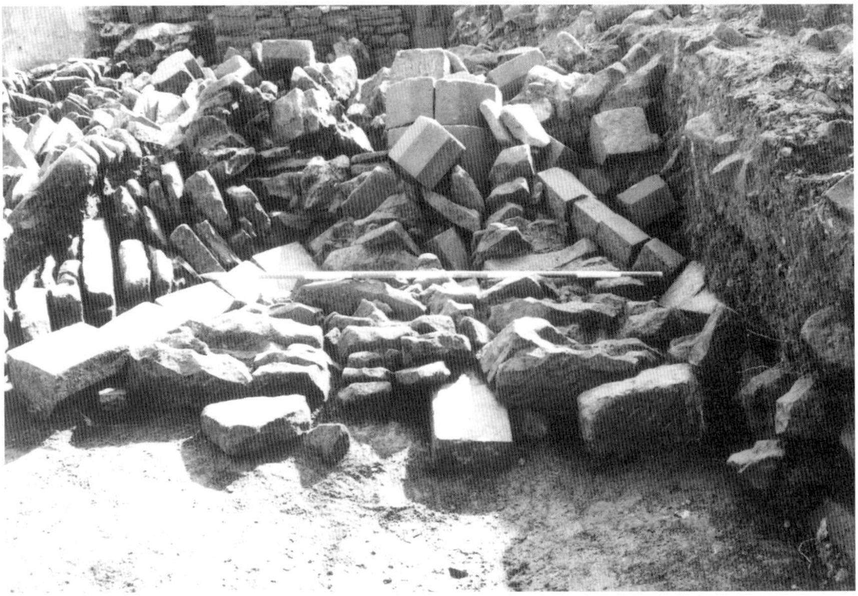

FIG. 5. St Mary's Cathedral Priory: the tumbled vaults of the refectory undercroft. An octagonal pier is visible in the centre: scale 2m

Photo, author, 2000

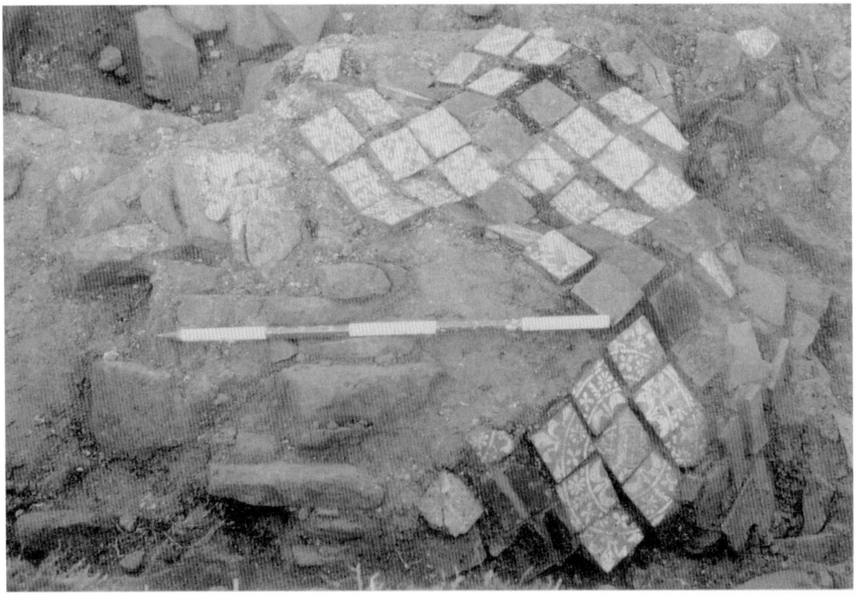

FIG. 6. St Mary's Cathedral Priory: the 14th-century tiled floor of the refectory, as excavated in 2000; scale 1m

Photo, author

apparently added in the 14th century. Practically no remains of the porch survived, except for a telltale spread of recorded finds which charted its former location.

The conventual buildings were equally massive, cut into the terraced hillside north of the church. The west range contained cellars which probably removed all but the merest vestiges of the first phase range, while that to the east comprised a complex of basements, undercrofts and courtyards which have been preserved as 'The Priory Undercrofts' under the new Youell House. The north refectory range also survived only as undercroft, its north wall facing out towards the priory mill. Just outside lay a kitchen garden,[21] while indoors, even the Dissolution had failed to remove traces of the carbonised doors and door-frames between the bays of the tumbled refectory undercroft (Fig. 5). The vaults and ribs which supported the upper floor of the range, including the last tiled floor of the refectory, lay collapsed but across the undercroft (Fig. 6 and Col. Pl. IIB in print edn). The early 16th-century rubbish beneath spoke of a monastic community which existed in solid sufficiency up until the day it was dissolved.

Many questions inevitably remain and in the cut-and-fill of the hillside, there is a distinct lack of the principal ground-floor and upper rooms around the cloister, but for traces of the refectory and the plan of the chapter-house.[22]

The Castle

THE castle of the earl of Chester at Coventry may have been built about 1100, or possibly as early as the 1080s, playing a prominent role during the Anarchy of Stephen and Matilda. Covering the area from Broadgate across Hay Lane to Bayley Lane (Prelim., Plan C), it seems to have been abandoned some time in the later 12th century, probably after the rebellion by Hugh Kevelioc, 5th earl of Chester (1153–81) against Henry II in 1173–74. However, isolated buildings, such as the bakehouse and prison, and possibly the castle chapel (perhaps eventually to become the earl's church of St Michael) continued to be used for their intended purpose for some time.

Excavations which took place on Bayley Lane in 1988 purported to have located one of the bailey ditches,[23] in the backfill of which had been constructed later cellars and deep stone-lined pits. However, the historical record suggests there was a quarry, or 'stoneydelph', at about the same location which might also result in a similar cutting. The evidence here remains equivocal since the excavation only exposed one side of this immense cutting. Castle ditches had first been suggested when the edge of a very large ditch-like feature was uncovered at the edge of the Broadgate excavations in 1974–75. The name Broadgate has always been related to the earl's castle, whose *porta lata* or main 'broad gate' it recalls.[24] The same feature was looked for, unsuccessfully, on the adjacent Derby Lane in 1982–84 (Fig. 1).

In the last quarter of the 19th century, the steeple of St Michael's church had to be underpinned, because it was apparently subsiding into an earlier archaeological cutting. Castle-advocates cried 'ditch', while the more sceptical said 'quarry'. Nearby the best candidate for a castle ditch found so far was in 1990 on the corner of Bayley Lane and Hay Lane ('hay' meaning ditch), only 30m from St Michael's steeple. Beneath a basement on the corner lay the deep, wide profile of a massive ditch (still 9m wide at 3m below the modern ground surface). It contained thick, black organic sediments and rubbish of 13th-century date and its alignment seemed to be along Hay Lane and turning into Bayley Lane, towards St Michael's.

One of the longest-lived elements of the former castle was the bakehouse, which retained its name as 'castelbachous' as late as 1410–11.[25] Corroborating good documentation, this was located in 1990 adjacent to St Mary's Hall.[26] Here a seemingly open-fronted building with 13th-century rubbish-pits stood over a pair of stone bread-ovens set into an earthen floor, each still containing the charred bread-wheats of their last firings (Fig. 7). Subsequently the building over these ovens burnt down, the area littered with pieces of charred timber-frame and strewn with roof-tiles. The structure was rebuilt more substantially, being given a new mortar floor, although its subsequent function may have changed since there were no new ovens within the excavated area.

The tradition that Caesar's Tower in St Mary's Hall was a relic of the castle's fortification seems possible, but unfortunately it is a rebuild after heavy bomb damage in 1940 (Fig. 8). The evidence remains equivocal, but documents suggest a major ditch-line connected with the castle is aligned close to that spot, lying at the rear of former high-status medieval properties along Earl Street. The ground level hereabouts has been lowered by the construction of the Council House during the First World War, but some further important evidence may yet survive towards Hay Lane in one direction or towards St Mary's Street, in proximity to the Bayley Lane excavations of 1988.

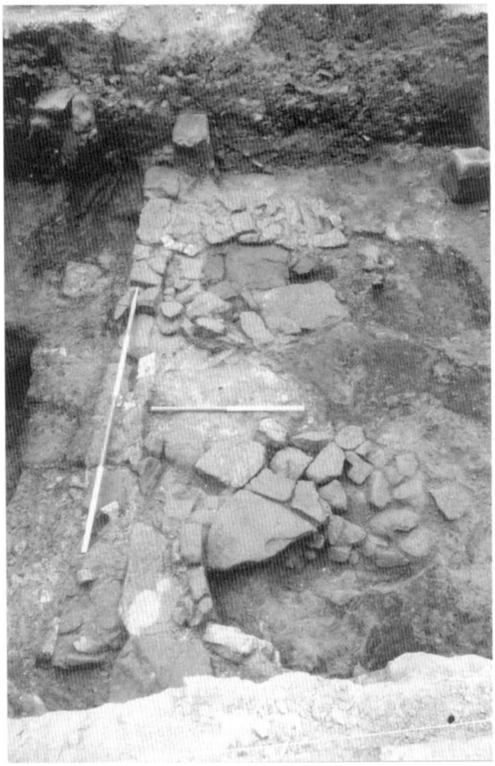

FIG. 7. Coventry Castle: the bakehouse ovens, excavated 1990; scales 1m and 2m

Photo, author

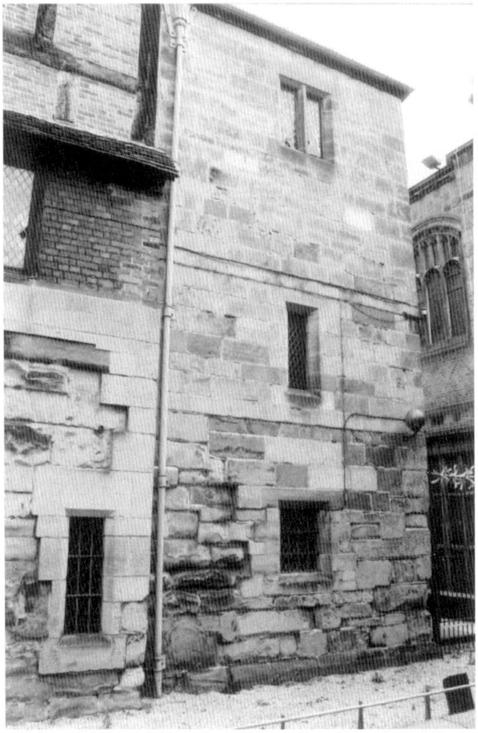

FIG. 8. St Mary's Guildhall, Caesar's Tower, west elevation: possibly part of the castle, but later the guild muniment room

Photo, author

Cheylesmore Manor, seat of Coventry's later lordship

EXCAVATIONS in 1992 laid bare the site of the earl of Chester's manor house at Cheylesmore (Prelim., Plan B).[27] Dated excavated remains indicate that this may have been first built for the 6th earl, Ranulf de Blondeville (1189–1232), probably to replace his father Hugh's defunct castle.[28] It included a fortified hall-house as the south range of a rectangular court, with walls 2.6m thick (on a wider batter) and defensible arrow-loops at ground-floor level. It may have stood as late as the 16th century, but had been compromised by the construction of the town wall in the 1380s.

Much of the manor was rebuilt and expanded by the earl's successors, particularly the de Montalt family and thereafter the crown, to which it devolved in the early 14th century. The east range, originally of relatively flimsy post and interrupted sill-beam construction, was rebuilt as a stately framed building at least 22m long on dwarf ashlar walls; it had a semi-basement, wide flights of stone stairs up to first-floor apartments, with a crown-post roof. This range survived, with many alterations and the addition of a brick skin, until demolished in the 1950s. The 14th-century north

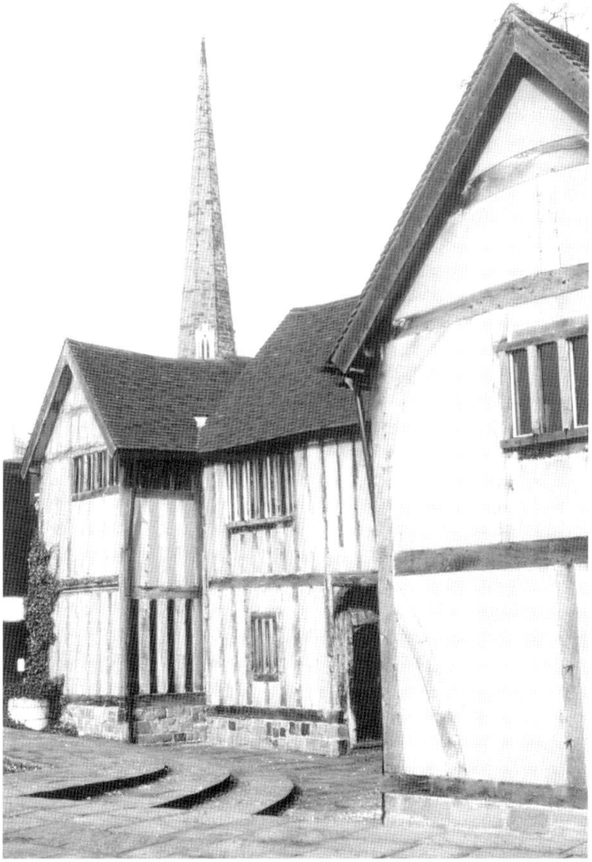

FIG. 9. Former Cheylesmore Manor, north range, now the City Register Office: courtyard elevation, with the spire of the Greyfriars behind

Photo, R. K. Morris, 1982

range of the manor, formerly the gatehouse, is today the city's Register Office (Fig. 9 and Col. Pl. IIA in print edn). Although much restored in the 1960s, it retains something of the manor's former character.

Despite eventually coming within the town walls, the manor remained individually moated and references to the former moat and drawbridge are traceable in documents through the later medieval period. The bridge is still visible in 19th-century drawings, by which time it had been rebuilt and acquired brick side-walls. The moat has never been investigated archaeologically on any side of the manor but is likely to be an organically rich environment.

The manor house remained at the centre of a fine hunting park (Prelim., Plan B), excavations recovering a much wider variety of meat at table than domestic sites in the city, testament to the acquisitive power which true wealth brought with it. Within the park also lay stone quarries and clay pits, rabbit warrens, deer houses, Quinton Mill and the so-called 'pest-houses', used for the quarantine of plague victims. While much of the former area of the park is given over to housing today, and the ring road separates it from the manor, some aspects are still discernible, such as the quarries landscaped in the 19th century into the London Road cemetery.

Growth and the monastic city in the 13th and 14th centuries

IN 1232 the Franciscan friary, or Greyfriars, was founded by the ailing Ranulf, 6th earl of Chester. In terms of its archaeology, it remains largely unexcavated, hampered by its location in a prominent open space with the former monastic cloister and precinct broken up by a sequence of busy main streets surrounding its crossing and spire — the third of Coventry's three surviving spires (Fig. 10).

The 13th century was a time of economic growth and it was in the second half of the century that the city became the main market for innovative pottery from nearby Nuneaton, while its own clays were used in a successful floor-tile industry for over 300 years, exporting all over the midlands. The various products from Nuneaton provide the basic dating sequence in most of the city's medieval excavations. A recent opportunity at Far Gosford Street (2006) to test this against dendrochronology and a plethora of coins, including a hoard of *c.* 1334, has shown just how reliable Coventry's ceramic sequence actually is.[29]

In the same period the Cistercians at Combe Abbey, east of the city, were building a sound economic base and consecrated their church in 1251. Excavations around the cloister in 1991–94 added to 19th-century recording of the church. Extensive internal building recording in 1993 provided further details for the nave and north transept and added a number of other structures around the cloister, although the medieval plan has been smothered by the increments of the post-medieval great house between the 1580s and the 1860s (Fig. 11).[30]

The 14th century was arguably the making of Coventry. From the late 13th century the Warwickshire Hundred Rolls and other documents indicate a massive influx of people from rural areas, who bear the names of their villages of origin. A successful move during the reign of Edward III by a Welsh immigrant, William Walssheman, to transfer cloth purchases for the Royal Wardrobe from London to Coventry, brought a leap in trade. The fame of the city's blue-dyed woollen cloth, sought across the cities of the Hansa, can be traced to this period and excavations have produced dozens of stone moulds for casting metal costume accessories for growing consumption.

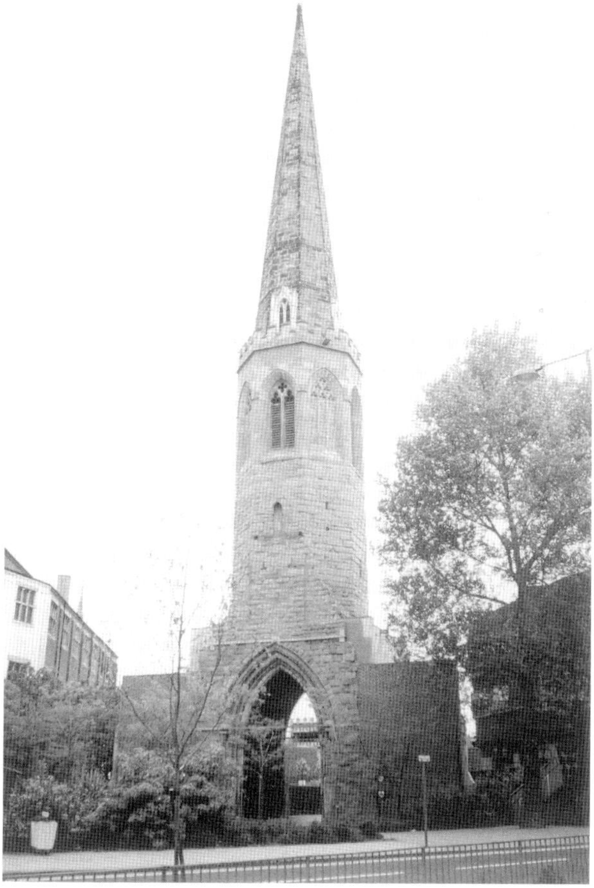

FIG. 10. Greyfriars: the crossing tower and spire, looking east
Photo, R. K. Morris, 1974

The Black Death wreaked havoc in 1349 on the city, with a mortality rate in excess of 50%. Plague returned in the 1360s and again in 1386, the latter in the so-called 'Great Plague of Coventry', related by William of Worcester, whose grandmother was a plague-refugee from the city. Nevertheless, archaeology suggests that progress of existing building projects continued, while new ones were also begun in the plague's aftermath. Stone quarries abound, some visible in documents, such as at the outer end of Hill Street, Primrose Hill (supplying Combe Abbey) and within Cheylesmore Park (supplying Cheylesmore Manor, Whitefriars and the town wall); others found in excavation, such as Bayley Lane (1988) and Whitefriars Street (2004).

Amongst the building projects was the town wall commenced in the 1350s, with a royal licence to crenellate in 1363. A 45m-long early section of the wall foundation and a defensive tower were excavated at The Cheylesmore in 1991 (Fig. 12).[31] Nearby the wall was built to encompass Cheylesmore Manor, at royal request. Evidence showed the steady, measured progress of each construction season, drawing to the winter's break with a stopped end, ready to begin afresh the following year. The wall is often said to have been primarily for show, but the projecting tower excavated here showed

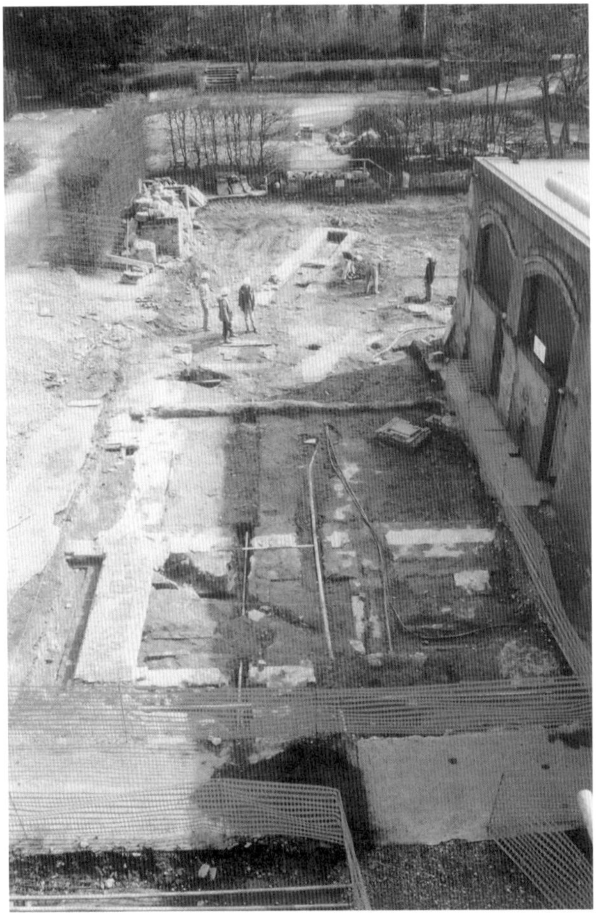

FIG. 11. Combe Abbey, 1993 excavations: the site of the north range (part of the sub-dorter), looking east
Photo, author

straightforward understanding of simple ballistics, its design incorporating rounded inner corners to reinforce the forward projections of the wall. Although the actual wall face in this part of the circuit was almost completely robbed out, nearby around Cheylesmore Manor it was of ashlar of the finest quality, with barely room to fit a trowel into the mortar-gaps after 600 years. While the Cheylesmore section of wall remains arguably the longest part so far excavated,[32] there still lies a 3.6km circuit which retains huge potential for the future.

The excavated street frontage sites of the city show steady occupation throughout the period. At numerous sites excavated since 1970,[33] the pattern is universally one of growth and expansion, in some punctuated by startling periods of setback; each a discernible hiatus in the archaeological record as periods of abandonment, destruction, or simply a sudden absence of finds or a change in their distribution.[34] The introduction of refuse collection in the 16th century tends to lend some confusion to patterns, but it is unclear how much of the city was taken in by this provision at any one time. Goddard's work on documentary sources may add considerably to our understanding of the ebb and flow of the city's economic fortunes.[35]

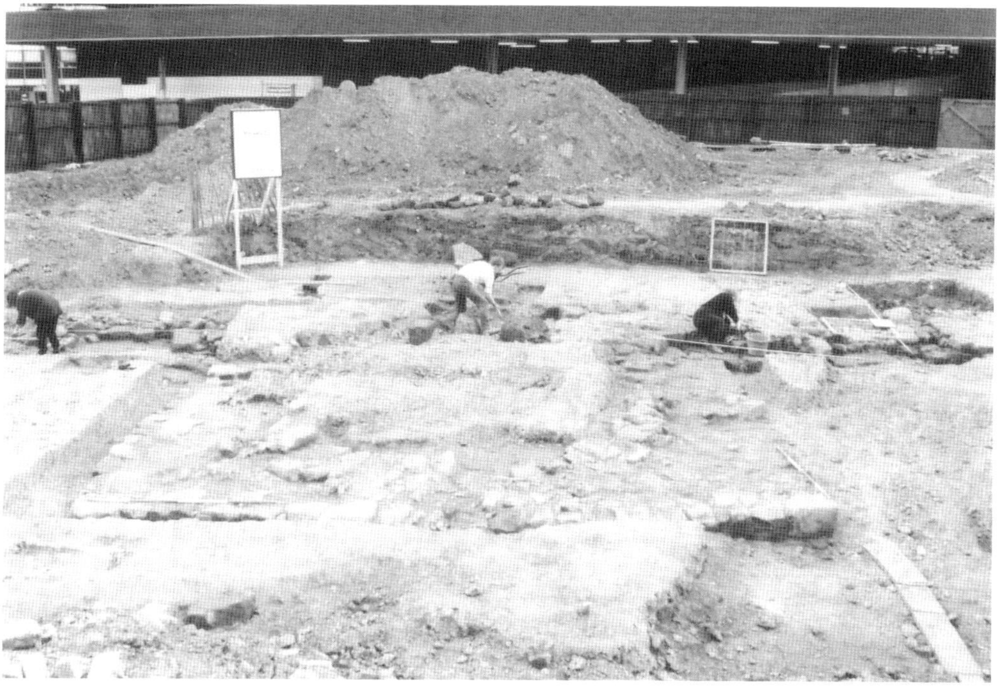

FIG. 12. The Cheylesmore, 1991 excavations: the town wall and an interval tower (centre foreground)
Photo, author

The new 14th-century monastic sites of the city are perhaps the best understood, although numerous surprises still occur. At Whitefriars (Prelim., Plan B), Charmian Woodfield's excavations and recent monograph have demonstrated the excellence of artistic and architectural endeavour which was lavished on the Carmelite house between 1341 and 1538.[36] Excavation was undertaken in the 1960s, with successive additions in the 1970s, all ahead of development and landscaping. How much more extensive would have been our knowledge had it been possible to plan the work without the imminent threat of the inner ring road, on the drawing board as early as 1942 and inevitable by the time of excavation.

At Charterhouse (Prelim., Plan B), home of the last of the monastic orders to arrive in Coventry in 1381, the excavation of a row of four cells in 1981 and the church in 1984–87 is the most widespread excavation of a Carthusian house in England (Fig. 13).[37] The work has drawn favourable comment in national overviews of the order,[38] and it has continued to generate papers in academic journals and monographs.[39] The church, constructed in five phases, was characterised by an apparent lack of foresight as it grew organically within a restricted site and within the strict requirements of the Carthusian Order (Fig. 14). Fifty-five intra-mural burials of benefactors attest its popularity locally, and include priests and minor local gentry, as ever buried beneath floors of locally made stamp-decorated ceramic tiles. The locations have been identified of at least five chantry altars in the nave and a side-chapel, in addition to the high altar.

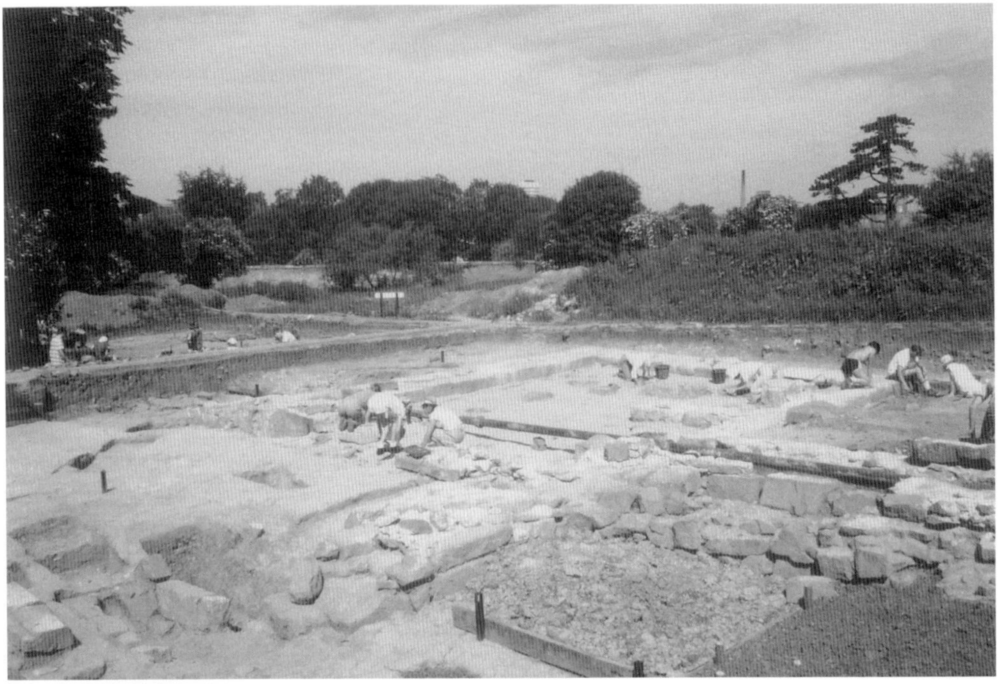

FIG. 13. Charterhouse, 1987 excavations: view north across the church and outer court towards the city centre
Photo, author

The monks' cells were separated around the cloister, in accordance with the Carthusian Rule. Excavation showed, however, that the internal arrangements of the cells and the 'gardens' attached were left much more to the whim of the occupant, such that, while one preferred gardening, another seems to have been engaged in metal-working, while another may have pursued the preparation of manuscripts. Unlike most other charterhouses where water is carefully managed, water-supply may have been haphazard, with no evidence of the individual garderobes and flushing cisterns seen, for instance, at Mount Grace (Yorks.), or the supply from a central source there and at London. Here wells seem to have sufficed, while a communal garderobe was supplied in the outer precinct. While monks were encouraged to eat individually in their cells from food prepared elsewhere by lay brothers, at Coventry more leeway seems to have been allowed — a number of cells producing evidence for both the preparation of food and service at table, rather than just consumption. Two cells retained strong evidence of floorboard-joists on the ground floor, denoting the warmer living-quarters of the monk, as opposed to a tiled lobby.

The excavations so far have been limited to the surrounds of the Great Cloister and recording limited to the standing building of the former refectory. Beyond these there lie large open areas which formed more open outer courts, guest accommodation, kitchens, stables and ancillary structures. The fourteen-acre site, still partly fringed by its original precinct wall, remains a semi-rural haven amidst the urban sprawl and offers great rewards for future investigation.

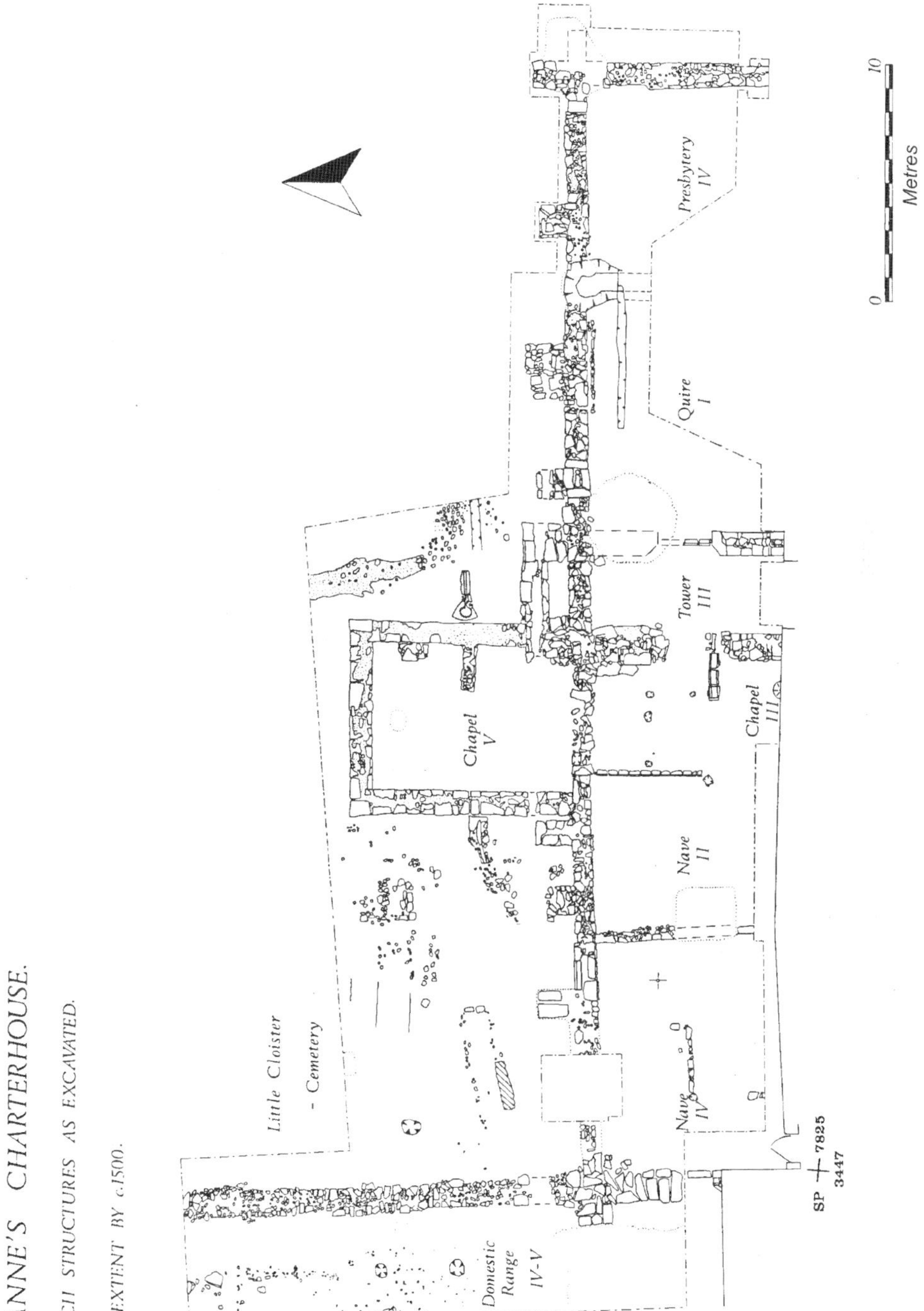

FIG. 14. Charterhouse: plan of St Anne's church, excavated 1984–87
Drawing, author

Decline and the Dissolution

FIFTEENTH-CENTURY economic success gave way to a period of decline, in no small part due to the collapse of Coventry's cloth trade from the 1460s and an ambivalent stance throughout the Wars of the Roses which saw it buy off whoever was in the ascendant, draining its reserves. Exacerbating economic difficulties, plague returned to the city in 1403–04, and in 1467–68 when papal support was secured for an altar to be set up in St Michael's to pray for the suffering city.[40] Again, in 1475, a later document attests 4,500 dead, surely an exaggeration but testament nevertheless to a difficult period in which much property lay vacant.[41] The situation barely recovered in the early 16th century and in 1522 a survey noted 500 empty properties.[42]

It was nevertheless a period of great opportunity and a few wealthy individuals grew even wealthier. During this period the reins of government began to be loosened as the ailing religious trading guilds lost power, while the monasteries became the butt of public cynicism. Benefaction to the monastic houses in the first three decades of the 16th century was piecemeal and funded very little new building. Reformation and the Dissolution, when they came, destroyed the spiritual fabric of the city and changed its medieval skyline forever. Seven stately spires were reduced to three,[43] and it was the one English city which lost its cathedral.

Ironically, the Dissolution has proved a rich vein for archaeologists, since so much fieldwork has been directed to the monastic sites of St Mary's, Whitefriars, Charterhouse and Combe Abbey, both in terms of excavation and building recording. The artefacts recovered attest to a dozen highly organised industries in and around the city, not least the makers of floor tiles in nearby Stoke, glaziers, alabaster carvers, tomb-brass makers,[44] masons and architects. The church-building in Coventry spanned many generations and kept the city at the forefront of masonry construction in the midlands. All the supporting industries ailed in the wake of 1539; some even came to an end. When the city contracted to build a new market cross in 1542, it employed masons from neighbouring counties and specified stone to be robbed from the cathedral priory. So great, however, was the available volume of materials to reuse and a waning demand that the ruins of the monastic sites remained as impromptu quarries for a further century. Coins of the mid-17th century have been found amongst the rubble of the Charterhouse, while documents indicate repairs to the town wall with stone at the Franciscan friary in 1636. At the cathedral priory, the nearby butchers were summonsed in the early 17th century for dumping their waste on the former nave, an area which produced hundreds of sheep bones in the excavations of 1999–2000.

CONCLUSION

COVENTRY remains today a challenging and innovative place to work, now facing a new round of redevelopment to parallel that of the post-war years. For the medieval archaeologist the city holds many more challenges and many more rewards. It must be remembered that the majority of the bombing of Coventry in 1940 was incendiary, leaving the remains below-ground relatively undamaged. Some major sites still have received precious little attention, such as the Greyfriars and the two parish churches of St Michael's and Holy Trinity. Among the city streets the relative medieval wealth of Bishop Street remains untapped, as do a host of other thoroughfares, such as Spon Street, Hill Street, Little Park Street and Smithford Way. More than 90% of the town wall and ditch awaits future excavation and the castle remains a little-understood enigma at the heart of the city.

ACKNOWLEDGEMENTS

Inevitably, my familiarity with the above-mentioned excavations is greatest with those for which I have been responsible in some form or another in the years during which I was employed by Coventry City Council and otherwise for Northamptonshire Archaeology. In my quarter of a century close to Coventry's archaeology, Margaret Rylatt was ever my most stimulating companion, and my gratitude must also be extended to the many who have been my predecessors, successors and companions along the way — in particular John Bateman (1975–78), Mark Redknap (1975–78), Jeff Perry (1982–84), Nick Digby (1989), Ray Wallwork (1988–89), J. Edward Dickinson (1991–95), Myk Flitcroft (1995–96), Paul Thompson (1996–2000), Chris Patrick (2004–present), Paul Mason and Danny McAree (2000–present) and the late, much-missed Mike Stokes (1974–89) who died in 2005. It is to Mike's memory that I dedicate this paper.

NOTES

1. Dugdale, *Warwickshire* (1656, later edns 1730, 1817).
2. Mr Percy's first name is not recorded. The excavations were first mentioned in Dugdale, *Warwickshire* (1817 edn), 327, when work was ongoing. See also T. Sharpe, *Epitome of the County of Warwickshire* (London 1835), 151; Revd Blythe, *History of Stoke* (1897), 5, who also made detailed notes (6, 286) of other remains then known there.
3. A neat archaeological trench was relocated during works on a cell garden in 1986. It was presumed to be the work of Wyley since it bore no relation to fully documented work in 1968, 1973 or 1980–87. Wyley died in 1941. Although his legacy was initially secured, his house contents were later auctioned off and records of his antiquarian interests largely lost.
4. M. Rylatt and A. F. Adams, *A Harvest of History: the life and work of J. B. Shelton MBE* (Coventry n.d., *c.* 1983; 2nd edn, Rylatt and M. Montes 1998). John Shelton published idiosyncratic notes on his pre-war work in *Austins Monthly Magazine* 25–31 (Nov. 1932–June 1939). However, his wartime and post-war work was not similarly summarised.
5. Hobley, 'Cathedral Excavations'; ibid., 'A Neronian-Vespasianic military site at "The Lunt", Baginton, Warwickshire: first interim report', *TBWAS* 83 (1969), 65–129; ibid., 'Second interim report', *TBWAS* 85 (1973), 7–92; ibid., 'Final report', *TBWAS* 87 (1975), 1–56.
6. A note on the excavation appeared as an Appendix in E. Gooder, *Coventry's Town Wall*, Coventry and North Warwickshire History Pamphlet, 4 (2nd edn 1971).
7. See Harris ed., *Dr Troughton's Sketches*, pls XIX–XXXIX.
8. M. Rylatt, *City of Coventry: Archaeology and Redevelopment* (Coventry Museums 1977, 2nd edn 1981).
9. www.iaa.bham/research/fieldwork_research_themes/projects/wmrrfa/sem5.htm.
10. Bassett, *Anglo-Saxon Coventry*.
11. M. A. Stokes, 'Cofa's Tree: development of Coventry's Anglo-Norman townscape reviewed', in *True as Coventry Blue: papers presented to Margaret Rylatt*, ed. I. Soden (Northants County Council 2000), 62.
12. Rylatt and Mason, *Cathedral Priory*, 12–15.
13. Bayley Lane's possible bailey ditch (1988–89), and the castle bakehouse and probable motte ditch (1989–90). See I. Soden, 'Excavations behind Hay Lane 1989–90' (unpublished report, Coventry Museums, 1990); CBA *WM Archaeology* 32 (1989), 95–6; 33 (1990), 94–5.
14. On Much Park Street, 114–15 Gosford Street and beneath Cheylesmore Manor.
15. See further Soden, *Hidden History*, ch. 3; and Plant, this volume.
16. Rylatt and Mason, *Cathedral Priory*, 8, 35–44.
17. Ibid., 16–19.
18. The traditional foundation date of Copston's Chantry is 1291 and its dedication is given as St Clement in Dugdale, *Warwickshire* (1730), I, 165; he also gives its location *iuxta porticum ecclesiae*. The earliest mention I have found is 18 July 1299 in *The Register of Walter Langton: I, 1296–1321*, ed. J. B. Hughes (Canterbury and York Society 2001), 100, which also records the location. It is mentioned again in 1313; ibid., 649. Although Hobley, 'Cathedral Excavations', pl. 9a, published a piscina from the floor here, in 2000 the archaeological remains hereabouts were very damaged. If the Copston/St Clement's association is correct, this

is not surprising as the functions of the chantry (and presumably the altar, tombs, etc.) were moved at the Dissolution to nearby St Michael's Church.

19. Named as Leicester's, Copstone's, Poley's, Blaby's, Brewoode's, Wedon's, Preest's, Wentbridge's, Shirland's and Marshall's in Dugdale, *Warwickshire* (1730), 164–5, and ibid., *Monasticon Anglicanum* (London, 1817–30 edn), III, 186–8. See also N. W. Alcock, 'The Catesbys in Coventry: a medieval estate and its archives', *Midland History* 15 (1990), 13, 17.

20. For the mullions reused in the steps, see Morris, 'The Worked Stones', in Rylatt and Mason, *Cathedral Church*, 22.

21. Evidence of the kitchen garden comes from the buried cultivation soils in the angle of the north cloister range and the kitchen. A simple stone bench rested against the north wall where pottery sherds were all just pre-Dissolution; I. Soden, 'Excavations in the frater undercroft, St Mary's Benedictine Priory, Coventry, March-April 2000' (unpublished report, Northamptonshire Archaeology, Oct. 2000), 7, figs 2–3.

22. See further Morris, 'Priory', this volume, 82–92.

23. No excavation report was completed. The castle ditch identification is that of the excavators at the time; the evidence remains equivocal.

24. For *Porta lata*, see N. W. Alcock, 'Documentary records', in *Excavations at Broadgate East, Coventry, 1974–5*, ed. M. Rylatt and M. A. Stokes (Coventry Museums Monograph, 5, 1996) 1, 8.

25. TNA, Coventry Priory Register, E164/21, 31.5.

26. Soden, 'Hay Lane' (as n. 13).

27. CBA *WM Archaeology* 35 (1992), 67–9; also M. Rylatt, I. Soden and J. E. Dickinson, 'Excavations on Manor House Drive, Coventry 1992, SP 333786' (unpublished report, Coventry Museums 1992).

28. I. Soden, *Ranulf de Blondeville: the first English Hero* (Cirencester 2009).

29. P. Mason and I. Soden, 'Excavations at the Astleys site, Far Gosford Street, Coventry 2006' (unpublished report, Northamptonshire Archaeology, 2008); for publication in P. Mason, D. McAree and I. Soden, *Coventry's Medieval Suburbs* (Northamptonshire Archaeology monograph, in preparation).

30. I. Soden, 'Building analysis at Coombe Abbey, Warwickshire 1993–94', *Post-Medieval Archaeology* 40/1 (2006), 129–59; and Rodwell, this volume.

31. CBA *WM Archaeology* 35 (1992), 67–9.

32. A similar length excavated at Godiva Street in 1970 remains unpublished.

33. Much Park Street (1970–74), Broadgate (1974–75), Derby Lane (1982–84), through many small interventions such as 114–15 Gosford Street (1987) and more recently at Hill Street (Bond's Hospital, 2003; Belgrade Plaza, 2005–07) and Far Gosford Street (2006).

34. For example, the destruction of houses to create the town's defences. Such destructions are recorded for Hill Street in 1403, TNA, Cartulary of St Mary's Priory 1410–11, E164/21, 128.1; this reference is courtesy of Professor Peter Coss, who is preparing a new edition of the Cartulary. Recent excavations confirm the extent of damage there, for which see P. Mason, D. McAree and I. Soden, 'Excavations at Belgrade Plaza 2005–7' (unpublished report, Northamptonshire Archaeology, 2008), for publication in Mason, McAree and Soden, *Coventry's medieval suburbs* (in preparation).

35. See further Goddard, this volume.

36. Woodfield, *Whitefriars*.

37. Soden, *Charterhouse*.

38. G. Coppack and M. Aston, *Christ's Poor Men: the Carthusians in England* (Stroud 2002).

39. I. Soden, 'The propaganda of monastic benefaction: statement and implication in the art of St Anne's Charterhouse, Coventry', in *Meaningful Architecture: Social Interpretations of Buildings*, ed. M. Locock (Aldershot 1994), 147–66; id., 'The planning and development of a Carthusian church — the example of St Anne's Charterhouse, Coventry', in *Monastic Archaeology*, ed. G. Keevill, M. Aston and T. Hall (Oxford 2001), 161–4; id., 'The conversion of former monastic buildings to secular use: the case of Coventry', in *The Archaeology of Reformation 1480–1580*, ed. D. Gaimster and R. Gilchrist (Leeds 2003), 280–9.

40. *Cal. Papal Reg.*, XII (London 1933), 644.

41. CA, PA 201/1; see also Goddard, this volume, 42–4.

42. M. Hulton, *Coventry and its people in the 1520s*, Dugdale Society (Oxford 1995).

43. The three surviving spires belong to St Michael's, Holy Trinity and the Greyfriars. A putative three were lost from the cathedral, and another from the central tower at the Whitefriars.

44. For alabaster working, see VCH *Warwickshire*, VIII (1969), 151–7 and n. 130; E. M. Carus-Wilson, *Overseas Trade of Bristol in the later Middle Ages* (Bristol Record Society, 1937), 41. For brass-makers, S. Badham, 'Evidence for the Minor Funerary Monument Industry 1100–1500', in *Town and Country in the Middle Ages: contrasts, contacts and interconnections 1100–1500*, ed. K. Giles and C. Dyer (Leeds 2005), 170, 189 and n. 23; R. Hutchinson, 'Tombs of Brass are Spent: Reformation Reuse of Monumental Brasses', in *Archaeology of Reformation*, ed. Gaimster and Gilchrist, 456–7, 466–7.

Recent Archaeological Work in Medieval Coventry and Future Opportunities

CHRIS PATRICK

The redevelopment of large areas of Coventry's historic city centre since 2004 has resulted in a series of major developer-funded archaeological investigations being carried out as a condition of planning consent. This paper will review some of the findings made during this recent fieldwork, and will also consider the priorities and opportunities for future research into the city's archaeology.

SINCE the 1950s, the city of Coventry has been the subject of over 300 archaeological investigations ranging from watching briefs to major open area excavations. The majority of these investigations have focused on the medieval city centre, so that in 2008 approximately 2.5 per cent of the 72 hectares (178 acres) of land lying within the medieval walls has been the subject of some degree of investigation. A vast body of information on the city was built up almost solely due to the efforts of staff at the Herbert Art Gallery and Museum and local volunteers, but in the last ten years the work has increasingly become the territory of archaeological contractors employed by developers to fulfil the obligations of their planning permission.

Funding archaeology through the planning system certainly has it advantages. Developers are now required to employ archaeologists to record archaeological remains before they are destroyed with provision for adequate time and money to do so. However, it does lead to a certain degree of bias in the data, as the sites chosen for excavation will depend on the developer's proposal. As a result, archaeology is governed by availability of development sites rather than research priorities, but when they coincide they offer excellent opportunities to discover more about the city. Parts such as Bayley Lane and Hill Street are now reasonably well understood due to recent work, but on the other hand many large areas of the city have received little or no archaeological investigation. These include major streets such as Smithford Street (Shopping Precinct) and areas to the north of the River Sherbourne near Bishop Street (Prelim., Plan B).

The archaeology of other areas of the city, such as Broadgate and Butcher Row, are now considered to have been lost forever due to extensive basement building in the 1930s and 1950s, whilst the origins and development of Holy Trinity Church and St Michael's are only likely to be resolved by targeted research excavations.

Where it does survive, with the exception of the areas close to the river, Coventry's archaeology tends to be relatively shallow without the deep stratigraphy that characterises other medieval cities. The character of the city's archaeological deposits is derived partly from the city's rapid growth from the 12th century onwards, and partly due to the uneven nature of the city's post-medieval development. Across large areas of the city, buildings from the 15th and 16th centuries survived into the early 20th century, to be eventually removed by either the remodelling of the city centre in the 1930s, the German air raids of the Second World War or the radical replanning of the 1950s and 1960s. The rebuilding of the Georgian and Victorian periods that can be seen in other cities did not take place to the same extent in Coventry, with the result that sandstone and timber-framed structures were often replaced by reinforced concrete with no intermediate phase. The redevelopment of the post-war period and the partial abandonment of the city's historic street pattern mean that many lengths of medieval street now lie under areas of landscaped civic gardens surrounding council office blocks or under car parks. The latter are often little more than sites damaged in wartime that have been tarmacked over. Many of these now provide prime development opportunities: with the archaeological deposits frequently lying just below the tarmac, preservation of these remains *in situ* is often problematic and mitigating the impact of these developments frequently results in their full excavation.

By contrast, deeply buried deposits do exist along the valley of the River Sherbourne, which has long been recognised as having considerable archaeological potential. The area between The Burges and the Priory Mill, where the River Sherbourne meets the Radford Brook, is an area of immense interest due to it being a waterlogged dumping ground for rubbish from the medieval city (see map, Soden, Fig. 1). This was sealed by 3m of reclamation deposits dumped in the 1840s to create Hales Street. The Coventry antiquarian J. B. Shelton first highlighted the potential of the area in the 1930s: he collected a large quantity of artefacts that would become the core of the Herbert's archaeology collection, whilst observing the construction of the river culvert.[1] In 2005 Worcestershire Archaeology Service undertook an evaluation of a site on Hales Street ahead of the construction of an extension to the Coventry Transport Museum,[2] with the intention of using pollen and plant remains to ascertain changes in the landscape. The anticipated depth of the deposits and the restricted space available meant the site was evaluated using coring rather than conventional trenches. The carbon-14 dating of fragments of wood taken from the base of the core gave a mean calibrated date of 985. Pollen taken from this 10th-century deposit showed an occupied rural landscape of grassy meadowland, with oak and birch woodland on the surrounding slopes above and cereal cultivation in nearby fields. The dating was broadly contemporary with the late Saxon burials and structures found in the earliest phases of St Mary's Priory excavations,[3] and would seem to corroborate the theory that settlement was centred on the Hill Top area and surrounded by farmland. The presence of dumped rubbish and changes in the pollen profile suggest that the urban area had expanded down the hill into the Hales Street area from the 12th century onwards. The evaluation at both Hales Street and, adjacent to the Sherbourne, at Far Gosford Street have consistently demonstrated an accumulation of alluvial deposits in the river valley from around 1000.[4] This may be because of the building of water mills obstructing the flow of the Sherbourne at a time when more land upstream of Coventry was being brought into cultivation with the resultant wash-off of soils.

There have been no pre-Conquest discoveries since the late Saxon skeletons at the priory in 1999, but an interesting development was the discovery of a Romano-British ditch and artefacts at Priory Street in 2006.[5] The ditch was filled with orangey-red sandy silt that was barely discernable from the natural geology. The finds are significant in two ways; first, in demonstrating a low level of Roman period occupation in what became the city centre and, secondly, in showing that remains from Coventry's earliest periods may not be as obvious as the later medieval remains and so could be easily missed in a narrow evaluation trial trench.

The excavations at Priory Street and the adjoining site at Bayley Lane were undertaken by Birmingham Archaeology between 2004 and 2006 and have provided a valuable insight into the development of this area of the city.[6] The earliest phases of occupation consisted of the post-holes of a relatively short-lived, but substantial, wooden building dating to the 12th century, followed by its disappearance in the early 13th century and the accumulation of a cultivation soil across the site. These phases are interpreted as corresponding with the construction and abandonment of the earl of Chester's castle and suggest that the Bayley Lane area was a neglected and marginal part of the city prior to it being redeveloped and divided into plots in the late 13th century. An artefact of particular interest was a bone chess piece, which came from a pit of this reoccupation phase (Fig. 1 and Col. Pl. IIIA in print edn). The chess piece is cylindrical and 50mm tall with an inverted V-shape incised on the front representing a throne, all suggesting that the piece was a king or a queen, whilst on the rear it is decorated with an incised ring-and-dot motif. The finding of the chess piece in what appears to have been a relatively humble neighbourhood is perhaps surprising and it may be that the piece is residual, dating from the higher-status 12th-century activities associated with the castle. The late 14th century and the early 15th century witnessed a major phase of construction as a series of substantial buildings, including some with stone undercrofts, were erected close to the Bayley Lane frontage (Fig. 2). Some of the buildings may have been set back from the street frontage in a similar arrangement to that of the Stone House on Much Park Street.[7] The building of fine stone houses and undercrofts is apparent elsewhere in the city in this period and it seems to be coincident with the boom period of church building that was also taking place, as Coventry's merchant class spent their wealth in a time of economic optimism.[8]

In March 2008, further substantial stone buildings of the 14th and 15th centuries were excavated to the rear of the Drapers' Hall in Bayley Lane by Birmingham Archaeology. [9] Of particular interest were substantial 14th century foundations that appeared to be subsiding into a large feature immediately to the south, and which has been interpreted as the ditch of the earl's castle. Access and depth precluded further

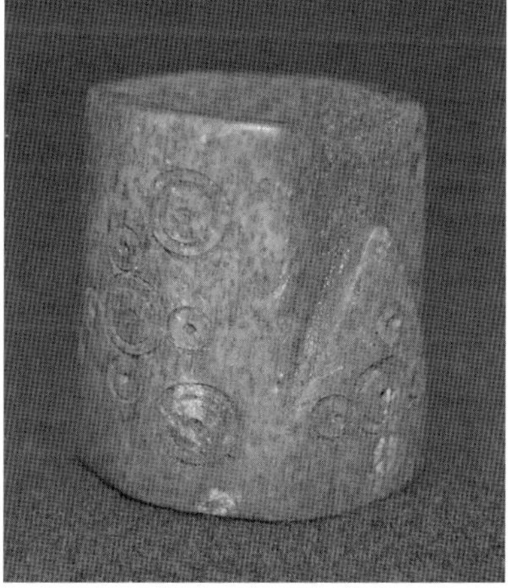

FIG. 1. Chess piece from the Bayley Lane excavation (2006), possibly 12th-century; Herbert Art Gallery, Coventry
Photo, P. Thompson

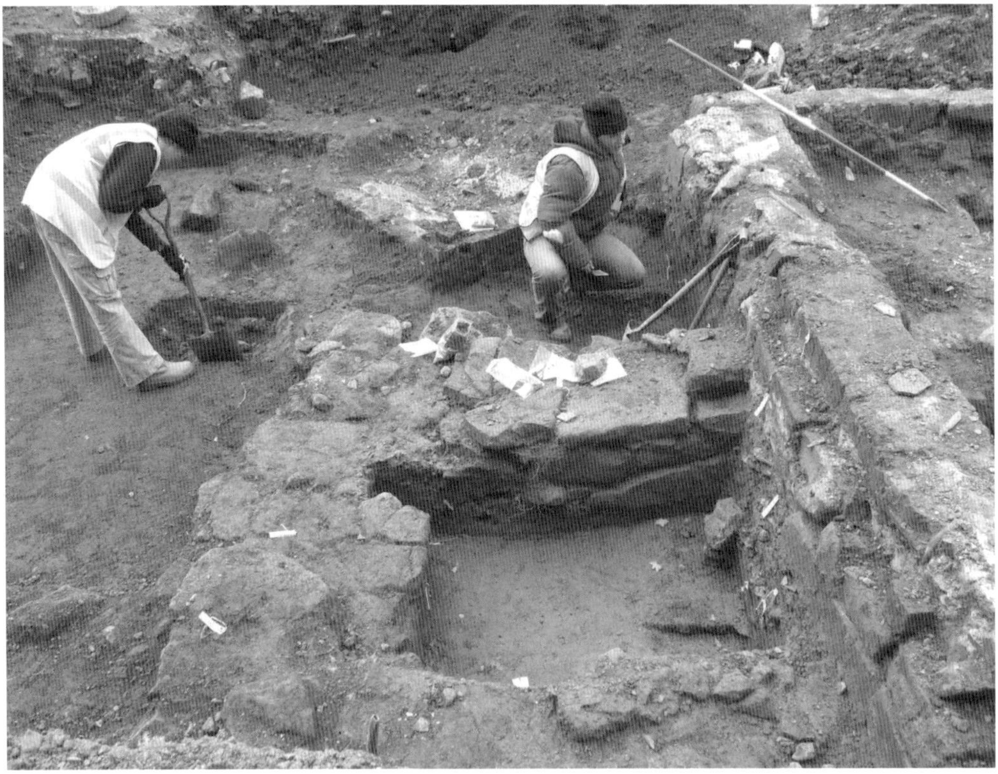

FIG. 2. Excavation of late 14th- or early 15th-century house foundations in Bayley Lane, Coventry (2006)
Photo, author

excavation, but the use of an auger showed the feature to be at least 4m deep with a clay lining and to contain dark brown peat, suggestive of a body of standing water like a moat. The position of the feature, in relation to the postulated ditch found in the 1988–89 Bayley Lane excavation,[10] suggests a large linear feature turning north from Earls Street and continuing towards the east end of St Michael's, a proposition that is supported by archaeological observation, borehole evidence and structural defects on local buildings. It has been debated whether the feature found in 1988–89 was the castle ditch or simply a quarry as suggested by the plot name Stoneydelph, or even both.[11] The opportunities to investigate the castle further will always be limited in the Bayley Lane and Hill Top area due to the fortunate existence of several major listed buildings: instead, we may be dependent on advances in remote sensing techniques, such as ground probing radar, before the location and extent of the elusive 12th-century castle can be confidently mapped.

In recent years several extensive investigations have taken place in Coventry's medieval suburbs. Excavations by Northamptonshire Archaeology in Far Gosford Street between May and July 2006 revealed a well-preserved sequence of street frontages dating between the 14th and 19th centuries.[12] The medieval reclamation of this wet, riverside site, located between the River Sherbourne and the Springfield Brook, resulted in the ground levels being repeatedly raised to avoid flood events, so that each episode of dumping sealed the previous occupation phase. The earliest excavated evidence from the site was a large timber post, dated by dendrochronology to 1162–1212. The post could have been part of the bridge that was first documented here in the 1260s, which had succeeded the earlier 'Goose' ford. By the early 14th century the ground level had been raised to create a causeway across the wetland, and the street frontage was lined with homes and workshops. The sandstone plinths and beaten earth floors of these early structures were found by the excavation (Fig. 3). Found buried in the floor of one of these houses was a cylindrical wooden receptacle containing thirty-eight silver coins. The coins were principally long cross pennies from the reigns of Edward I and Edward II, but the inclusion of a single coin from early in the reign of Edward III showed the frontage was occupied by housing from at least the 1330s.

A variety of craft and industrial activities appear to have taken place on the site in the 13th and 14th centuries including smelting and smithing, along with bone and horn working. Soil samples taken from pit fills and occupation layers found pollen and plant remains indicating that textile manufacture was also taking place on site. The presence of flax pollen and capsule fragments indicate that the plant was being locally cultivated and processed into fibres on, or near, the site. Hemp also appears to have been processed on site in the 14th and 15th centuries and many of the wood-lined pits found behind the frontage may have been used for retting. Evidence for dyeing came from a pit close to the riverside, which was found to contain seeds of weld or dyer's rocket, which was often used to produce a bright yellow dye. The textile trade is often invisible from Coventry's archaeological record and the Far Gosford Street excavations demonstrate how information derived from pollen and plant macrofossils can play an important role in revealing it and interpreting the functions of otherwise ubiquitous medieval pits.

The street frontage underwent a major phase of rebuilding in the early 15th century; fitting in with the pattern of rebuilding that was also seen at this time in the Bayley Lane area. The rebuilding in this location, however, may owe more to the engineering works associated with the arrival of the town wall in the 1430s. Replacement frontage buildings appear to have remained until 1643 when they were cleared in preparation for the reinforcement of the city's defences during the Civil War.

The excavations at Far Gosford Street demonstrated the archaeological potential of sites where historic streets cross a river valley and where material has been imported to raise the ground level, sealing earlier phases (Fig. 4). Sites similar to Far Gosford Street that potentially exist elsewhere in the city, include Fleet Street, The Burges and Cox Street.

Further riverside industrial activity was found up stream of Far Gosford Street at Birmingham Archaeology's excavations at Lower Ford Street in 2005.[13] The excavation showed 13th-century expansion into a peripheral area of the city previously thought to be unoccupied. Like Far Gosford Street, the site seemed to show an investment in infrastructure with the construction of flood defence banks. These may have provided protection from the river, for what appears to be horse knackering and tanning activities, before the area was abandoned in the mid-13th century.

Other suburbs have been investigated on the north-west side of the city at Upper Well Street by Birmingham Archaeology,[14] and Hill Street by Northamptonshire Archaeology,[15] making this one of the better understood areas of the city. Both suburbs

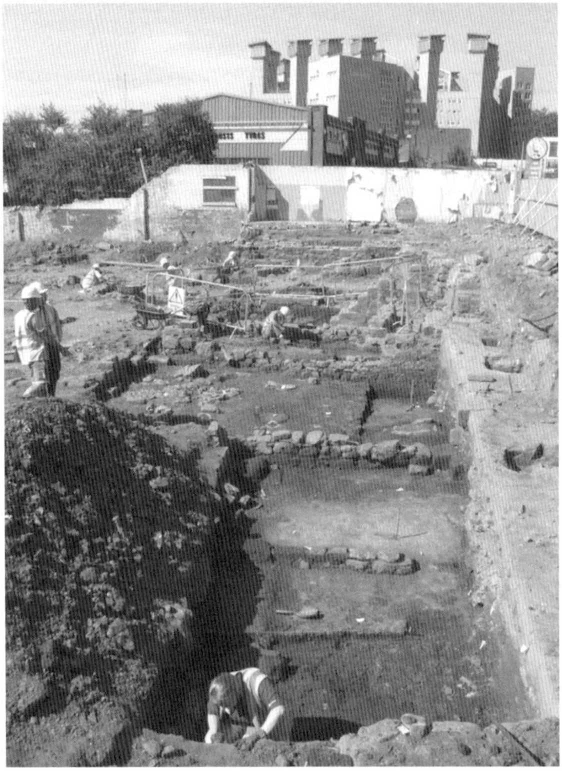

FIG. 3. Excavation of the early 15th-century street frontage at Far Gosford Street, Coventry (2006)

Photo, author

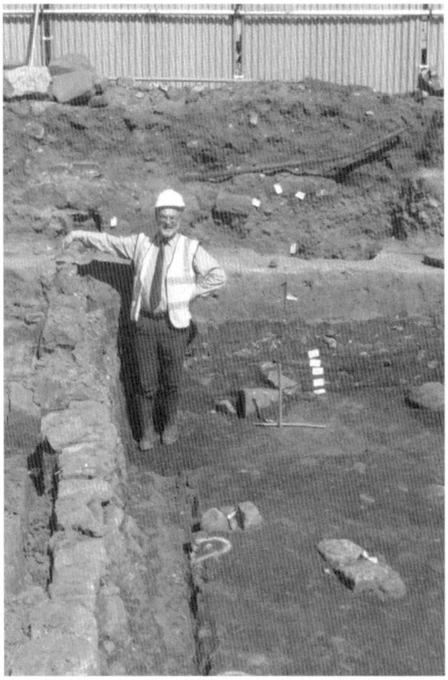

FIG. 4. George Demidowicz standing on the floor of an early 15th-century house at Far Gosford Street, Coventry, during the 2006 excavations, showing the raising of the street level and the fossilisation of medieval property boundaries

Photo, author

appear to have been laid out in the 13th century, and seem to have been dominated by leather-working industries throughout the medieval period.

As well as examining the nature of the suburb, the Hill Street excavations also allowed one of the most extensive excavations of the town's defences, with the exposure of a 50m length of the 15th-century town ditch, running parallel with Bond Street (Fig. 5 and Col. Pl. IB in print edn). An almost complete profile of the ditch was exposed in three sections, showing this major feature to have been at least 12m wide and approximately 3m deep; with the town wall buried below the adjacent Bond Street.[16] Clearly, the defensive ditch was not regularly maintained, and the presence of capping stones from the demolition of the wall in the upper fills indicates that the ditch was almost entirely backfilled by the late 17th century. Lack of cleaning provided a rich source of evidence for the late medieval suburb: most notably a collection of at least 120 leather shoes, mostly dating from the 15th century, and which was interpreted as representing the waste from a cobbler's workshop. The town ditch would have been present for much of the 3.5km (2.17 miles) length of Coventry's defensive circuit, but only a tiny fraction of it has so far been sampled. The ditch is likely to contain a wide range of artefactual and ecofactual material, and further investigation of the circuit

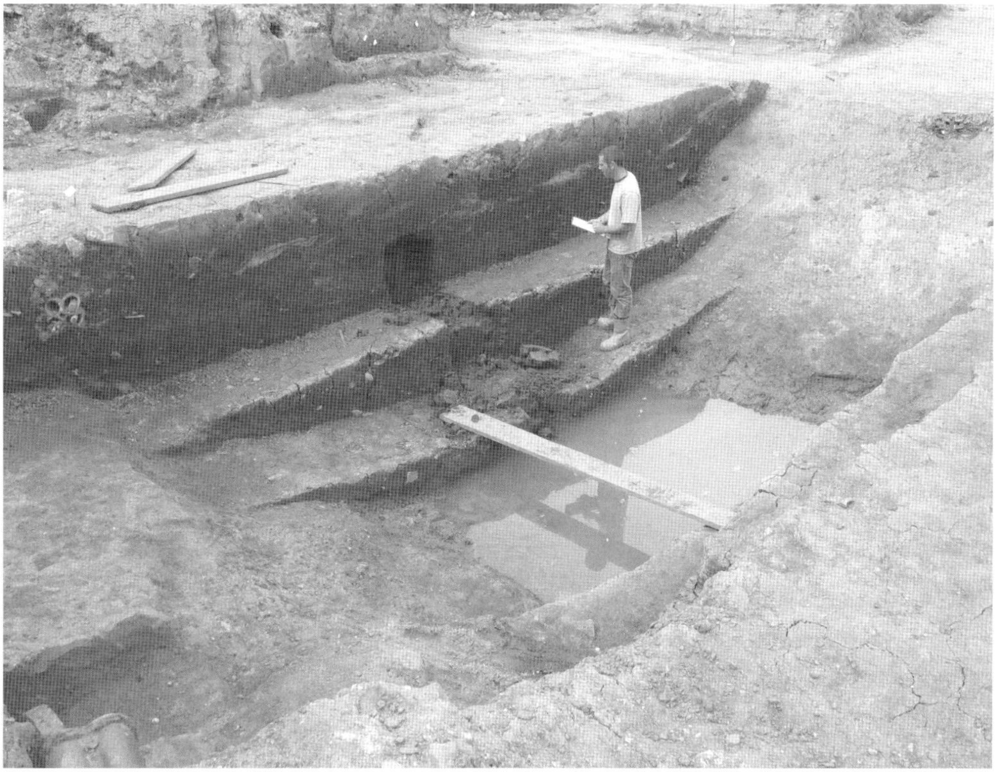

FIG. 5. Recording a section across the Coventry town ditch during the Hill Street excavation (2005)
Photo, author

should provide a wealth of information on the environment and activities taking place in different parts of the late medieval city.

Evidence for an earlier defensive circuit, as suggested by the excavations at Upper Well Street in 1960,[17] remains speculative, but a substantial 14th-century ditch, measuring 5.5m wide and 1.75m deep, was found on the western side of Hill Street in an investigation by Warwickshire Museums Field Archaeology Service at Bond's Hospital.[18] However, at present it is hard to see these isolated lengths of ditch as forming a single defensive circuit for the northern part of the town.

Unsurprisingly, much of the archaeological investigation which has been carried out in Coventry has been directed at the city's religious houses. The thorough investigation and publication of St Mary's Priory and the Whitefriars has revolutionised our understanding of their layout and development, while the Greyfriars by comparison, still awaits attention. This may come its way with the next round of city centre remodelling. However, where development-led investigation is not forthcoming other opportunities must be grasped, which can often make substantial contributions to the understanding of even well-investigated sites. An example is the trial pit that was excavated by the City Council's Conservation and Archaeology Team at 7 Priory Row in 2004.[19]

Repair work to the listed building involved the temporary removal of the floor in a rear ground-floor room. This room coincided with the assumed position of the priory's eighth pier in the nave south arcade (pier S8, see Prelim., Plan A), and an opportunity was presented to locate this pier by excavation. The room was built as an extension to the building in 1909 and the local newspaper had reported the discovery of medieval fabric at the time.[20]

Based on the locations of the surrounding piers, as discovered during the Phoenix Initiative excavations of 1999–2000, a test pit was opened in September 2004 and was positioned to locate pier S8 (Fig. 6). Demolition deposits from the cathedral consisting of densely packed pink-orange coloured mortar and sandstone were found 0.5m below ground level, with the top of the pier located a further 0.4m deeper.

The trench coincided with the south-east quadrant of the pier, which had been built with an ashlar facing and a rubble and mortar core. Attached to the eastern side of the pier was part of a drum, that probably originally stretched across the whole of the eastern side; a half-round shaft was centred on its southern side (Fig. 7). The drum would have supported the arch that connected eastwards with the larger south-west pier of the central crossing. Although it was only possible to dig 0.4m down the southern side of the pier, this was enough to show that the stone still retained traces of limewash that had covered the cathedral's interior. The equivalent pier of the north arcade (pier N8), which was found during the 1999–2000 excavations, was also Romanesque (Prelim., Plan A); the pier had only been seen on its north-west side and displayed an entirely different arrangement of shafts linking westwards to pier N7 (see Plant, Fig. 2).[21] Directly attached to the drum of pier S8 was a masonry structure running eastwards, which may have been part of the screen that separated the aisle from the choir; none of the facing stonework had survived and only the rubble and mortar core work remained.

The investigation suggests that areas of the eastern end of the nave, the crossing and the western half of the chancel may survive in a good state of preservation beneath the houses and gardens of the properties facing on to Priory Row. This is significant, as the majority of the nave, which was exposed in the 1999–2000 excavations, had been damaged by grave digging when the area was used as a cemetery in the 18th and 19th centuries. It is possible that pier S8 still stands as much as 3m high on the floor of the cathedral. Cellars located below the Priory Row properties will have caused extensive damage, but a burial in a stone coffin which was found to the east during the replacement of the cellar floor of number 10 Priory Row in 1987 has shown that even denuded areas of the cathedral are still of archaeological potential.[22]

The majority of the recent archaeological work has concentrated on the city centre, but much work still remains to be carried out in the surrounding modern suburbs. Coventry was Britain's fastest growing city in the inter-war period and vast areas of countryside rapidly disappeared under the motor factories or streets of semi-detached housing which still characterise much of the city. Today, former village centres and monastic granges lie in the gardens of these houses and are unlikely to be investigated as a result of the development process. More promising are sites located in parks, school grounds and public open spaces that are likely to be both better preserved and also unaffected by development. Moreover, they offer the opportunity for research excavations, should the circumstances arise. As no development usually means no

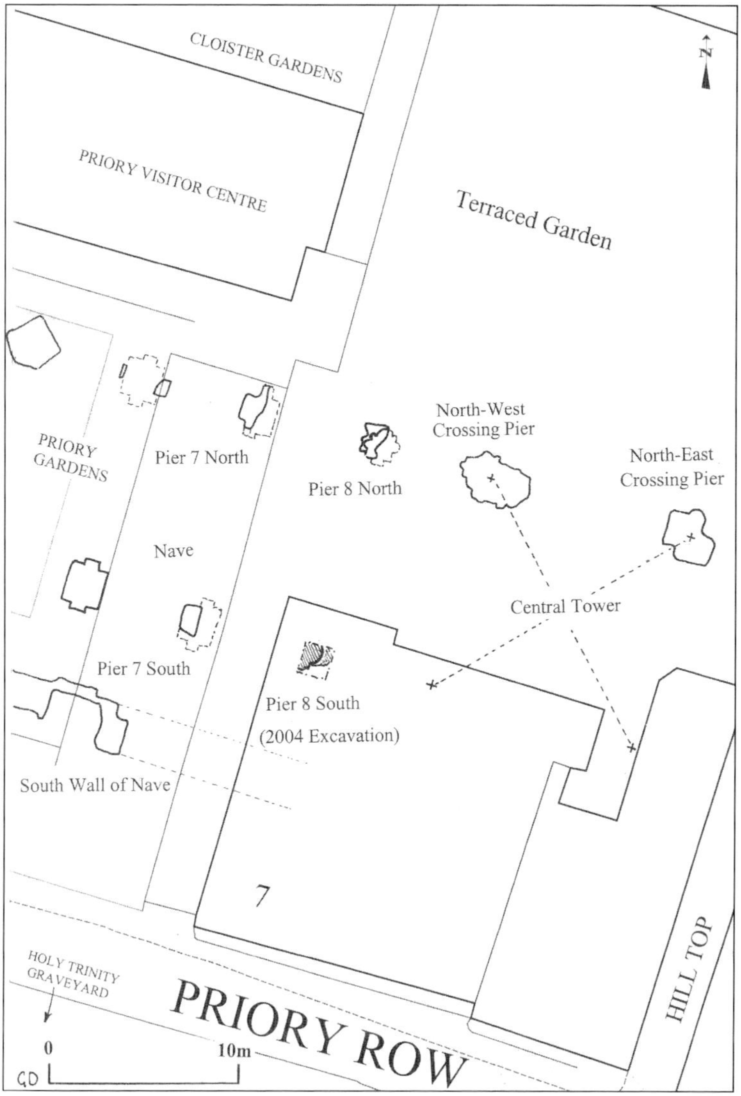

FIG. 6. Coventry, St Mary's Cathedral Church: plan of the pier locations towards the east end of the nave

Drawing, G. Demidowicz and author

archaeology, it is perhaps here on unthreatened sites that the role of the local volunteer archaeologist comes to the fore to fill these inevitable gaps.

In 1977 Coventry Museums published an assessment of recent archaeological work in the city.[23] This also outlined fifteen priority questions on Coventry's history, and identified key sites in the city where excavation could potentially answer them. Progress has clearly been made towards some of the answers, particularly those concerning the priory and the suburbs; but many questions, from the nature of the pre-conquest settlement to the severity of the city's decline in the 15th century, are still as relevant today as they were thirty years ago. Archaeology alone will not provide all the answers and documentary research and the study of standing buildings will have equal

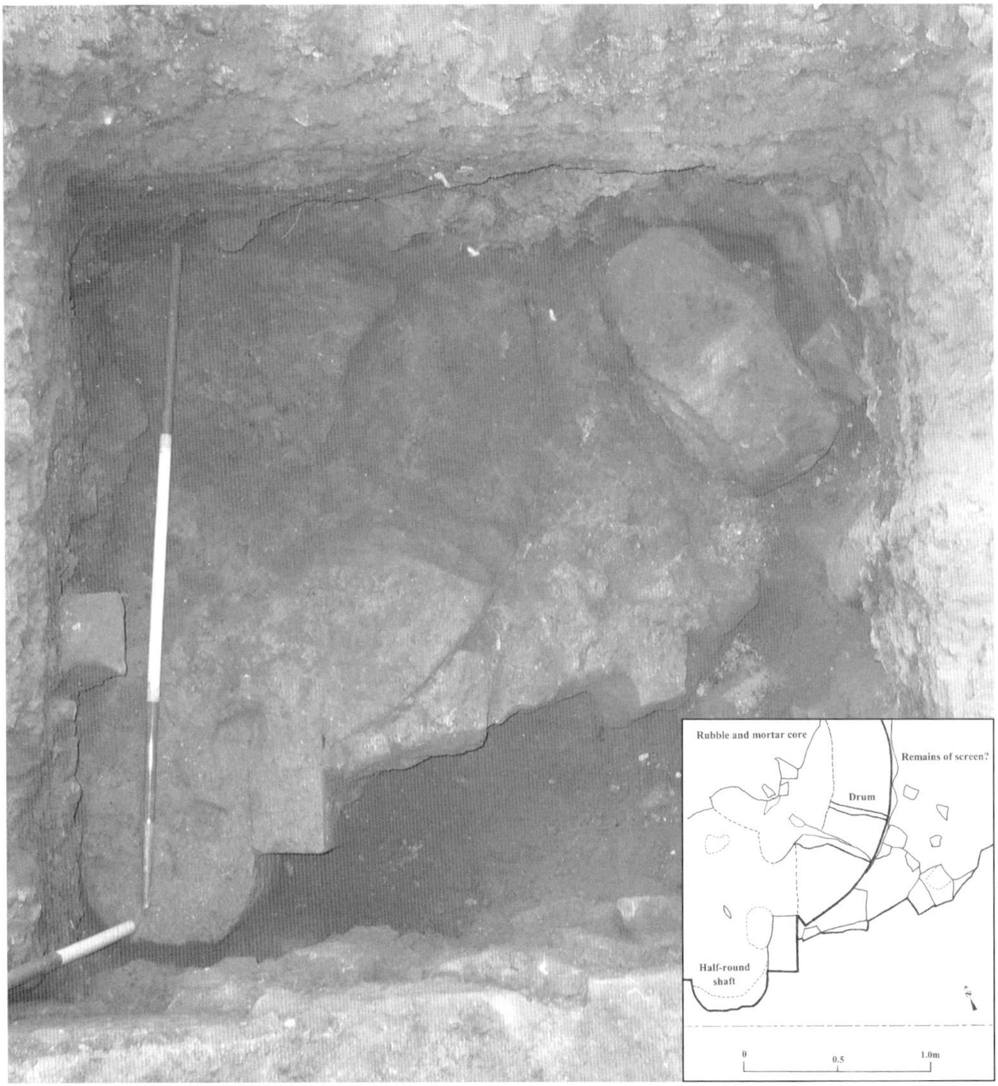

FIG. 7. Coventry, St Mary's Cathedral Church: a test pit excavated to locate nave pier S8 under 7 Priory Row, Coventry (2004). North is at the top of the picture
INSET: plan of the pier
Photo and drawing, author

contributions to make. The results of historical research now sit side by side with archaeological fieldwork data in the Coventry Historic Environment Record but there is still need for a modern synthesis of Coventry's archaeology to guide future research.[24] In some instances there is also a need to return to earlier investigations: The analysis and publication of the Shelton Collection and the important 1988–89 Bayley Lane excavation are particular priorities.[25] Perhaps most importantly, a great deal of thought needs to be given to how we display and communicate the results of our work to our principle audience, the people of Coventry, whose interest and enthusiasm are vital to successfully tackling the challenges that lie ahead.

ACKNOWLEDGEMENTS

The author would like to thank the staff of Birmingham Archaeology, Northamptonshire Archaeology, Warwickshire Museum Field Services and Worcestershire Historic Environment and Archaeology Service for their assistance with this paper, and to George Demidowicz, Richard Goddard and Cathy Patrick for their helpful comments.

NOTES

1. M. Rylatt and A. F. Adams, *A Harvest of History: the life and work of J. B. Shelton MBE* (Coventry n.d., *c.* 1983; 2nd edn, Rylatt and M. Montes, Coventry 1998).
2. K. Head and K. Wilkinson, 'Environmental Remains From Coventry Transport Museum, Hales Street, Coventry 2005' (unpublished planning report, Worcestershire Historic Environment and Archaeology Service Report 1370).
3. Rylatt and Mason, *Cathedral Priory*.
4. K. Head and K. Wilkinson, 'A Palaeoenvironmental Assessment at Far Gosford Street, Coventry, 2006' (unpublished planning report, Worcestershire Historic Environment and Archaeology Service Report 1455).
5. J. Halstead, 'Land off Priory Street, Coventry, Archaeological Excavations 2006: Post-Excavation Assessment and Updated Research Design' (unpublished planning report, Birmingham Archaeology Project 1417).
6. K. Colls and E. Hancox, 'Excavations at the Herbert Art Gallery and Museum, Coventry, 2005–6: Post-Excavation Assessment' (unpublished planning report, Birmingham Archaeology Projects 1266 and 1402).
7. S. Wright, 'Much Park Street, Coventry, the development of a medieval street: excavations 1970–74', *TBWAS* 92 (1982), 49–81.
8. See Goddard, this volume, 38–42.
9. B. Burrows and K. Colls, 'Land to the rear of Drapers Hall, Coventry: Archaeological Evaluation 2008' (unpublished planning report, Birmingham Archaeology Project 1767).
10. An archaeological excavation was undertaken on the west side of Bayley Lane in 1988 and 1989 under the direction of Ray Wallwork. The excavation found stratified deposits extending to a depth of over 7m, which were interpreted as being the castle ditch. There was no funding available for post-excavation analysis and no report has yet been produced.
11. Soden, *Hidden History*, 41–9.
12. P. Mason and I. Soden, 'Archaeological excavations at the former site of Astleys, Far Gosford Street, Coventry, May–July 2006' (unpublished planning report, Northamptonshire Archaeology Report 08/42).
13. M. Duncan and K. Colls, 'Lower Ford Street Post-Excavation Assessment 2005' (unpublished planning report, Birmingham Archaeology Project 1338).
14. E. Hancox, 'Upper Well Street, Coventry: an Archaeological Excavation, 2004, Post-Excavation Assessment Updated Project Design' (unpublished planning report, Birmingham Archaeology Project 1067).
15. P. Mason, D. McAree and I. Soden, 'Archaeological Excavations at Belgrade Plaza, Coventry 2005–2007' (unpublished planning report, Northamptonshire Archaeology Report 08/096).
16. P. Mason, A. Thorne and T. Webster, 'An Archaeological Watching Brief at the Belgrade Theatre, Coventry, February to October 2005' (unpublished planning report, Northamptonshire Archaeology Report 05/154).
17. E. Gooder, C. Woodfield and R. E. Chaplin, 'The Walls of Coventry', *TBWAS* 81 (1966), 102–6.
18. C. Jones and C. Coutts, 'Archaeological Recording at Bond's Hospital Extension, Hill Street, Coventry' (unpublished planning report, Warwickshire Museum Field Services Report 0619).
19. G. Demidowicz and C. Patrick, 'Excavations at 7 Priory Row, 2004', CBA *WM Archaeology* 47 (2004), 7–15.
20. Morris, 'Cathedral Church', 20.
21. See further Plant, this volume, 55–60.

22. G. Demidowicz, pers. comm.

23. M. Rylatt, City of *Coventry: Archaeology and Redevelopment Plan* (Coventry Museums 1977).

24. The Coventry Historic Environment Record (HER) is a computerised database linked to GIS mapping containing information about archaeology, historic buildings and documentary research. The HER is an ongoing project funded by the Coventry City Council.

25. The Shelton Collection is the large quantity of artefacts collected in Coventry by John Shelton from the late 1920s until his death in 1958. The collection has been highlighted as being of particular regional importance in the West Midlands Regional Research Framework for Archaeology. See further, Soden, this volume, 1–2.

The Built Environment and the Later Medieval Economy: Coventry 1200–1540

RICHARD GODDARD

The hypothesis under investigation here is that periods of extensive urban construction, both of church and private building in the middle ages, tend to coincide with periods of commercial vitality and a booming economy. During periods of economic recession far less construction takes place. Coventry's rich architectural and archaeological heritage is compared to local economic historical data for the period 1200–1540 to attempt to evaluate this relationship systematically. The juxtaposition of artefact and economic cycle in medieval Coventry is striking.

THIS paper uses the historical, architectural and archaeological evidence from medieval Coventry to discover if a relationship between commercialisation and construction can be identified within the later medieval city. The period 1050–1500 is considered a profound period of commercialisation.[1] After 1200 few people lived more than a day's walk from a market. All levels of society from the poorest agricultural smallholder to the greatest magnate became increasingly orientated towards producing for the market, and by 1300 the populations of towns like Coventry were higher than at any other period of the middle ages. These towns were the foci of this commerce — for the buying and selling of agricultural produce, the manufacture of all kinds of goods, the supply of all manner of services and the centre of the infrastructure for local marketing. All towns, regardless of their size, had markets, shops, manufacturing and industrial premises, merchants and shopkeepers. Towns were places where buyers and sellers could transact business more easily. This commercialised economy grew and contracted during the middle ages.

Episodes of economic growth were (and continue to be) followed by episodes of decline. In modern economies these are referred to as business cycles. They are neither regular nor predictable, but they are identifiable historically.[2] Long business cycles, sometimes referred to as 'Kondratieff Cycles' (lasting between fifty-four and sixty years), can be identified in the middle ages. Whilst their exact dates are contested, the later medieval English economy comprised, very roughly, four main phases.[3] The period 1150–1250 is considered an episode of particularly rampant economic expansion; another short burst of commercial expansion followed the Black Death; a short episode of severe economic depression extended from the early decades of the 15th century until the 1480s and a fourth period of recovery and economic expansion is posited for the 1520s.[4] Can an understanding of these later medieval economic cycles help us interpret changes in material culture and the built environment? The concept of a loosely cyclical pattern for monastic building projects has been discussed in general terms, although not in relation to Coventry.[5] John Langdon has recently suggested that investment in medieval building projects might be used as a guide to vitality or robustness of the English economy.[6]

The commercial evidence used in this analysis reveals the chronology of these commercial phases in medieval Coventry. The first tracks the chronology of debt with reference to credit and loan transactions enrolled at Coventry's Statute Merchant court.[7] Many of these debts were used to fund business ventures, and trends in the volume of credit in Coventry can inform us about the changes in, and the health of, the local economy (Fig. 1, Tables 1 and 2). Credit is crucial to the functioning of all trade, and the middle ages is no exception. The Statute Merchant system was introduced by the crown in 1284 in order to allow merchants to enrol their business debts for greater security and, if the debt remained unpaid on the due date, recover their money through chancery.[8] The system remained in use, largely unaltered, until 1532.

Beyond debt evidence, this analysis will use the documents originating from Coventry's busy medieval land market (deeds and leases) to identify periods of high migration and investment (Figs 2–4). During periods of commercial expansion, people migrated to cities like Coventry looking for work and profit. In some cases between one quarter and one half of a city's population in the 13th century was made up of recent immigrants.[9] It was Coventry's successful economy, particularly in the 13th and 14th centuries, that attracted new blood and new business into the city. This was reflected in a more vigorous and dynamic local market in urban property as these individuals sought places to live and work. In the 13th century the value of medieval urban land was a combination of down-payment and rent. The rent, being perpetual and generally unchanging, was not a flexible enough tool to reflect changes in the demand for property and this function seems to have been conferred, presumably by market forces, onto the down-payment. In Coventry down-payments of this sort were very common, occurring in over 80% of 13th-century transfers. The down-payment was affected both by the size of plot and by its location: plots in busy commercial areas such as Earl Street or the market area were considerably higher than those in other areas of the city.[10] Down-payments tended to change every time properties were re-granted, suggesting some reactivity to market conditions (Fig. 2).[11] For the 14th and

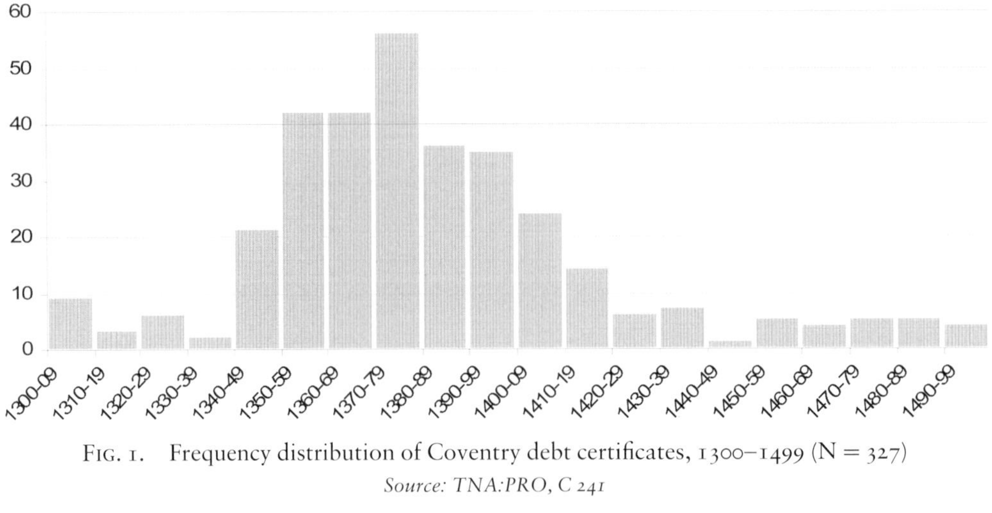

FIG. 1. Frequency distribution of Coventry debt certificates, 1300–1499 (N = 327)

Source: TNA:PRO, C 241

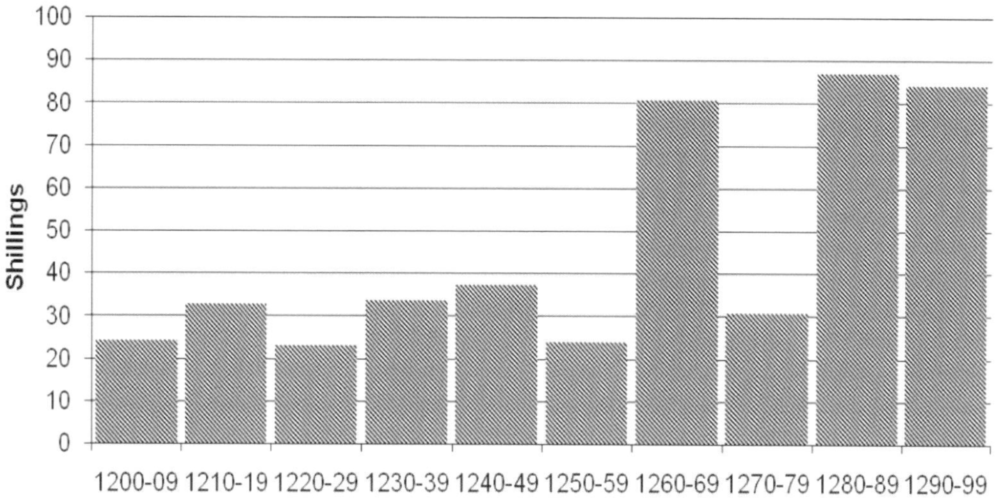

FIG. 2. Decennial trends in Coventry property down-payment means, 1200–99 (N = 283)
Sources: CA BA, TNA:PRO, E 40

15th centuries, both the decennial trends in the quantity of surviving Coventry messuage leases (Fig. 3) and the mean leasehold rents of shops (Fig. 4) have been used to track changes in the demand for city property. These leasehold agreements are instructive because the agreed rent embodies what landlords thought they could get away with charging in that particular year.[12] This decision was presumably made with reference to local economic conditions and future return on the landlord's investment. Trends in rents of 14th-century shop leases therefore give us an insight into the amount Coventry

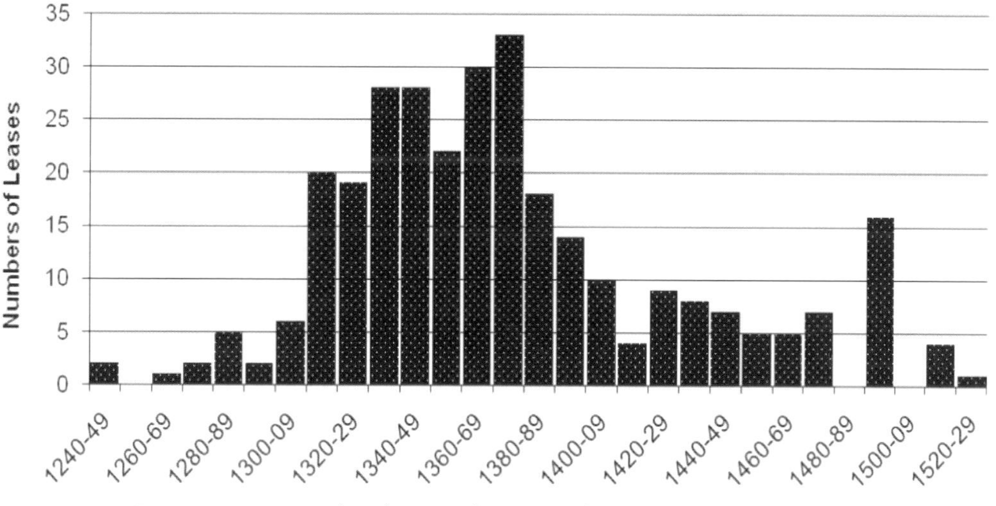

FIG. 3. Frequency distribution of Coventry leases, 1240–129 (N = 306)
Sources: CA BA, TNA:PRO, E 40

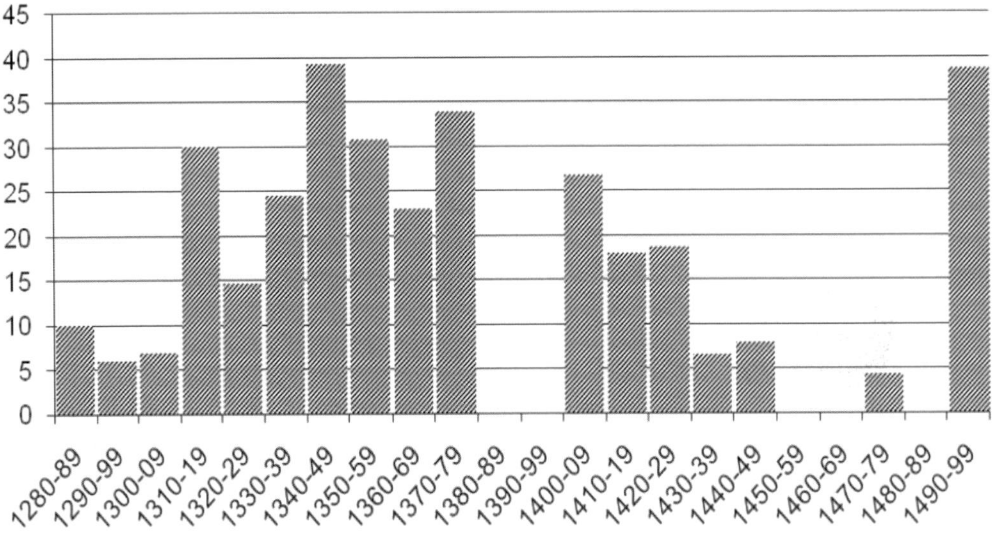

FIG. 4. Mean leasehold rent of individual shops and selds, Coventry, 1280–1499 (N = 62)
Sources: CA BA, TNA:PRO, E 40

shopkeepers were willing to spend on property and, as such, suggest much about their perception of local economic conditions at that time.

This analysis will be divided into three main sections. The first will examine the evidence for building in Coventry during periods of commercial growth particularly in the 13th and early 14th centuries; the second will look at the period from the arrival of the plague in the city in 1349 until the early decades of the 15th century and the third will examine the period of the economic decline, and later recovery, from the mid-15th century until *c.* 1540.

1200–1349: EXPANSION

THE long period from the late 11th to the end of the 13th century is well known as one of relative peace, significant population growth and economic expansion. At the time of Domesday survey in 1086 the English population is estimated to stand at about 2.5 million.[13] By 1300 it had exploded to about 6 million.[14] This period was also one of dramatic commercial expansion. Hundreds of new markets and fairs were set up between *c.* 1100 and the mid-13th century, suggesting a major increase in the number of transactions within the economy, and the money supply expanded dramatically, greasing the wheels of medieval commerce. In terms of locations for commerce, this period has also been recognised as a one of dynamic urban growth. Not only did older towns, like London and Gloucester considerably expand, but between *c.* 1050 and 1300 about 500 new urban settlements were established. Each of these was a centre of a commercial network. The proportion of the English population living in towns is thought to have doubled in that period to about 20%.[15] Furthermore, the number of ports increased particularly in the second half of the 12th century, as did exports from these ports, particularly of high quality English wool.[16] Other commercial enterprises such as mills also increased in number, especially in the first half of the 13th century along with large numbers of bridges being built in the period before 1250, which helped to facilitate trade by lowering transport costs.[17] Thus, for most of the English population, the years from Domesday to *c.* 1300 were a 'hot' period of commercialisation.

Coventry certainly grew before 1200.[18] For the opening years of this study, archaeological evidence suggests that the plots in West Orchard had been occupied by the early 13th century and the charter evidence indicates that at the same time the plots on the corner of Cross Cheaping contained stalls and selds (groups of covered stalls resembling a bazaar) (Prelim., Plan C for street names). Archaeological and documentary evidence for Well Street also suggests early 13th-century habitation and it clearly possesses a planned layout probably from that period. The land market evidence for Coventry in the 13th century tends to confirm this impression of a growing and commercially vibrant city that attracted people looking for work and landlords seeking profitable investments. A timber of a bridge that once spanned the Sherbourne at Gosford Street has been dated dendrochronologically to 1162–1212, indicating urban development in that area; also industrial premises dated to between *c.* 1150–1250 have been excavated at the other end of the city at Lower Ford Street.[19] The decennial trends in average down-payments (Fig. 2) rose throughout the century, suggesting that demand for property steadily grew throughout the first half of the century as landlords raised the down-payments on their properties in response to new tenants arriving in the city. Development continued in Bishop and Cook Streets during the 13th century. By the 1220s, the southern or earl's half of the city already contained characteristic long, thin burgage plots filled up with messuages and halls. During this period of urban expansion, the largest building in Coventry, the cathedral priory church, was completed. The masonry evidence dates the nave and the renovated cloister of this impressive and expensive undertaking to the second half of the 12th century and the early decades of the 13th century;[20] the first Franciscan church was built in the 1230s;[21] Holy Trinity was rebuilt after a fire in the mid-13th century. [22]

In the second half of the 13th century the average down-payments increased quite dramatically (except in the 1270s), suggesting that the demand for property increased still further and that Coventry was perceived to be a profitable place to invest in property. By the 1280s the earl's half contained at least 116 burgages.[23] There is also archaeological evidence of 13th-century building on Derby Lane and Much Park Street, with early construction on Bayley Lane dating from the 1250s.[24] Indeed, Soden believes that the majority of Coventry's buildings were first constructed as one- or two-storeyed timbered buildings in the 13th century.[25] The nave of St Michael's church is thought to have been rebuilt during the late 13th century. By the 13th century the city had developed into the largest town and the principal commercial and manufacturing centre of the midlands, and it was also the centre for the marketing of textiles from a large hinterland and an important centre for the manufacture of luxury goods. Not only did average down-payments rise, but also, from the 1270s, the number of surviving grants doubled from about twenty-two per decade between 1220 and 1240 to about forty-four per decade at the end of the century. This must also reflect local economic conditions peculiar to the city itself which seems to have experienced particular commercial growth in the later 13th and early 14th centuries. Levels of later 13th-century migration were very high and the city attracted immigrants from considerable distances.[26] By the end of the century the northern half of the city had grown to its 15th-century extent.

This period of pronounced commercial expansion continued into the 14th century. The evidence of the Statute Merchant certificates clearly reflects this and points particularly to a surge of economic vibrancy in the 1330s and 1340s (Fig. 1, Table 1). Although many debt recognisances were enrolled at the borough court in the early 14th century, Coventry's official Statute Merchant court was established in 1345 during the opening phases of the city's commercial apotheosis.[27] Many of these debts were for high amounts, commonly greater than £20 and often more than £100.

The increase in the numbers of surviving leases (Fig. 3) and the sharply rising trend in leasehold rents for shops (Fig. 4) in the late 13th and early 14th centuries further confirms the commercial expansion during the early 14th century, with the property market trends shadowing this rapid and dramatic expansion in credit in the 1330s and 1340s. Between 1300 and 1349, there was a general increase in the amount of land that changed hands in Coventry. In the ninety-nine years between 1200 and 1299 there is evidence of 604 deeds transferring property, including both leases and grants, whereas in the fifty-five years between 1300 and 1355 there are 1,193 such survivals for the city, many of them deeds for land which had not been transferred officially before.[28] That is almost twice as many deeds for a period that was half as long. Once again this indicates a dynamic land market and a heavy demand for city properties resulting both from immigration and continued investment in remunerative urban property by landlords. The soaring demand for shops in this period, reflected in the rising leasehold rents being charged for them by landlords, confirms the impression of Coventry as a highly prosperous commercial centre at this time. City property was a valuable asset to those, like the cathedral priory, who invested in it to increase their rental income in the 13th and early 14th centuries. Between 1284 and 1299 the priory acquired over £7-worth of city rents: between 1305 and 1349 they acquired ninety-three new city properties and a further £5 in rent, showing that the priory sought to take advantage of the strong demand for Coventry properties in this period.[29] In particular it profited from the rents of migrant tenants in search of work in the city.

Correlating with this is the evidence for physical development of the city. Recently it has been argued that a whole new suburb, lying south of Much and Little Park Streets, was planned, but not executed, in the late 1340s.[30] This speculative development is witness to the confidence that rent-paying tenants would be attracted to the city during the prosperous decades of the 1330s and 1340s. Indeed, the archaeological evidence indicates that many private city buildings were redeveloped by their owners or landlords in the later 13th or 14th centuries.[31] The small coin hoard found beneath the floor level of a late 13th-century building (possibly a dyeing works) in Far Gosford Street has been dated to 1327–35 and further suggests a period of thriving commercial

TABLE 1. Frequency distribution of Coventry Statute Merchant debt recognisances, 1300–49

1300–09	1
1310–19	0
1320–29	3
1330–39	14
1340–49	25

Source: TNA: PRO C 241, CA Borough Archives (BA/), WCRO DR 429 activity.[32] Other building activity of this period included the construction of the priory's chapter-house and the refenestration of the cathedral church's nave; the first phase of the construction of the Whitefriars (1340s) and the first works on the collegiate church of St John the Baptist.[33]

1349–*c.* 1420: EXPANSION

THE above analysis certainly suggests a tangible link between commercial growth and urban expansion before the Black Death. But most commentators attribute the real boom in building, especially church building, to the later 14th and early 15th centuries, in a period associated with catastrophic demographic collapse, declining agricultural production, vacant holdings, lapsed and falling rents, rising wages resulting from labour shortages and shrinking money supply.[34] The English population is thought to have fallen to perhaps under three million in 1377 and down to about two million in the 1520s.[35]

The plague arrived in Coventry early in April 1349.[36] Whilst this had a short-term disruptive impact upon local economy (and ignoring the devastating human cost), it is clear from all evidence that the city's economy recovered very quickly. In this, Coventry was not unique. Similar expansion has been seen in other cities as they serviced the demand resulting from a temporary rise in *per capita* wealth (from increased wages and inheritances) and consumption (survivors choosing to spend more than their predecessors). The textile industry grew rapidly, with huge increases in cloth exports and a considerable expansion of domestic production, and Coventry's merchants greatly benefited from the growth of the cloth market.[37] Thirty-six per cent (the largest single group) of occupational titles of Coventry's Trinity Guild membership in the late 14th and early 15th centuries related to textile production or marketing.[38] All of the evidence suggests that the city's commercial high point was reached in the decades following the plague.

This post-plague boom is revealed clearly by the number of debt certificates, which increase between the late 1350s and the 1380s (Fig. 1), with the 1370s recording the highest number of Coventry debt certificates within the medieval period. It can be inferred from this that Coventry merchants very quickly regained sufficient confidence to lend money to fund profitable, possibly cloth-related, business opportunities. Certainly many of those who lent money in this period were involved in the region's cloth trade.[39] Additionally, large numbers of credit agreements continued to be enrolled at Coventry's Statute Merchant court until the end of the 14th century (Table 2).

TABLE 2. Frequency distribution of Coventry Statute Merchant debt recognisances, 1392–1456

1390–99	127
1400–09	111
1410–19	49
1420–29	8
1430–39	25
1440–49	1
1450–59	5

Source: CA BA/E/C/7/1–31[40]

The recurrent epidemics caused a number of city plots to be abandoned, particularly between 1371 and 1417.[41] However, what the land market evidence indicates is that during this period there was enough demand for Coventry land for these plots to be leased to new tenants fairly quickly. For example, in 1371, the new tenant of a vacant plot in 'Between the Bridges' was required to build a new house there.[42] Furthermore, the land market saw a considerable expansion in the leasing of messuages between 1360 and 1379 (Fig. 3), as immigrants swarmed into the city looking for opportunities away from the plague-ravaged and economically stagnant countryside. Likewise, shop rents remained very high in the 1370s (Fig. 4), showing that Coventry's merchants and shopkeepers wanted to take advantage of the profitable opportunities. They were prepared to pay high rents to allow them to sell from permanent shops rather than weekly market stalls. The Catesby family were landlords in Coventry in the 14th and 15th centuries. Their archive indicates that their modest urban estate was at its most extensive, and bringing in most rent (£36 11s.), in 1360, again confirming the image of high levels of post-plague migration and a confident economy.[43] Both the debt and the land-market evidence suggest that this post-plague boom lasted only until the 1420s at the latest (Figs 1, 3 and 4).

Many of those lending money during this optimistic commercial expansion were merchants. Of particular significance to Coventry's built environment were the Botoners, Adam and his younger brother, William, both of whom used the credit market to finance their mercantile business.[44] These two are generally credited with funding the new tower of St Michael's church in 1373,[45] quite early in their business careers (their first recorded debt being enrolled in 1377), as well as acting as patrons to other religious institutions in the city. The later 14th century in Coventry has been described by Morris as a 'church-building boom'.[46] According to Monckton's analysis of St Michael's, the large-scale rebuilding of the church began in the late 14th century and continued well into the 15th century. The east end of the church has been dated to the end of the 1390s, with work continuing into the 1420s. The clerestory was added before *c.* 1435.[47] Coventry's town wall was begun in 1355, with most of the southern half of the city up to Radford Brook in the east having been enclosed by the turn of the 15th century, with the Whitefriars' section of wall completed in the 1420s. Holy Trinity's nave arcades were rebuilt in the later 14th century, and the chancel — which had become ruinous — was extended then, too; a new chancel south aisle and a nave clerestory were added and finished before 1430.[48] The Greyfriars' church was being rebuilt in the early 1360s and the new Charterhouse was established in the early 1380s, where ceiling beams from the house have been dated to the early 15th century.[49] The Whitefriars' chapter-house was built in the late 1370s and the church's nave bays and Lady's Tower were completed by the 1420s.[50]

Major building projects continued to be undertaken, despite declining 14th-century seigneurial incomes and a doubling of wages for building workers resulting from the plague-related labour shortages.[51] Work carried out by the priory in the 14th century seems to have required extra external funding as, for example, in the forty-day indulgence granted during the early 1320s and in the late 14th-century agreement between Prior James de Horton and the parishioners regarding the rebuilding of Holy Trinity's crumbling chancel.[52] The chancel was to be extended by 24 feet and was afterwards to be maintained at the joint charge of the parish and priory, hinting at a possible shortage of priory funds. It is possible, too, that these works were part-funded by aristocratic patronage — the Beauchamp heraldry on floor-tiles of the priory's refectory might be a reflection of this. Building works therefore continued on the priory's conventual buildings: the refectory was extensively rebuilt between the 1340s and 1380s, and the refurbishment of the priory cloister has been dated to *c.* 1400. In the cathedral church, the new extended east end was probably started in the later 14th century and continued into the 15th century, a major refenestration of the western parts of the nave has been identified about 1370–90, and a new high vault in the transept dated around 1400.[53] Thus, despite rising wages and falling seigneurial incomes, the benefits of the economic boom — a rise in aggregate wealth in the region — meant that building continued.

The chief beneficiaries of Coventry's commercial boom were merchants who, whilst their commercial ventures prospered, were capable of funding church-building projects. The Botoners and their tower are the prime example, but others exist. This building boom, and its connection to the merchant elite, can be seen most clearly in St Michael's church. The first chantry was founded in the church in 1323 by the wool merchant, Hugh de Merynton. He endowed it with rents worth £8 for two priests to sing daily mass for him and his wife.[54] Whitefriars was founded by John Pulteney, a man from a wealthy Coventry merchant dynasty who later became lord mayor of London. It is likely that he funded some of the building there. In the 1350s, other members of Coventry's mercantile elite donated further plots of land for extending the friary.[55] It is also well known that much English building of the later 14th and 15th centuries was financed by donations, fundraising events by parishioners and bequests.[56] The role of the parishioners in the rebuilding of St Michael's church can be seen in the 15th-century petition to the pope, instigated by Coventry's Drapers' Guild, concerning liturgical duties in their chapel within the new church.[57] This states that it was the parishioners themselves (rather than the prior) who wished to enlarge the church. Merchants generally feature amongst the most munificent benefactors to churches, but bequests which assigned sums of money to the fabric of a church were of equal importance. Thus, for example, John Prest, a Coventry merchant of middling status bequeathed, amongst other things, 40s. to the fabric of the cathedral church, 26s. 8d. to the fabric of St John's Hospital (where he was to be buried) and 6s. 8d. to the fabric of the suburban church of St Nicholas in his will of 1361.[58] This money was thus expressly earmarked for building or repair work. Bequests of this type were extremely common and took advantage of the propitious commercial climate to help towards funding building projects. It is not difficult to see how the combination of a wealthy and successful mercantile elite, in a period infamous for ornate and ostentatious display combined with a general fear of the agonising pains of Purgatory during repeated deadly epidemics, might lead to increased lay patronage of spectacular religious architecture.

But it was not just the churches that were rebuilt. Much of the private building indicated by archaeology must have been undertaken by artisans and others whose incomes had been swelled by high demand for their goods and services and rising wages. Many must have felt that this was an opportune time to upgrade their workshops and houses. Many of the city's cellars were built in this period, such as the one at Bayley Lane dated to between 1380 and 1410. Many of the medieval house plots that have been excavated, such as that in Much Park Street, seem to have been rebuilt, often in stone, in the late 14th or early 15th centuries. For example, a house in Far Gosford Street was rebuilt between 1400 and 1425; Cheylesmore manor and its mill were repaired between the 1360s and the early 1420s.[59] Once again there seems to be a close correlation between building activity, in this case by both lords and their tenants, within this period of post-plague commercial boom. This is seen clearly in the history of St Mary's Guild (later amalgamated into the Trinity Guild). In 1347 Henry de Deodenhale, another Coventry merchant, granted a large number of tenements and rents from all over the city to this guild. These properties had been accumulated previously, probably with the express purpose of donating them to the guild in one go. The first plot cited in the grant, described as a newly built messuage, was the guild-hall itself, 'Seynte Marie Halle'.[60] The membership of the Holy Trinity Guild was composed of all levels of business people from Coventry and beyond,[61] and it built up huge numbers of properties in the city during the later 14th century. In 1392, for example, it acquired 153 city messuages and over £22 in rent; by the end of the 15th century its urban rents totalled £318 12s. 6d., making it the principal landholder in Coventry.[62] The combination of a buoyant economy with a successful mercantile membership, eager to display their prosperity in stone and in large numbers of remunerative rents, allowed the guildhall to be refashioned into its current form between *c.* 1392 and 1414.[63]

c. 1420–1540: DECLINE AND RECOVERY

THIS period of commercial growth was, however, unsustainable. Coventry's post-plague expansion began to fade in the early 15th century.[64] Nationally, by the mid-15th century, a severe recession had materialised in almost every branch of the economy as it adapted to the demographic realities of post-plague England.[65] The combination of reduced immigration and the emigration of mercantile elites resulted in the contraction and decay of many of England's larger towns, like Boston and Lincoln, in the 15th and early 16th centuries.[66] The commercial foundering of this period in Coventry can be seen graphically in Figure 1 and Table 2, with the precipitous fall in the number of debts enrolled in the city from the 1420s. The situation continued unabated until the end of the century: Coventry merchants did not feel confident enough to lend money or extend credit on their goods for much of this period. They feared that, in those inauspicious economic circumstances, their customers would have been unable to repay those debts. Between 1420 and 1490 the leasehold market virtually collapsed as migrants spurned Coventry and landlords decided not to invest in property (Fig. 3). There were more than six times as many surviving messuage leases for the decade of the 1370s when compared to the 1450s. The rents for Coventry shops also declined, particularly in the 1430s and 1440s (Fig. 4) as the city economy contracted to its new equilibrium point. From the 1440s all of Coventry's landlords — the priory, the guilds, the corporation and smaller landlords like the Catesbys — experienced growing difficulties in attracting tenants to their properties and high levels of rent arrears. For example, the archives of the Catesby's urban estate, centred on Ironmonger Row, reveal increasing numbers of vacancies and declining rents from the 1440s. By the late 1470s and early 1480s, more than half of their city properties were not paying their full rent. In 1473, the city's government insisted that any ruinous buildings should be demolished on pain of a fine. Clearly, nobody thought that these houses were going to be reoccupied in the near future, rather they now represented little more than a danger to passing traffic. In 1485, the Trinity Guild's rental reveals that 34% of its city tenements (roughly 135 properties) were standing empty. The majority of these had remained so for over a year. That year the guild faced rental arrears equalling approximately 22% of its yearly rental income. Thus, in the 1470s and 1480s most of Coventry's streets, both in the periphery and in the centre, had tenements and cottages that were standing empty. This, of course, suggests a significant and long-term fall in population — one of the defining features of urban decay.

Coventry's economic stagnation and contraction had a discernable impact upon the built environment of the city. The suburban areas at Hill Street and Well Street contained 'rows' — blocks of timber-framed terraced cottages possibly built in the 14th century. Both the cathedral priory and the Holy Trinity Guild rented these to tenants from the late 14th century. The buildings survived until the 16th century by which time many were converted into barns.[67] This suggests that the declining population in the 15th century resulted in a physical contraction of the city with suburbs returning to agricultural use, a classic indicator of urban decline. With regard building evidence, Morris points out that one of the problems of studying this period in Coventry is the lack of 15th-century evidence when compared to the abundance of datable material from the 14th century.[68] This may reflect the lack of actual building undertaken at that time. There appears to be no firmly dated evidence of major building activity at the cathedral church after *c.* 1420. The northern section of the town wall was built in fits and starts during the 15th and early 16th centuries, finally limping to a conclusion in 1538. This painfully slow process suggests that the corporation found these building works difficult to fund during the recession. This can be seen in the disputes in the 1480s between the prior and the corporation over the prior's contribution to murage (the tax granted to pay for the wall). The prior declared that his income had been greatly reduced since the early 15th century and thus could not contribute to the murage. The northern section of the wall took twice as long to build (over a hundred years) during the recession when compared to the southern section (about fifty years), which was built during the boom period of the later 14th century. But, in general, large-scale, expensive building work was not a common feature of the decline phase of Coventry's medieval economy. The archaeological and architectural evidence suggests that most buildings, rebuilt or improved in the later 14th century, remained unaltered during much of the 15th century.

Building in the city did not cease completely, however. Indeed, building work at St Michael's during the recession of the 15th century seems to invalidate any theoretical relationship between the performance of the urban economy and the built environment. The construction of the main body of the church continued into the late 1440s and is described in the papal petition of 3 January 1450, immediately following the worst years of the recession, as 'newly built'.[69] Furthermore, according to Sharp's testimony, the three 15th-century chapels there — St Andrew's (the Smiths' Chapel), St Thomas's (the Cappers' Chapel) and the Dyers' Chapel — had all been completed and were in use by the end of the 1450s or early 1460s at the latest, decades that, according to the economic evidence, witnessed a severe local economic downturn (see Figs 1, 3 and 4).[70] This apparent contradiction is not difficult to explain. This phase of building needs to be understood, not as new work, but simply as a continuation of earlier building work on the site. The most extensive and expensive work, the nave, was completed by the late 1440s. But this must have been planned much earlier, probably in conjunction with the east end of the church which was completed *c.* 1400. Thus, this impressive parish church was conceived during the boom period and financed by gifts and donations from wealthy individuals and guilds whose businesses remained solvent and profitable during the commercial euphoria of the late 14th and early 15th centuries. They could not have predicted the crash that occurred during the 1420s and 1430s. St Michael's, a jewel of parochial architecture, could not have been abandoned as a half-completed ruin. Further money must have been found to finish the building. Exactly similar circumstances exist in the modern world. Many of the tallest skyscrapers of the 20th century are visual manifestations of economic booms. The Empire State Building was a product of the American speculative boom of 1928: construction commenced in 1929, just as stock market prices collapsed and the depression of the 1930s began. The story of St Michael's church is the medieval equivalent in Coventry.

However, between 1470 and 1520 England experienced a recovery and expansion of the population.[71] Immigration into towns like Coventry increased, so wages fell and agricultural prices rose as more mouths had to be fed. Agriculture prospered and this was of great benefit to towns which acted as the central market places for rural commodities. At the same time cloth exports increased dramatically and this was combined with a significant increase in the money supply and a rising volume of national credit transactions by the mid-16th century. In Coventry, a limited revival in its credit market might have begun in the 1470s and 1480s as more certificates were sent to chancery (see Fig. 1), suggesting a possible resurgence in Coventry's long-distance trade. Furthermore, Coventry's land market became considerably more active from the 1470s, with over three times as many messuage leases surviving for the 1490s when compared to the market's low point in the 1450s (Fig. 3). The leasehold rents for shops, many of them little more than converted stalls in the Drapery,[72] increased dramatically in the 1490s after sixty years of stagnation (Fig. 4). These signs of tentative commercial recovery might have made the mercantile community more willing to contribute to building projccts. Once again the architectural and archaeological evidence to some extent bears this out. At Holy Trinity, the Lady Chapel and the Jesus Chapel were added in the 1470s.[73] The granting of indulgences to the Lady Chapel in 1477 further suggests that it was the parishioners, rather than the priory, who contributed financially towards the building. Dendrochronological evidence from the roof timbers from the east range of the Whitefriars cloister reveal a reroofing campaign that took place between 1474 and 1500. In 1506, Thomas Bonde, another member of Coventry's ruling elite, bequeathed 20 marks to the White Friars in order that they might finish building their cloister.[74]

Excavations at the suburb of Far Gosford Street indicate that new occupation began in that area in the 16th century, suggesting that a resurgent population had begun to take up suburban land that had previously been abandoned. Furthermore, a timber-framed property in Much Park Street was completely rebuilt in the 16th century, suggesting a renewed programme of private building within the city. Excavations at Lower Ford Street found evidence implying renewed occupational activity and heavy use on previously abandoned land, particularly after 1480. In Bayley Lane, archaeological evidence indicates a significant increase in activity, which included the building of stone cellars, between the 1480s and the 1520s.[75] Phythian-Adam's seminal work on Coventry, of course, suggested that the city was still in the vice-like grasp of economic decline in the 1520s, but recent work has challenged the ferocity and severity of this decline.[76] Nationally, the late 1520s appear to have been a period of considerable economic expansion and commercial confidence. In Coventry too debts began to be enrolled once more in the city's Statute Merchant court in 1523, again suggesting a recovery of high value trade.[77] At exactly this time the Marler Chapel was added to Holy Trinity.[78]

CONCLUSION

ONE of the inherent obstacles to an analysis of this sort is the problem of dating. The early 13th-century documentary evidence, along with the topographical, architectural and archaeological data, all suffer from a similar inexactitude for different reasons.

Perhaps firmer conclusions might be achieved by comparing the debt and land market evidence with dendrochronological data. Whilst this brief survey has only skimmed the surface of the archaeological and architectural evidence for the city, much of the above suggests that, perhaps unsurprisingly, there is a rough correlation between periods of commercial expansion, or at least between a perceived confidence in a brighter business future and building activity. The period of local economic growth certainly began before 1200 and continued at a fairly leisurely pace throughout the 13th century, to be followed by a dynamic and sustained phase of commercial growth between *c.* 1280–1400, just the period in which much of the later medieval building took place. Whilst those who funded the pre- and post-plague building programmes may have been different, the end result was similar. Buildings were constructed whilst the local economy thrived. The opposite also appears true: that during periods of recession, fewer buildings were built. This period of recession lasted from *c.* 1420 to 1480, during which time far less construction took place. From *c.* 1500, there is some evidence of a recovery and almost immediately building recommenced.

ACKNOWLEDGEMENTS

I would like to thank Richard Britnell for helpful and constructive comments on an earlier draft of this paper; Chris Patrick for his help with Coventry's medieval archaeology; Jeremy Ashbee for allowing me to read his unpublished work on Coventry's town wall; Richard K. Morris for his comments on the dating of Coventry's medieval buildings; and particularly to Linda Monckton for her encouragement, support and generosity in sharing her research on St Michael's with me.

NOTES

1. See particularly R. H. Britnell, *The commercialisation of English society, 1000–1500* (Manchester 1993).
2. For an historical examination of business cycles in the period 1787–1842, see J. A. Schumpeter, *Business cycles: a theoretical, historical and statistical analysis of the capitalist process* I (New York 1939), 220–96; id., 'The analysis of economic change', in *Joseph A. Schumpeter: essays on entrepreneurs, innovations, business cycles and the evolution of capitalism*, ed. R. V. Clemence (New Brunswick and London 2008), 144–5.
3. For a recent summary of these phases, see R. H. Britnell, *Britain and Ireland, 1050–1530* (Oxford 2004), 71–95.
4. J. Langdon and J. Masschele, 'Commercial activity and population growth in medieval England', *Past and Present* 190 (2006), 54–68; J. Hatcher, *Plague, population and the English economy* (London 1977), 31–5, 64–5; J. Hatcher, 'The great slump of the mid-fifteenth century', in *Progress and problems in medieval England*, ed. R. Britnell and J. Hatcher (Cambridge 1996), 237–72.
5. R. Morris, *Cathedrals and Abbeys of England and Wales: the Building Church, 600–1540* (London 1979), 177–236.
6. J. Langdon, J. Walker and J. R. Falconer, 'Boom and bust: building investment on the Bishop of Winchester's estate in the early fourteenth century', in *The Winchester Pipe Rolls and Medieval English Society*, ed. R. H. Britnell (Woodbridge 2003), 147.
7. *Statute merchant roll of Coventry 1392–1416*, ed. A. Beardwood (Dugdale Society Publications 1939); CA BA/E/C/7/1–31; TNA:PRO C 241.
8. The writ copies given to each party to the transaction are known as recognisances, and the writs that were sent to chancery are known as certificates.
9. D. Nicholas, *The growth of the medieval city* (London 1997), 181. For migration in general, see P. McClure, 'Patterns of migration in the late middle ages: evidence of English place-name surnames', *Economic History Review* 32 (1979), 167–82.
10. Goddard, *Coventry 1043–1355*, 192–5.
11. See, for example, CA B/P/138/1–3 (1270s–80s); CA H/H/77/1–2 (1280s–90s); CA H/H/86/1–2 (1280s–95).

12. Goddard, *Coventry 1043–1355*, 235–8.
13. Medieval population estimates are an inexact science; see Britnell, *Britain and Ireland*, 81.
14. The population evidence is usefully summarised in Langdon and Masschele, 'Commercial activity', 54–68.
15. Britnell, *Britain and Ireland*, 139–40; C. Dyer, *Making a living in the Middle Ages* (London 2002), 187.
16. E. M. Carus-Wilson and O. Coleman, *England's export trade, 1275–1547* (Oxford 1963).
17. The commercial evidence is summarised in Langdon and Masschele, 'Commercial activity', 42–52.
18. Goddard, *Coventry 1043–1355*, 43–6, 56–61.
19. Patrick, this volume, 24–5.
20. Rylatt and Mason, *Cathedral Priory*, 30, 65, 68–9, 71–2; Morris, 'Cathedral Church', 48–54; Bassett, *Anglo-Saxon Coventry*.
21. Soden, *Hidden History*, 222; VCH *Warwickshire* VIII, 342.
22. VCH *Warwickshire*, II, 103; Soden, *Hidden History*, 158.
23. Goddard, *Coventry 1043–1355*, 68–71.
24. Patrick, this volume, 23–4.
25. Soden, *Hidden History*, 24–5, 29.
26. Goddard, *Coventry 1043–1355*, 145–55.
27. Goddard, *Coventry 1043–1355*, 275.
28. Goddard, *Coventry 1043–1355*, 234.
29. R. Goddard, 'Church lords and English urban investment in the later middle ages', in *Rodney Hilton's Middle Ages*, ed. C. Dyer, P. Coss and C. Wickham (Oxford 2007), 159.
30. N. W. Alcock, 'Queen Isabella's new suburb in Coventry in 1348', *Midland History* 33 (2008), 240–8.
31. Soden, *Hidden History*, 24–5, 29.
32. Patrick, this volume, 25.
33. Rylatt and Mason, *Cathedral Priory*, 21–2, 30, 64–5, 71; Woodfield, *Whitefriars*, 3, 23–4; Morris, 'St. Mary's Hall', 9, 13.
34. For example, see Morris, 'St. Mary's Hall', 13–22; Demidowicz, 'Hall', this volume, 171–7; Monckton, this volume, 143–60.
35. Britnell, *Britain and Ireland*, 81.
36. R. A. Davies, 'The effect of the Black Death on the parish priests of the medieval diocese of Coventry and Lichfield', *Historical Research* 62 (1989), 85–90.
37. Hatcher, *Plague, population and the English economy*, 34; Britnell, *Britain and Ireland*, 351–3.
38. *Guild Register*.
39. See, for example, TNA:PRO C 241/158/30, 188/81, 156/96.
40. The first section of this is *Statute merchant roll 1392–1416*, ed. Beardwood.
41. For example, CA BA/B/16/402/7, BA/B/16/150/1, BA/B/16/247/1.
42. TNA:PRO E 40 4358.
43. N. W. Alcock, 'The Catesbys in Coventry: a medieval estate and its archives', *Midland History* 15 (1990), 7, 15.
44. TNA:PRO C 241/156/96, 162/117, 170/56, 170/57, 182/53, 176/33, 187/48.
45. See further Monckton, this volume, 143–4.
46. Morris, 'St. Mary's Hall', 14.
47. Monckton, this volume, 148–57.
48. VCH *Warwickshire* VIII, 343.
49. Soden, *Hidden History*, 158.
50. Woodfield, *Whitefriars*, 4, 25–7.
51. C. Dyer, *Standards of living in the later middle ages: social change in England, 1200–1520* (Cambridge 1989), 41–4; J. H. Munro, 'Wage-stickiness, monetary changes and real incomes in late medieval England and the Low Countries, 1300–1500: did money matter?', *Research in Economic History* 21 (2003), 243.
52. VCH *Warwickshire* II, 55; *Register of Roger de Norbury*, ed. Bishop Hobhouse (Collections for the History of Staffordshire 1, 1880), 253, 256, 271.
53. Rylatt and Mason, *Cathedral Priory*, 49, 71–2; Morris, 'Priory', this volume, 70–3, 82–96; Morris, 'Cathedral Church', 18, 57–62.
54. Goddard, *Coventry 1043–1355*, 250.
55. Woodfield, *Whitefriars*, 2–3.
56. Morris, *Churches in the landscape*, 355–7.
57. The drapers are described in the petition as, '*sociorum artis sive mistere panariorum draperskinste vulgariter*'; *Cal. Papal Reg.* X, 202–3.
58. TNA:PRO E 40 11564; Goddard, *Coventry 1043–1355*, 216–18.

59. Soden, *Hidden History*, 23, 25, 157.
60. Goddard, *Coventry 1043–1355*, 247–8.
61. Harris ed., *Guild Register*.
62. Goddard, 'Church lords', 154.
63. Demidowicz, 'Hall', this volume, 171–7.
64. R. Goddard, *Commercial contraction and urban decline in fifteenth-century Coventry*, Dugdale Society Occasional Papers 46 (2006).
65. Hatcher, 'The great slump', 237–72.
66. A. Dyer, *Decline and growth in English towns, 1400–1640* (Basingstoke 1991), 29–42.
67. Soden, *Hidden History*, 34–5.
68. Morris, 'St. Mary's Hall', 20.
69. *Cal. Papal Reg.* X, 202–3; Monckton, this volume, 151, 155, 157.
70. St Andrew's had been established by 1449; St Thomas's was in use by 1458, according to the accounts of the Trinity Guild, and a priest was operating in the Dyers' Chapel by 1463. See Sharp, *Papers* 29 (footnote), 32.
71. C. G. A. Clay, *Economic expansion and social change: England 1500–1700* (Cambridge 1984).
72. CA BA/B/16/119, 122–6, 127/1.
73. VCH *Warwickshire* VIII, 344.
74. Woodfield, *Whitefriars*, 5, 29.
75. Soden, *Hidden History*, 29, 36; Patrick, this volume, 23.
76. C. Phythian-Adams, *Desolation of a city: Coventry and the urban crisis of the late Middle Ages* (Cambridge 1979); M. Hulton, *Company and fellowship: the medieval weavers of Coventry*, Dugdale Society Occasional Papers 31(1987); M. Hulton ed., *Coventry and its people in the 1520s*, Dugdale Society Occasional Papers 28 (1999), 4–54.
77. CA BA/E/C/7/32.
78. VCH *Warwickshire* VIII, 345.

The Romanesque and Early Gothic Cathedral of St Mary, Coventry

RICHARD PLANT

The Romanesque and early Gothic parts of the priory church of Coventry Cathedral have, until very recently, been poorly understood. However, over the past ten years clearer evidence of the nave and crossing piers has been uncovered, revealing a surprising complexity of design. This paper, focusing on the less-known Romanesque material, will try to set the scant remains of the building in the wider context of English architecture in the 12th century.

OF the medieval cathedrals of England, none has disappeared so thoroughly from view as that of Coventry. The remains of the building, now in a sunken garden west of the modern cathedral, constitute a few courses of the western wall, the base of a western tower, and a few fragments displayed over the site of excavated pier bases. The situation is, however, rather better than it was twenty years ago, before a number of archaeological campaigns put our understanding of the fabric on a firmer footing. The site was investigated spasmodically in the later 19th and early 20th centuries, with a more thorough investigation undertaken in the 1960s.[1] In the late 1990s and early this century, a sustained campaign of excavation brought to light much of the nave and monastic complex, with one further small investigation in 2004 adding further information.[2]

HISTORICAL BACKGROUND

THE early history of the church or churches in the centre of Coventry is somewhat unclear. What is certain is that an abbey church was consecrated in 1043 following foundation or refoundation by Earl Leofric and his wife Godiva. This probably supplemented earlier minster churches, the site of one of which perhaps lies under Holy Trinity Church.[3] The monastery may indeed have been instrumental in developing the city.[4] The process whereby the monastery came to house the bishop's seat was part of the most complicated of the post-Conquest resettlements of diocesan centres. The see was at Lichfield during the Anglo-Saxon period, was moved to Chester in 1075, and then moved to Coventry. Later bishops, however, divided their interest between the Lichfield and Coventry, with a number favouring Lichfield even during the construction of the cathedral.

In 1102 Bishop Robert de Limesey (1085–1117) gained permission from the pope to raise the abbey to cathedral status, but since this date marks the papal confirmation, and was given at the same time as other well-established transferrals were confirmed, the transferral to Coventry may have taken place somewhat earlier.[5] Indeed, the bishops of Chester seem to have asserted their authority over the monastery as early as the 1080s, lodging the episcopal *familia* in the monks' buildings.[6] The move to Coventry may have been prompted both by the wealth of the city and by the lack of rival institutions there in comparison to Chester.[7] William of Malmesbury noted Bishop Robert's depredations of the monastery and that he was no supporter of the monks, even claiming that '... he never saw to the endangered roofs, which were threatening to fall in'.[8] Despite this, Bishop Robert was buried at Coventry, which William claimed was to aid the claims of his successors to the church.[9] There was a vacancy following his death, before the short episcopacy of Robert Peche (1121–26), who was followed by Roger de Clinton (1129–48), a bishop who seems to have favoured Lichfield, the division of interests which was ultimately to prove disastrous for the cathedral at Coventry.[10]

A number of early sources report that in 1143 the buildings were fortified as part of the siege of Coventry during the Anarchy. This may well have left an archaeological record; a ditch was discovered which ran north–south under the foundations of pier N2 and the north aisle wall of the church, and turned east at about the mid-point of the nave.[11] At the points where it survived best it was 1.58m deep and 7.5m wide. It appeared to have been open for a relatively short time, and was backfilled with material containing ceramics dating to the middle of the 12th century.[12]

Later in the 12th century Bishop Hugh de Nonant (1185–98) attempted to replace the monks with a secular chapter, a move which was ultimately unsuccessful but which resulted in the expulsion of the monks from 1189–97. Far from signalling a pause in construction, Bishop Hugh is reported to have to have spurred building on, using materials from the monastic buildings which he had destroyed for the 'unfinished church of that house'.[13] A royal grant of twenty oaks was made in 1247–51, during a period of financial difficulty for the priory, which may have been for roofing or spires.[14] Certainly, this date fits well with the stylistic evidence discussed below. Following the suppression of the cathedral in 1539 the majority of the buildings, apart from the western towers, appear to have been destroyed within about fifty years.[15]

This does not give a very clear chronology for the building. 1102, the date of papal confirmation for cathedral status at Coventry, has frequently been used as a *terminus post quem* for construction of the cathedral, but since it may simply confirm pre-existing arrangements it is of little help. It is also conceivable that the monastic community could have initiated the reconstruction before the church became a cathedral, as happened at Ely (from *c.* 1082) and St Alban's (from *c.* 1077). From the actions of Hugh de Nonant, however, it is clear that he, at least, regarded the construction of the new church as an episcopal responsibility. Of the earlier bishops, Roger de Clinton is perhaps an unlikely candidate as he seems to have favoured Lichfield, establishing new prebends at that cathedral using Coventry lands.[16] Robert de Limesey has, however, been credited with the reconstruction of the churches at his two other episcopal centres. At Lichfield, William of Malmesbury claims Robert 'began great buildings', a view which the archaeological evidence seems to support. At Chester, the architectural remains also seem to support a date of *c.* 1100.[17] William's silence on building work at Coventry may be because of his desire to present Robert as a persecutor of the monks, and Robert's burial at the church suggests him as the most likely patron.[18]

Clearly, the west end of the church was incomplete by 1143, when the ditch was dug, was still incomplete in 1189 when Bishop Hugh expelled the monks, and may indeed only have been completed *c.* 1250. This is a remarkably slow rate of construction. No other English cathedral which we know of seems to have taken so long to complete. A number of factors may have contributed to this: the disruption to building during the Anarchy, poor relations between the monks and the bishop, the division of interest between Coventry and Lichfield, and possibly that the cathedral seems to have had no parochial role, lying itself in the parish of Holy Trinity.[19]

SURVIVING AND EXCAVATED EVIDENCE FOR THE CATHEDRAL CHURCH

THE remains of the church lie a short distance north of the church of Holy Trinity, and downhill from it. This suggests that some other institution occupied the summit of the hill, perhaps an earlier minster church. The site required terracing and some making up of the ground to build the church and conventual buildings. The first terrace was just outside the south aisle wall, while the north arcade stood partly on made-up ground.[20] During the excavation of the nave, some rather enigmatic foundations of what was possibly a late-Saxon church were found under the north arcade, below and to either side of pier N6. The foundations were aligned east/west, and to the west of pier N6 part of a round feature was uncovered, with its curvature facing west.[21]

From successive excavations fragmentary remains have been revealed of the east and west crossing piers on the north side, a pier for an arcade on the east side of the north transept, the arcade piers on the north side of the nave, and most of those on the south side (Fig. 1 and Col. Pl. IA in print edn). The only two piers from the nave which retained any cut stonework were the easternmost piers on the north and south sides

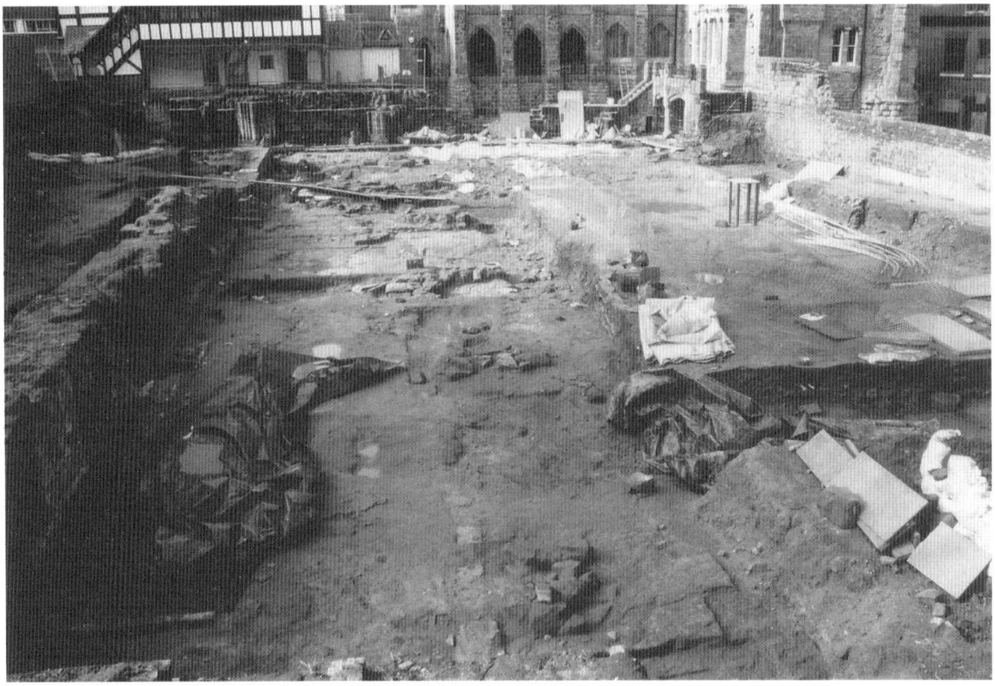

FIG. 1. Coventry, Cathedral Church: nave site as excavated, looking west along the south arcade pier foundations

Photo, March 2000, R. K. Morris

(N8 and S8; Fig. 2). Simple pilaster buttresses are visible against the remaining courses of the south aisle wall, which survive exposed from the east side of the west tower to a point just east of pier 6. Opposite pier S3 there is the base with a type of water-holding profile, different from those further east (Fig. 3). The interior of the west wall, uncovered in the 19th century, stands revealed in the present sunken garden with evidence for a central western door, responds for the arcades and larger west-facing responds for the western towers. The architectural fragments currently encased on top of the pier footings, however, do not relate to the piers which once stood above the footings. In summary, there is evidence for a nave of nine bays, a crossing, a transept with an eastern aisle, at least on the north side, and a west front with towers standing outside the aisles. Evidence for the length of the transept is somewhat circumstantial, and there is none for the choir in the Romanesque and early Gothic period.

The protracted building campaign is evident from the change in pier form. To the east their foundations were mostly essentially cruciform, but lozenge-shaped further west (Prelim., Plan A). The former seem to have been, broadly speaking, of Romanesque

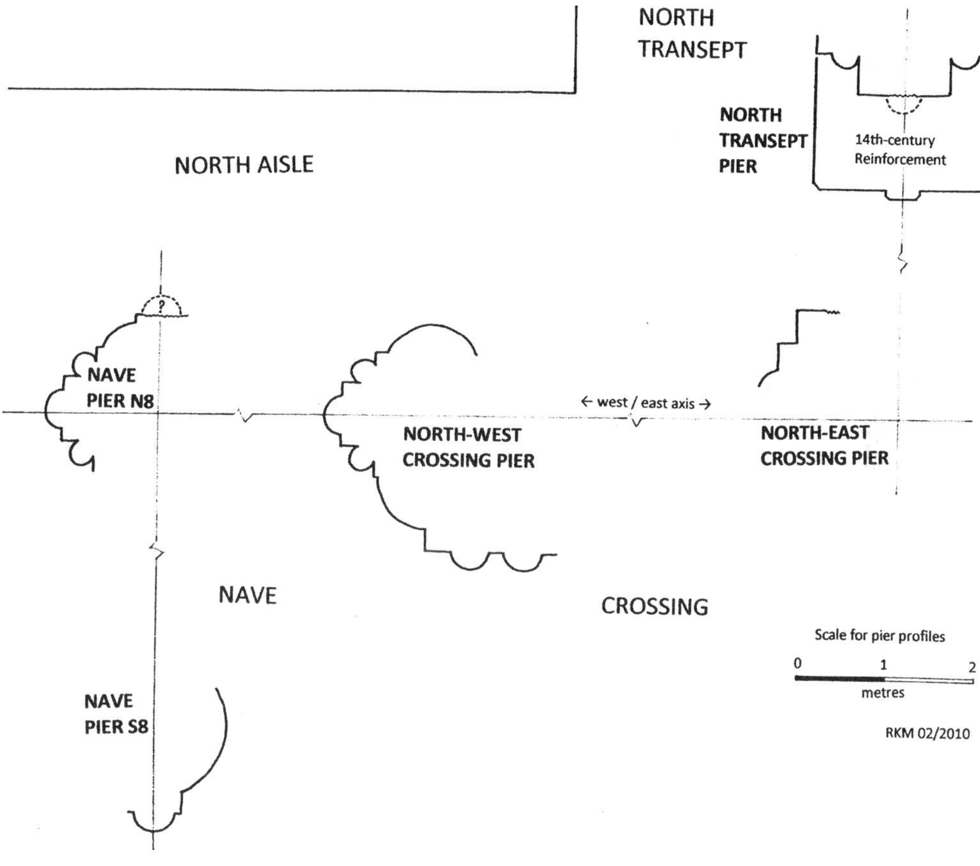

FIG. 2. Coventry, Cathedral Church: profiles of excavated piers which retain worked stonework, in the north transept/crossing/east bay of the nave

Drawing, R. K. Morris

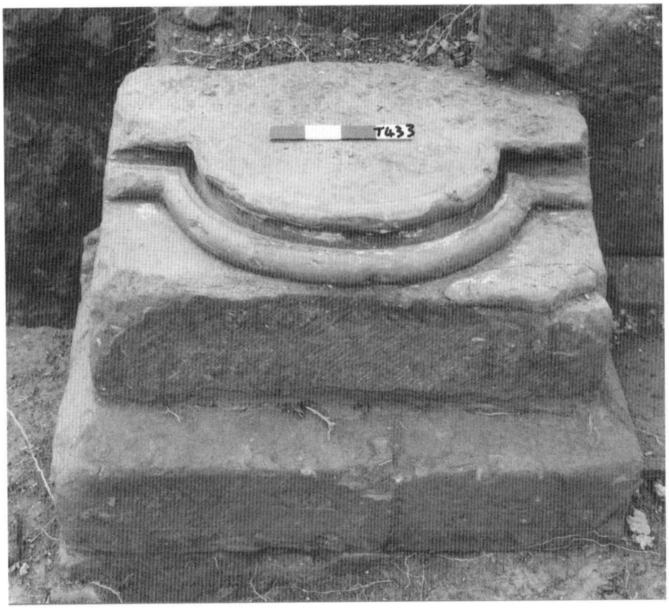

FIG. 3. Coventry, Cathedral Church: south aisle, the base of the respond opposite nave pier S3 (scale 20cm)
Photo, R. K. Morris

type, the latter early Gothic. The surviving evidence for the Romanesque piers was best preserved at the east end of the nave, and is no longer exposed, while the Gothic piers are best understood by reference to the western responds (Fig. 4). The change in pier type occurs at pier N5 on the north side, and somewhat further west on the south side, where only the westernmost two piers are lozenge-shaped.[22] The conjunction of early Gothic western bays to Romanesque eastern bays occurs at a number of other English great churches, Selby Abbey (Yorkshire) and Romsey Abbey (Hampshire), for example,

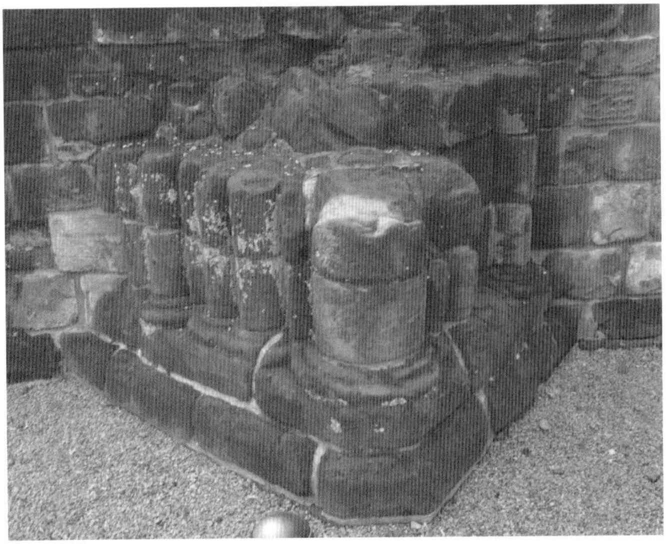

FIG. 4. Coventry, Cathedral Church: nave north arcade, west respond
Photo, author

but the disjunction between north and south arcades is more unusual. The change in form cannot be easily put down to any particular historical circumstance, and indeed seems to represent a change of heart quite late in construction. Beneath pier N2, the pier which overlies the ditch associated with the defences built during the Anarchy, the foundation trench for what might have been part of a cruciform pier was found (Prelim., Plan A). While no other indications of the setting out of cruciform piers were apparent in piers N3, N4 and N5, this may only be because the evidence was destroyed.[23] It is possible that structural instability caused the north side piers to be rebuilt, though there is no evidence to suggest to what extent, if at all, the piers had been built to a cruciform shape, and none to suggest that the church had been completed in a Romanesque style and then reconstructed.

CHOIR

NOTHING can be assumed about the form of the choir, whether apse ambulatory or apse echelon, or its length, since a nave of similar dimensions produced choirs of two, three and four bays at Tewkesbury Abbey, Gloucester Cathedral and Durham Cathedral respectively. At Durham the liturgical choir seems to have been placed entirely to the east of the crossing, while the possible evidence of a screen attached to the pier S8 uncovered in 2004 (see below) might indicate that this was not the case at Coventry. A shorter eastern arm might therefore be expected, and the suggestion that the partially surviving Gothic chapels at the east of the cathedral were simply added to a Romanesque east arm of a similar length is unlikely.

Likewise we can say little about the nature of the supports. In other churches where there is an aisle only on the eastern side of the transept, such as Durham and Peterborough, the pier forms tend to follow those of the eastern arm; in this case this would indicate that the eastern arm had an elevation based on cruciform piers.[24] However, this can hardly be stated as a firm rule. There were probably columnar supports, mixed with piers, in the eastern arm of Winchester Cathedral, where the transept piers (found on both east and west sides) are all compound cruciform.[25]

Robert de Limesey, the putative patron of the earliest phase of the building, which should have included the eastern arm, may have two other fragmentary eastern arms to his credit at the other sites most closely associated with his see. The church of St John, Chester and Lichfield Cathedral seem both to have had columnar arcades, but there the similarities between the two end. At Chester there remains a flat eastern wall which was penetrated by openings to an eastern apse in the centre and two flanking chapels, while at Lichfield there seems to have been an apse with an unusually narrow ambulatory.[26] Either or neither could have been employed at Coventry. Both, moreover, display greater affinities with the Romanesque architecture of western England, while Coventry, as shall be seen, finds close parallels in its pier forms with eastern England.[27]

TRANSEPT

THE limits of the transept are also poorly known: a fragment of wall was uncovered in 1825, giving an unusually short north/south length.[28] This was corroborated by the 1960s excavations which discovered the south wall of the chapter-house, with a weathered plinth demonstrating that it had been external.[29] Allowing for a passage between chapter-house and transept (surely a covered slype is precluded by the 'badly weathered' state of the plinth) the current reconstruction of the transept has an internal length of only about 35m (Prelim., Plan A). The 19th-century evidence relating to the transept was not recorded with standards of modern accuracy, which has raised doubts about whether the transept was symmetrical, though this is perhaps unnecessarily compounding irregularities in the building.[30] As to why such a modest transept should have an aisle, we can again only speculate. One reason might be to provide additional altar space, which would, in turn, require there to be a gallery in the transept at least. This may have implications for the elevation of the whole church, though there are a number of churches with galleries in the eastern arm but not the nave, such as Gloucester and Hereford cathedrals and Tewkesbury Abbey.

PIERS

DESPITE the best efforts of the archaeologists, the evidence for the Romanesque piers is very scrappy, and cut stone was revealed only for the north transept pier, north-east and north-west crossing piers, and the nave piers N8 and S8. None can be fully reconstructed with complete certainty, as in no case was more than half the pier recovered, and in no case was the surviving part of the pier facing the surviving part of the adjacent pier. All are now reburied. The piers present a bewildering variety of forms, which makes reconstruction of the elevation of the church highly problematic. Each pier, however, can be paralleled at other buildings of the late 11th and early 12th centuries, particularly buildings in East Anglia. Furthermore, the bases found *in situ* on the north-west crossing pier and nave pier N8 are of a type described by Stuart Rigold as 'markedly eastern' in distribution, with reduced upper and lower rolls flanking an elongated central band, and with comparative examples mostly dating from *c.* 1110–30.[31]

The transept pier (Figs 2, 5) was uncovered on its southern face, which had a later medieval addition. The pier appears to have been roughly cruciform, longer east/west,

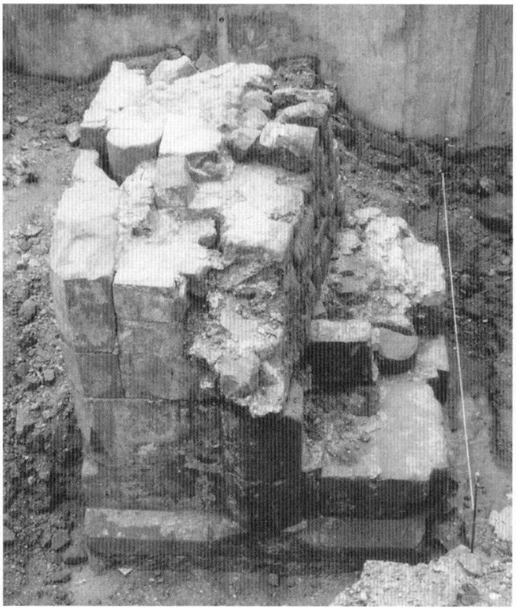

FIG. 5. Coventry, Cathedral Church: north transept pier, from the south, with the masonry reinforcement added in the 14th century
Photo, R. K. Morris

with the southern pilaster probably having a half-shaft on the southern face, the eastern and western pilasters flanked by half-shafts.[32] The shape of the pier can be compared to a number of examples, such as the strong (fully compound) piers in the north transept at Ely Cathedral (probably before 1093) or in the nave of Thorney Abbey (Cambridgeshire, late 11th and early 12th century).[33] One would expect, following those examples, that a pier of this form would support an arcade of two orders, the outer order on the flanking half-shafts, supporting a wall just under 2m in thickness.

Of the north-eastern crossing pier only the north-western corner was found, stepped, with a half-shaft (perhaps one of a pair) on the western side (Figs 2, 6). The north-western crossing pier revealed more cut stone, in this case on the southern and western faces: two half-shafts, perhaps out of three, on the southern face and a quadrant roll in the angle between the south face and the west respond, which had a central half-shaft flanked by angle-shafts (Figs 2, 7). The pier was asymmetrical, as there was a substantial half-columnar feature on the northern, aisle, side. Leaving this latter feature aside, the form of the pier with three shafts projecting from a quadrant feature can be best paralleled at Dunstable Priory (Bedfordshire), founded in 1131 by King Henry I, but dating in its surviving western parts from later in the 12th century (Fig. 8).[34]

The stonework of nave pier N8 survived, frustratingly, on its north-west quarter, not that facing the crossing pier (Figs 2, 9). On its western face it had a central pilaster with a half-shaft flanked by angle shafts, like that of the crossing pier, and had a quadrant element between this and the northern face, but of much smaller dimensions than that of the crossing pier to its east. If this is reconstructed as a fully symmetrical pier, with a half-shaft and pilaster on the north and south faces, quadrant rolls in all four corners and triple shafts east and west, one can find slightly simpler parallels in the weak (partly columnar) piers in the nave of Peterborough Cathedral, begun probably in 1118, but not completed until the second half of the 12th century.[35] However, it is possible that it might not have been a symmetrical pier, as will be argued below.

To complete this mismatched group, the equivalent nave pier S8 in the south arcade was uncovered in a separate excavation in 2004 (Fig. 2; Patrick, Fig. 7).[36] Only the south-east quarter was found (surviving at a height of perhaps 3m above the floor, and not investigated to its base), but this was columnar, with a shaft to the south, towards the aisle. Abutted to the east face were masonry remains, interpreted by the

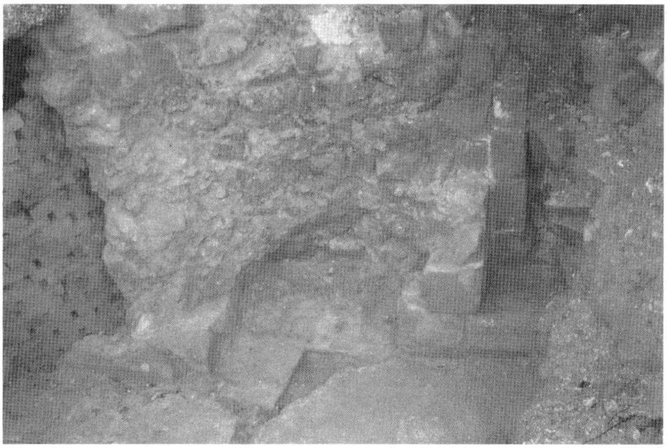

FIG. 6. Coventry, Cathedral Church: remains of the north-east crossing pier, from the north
Photo, R. K. Morris

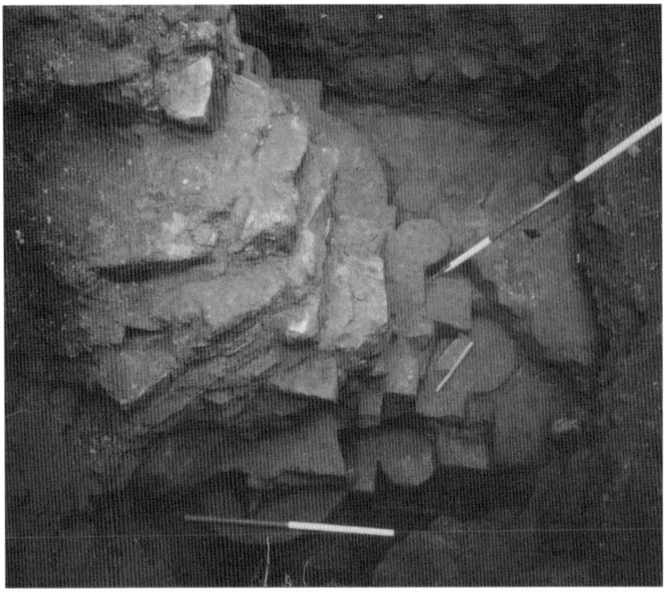

FIG. 7. Coventry, Cathedral Church: north-west crossing pier, north and west faces
Photo, R. K. Morris

archaeologists as the remains of the screen separating the liturgical choir from the aisle.[37] This interpretation is supported by reports from 1909 of the discovery of this pier, and another 'a little to the north', which would have formed part of the north–south return of the screen forming the western enclosure of the choir.[38] We have no evidence of the north face of the pier, and therefore cannot know whether it had a shaft to match that on the south side. If it did not, and is reconstructed as a symmetrical pier, it can be paralleled to the columnar piers in the Ely transept; if it did have a half-shaft, it compares to the weak piers of Thorney Abbey or (in a slightly more elaborate form) to the weak piers in the nave of Ely Cathedral (after 1100; Fig. 10).

The pier forms discovered can be reconciled into a regular arcade only with the greatest difficulty, but a case should be made for the most orderly possible arrangement of the piers, even if it is neither demonstrable at present, nor entirely convincing. The first consideration is that the piers should match across the nave. Even at Castle Acre Priory (Norfolk; Fig. 11) and at Rochester Cathedral, where each pier differs from the next, the piers match across the nave in the north and south elevations, as always seems to have been the case (except with minor variations) when the work was constructed during one stylistic phase. It may be, of course, that Coventry provides an exception to this rule, and that this might not be the case when there is a substantial stylistic shift, as demonstrated by Coventry itself in the western part of the nave. There is, however, no evidence of such a shift directly west of the crossing. One would expect in a reasonably orderly building campaign that the east end of the nave would be completed in a single campaign, especially if it formed the west end of the choir; breaks being most often evident to the west of the first bay.[39] This would only be possible if the missing parts of the piers somehow matched up, so that the east side of pier N8 would match its counterpart on pier S8, and the west side of the latter would in turn match its counterpart on pier N8. Such a solution is not impossible, and has a certain precedent in English Romanesque both in the crossing of Peterborough Cathedral and at Castle

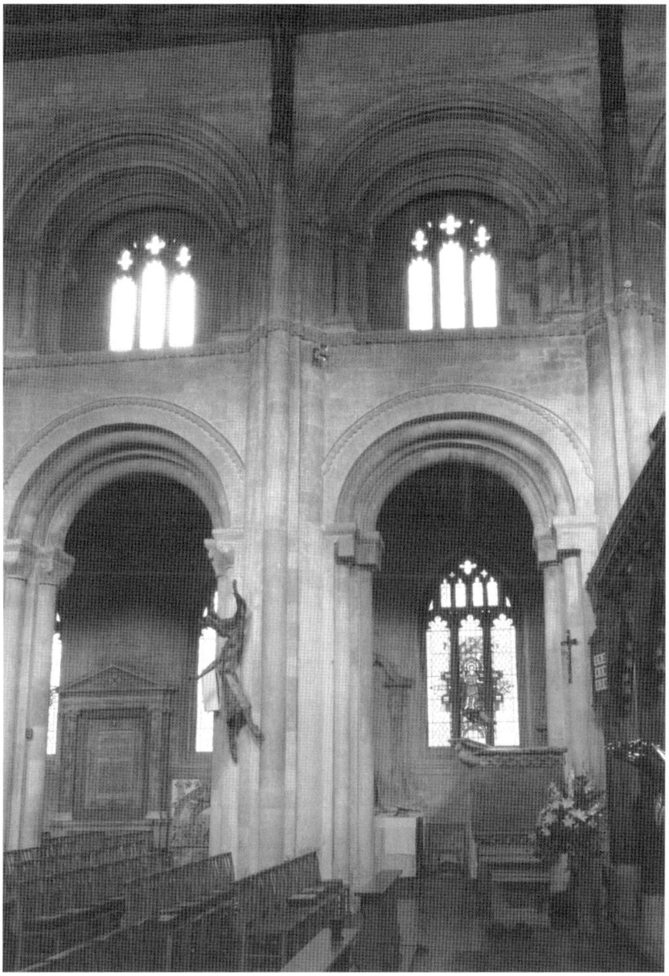

FIG. 8. Dunstable Priory: the east bays of the nave, north elevation
Photo, author

Acre Priory, where the piers are asymmetrical on a north/south axis, but the faces match within each arcade bay (Fig. 11).[40]

This reconstruction, therefore, requires both eastern nave piers to have a columnar eastern face and compound western face (Fig. 12). While it might be objected that the west face of the north-west crossing pier does not match the east face of pier S8, this situation is not unknown elsewhere; for example, at Romsey Abbey, the west face of the compound crossing pier does not match the columnar easternmost pier of the nave. There is, however, also a problem with the correlation between pier N8 and the north-west crossing pier, which might encourage the reconstruction of pier N8 as asymmetrical. On their surviving (west) sides, both had a group of three shafts, similar to, but narrower than, the three shafts which probably supported the arcade on the transept pier (Fig. 12).[41] Both had a quadrant roll flanking the three shafts, but that of the crossing pier was substantially larger than that of the nave pier (with a radius of 530mm against the 330mm of the nave pier). Indeed, the projection southwards of the quadrant

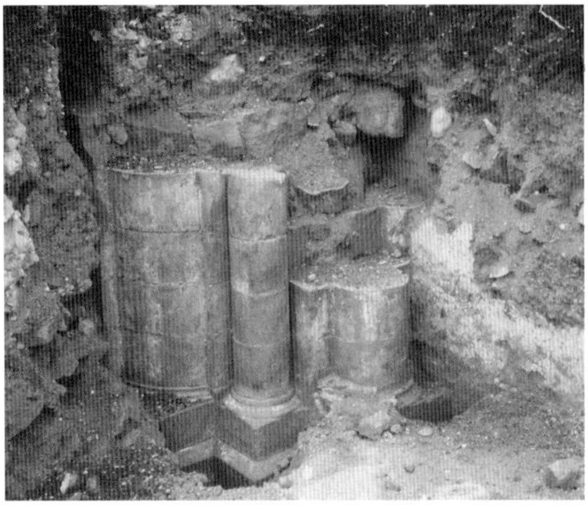

FIG. 9. Coventry, Cathedral Church: nave pier N8, from the north-west
Photo, R. K. Morris

roll of the crossing pier into the main vessel of the nave would appear to be the equivalent of all the elements of the nave pier N8, if N8 were to be reconstructed as a fully symmetrical pier. This raises the question as to what, if anything, it would have supported. At Dunstable, the comparative example cited above for the north-west crossing pier, the quadrant supports a giant order which encompasses the arcade and gallery above (Fig. 8). On the Peterborough piers, perhaps closer to the nave pier, the quadrant sections support the outer order of the arcade. Two solutions for the elevation on the north side therefore suggest themselves.

The first has the quadrant section of the crossing pier supporting a feature which rises straight up the elevation, not forming part of the nave arcade. A comparable solution can be seen at Carlisle Cathedral, where a shaft is found in the angle of the crossing pier and the east respond for the nave arcade.[42] The quadrant roll of the nave pier finds no answering element in the crossing pier, and it could either support an element which rises through the elevation, or support an outer order of the arcade (or a giant order) which somehow dies into the quadrant element of the crossing pier, while the inner two orders are supported on the group of three shafts. The advantage of this reconstruction is that it results in a symmetrical pier N8 as part of a regular system with what (little) is known of the other Romanesque piers of the nave, with their roughly cruciform plinths. The disadvantage, apart from the potentially messy junction with the crossing pier, is that it ignores the evidence of nave pier S8.

Therefore a second solution would be to reconstruct the east side of pier N8 as columnar, like S8. This might, when coupled with the quadrant element of the crossing pier, give a different character to the east bay of the nave, one in which columnar elements predominate. They may have risen through the elevation for a giant order, as at Romsey and Dunstable, or may have been confined to the arcade level. We have no evidence for the south-west crossing pier, so any problems with its alignment can only be guessed at, but on its north side the elevation would project further into the main vessel in this bay than it would in those further west. In favour of this possibility is the apparent similarity of the Coventry pier forms to piers in eastern England, where asymmetrical piers are known at Castle Acre Priory (Fig. 11).

Differences in pier design and elevation in the eastern bays of the nave, compared to the western bays, have often been noted elsewhere in English great churches. They are

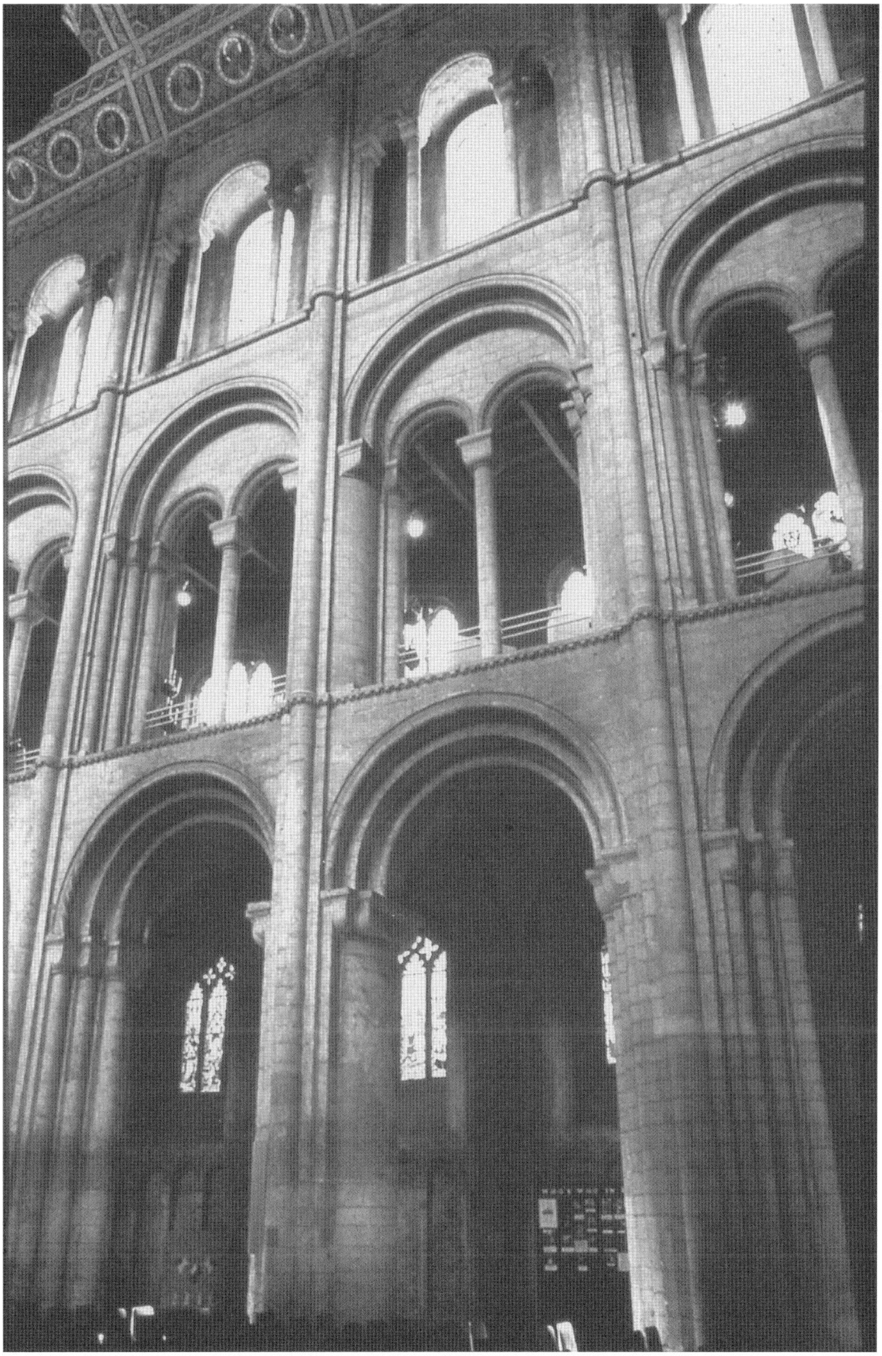

FIG. 10. Ely Cathedral: nave north elevation, from the east
Photo, author

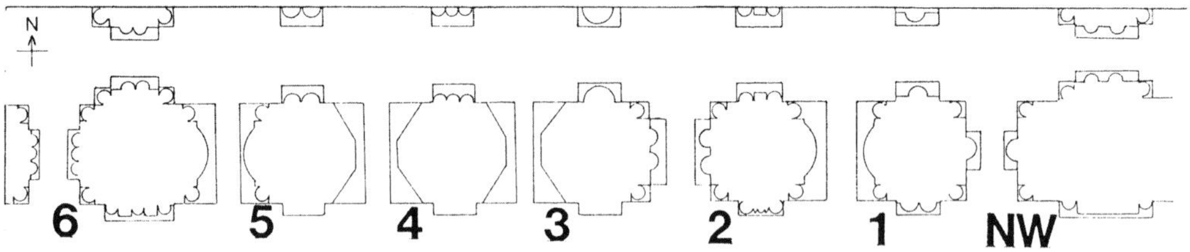

FIG. 11. Castle Acre Priory: schematic reconstruction of the nave pier system, north arcade (NW = north-west crossing pier)

JBAA, 1978, drawing courtesy of B. Cherry

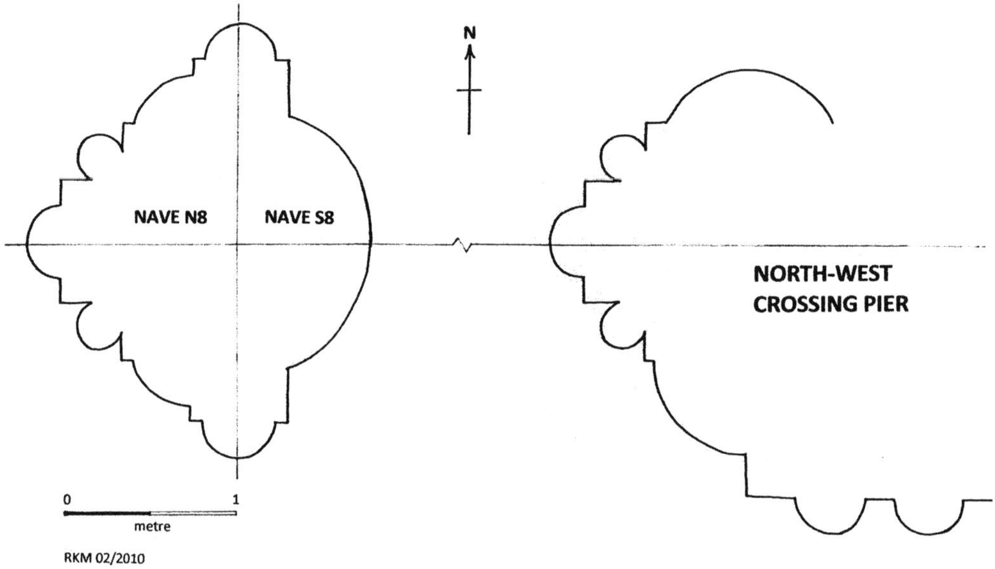

FIG. 12. Coventry, Cathedral Church: nave pier N8, a possible reconstruction in relation to the north-west crossing pier

Drawing, R. K. Morris

now usually interpreted as planned variants, associated with the presence of the west end of the choir and the nave altar.[43] Columns in particular are often associated with purposeful change of support, for example, at Norwich Cathedral and Romsey Abbey. This view has gained currency against the traditional interpretation of the changes being caused by building breaks and an alteration in the design. Of course, it is possible that both might coincide. At Lenton Priory (Nottinghamshire), there were columnar elements to the piers in the eastern bays, coinciding with the position of the west end of the choir and the nave altar, but a break in the foundations between the westernmost of these and the first fully compound pier was also found.[44] The evidence for the piers at Coventry is so exiguous that a number of other explanations are possible. For example, since the piers were found at different heights, pier N8 could have changed to a columnar form below the height at which its southern counterpart was discovered.[45]

Thus, on the available evidence, no straightforward solution can be offered for reconstructing the Romanesque nave and crossing piers. The simplest explanation would be that the monks of Coventry lived for 400 years with mismatched piers, but the appearance would have been so odd that it does not seem the most likely.

WESTERN BAYS

AS mentioned above, piers S3–S7 on the south side and N6–N8 on the north had cruciform foundations. Piers S1 and S2 and N1–N5 were lozenge shaped, although there appeared to be a foundation trench of a cruciform pier under pier N2. There is little evidence for the piers themselves (though loose fragments were discovered in the excavation and are discussed below), but it is tempting to assume that the cruciform piers resembled the exposed part of pier N8 (Fig. 2), and the lozenge piers the responds against the western wall (Fig. 4). A base for the respond opposite pier S3 survives *in situ* (Fig. 3) and is of the water-holding type also found on the 13th-century west front for the shafts of the centre and north doors.[46] However, the profile of the respond base is different to those of the west front, being closer to 'neo-attic' designs found elsewhere in the later 12th century, and therefore likely to pre-date them.[47] The pier it faces was of the earlier cruciform type. The best-preserved, and best-known, evidence for the whole cathedral is provided by the wedge-shaped responds on the west front (Fig. 4), the smaller ones facing towards the arcade, the larger ones across the projecting bays which supported the western towers. These consist of a semicircular shaft on the axis flanked by groups of keeled shafts, sitting on double roll bases.[48] On the aisle side of the responds to the arcades the central shafts were detached, and are now lost. The affinities of the forms used on the west front are fairly widespread, but the most pertinent stylistic comparisons for their detail are perhaps with the transepts of Lichfield Cathedral, complete or nearly complete by 1241.[49] Coventry and Lichfield shared a base type, used mixed coursed and detached shafts and have similar polygonal buttresses on the exterior.[50]

The west front was evidently a splendid structure; a screen façade with towers over projecting bays, as was eventually constructed at Wells Cathedral but belonging to a tradition going back to the early 12th century where it is found at St Botolph's Priory, Colchester (Essex).[51] The readily appreciable architectural ambition of the façade should remind us that what we have lost of the building would once have matched its splendour.

LOOSE STONES

LARGE numbers of architectural fragments were recovered from the nave and transept during excavation.[52] A selection of the best are on display in the Priory Visitor Centre and many more are in a store off the Priory Undercrofts. A number once formed parts of Romanesque half-shafts, some of which still retain a good deal of limewash.[53] There are also parts of shafts, both coursed and free-standing from the Gothic phase; keeled triple shafts, as are found on the standing responds at west end, along with annulets which presumably belonged to free-standing shafts. From the same period there are fragments of stiff-leaf capitals.[54] These give us a further indication that the piers of the western parts of the nave would probably have resembled the western responds.

A Romanesque voussoir found in the north transept, close to the north-east crossing pier, was from a large arch, either arcade or crossing. It had a roll on the angle with a quirk on the face.[55] A further, smaller, Romanesque voussoir with similar mouldings was found in the nave, its size suggesting it came from openings in the middle storey or clerestory.[56] The early Gothic voussoirs are more interesting, again likely to come from the middle story, as a large double-springer block was found, suggesting paired openings (Fig. 13). This, and its associated voussoirs, had complex mouldings: beak, roll-and-fillet, and a beaked roll-and-fillet.[57]

Two sets of stones from rib-vaults were found fallen into the aisle bays over which they had stood. The earlier set, found in bay 7 north, were square in section with chamfered corners and showed the diagonal tooling characteristic of Romanesque masonry (Fig. 14; Morris, Fig. 6C, T565). Quite a few have excellent masons' marks on their reveals. The stones found included the key-stone, with a linked foliate pattern (Fig. 15).[58] The later ribs, from bay 2 south, are more delicate versions of these, narrower in section and with chamfers in the corners (Morris, Fig. 6C, T500). While

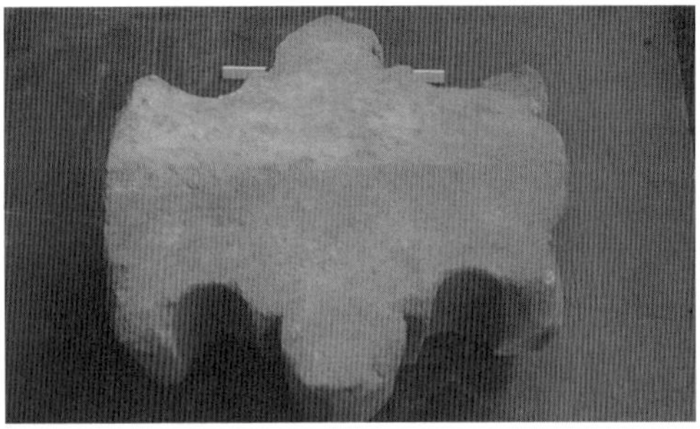

FIG. 13. Coventry, Cathedral Church: early Gothic voussoir
Photo, author

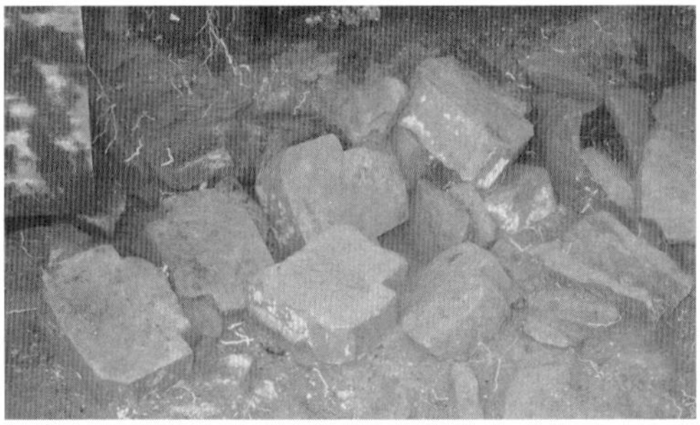

FIG. 14. Coventry, Cathedral Church: square-section rib-stones, as found in nave bay N7
Photo, R. K. Morris

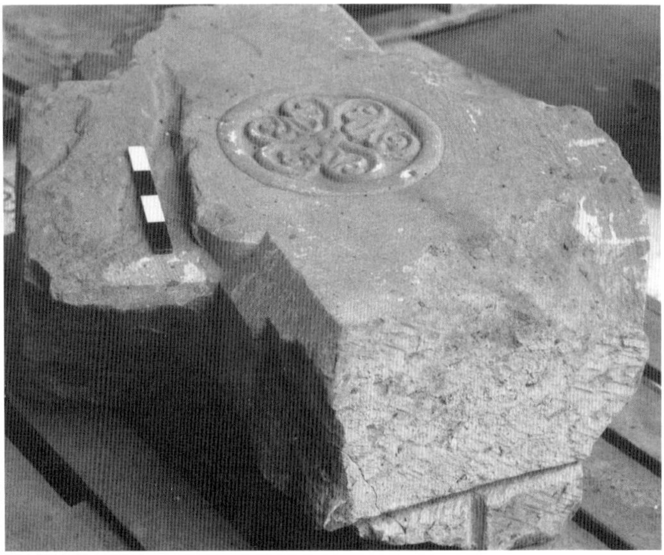

FIG. 15. Coventry, Cathedral Church: the key-stone for a vault with square-section ribs (scale 20cm)
Photo, R. K. Morris

these are hard to parallel elsewhere, they were presumably developed out of the local Romanesque prototype.[59] Square-sectioned ribs could be viewed as an early form, occurring as they do in the south transept chapel at Tewkesbury Abbey (*c.* 1100).[60] At Coventry, the evidence is ambivalent. On the one hand, the rib-stones in bay 7 north were supported on the pier N6 which had a skeleton under it dated to the mid-12th century.[61] On the other hand, the key-stone was found further east, adjacent to pier N8, which could suggest that this type of rib was in use earlier in the building works.[62] A number of square-sectioned ribs occur in Warwickshire, evidently also from a period well into the 12th century; in the crypt of St Mary's, Warwick, in the crypt of Berkswell parish church and in a rebuilt form at Beaudesert church.[63] All three share a peculiarity of construction: the diagonal ribs fall on corbels angled approximately in line with the ribs (Fig. 16). In each case the arrangement gives the air of improvisation.[64] No shaft or respond is underneath the corbels, and the corbels themselves, in each case scalloped, do not seem particularly shaped to their function. The impression is of an unplanned imposition of a rib-vault on a pre-existing structure, though it would be surprising if a change of plan actually occurred at all three sites. Indeed, at Warwick the central piers of the crypt have ample half-shafts to receive the diagonal ribs, indicating that the vault was planned. However, there is no sign of provision for ribs on the cathedral aisle walls either; the surviving respond base sits on a pilaster with no shafts flanking it to receive diagonal ribs. Thus it may be that the unusual form of springing of these Warwickshire rib-vaults reflects a practice which was also once found at the cathedral church.

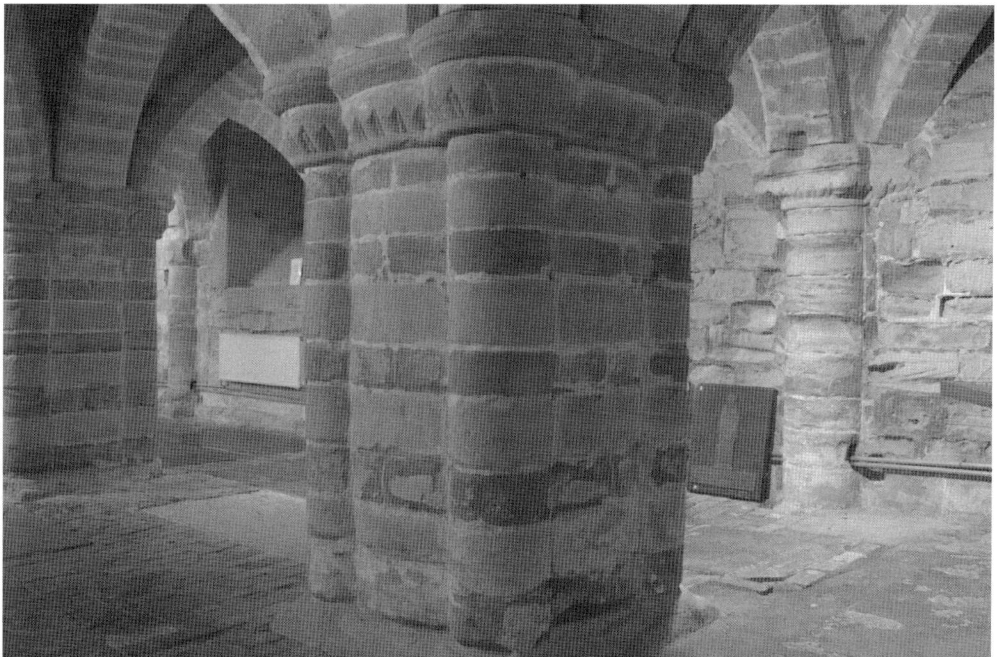

FIG. 16. Warwick, St Mary's church: the crypt
Photo, author

CONCLUSION

WHILE excavation has revealed a great deal of material from the medieval church, St Mary's Cathedral remains something of a mystery. However, we can be more certain of the dates of the fabric, as the forms found around the crossing reflect other works from the early decades of the 12th century, and the west front seems closely related to Lichfield in the second quarter of the 13th century. Whether the stylistic change from Romanesque to Gothic coincided with the attempt of Bishop Hugh de Nonant (1189–97) to complete the church, or came soon after, cannot be decided on the limited stylistic evidence available. It is clear, however, that the earlier parts of the building derived their repertoires of forms from East Anglia, not something that would have been known before the excavation, and in contrast to the other major buildings of the diocese, at Lichfield and Chester. Further investigation might solve some questions, for example about the anomalies of the nave supports, or the original form of the choir, but sadly most are destined to remain unanswered.

ACKNOWLEDGEMENTS

My thanks to Richard K. Morris, both for inviting me to speak at the conference, and for his encouragement and advice, and to Duncan Givans for his company and driving around Warwickshire.

NOTES

1. Poole, *Antiquities*, 14, 18; T. F. Tickner, 'The Cathedral and Priory of St Mary of Coventry and an Approximate Restoration of the Plan of the Church', *JBAA*, n.s. 25 (1919), 24–38; Hobley, 'Cathedral Excavations'. A summary and interpretation of what was known by the early 1990s is found in Morris, 'Cathedral Church', 19–42.

2. The main campaign of excavations was published in Rylatt and Mason, *Cathedral Priory*, preceded by a preliminary report by Northamptonshire Archaeology, *Excavations at the Cathedral Church of St Mary, Coventry 1999–2000: Summary Report* (Northampton n.d). The archive of this campaign is kept at the Herbert Art Gallery and Museum, Coventry. For the later excavation, see G. Demidowicz and C. Patrick, 'Excavations at 7 Priory Row 2004, The Cathedral of St Mary, Priory Row, Coventry (SP 3354 7909)', CBA *WM Archaeology* 47 (2004), 7–14.

3. Bassett, *Anglo-Saxon Coventry*.

4. Goddard, *Coventry 1043–1355*, 21–48.

5. M. J. Franklin ed., *Coventry and Lichfield 1072–1159*, English Epicopal Acta 14 (Oxford 1997), xxxii–xxxvi.

6. Ibid., xxxi.

7. A. Thacker, 'The Early Medieval City and its Buildings', in *Medieval Archaeology, Art and Architecture at Chester*, ed. A. Thacker, *BAA Trans.* XXII (Leeds 2000), 23–4.

8. William of Malmesbury, *Gesta Pontificum Anglorum: the History of the English Bishops*, I, *Text and Translation*, ed. and trans. M. Winterbottom and R. M. Thomson (Oxford 2007), 468–71.

9. *Gesta Pontificum*, 470–1.

10. For Roger de Clinton, see Franklin, *Coventry and Lichfield 1072–1159*, xxxviii–xlvii; for the dissolution of the priory at the Reformation, J. J. Scarisbrick, 'The Dissolution of St Mary's Priory, Coventry', in Demidowicz ed., *First Cathedral*, 158–68.

11. The piers of the north arcade are titled N1, N2, et.c, and those of the south arcade S1, S2, etc., both counting from west to east (Prelim., Plan A); the bays are numbered 1 to 9, also from west to east.

12. Rylatt and Mason, *Cathedral Priory*, 16–19 and fig. 5.

13. M. J. Franklin ed., *Coventry and Lichfield 1183–1208*, English Epicopal Acta 17 (Oxford 1998), xxx–xxxv. The quote is from Richard of Devizes, *The Chronicle of Richard of Devizes of the Time of King Richard the First*, ed. and trans. J. Appleby (London 1963), 70.

14. M. W. Lambert, 'The History of the Benedictine Priory of St Mary', in Hobley, 'Cathedral Excavations', 62–3.

15. Rylatt and Mason, *Cathedral Priory*, 25–8, 141.

16. VCH *A History of the County of Stafford* III, ed. M. W. Greenslade and R. B. Pugh (London 1970), 142.

17. *Gesta Pontificum*, 470–1; W. Rodwell, 'The Development of the Choir of Lichfield Cathedral: Romanesque and Early English', *Medieval Art and Architecture at Lichfield*, ed. J. Maddison, *BAA Trans.* XII (Leeds 1993), 20–2; R. Gem, 'Romanesque Architecture in Chester, *c.* 1075–1117', in Thacker ed., *Medieval Archaeology at Chester*, 38–41.

18. His account contains some notable inconsistencies. At the outset of his account of the diocese, he writes: 'The church [at Lichfield], on its cramped site, gave a good idea of the moderation and restraint of the ancients; our modern bishops would not think it a fit place of residence for episcopal dignity', and concludes with the 'great buildings' there begun by Robert. Robert himself was 'a man by no means of ill repute, taking him all in all', despite William's earlier accusations of bribery. *Gesta Pontificum*, 464–5, 468–71.

19. Bassett, *Anglo-Saxon Coventry*, 12.

20. Rylatt and Mason, *Cathedral Priory*, 20.

21. Rylatt and Mason, *Cathedral Priory*, 12–15.

22. The pier foundation (pier S4), reconstructed by Hobley as a columnar pier, proved to be cruciform; Hobley, 'Cathedral Excavations', 93 and fig. 4.

23. Rylatt and Mason, *Cathedral Priory*, 20.

24. Durham has alternating columns and piers, Peterborough columns and polygonal columns. An alternating system is less likely at Coventry because the (sole) compound pier in the transept is adjacent to the compound crossing pier.

25. For definitions and further information on pier types, see E. Fernie, *The Architecture of Norman England* (Oxford 2000), 258–61, 316.

26. Gem, 'Romanesque Architecture in Chester', 38–41; Rodwell, 'Development of the Choir of Lichfield', 20–2.

27. This division is used for great churches in Fernie, *Norman England*, 102–76. Notable differences are in a preference for complex piers in the east, as against columnar piers in the west, though such a distinction is by no means absolute. For piers in eastern England, see B. Cherry, 'Romanesque Architecture in Eastern England', *JBAA* 131 (1978), 1–29.

28. Poole, *Antiquities*, 18.

29. Hobley, 'Cathedral Excavations', 92 and figs 2 and 5.

30. Morris, 'Cathedral Church', 25–7, raises the possibility of an enlarged south transept housing the cult of St Osburg; see also Morris, 'Priory', in this volume, 70.

31. S. Rigold, 'Romanesque Bases in and South-East of the Limestone Belt', in *Ancient Monuments and their Interpretation; Essays presented to A J Taylor*, ed. M. Apted (Chichester 1977), 119–20 and fig. 5. Each worked stone has been given a T (type) number in the Worked Stones Catalogue; see further, Rylatt and Mason, *Cathedral Priory*, 64. The records for the north-east crossing base are T475–8, and T471–2 for nave pier N8.

32. All the *in situ* Romanesque stonework is discussed briefly in Morris, 'The Worked Stones', 80.

33. E. Fernie, 'The Architecture and Sculpture in the Norman Period', *A History of Ely Cathedral*, ed. P. Meadows and N. Ramsay (Woodbridge 2003), 97–9; J. Ayton, 'Thorney Abbey: An Architectural Analysis of a Romanesque Fen Abbey-church' (unpublished MA dissertation, University of London, 1998).

34. N. Pevsner, *Bedfordshire and the County of Huntingdon and Peterborough*, B/E (1968), 75–7.

35. Cherry, 'Romanesque Architecture in Eastern England', 15–17.

36. Demidowicz and Patrick, 'Excavations at 7 Priory Row', 7–14.

37. See further Patrick in this volume, 29–30.

38. Demidowicz and Patrick, 'Excavations at 7 Priory Row', 9, 11.

39. Fernie, *Norman England*, 294–5.

40. Perhaps begun at the end of the 11th century, but evidently, from the detailing of the west front, not completed until the later part of the 12th century. See M. Thurlby, 'The Influence of the Cathedral on Romanesque Architecture', in *Norwich Cathedral: Church, City and Diocese, 1096–1996*, ed. I. Atherton, E. Fernie, C. Harper-Bill and H. Smith (London and Rio Grande 1996), 138–42; Cherry, 'Romanesque Architecture in Eastern England', 12–15, with the possible additional example of Thetford, 11–12; L. Reilly, *An Architectural History of Peterborough Cathedral* (Oxford 1997), 30–1.

41. The width of the feature in the transept is 1940mm, whilst on the crossing pier and pier N8 it is 1320mm.

42. R. Plant, 'The Romanesque Fabric of Carlisle Cathedral', in *Carlisle and Cumbria: Roman and Medieval Architecture, Art and Archaeology*, ed. M. McCarthy and D. Weston, *BAA Trans.* XXVII (Leeds 2004), 95–7.

43. E. Fernie, 'The Use of Varied Nave Supports in Romanesque and Early Gothic Churches', *Gesta* 23 (1984), 107–17.

44. B. W. Beilby, 'Excavations at the Cluniac Priory of the Holy Trinity, Lenton, 1962–64', *Transactions of the Thoroton Society* 70 (1966), 55–62. My thanks to Richard Halsey for drawing this building to my attention.

45. The best-known English pier which changes form as it rises is pier 11 in the Canterbury Cathedral choir; P. Draper, 'Interpretations of the Rebuilding of the Canterbury Cathedral, 1174–1186: Archaeological and Historical Evidence', *Journal of the Society of Architectural Historians* 56 (1997), 184–203.

46. The respond base is T433; the relevant west front profiles are T410, T413.

47. R. K. Morris, 'An English Glossary of Medieval Mouldings: with an Introduction to Mouldings *c.* 1040–1240', *Architectural History* 35 (1992), 10.

48. Morris, 'Cathedral Church', 50–4.

49. M. Thurlby, 'The Early Gothic Transepts of Lichfield Cathedral', in Maddison ed., *Medieval Art and Architecture at Lichfield*, 50–64.

50. Morris, 'Cathedral Church', 54; Thurlby, 'Transepts of Lichfield Cathedral', 56.

51. J. P. McAleer, 'Particularly English? Screen Facades of the Type of Salisbury and Wells Cathedral,' *JBAA* 141 (1988), 124–58, esp. 137–40 and 142–3.

52. They are all recorded in the Worked Stones Catalogue compiled by Richard Morris, a copy of which is in CA; its findings are summarised in R. K. Morris, 'The Worked Stones and Architectural Stonework', in Rylatt and Mason, *Cathedral Priory*, 63–82.

53. For example, T508 and T509.

54. Triple shaft T523; annulet T536; capitals T604; triple capital T503, perhaps from one of the exterior buttresses. Morris, 'Worked Stones', 71.

55. T915; Morris, 'Worked Stones', 76. The stone could not be retrieved and was left *in situ*; my thanks to Richard Morris for sharing his drawings of this with me.

56. T613. Other excavated pieces cannot be assigned securely to the church itself rather than the monastic buildings, e.g. T758, a chevron voussoir found in Trench 10 (east range of the cloister bordering the north transept).

57. T591, with which belong eleven pieces of T638; Morris 'Worked Stones', 71, dates it to *c.* 1200 or early 13th century. See also Morris, 'Glossary of Medieval Mouldings', 5.

58. Rylatt and Mason, *Cathedral Priory*, 20; Morris 'Worked Stones', 71. The ribs are T565 and the key-stone, displayed in the Priory Visitor Centre, is T699.

59. T500; Morris, 'Worked Stones', 71.

60. M. Thurlby, 'The Norman Church', in *Tewkesbury Abbey: History, Art and Architecture*, ed. R. K. Morris and R. Shoesmith (Little Logaston 2003), 93.

61. A radiocarbon dating of *c.* 1160; Rylatt and Mason, *Cathedral Priory*, 12.

62. Rylatt and Mason, *Cathedral Priory*, 20.

63. For Beaudesert, Berkswell and Warwick, see N. Pevsner and A. Wedgwood, *Warwickshire*, B/E (1966), 88–9, 90–1 and 443 respectively. Both Berkswell and Beaudesert use fleshy-leafed capitals related to water-leaf capitals.

64. At Beaudesert the capital and corbels supporting the ribs appear to be medieval.

The Gothic Architecture of Coventry Cathedral and Priory: Keeping Up Appearances?

RICHARD K. MORRIS

The Phoenix Initiative excavations of 1999–2003 produced extensive new physical evidence for the buildings of the lost cathedral priory of St Mary, Coventry, and this paper is a brief account of the main findings relating to the Gothic architecture. In the cathedral, the picture was a fairly typical one of keeping up appearances in an ageing Romanesque great church — piecemeal new fenestration of the nave through the 14th century, structural problems with the crossing tower (perhaps newly built) in the mid-14th century, and a new transept vault around 1400. However, investigation of the conventual buildings revealed a much more pro-active story. Most of the accommodation around the cloister was reconstructed in the second and third quarters of the 13th century, as evidenced by the partial survival of a fine series of undercrofts, including one with the earliest known tierceron rib-vault in Coventry. Then, in the next century, two impressive new ceremonial rooms were created with the rebuilding of the chapter-house (c. 1310–30), later to be embellished with a cycle of Apocalypse paintings, and of the refectory (c. 1340) with a polychromed stone pulpit of the same date. In the early 15th century, an ambitious renovation of the cloister was undertaken on the model of that at Gloucester, but by then more limited resources would not stretch to vaulting its alleys in stone.

WHEN my preliminary assessment of 'the Cathedral Priory church' was published in 1994,[1] little could I have imagined that so much more of the physical evidence for St Mary's cathedral priory would be discovered so soon afterwards, primarily as a result of the Phoenix Initiative excavations (1999–2003).[2] So the opportunity has been created for this second paper, providing a review of the Gothic architecture of the cathedral church and conventual buildings in the light of this new evidence.[3]

THE CHURCH

THE account of the cathedral priory church in my 1994 paper now requires some updating. The available evidence from the fabric up to 1994 was relatively modest and much of it derived from poorly documented excavations.[4] However, the excavation of the nave in 1999–2000 proved more fruitful, even though relatively little evidence for later medieval work was found because the rubble had been almost entirely removed between after 1545 (see Plant, Fig. 1), in contrast to the rich deposits of worked stones which survived on the terraced site of the conventual buildings (Fig. 1). Over 100

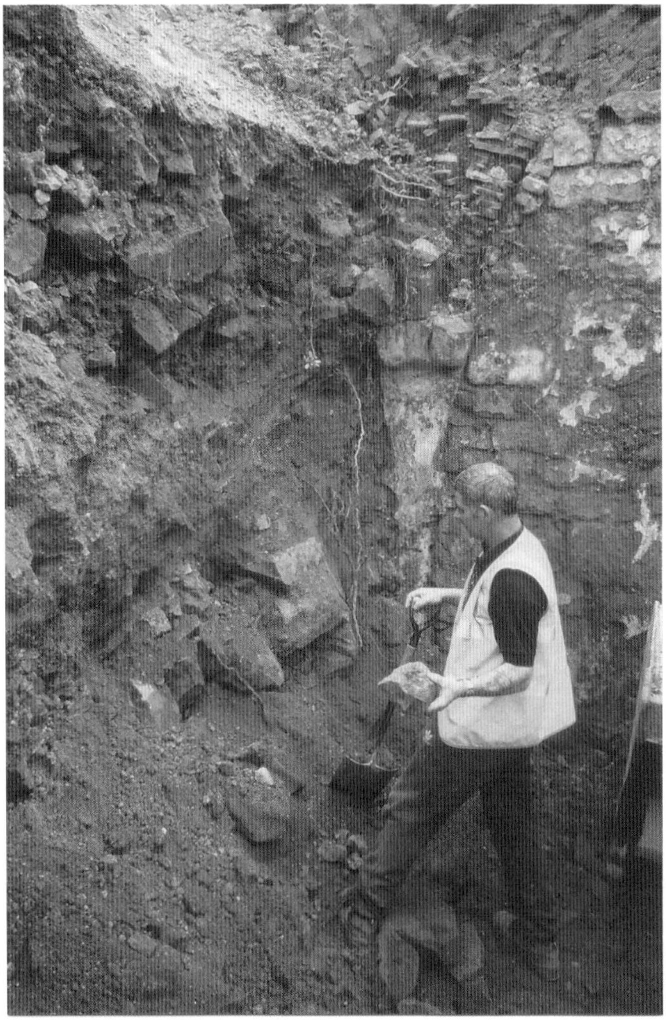

FIG. 1. Coventry Priory site: excavations in Trench 10, April 2002. Demolition rubble, mainly from the chapter-house, fallen into the eastern part of the east–west undercroft; note the respond for the undercroft vault, right of centre
Photo, author

fragments of window tracery were recovered which provide evidence for the modernisation of the 12th-century nave.[5] At least seven different designs of mullion profile can be identified amongst the tracery pieces, all of which seem to belong to the 14th century. Eight pieces of type T579[6] employ the design of an axial roll-and-fillet with lateral hollow chamfers (Fig. 2A),[7] generally comparable to the mullion profiles of the chapter house (*c.* 1310–30, see below). In another related design, T586, one half of the profile includes a small hollow and demi-roll-and-fillet (Fig. 2B),[8] an unusual feature for a mullion and with a distribution at sites in the east and south-east of England from the late 13th century to the mid-14th century.[9]

Generally, the surviving pieces are too fragmented to permit the reconstruction of tracery patterns, but T586/1 shows that this tracery included a light with an unframed trefoiled head, perhaps with an impaled foiled figure above as part of an intersecting

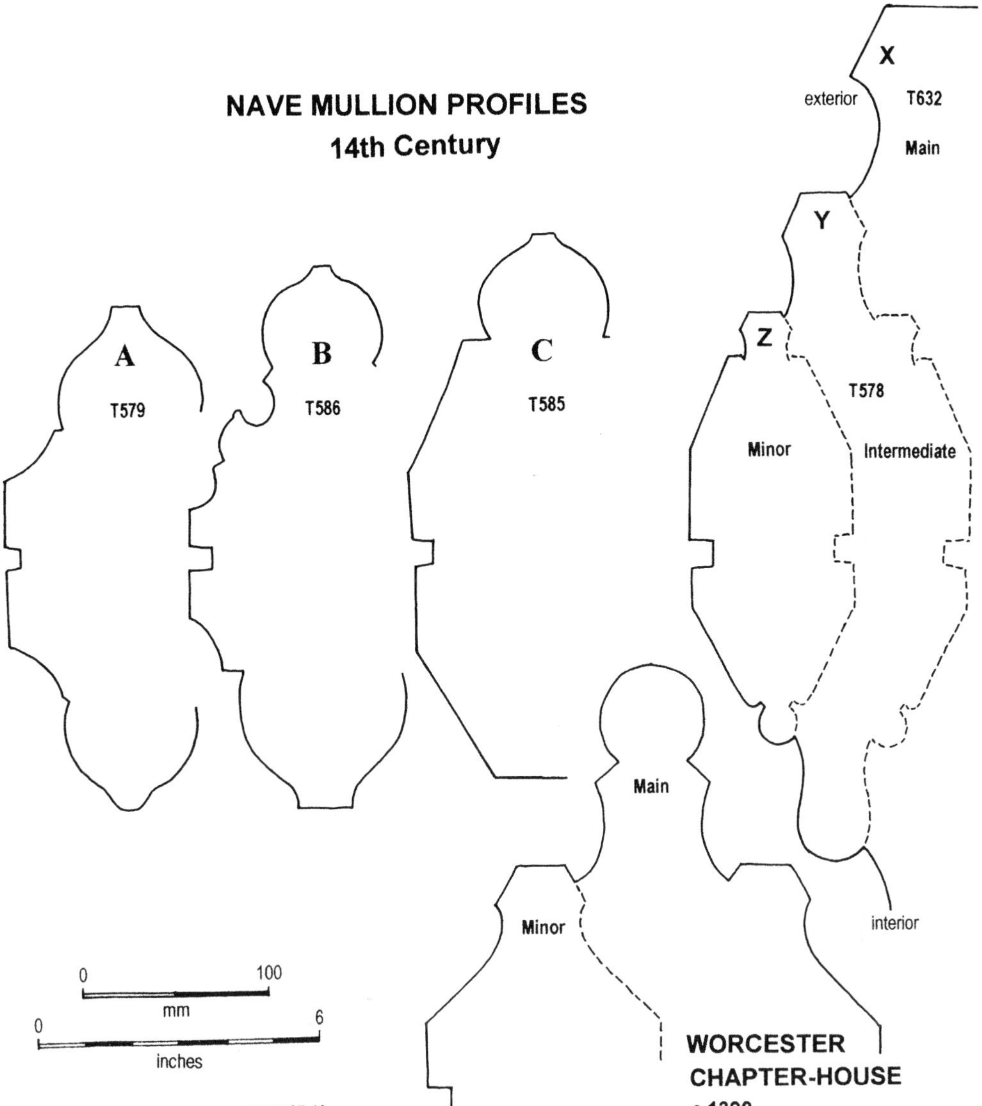

FIG. 2. Coventry Cathedral Priory: 14th-century mullion profiles from the nave. All moulding profile Figures are at ¼ scale, unless indicated otherwise

Drawing, author

tracery composition typical of some early Decorated windows of *c.* 1290–1325 (e.g. Old Arley, Warks., east window). In contrast, the cusping on T585, which has a different mullion profile (Fig. 2C), is ogee-foiled and indicative of a later date probably in the 1320s or 1330s.[10] Ogee foils originate in various delicate tracery designs developed in the Kentish court style of south-east England in the 1290s,[11] and which seem to have found their way into masons' pattern books elsewhere by the high Decorated period. At Coventry it is a possibility that the designer was the royal mason, Master Hugh de Titemersshe (Tichmers), who was granted a corrody at the priory in 1312.[12]

The impression is gained that the cathedral church had a variety of new windows introduced at various dates in the first half of the 14th century, which is in tune with the Decorated aesthetic for invention, as famously exemplified in the windows of Exeter Cathedral (*c.* 1280–1340). However, in contrast to the uniformity of the mullions at Exeter,[13] the number of different mullion profiles at Coventry suggests a more piecemeal succession of works,[14] some of which probably occurred in the time of Prior Henry Irreys (1322–42), when indulgences were granted to contributors to the fabric.[15]

More information can be gleaned from piece T632/1 than from any other tracery piece found on the nave site. It is a 'V-shaped' springing stone, almost 3 feet high (850mm max.), which sat on top of the centre mullion of a large window with a sub-arcuating tracery pattern (Fig. 3A).[16] The best-preserved face incorporates three successively larger mullion profiles, each with an axial polygonal moulding (Fig. 2, XYZ respectively). A similar hierarchy formerly existed on the other face (Fig. 2).[17] In the midlands, large axial polygonal mouldings for window tracery first made a significant appearance in the Perpendicular remodelling of Gloucester Cathedral (then St Peter's Abbey) from *c.* 1330, and the profiles which approximate most closely to T632 are those of the second phase of Gloucester cloister (1381–1412)[18] and comparable mullions at Worcester Cathedral chapter-house (*c.* 1390) and Tewkesbury Abbey cloister (*c.* 1400, Fig. 2). Therefore, overall, T632 seems to belong to the second half of the 14th century, perhaps to the decades *c.* 1370–90, and was part of a major window or set of windows probably at the west end of the church.[19] The size of springer T632/1 and the large curvatures implied by its major mullion profile suggest a sub-arcuated window of at least six lights (3 + 3), so the main west window must be a possibility.[20] The south window in the south transept of Gloucester Cathedral is an important early exemplar of a sub-arcuated window in an end elevation (*c.* 1335, 4 + 4 lights),[21] and prominent later examples in Coventry include the apse windows of St Michael's, *c.* 1400 (2 + 2; see Monckton, Fig. 13), and the 15th-century south transept window at St John the Baptist's (4 + 4, heavily restored).

Towards the middle of the 14th century, a structural problem had evidently developed with the central crossing, such that one or more of the Romanesque piers required reinforcement. The main evidence comes from the north transept pier, which had received a massive ashlar abutment against its south face, presumably reciprocated in the lost north face of the north-east crossing pier (Plant, Figs 2, 5). The second or third quarter of the 14th century is the most likely date for the reinforcement, on the basis of the style of the part-polygonal stoup T486,[22] integral with the west face of the new masonry. It is impossible to know for certain whether other areas of the crossing received similar treatment, because of a dearth of appropriate information about the other crossing piers.[23] However, nave south arcade pier S8 had the core of an abutment against its east face, which has been tentatively interpreted as part of the screen for the monks' choir,[24] but which perhaps might rather (or as well) be a reinforcement running east for the south-west crossing pier.

Almost certainly the cause of the problem was a heightening of the central tower, or possibly an entirely new tower — a scenario familiar from several other contemporary examples, of which that at Hereford Cathedral is especially comparable (tower erected *c.* 1305–15, structural failure by 1319).[25] Unfortunately, no pictorial evidence or

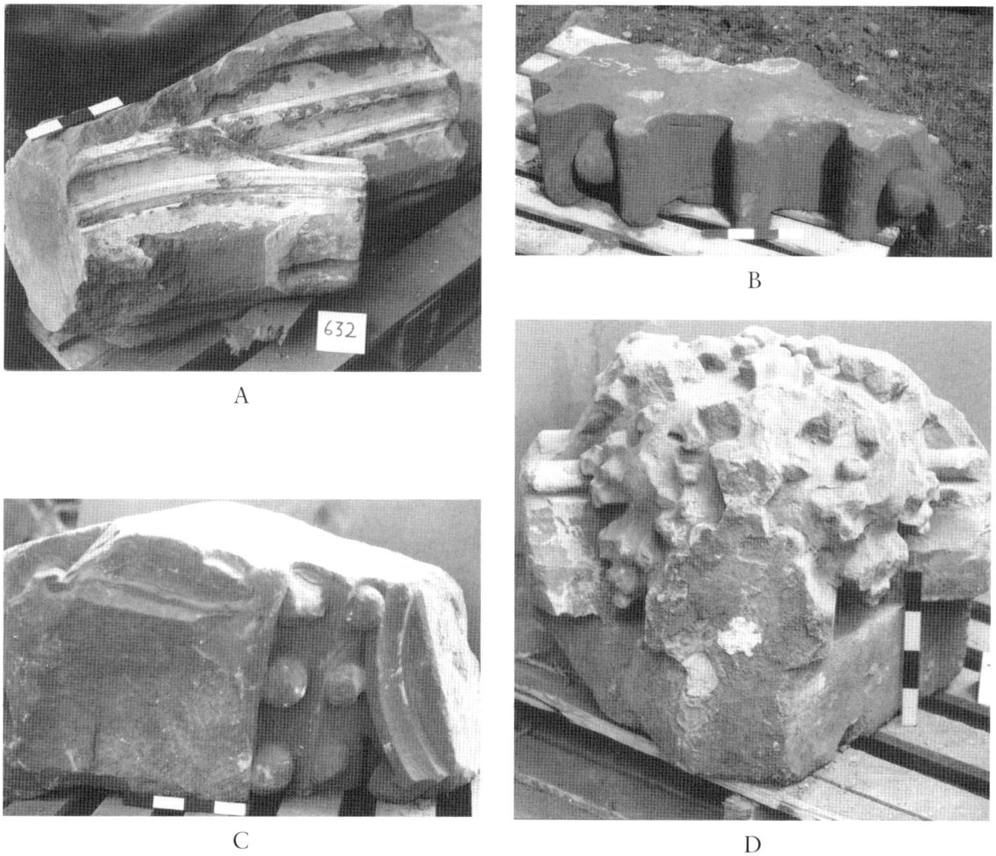

FIG. 3. Coventry Cathedral Priory: worked stones (scale 20cm). A. Tracery stone T632/1, perhaps from the nave west window; B. Buttress piece T345/1, perhaps from the crossing tower; C. T785 with blind tracery and ball ornament, perhaps from the crossing tower; D. Vault boss T795 from the north transept

Photos, author

surviving fabric can be associated with certainty with Coventry's central tower. It has been identified with the tower second from the right in William Smyth's view of Coventry (*c.* 1576), which would appear to show an octagonal tower of two stages (Demidowicz, 'Priory', Fig. 2).[26] However, it could equally be argued that this tower is that of the Whitefriars.[27] The reality is that Smyth's drawing is no more than an indicative representation of the city's skyline, done from memory, and that no conviction can be placed on its details.

Several large stones were found during the excavations which might have come from the central tower. The most dramatic was a large chunk of masonry forming the angle of an octagonal feature, which had apparently fallen from some height onto the north transept.[28] This raised expectations that it might be part of a stone spire. Almost certainly the central tower must have been crowned by a spire,[29] given the propensity for spires both in the city churches and at Lichfield, though whether constructed in stone or timber cannot be known.[30] However, the solid mass of the angle masonry was more likely to have been part of a corner turret or spirelet. The other stones are all carved with ball-flower or ball ornament, a motif found in profusion in the first quarter of the 14th century on central towers at Hereford, Salisbury and Lincoln cathedrals, and on the west towers at Lichfield.[31] A large block decorated with ball ornament (T345/1) must derive from an angular buttress, and the simplicity of its mouldings and the large size of the ornament implies that it was probably located high up, where small detailing was superfluous (Figs 3B, 4).[32] Its similarity of design to the cut-water buttresses on the corners of the Hereford tower is striking (Fig. 4). Another stone with ball ornament, T785, is from the head of a panel with blind cusped tracery, reminiscent of the blind windows in the Hereford tower (cf. Figs 3C, 4, 5). Thus, a case might be made for reconstructing a crossing tower with resemblances to that at Hereford,[33] but unfortunately some of the relevant stones were found in the excavation at some distance from the church and are unhelpful in corroborating this hypothesis.[34]

The partial exploration of the north transept site also provided new evidence for rib-vaulting in the eastern parts of the church in the late Gothic period. The key find was a large stone roof-boss (T795) with foliate carving, 16 inches (410mm) in diameter. A boss of this size would have come from a high vault, at a point where two tierceron ribs met a ridge-rib, as indicated by the positions of the four rib-stubs (Figs 3D, 11D). Tierceron 'star' vaults had appeared in Coventry in the 13th century (e.g. St Michael's,

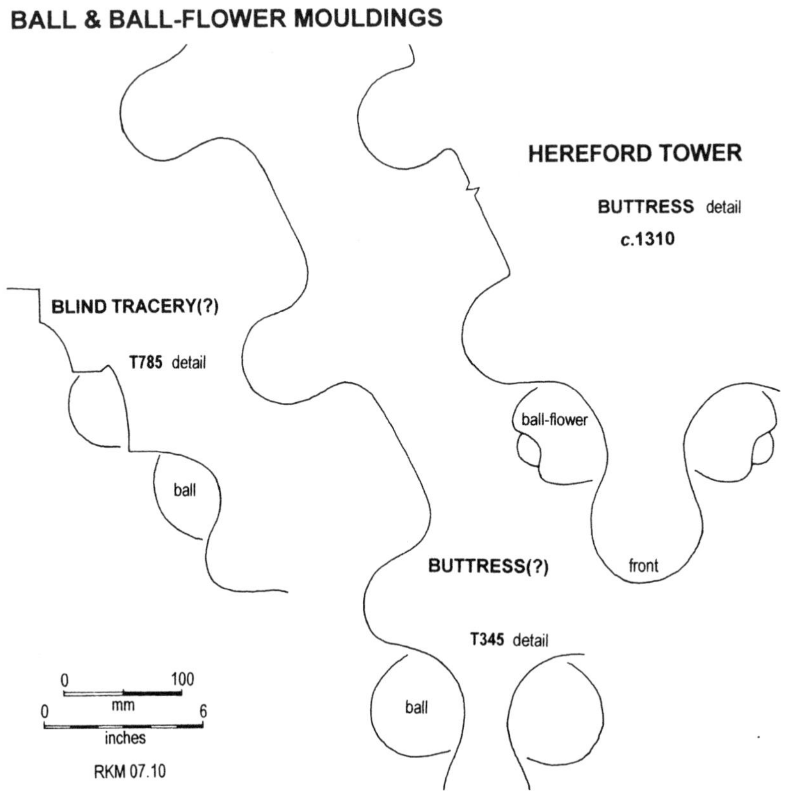

FIG. 4. Coventry Cathedral Priory: ball and ball-flower mouldings (from a former crossing tower?). ⅙ scale
Drawing, author

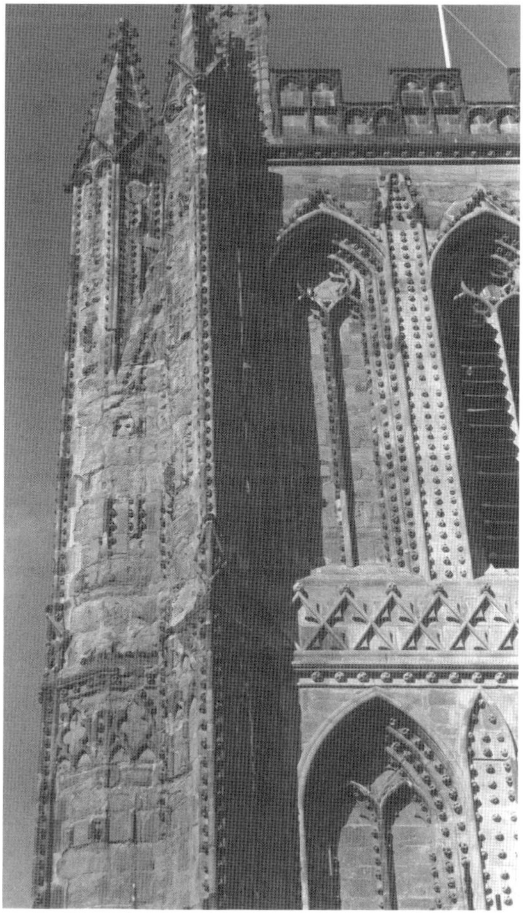

FIG. 5. Hereford Cathedral: crossing tower, detail
Photo, author

south porch; see Monckton, Fig. 5) and generally remained the basis for vault patterns in the later middle ages in the city and the midlands.[35] In Coventry, the comparisons for this style of high vault are restricted to lantern towers, but the structural problems with the cathedral's crossing, described above, make the central tower a less likely provenance for these vault pieces, which stylistically definitely post-date the Decorated 'ball' stones and quite probably the pier reinforcements as well. They are more likely to belong with a new vault inserted into the old transept, a process undertaken at a number of midland cathedrals in the period.[36] Though the heaviest piece of the vault, the boss T795, was found on the north transept site (Trench 3), the other fragments were spread over quite a large area (Trenches 3, 6, 10) and provide strongly suggestive evidence not only for the use of the cloister garth as a processing and distribution yard, but also for the sequence of demolition.[37] In Trench 10, the vault pieces were generally found on top of the rubble from the collapsed chapter-house, indicating that the conventual buildings had been despatched promptly after the 1539 Dissolution, but that the church had followed suit only after it was deemed redundant in 1545.

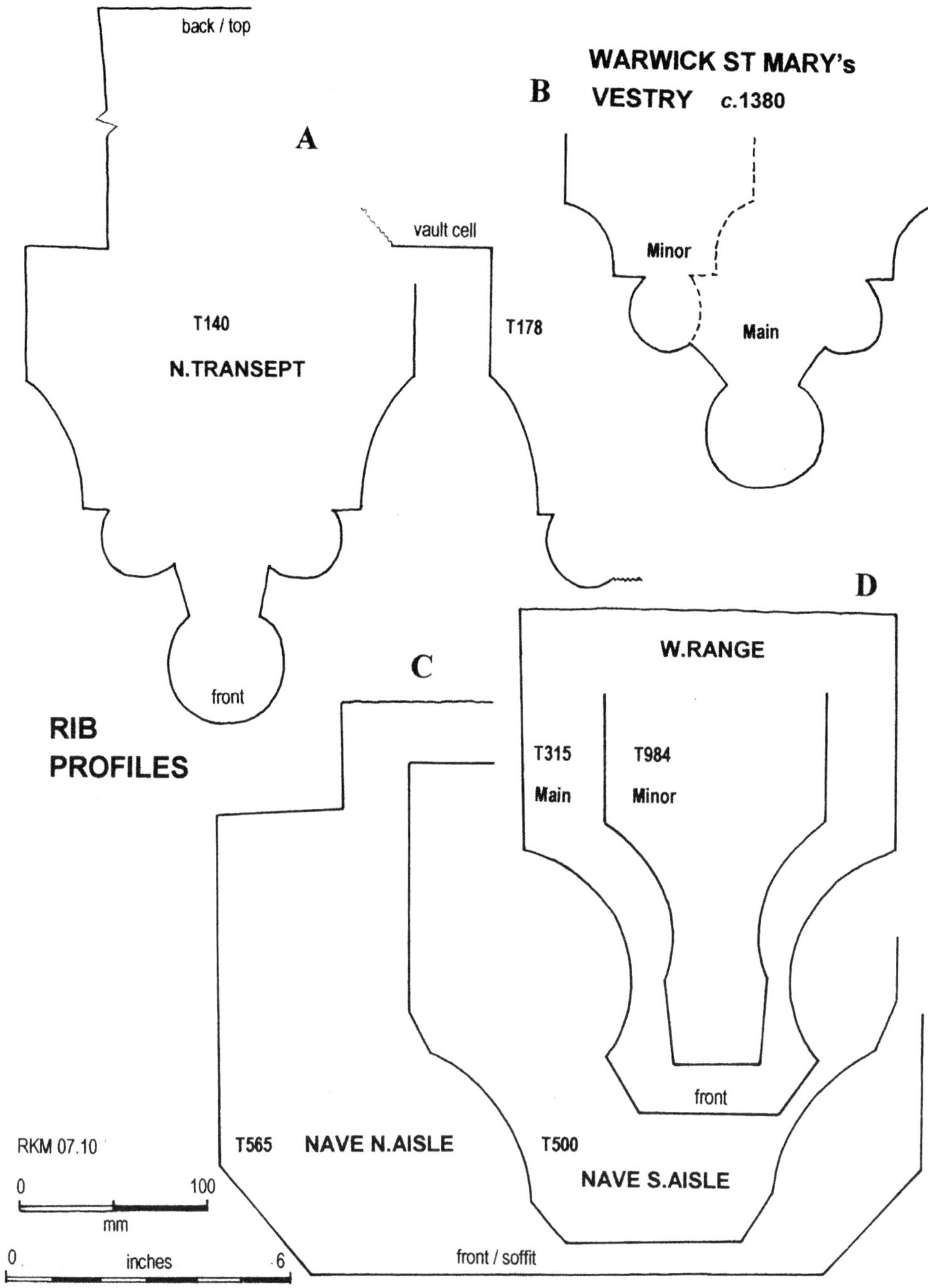

FIG. 6. Coventry Cathedral Priory: vault rib profiles from the cathedral church and west range
Drawing, author

The style of the boss T795 and its associated rib profile (T140)[38] suggests that the vault should be dated no earlier than the last quarter of the 14th century. The carved leaves can be compared with some of the foliage carving on the misericords from the Coventry Whitefriars (mid-1380s),[39] especially the handling of the trefoiled tips (Fig. 3D), though this style of foliage continues well into the Perpendicular period. The 'keyhole' profile of rib T140 consists of an axial roll linked by a wedge-shaped piece to a roll and hollow chamfer on each side (Fig. 6A). This profile became fashionable in the last quarter of the 14th century, in works in the south of England generally linked to major master masons with experience of the royal works, and usually for window mullions as, for example, in William Wynford's chapel at New College, Oxford (1380–86).[40] It became a classic moulding of the Perpendicular style, but it is rare in the midlands, except for an early example at St Mary's collegiate church, Warwick, in the vestry rib-vaults (1370s or 1380s).[41] The nave aisle vaults of Winchester Cathedral (after 1394) provide another early case of its employment for a rib, and both this and the Warwick example demonstrate that the design incorporates a minor rib profile for liernes and lesser ribs (Fig. 6B).[42] Thus the priory vault design almost certainly included liernes (Fig. 11D), as does the west porch vault of St Michael's (*c.* 1440), the only vault surviving in the city which mimics the rectangular bay pattern of a high vault.[43]

Thus, the recent finds on the cathedral's north transept site have increased our appreciation of the potential significance of Coventry's churches for major vaulting commissions in the late middle ages. The transept vault probably should be linked to the general revaulting of the eastern arm, for which in 1994 I proposed a date in the first half of the 15th century, relating it to the documented 'new work' of 1409.[44] It is doubtful that it could be as early as the work at St Mary's, Warwick, despite the similarity of rib design, because one fragment of the T140 group (T178) has the cell and rib cut from the same stone (Fig. 6A), suggesting a vault incorporating jointed masonry construction, as noted also in the stones attributed to the vault of the east arm, discovered in 1955.[45] Very precise cutting of the cell-stones is also indicated by the octagonal back-plate for the boss T795 (Fig. 3D).[46]

THE CONVENTUAL BUILDINGS

ONE should visit Gloucester and Worcester cathedrals to gain an idea from their surviving conventual buildings of what has been lost at Coventry. Hobley's excavations of 1965–66 were the first to elucidate the plan of the cloister and reveal the fabric of some of the buildings,[47] and the Phoenix excavations have added very considerably to our knowledge, particularly of the refectory, chapter-house and elements of the west range.[48] What Hobley had interpreted as an unusually massive square dormitory block has now been clarified as a series of undercrofts grouped around a small courtyard, probably with a dormitory range in an L-plan on the upper floor (Prelim., Plan A).[49] Very little physical evidence of the Romanesque monastic buildings was recovered in the recent excavations.[50] This would appear to substantiate that Bishop Nonant destroyed conventual buildings when he expelled the monks from the priory in 1189,[51] especially as there is clear evidence for extensive rebuilding of the undercrofts in the 13th century. However, the lack of early fabric must also result from the series of extensive new works carried out through the 14th century. The chronological development of the excavated buildings has been well summarised by Rylatt and Mason, so this short account will focus primarily on any differences of interpretation and on new information derived from study of the worked stones.

The undercrofts

THE earliest surviving Gothic fabric is found in the 13th-century remains of the undercrofts around the northern parts of the cloister, partly preserved as the 'Priory Undercrofts' (Demidowicz, 'Priory', Fig. 25). This incorporates an east–west undercroft and a north–south undercroft so, together with those under the former refectory and in the northern part of the west range, there are four recently excavated undercrofts to be considered (Fig. 7; Prelim., Plan A). Archaeological stratigraphy and evidence such as pottery deposits have allowed Rylatt and Mason to construct a relative chronology,[52] whereas the forms of the architecture are less helpful. A striking feature is the lack of exact repetition of details between the various undercrofts, which implies a piecemeal rebuilding through the century rather than one concerted campaign (Fig. 8B, C). For example, the plain chamfered ribs differ in their dimensions and, whereas one was designed using the geometry of an isosceles triangle (T453), the other two employ a different triangulation which produces a deeper, narrower profile (Fig. 8C). As the latter is used in the two earliest undercrofts, I must accept that my previous rule-of-thumb, that 'deep' profiles appeared only from the 14th century, is no longer tenable for chamfered ribs.[53] However, there are no repeats of template between the cathedral priory ribs and those of other vaulted crypts and undercrofts in Coventry and its

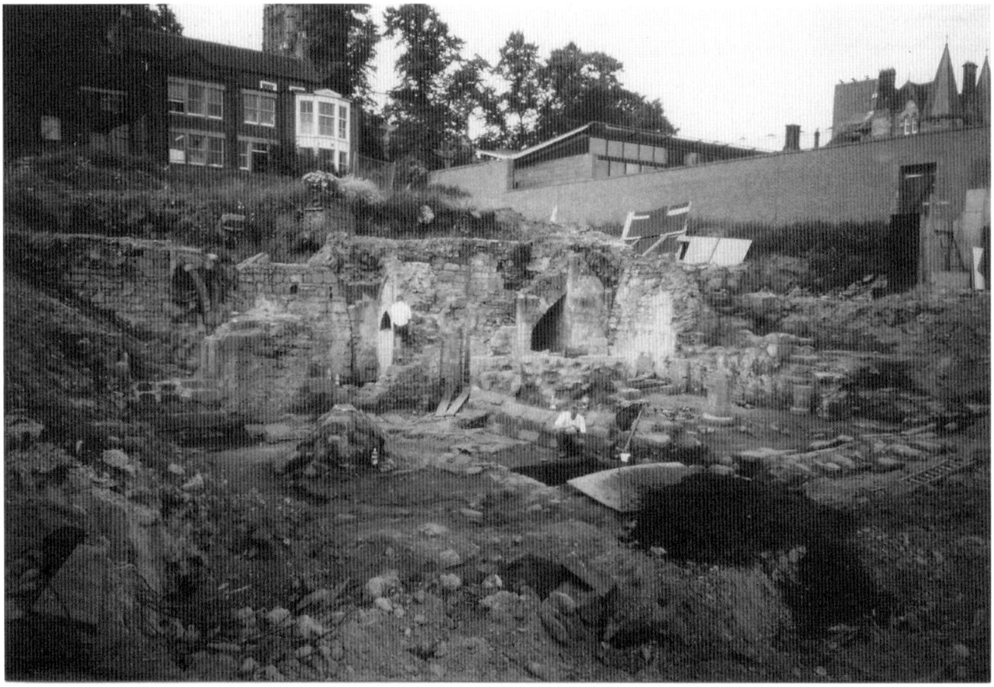

FIG. 7. Coventry Priory site: the undercrofts after excavation, looking south, July 2001. Courtyard (foreground) with a large lump of masonry fallen from the chapter-house vault. East–west undercroft (middle distance), with the 'great wall' and chapter-house site beyond. North–south undercroft is to the right

Photo, author

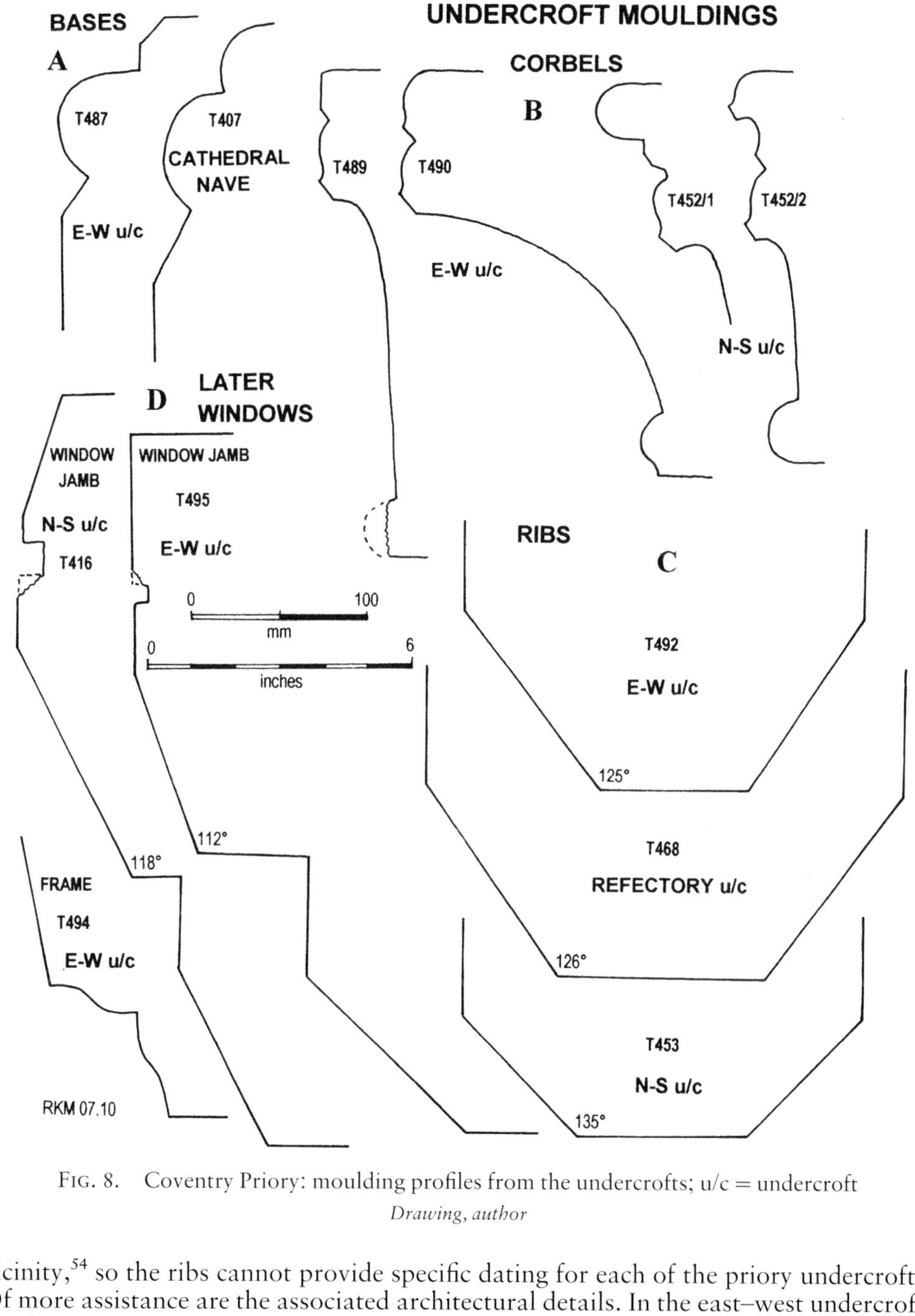

FIG. 8. Coventry Priory: moulding profiles from the undercrofts; u/c = undercroft
Drawing, author

vicinity,[54] so the ribs cannot provide specific dating for each of the priory undercrofts. Of more assistance are the associated architectural details. In the east–west undercroft, the demi-roll-and-fillet moulding of the respond capital and vault corbels (T489, 490) is unlikely to be much earlier than *c.* 1220 (Fig. 8B),[55] nor is the double-roll base on the respond (T487), which is also used at the west end of the cathedral nave (Fig. 8A).[56] Also, the triple lancet window uncovered in 2003 in the easternmost bay of this undercroft may be compared with the triple windows in the choir clerestory at Pershore Abbey (*c.* 1220–39) in the way the vertical elements articulate the blind wall below the window apertures (Fig. 9). Thus the east–west undercroft would appear to be the first to be built, but no earlier than the 1220s, and so was not rebuilt immediately after the removal in 1198 of the anti-monastic Bishop Nonant.

The undercroft under the refectory must have been rebuilt next, probably around the mid-13th century, not in the 14th century as previously thought.[57] This was a much larger undercroft, with an intermediate row of octagonal piers and two parallel aisles with rib-vaulting, part of which was discovered in 2000 just as it had collapsed after the Dissolution (Soden, Fig. 5).[58] The rib profile (T468) shares the same geometry as that of the east–west undercroft (Fig. 8C),[59] but the more significant feature is the style of the carved head corbels, which is quite compatible with a mid-13th-century date (Fig. 10A). The last of this sequence was the north–south undercroft, which post-dates the refectory undercroft because its construction blocked Gothic doors in the east wall of

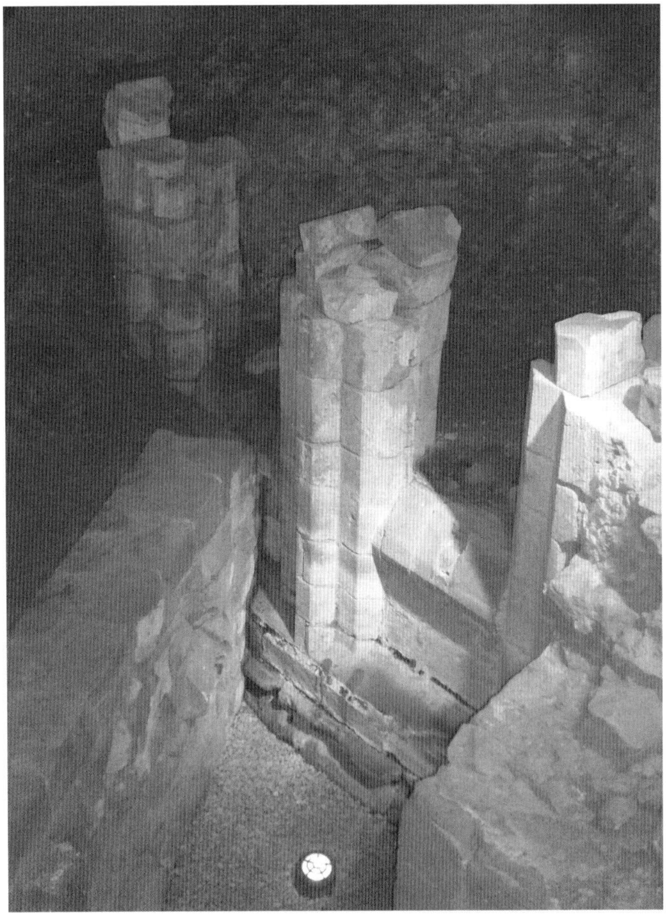

FIG. 9. Coventry Priory: east–west undercroft, 13th-century triple-light window
Photo, author

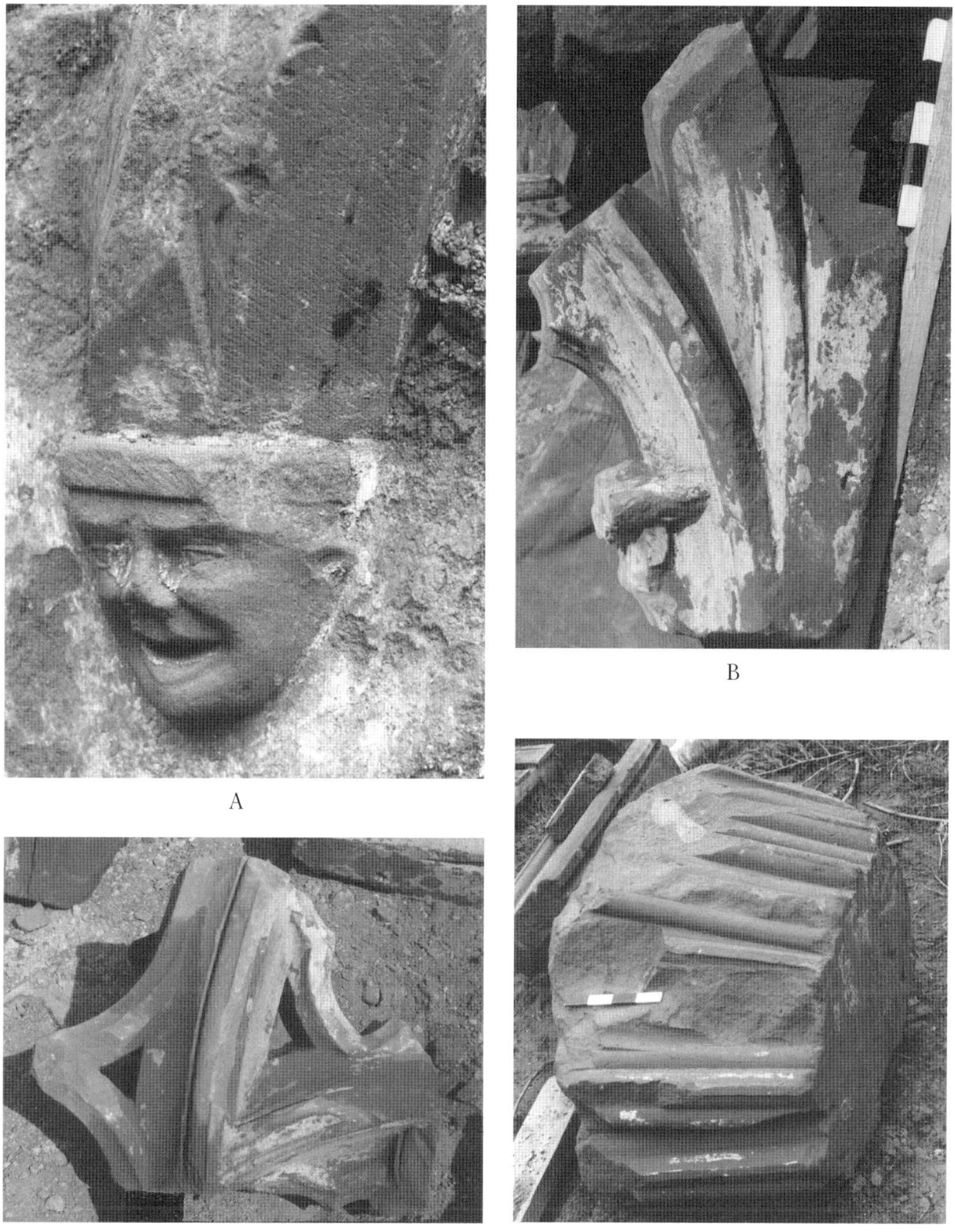

FIG. 10. Coventry Priory: worked stones. A, Refectory undercroft, corbel T469; B, Chapter-house, tracery piece T727/26 (scale 25cm); C, Chapter-house, tracery piece T727/25; D, Chapter-house, vault springer 343/1 (scale 20cm)
Photo, author

the latter.[60] It is vaulted in two aisles like the refectory undercroft, but is smaller in size and accordingly the octagonal piers are narrower (Fig. 7, right; Demidowicz, 'Priory', Fig .25, right). The use of the demi-roll-and-fillet moulding in the vault corbels (T452) dates it to the 13th century, probably in the third quarter (Fig. 8B).

The function of the northern undercrofts, and the form and function of the buildings they supported, is open to conjecture. Nothing survived of the fabric of the rooms above the east–west and north–south undercrofts. The only certainty is the location of the refectory and the probability that its undercroft was used for storage.[61] The western extension of the refectory range was probably part of the prior's accommodation, continuing on round into the west range, and might have included his chapel. A most important discovery in this area was an assemblage of stones from an early tierceron rib-vault, including two springers (one for an octagonal pier) and four bosses with excellent decorative carvings.[62] The vault pattern can be confidently reconstructed from these pieces (Fig. 11A), and the fact that it necessitated one or more exceptionally large central piers could imply that it occupied an undercroft location, perhaps the lower floor of a chapel.[63] It probably dates from the third quarter of the 13th century, on the basis of the combined evidence of its stiff-leaf foliage, the animated figure carving, the vault pattern and a distinctive rib profile with a polygonal termination (Fig. 6D).[64] An interesting detail of the tierceron vault is that it incorporates a smaller, minor profile for the ridge-ribs (Figs 6D, 11A), a differentiation found also, for example, in the high vaults at Lichfield Cathedral.[65] The earliest surviving tierceron vault in Coventry is in the south porch of St Michael's of the late 13th century (Monckton, Fig. 5), and thus probably after the priory example.[66]

The undercrofts at the north-east corner of the cloister are unusual in being set below a terrace, which makes the identification of their functions more problematic.[67] To the north, the priory undercrofts have their backs to the terrace (the 'great wall'), but to the south and east they open onto a small courtyard (Fig. 12; Prelim., Plan A). It has been assumed that the east–west undercroft was subsequently converted to accommodation, possibly for corrodians, during the 14th century.[68] The main evidence is the presence of two secondary windows in the north wall, the few surviving details of which are unlikely to be earlier than the 1330s (Fig. 8D).[69] Locally their 'deep' chamfer profile is used, for example, in the window jambs of the undercroft of John of Gaunt's great hall at Kenilworth Castle (*c.* 1373–80), and the double-ogee in his great hall and in the gatehouse of Kenilworth Priory (*c.* 1361–75).[70] However, the presence of the 13th-century triple lancet window in the next bay of the east–west undercroft suggests that it incorporated accommodation before the 14th-century (Fig. 9).[71] The infirmary was nearby to the east (Prelim., Plan A).

The north–south undercroft also apparently had a domestic purpose from the start because the fireplace in its east wall seems to be primary, and a function as the monks' warming-house has been proposed.[72] It, too, has had new windows with deep chamfer profiles inserted in the 14th century (Fig. 8D, T416), probably replacing smaller apertures in the east wall, and involving a reduction in the size of the fireplace.[73] Interestingly, none of the surviving details of the 14th-century windows in both undercrofts is identical, implying that their insertion was a piecemeal process, as required (Fig. 8D). The improvements in the north–south undercroft may indicate that its original function had changed — perhaps to a common hall for corrodians — and that the warming-house had moved elsewhere, possibly to the floor above.[74] Regarding the east–west undercroft, assuming that it had an upper floor, the most usual designation for a room adjacent to the chapter-house would be an inner parlour.[75] It is

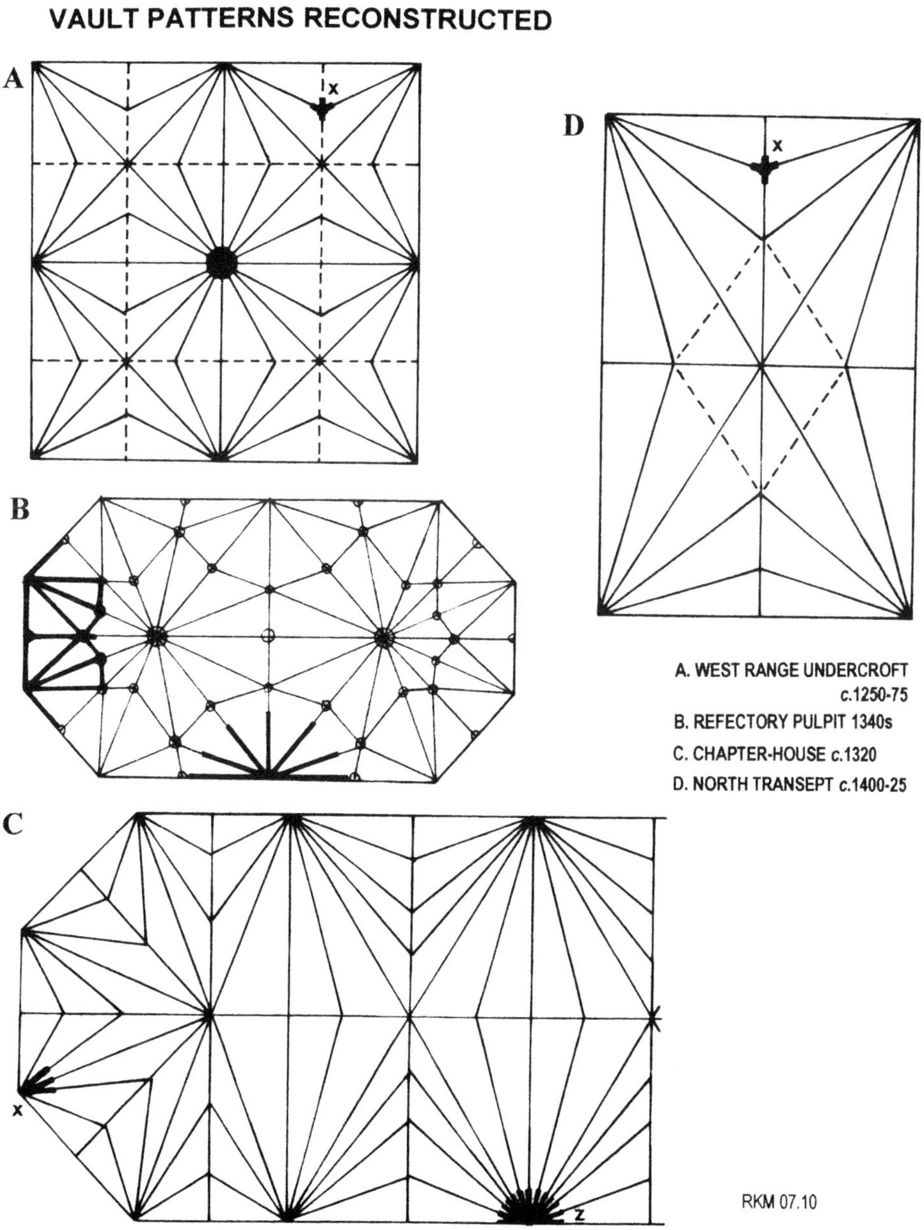

FIG. 11. Coventry Cathedral Priory: conjectural reconstructions of rib-vault patterns, not drawn to the same scale. In A, the centre pier is stone T977; x = boss T984; dashed lines = minor ribs. In B, extant rib patterns (from T344 and T640/1) are in bold. In C, x = springer T343/9; z = springer T343/4. In D, x = boss T795; dashed lines = possible lierne ribs

Drawing, author

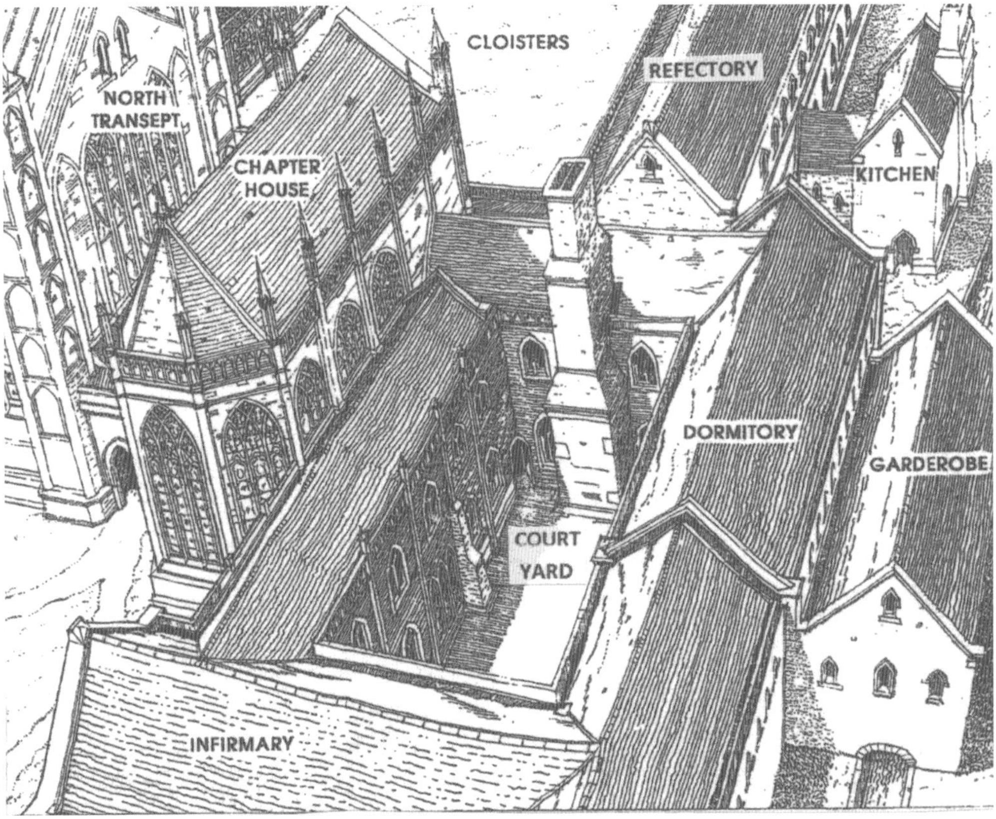

FIG. 12. Coventry Priory: reconstruction view of the conventual buildings at the north-east corner of the cloister ('Priory Undercrofts')

2003, © Bremner & Orr Design Consultants Ltd

also possible that it was remodelled as additional private accommodation in the later middle ages, for which a general parallel exists on two floors of the south range of the cloister at Cleeve Abbey (Som.), rebuilt in the later 15th century.[76]

The chapter-house

AMONGST the lost conventual buildings, the early 14th-century chapter-house is the only major room for which a reconstruction can be ventured, thanks to the large deposit of architectural fragments recovered mainly from the undercrofts area to the north, into which they had toppled during the demolition after the Dissolution (Fig. 1).[77] This impressive room, internally about 22m long and over 8m wide (72ft by 26ft),[78] would have borne a general resemblance to the interior of the Lady Chapel at Lichfield Cathedral (Fig. 13). The demolished eastern Lady Chapel at Tewkesbury Abbey (70ft by 25ft 6in.) is also related, all three terminating in a part-octagonal apse.[79]

It is virtually certain that the chapter-house was rebuilt on the thick-wall foundations of its Norman predecessor, and that the lower parts of the lateral walls were reused.[80]

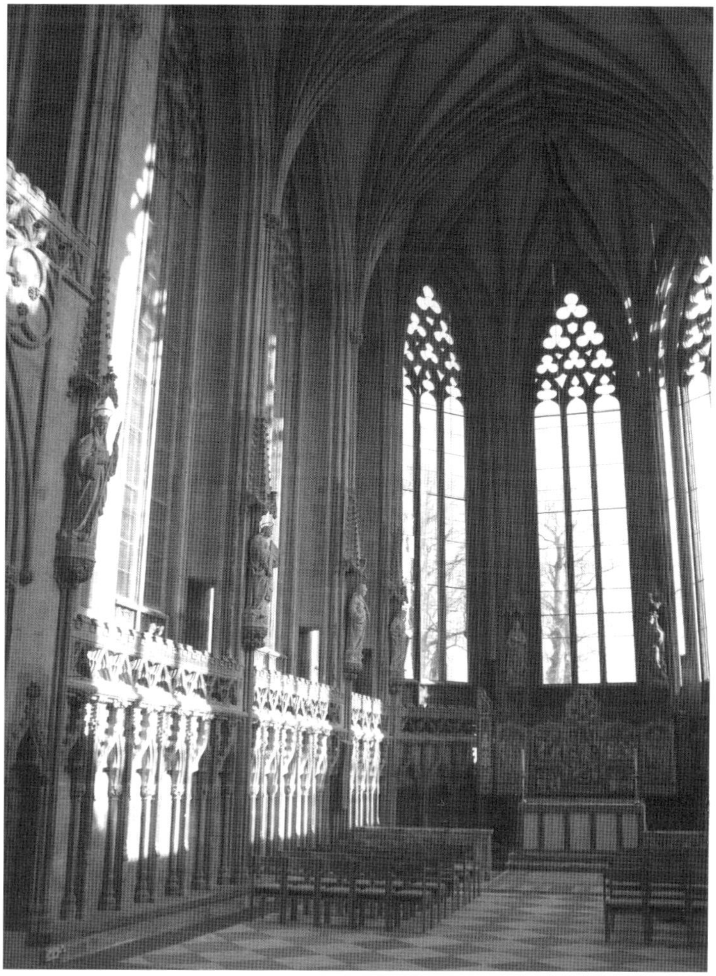

Fig. 13. Lichfield Cathedral, Lady Chapel, interior
Photo, author

Nonetheless, the foundations were reinforced on the north side, where the ground level dropped to the undercrofts, by thickening the south wall of the east–west undercroft (Fig. 1, right).[81] This measure may reflect the more ambitious nature of the new chapter-house compared to its predecessor, in terms of its height and vaulting (Fig. 12). Provisional reconstructions of its interior and a bay of its sedilia have previously been published, in conjunction with the cycle of Apocalypse paintings which was added *c.* 1360–70.[82] So the main aim of this section is to discuss further some features of the windows and the vault.

The window apertures were treated internally with elaborately moulded frames and rere-arches, incorporating alternating roll and hollow mouldings (Fig. 14C, D). The main mullion type had an axial roll-and-fillet and hollow chamfer profile to the interior (Fig. 14B).[83] All these mouldings suggest an architectural affinity with east and north-east England, at centres such as York and Lincoln,[84] though similarities with the window-frame profiles can also be cited in the Lady Chapels at Lichfield and

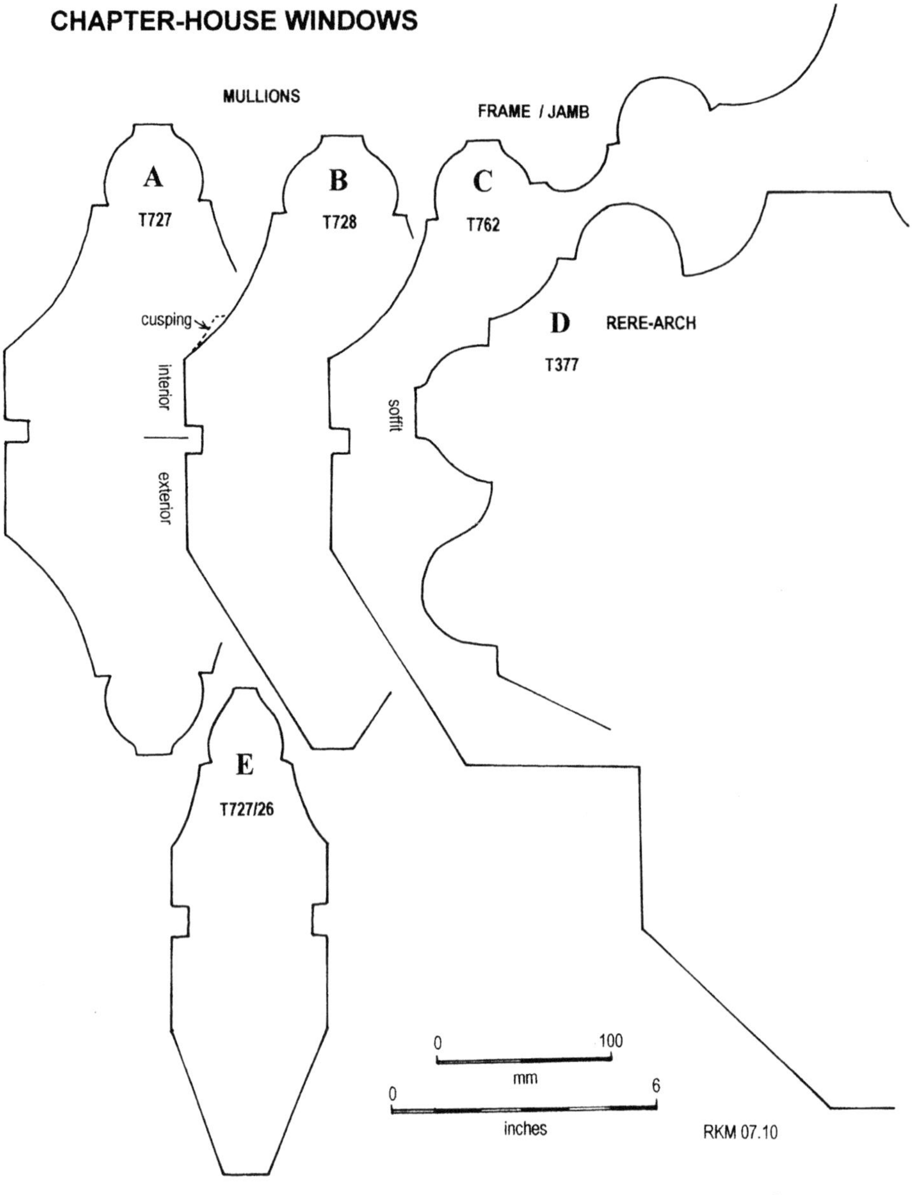

FIG. 14. Coventry Priory: mouldings from the chapter-house windows
Drawing, author

Tewkesbury. Indeed, the chapter-house rib profile, which survives in the key-stone of a window head T377, has returned beak mouldings characteristic of Decorated vaults at Tewkesbury Abbey and in the lower Severn valley (Fig. 19B, C).[85] The use of plain chamfers for the exterior mullion profile and the exterior frames of the chapter-house windows (T762, Fig. 14C) implies that they were not easily visible and thus these pieces probably derive from the lateral clerestory windows above other buildings.[86] One fragment of window frame (T762/2) shows the weathering crease for the roof of an adjoining building. On the other hand, several fragments have the roll-and-fillet/hollow chamfer profile returned on the exterior (Fig. 14A), suggesting a more prominent location, quite possibly the west window, visible from the cloister.[87]

The windows were probably of three lights in the apse, four lights in the lateral apertures and five or six lights for the west window, judging from the widths available in their respective bays.[88] The exact forms of their tracery patterns remain elusive, despite the recovery of over forty pieces of tracery. However, a number of features indicate patterns of some complexity and significance, post-dating displays of geometrical tracery in the area, such as Temple Balsall (*c.* 1300), but pre-dating the full use of curvilinear tracery, as at Astley (*c.* 1343). One piece of frame from the springing point of a window head (T727/26) indicates a design that was sub-arcuated, probably as two pairs of lights in a four-light window, as this stone should belong to the north lateral windows (Fig. 10B).[89] T727/26 also shows the stub of a minor mullion diverging from the archlet of the light and almost certainly framing the bottom of an impaled trefoil, a motif borrowed from intersecting tracery, a common local pattern in these decades (e.g. Stoke Golding, Leics.; Fig. 15, right).[90] Most of the stones show the use of

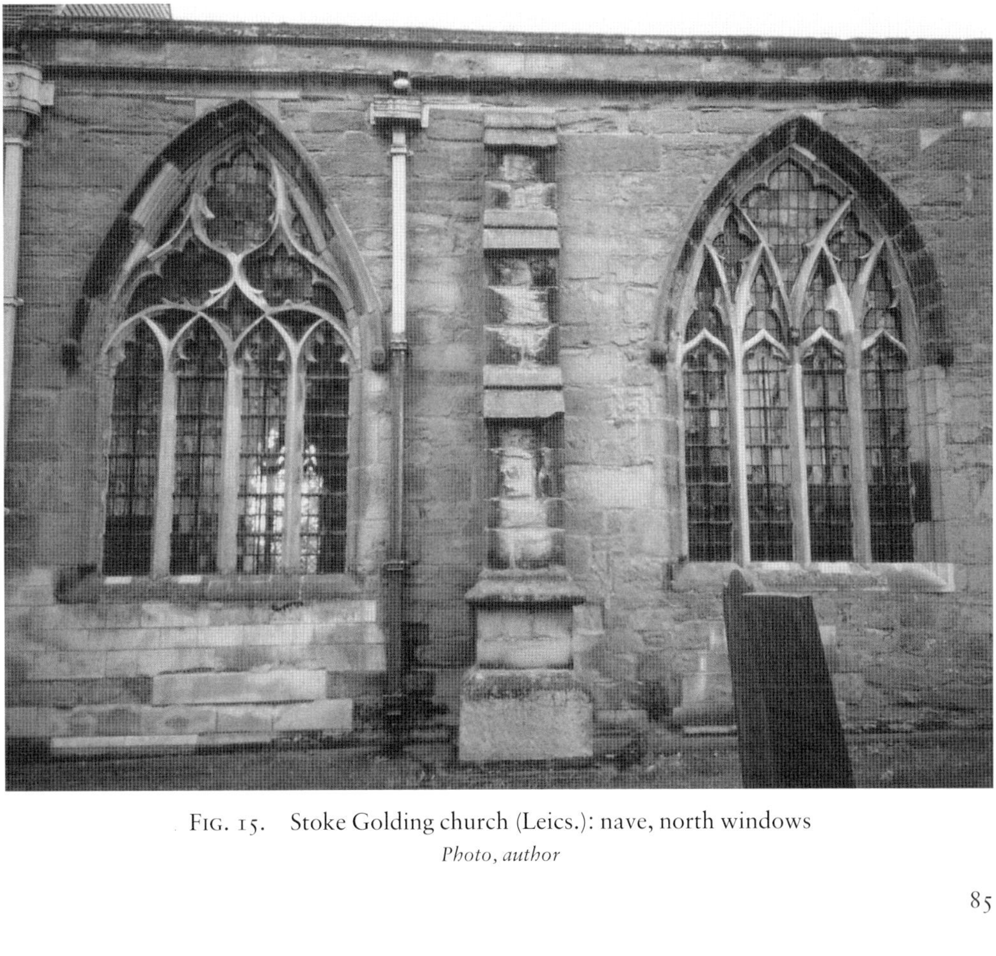

FIG. 15. Stoke Golding church (Leics.): nave, north windows
Photo, author

the minor mullion profile (Fig. 14E), and three other pieces indicate the presence of sub-cusping too (T729/1–3). This rendition of the tracery in layers (main mullion, minor mullion, cusping) is usually applied only to grander windows, and the use of sub-cusping is rare, for example in the west window of the former eastern Lady Chapel at Tewkesbury Abbey (*c.* 1315–25). Exactly how the heads of the four-light windows were filled is unclear, but the presence of impaled trefoils together with extensive cusping (often placed asymmetrically) might suggest a foiled figure above each pair of lights and a group of several foiled figures in the main head, resembling the blind tracery pattern on a 14th-century fireplace lintel from Coventry (Fig. 16).

Other fragments indicate different window designs, some incorporating lights of staggered height (e.g. T727/15, T728/2) and others with the archlets of adjacent lights treated differently — one with an impaled figure, the next without (e.g. T727/27, T728/5). Both these features would be appropriate in a window with an odd number of lights.[91] Considered together with the asymmetry of several of the tracery pieces (e.g. T727/25, T728/1; Fig. 10C), the chapter-house windows of *c.* 1320 could have been prototypes for the rather loose, more curvilinear patterns found in the second quarter of the century, for example in the city at St John's Hospital (east and west windows, Fig. 17), and in its hinterland, for example at Crick (Northants., lateral windows of the chancel) and Stoke Golding (Leics., nave north windows, Fig. 15, left).

As an additional embellishment, there is evidence that the tracery might have incorporated small carved figures, like that of a prophet (T919) recovered in the excavation (Fig. 18A and Col. Pl. IIIB in print edn).[92] The back of T919 shows that it was integral with a larger block of stone yet almost freestanding from it (Fig. 18B). Similar statuettes attached to mullions may be seen in the Lady Chapel of St Albans Abbey (now cathedral, 1308–27) and the chancel windows at Dorchester Abbey (Oxon., *c.* 1330–40).[93] Furthermore, T919 appears to have been standing on a carved foliage stem, a motif used in the Tree of Jesse window at Dorchester.

The crucial evidence for reconstructing the pattern of the vault (Fig. 10C) derives from twelve pieces of vault springer (T343) recovered from demolition debris in the area of the chapter-house.[94] The springer stone T343/9 describes one of the angles of a semi-octagonal apse, the plan found in the eastern termination of the chapter-house. The two best-preserved examples from the main vessel, T343/4 and T343/11, indicate that no less than thirteen ribs (including wall-ribs) sprang from the intermediate points along the lateral walls (Figs 11C, 19A). However, the springer segment T343/9 appears to show only five ribs, whereas it is hard to believe that there would not have been at least seven to complement the thirteen ribs of T343/4. So the angles of the apse have been reconstructed with seven ribs each, including wall-ribs (Fig. 11C). No bosses or complete rib-stones have been identified from the main structure of the vault.[95] In the absence of such evidence, all the ribs which are not diagonal or transverse ribs have been reconstructed as tiercerons.

Thus, the chapter-house was a work of considerable architectural ambition, with a vault with as many ribs per springer as the most elaborate tierceron vaults in England, in the high vaults at Exeter and the octagon at Ely. The sedilia and the window mouldings appear to be influenced by works around 1300 in the north-east (York, Lincoln), but similarities have also been noted with Tewkesbury and Lichfield. Nothing in the sources and parallels contradicts a date-span of *c.* 1310–30, which has also been suggested for the stained glass found on the site in the 1960s.[96] Although the chapter-house appears as a synthesis of various ideas, in practice these may represent several

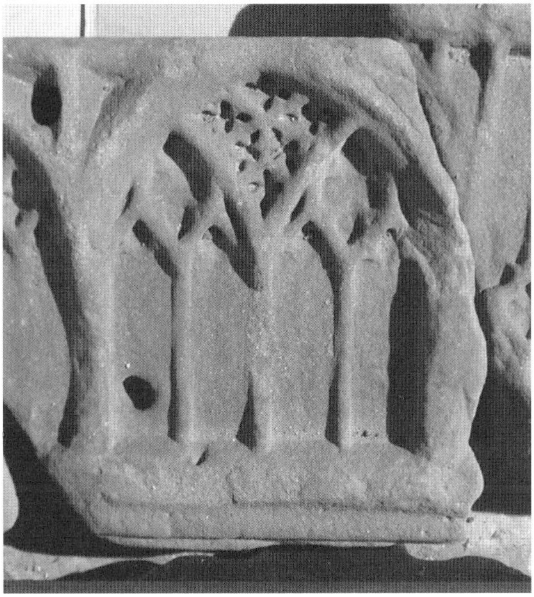

FIG. 16. 14th-century fireplace lintel from Coventry, detail, micro-tracery; Herbert Museum, Whitefriars store
Photo, author

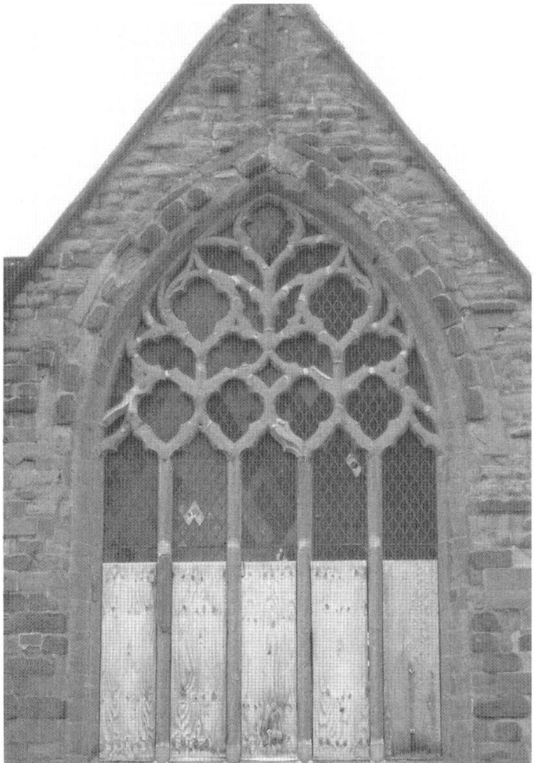

FIG. 17. Coventry, former St John's Hospital: west window
Photo, author

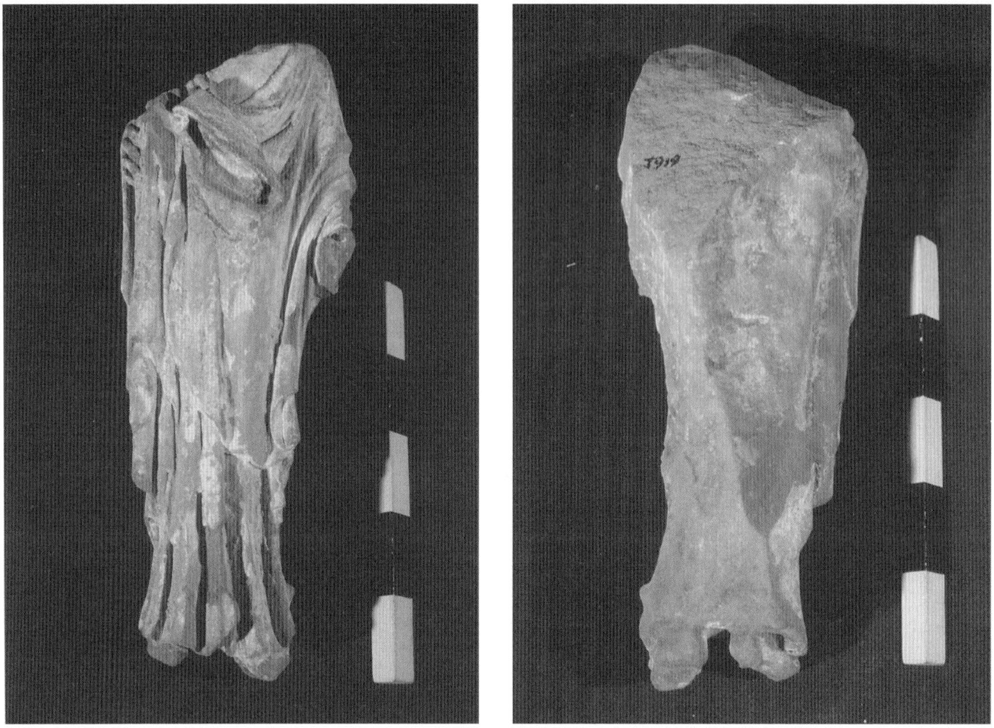

A B

FIG. 18. Coventry Priory: statuette T919, from the chapter-house(?)
A, front; B, back (scale 25cm)
Photos, author

consecutive phases and could actually pre-date the lady chapels at Tewkesbury and Lichfield, being a key work in transmitting architectural features from the north-east to them both.

The Refectory

THE main hall of the refectory was rebuilt or very substantially remodelled at some time between *c.* 1340 and 1370, retaining the mid-13th-century undercroft. The dating evidence for the new work relies almost entirely on a stylistic assessment of the worked stones found fallen on top of the collapsed undercroft.[97] These are not as numerous as those recovered from the chapter-house so it is difficult to assess how total was the remodelling, but the fact that we also have evidence for a new 14th-century pulpit and tile pavement suggests that the work was considerable; probably comparable in extent to the refectory hall at Worcester Cathedral Priory (1330s).[98] The main architectural feature that can be identified is a massive jamb-stone, T287, from one of the lateral windows (Fig. 20C). The window was apparently framed internally by a hoodmould describing an ogee arch and topped by a fine foliate finial, T331 (Figs 20A, 21A).[99] Four excellent carved heads from the refectory site fit with this hoodmould and would have

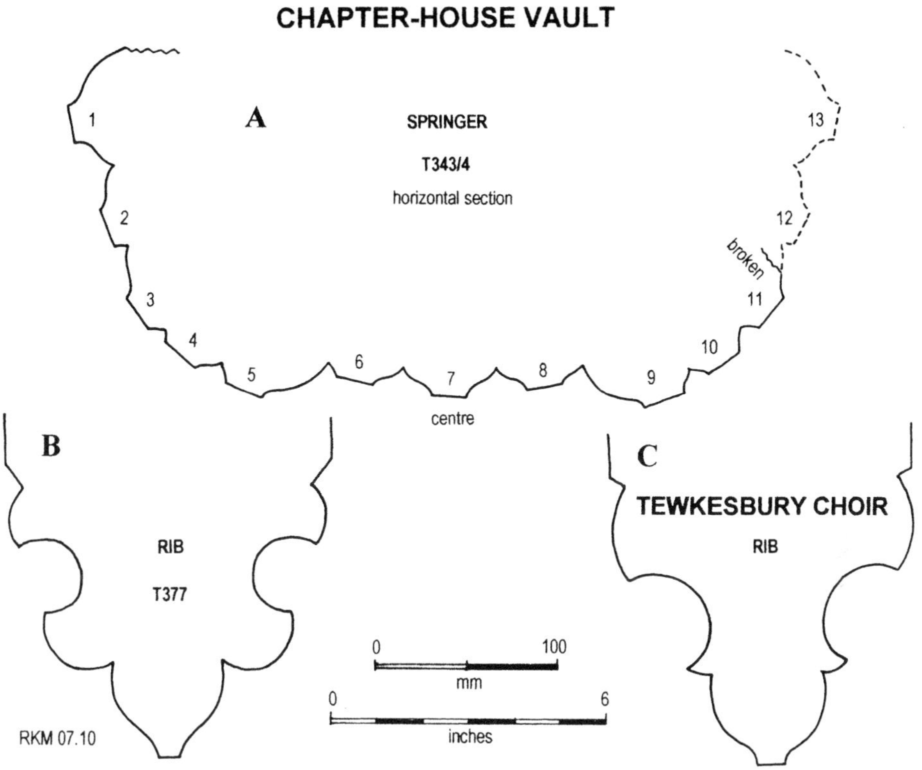

FIG. 19. Coventry Priory: moulding profiles relating to the chapter-house vault. In A, the emerging rib profiles are numbered (12 and 13 are reconstructed to complete the stone); note how 3, 4, 5 and 9, 10, 11 are closely grouped

Drawing, author

formed the headstops.[100] Another huge stone, T290, is from a large aperture with an elaborate frame of roll and hollow mouldings, probably from the entrance door or an internal opening (Fig. 20B).[101] Its hoodmould is a larger version of that for the windows (Fig. 20A).[102]

Dating the new refectory more precisely within the second and third quarters of the 14th century is tricky. Comparisons are hard to come by, partly because of its building type and partly because of the limited range of its mouldings. It is tempting to place it close in date to the fine heraldic tile pavement, which has been assigned to the later 14th century (Soden, Fig. 6).[103] However, on balance, the evidence suggests that the new architectural work may be earlier, in the 1340s, following on from the chapter-house. Beyond the priory, the only parallel for the refectory mouldings in the city occurs in the nave of St John the Baptist's church (begun *c.* 1375),[104] but in combination with other details derived from the early Perpendicular works at Gloucester Cathedral (*c.* 1329–60s) and Windsor Castle (cloister works, 1350–56), which first appeared in the area in the new chancel of St Mary's, Warwick, in the late 1360s (Fig. 20D, x).[105] The absence of these details from T290 suggests that it pre-dates the 1360s, that its

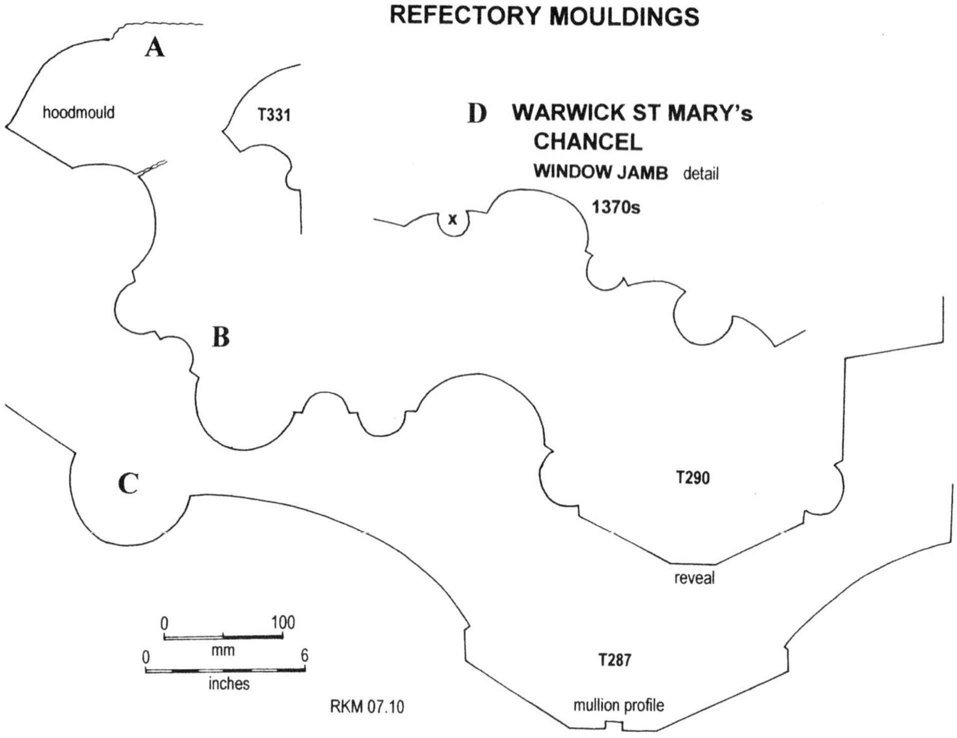

FIG. 20. Coventry Priory: refectory, moulding profiles; in D, x = the Gloucester-derived detail of a small roll ('bowtell') set in a shallow hollow moulding ('casement'). ⅙ scale
Drawing, author

alternating rolls and hollows represent continuing influence of the Decorated style of the north-east midlands. The ogee hoodmoulds on the Lady Chapel windows at Lichfield and the chancel windows at Astley church (Warks., *c.* 1343) may provide a useful clue to the appearance of the refectory hoods, and perhaps to their date as well.[106]

The best evidence for a pre-Black Death date for the refectory lies in the style of its pulpit. This exciting discovery, which can be partly reconstructed from numerous fragments, is an exceptional example of a monastic fitting which survives only rarely, and is distinguished by the survival of its stunning polychromy (Fig. 22 and Col. Pl. VIIIB in print edn).[107] It was an elongated octagonal structure in plan, corbelled out from the wall like the examples at Beaulieu and Shrewsbury abbeys, and with an elaborate miniature vault (Fig. 11B).[108] In general form, it should be placed amongst the group of stone antecedents to the wooden choir stalls at Lincoln (1363–72) outlined by Joanna Allen,[109] and its detail is convincingly from the north-east midlands, but earlier. The most diagnostic detail is the profile used for the miniature vault rib and the mullion of the openwork tracery (Fig. 23B, C). This unusual design is characteristic of the north-east midlands in the first half of the 14th century at Lincoln (*c.* 1300–10) and at Hawton (Notts.) and Heckington (Lincs.), both *c.* 1320–40.[110] In addition, the refectory pulpit shares with these works, and others like the Luttrell monument at

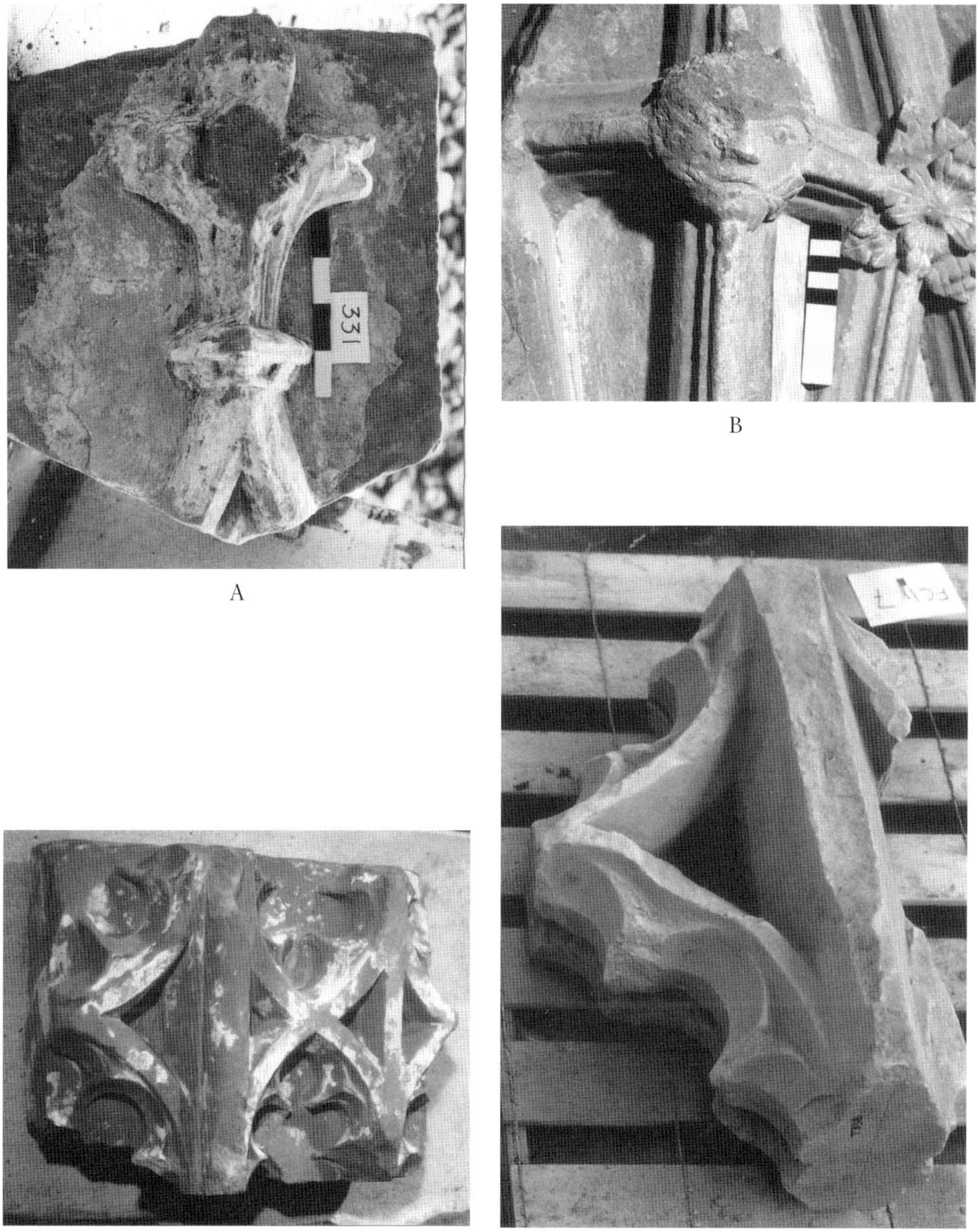

FIG. 21. Coventry Priory: worked stones. A, Refectory finial T331 (scale 20cm); B, Refectory pulpit, vault boss (scale 10cm); C, Cloister, panelling, blind tracery T261; D, Cloister, garth tracery piece T338

Photos, author

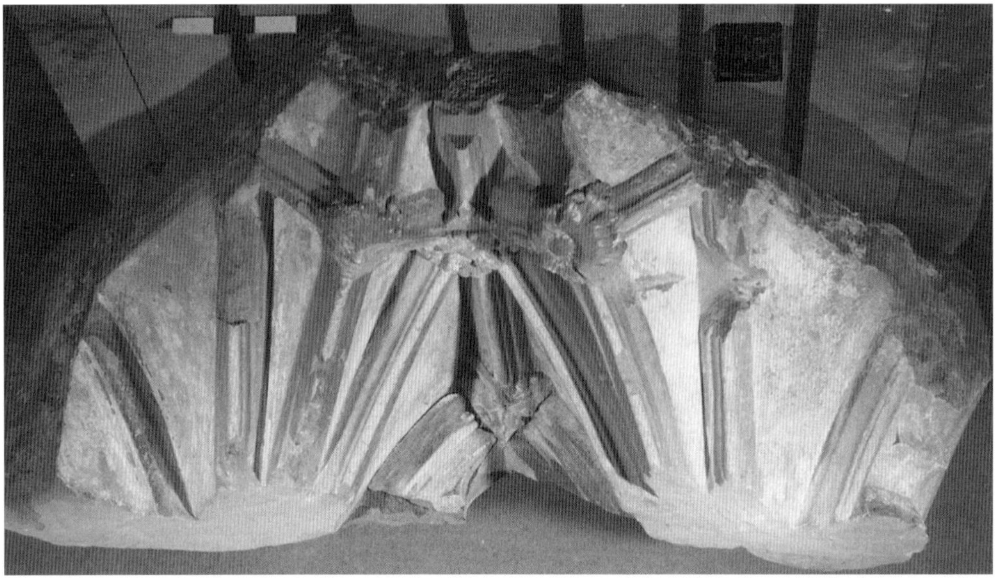

FIG. 22. Coventry Priory: refectory pulpit, piece T640/1, underside, miniature vault with original polychromy (scale 25cm)
Photo, author

Irnham (Lincs., *c.* 1340), a decorative vocabulary of gables, miniature crenellation and exquisitely detailed miniature vault bosses, though these similarities are more generic (Figs 21B, 24).[111] The main difference is that the application of ornament is markedly more restrained in the pulpit, which may reflect its context, or it may suggest that it is later. Certainly, the bell profiles of its bases are unlikely to be earlier than the 1330s, being associated more with early Perpendicular (Fig. 23A).[112]

It is unlikely that the pulpit would have been introduced into the refectory before the major rebuild, and thus it provides a guideline for the date of the main work. Indeed, it is possible that the same craftsmen may have been engaged on both, judging from details like the foliate ornament on the necking moulding of finial T331, a favourite device of the Lincolnshire/Nottinghamshire carvers (Fig. 21A), and the general similarity between the carved heads of the refectory and pulpit, with well-defined eyes and pursed lips (Fig. 21B). Quite possibly parallels for the headstops should be sought in Lincolnshire, too, for example in the many heads decorating the steeple at Anwick (Fig. 25).[113]

The Cloister

THE remodelling of the cloister is the last major medieval work on the conventual buildings for which we have evidence, in the form of almost 100 pieces of worked stone.[114] They were found in the Phoenix excavations in the areas of the north, east and south walks, implying a fairly thorough renovation of the previous cloister.[115] The work consisted of refacing the back walls of the walks with carved stone panelling and

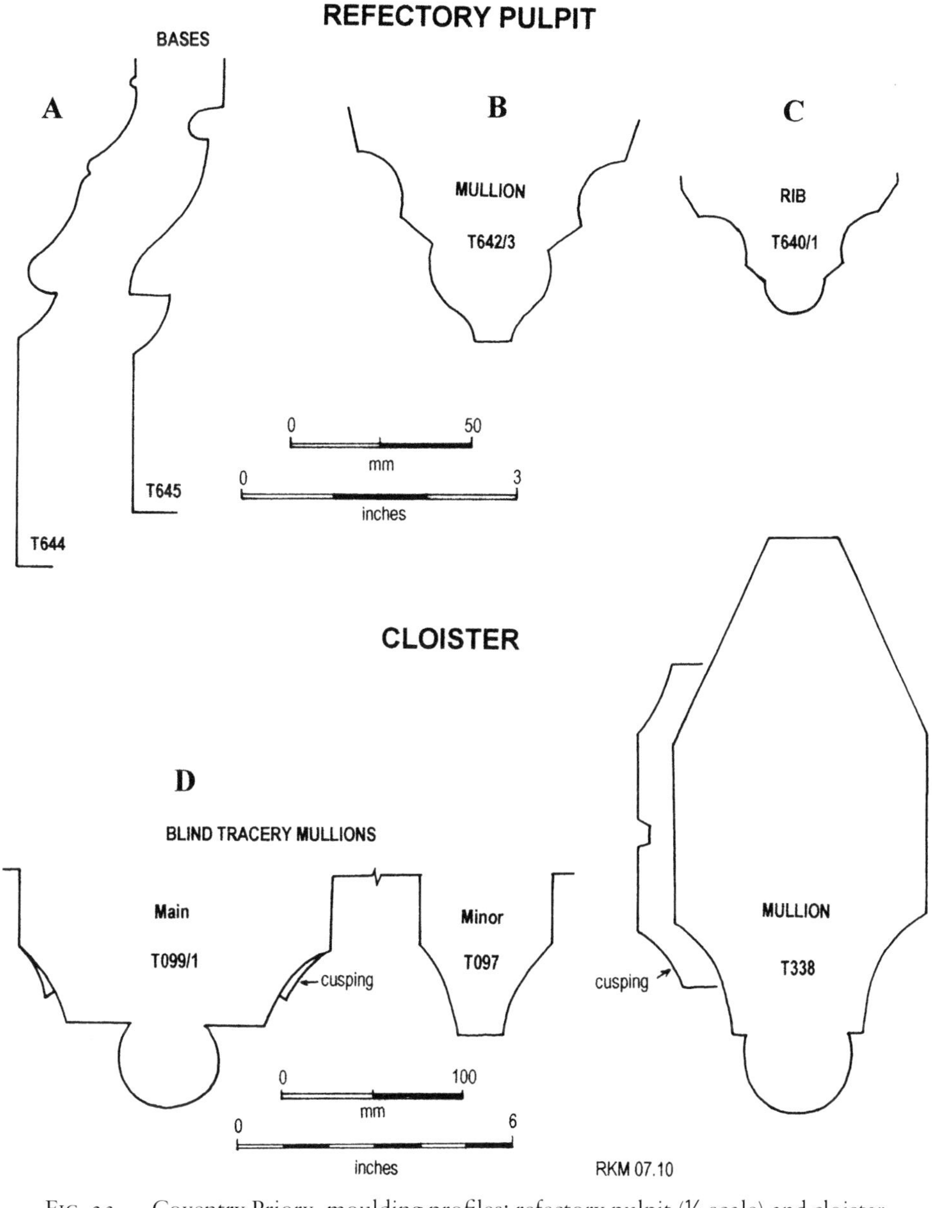

FIG. 23. Coventry Priory, moulding profiles: refectory pulpit (½ scale) and cloister
Drawing, author

constructing new glazed windows to the garth. No conclusive evidence has been identified for stone vaulting, so presumably the walks were wooden ceiled.[116]

This is not the place to attempt a reconstruction of the cloister, and the main aim here is to review the stylistic evidence for its dating, in the absence of any

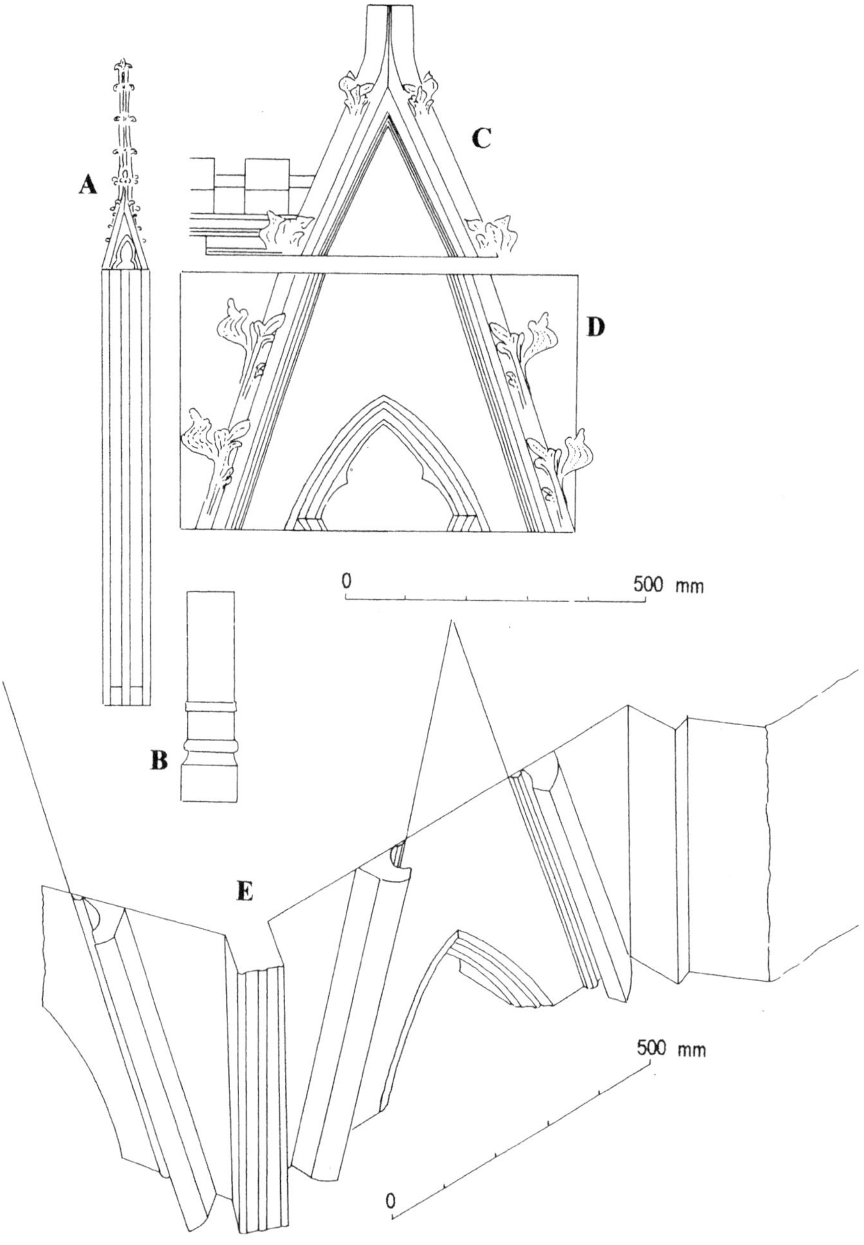

Fig. 24. Coventry Priory: refectory pulpit canopy, reconstruction details. A. Pinnacle from T641 over a side-shaft (they do not belong together); B. Base of a side-shaft from T644; C. Top of a gable, probably from the large central opening (not from D); D. Elevation of the gable and tracery of T640; E. Partial isometric drawing of T640/1, with a straight side (centre) adjoining a diagonal side (left) and leading to the wall (right)

Drawings, Jamie Preston

documentation. The predominant pattern for both blind and glazed tracery consisted of panels with cinque-cusped lancet archlets, with the unusual feature of reversed archlets, producing a form of 'latticed' transom horizontally (Fig. 21C, D).[117] The panels or lights were stacked in vertical grids, without any evidence for sub-division into batement lights, nor for the use of alternate (or reticulated) tracery which was such a characteristic in the cloister walks of Gloucester, Tewkesbury and Wells (Fig. 26). Judging from stones like T286, the panels were about 14 inches (360mm) wide, but it is unclear whether the tracery was six or eight lights in width, though the latter is more likely because of the relative narrowness of the lights and the type of tracery pattern.[118]

Gloucester's cloister (1351–1412) is the obvious comparison for the priory cloister, with its walls lavishly panelled with blind tracery (Fig. 26), in contrast to the plain walls in the renovated cloisters at Worcester (*c.* 1385–1438) and Wells (*c.* 1420–1509).[119] A few details hint at a familiarity with Gloucester, such as the lights with reversed archlets (Fig. 26),[120] and the latticed transom effect which appears in the east walk (only) at

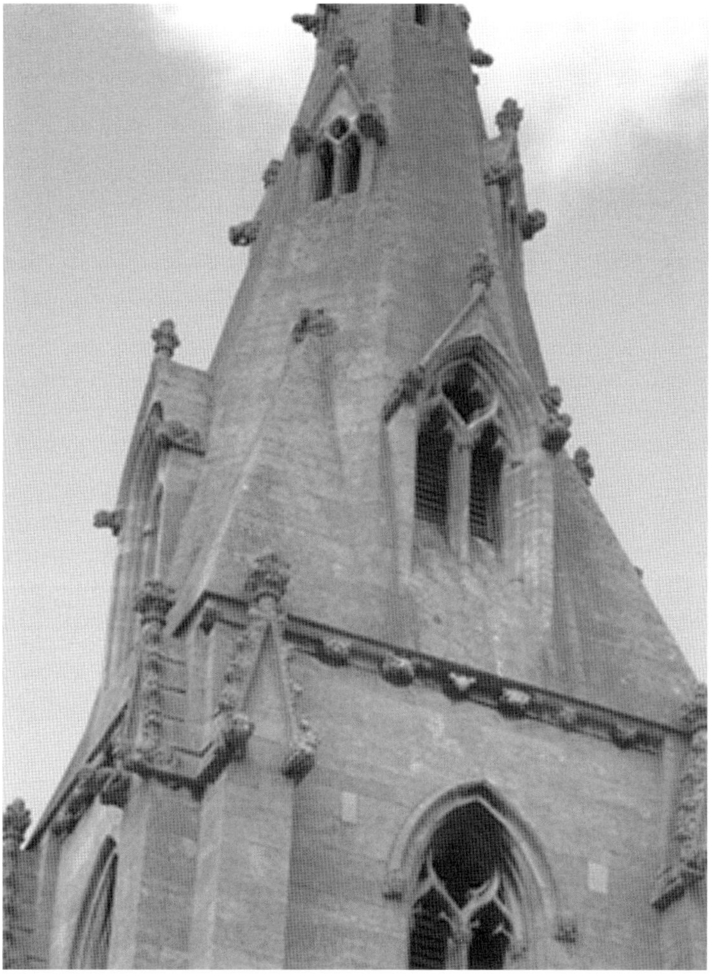

FIG. 25. Anwick (Lincs.), St Edith, steeple, detail
Photo, author

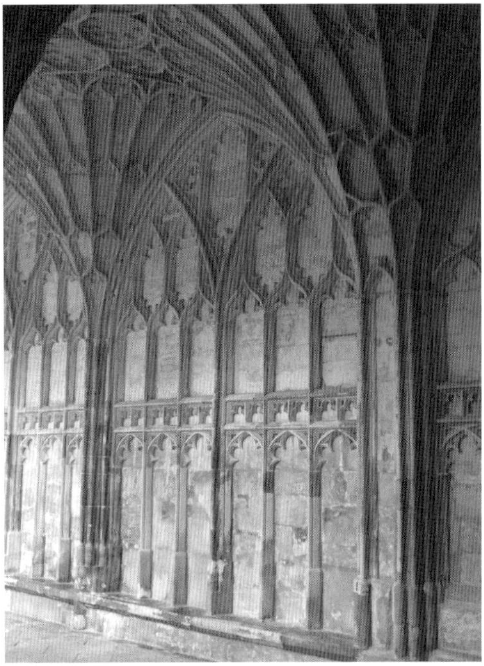

FIG. 26. Gloucester Cathedral: cloister north walk, blind tracery

Photo, author

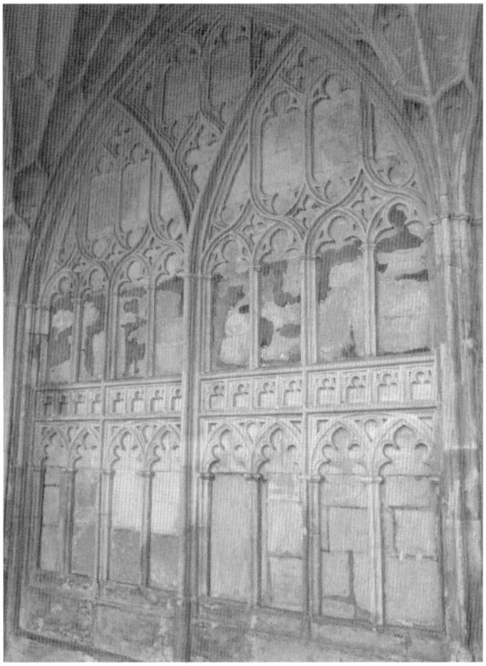

FIG. 27. Gloucester Cathedral: cloister east walk, blind tracery

Photo, author

Gloucester, but with the rhythm of the main mullions imposing an alternate pattern on the tracery lights (Fig. 27). Coventry is clearly not a clone of Gloucester, however, and the Coventry mullion profiles bear no relationship to those of the latter (Fig. 23D). In fact, the Coventry pattern of full-width stacked lights in combination with reversed archlets and latticed transoms is seldom found. One may note the east walk tracery of the bishop's cloister at Hereford Cathedral (*c.* 1412),[121] and more so the tracery of the nave and transept clerestory windows of St Mary's church, Nottingham, which is the closest parallel for the Coventry pattern known to the author; unfortunately undated but probably c. 1425–50 (Fig. 28).[122] Nothing exactly similar is found today amongst the churches of Coventry, but the panelled interior elevation of the chancel of St Michael's (*c.* 1390–1420) comes closest in effect, together with the window tracery of the St Laurence's Chapel in the north chancel aisle.[123] Overall, therefore, the cloister tracery pattern seems to fit best in the first half of the 15th century, probably in the early 1400s.

CONCLUSION: 'KEEPING UP APPEARANCES?'

IN the 13th and 14th centuries, the pressure on the cathedral priory to 'keep up appearances' in its building stock was enormous. Impressive new churches and convents appeared with the arrival of the Greyfriars and Carmelites, and the chapter at Lichfield was completely remodelling Coventry's twin cathedral throughout the period. More

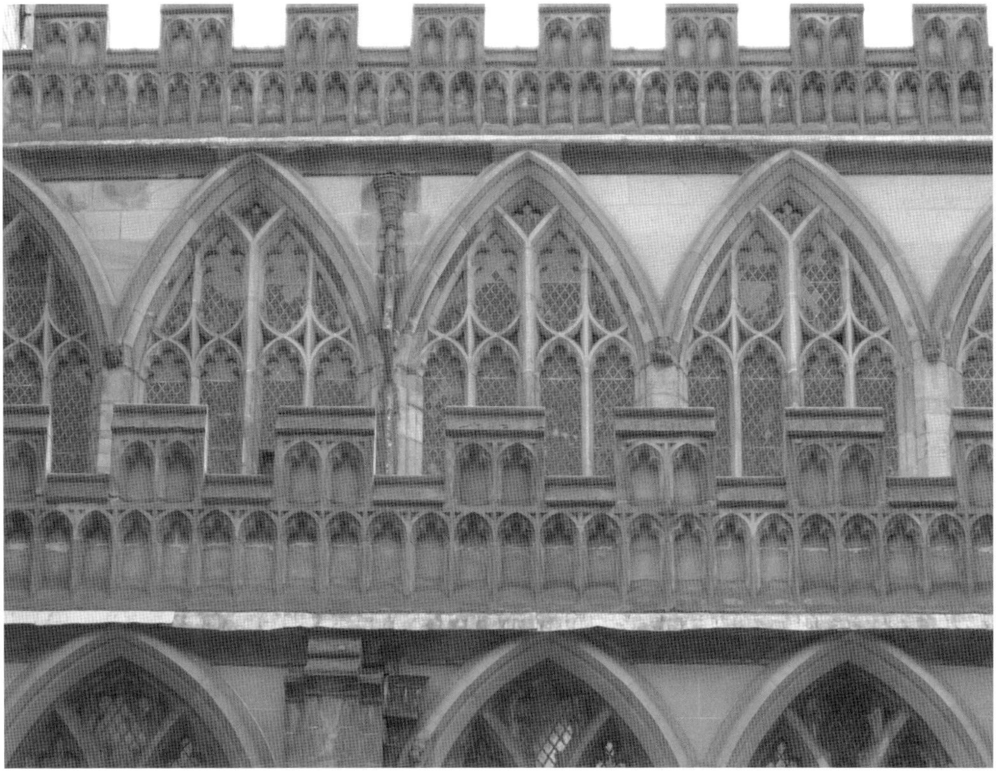

FIG. 28. Nottingham, St Mary's church: nave clerestory tracery
Photo, author

so, the prior had lost out politically and financially to the rising power of the burgesses, symbolised architecturally in the new St Mary's Guildhall and the breathtaking final rebuild of St Michael's parish church.[124] Nevertheless, the priory's financial position remained reasonably buoyant through the vicissitudes of the 14th century, as Richard Goddard has shown.[125]

In the cathedral church, the refenestration of the nave is a typical example of keeping up appearances in older great churches in the 14th century. What is harder to assess, because of the almost total loss of comparable windows in other Coventry buildings, is to what extent the cathedral priory workshop led the city in architectural design in the Decorated period, or was merely reactive to developments elsewhere.[126] Certainly, beyond the city one should take account of the significant works of the earls and dukes of Lancaster at Kenilworth Castle and in Leicester.[127] Towards the end of the 14th century or early in the 15th, the priory embarked on what was apparently a much more ambitious remodelling of the east end of the cathedral church, but the recent excavations provided no new information about this, except that the north transept was also vaulted about this time.[128]

However, the Phoenix excavations uncovered exceptional evidence from the conventual buildings, showing that in the 13th century a major investment was made in new accommodation with fine undercrofts, and that the rebuilding of the chapter-house and refectory in the 14th century created prestigious new ceremonial rooms. The prior may have been motivated by knowledge of new Benedictine chapter-houses rising elsewhere, for example locally at Evesham Abbey (*c.* 1296–1318),[129] but the general form of the chapter-house is evidently closely linked with the contemporary new Lady Chapel at Lichfield, and probably deliberately so. Coventry had a longstanding dispute with the secular chapter at Lichfield about episcopal elections, and in 1321 the Coventry monks were promoting the candidacy of their prior, Henry of Leycester, for bishop.[130] The new refectory, probably begun about 1340 but apparently not fitted out until after the Black Death, was in part more of a secular space, a great hall to impress important visitors to the priory. Its quality is now best judged by the remains of the pulpit and tiled pavement, the latter emblazoned with the arms of the Beauchamp earls of Warwick, powerful allies in the changing world of the 14th century. These two works do more than keep up appearances: they are bold statements of conviction in the power and rights of the priory, made at the very time that they were under threat. On the other hand, the last major conventual work, the new cloister of the early 15th century, may be read as a sign of over-reaching ambition. Clearly inspired by the stunning new cloister at Gloucester, it was in this respect a cut above other contemporary cloisters at Worcester and Wells. But it was apparently never stone-vaulted,[131] an omission implying that the priory's resources were finally becoming stretched.

ACKNOWLEDGEMENTS

Having had the opportunity before to acknowledge many people who helped me with the stones catalogue of the Phoenix excavations (see Rylatt and Mason, *Cathedral Priory*, 64), here I should like to thank sincerely the following: Nicola Coldstream for advice about sculpture, David Kendrick for helping me take a second look at some of the stones, Paul Thompson for assistance with photographs, the staff of the Priory Visitor Centre for access to the store, and most of all George Demidowicz for his sustained interest and encouragement.

NOTES

1. Morris, 'Cathedral Church', 17–66. I am very grateful to Canon Michael Sadgrove for the initiative which led to this publication.

2. Report in Rylatt and Mason, *Cathedral Priory*. Praise is due to Chris Beck (Project Director), George Demidowicz (Conservation Officer) and Margaret Rylatt (City Archaeologist) in seizing the archaeological potential of this redevelopment project.

3. This short paper deals only with monumental architecture, and excludes fittings and statuary, for some idea of which see R. K. Morris, 'The Worked Stones and Architectural Stonework', in Rylatt and Mason, *Cathedral Priory*, 63–82 (passim) and pl. 2, fig. 53.

4. The exception is Hobley, 'Cathedral Excavations', of 1965–67.

5. For other examples of comparable refenestration in the midlands, note the transepts of Lichfield Cathedral, parts of the nave at Gloucester Cathedral, and the nave of Great Malvern Priory.

6. The T579 group also includes T532, T702 and T 856. Numbers like 'T579' ('T' denotes a Type-stone) refer to the entries in the author's multi-volume catalogue, listing and illustrating all the worked stones, a copy of which is held in the Coventry Archive at the Herbert Art Gallery and Museum.

7. For the context for this roll and chamfer design, see R. K. Morris, 'The development of later Gothic mouldings in England c.1250–1400, Part II', *Architectural History* 22 (1979), 3, 7 ('Mullions, First Family, second variety').

8. There are ten pieces of T586.

9. See Morris, 'Later Gothic mouldings, Part II', 4 ('sixth variety'). An early example to be added to this list is Lincoln Cathedral Angel Choir, in the heads of the aisle windows (1256–80).

10. Apparently from the same source as a tracery piece recorded by N. Troughton, presumably found towards the west end of the nave site when the Blue Coat School was built there in 1856–57; Troughton IX.19.

11. For ogees, see J. Bony, *The English Decorated Style: Gothic Architecture Transformed* (Oxford 1979), 166–7.

12. Lambert in Hobley, 'Cathedral Excavations', 65; for his career, see J. H. Harvey, *English Mediaeval Architects: a Biographical Dictionary down to 1550* (rev. edn, Gloucester 1984), 299 ('Tichemers, Hugh de'). See also Morris, 'Kenilworth', this volume, 347.

13. See R. K. Morris, 'Thomas of Witney at Exeter, Winchester and Wells', in *Medieval Art and Architecture at Exeter Cathedral*, ed. F. Kelly, *BAA Trans.* XI (Leeds 1991), 62, 71–2, for the mullions and tracery.

14. More comparable to the Decorated works at Tewkesbury Abbey of *c.* 1315–40; R. K. Morris and R. Shoesmith ed., *Tewkesbury Abbey: History, Art and Architecture* (Little Logaston 2003), 117–21.

15. Hobley, 'Cathedral Excavations', 65.

16. For tracery terminology, see J. H. Harvey, *The Perpendicular Style 1330–1485* (London 1978), 70–2.

17. Judging from other examples, especially of Gloucester-style work, it would seem that the face with polygonal mouldings was exterior and that with the bowtells was interior, even though the former still preserved extensive traces of limewash. The glazing slot is generally closer to the interior face, which in the intermediate mullion is the one with bowtells (Fig. 2Y). Presumably the interior face was badly damaged when piece T632/1 fell to the church pavement.

18. In the abbacy of Walter Froucester; see W. C. Leedy, *Fan Vaulting: a Study of Form, Meaning and Technology* (London 1980), 166–7.

19. At least 68 pieces have been identified, the majority in the western part of the nave. They include types T578, T581, T639; a piece found in a 1998 trial pit in the nave north aisle adjacent to the north-west tower (NNW/1998, WS1A and B); and two pieces apparently recovered in the 1850s when the Blue Coat School was built at the west end of the nave (T025, T027).

20. In which case, it may well be contemporary with the substantial deposit of painted window glass from beneath the west window, recovered in 1999–2000 and still awaiting analysis; Rylatt and Mason, *Cathedral Priory*, 96 and fig. 62a.

21. Harvey, *Perpendicular Style*, fig. 8.

22. More likely than a statue bracket, because of the extent to which the stone is hollowed out, which is unlikely to have been created entirely by post-Dissolution destruction (cf. Rylatt and Mason, *Cathedral Church*, 21).

23. The north-west pier showed no sign of reinforcement on its west face (the reciprocal east face of nave pier N8 was missing) but most of its north face and any nave north aisle respond were lost, and the south-east and south-west piers have not been excavated.

24. G. Demidowicz and C. Patrick, 'Excavations at 7 Priory Row 2004', CBA *WM Archaeology* 47 (2004), 21; also Patrick in this volume, 27–30.

25. R. K. Morris, 'The Architectural History of the Medieval Cathedral Church', in *Hereford Cathedral: a History*, ed. G. Aylmer and J. Tiller (London 2000), 220–2, 237–9.

26. See Demidowicz, 'Priory', in this volume, 107; also Rylatt and Mason, *Cathedral Church*, 26 and fig. 12 (caption).

27. Thus, the prospect would be taken more from the south-west, nearer Spon Gate. The Woodfields suggest that the right-hand steeple is that of the Whitefriars, but it is then hard to explain why the still existing steeple of the Greyfriars — one of Coventry's famous 'three spires' — is omitted; Woodfield, *Whitefriars*, 123 and fig. 32 (caption).

28. Found during the Time Team excavations (1999), Trench 2, but unfortunately not retained.

29. *Pace* George Demidowicz, this volume, 107.

30. All the surviving local examples are of stone, but the former spire at Hereford Cathedral was of timber and, like Coventry, was on a tower erected over a crossing with Romanesque piers; Morris, 'Hereford Cathedral Church', 239 and fig. 33.

31. Morris, 'Hereford Cathedral Church', 238.

32. Plain ball ornament is substituted for fully carved ball-flowers on parts of the Salisbury Cathedral spire, Pershore Abbey tower and the spires of the Lichfield Cathedral west towers.

33. For other stones which might have come from a tower, see Morris, 'Cathedral Church', 56–7.

34. T784 and T785/1 were found close to the crossing, on the north transept site (Trench 3), but T345 was in the area of the cloister north walk (Trench 5), and some other examples of T785 were in the area of the undercrofts north of the chapter-house (Trench 10).

35. For example, in the tower and west porch of St Michael's and the east arm and transepts of Lichfield Cathedral. St Michael's tower vault is a re-creation of 1890, but the surviving medieval rib stubs would have indicated the presence of tierceron ribs. Tierceron vaults also exist in the crossing towers of Holy Trinity (in timber, a restoration of 1854) and of St John the Baptist. At Lichfield, the east arm vaults are *c.* 1320–50 and the transept vaults probably early 15th century.

36. For instance, at Worcester (1385–86), Lichfield (*c.* 1400) and Hereford (south transept, *c.* 1430).

37. The distribution of pieces with a recorded location is — Trench 3, 2 pieces (including the boss); Trench 6 (cloister garth, east), 18 pieces; Trench 10 (undercrofts north of chapter-house), 8 pieces.

38. The full list of the T140 group is — T140/1–19 (rib), T141 (vault cell), T142 (springer), T143/1–6 (wall-rib), T178 (rib and panel) and T295/1–3 (rib like T140).

39. See C. Tracy, 'Choir-Stalls from the 14th-Century Whitefriars Church in Coventry', *JBAA* CL (1997), 76–95, e.g. pls XXVIc, XXVIIa (misericords HT VI and V respectively).

40. See further Morris, 'Later Gothic mouldings, Part II', 5; Harvey, *Perpendicular Style*, fig. 30, mullion profiles for Canterbury Cathedral cloister (*c.* 1395–1414), Westminster great hall (*c.* 1394).

41. The new east arm, including vestries and chapter-house, was begun by Thomas Beauchamp the elder before his death in 1369, and completed by his son by 1394, on the evidence of Dugdale; R. K. Morris, 'The Architecture of the Earls of Warwick in the Fourteenth Century', in W. M. Ormrod (ed.), *England in the Fourteenth Century* (Woodbridge 1986), 169–70.

42. Actually for tiercerons in the simple star vaults of the Warwick vestries.

43. The fragment of springer, T178, is unhelpful in providing additional evidence for the vault pattern, showing, unsurprisingly, at least three ribs at the springing point.

44. Morris, 'Cathedral Church', 33–4, 57–62.

45. Morris, 'Cathedral Church', 57–8; examples of major vaults using jointed masonry construction are unknown in the 14th century. An alternative explanation for T178 is that it derives from wall panelling contemporary with the vault.

46. Another jointed masonry vault apparently existed in the former crossing tower of the Coventry Whitefriars, rebuilt after a tower collapse of 1446 or 1447; Woodfield, *Whitefriars*, 4, 66, 80, 131.

47. Hobley, 'Cathedral Excavations', 95–100, figs 2, 5.

48. Rylatt and Mason, *Cathedral Priory*, 30–62.

49. See further Rylatt and Mason, *Cathedral Priory*, 44–5. Thus, the parallel previously drawn with the dormitory arrangement at Christ Church Canterbury is no longer applicable; Hobley, 'Cathedral Excavations', 46, and Morris, 'Cathedral Church', 50.

50. For the few Romanesque worked stones, see Morris, 'The Worked Stones', 67, 73–5, 78, 80.

51. The claim made by Richard of Devizes, cited by Lambert in Hobley, 'Cathedral Excavations', 57–8.

52. Rylatt and Mason, *Cathedral Priory*, 35–49.

53. See, for example, the discussion of geometry employed for ribs in Morris, 'The Architecture of the Earls of Warwick', 164–7. I contend that the chamfer criteria is still valid for window mullions.

54. Examples checked in Coventry are the Holy Cross crypt and Wyley Chapel at St Michael's, St Mary's Guildhall undercrofts and the remains of vaulting at the base of the cathedral priory's south-west tower. Elsewhere the eastern undercroft of Stoneleigh Abbey, the undercrofts of the great hall range at Kenilworth Castle and the residential range at Warwick Castle, and the eastern bays of the crypt of St Mary's, Warwick.

55. It is commonly used in capitals and corbels from the 1220s right up to *c.* 1300, e.g. in the new claustral buildings (mainly *c.* 1230–45) and church at Tintern Abbey (1269–*c.* 1300).

56. For dating the cathedral west end around 1220, see Morris, 'Cathedral Church', 51, though there is no independent dating evidence for this work. Jackie Hall has recently argued for its earlier use at Croxden (from *c.* 1200); J. Hall, 'Croxden Abbey Church: Architecture, Burial and Patronage', *JBAA* 160 (2007), 80–1, fig. 43.

57. Rylatt and Mason, *Cathedral Priory*, 46, '*c.* 1325–48', based on my preliminary dating of the chamfered rib T468 (the same profile as the many loose pieces, T320), now revised (see main text).

58. Hobley discovered another pier, though apparently wider ('70cm') than those found in 2000 (T467, 610mm); Hobley, 'Cathedral Excavations', 97, pl. 12a. The unmortared wall of massive blocks abutting this pier would appear to be post-dissolution rather than a medieval partition, *pace* Rylatt and Mason, *Cathedral Priory*, 46.

59. Probably rib T468 is wider because of the larger size of the refectory undercroft.

60. It has also been inserted into the west bays of the original east–west undercroft; Rylatt and Mason, *Cathedral Priory*, 37–9.

61. See further Rylatt and Mason, *Cathedral Priory*, 48.

62. Illustrated in Rylatt and Mason, *Cathedral Priory*, figs 49d, e, and 54d; the bosses (T316, 361, 696, 984) are currently displayed in the Visitor Centre. More bosses, apparently from the same vault, were recorded by Dr Troughton in the 19th century; reproduced in Hobley, 'Cathedral Excavations', pl. 29(b).

63. The pier would have been approximately 800mm wide, compared with 610mm for the refectory undercroft piers. A comparable example of an early decorative vault in an ecclesiastical crypt is at Glasgow Cathedral (1240s–50s); see C. Wilson, 'The stellar vaults of Glasgow Cathedral's inner crypt and Villard de Honnecourt's chapter-house plan: a conundrum revisited', in *Medieval Art and Architecture in the Diocese of Glasgow*, ed. R. Fawcett, *BAA Trans.* XXIII (Leeds 1998), 55–76.

64. See further Morris, 'The Worked Stones', 68, 79.

65. Only the nave vault at Lichfield is as early as the 13th century (*c.* 1270–80); there the differentiation is between the larger ridge-rib and the smaller diagonal and tierceron ribs. Elsewhere at Lichfield the ridge-ribs are smaller than the diagonal and tierceron ribs in the choir vault (*c.* 1340) and the vaults of the transepts (early 15th century). The differentiation is also found in the pioneering tierceron vaults at Lincoln Cathedral (e.g. the nave aisles, 1230s), though implemented by different rib profiles rather than by size.

66. See further Monckton in this volume, 139.

67. A topographical difficulty found occasionally elsewhere, as at Rievaulx Abbey (Yorks.), a spectacular example of terracing in its east and south ranges to deal with a sloping site; P. Fergusson and S. Harrison, *Rievaulx Abbey: Community, Architecture, Memory* (New Haven and London 1999), 103, 140–1.

68. Rylatt and Mason, *Cathedral Priory*, 36–7, 40. As early as 1312, the priory granted a corrody to the royal master mason, Hugh de 'Titemersshe'; Lambert in Hobley, 'Cathedral Excavations', 65.

69. The other one (west bay) is also an insertion, but is missing all its details except for part of its sill, which is another deep profile chamfer.

70. See further Morris, 'Kenilworth', in this volume, 351–2. For the double-ogee in general, see R. K. Morris, 'The development of later Gothic mouldings in England c.1250–1400, Part I', *Architectural History* 21 (1978), 35–9.

71. The window jambs incorporate a groove for glazing, which is probably secondary.

72. Rylatt and Mason, *Cathedral Priory*, 39.

73. Rylatt and Mason, *Cathedral Priory*, 40. Mouldings survive only for the southernmost window.

74. Nothing survived of the fabric of the rooms above the north–south and east–west undercrofts to provide guidance.

75. For example, Benedictine Chester Abbey (now cathedral) in R. Gilyard-Beer, *Abbeys: an illustrated guide to the abbeys of England and Wales* (HMSO, London, 2nd edn 1976), fig. 11. At Coventry, it is assumed that on the south side of the chapter house there was a slype, above which may have been housed a treasury or vestry (Prelim., Fig. A).

76. R. Gilyard-Beer, *Cleeve Abbey* (English Heritage guidebook, 2nd edn 1990), 47.

77. All the pieces attributed here to the chapter-house derive from Trench 10, unless stated otherwise.

78. Dimensions from Rylatt and Mason, *Cathedral Priory*, 32.

79. See Morris and Shoesmith ed., *Tewkesbury Abbey* (as n. 14), fig. 21.1, for the excavation plan of the Lady Chapel.

80. The Norman chapter-house may have had a semicircular eastern apse, judging from the evidence in Hobley, 'Cathedral Excavations', 95–6, fig. 6. I now consider the 'column' base which Hobley found in this location to be part of the 14th-century rebuilding; cf. Morris, 'Cathedral Church', 54–5.

81. Rylatt and Mason, *Cathedral Priory*, 39–40, fig. 29. There are no features in the fabric of the reinforcement to date it, so it cannot be certain whether it was a preventative measure when the new chapter-house was started or a reactive measure to deal with subsequent instability.

82. See Gill and Morris, 'Apocalypse', figs 6, 8; Rylatt and Mason, *Cathedral Priory*, 32–3, 77–8, pl. 4, fig. 52. Budget and time restraints on the interior reconstruction commissioned by Past Forward meant that it had to be finalised before all the information from the excavations was available and assessed.

83. Types T727 (39 pieces recorded) and T728 (17 pieces recorded); for the purpose of cataloguing, T727 was differentiated from 728 by the inclusion of cusping on the stones.

84. For example, York Minster chapter-house and vestibule (1280–90) and Little St Hugh's shrine at Lincoln Cathedral (1290s–1307); see further Morris, 'Later Gothic Mouldings, Part II', 1–4, 7–8. The bases at the chapter-house entrance also resemble those of Little St Hugh's shrine; illustrated in Hobley, 'Cathedral Excavations', pl .17b.

85. T377 is illustrated in Rylatt and Mason, *Cathedral Priory*, fig. 49c; for the Severn valley ribs, see Morris, 'Later Gothic Mouldings, Part II', 16.

86. On the north side one must assume that there was an upper floor (of unknown purpose) above the east–west undercroft (and thus at ground-floor level with the cloister walk and chapter-house).

87. Some of these pieces were recovered from the west end of the chapter-house, e.g. T040, T083, from BP99 Trench 1, excavated during the first Time Team visit.

88. The maximum internal width of the west front was 27ft 6in. (8.4m); the approximate internal widths of the lateral bays can be reconstructed at 17ft (5.2m) and of the apse bays at 11ft (3.4m).

89. A similar piece is 727/40, from a similar location, indicating more than one window of this design.

90. For example, Cubbington, Old Arley (both Warks.), Stoke Golding (Leics.), Stanford on Avon (Northants.).

91. Windows of three stepped lancet lights with cusping are found in contemporary local churches (e.g. Lapworth, Old Arley, Wroxhall), but the taller chapter-house windows are likely to have included additional tracery above in the head.

92. See Hobley, 'Cathedral Excavations', 124, fig. 18/7, for a similar fragment found near the chapter-house door.

93. For St Albans, see RCHME, *A Guide to St Albans Cathedral* (London 1952), 12, pls 2, 7; for Dorchester, W. Rodwell, *Dorchester Abbey, Oxfordshire: the Archaeology and Architecture of a Cathedral, Monastery and Parish Church* (Oxford 2009), ch. 7.

94. Mainly from Trench 10.

95. The one piece of a single rib profile (T310) retains only its front mouldings, and therefore could be broken off a springer. On the other hand, Hobley found what appears to be a chapter-house rib piece in the cloister south walk, which may be evidence for the movement off site of the debris from the main vault at the Dissolution; Hobley, 'Cathedral Excavations', 126, fig. 21/9 (erroneously identified as window mullion).

96. Peter Newton in Hobley, 'Cathedral Excavations', 110–11. Newton made comparisons *inter alia* with the chancel glass at Stanford on Avon, which he dated to *c.* 1315–26; see Marks, this volume, 192, suggesting a date after 1324.

97. For the stratigraphic evidence, see T. Hallam and I. Soden, 'Excavations in the Frater Undercroft, St Mary's Benedictine Priory, Coventry March–April 2000', Northamptonshire Archaeology (unpublished summary report, n.d.), 5–6, fig. 4.

98. U. Engel, *Worcester Cathedral: an architectural history* (Chichester 2007), 33.

99. 30 pieces of this design were identified, mainly fragments (from T287, 380, 381). The evidence for the ogee curve of the hoodmould comes from T368.

100. Illustrated in Rylatt and Mason, *Cathedral Priory*, pl. 2b–e. Unfortunately no pieces of tracery have been firmly identified for these windows, so the hope previously expressed by the author about the potential of the tracery stones from the CRU excavation has not been fulfilled; Rylatt and Mason, *Cathedral Priory*, 68. T329 is probably a length of mullion from these windows, but T338 belongs with the cloister.

101. Four pieces of T290 were identified, together with T370 (same feature) and T323 (hoodmould).

102. The T290 hoodmould is reconstructed from T323, and the T331(finial) hoodmould from T368.

103. See Rylatt and Mason, *Cathedral Priory*, 49, pl. 1. The heraldry provides a wide span of 1340–1401 (Thomas I and II Beauchamp), but Iain Soden (pers. comm.) sees a similarity of local manufacture with the Beauchamp tiles produced for the Coventry Charterhouse, 1381–85; for the latter, see Soden, *Charterhouse*, 100–5. He has variously dated the refectory pavement to 'the later 14th century' (Hallam and Soden, 'Excavations in the Frater Undercroft', 5) and to '*c.* 1360' (Soden, *Hidden History*, 179).

104. W. G. Fretton, 'The Collegiate Church of St John the Baptist, Coventry', *TBAS* (1876), 1–18. No parallels have been noted with other Coventry works of the second half of the 14th century (St Michael's tower, Holy Trinity nave, the Whitefriars, St Mary's Guildhall); nor with John of Gaunt's works at Kenilworth Castle, in contrast to my suggestion in Rylatt and Mason, *Cathedral Priory*, 68. For the dating of St John the Baptist's nave, see Morris, 'St Mary's Hall', 14.

105. For the Gloucester and Windsor mouldings, see Morris, 'Later Gothic Mouldings, Part II', 5–7; J. H. Harvey, *The Perpendicular Style 1330–1485* (London 1978), 79–84, fig. 10. For Warwick, Morris, 'The Architecture of the Earls of Warwick' (as n. 41), 169–71.

106. Though the ogee hood continued in Perpendicular works (e.g. St Michael's steeple, *c.* 1375–1430s).

107. For instance, at Beaulieu Abbey, Chester Cathedral (formerly St Werburgh's Abbey), Worcester Cathedral Priory and Shrewsbury Abbey.

108. For a fuller description, see Rylatt and Mason, *Cathedral Priory*, 68–9.

109. J. Allen, 'The Choir Stalls of Lincoln Cathedral, Chester Cathedral and St Mary's Church, Nantwich', *JBAA* 161 (2008), 108–11.

110. The miniature ribs of Little St Hugh's shrine at Lincoln and of the sedilia at Hawton and Heckington, and the mullions of Hawton chancel; see further Morris, 'Later Gothic Mouldings, Part II', 1–3, 'fourth variety' of mullion.

111. For a brief account of these works, see V. Sekules, 'A Group of Masons in Early Fourteenth-Century Lincolnshire: Research in Progress', in *Studies in Medieval Sculpture*, ed. F. H. Thompson (Society of Antiquaries of London, 1983), 151–64.

112. Bell bases are found at Lincoln Cathedral from the end of the 13th century, but the Coventry pulpit bases as a group look later, more like Irnham, *c.* 1340; see Morris, 'Later Gothic Mouldings, Part II', 26–9.

113. Sekules, 'A Group of Masons in Early Fourteenth-Century Lincolnshire' (as n. 111), pls LXII–IV. For context, see also N. Coldstream, 'Fourteenth-Century Corbel Heads in the Bishop's House, Ely', in *Studies in Medieval Sculpture*, ed. F. H. Thompson (Society of Antiquaries of London, 1983), 165–76.

114. The pieces are all in a distinctive greyish-green 'Warwick' type sandstone, also used at Coventry Whitefriars, mainly in the later 15th century, and probably quarried close to the city; Woodfield, *Whitefriars*, 125.

115. There was less excavation in the area of the west walk. For evidence for the earlier cloister fabric, see Rylatt and Mason, *Cathedral Priory*, 30–1.

116. Hobley, 'Cathedral Excavations', fig. 4 (bottom right) captions fallen masonry in the south walk as 'collapsed cloister ceiling', but inspection of an unpublished photograph of these stones in his excavation archive suggests they are from the wall panelling.

117. For latticed transoms and other tracery terminology, see Harvey, *Perpendicular*, 70–2. The standard solid transom was also noted on some stones (e.g. T097–099, T098, T240), whilst a transom piece decorated with miniature crenellations was found in the south walk in Hobley's 1965 excavations (from an unpublished photograph in his excavation archive).

118. Eight lights at 14in. would produce a reasonable bay of about 10ft (3m), whereas 6 lights would produce only about 7ft 6in. (2.3m). Comparable widths at Gloucester are about 12ft 6in. (3.8m) for 8 lights and 12ft (3.65m) for 6 lights, but in plan Gloucester's cloister is about 50% larger than that at Coventry. However, a stone illustrated by Troughton (Troughton IX, 17), which I attribute to the cloister, suggests lights grouped in threes, and six lights grouped 3 + 3 was the norm for comparable Perpendicular cloisters (e.g. Gloucester, all walks after the east walk; Tewkesbury *c.* 1400; Wells, after *c.* 1420). Possibly more than one tracery pattern was used around the walks, as at Gloucester: Troughton's piece may well have been found around the west part of the cloister (Blue Coat School excavations 1856–57), whereas the Phoenix excavations focused on the east, south and north walks. They also noted variations in the widths of the walks between 8ft to 10ft 6in. (2.40–3.20m); Rylatt and Mason, *Cathedral Priory*, 30.

119. For Gloucester, see Leedy, *Fan Vaulting* (as n. 18), 166–8. For English late medieval cloisters in general, see L. A. Monckton, 'Experimental Architecture? Vaulting and West Country Cloisters in the Late Middle Ages', *JBAA* 159 (2006), 249–83.

120. Reversed archlets appear first at Gloucester in the south transept south window, *c.* 1335. The tracery of the north, west and south cloister walks all use lights with cinque-cusped archlets top and bottom like Coventry, but with ogee heads because the tracery pattern is alternate.

121. Illustrated in Harvey, *Perpendicular*, fig. 12.9.

122. The Perpendicular rebuilding of the church spans *c.* 1400–*c.* 1475. The clerestory tracery was restored by Sir George Gilbert Scott 'in imitation of what had been there originally'. See D. J. Peters, *St Mary the Virgin, Nottingham: a Short History and Guide* (Newark 1974), 3–5. also E. Harwood, *Nottingham*, Pevsner Architectural Guides (New Haven and London 2008), 31–4, passim.

123. For dating evidence, see further Monckton in this volume, 148–52.

124. For which see this volume, Demidowicz, 'Hall', 171–7, and Monckton, 143–60.

125. Richard Goddard in this volume.

126. With the almost total loss of the Greyfriars and Whitefriars, and the Perpendicular rebuildings of the parish churches, Decorated-style windows survive only in the end windows of St John's Hospital, the nave north clerestory at St John Baptist's church and an ogee reticulated window in the north porch of Holy Trinity.

127. See further in this volume Morris, 'Kenilworth', and Goodall, 'Newarke'.

128. For the evidence for the new east end, see Morris, 'Cathedral Church', 27–34, 57–62.

129. Evesham was a ten-sided polygonal chapter-house; D. C. Cox, *Evesham Abbey and the Parish Churches* (Evesham 1980), 8–9.

130. See R. N. Swanson, 'The Priory in the Later Middle Ages', in Demidowicz ed., *First Cathedral*, 144–5.

131. Somewhat like the clone of Gloucester at Tewkesbury Abbey, where apparently only the east walk was vaulted; see further Morris and Shoesmith ed., *Tewkesbury Abbey* (as n. 14), 149.

The Redevelopment of the Cathedral Priory Site from the Dissolution to the Present Day

GEORGE DEMIDOWICZ

First, a new definition is presented of the geographical extent of the pre-Dissolution cathedral and monastic precinct of St Mary's Cathedral Priory, Coventry. Following the Dissolution, the demolition of the majority of the precinct buildings created a large area of derelict land within the town. Using a wide variety of documentary and cartographic sources, this paper chronicles how the rubble fields eventually came to be reclaimed and developed. By the mid-17th century socially distinct areas of housing had emerged. Continuity of industrial use characterised the north end of the precinct in the area of the medieval water mill and dye house. The 20th century witnessed the greatest changes when Coventry rapidly grew into a major industrial city. At the end of the century the Millennium celebrations gave the opportunity to reveal the site of the lost cathedral and priory. The Phoenix Initiative was the first time that comprehensive redevelopment in the city centre included as a first principle the laying out, display and interpretation of archaeological remains over an extensive area.

INTRODUCTION

THE demolition of the cathedral of St Mary, Coventry, was a unique event in the English Reformation. The cathedral was the only one in the country to be abandoned and have its site redeveloped. It was not unusual for a Benedictine house to be demolished after the Dissolution, even within a town, but the loss of both cathedral and its attached priory in Coventry was an upheaval of unprecedented magnitude. A centuries-old institution disappeared almost overnight, disrupting an already ailing economy and severely damaging the urban fabric. Rubble fields replaced the largest complex of stone buildings located within the medieval town. The manner in which this area was later redeveloped presents an intriguing story and has never been chronicled in any detail.

THE PRECINCT AT THE DISSOLUTION

THE Benedictine monks, a shrunken community of about thirteen, were expelled on 15 June 1539.[1] The first extant survey of the precinct was compiled after their eviction in the early 1540s.[2] By this time various buildings in the precinct had been leased out, including several stables, a water mill, the 'hawkes mewes', the 'yate howse', the porters lodge, the 'Slaught[er] howse over the running water', 'le malte howse' and 'le kylne'. Henry Over and Thomas Kevett rented the monastery, and the mayor and aldermen 'certain habitations'. Not unexpectedly, there was some open land within the precinct, for example, 'le utt[er] courte', some gardens, an orchard and 'le hoppeyarde', and also water: St Osburg's Pool, the mill waterworks and another pool. The evidence suggests a different line for the precinct boundary than those proposed in earlier reconstructions, none of which appear to have used this survey.

The plan published by Brian Hobley defines areas 'directly occupied by the priory' as including many Coventry streets that could never have been within the precinct. The precinct wall delineated by Joan Lancaster's in *The Historic Town Atlas* has the advantage of defining a more compact area, including the priory mill, but embraced Holy Trinity church, the bishop's palace and Bastille House, certainly not in the precinct in the 16th century. Lancaster placed the dye house in the correct position, but Lilley re-interprets it as the prior's chamber, moving the dye house to a position to the south west of the mill. He excluded the mill from the precinct, contrary to the evidence of the Dissolution survey.[3]

All three interpretations have the later Miller's Alley leading to Bastille House as the eastern precinct boundary (Fig. 1 and Col. Pl. IV in print edn). The 16th-century evidence suggests, however, that the boundary was much closer to the cathedral's east end, running in a line roughly north of the bishop's palace to immediately east of the dye house (Fig. 1). This would exclude an area of open ground that was used for tentering cloth in the 16th century and which had been leased from the priory to Gelinus (Julines) Nethermylle, a draper and mayor of Coventry in 1522.[4] In 1578 the lease of the eastern end of the precinct, including the site of the chancel, mentioned an 'old stone wall' forming the eastern boundary with the land of John Nethermylle, son of Julines.[5]

The south boundary of the precinct ran from the rear of the bishop's palace, past the east end of the cathedral, probably meeting the south-east corner of the south transept. Here a wall enclosed the monks' cemetery and an area known as the 'well yard'[6] (Fig. 1). The cathedral itself (south transept, nave and south-west tower) formed the boundary with Holy Trinity churchyard. The remainder of the south precinct boundary, west of the south-west tower, and the first part of the west precinct boundary was formed by the cathedral forecourt wall in which there was a gate, the 'foregate' (Fig. 1). The position of the gate has been precisely located.[7] This gave access from the town to the forecourt, the outer court and the remainder of the precinct. From the north-east corner of the forecourt the precinct wall then descended, more or less, in a straight line northwards to the River Sherbourne, which functioned as the head race and pool for the priory mill. Stables were probably built along the wall on the interior of the precinct and this line survived as a property boundary well into 19th century.

At the bottom of the slope at the Sherbourne the precinct turned east and followed the river on its north bank to its confluence with the Radford Brook. Immediately to the north, on the line of the precinct wall, was the 'rear gate' (Fig. 1), which was replaced by Priory Gate (later Swanswell Gate) when this section of the town wall was constructed in the later 15th century (Fig. 1). The timber-pile base of the original gate was discovered when a new Sherbourne culvert was being constructed in the late 1930s.[8] From here the precinct boundary probably followed the south side of a curving channel, giving the appearance of a natural water course, but which acted as the side race or storm water channel once the mill had been constructed. Farther east this channel was eventually met by the tail race from the mill; the precinct boundary following the combined waters to the dye house and the north-east corner of the precinct.

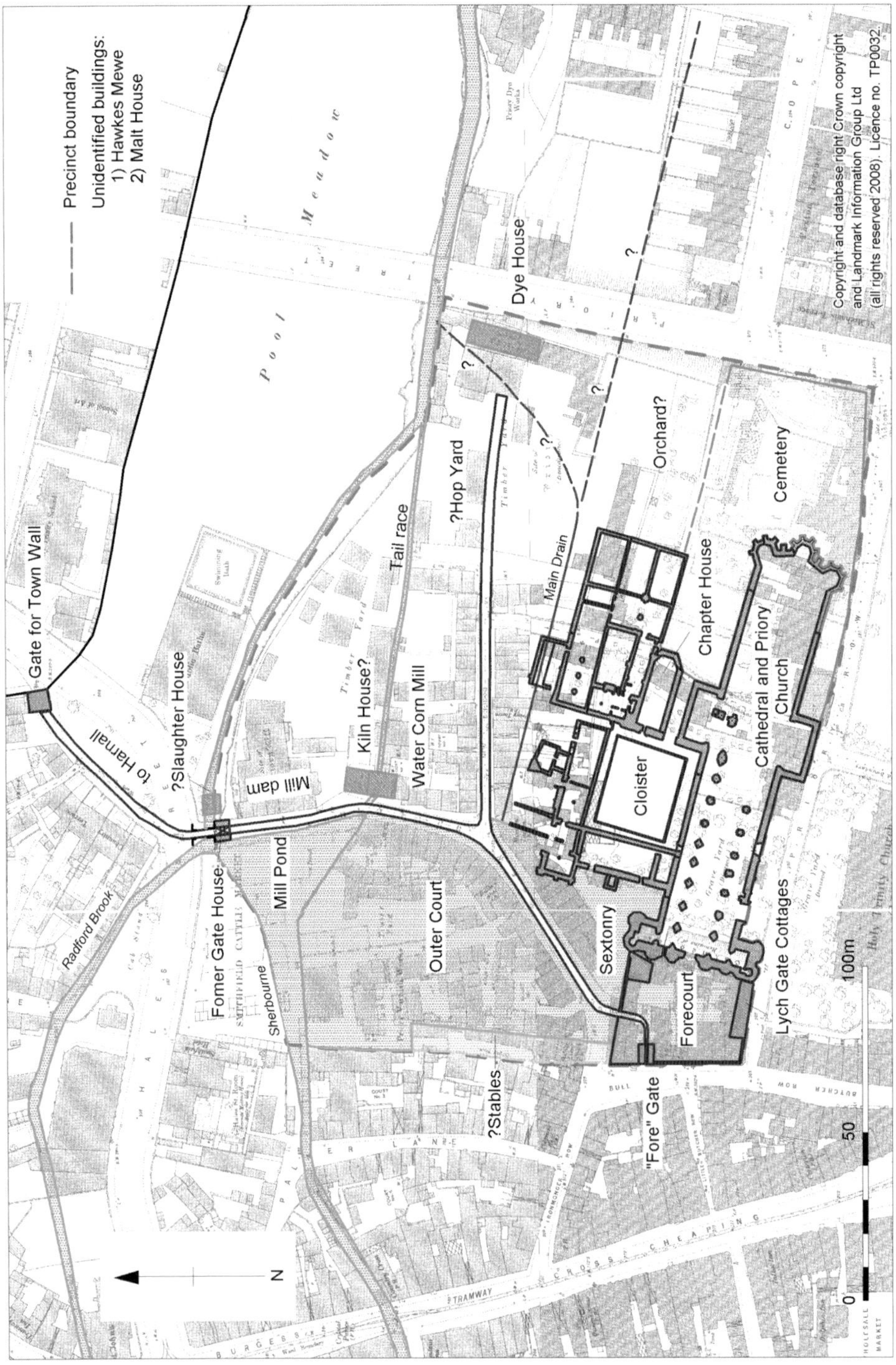

FIG. 1. The priory precinct *c.* 1540, laid over Ordnance Survey map 1:500, 1st edition 1886

Drawing, author and Historic Environment Record, Coventry City Council

CHANGES TO THE PRECINCT IN THE LATTER HALF OF THE 16TH CENTURY

IN 1545 the precinct and a considerable amount of former property in and beyond the town were sold to John Hales via his agents.[9] Attempts had been made by the city authorities to save the cathedral, but these had come to nothing, and in truth the city was unwilling to pay the hefty asking price for a building that would have no obvious future use.[10] It is likely that from 1545, after five years of respite, the buildings were set upon to remove the more valuable of these materials and in the process transformed into ruinous hulks.

The more difficult structures to demolish survived longer, such as the two west end towers and the central tower. There are no known illustrations of the cathedral and priory before the Dissolution, but there is a view of Coventry taken at some distance from the south by William Smyth, herald to Queen Elizabeth and dated about 1576.[11] Smyth appears to have relied on his memory to produce the drawing, as the main churches are not in correct geographical relationship with each other (Fig. 2). Nevertheless, the large tower can be interpreted as St Mary's, and, significantly, it has no spire. It is possible that the central crossing never supported one; the drawing has the tower parapet pinnacles still in place, not likely if the spire had recently been demolished.

We can only guess about the progressive devastation of the precinct during the quarter-century it was owned by Hales. In the undercrofts on the north side of the chapter-house and cloister, the rubble that accumulated like scree slopes preserved walls to a height of five metres immediately north of the cloister terrace. This accident of preservation can be seen clearly in the priory undercrofts, exposed in excavations during Coventry's Millennium scheme. Parts of the north wall of the chapter-house fell into the undercrofts, including fragments of a glorious 14th-century Apocalypse cycle, one of which is on display in the Priory Visitor Centre.

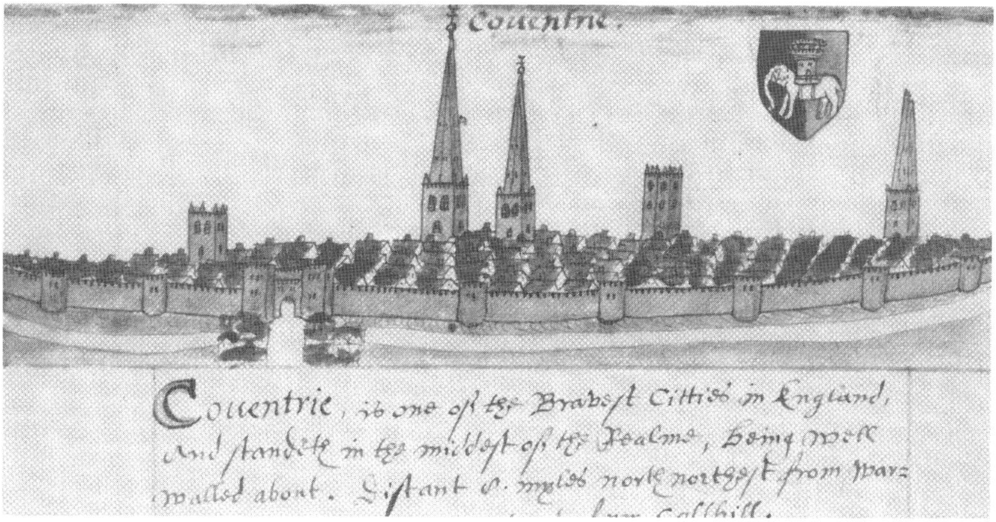

FIG. 2. View of Coventry from the south, William Smyth, *c.* 1576

Photo, Coventry City Council

The forecourt of the cathedral, however, escaped the devastation. This was an area capable of being developed, as it faced the town and the busy Great Butcher Row. It was sold through the crown directly or via John Hales and two of the families who bought property there are known: the Saunders family, butchers and graziers, and the Hopkins family.[12] Most of the west wall was demolished, but not its 'foregate', and a row of houses on either side of the gate was constructed with small yards backing onto the west front of the cathedral. The gate was still needed to maintain access to the precinct from the town, the corn mill and the area of the former stables that had probably been built against the west precinct wall. Within the forecourt walls the monastic Sextonry (the sacristan's building) managed to survive, situated against the north-west tower.[13] The name became corrupted to 'Sextry or Sextrie'.

John Hales died in 1571 and in 1575 his family sold the priory site, with its corn mill and dyehouse, to the corporation for £40 and the dyehouse equipment for £400.[14] The disparity in price may exaggerate the difference in value between the ruinous and rubble-filled precinct land and the going concern that the dyehouse must still have been, but it nevertheless illuminates the contrasting fates of the buildings. The Hales family had exploited those resources on the site that could yield an income and continuity of use was thereby assured for the water mill and dyehouse.

Although the crown had retained the stone for its own disposal many years before, there was plenty left for the corporation to sell. The rubble fields would have provided little return on the corporation's investment otherwise and could not be leased in the long term until properly cleared and levelled. Unfortunately for the corporation, the stone salvagers were not so willing to pay their bills and a long list of debtors compiled in the 1570s and 1580s reveals that a substantial part of the cathedral was still standing at this time. George Keyvett (Kevett) had still not paid £40 for the 'Chancell' and the 'Rammell [Rubble] in the Churche' and George Gardiner owed 30s for two 'Arches of Stone'.[15]

In 1577 the dyehouse and much of the precinct was leased by the corporation to Peter Demetrius, a 'doctor of physic'. He quickly sub-let the dyehouse to Thomas Eybourne, a dyer, and some ground in the south-east corner of the precinct at the east end of the cathedral to Richard Denton. It appears that Denton had already set about clearing this area 'beynge before a stoney and graveleye grounde full of rammell stone and fundac[i]ons of olde walles'.[16] For his efforts he was rewarded with a separate lease of the ground around which new boundary walls had been constructed, perhaps from the rubble of the cathedral. This action represents the next stage of the development of the precinct when leases could be granted following the removal of buildings and the levelling of the ground. Initially only gardens were created, enclosed by stone walls built from the rubble of the demolished buildings.

The corporation commissioned a survey of all its property in 1581, including the priory site where the dyehouse, the mill ('pryorie myln') and the foregate ('gate howse') were specifically listed.[17] The dyehouse and dwelling house contained seven bays and a lean-to, and adjacent were a two-bay barn and stable and a three-bay stone building. These buildings all appear to have survived into the 20th century (see below). The corn mill housed two water wheels, one overshot and the other breast shot. It was noted that there was 'stone which ys lefte of the steeple and Church there worthe xl poundes'. This must have been concentrated around the west end towers and the central crossing tower. The boundaries of the precinct were given as Mr Nethermyll (east and south), the Sherbourne (north), the churchyards of Holy Trinity and St Michael's (south) and John Saunders' land (west).

THE PRECINCT IN THE 17TH CENTURY

THE cathedral site lying adjacent to the burial grounds of Holy Trinity and St Michael's had the most potential for development, as it fronted a road that skirted the north side of the cemeteries, later known as Priory Row (Fig. 3). The timber-framed Lych Gate cottages are the only survivors of the medieval precinct.[18] It was to be another two centuries before any other domestic buildings were constructed to face the two graveyards. In 1611 a lease of the former nave was granted to Henry Sewell, the document confirming that at least two central crossing piers were still standing at this time, and Speed's map also shows a pile of rubble at this location (Figs 3, 4). The forecourt area to the west, described as the 'Sextree', was separated from the nave by the surviving north- and south-west towers.[19] The strip of land immediately south of the nave was already in the tenure of the Sewell family, later to be developed with housing. By 1611 a new route into the precinct had been established across the east part of the transept, the origin of the present Hill Top alley (Fig. 4). This gave an alternative access from the town to the former priory mill, renamed Aston's Mill after the tenant.

By 1637 a house had been built by William Wilkes, a doctor of divinity, on the Priory Row frontage near the corner with Hill Top. A new lease of this house and its garden to Philip Adams, a draper, in this year mentioned a stone pillar, 'newly erected', and a lead cistern. Thomas Sargenson, a mason, and Bartholomew Bewley, a plumber, had erected a cistern 'at the highest part of the city' under an agreement made in 1632 with the corporation.[20] The converted central piers of the crossing would have provided a ready-made high point to which the water could be to pumped from a waterwheel at Swanswell mill below to the north (New Mill). East of the Adams' house, the remainder of the Wilkes' lease, an enclosed garden fronting St Michael's graveyard, eventually came into the hands of the Brownell family.[21]

The Grascombe family of butchers took over the Sewell lease of the nave, which was then apparently used by them to 'keep hogs in'.[22] Eventually the north-west tower itself was put to a new use: in 1644 the lease was sold to the Revd John Bryan, vicar of Holy

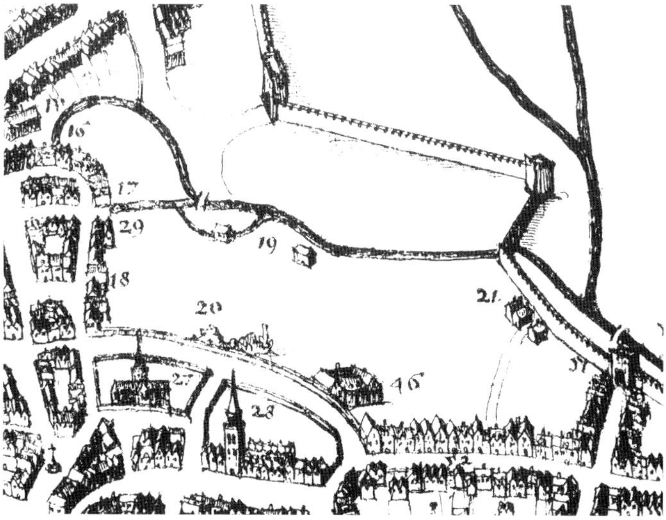

FIG. 3. Map of Coventry, John Speed, *c.* 1620; detail of the precinct area. 20 is the Priory ruins, 27 is Trinity Church, with Priory Row in between

Dugdale, Antiquities of Warwickshire, *1656*

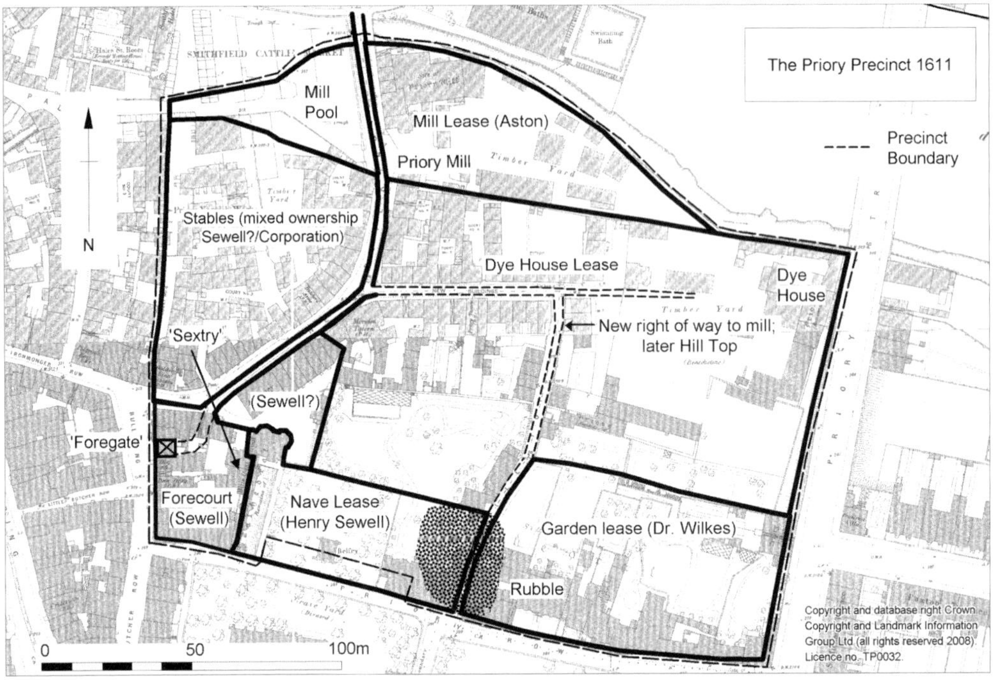

FIG. 4. The priory precinct, 1611

Drawing, author and Historic Environment Record, Coventry City Council

Trinity, and in the next few years he transformed the area, 'making dwelling houses on the bottom of the two steeples [the west end towers]' and cleared the ground of ruins, creating a garden (Fig. 5). He converted the north-west tower into his own home, calling it 'Tower House', and the south-west tower into a gatehouse.[23] The corporation eventually granted Revd Bryan the freehold of the towers and nave site for his endeavours. It is likely that this action helped preserve the medieval north-west tower and it was converted into a school in the early 18th century. By 1652 the street frontage south of the nave, and opposite Holy Trinity church, had also been developed and contained about six houses.[24]

Houses had also been built farther to the north in response to Civil War requirements. In 1643 many properties outside the main gates of the town were pulled down to create a clear line of fire and their inhabitants were moved within the walls and provided with new houses 'in places where there were none before'.[25] One of the locations chosen was within the precinct, immediately west of the dyehouse. John Barker, mayor in 1644–45, obtained a lease of the dyehouse from the corporation and its land with the promise that he would build houses there to the value of £500.[26] Most of the houses were laid out on either side of an existing road that ran west to east to the dyehouse, skirting the north side of the former monastic buildings. This branched off the main link between the former cathedral forecourt and Aston's mill. Both of these routes probably originated in the monastic period as internal precinct roads and eventually became known as New Buildings. It is possible that the link into the south end of Great Butcher

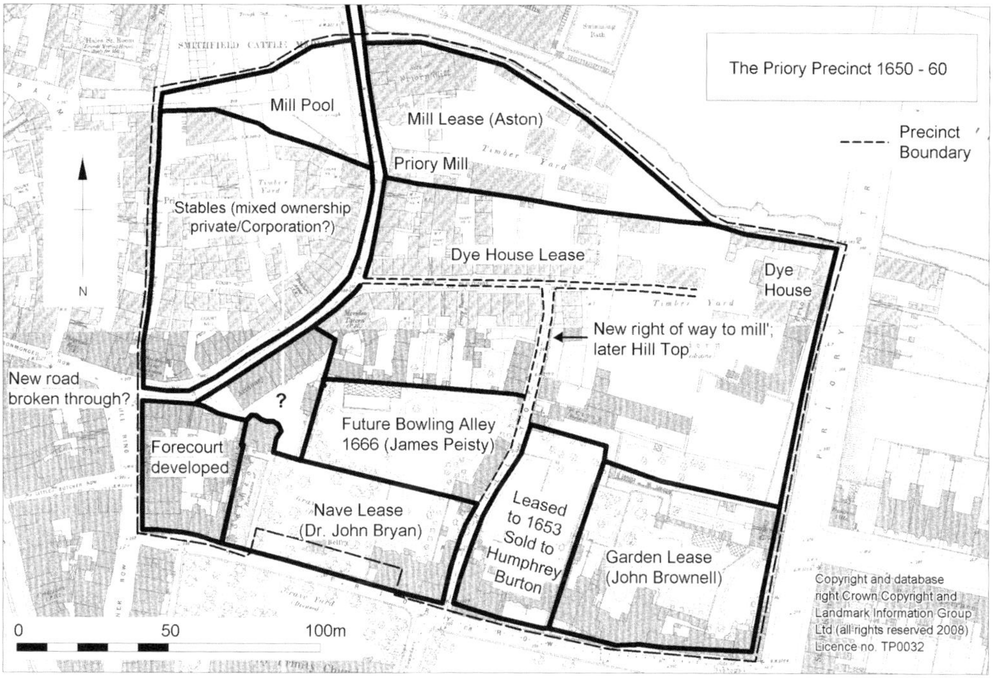

FIG. 5. The priory precinct, 1650–60
Drawing, author and Historic Environment Record, Coventry City Council

Row, later Bullring, was broken through at this time, avoiding the constriction of the former priory gate and what remained of the forecourt.

The south side of the dyehouse road needed to be cleared of rubble and levelled. This created an unstable cut in the undisturbed monastic remains. A high sandstone retaining wall was built from the rubble to form the rear boundary of the new plots (Figs 5, 26). This wall ran parallel to the roadway and was slightly out of alignment with the orientation of the former claustral complex. Its construction gave the opportunity to improve the land immediately above it, corresponding roughly with the former cloister area, and by 1666 James Peisty had laid out a bowling green with his house and garden.[27] Much of the sandstone (and later brick wall) was replaced during the Phoenix Initiative (1999–2003) and now partly corresponds with the large viewing window into the priory undercrofts and the adjacent water cascade.

By 1652 at least ten houses had been constructed along the two branches of New Buildings.[28] In the same year about thirty-five stables were recorded, lying in the area between the New Buildings roadway leading to Aston's Mill and the west precinct boundary. The humbler dwellings erected here for the displaced extra-mural residents created an early social distinction between the housing in upper and lower precinct area. In 1649 Humphrey Burton (town clerk, 1636–82) took out a new lease of Philip Adams' house on the east corner of Hill Top and Priory Row.[29] It is likely that the house he occupied reflected his status, although it was overlooked to the west by a pillar of stone surmounted by the lead cistern that supplied the town with water.[30] To the east, as far as the former bishop's palace and tenter grounds, the Priory Row frontage remained undeveloped but cultivated as a walled garden (Fig. 5).[31]

In the late 1650s, lower down in the precinct, the dyehouse was re-let to a silk dyer and was taken over in 1670 by Richard Stretton, a tanner, and continued to be used for tanning until at least 1685.[32] In the meantime Aston's Mill continued to grind corn, renamed Perkin's Mill by 1666 when it contained three sets of stones grinding wheat, maslyn (a mixture of rye and wheat), and malt. By 1687 it was known as Chaplin's Mill and the buildings were in an extremely dilapidated state.[33]

THE PRECINCT IN THE 18TH CENTURY

AT the turn of 18th century the corporation found itself in severe financial difficulties, not helped by a pervasive culture of corruption. Various methods of raising revenue and cutting expenses were initiated, including the drastic measure of selling off part of the corporation lands and properties.[34] Most of its houses in New Buildings were sold between 1703 and 1744 (Fig. 6). The water mill, which had been rebuilt in about 1688, was disposed of in 1731, but the corporation retained the dyehouse until well over a century later.[35] By 1765 it had been converted to paper making.[36] Even in the first half of the 18th century the section of New Buildings leading eastwards to these premises was not heavily built up, with plots still containing 'waste ground', barns, stables and a muckhill (Fig. 6). The appearance of the New Buildings between Great Butcher Row and the mill is not so clear.[37] It is assumed the area was dominated by stables in 16th and 17th centuries, and it is possible that some houses had been built during the Civil War on this land. The site of the later ribbon factory, immediately north of Tower House, had come into the hands of the prominent Hopkins family by 1757.[38] By the end of the century their tenant, Joseph Downes, was building new tenements and a stable on the site.[39]

Samuel Bradford's map of 1748–49 shows New Buildings for the first time, then called Priory Lane (Prelim., Plan C). The west side from Great Butcher Row to the mill had been completely built up, probably leaving some stables behind a solid street frontage of houses. Houses also lined the south side of the link to the former dye house, but the north side was still relatively open. On Priory Row (not then named, but otherwise known as 'Church Yard Lane') buildings lined the street opposite Holy Trinity Church as far as Hill Top. One of the houses was of sufficient status to contain a mount in its garden, no doubt raised from the rubble of the cathedral nave in which it stood.[40] About 1714 Tower House and its associated former 'Sextrie' building was converted into a school for orphaned girls, which became known as the Blue Coat School (Fig. 7).[41]

East of Hill Top a house set back from the street, which survives today as the cathedral Deanery, appears on Bradford's 1748–49 map (Prelim., Plan C). The previous building was sold in 1721 by Humphrey Burton III to David Wells, a wine cooper for £1,725.[42] He appears to have flourished in this trade, demolished Burton's house and had erected a town house of considerable architectural pretension, with a giant order of fluted Ionic pilasters, generally reminiscent of the work of the Smith Brothers of Warwick.[43] The 'new mansion house' was sold in 1741 by David Wells to John Hollyer, a vintner. [44] In 1744 John Hollier (*sic*) purchased from the corporation the garden that lay to the east of the house. This was partly over the site of the cathedral chancel and had previously been leased to the Bott family of apothecaries.[45] John Hollyer intended to build a house, beginning the row that would eventually stretch along Priory Row as

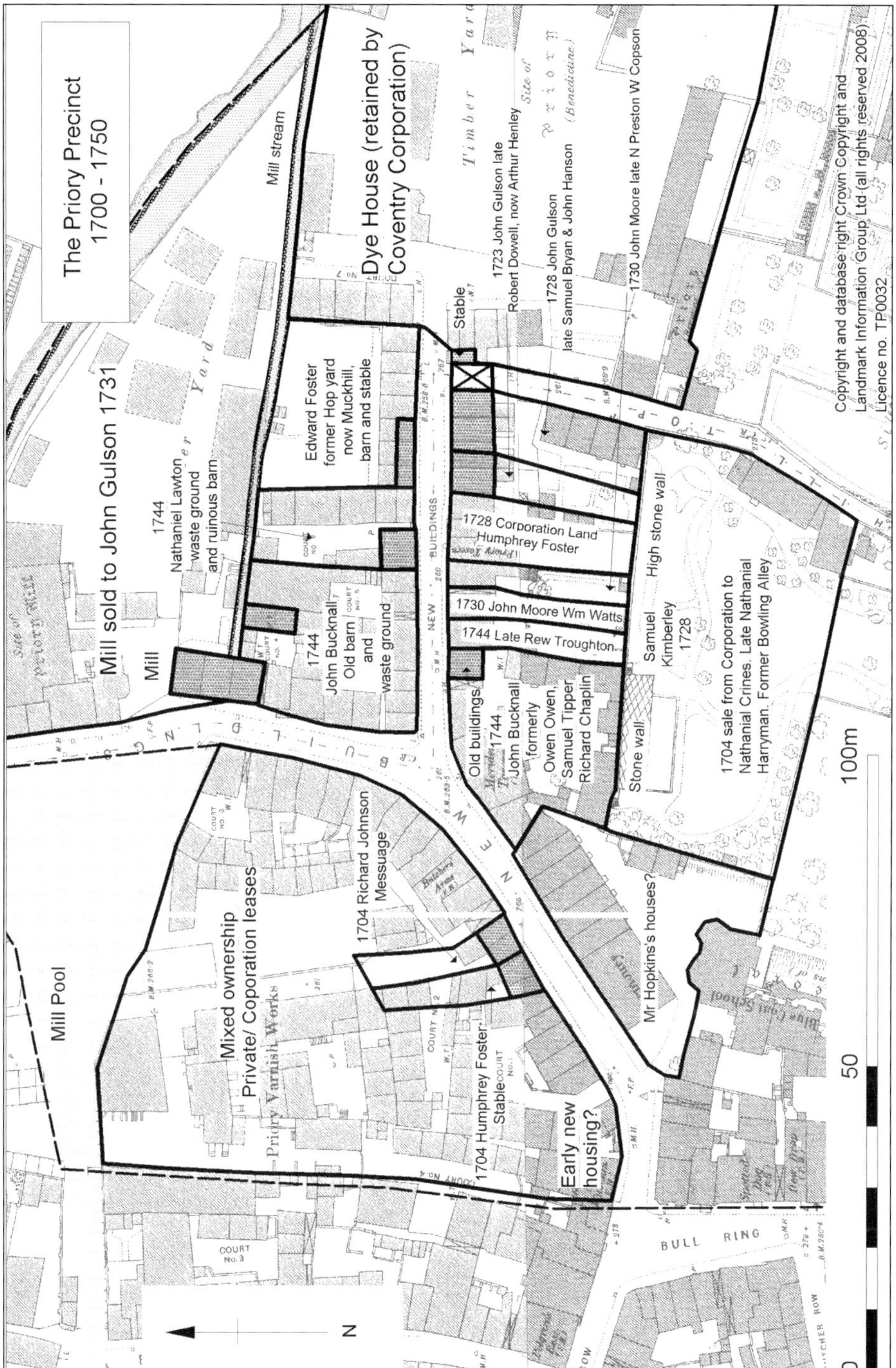

FIG. 6. The priory precinct, 1700–50
Drawing, author and Historic Environment Record, Coventry City Council

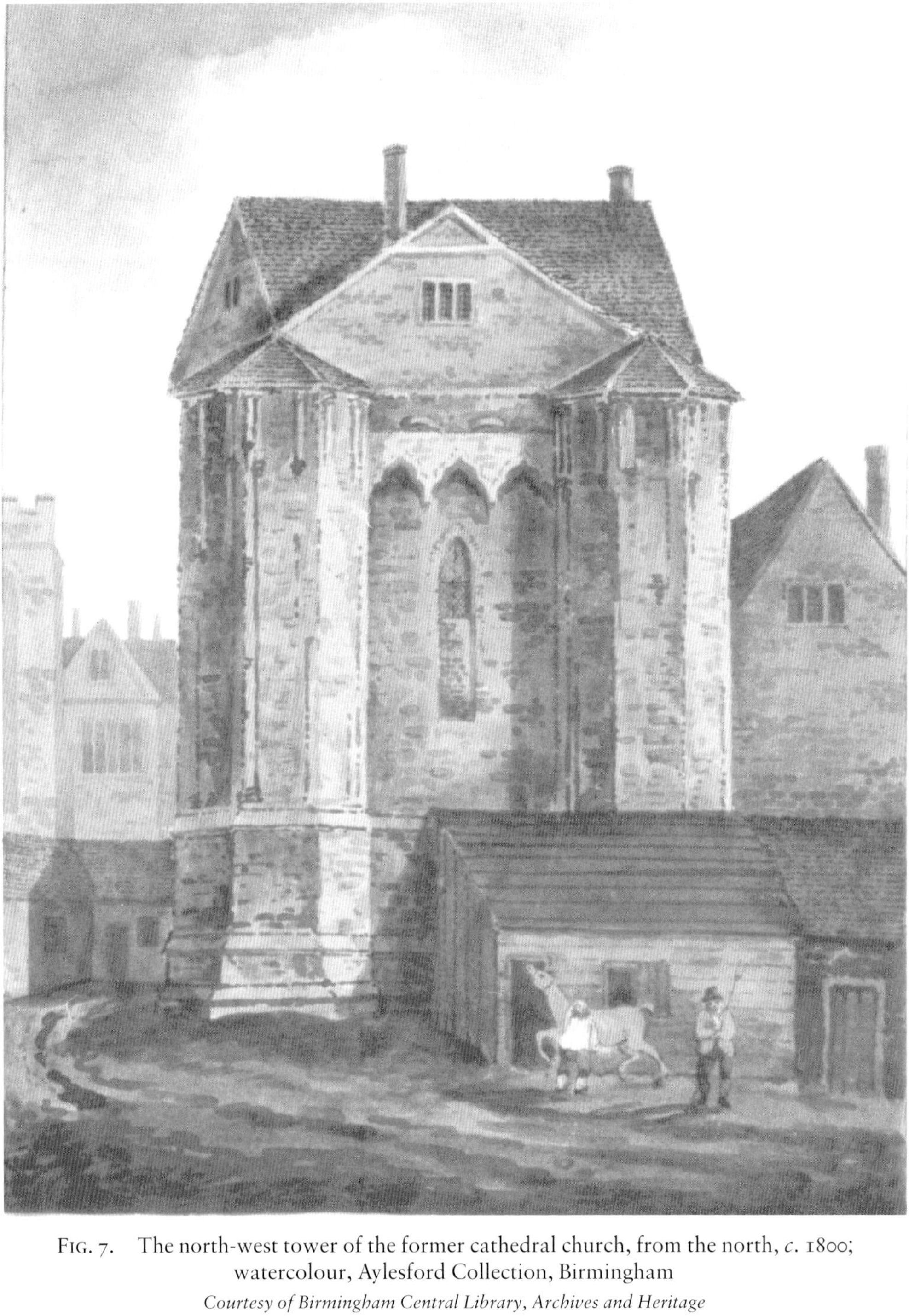

FIG. 7. The north-west tower of the former cathedral church, from the north, *c.* 1800; watercolour, Aylesford Collection, Birmingham

Courtesy of Birmingham Central Library, Archives and Heritage

far as the east end of St Michael's church, but this did not begin until the house and garden were sold by John Hollyer's son to John Watts in 1751.[46] The fact that in the latter part of the century the house was known as 'The Priory' reflects the continuing awareness that the monastery had stood close by.[47]

In about 1704 the 'foregate' was demolished, an event noted several years later by Browne Willis.[48] The appearance of Priory Row was dramatically altered in the early 1770s when part of the 17th-century row of houses was demolished.[49] The land was acquired for an extension to Holy Trinity burial ground, the existing graveyard surrounding the church having become severely overcrowded and a public health risk. A wide gap was opened, re-exposing Blue Coat School to view. A section of the original row of houses stretching eastwards to Hill Top was left. The houses on this site today, belonging to Coventry Cathedral and Diocese, appear to have been erected *c.*1800, no. 18 having been built by Richard Goodall, a banker, around 1812.[50]

THE PRECINCT IN THE 19TH CENTURY

BY the early 19th century the socially distinct area of middle-class housing on Priory Row and artisan dwellings on New Buildings was emphasised with the completion of a row of generously proportioned houses eastwards of the present Deanery. This had necessitated realigning a section of the road that surrounded the north-east corner of St Michael's cemetery. Priory Row was straightened, the cemetery expanded, and the much-altered surviving fragment of the bishop's palace found itself directly on the street frontage, causing a minor obstruction.[51]

The survival of the former priory dyehouse, later a paper manufactory, and the water mill into the 19th century stimulated the industrialisation of the north part of the precinct. The dyehouse probably returned to its original function in the 1780s and in 1811 the corporation leased it to William Browett, a cotton manufacturer. He had converted a former warehouse and stable at the southern end of the site into a calico factory (Fig. 26).[52] The venture did not last long and by 1814 Thomas Moy, a timber-merchant, had taken over the site for a wood yard, but he converted a surviving medieval building at the entrance into dwellings, previously used as stables (see below). He also sub-let the redundant cotton works to Thomas Cope, a silkman, who in 1813 had acquired a considerable area of the former tenter yards and Bastille House (then a dye works) to the east.[53] By 1845 his son, also named Thomas, had entered into a partnership with Stephen Hammerton as ribbon manufacturers using the same premises, where a steam engine had been installed, but gave them up in 1849.[54]

This area of the precinct was developing as an enormous timber yard with the factory purchased from the corporation in 1861 by W. S. Boothe and G. Earle, timber merchants.[55] In the same year they also purchased the former dyehouse site (wood yard) adjoining to the north, except for the two rows of cottages on either side of the gates, which the Corporation had sold separately two years before.[56] Thomas Moy had continued in his business as a timber merchant, but by the time of his death in 1848 had allowed his buildings to deteriorate seriously, and the lease was taken over by another timber merchant, William Dickenson.[57] The appearance of this area is well illustrated in an oil painting of 1861, which also shows the new road, Priory Street, which had been cut in 1857–58 through Thomas Cope junior's land, roughly along the former east boundary of the precinct (Fig. 8 and Col. Pl. VA in print edn). It demolished what was left of the bishop's palace and a ribbon factory belonging to Thomas Cope that had stood behind it (Fig. 26).[58]

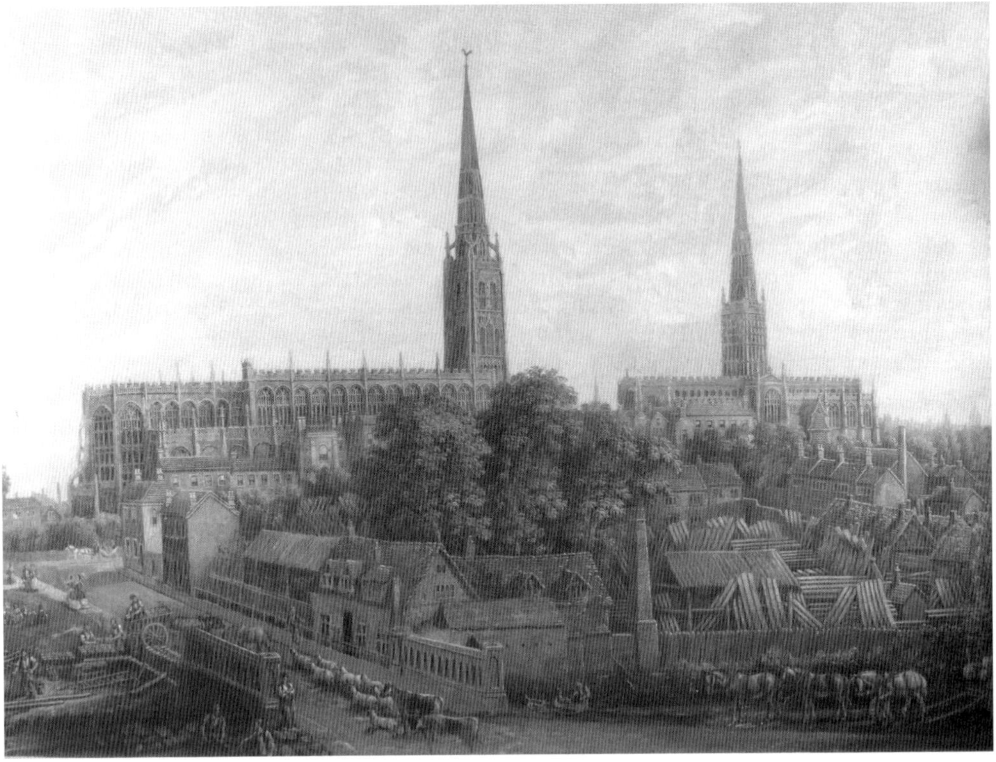

FIG. 8. View of St Michael's, Holy Trinity and the former priory precinct (foreground) from the north-east. David Gee, 1861, oil painting

Courtesy of The Herbert Art Gallery and Museum, Coventry

The wood yards were undoubtedly a response to growing demand for timber for new houses that were being built at a rapid rate, particularly to the north of Coventry. The water corn mill to the west struggled on for another half century, some of the buildings converted into dwellings. The mill was removed under a local act of parliament around 1849 as a serious obstruction to the flow of water: its mill pool, a 'noisome and pestilential reservoir', considered a threat to public health, was drained. The site of the pool became the new cattle market, called Smithfield, solving another public nuisance problem of stock markets held in streets.[59] Priory Mill was replaced by a steam-driven saw mill located immediately to the north on the land that lay between the mill tail race and the River Sherbourne. It was probably established by William Newark (later William Newark and Sons), conveniently serving the adjacent expanding wood yards in New Buildings.[60]

Steam power had also been introduced about thirty years earlier by Josiah Beck to run silk ribbon looms. Beck built his factory at the end of an alley on the opposite (west) side of New Buildings alongside the mill pool, which had not yet been drained. In about 1833 local weavers, used to working with hand looms, sensed a threat to their precarious livelihood and marched on the factory, destroying the machinery and throwing the debris into the mill pool (Fig. 26).[61] The mill survived the attack and was

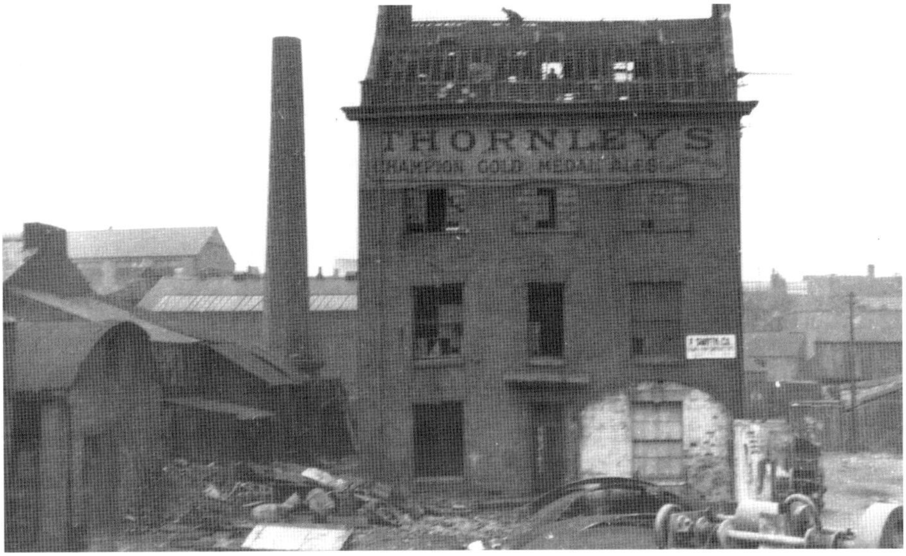

FIG. 9. Josiah Beck's factory, *c.* 1937
Photo, courtesy of Coventry History Centre

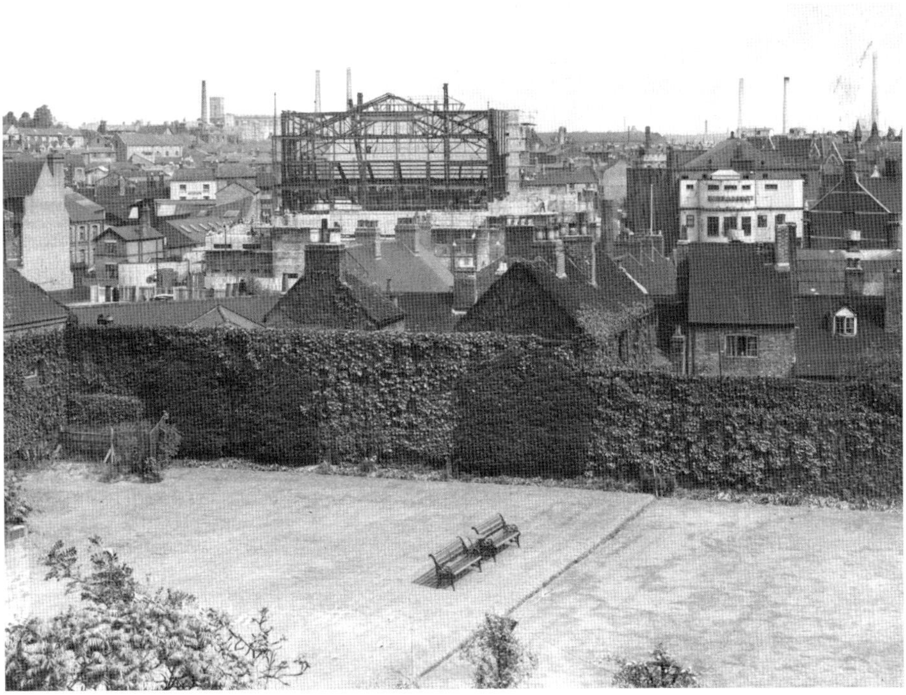

FIG. 10. View over the garden of 7 Priory Row and New Buildings, *c.* 1938
Photo, courtesy of Coventry History Centre

still standing when cleared for the new Trinity Street in 1937 (Fig. 9). The introduction of steam-powered ribbon weaving could not be halted, however, and in about 1849–50 a factory was built on a site fronting New Buildings itself, owned jointly by the Northey and Hopkins families, and which had also become known as 'The Wood Yard' through its more recent use.[62] By 1850 the density of housing in New Buildings had increased significantly; terraces of houses built in cramped rear courts had ousted the stables that had occupied the west side of street for so many centuries.

The contrast in housing density between the upper and lower part of the lower precinct could not be better illustrated than at the boundary between the two, the high sandstone wall that had been constructed in the mid-17th century (Fig. 10). To the south the area of the former bowling alley had been incorporated into the garden of John Gulson's house at 7 Priory Row, immediately west of Holy Trinity's burial ground (Fig. 11 and Col. Pl. VB in print edn).[63] The philanthropist lived in the house from 1837

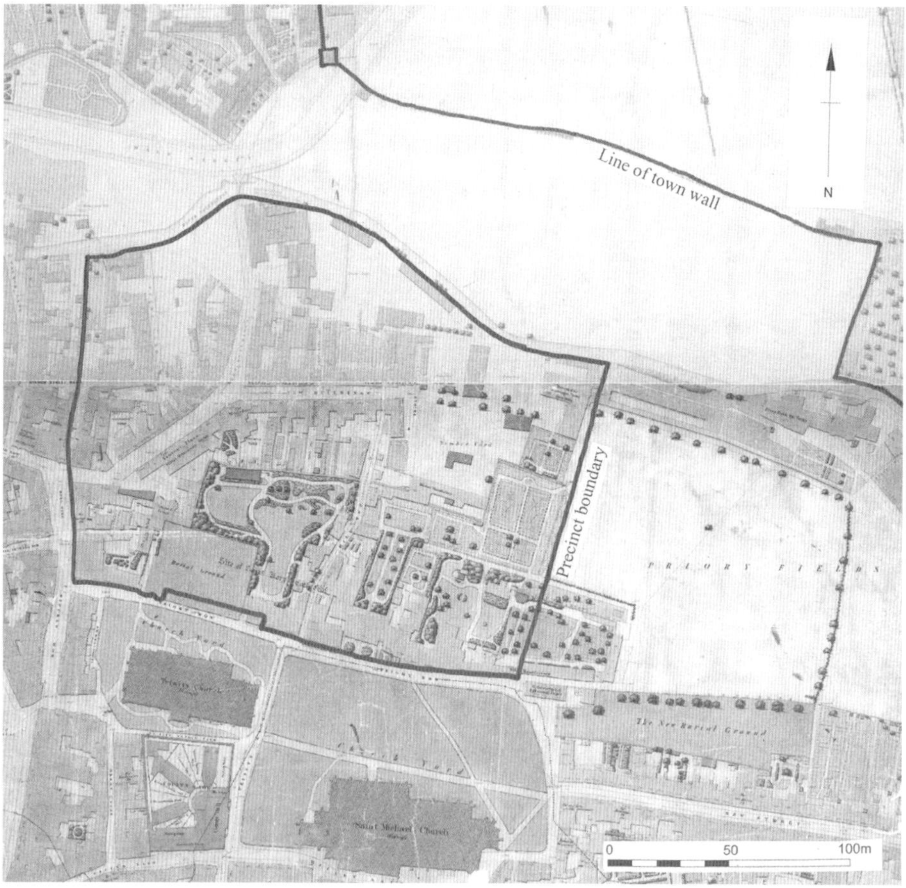

FIG. 11. Board of Health Map, Coventry 1850: detail, overlain with the priory precinct boundary

Photo, courtesy of Coventry History Centre

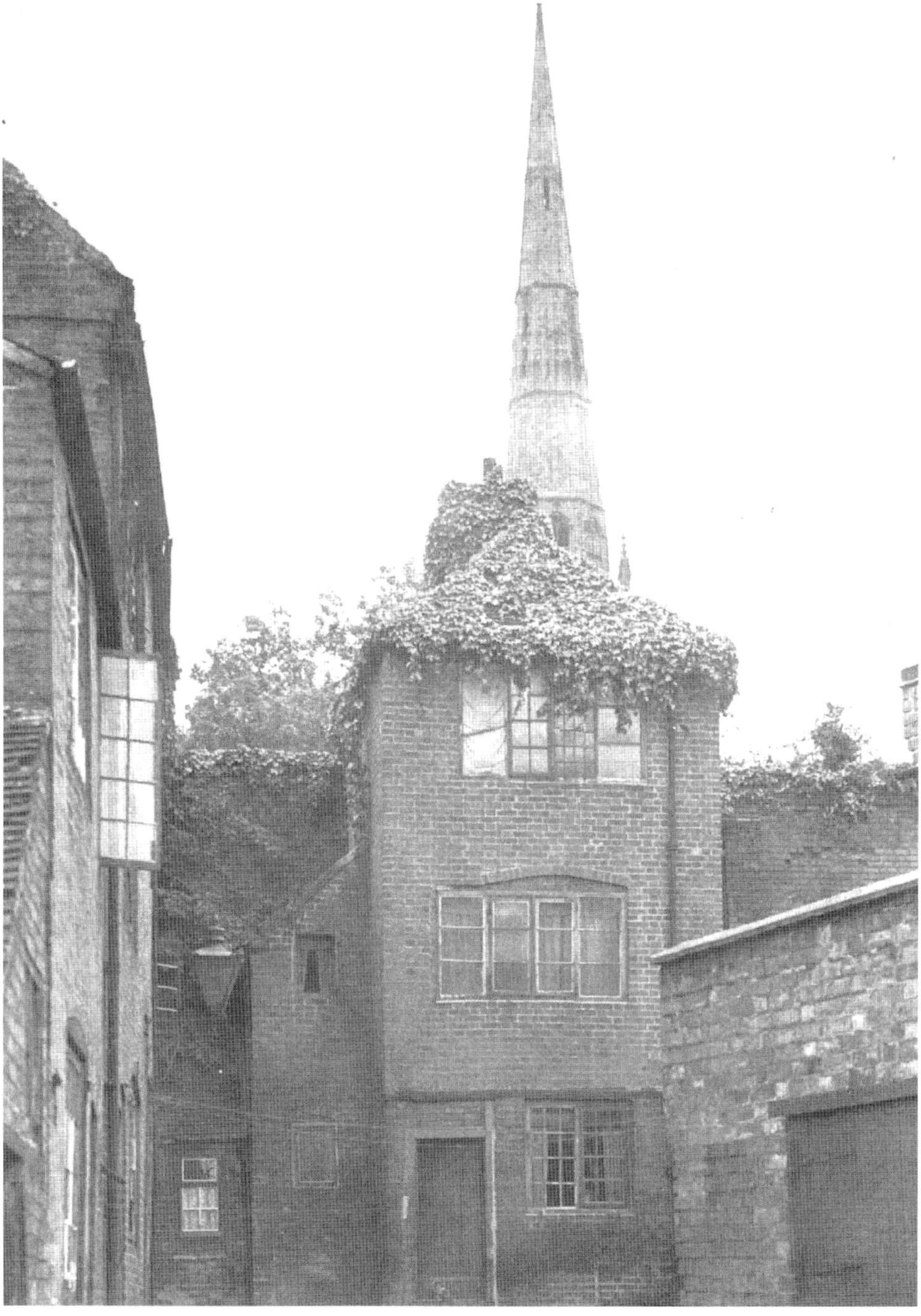

FIG. 12. View of a cottage against 17th-century boundary wall, south side of New Buildings
Photo, courtesy of David McGrory

to 1904 and its combined garden formed an extensive area of shrubbery and lawn that overlooked the small rear yards and gardens of houses below to the north. Two short terraces of houses had been constructed into these overshadowed yards that met the sandstone wall at their gable end. One house was built with its back against the wall itself (Fig. 12). Rich and poor therefore lived cheek by jowl in a way that would be considered unusual in more recent times.

At the east end of Priory Row the archaeology of the cathedral was exploited by a business that established itself below the houses that had been built in the 18th century. Each was furnished with a cellar that was excavated into the loose sandstone rubble of the cathedral, during which an awareness of the site's antiquity must have been aroused, as many tons of moulded and limewashed stone were encountered and disposed of.[64] Some time in the 19th century the firm of D. Collins, wine merchants, moved into the cellars below the now demolished 12 and 13 Priory Row (the present cathedral car park) and gradually spread westwards into the cellars of the adjoining houses as far as the corner with Hill Top (Fig. 13).[65] Here, in the former south transept, a two-storey cellar had been constructed under 9 Priory Row. An independent entrance to the wine cellars was created below 13 Priory Row, which had its narrow forecourt partly filled with a low flat-roofed structure functioning as the firm's office (Figs 14, 26).

At the other end of Priory Row the buildings that had housed Blue Coat School had become decrepit and were mostly demolished, replaced by a new school built between the years 1856 and 1857 to a design by James Murray. During the demolition the substantial foundations of the west end of the cathedral were uncovered. In the light of the growing awareness of the antiquity of the site, the significance of this discovery was quickly understood. The position of the main school room may have been deliberately

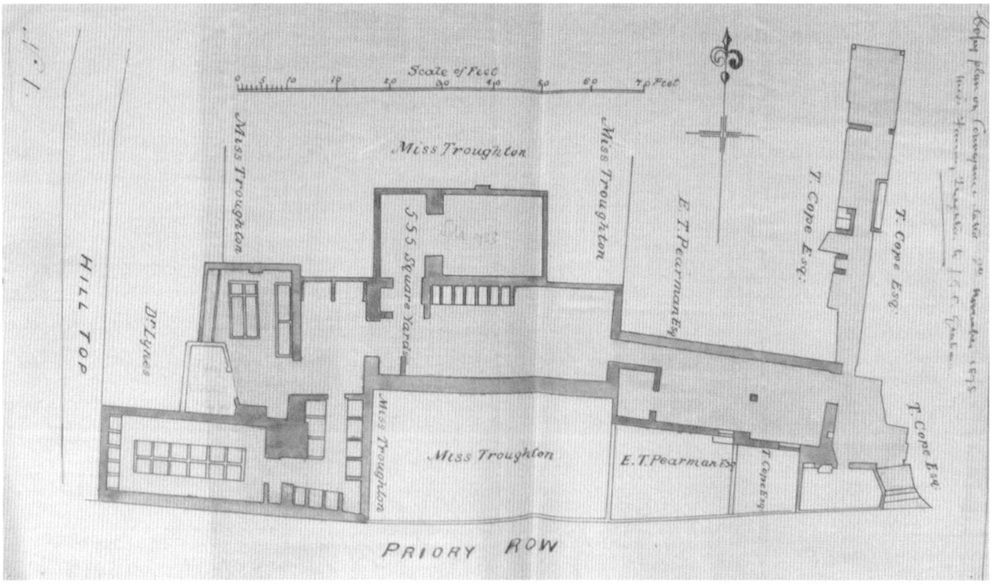

FIG. 13. Plan of cellars under 8–11 Priory Row, 1878

Drawing, courtesy of Coventry Cathedral

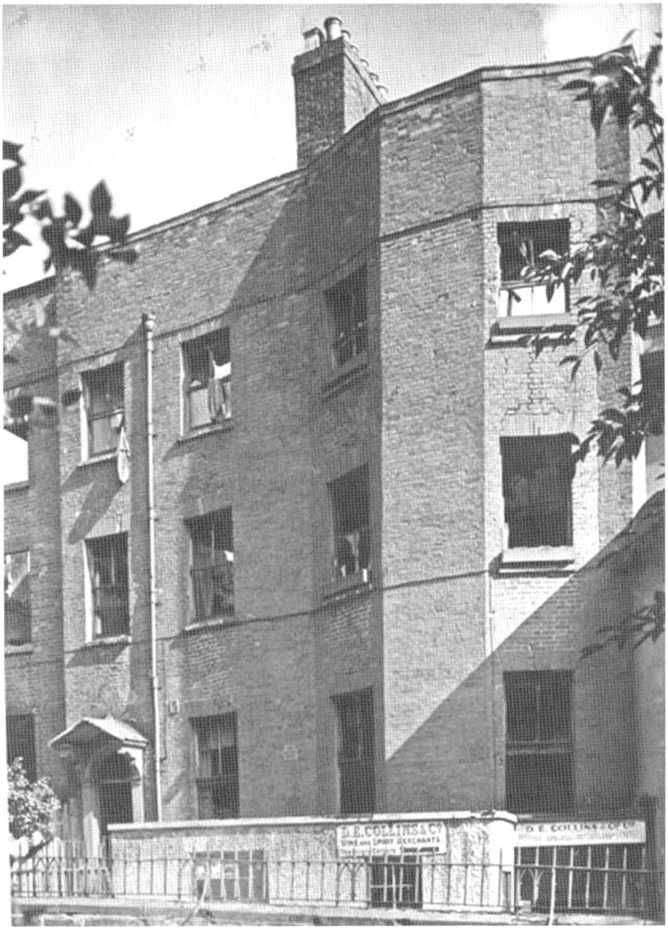

FIG. 14. Entrance to Collins' cellar, 13 Priory Row, late 1940s
Photo, courtesy of Coventry History Centre

moved westwards to enable the interior of the west end to be exposed permanently to view. The west end ruins were left in a deep trench and the approach path from Priory Row laid out along the top of the bank that ascended from the medieval masonry. The architect's original intention was to save as much of the north-west tower as possible, but during the contract much was demolished and only the lower three metres (the plinth) survived intact to be incorporated into a cellar.[67]

THE PRECINCT IN THE 20TH CENTURY

THE most dramatic changes to the urban topography of the former precinct took place in the last century. By 1900 the economic rebirth of Coventry as a major manufacturing centre had an immediate impact on the extensive area of wood yards dominating the corner between the River Sherbourne and Priory Street (Fig. 15). In 1896 William Booth, timber merchant and survivor of the Booth and Earle partnership, dissolved in

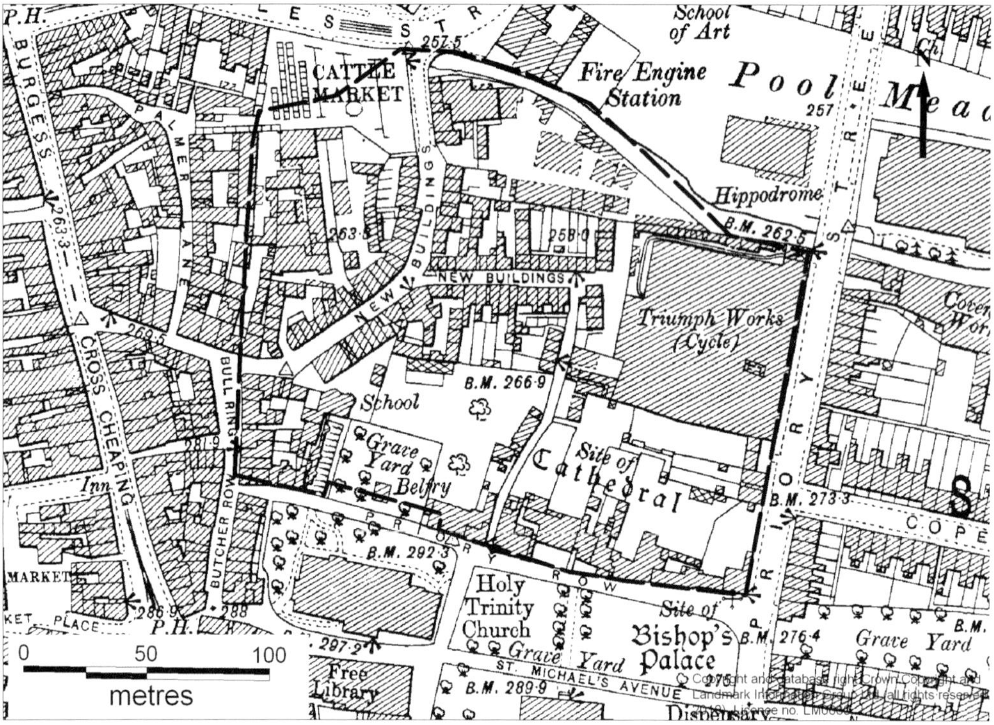

FIG. 15. Ordnance Survey map 1:2500, 1906 edition, overlain with the priory precinct boundary

1873, sold the Priory Wood Yard and the ribbon factory at the south end to the Triumph Cycle Company.[68] By 1903 Triumph had built one of the largest factories in Coventry at the time, removing the medieval remains of the dyehouse and covering most of the site with a multi-storey block on the Priory Street frontage and extensive north-lit sheds.[69] In 1907 Triumph acquired the two terraces of houses just outside their gates and another terrace fronting the north side of New Buildings.[70] A photographic survey, made by the company at the time, reveals that the south-side terrace had probably been a medieval priory building, which it demolished to make way for a new building (Figs 16–18).[71] The east elevation of this priory building had been rebuilt in brick to accommodate the four cottages. Another photograph demonstrates an intriguing juxtaposition of medieval and steam engine fabric (Figs 18, 26). Triumph retained the west part of the ex-ribbon factory located near Hill Top, presumably for its power house. A century earlier the sandstone wall behind the chimney had attracted the attention of artists with its tiers of pointed arches (Figs 19, 26).[72]

By 1923 Beck's ribbon factory, long out of use, had been incorporated into a varnish works.[73] The ribbon factory fronting New Buildings itself, adjacent to Blue Coat School, had ceased production in the late 1850s when silk ribbon weaving collapsed due to competition from abroad. John Gulson purchased the factory in 1858 and opened it as a Ragged School in 1860.[74] In 1905 John Gulson's trustees sold the factory to the Coventry Ragged School, and it was still operating as a Sunday School in 1923.

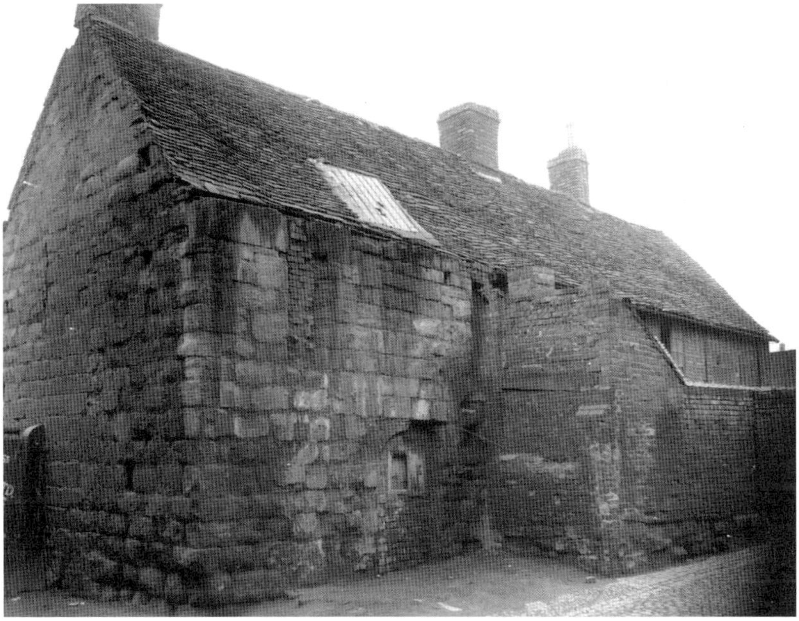

FIG. 16. Rear of an early sandstone building, perhaps part of the priory, later converted to cottages, photo *c.* 1908

Photo, courtesy of Coventry History Centre

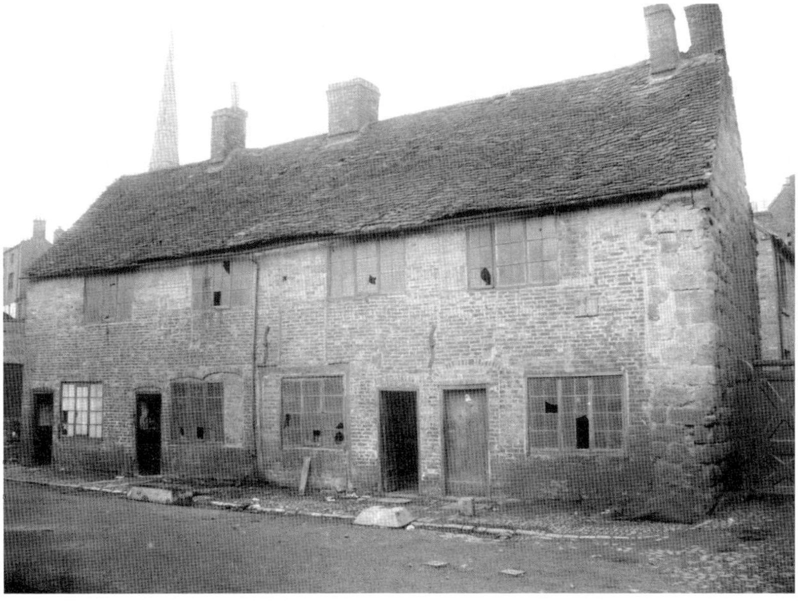

FIG. 17. Frontage of the cottages in Fig. 16, photo *c.* 1908

Photo, courtesy of Coventry History Centre

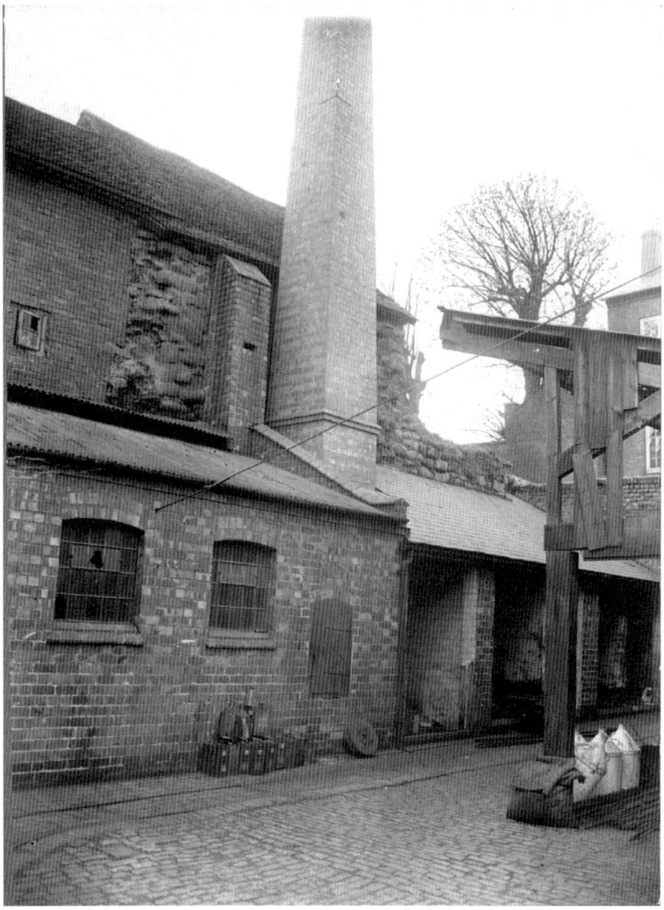

FIG. 18. Steam engine chimney constructed against a priory wall; Hill Top alley in background, photo *c.* 1908
Photo, courtesy of Coventry History Centre

By 1874 the house attached to the south-west side of the factory had became an armoury for the Rifle Volunteers corps, which used the factory as a drill hall during the week.

Coventry grew rapidly in the 1920s and 1930s, and the city council, in an attempt to develop a city centre to serve the burgeoning suburbs, demolished a large part of the historic town in the area of Great and Little Butcher Row. A new shopping street connecting Broadgate to Hales Street was laid out (Fig. 20). Demolition along the route of the new Trinity Street removed the ancient buildings constructed on the cathedral forecourt in the immediate post-Dissolution period and later buildings on the west side of New Buildings.[75] A steel-framed building cloaked in mock Tudor timber-framing was erected on a new building line so that the site of the priory 'foregate' found itself in the pavement in front (Fig. 26).[76] Apart from the devastation that preceded the construction of Trinity Street in 1938, there was relatively little change in the remainder of the former precinct area up to the outbreak of the Second World War.

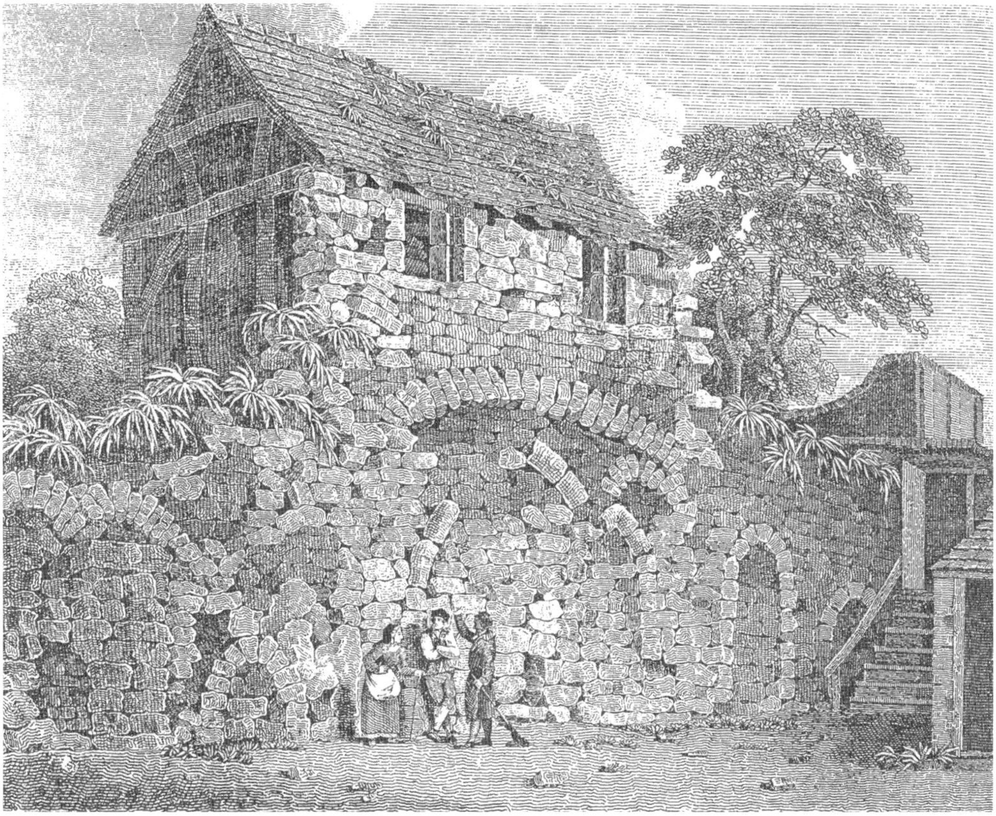

FIG. 19. View of a priory wall with arches, David Gee, before 1830, engraving
Courtesy of the Herbert Art Gallery and Museum, Coventry

The precinct area did not escape the Blitz of 1940 and the houses from 11 Priory Row eastwards to 16 Priory Row were seriously damaged, including the great Georgian town house at No. 11, now the Deanery. Farther to the north the Triumph works, producing motorcycles from 1936, was entirely destroyed.[77]

After the war the decision to build a new cathedral adjacent to the burnt out St Michael's would have a profound affect on the future appearance of the east side of the former precinct. The parish church had been elevated to cathedral status in 1918. The new cathedral would brush past the east end of the medieval cathedral of St Mary's, whose exact position was not then known. In the late 1940s and early 1950s the ruined houses and gardens on Priory Row were acquired and only No. 11 was saved, presumably due to its architectural merit.[78] In 1951 Basil Spence won the architectural competition for a design, with recognisable liturgical east and west ends, but on a north–south alignment.[79] Work began in 1955 and the foundation operations accidentally discovered the east chevet of the medieval cathedral that had lain buried for perhaps four hundred years (Fig. 21). On 25 May 1962 the new cathedral was consecrated and Coventry became unique in this country in having three cathedrals,

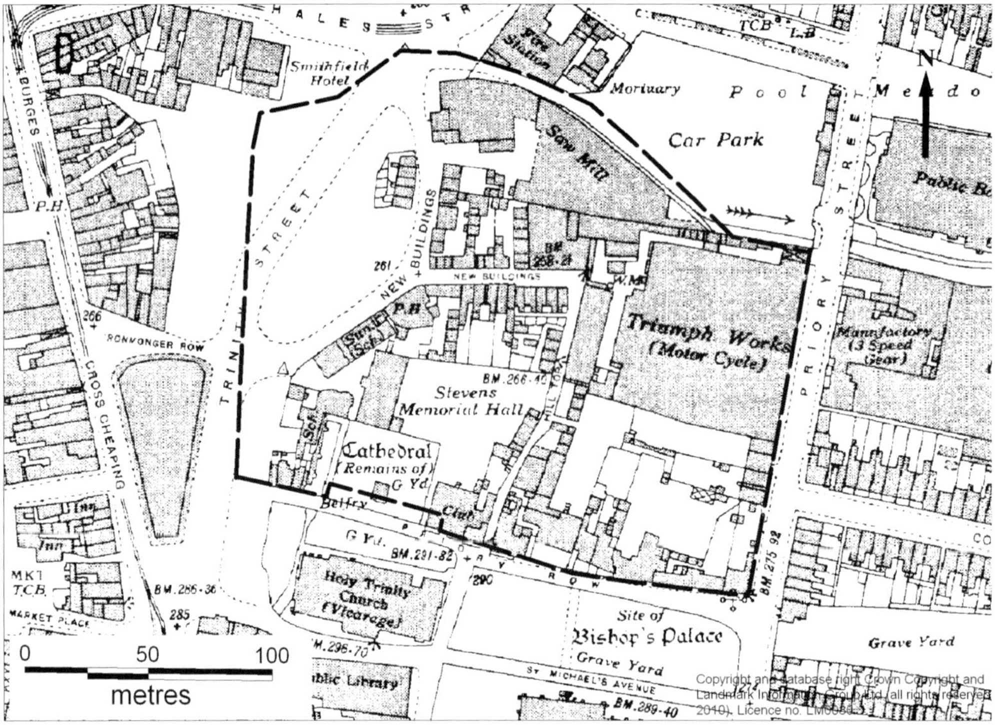

FIG. 20. Ordnance Survey map 1:2500, 1937 edition, overlain with the priory precinct boundary

not only in one place, but almost in contact with one another by the fortuitous interconnecting link of the new St Michael's (Fig. 22 and Col. Pl. VI in print edn).

Other buildings constructed within the precinct area were not so inspirational. Sainsbury's moved into a new three-storey building in the early 1960s completing a site that had been created just before the war between New Buildings and Trinity Street (Fig. 23). In the mid-1960s Fairfax Street was cut through from Cox Street to Hales Street as part of the new inner circulatory road. Its route followed the former course of the Sherbourne and the tail race from the priory mill, swinging at its western end across the site of Newark's saw mill and yard. Houses that had survived the war along the south side of New Buildings and into Hill Top were demolished, leaving only the former ribbon factory and the Meriden Tavern (later the Alhambra public house) as buildings of any antiquity in New Buildings. A large multi-storey car park with shops lining Fairfax Street (1968–69) was the cause of the demolition, attaching itself to Sainsburys over the site of the mill, thereby blocking the ancient precinct route for the first time.[80] East of Hill Top a new hotel was constructed in the early 1970s (the De Vere, now the Britannia) at the western end of the Triumph site, the remainder of which was laid out as an open space, Cathedral Square, overlooked by the high wall and cross of the north end of the new cathedral. Student accommodation for the then Lanchester College was constructed on the north side of the square, continuing eastwards across Priory Street to the new municipal swimming baths (1962–66).

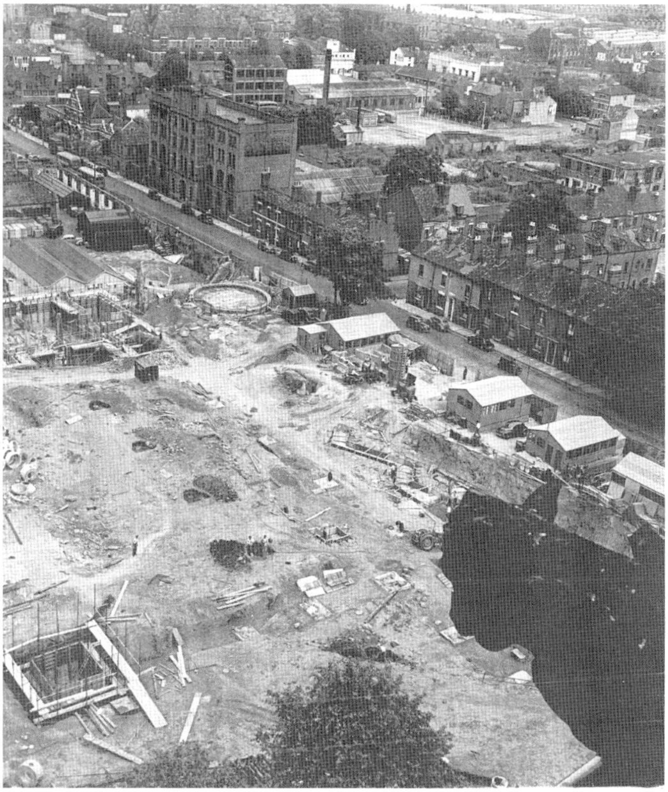

FIG. 21. Spence's new cathedral under construction on the site of demolished Priory Row houses, *c.* 1955
Photo, Conservation and Archaeology, Coventry City Council

Had it not been for the approach of the Millennium, there was every likelihood that the precinct area would not have changed for some time to come. The Phoenix Initiative of the years 1996–2003 represented Coventry's Millennium scheme and its intention was to create a new link between the cathedral 'quarter' and the Motor Museum (Fig. 24 and Col. Pl. VII in print edn).[81] It so happened that the direct route led across the site of the Cathedral Priory of St Mary and it was quickly realised that here was an opportunity once and for all to revive the memory and the physical presence of the lost medieval site. For the first time historic building conservation and archaeology would determine the layout and appearance of a comprehensive redevelopment in the city. Four new squares were laid out following extensive excavations, which concentrated on the nave of the cathedral and the claustral complex. The first square, Priory Gardens, closely follows the form of the nave and includes fourteen of the sixteen piers of the arcade, though only ten are now visible or represented. The west end ruins revealed in 1856 were integrated with the new square, which forms a sunken garden created by the excavation down to the cathedral floor. Next on the descent is Priory Cloister, a more secluded space, with sandstone walls closely approximating the original plan of the cloister. Constructed in its south walk is a modern visitor centre in which some of the best artefacts and architectural fragments found in the excavations are displayed. Alongside these two squares the former Blue Coat School and ribbon

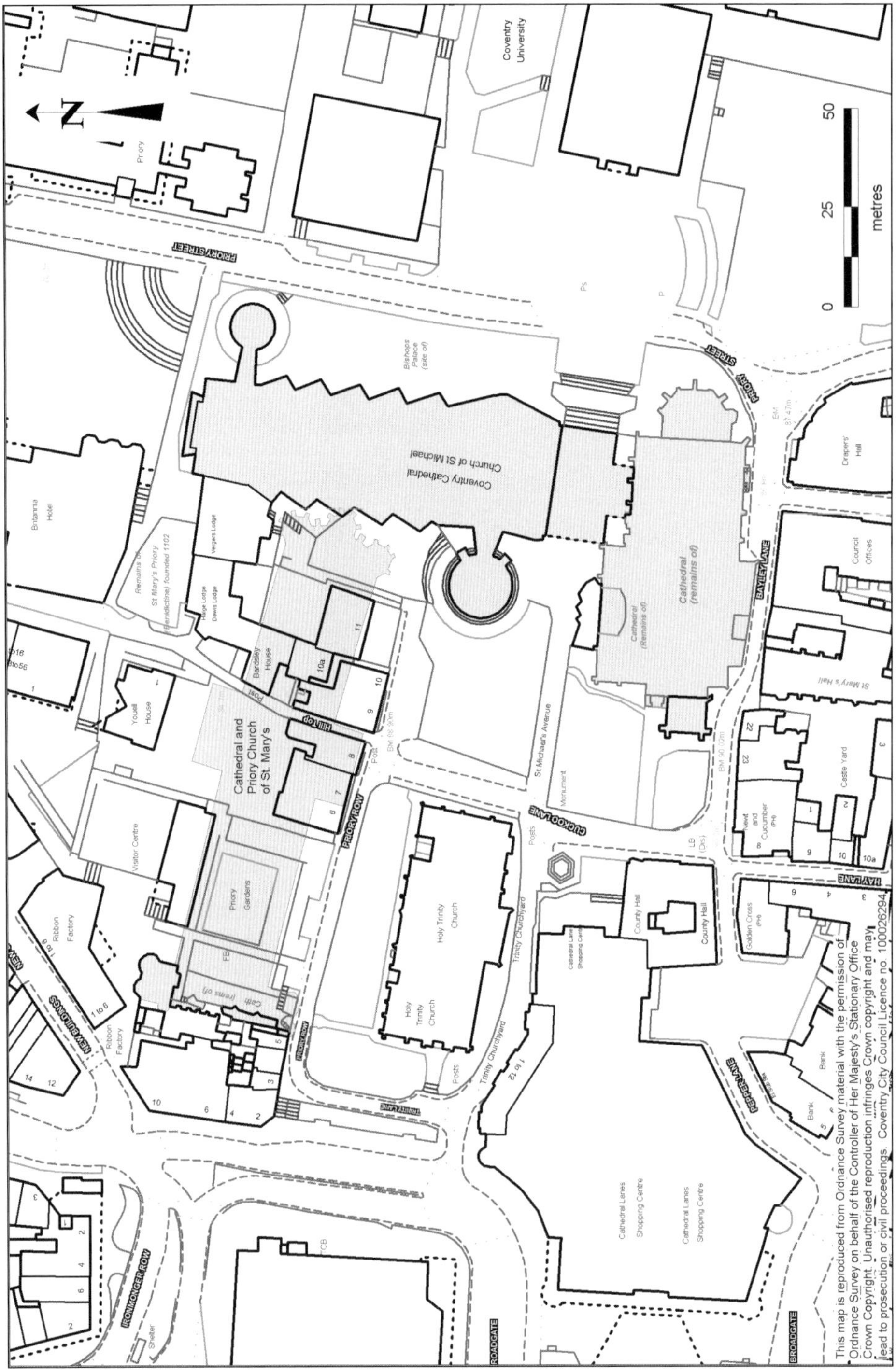

FIG. 22. Plan of the three cathedral sites, Coventry
Drawing, author

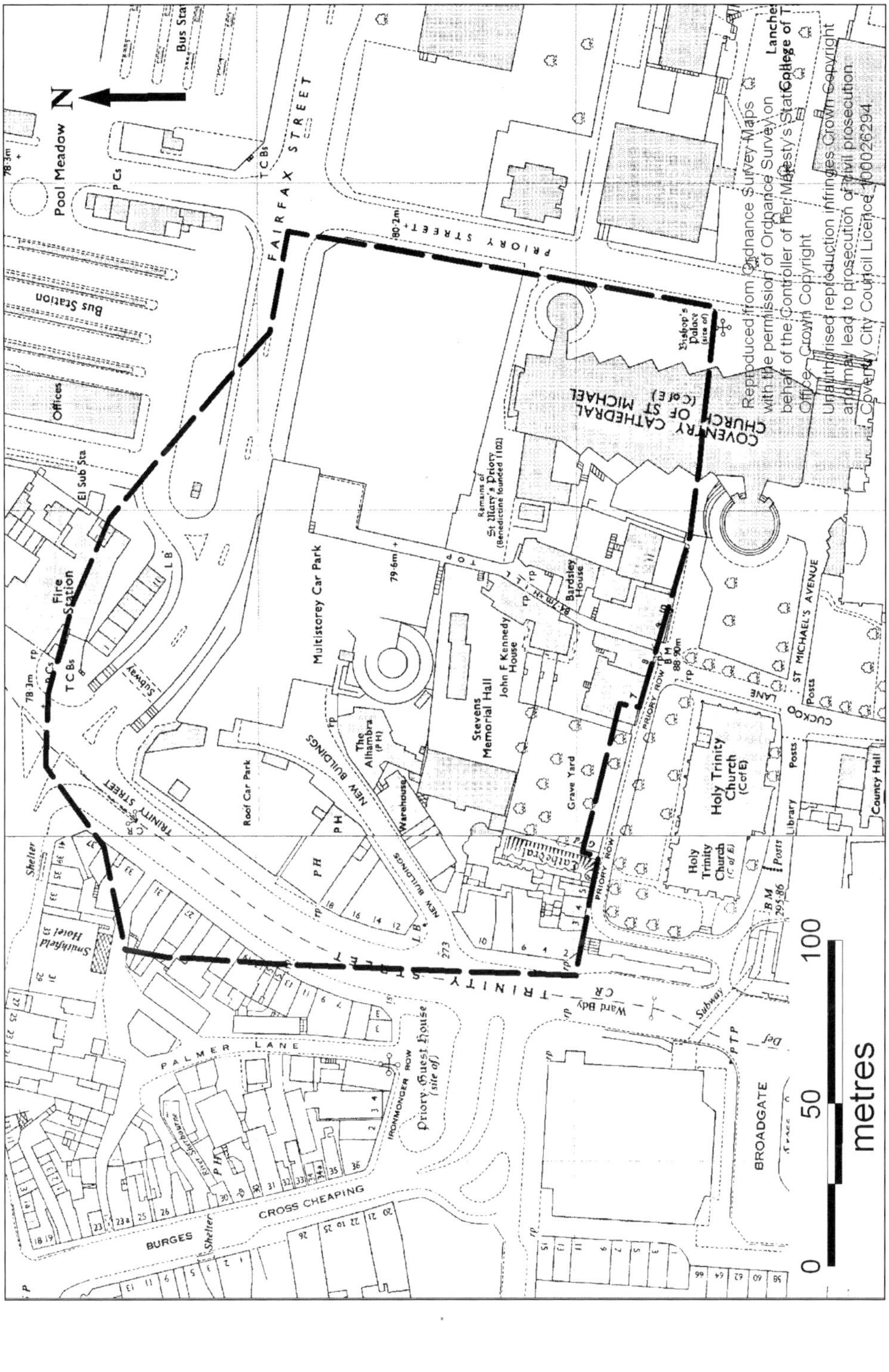

FIG. 23. Ordnance Survey map 1:1250, 1971, overlain with the priory precinct boundary

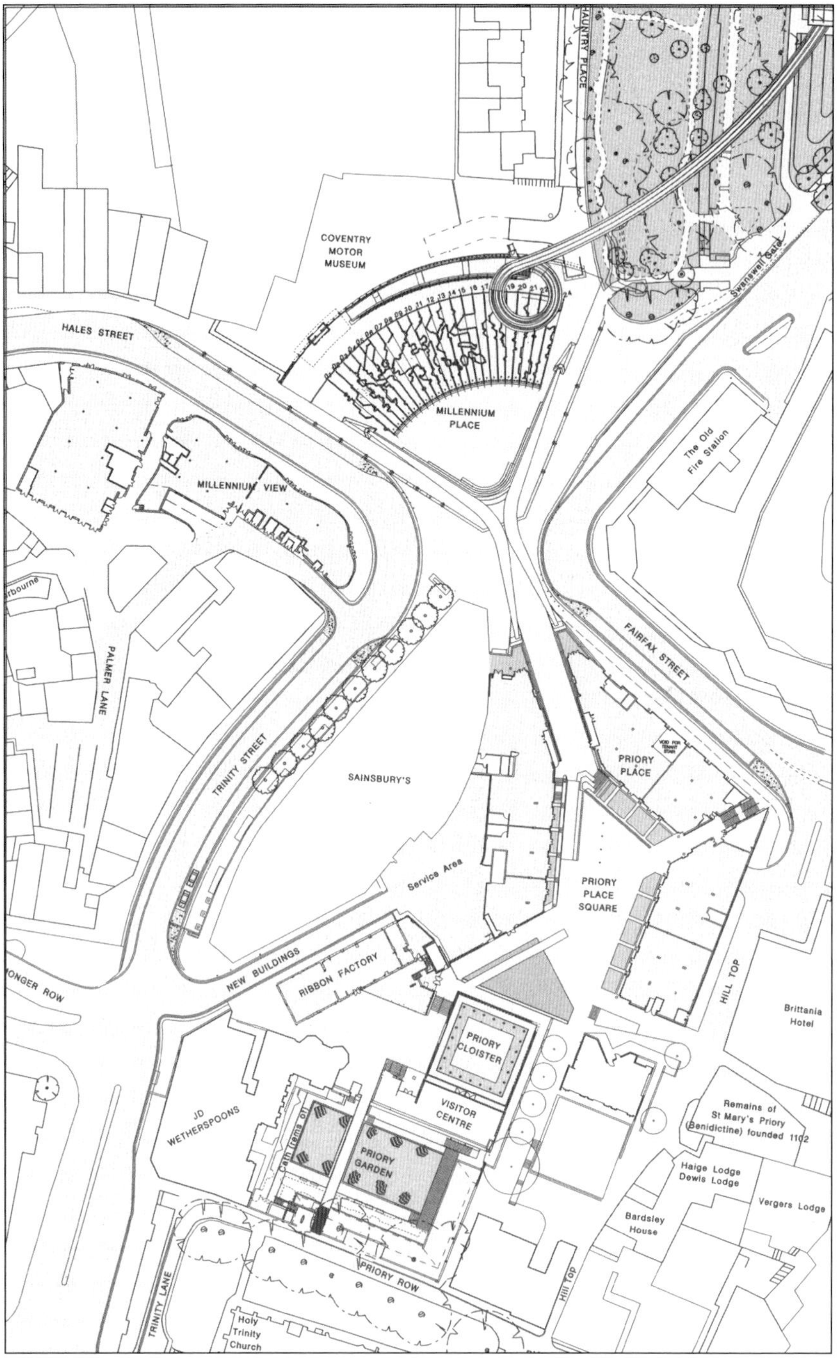

FIG. 24. Plan of the Phoenix Initiative project (*c.* 2000)
Drawing, Coventry City Council

factory, both of which had reached a serious state of dereliction by the 1990s, were restored and are now in use as the Holy Trinity church centre, and a restaurant and flats respectively. An unexpected major discovery was the undercrofts situated north of the chapter-house on the next level below the claustral complex. Beneath the new cathedral building (Youell House) that prompted the excavation, a great cavern contains the priory undercrofts. These can be permanently viewed through a large glass screen and visited by organised tour (Fig. 25 and Col. Pl. IIIc in print edn). The site of the priory mill and the foregate have been interpreted 'on the ground' (Fig. 26). Other parts of the site have been interpreted using the vast amount of new information that came to light during the excavations and in further research.[82]

The history of the precinct site after the Dissolution has turned full circle. The destruction of a large medieval cathedral and priory complex was replaced over time by the much finer grain of domestic-scale buildings. In turn the 20th century witnessed the loss of most of the dwellings, except on Priory Row, and the construction of a wide variety of large buildings, some architecturally impressive, restoring some grandeur to the site (Prelim., Plan A). The advent of the Millennium created an extraordinary opportunity to rediscover the lost precinct of the cathedral and priory of St Mary.

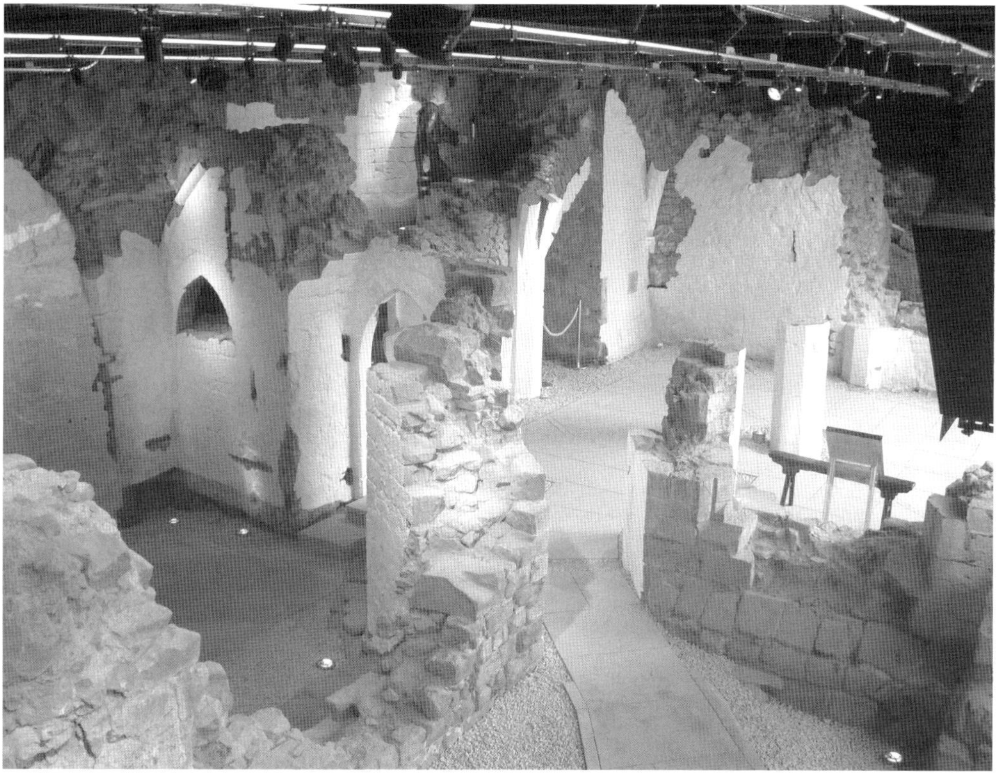

FIG. 25. The priory undercrofts today, interior looking south-west; the east–west undercroft is in the left foreground, the north–south undercroft with its pier to the right

Photo, author

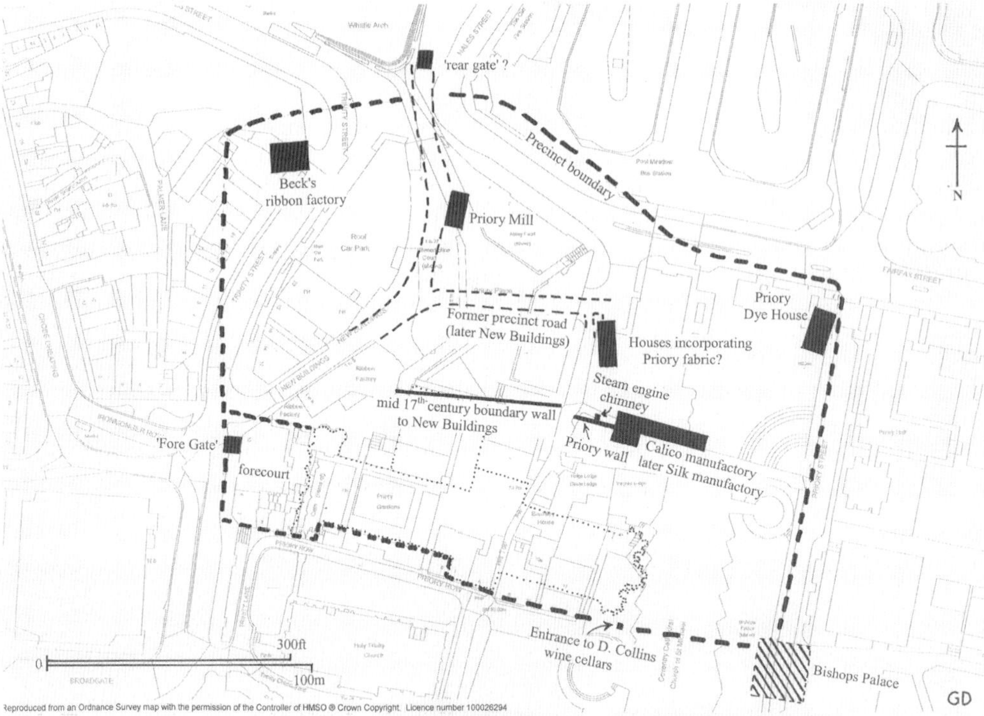

FIG. 26. Lost pre- and post-Dissolution sites overlain on the current Ordnance Survey map

Drawing, author

ACKNOWLEDGEMENTS

I should like to thank all the staff of the History Centre, Coventry (formerly Archives and Local Studies) for all their help, and particularly Michael Hinman, whose recataloguing of the borough archive made tracking down relevant deeds and other material so much easier. I am also grateful to Coventry Cathedral for providing access to its own deeds collection. Anna Wilson and Alex Thompson, Historic Environment Record Officers at Coventry City Council, have patiently converted my sketch drawings through numerous revisions into computerised versions. I am indebted as well to the joint editors for their forensic reading of my original text.

NOTES

1. J. J. Scarisbrick, 'The Dissolution of St Mary's Priory, Coventry', in Demidowicz ed., *First Cathedral*, 158–68.
2. TNA, LR2/181.
3. Hobley, 'Cathedral Excavations', fig. 8; J. C. Lancaster, chapter on Coventry, in *The Historic Towns Atlas*, ed. M. Lobel, II (London, 1975), Coventry chapter; K. D. Lilley, 'Coventry's Topographical Development: the Impact of the Priory', in Demidowicz ed., *First Cathedral*, 80–8 and fig 2.
4. TNA LR2/181 109v; Coventry Record Office Index: Person/14/89.
5. CA PA56/99/2.
6. CA BA/F/A/23/f99, Tripartite Agreement; Dugdale, *Warwickshire* (1730), 163.

7. G. Demidowicz, 'Coventry — A New Beginning?', in Demidowicz ed., *First Cathedral*, 11–13. The term 'foregate' has been coined by the author for convenience; there is no evidence that it ever had this name.
8. J. B. Shelton, *Austin's Monthly Magazine*, nos 332–4, Feb.–April 1935; the term 'rear gate' has also been coined by the author.
9. *Letters and Papers, Henry VIII*, XX, pt1, no. 51.
10. Scarisbrick, 'The Dissolution', 158–68.
11. View of Coventry by William Smyth, 1576; in William Smith, *The particular description of England, 1588*, from the original manuscript in the British Museum with an introduction by H. B. Wheatley and E. W. Ashbee (London 1879).
12. CA BA/A/D/53/3.
13. G. Demidowicz, *A History of the Blue Coat School and the Lych Gate Cottages, Coventry* (Coventry 2000), 11–14.
14. CA PA56/99/5; PA/96/12/1.
15. CA BA/A/A/17/1 ff. 1–2.
16. CA PA56/99/2.
17. CA BA/A/1/2/3.
18. Demidowicz, *Blue Coat School*, 16–21.
19. CA BA/B/A/25/1.
20. CA BA/B/1/25/3; PA244/32/1.
21. CA BA/B/1/27/1.
22. CA BA/B/24/4; City Annals 1648 quoted in Poole, *Antiquities*, 13.
23. Corporation leases, 18 Feb. 1647, CA BA/B/A/25/5, 2 Aug. 1654, CA BA/B/A/25/8; City Annals, 1648. In 1652 Revd Bryan had a house next to the 'water house' and another in the tenure of John Hix (CA BA/B/G/5/1, fol. 40). John Hix's shop and the 'waterwork' was reserved by the corporation under the 1647 lease.
24. WCRO CR564/1(b); CA BA/B/G/5/1.
25. City Annals 1643.
26. CA BA/H/3/17/2, fol. 47v quoted in VCH *Warwickshire* VIII, 32.
27. CA BA/A/A/26/3; Demidowicz, *Blue Coat School*, 25.
28. CA BA/B/G/5/1, ff 38v–39v.
29. CA PA56/83/1–2. Hill Top was still a private route reached by a door in Humphrey Burton's curtilage and provided access to the Aston's Mill and to Sargeson and Bewley to maintain the waterworks.
30. Humphrey Burton's house was rated at 6s. 6d. in comparison with the much lower rates of the New Buildings houses, mostly between 1s. and 2s. 6d.; CA BA/B/G/5/1, ff. 38v–40. In 1653 he acquired the freehold of his house and garden from the corporation, CA PA56/83/4.
31. CA BA/B/1/27/1, 3; the garden was leased by John Brownell in 1649 and reassigned to Septimus Bott, an apothecary in 1677.
32. CA BA/A/A/26/3; BA/B/1/26/2. Christopher Davenport had leased the dyehouse before 1658 and gave it up in 1666, Birmingham Central Library, Archives and Heritage, 257427; CA PA55/99/7; BA/B/1/26/3.
33. G. Demidowicz, 'The Priory Mill', in Rylatt and Mason, *Cathedral Priory*, 55–6; CA BA/B/A/28/1, lease to Frances Perkins; BA/H/C/17/2, ff. 338–9, Richard Chaplin tenant.
34. VCH *Warwickshire* VIII, 267.
35. CA BA/A/A/12 (Cross Cheaping Ward sales); PA90/9,10,13, 14,15, 16, 18, 19, 22; WCRO CR1709/206/6–7; CA PA1896/10/5/7.
36. CA PA56/99/9.
37. Only a small part had been in council ownership; CA CCA/2/3/423/1–2.
38. Deeds for New Buildings ribbon factory, private collection; CA Persons/8/1352; PA194/12/5. This branch of the Hopkins family inter-married with the Northey family, taking the name Northey Hopkins.
39. CA PA362/8.
40. WCRO DR564/I(b) 6.
41. Demidowicz, *Blue Coat School*, 26–33; CA PA145/1. The buildings were probably sold by Samuel Bryan, son of John Bryan, to the Belcher family
42. CA PA56/83/7–8.
43. G. Demidowicz, *A Guide to the Buildings of Coventry: An Illustrated Architectural History* (Stroud 2003), 66–7; A. Gomme, *Smith of Warwick: Francis Smith, Architect and Master Builder* (Stamford 2000), 395–6.
44. CA PA56/83/9–10.
45. CA BA/B/1/27/3; PA 90/24; PA56/83/20–1. The apothecaries had probably used the garden for growing herbs, though it was last occupied by a china man, John Taylor.
46. CA PA56/83/24, 26–7.

47. S. Kelly ed., *The Life of Mrs Sherwood chiefly autobiographical with extracts from Mrs Sherwood's Journal* (London 1857), 41.

48. B. Willis, *A History of the Mitred Parliamentary Abbeys and Conventual and Cathedral Churches* (London 1718–19); Demidowicz ed., *First Cathedral*, 11–15.

49. Demidowicz, *Blue Coat School*, 31, fig. 16; WCRO DR564/I/(b), DR340/85; DR1063/3/1–3; DR801/32.

50. Coventry Cathedral Deeds (private collection) CC/B/26.

51. Thomas Sharp's plan of Coventry, 1807; Board of Health map of Coventry, 1851.

52. CA PA56/99/9–11.

53. CA PA56/99/12–14. Thomas Cope took out a lease of the factory direct from the corporation in 1829, CA PA56/99/15.

54. CA CCA/TC/19/9; PA1896/10/3/2.

55. CA PA1896/10/3/4.

56. CA PA1896/10/2/5.

57. CA PA5699/21–6.

58. VCH *Warwickshire* VIII, frontispiece, 31; Plan of Thomas Cope's land, April 1854 PA415/1; painting by David Gee, 1861, Herbert Art Gallery and Museum, VA/1960/0036.

59. VCH *Warwickshire* VIII, 282, 291.

60. The date that William Newark established the saw mill is not precisely known, but, judging by directory evidence and the Board of Health map of 1851, it was in existence by 1850.

61. V. E. Chancellor ed., *Master and Artisan in Victorian England: the Diary of William Andrews and the Autobiography of Joseph Gutteridge* (London 1969), 101–2.

62. Deeds, private collection. A plan to build a terrace of houses was abandoned; CA PA362/12/1–4; PA194/12/21; Poole, *Antiquities*, 14.

63. J. E. Short, *The Gulson Story* (Kineton 1978), 6, pl. 3.

64. The more interesting stones were retained, such as a statue of a 'nun and a king' that had been placed in the rear garden of ' The Priory' (11 Priory Row) by the late 18th century; S. Sherwood, *The Life of Mrs Sherwood* (London 1857), 41.

65. *Coventry 'Up-to Date', Views and Reviews* (London [1896]), 181. The firm purchased the cellars in 1878; Coventry Cathedral deeds (private collection), CC/B/12, plan on deed of 1878.

66. Demidowicz, *Blue Coat School*, 38–48.

67. An irregular area of medieval red sandstone above the plinth was also saved and contrasts with the grey sandstone of the new fabric.

68. CA PA1896/10/3/6; PA1896/10/5/10, 15–17.

69. Ordnance Survey map, 1:2500, 2nd edn, surveyed 1903–05, published 1906; P. Collins and M. Stratton, 'A Survey of Coventry Car Factories 1894–1994', for Coventry City Council (Oct. 1994) 125–6, T.02.

70. CA PA1896/10/1/40–2; PA1896/10/2/16–19 (51 New Buildings and 1–8 Priory Yard, 44–50 New Buildings).

71. Ordnance Survey map, 1:2500, 3rd edn, surveyed 1912, published 1914.

72. The wall probably formed the north wall of the priory infirmary and disappeared entirely from view when Triumph expanded its works between the wars. It may survive today below ground on the boundary between the cathedral car park in Hill Top and the footpath that leads to Priory Street. It is marked on Brian Hobley's plan as 'Carter's Wall'; Hobley, 'Cathedral Excavations', 84, figs 5 and 22.

73. Ordnance Survey map, 1:2500, 4th edn, surveyed 1923, published 1925; 1874 Street Directory of Coventry, Edward Powers & Co., varnish and japan manufacturers.

74. Deeds, private collection; Short, *The Gulson Story* (as n. 63), 15–16, 29.

75. Ordnance Survey map, 1:2500, 5th edn, 1937 revision.

76. Demidowicz ed., *First Cathedral*, 11–15, fig. 5; the building is currently occupied by Wetherspoons.

77. Collins and Stratton, 'Coventry Car Factories', 126. Production was transferred temporarily to Warwick and then permanently to Meriden by 1942; www.ianchadwick.com/motorcycles/triumph/time02.html

78. Coventry Cathedral deeds (private collection).

79. J. Thomas, *Coventry Cathedral* (Cambridge 1987), 89, 110.

80. G. Lewison and R. Billingham, *Coventry New Architecture* (Warwick 1969), 19.

81. G. Demidowicz and I. George, 'From the Ashes? The Coventry Phoenix Initiative', *The Archaeologist* 55 (Winter 2005), 34; H. Broughton, 'Coventry's Path to Reconciliation', *The Architects' Journal* (2/9 August 2001), 28–37; L. Campbell and R. Cork, *Phoenix: Architecture Art Regeneration* (London 2004).

82. Rylatt and Mason, *Cathedral Priory*.

St Michael's, Coventry: The Architectural History of a Medieval Urban Parish Church

LINDA MONCKTON

The three churches of St Michael, Holy Trinity and St John the Baptist are amongst the most telling reminders today of Coventry's medieval past. Their architectural fabric is almost entirely late medieval, part of an explosion of building and rebuilding within the city from the late 14th century onwards. St Michael's was by far the most impressive, both in terms of scale and the nature of patronage that allowed for a complete reconstruction of the church. Little is recorded of its construction dates and since its partial destruction in 1940 its architecture has been largely overlooked. This article aims to reassess its history, placing it in a local and national context. Almost everything above ground was the result of two reconstruction programmes in the later middle ages, carried out in stages from c. *1370 to* c. *1450. Usually interpreted as a single campaign, this paper will show how the 13th-century church, itself a significant building, was adapted and altered before the wholesale reconstruction of the nave and chancel, and how the evolution of the church cannot be divorced from the circumstances of the economic, social and topographical development of Coventry.*

INTRODUCTION

Once travelling in an express train between Nuneaton and Rugby, I glanced out to the west, and by some accident which had cleared the atmosphere, Coventry appeared like a crystal city in the brilliant sunshine, set upon its hill. And dominating it, above its two attendant spires, soared the 300 feet of St Michael, portentous as its namesake's sword. It has never been my fortune to see it thus again, but the memory remains to prove that the possession of one masterpiece can make even Coventry glorious as the New Jerusalem.[1]

JOHN HARVEY's assessment of St Michael makes clear the impact of the late medieval church of St Michael's on the townscape of Coventry and its place on the hill-top location that was home to the city's earliest religious foundations (Fig. 1). Even in its ruined state, the scale and architectural pretension of St Michael's is evident. The circumstances of its reconstruction form the subject of this paper.

BACKGROUND

ST MICHAEL's was used as a seignorial chapel in the 12th century. This is demonstrated, first, by its proximity to the earl of Chester's castle.[2] The precise topography of the area is not clear,[3] although the presence of Bayley Lane must relate at least approximately to the northern castle boundary, and it is likely that the chapel abutted this (Soden, Fig. 1).[4] Secondly, a reference of the 1190s makes it clear that the chaplain

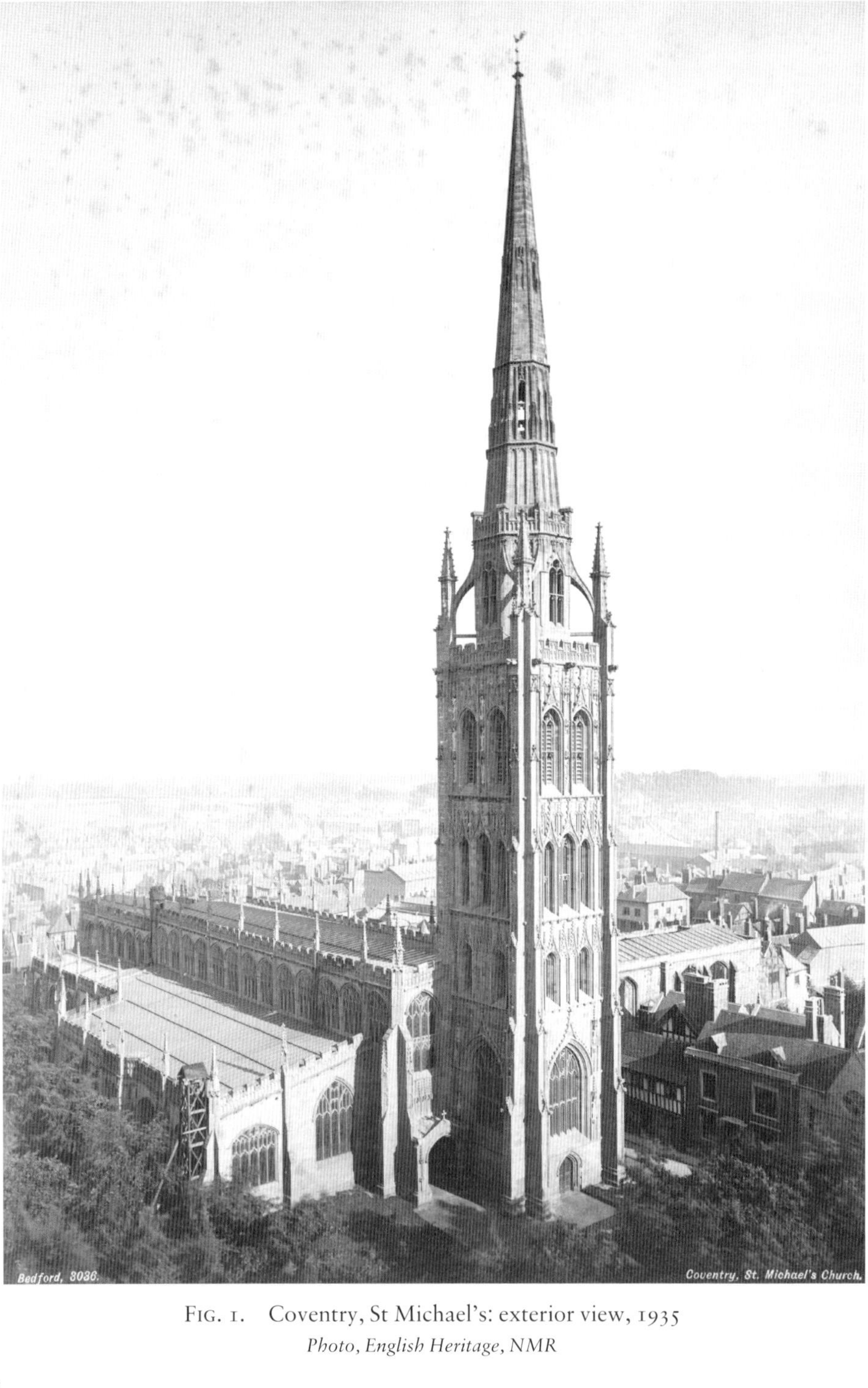

FIG. 1. Coventry, St Michael's: exterior view, 1935
Photo, English Heritage, NMR

of Ranulf III, earl of Chester, was the incumbent of the chapel of St Michael.[5] The castle still existed in the late 12th century and it appears that the two buildings were closely related functionally and physically.

Despite this status as the seigniorial chapel, Ranulf II allegedly restored the tithes of St Michael's to the prior in 1153, a situation confirmed during the period of his successors Hugh II and Ranulf III in 1183–84 and 1192 respectively. Conflict over the tithes and parochial rights of St Michael's lasted for at least a century, and ultimately resulted in its full appropriation by the priory.[6] St Michael's was evidently worth wrangling over, most likely because of its value (it was valued at £33 6s. 8d. in 1291)[7] and its position as a mother church over the souls of the entire earl's half of the town and the lands of the earls beyond. The prior was apparently keen to maintain control over ecclesiastical jurisdiction and the income of the region.

The earl of Chester began developing his half of the town in the 12th century, most significantly with the creation of burgage plots along Earl Street, which was the opposite side of the castle to St Michael's (see Prelim., Plan C). This street was to become the most important for mercantile and commercial property in the city and it connected to the south end of Broadgate, where the market established by the prior was held on a Friday.[8] After this, the decline of the castle and the development of Bayley Lane (see below) fundamentally altered the immediate physical environs of St Michael's (Prelim., Plan C).[9]

The formalisation of parish boundaries and associated parochial status for St Michael's came in the 13th century. It is variously referred to as 'church' or 'chapel' from the 1220s to 1260s.[10] The shift in terminology from chapel to church may be a formal acknowledgement of its status within the developing urban environment at a time when the priory was moving close to a position of full appropriation. This finally occurred in 1249, when a more momentous and significant transfer of property was granted by Roger Montalt, earl of Chester,[11] including the rights of the advowson of St Michael's and its ten dependent chapels.[12]

The chapel of St Michael's had sat on the periphery of an area of decline in the late 12th and early 13th centuries with the abandonment of the castle and Bayley Lane. The latter shows signs of redevelopment in the 1220s but with visible signs by the 1260s.[13] The development of the church cannot be separated from the shift in focus to the earl's half, which showed signs of planned development by the end of the century, and in which most of the mercantile elite resided. Tension between the merchants and the prior concerning control of the town's trade is well documented in the early 14th century.[14] The inheritance of the earl's half by Queen Isabella shifted the dynamic and eventually led to the granting of the Charter of Incorporation in 1345,[15] providing a communal self-government instead of the lordship of the prior, and the Tripartite Indenture of 1355, which redefined the boundaries between the two halves, resulting in her gaining control of much of the prior's half, including most of the market and Cross Cheaping. All of these new rights and land holdings she transferred to the burgesses in 1346.[16] Alongside this sea change in the organisation of trade and property in the city, the first guild merchant was formed in 1340 and from the mid-1350s the guilds began a policy of acquiring property.[17] By the mid-14th century the burgesses were a powerful force in a city with a rapidly expanding economy. They were the most significant class in both number and the amount of service rendered among Coventry's justices of the peace. In essence they constituted the dominant ruling class.[18] It is against this backdrop that the history of St Michael's must be understood.

THE REBUILDING PHASES OF ST MICHAEL'S

The 12th century

WITHOUT excavation, the early form of the chapel of St Michael must remain wholly speculative. Holy Trinity, with its prime location and its probable scale, even before its 13th-century rebuilding, most likely overshadowed its surrounding dependent chapels, of which St Michael's was one. Blair has commented that it is not uncommon for ex-minsters to maintain a 'residual pre-eminence in their former territories', and this certainly appears to be the case in Coventry.[19] One might assume that the dependent chapel was a one- or two-cell building and Chatwin presented a theory on the 12th-century church in 1928, which is now generally accepted (Fig. 2).[20]

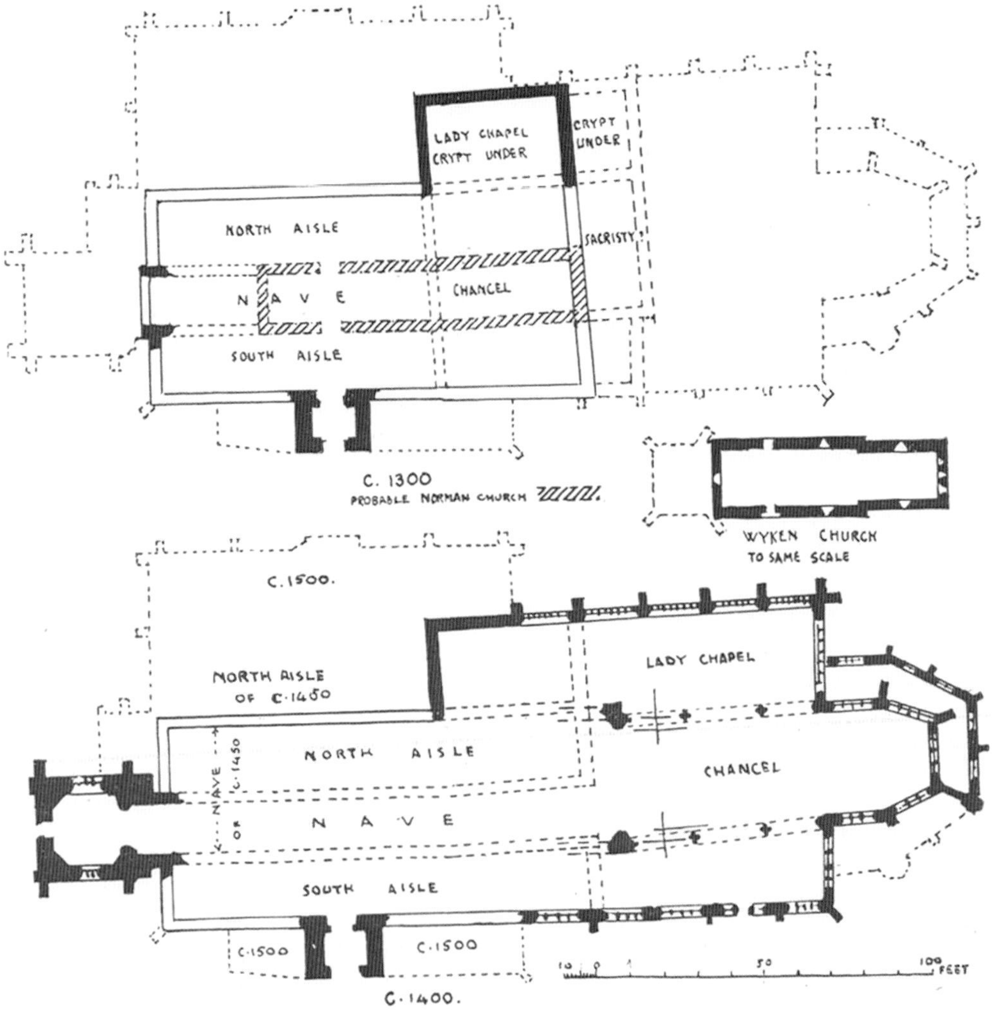

FIG. 2. Coventry, St Michael's: plan form of the 12th-century church, as proposed by Chatwin *TBAS*, 1928

Chatwin highlights the misalignment of the chancel and the nave as one of the church's particular puzzles: the chancel diverts slightly to the north. He suggests that 'the western end of the [Lady] chapel marks the line of division between the nave and the chancel'.[21] It seems much more likely, however, that the current chancel retains an ancient alignment for the building, presumably Anglo-Saxon, a proposal confirmed by the fact that the chapel of St Mary follows the same alignment as the chancel. The change of alignment relates directly to Bayley Lane as a southern boundary and enabled a longer nave to be erected than one that simply continued the old chapel's alignment; whether this was introduced in this phase or in the 13th century is uncertain. Much of Chatwin's evidence relies on interpretation of features that relate to the next building phase of the church in the late 13th century, but without further evidence coming to light his hypothesis cannot be validated.

The 13th century

PHYSICAL evidence from the 13th century provides the first clear sign of an expansion of the church's size and architectural pretensions. The maximum northern and southern extent of the building is set respectively by the presence of the northern crypt (and henceforth referred to as the drapers' crypt)[22] and the surviving south porch (Fig. 3). The latter is commonly ascribed to *c.* 1300: its main features are a large trefoiled arch for the outer entrance (Fig. 4) and a rib-vault of tierceron design inside (Fig. 5). It must have related to a nave of considerable proportion. Its prominent opening onto Bayley Lane suggests a relationship between the developing urban parish centre and the church, and one that supplanted its earlier direct relationship to the castle. The monumental trefoil opening, supported by four shafts is of a type hard to parallel but limited evidence suggests a date earlier than 1300. In overall form it can be compared to the interior dado of the Lady Chapel at Winchester Cathedral, which was completed by 1238 (Fig. 6).[23] Its use in Coventry is simpler and it is likely to come after the cutting edge design at Winchester, but, even taking this into account, it would push the date back to the mid-13th century, contemporary with the development of Bayley Lane. On the other hand, the rib-vault appears to be an insertion of *c.* 1300.

Both the reinvestment in this area of the town and the rebuilding of St Michael's may well be related to a combination of events in the early 13th century. On a general note, the Fourth Lateran Council (1215) had demanded better provision for the saying of mass and stimulated a number of rebuilding projects. Furthermore, it is not uncommon for an appropriation of ownership to stimulate a rebuilding campaign in order to demonstrate patronage,[24] and just such an appropriation occurred in Coventry in 1249 when the prior took control of both halves of the city. The formal recognition of the full parochial status of the church also occurred at about this time. It is extremely likely, therefore, that the church was reconstructed soon after 1249, and for the first time St Michael's appeared architecturally as a grand urban parish church rivalling Holy Trinity.

Precise dating of the drapers' crypt is difficult, with its relatively simple details, but it would fit with a documentary reference to the construction of a Lady Chapel for the drapers about 1300 (Fig. 7). The records of the Drapers' Guild state that 700 indulgences were granted for 720 days for building the chapel and charnel house of St Michael's, Coventry.[25] In the later middle ages, the Drapers' Chapel is known to be synonymous with the Lady Chapel, so it is assumed that the extant crypt does indeed relate to this

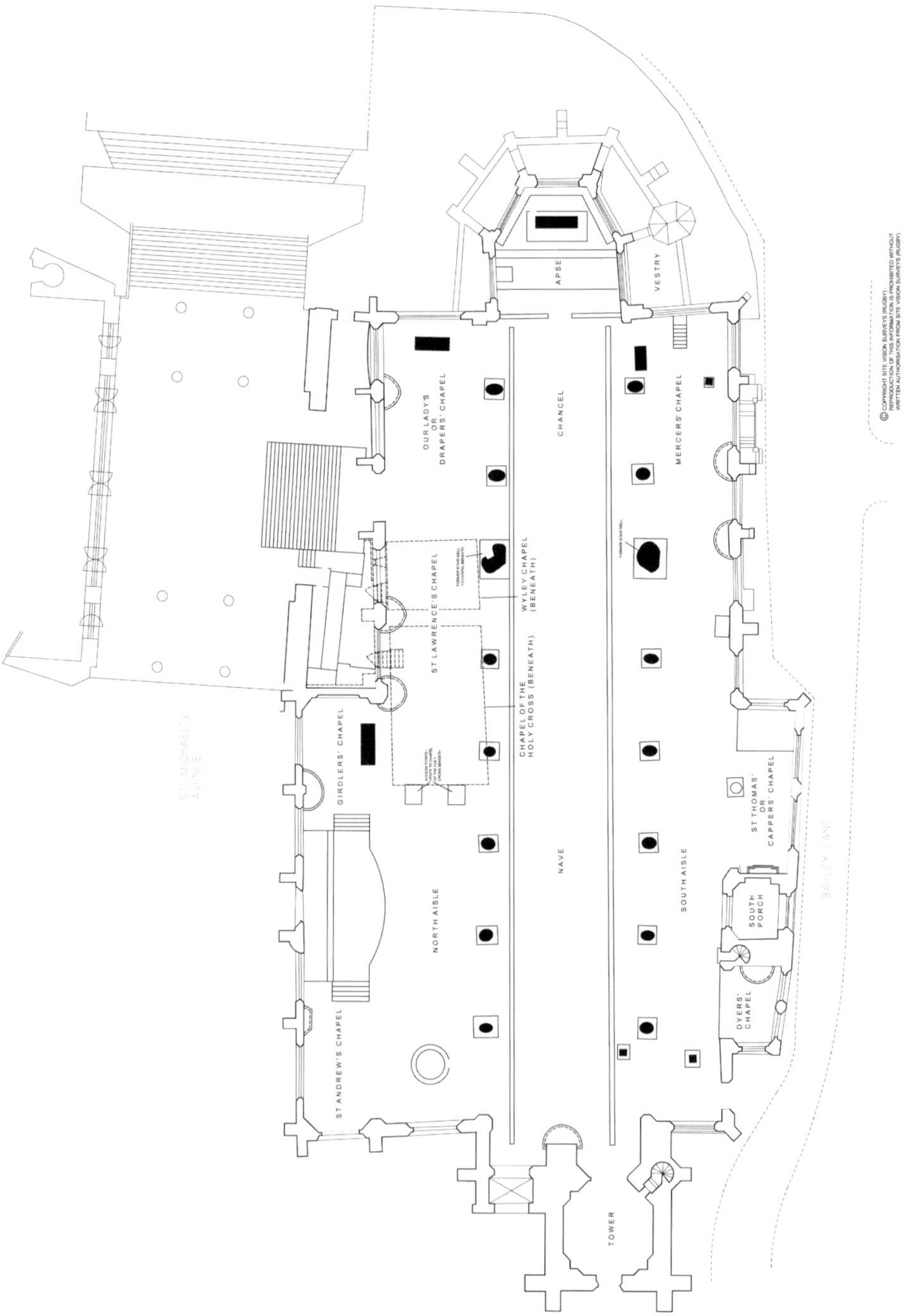

FIG. 3. Coventry, St Michael's: ground-plan
© Site Vision Survey, Rugby

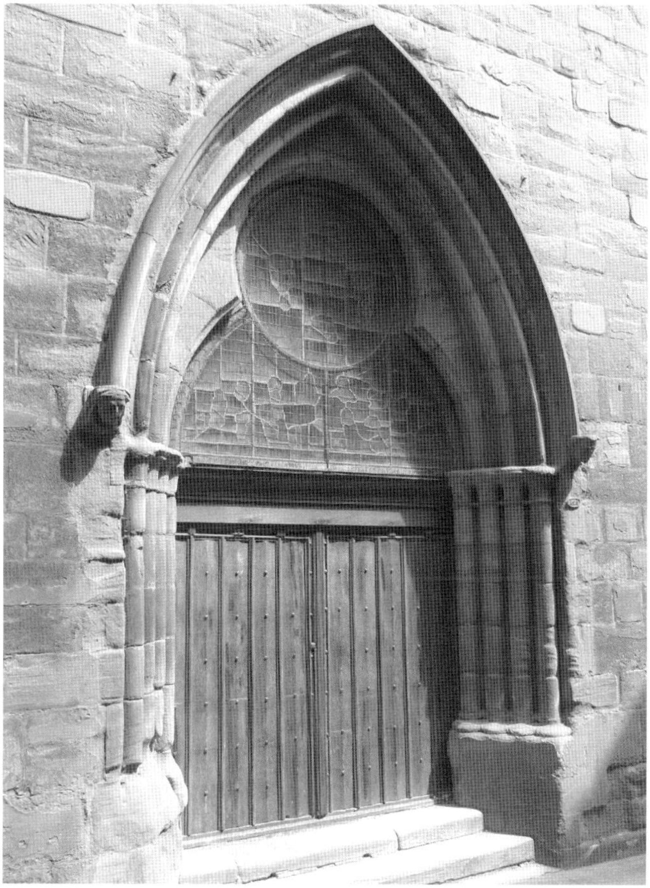

FIG. 4. Coventry, St Michael's: south porch
Photo, author

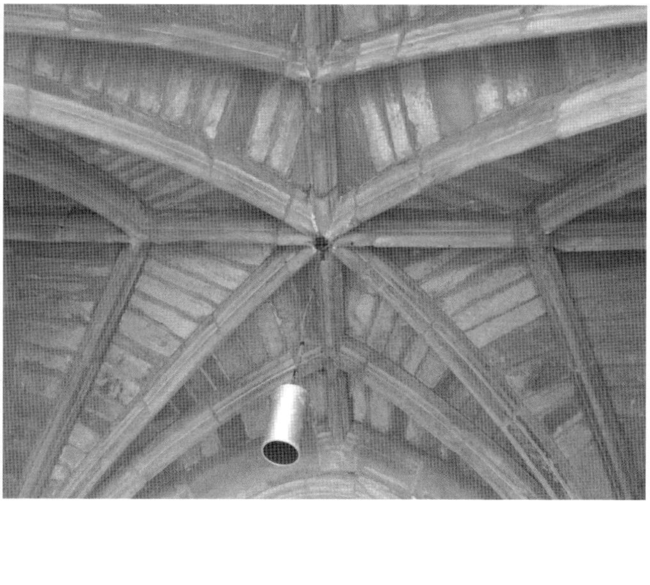

FIG. 5. Coventry, St Michael's: south porch, vault
Photo, R. K. Morris

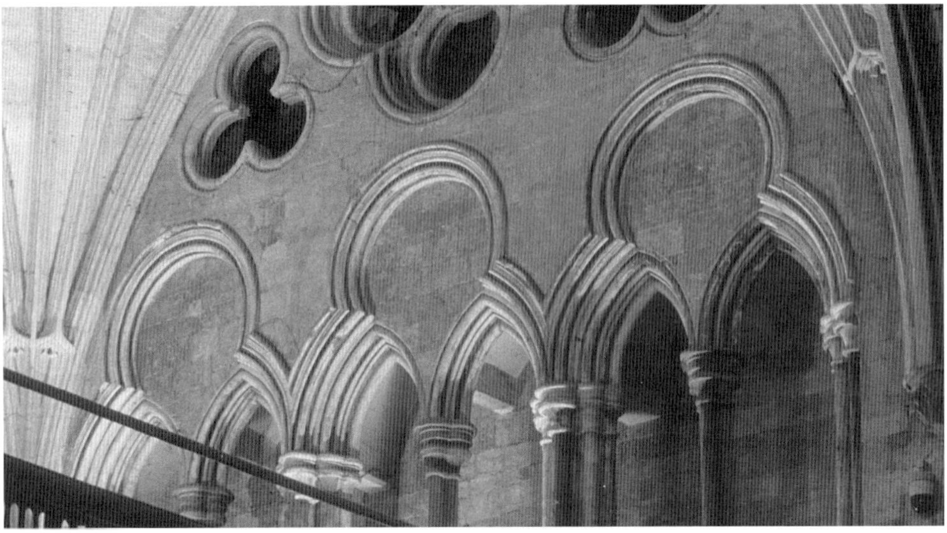

FIG. 6. Winchester Cathedral: Lady Chapel, detail
Photo, J. McNeill

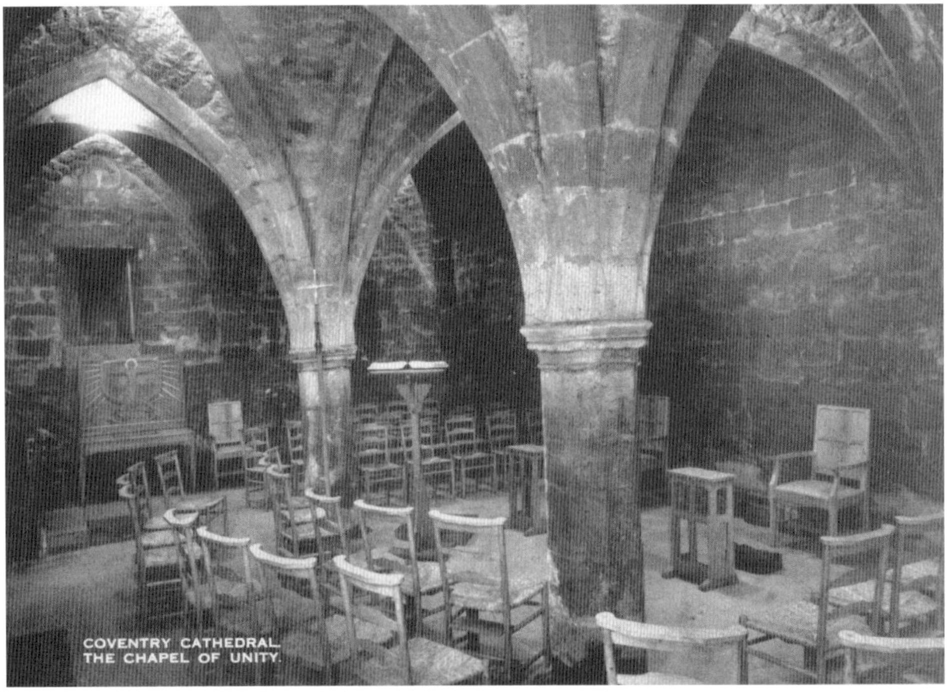

FIG. 7. Coventry, St Michael's: the 'drapers crypt' (Chapel of the Cross, formerly Chapel of Unity)
Photo, by kind permission of Coventry History Centre

building. This may also explain why its alignment reflects that of the chancel, not that of the nave which was being constructed at a similar time.

The drapers had an increasingly prominent presence in the area close to St Michaels, which culminated in the relocation by 1360 of their hall from Broadgate, where it faced onto the prior's market, to Bayley Lane opposite the south side of the church by 1360.[26] Their possible appropriation of an ancient chapel — which Bassett assumes was one of the four hill-top chapels constituting the original minster complex — may be the first sign of the Coventry merchants investing significantly in their parish church, an association which was maintained throughout the later middle ages. It is known that in 1455 cloth was sold from the south porch of the church, although it is not clear how early this practice began.[27]

The 14th century

FROM 1300, the connections between local merchant parishioners and the church grew, with its first recorded chantry founded in 1323 by Hugh de Merynton for two priests to sing mass daily for him and his wife Agnes. Other chantries and bequests are listed in the 1330s (Shepey family), in 1350 (merchant guild of St Mary), and in 1371 (Dilcock Chantry and others).[28] It was only after the emergence of the guilds and the achievement of power by the merchants that the church would become a real beneficiary of Coventry's economic boom. Whilst in the late 13th century the stage may have been set for the future of St Michael's as central to the urban development of the earl's half, nothing could prepare for the degree to which the church and its patrons would assert their dominance over the city from the late 14th century.

PATRONAGE AND DESIGN IN LATE MEDIEVAL COVENTRY

The late 14th century

TWO generations passed with no recorded major building work at St Michael's. In the rest of Coventry the building boom from the mid-14th century transformed the city and its religious establishments. Hill Top must have appeared like a building site for the last three decades of the century, including works at St Mary's Guildhall and Holy Trinity church. At St Michael's, the construction of a new tower in 1372 traditionally is said to have been funded by two merchants, Adam and William Botoner (Fig. 8). The established history of late medieval St Michael's relies heavily on selected extracts from the Coventry Annals. However, problems exist in ascribing significant value to many of its references, and a digression is necessary to discuss these in relation to the proposed dating for the late medieval campaigns.

The Annals, which in essence contain a list of mayors from the mid-14th century on, survive as a large number of transcripts ranging in date from the late 16th to the early 18th century. Variations in the date ascribed to the first mayor of Coventry in the 1340s results in related variations of dates for the late 14th- and 15th-century works to the church. In brief, the salient relating to St Michael's are as follows. The Botoners were responsible for the tower in 1372, 1374 or 1375 — some specify their death, some specify a twenty- or twenty-one-year campaign and some the cost of £100 per annum.[29] The steeple is said to have been begun in 1432, 1433 or 1435 and the bells hung in 1430, 1431 or 1433. At least one mentions the choir as being begun in 1433. However, the earliest available transcript, of 1588, includes no references to the construction

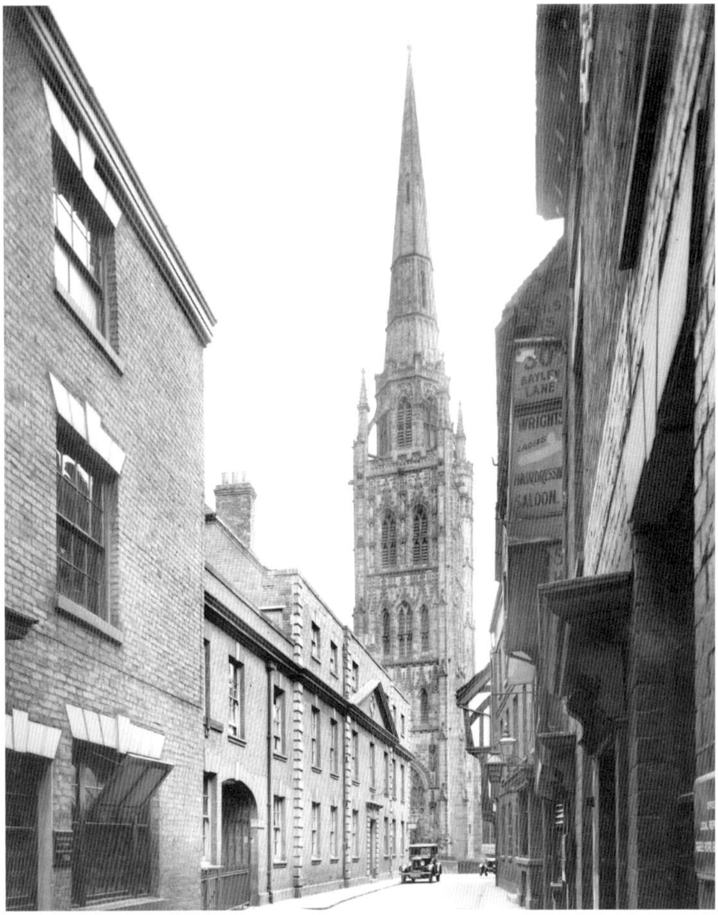

FIG. 8. Coventry, St Michael's: west tower, viewed from Bayley Lane
Photo, English Heritage, NMR

of the church or its patrons (except one — the tower being started in 1375).[30] The complete absence of attribution to individuals and of most of the dating in the earliest version does lead one to assume that folklore and tradition may be the sources for insertion of information in the later versions. One of the fuller versions, however, was relatively early (late 16th century), but was a victim of the fire in the Birmingham Reference Library in 1879. Previously it had been studied by Sharp and it may be the one also seen by Dugdale.[31] The possibility of lost documents on which many of these dates are loosely based must therefore remain. Even setting aside the thorny issue of 17th-century historians elaborating or tidying up building histories on the above basis, the Annals cannot be used as incontrovertible evidence for dating the building. However, alternative sources of information, such as wills and the Leet Book, do provide some information and this sets the parameters for the subsequent analysis.

The high quality of the tower represents a significant level of patronage and can only be ascribed to the city's elite. Both Botoner brothers were at various times mayors of Coventry, and that they had some role as individual or group patrons of the tower is probable;[32] a brass tablet formerly in the church had an inscription attributing the tower to the brothers.[33] The family was a prominent patron of a number of religious foundations in the city. Adam funded a cell at the newly founded Charterhouse,[34] and was later buried at the Greyfriars. William gave a parcel of land to the Whitefriars in the early 15th century, whilst John (mayor in *c.* 1409)[35] was one of the two main local benefactors for the Charterhouse, jointly funding three cells.[36] Regardless of the specific contribution of the Botoners, St Michael's construction, massive and impressive by any standards, cannot be separated from the general building boom in Coventry. Towers are commonly constructed to indicate both wealth and pride in the community and as such the construction of St Michael's may be linked, conceptually at least, to the contemporary construction of the city wall and the new guildhall.

West towers are frequently the last part added to a parish church, as in countless Somerset parish churches. The new tower at St Michael's was placed on axis with the 13th-century nave, and there is physical evidence that it was linked to it, although no doubt constructed outside its limits. There has been some debate as to whether its location indicates that it was intended to relate to the 13th-century church, but its sheer scale and architectural pretension have tended to contradict this assumption. As Wilson has pointed out, it owes more to the crossing towers on great churches like Lichfield Cathedral than anything seen within a parish context.[37] Its construction was surely a clear attempt to rival the towers and spires that already crowded Hill Top. One suggestion put forward to explain the tower's off-centre position in relation to the late medieval nave is the presence of a ditch to the north-west that caused problems with its foundations and prevented it from being built further north.[38] Other examples of subsidence associated with late 14th-century structures have been discovered in the locality, lending some weight to this theory and indicating a common pattern of infilling of the ditch and associated redevelopment.[39]

However, examples exist of towers constructed as status symbols almost out of scale with their churches do exist, such as St Botolph's, Boston (Lincs.), and Huish Episcopi (Som.). Various factors show conclusively that the tower at St Michael's was constructed in relation to a 13th-century church and that it was not the first phase of a total reconstruction plan. First, the straight sections of wall that stretch eastwards from the tower's eastern face show that it abutted a structure pre-dating the present nave. The tower, in plan, is effectively freestanding as its buttresses are independent from the church proper and no attempt to integrate the east wall of the tower with the west wall of the nave was made. Instead, straight walls that can only have existed if there was an earlier, smaller tower were extended to meet the new structure, as indicated by a straight joint in the masonry. The freestanding nature of the structure had advantages both for the construction process, which could take place outside the walls of the church, and for structural stability, bearing in mind the potential issues of subsidence.[40] Such a method of constructing a great western tower can be compared to that of Louth (Lincs.) in the 1440s.[41] Second, early fabric which clearly pre-dates the construction of the present tower survives in the west wall of the south aisle, confirming that the church already extended this far west (Fig. 9).[42] Third, one edition of the Annals differs from the rest in suggesting that 'William and Adam Botoner built St Michael's steeple to the battlements and then died. The church body and 2 side aisles were built before'.[43] Whilst the validity of this entry remains unresolved, it does imply that the tower was added to the earlier fabric, probably 13th century. Fourth, conclusive physical evidence confirming that the current nave was not conceived at the time of the tower's construction is shown in the latter's east wall. The roof line of the current building is clearly secondary, cutting awkwardly across the lower stage of the tower, with its

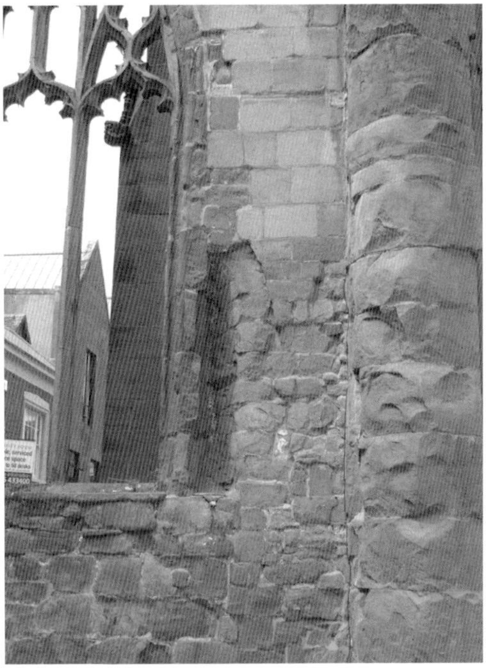

FIG. 9. Coventry, St Michael's: nave south aisle, west wall with remnant of earlier fabric

Photo, author

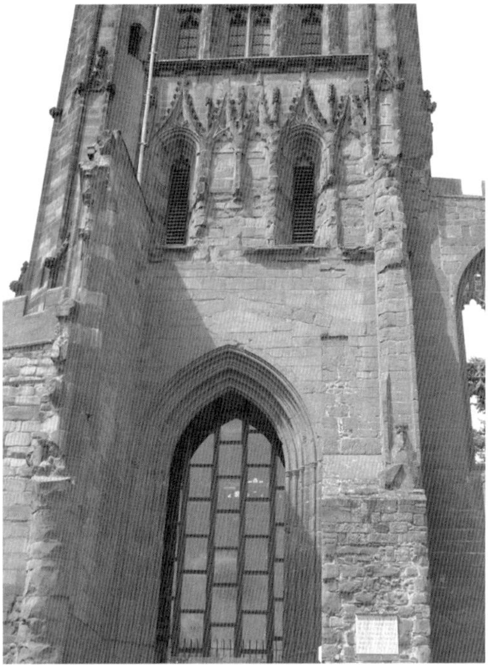

FIG. 10. Coventry, St Michael's: west tower, east elevation showing primary and secondary roof lines

Photo, author

weathering intersecting window and arch mouldings that were intended to be viewed externally (Fig. 10).

Furthermore, an earlier roof line appears on the east face of the tower lower down (Fig. 10). This was noticed by Chatwin, who, like other authors, has assumed that this relates to the 13th-century building. As a result, the history of St Michael's has been neatly divided into three clear rebuilding programmes — 12th-century Romanesque, 13th-century Early English, and late medieval Perpendicular: a model Rickmanesque sequence.[44] The scar shows the roof to have been low-pitched, which would have been inconceivable in a 13th-century building. And yet it seems to relate perfectly to the construction of the tower, sitting just below the first, external stage. No other early roof lines are in evidence, so this must represent the roof on the church when the tower was constructed.

It is proposed here, therefore, that the tower related directly to the plan and structure of a grand 13th-century church, but one which had been subject to re-roofing in the third quarter of the 14th century. Probably this was driven by a desire to heighten the building with a clerestory, and then covered by a lower pitched timber ceiling. It seems most likely that these two campaigns, to modernise the nave of the church and construct the tower, should be viewed together. Elsewhere it has been shown that the tower's upper stages were later additions, and it seems that the original height of the tower would have related to a newly heightened nave. This 1370s work marks the first phase of transition of St Michael's into a late medieval parish church, achieved at this stage by additions to the 13th-century church. Survivals of comparable, albeit later, additions to 13th-century naves exist to provide an impression of St Michael's appearance, for example at All Saints', Stamford (Fig. 11).

The parishioners, as patrons, were clearly aiming higher, both literally and figuratively, than those at Holy Trinity.[45] They most likely employed the master mason, Robert Skillington, known to have worked at Kenilworth Castle in the 1390s and who probably had trained under Windsor masons in the mid-14th century. Skillington was evidently a mason designing at the forefront of his craft and working for some of the wealthiest and most ambitious magnates in England.[46]

What is especially surprising, therefore, is the rapidity with which the decision to embark on complete reconstruction was then taken within a generation. Even as the upper stage of the tower was being completed, it seems that work to the east end of the building was commenced, making a reconstruction of the entire church inevitable. The comprehensive nature of this reconstruction reflects the ambition and wealth of the merchants who predominantly funded it. It also says something about the rapid pace of change within a community that had really emerged as a political and economic force only fifty years before. The 15th-century later medieval rebuilding of St Michael's can be interpreted as a symbol of the power, piety and optimism that characterised the newly constituted city.

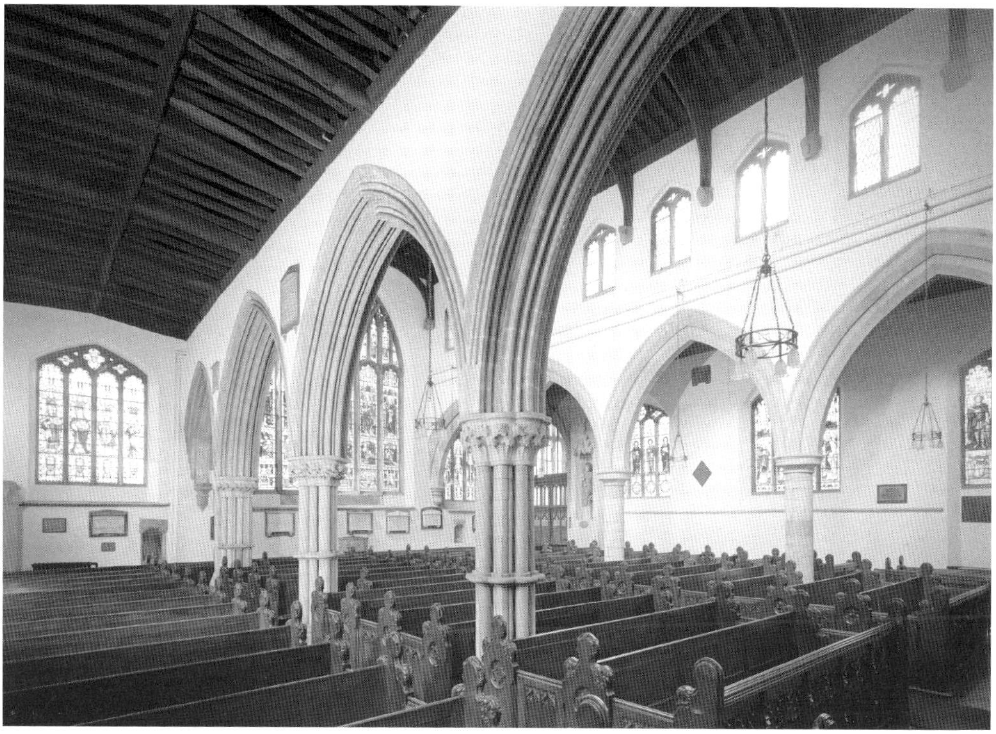

FIG. 11. Stamford (Lincs.), All Saints': nave, looking north-west

The 15th century

BEQUESTS for the church are to be found at the turn of the century. In 1392 the master of the Trinity Guild gave land with others in aid of works, and in 1401 Alice Wyschard bequeathed money for the fabric,[47] although the nature of the works in both cases is unspecified. That work at the northern boundary of the churchyard was carried out in the early 15th century is shown by an order in the Leet Book for the removal of a hovel against the 'drapery door' and the construction of a wall to enclose the churchyard.[48] These are but minor distractions from the main work in hand in the early decades of the 15th century.

By any standard, the rebuilding of the main body of St Michael's is an exceptional programme, providing a model for high status parish church designs for the rest of the century (Figs 1, 12). The design has a number of distinctive features that warrant analysis and help with dating. The chancel has a polygonal apsidal termination that extended its length to the maximum on the available plot of land. Huge windows fill the apse, with two transoms and drop tracery of sub-arcuated design in the head,[49] combining ogee-headed main lights with lights with two-centred trefoil heads (Fig. 13 and Col. Pl. IXA in print edn). Buildings with polygonal terminations have local precedents in the 14th century, notably the Lady Chapel at Lichfield Cathedral (*c.* 1315–30) and the chapter-house of Coventry Priory.[50] These could be seen as obvious general models, but the connection between these ideas and St Michael's comes

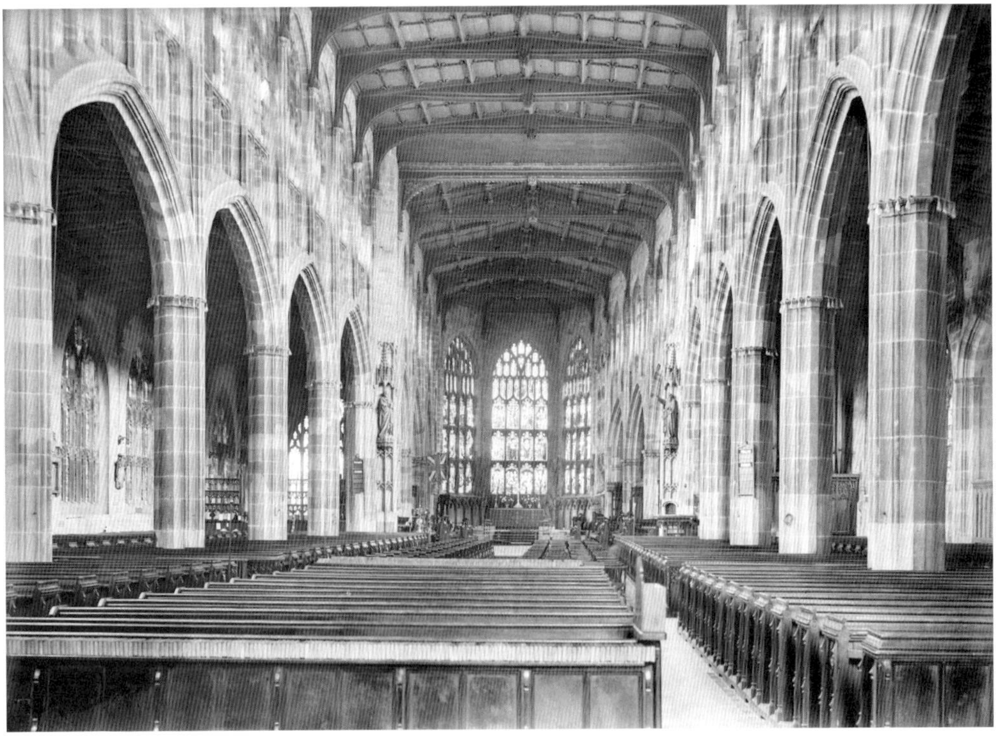

FIG. 12. Coventry, St Michael's: interior looking east, pre-1939
Photo, English Heritage, NMR

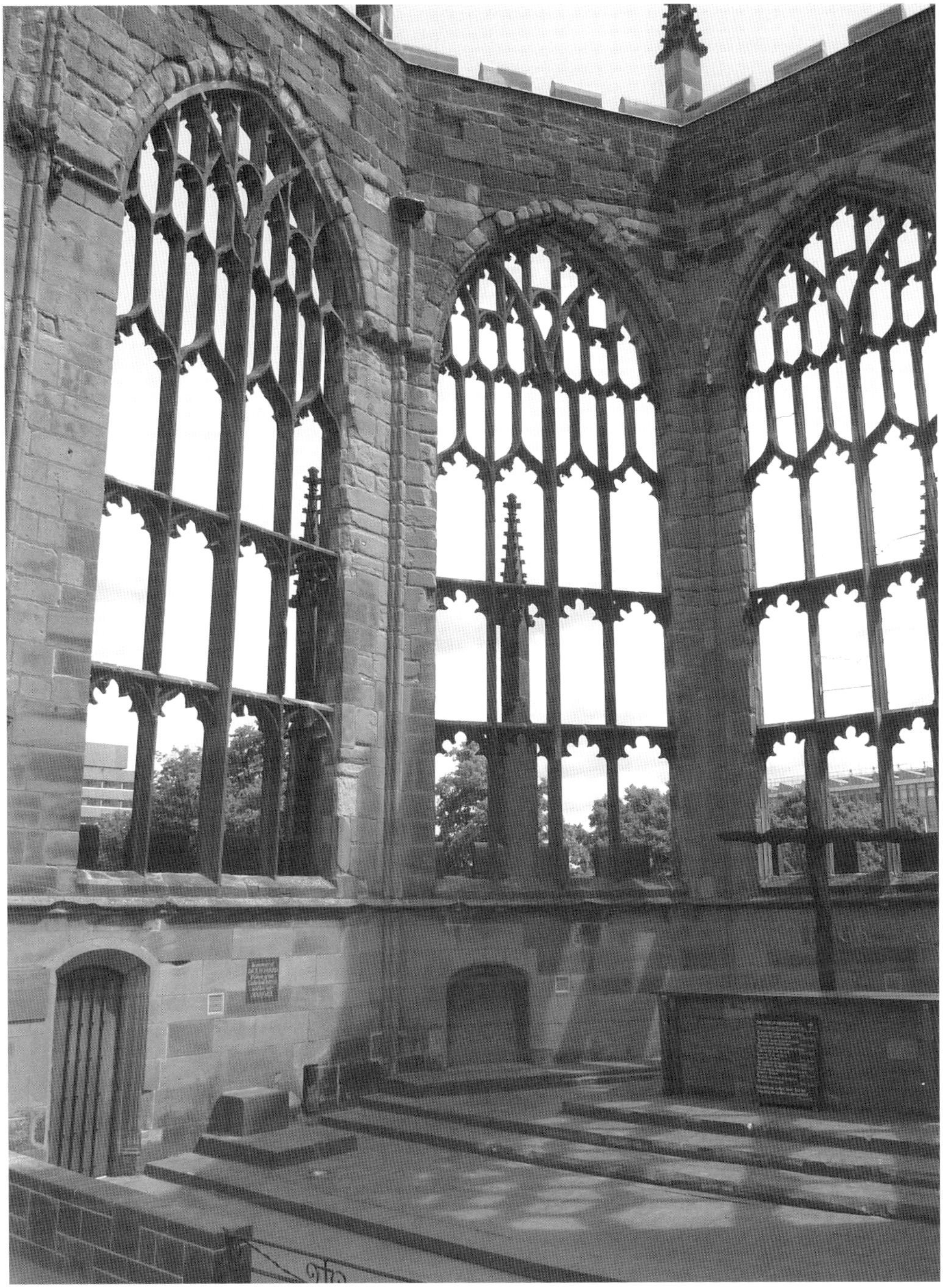

FIG. 13. Coventry, St Michael's: windows of the eastern apse
Photo, author

through their use in buildings of the 1370s constructed for the duke of Lancaster and the earls of Warwick at Kenilworth Castle and St Mary's Warwick respectively. The chapter-house of the latter is a small but elegant structure with a polygonal termination, with each window filled by a sub-arcuated and drop tracery design, as at St Michael's (Fig. 14). At Kenilworth, polygonal terminations are key elements of the palatial new hall and lodgings. Here also, in the windows of the great hall, a prominent main mullion creating a sub-arcuated design is also present (Morris, 'Kenilworth', Fig. 1). These double-transomed windows form the centrepiece of Gaunt's hall façade. The rarity of this feature in the 1370s and their architectural impact suggest that these are the source for the ambitious apse windows at St Michael's (Fig. 13).[51] Coventry Priory's interest in emulating these forms is evident in the new polygonal chevet with polygonal chapels at the east end of the cathedral church, under construction probably in the late 14th or early 15th century, no doubt close in date to the works to the chancel at St Michael's.[52]

Other details further demonstrate the influence of works for the earl of Warwick. The elevation of St Michael's bears comparison with the chancel of St Mary's,

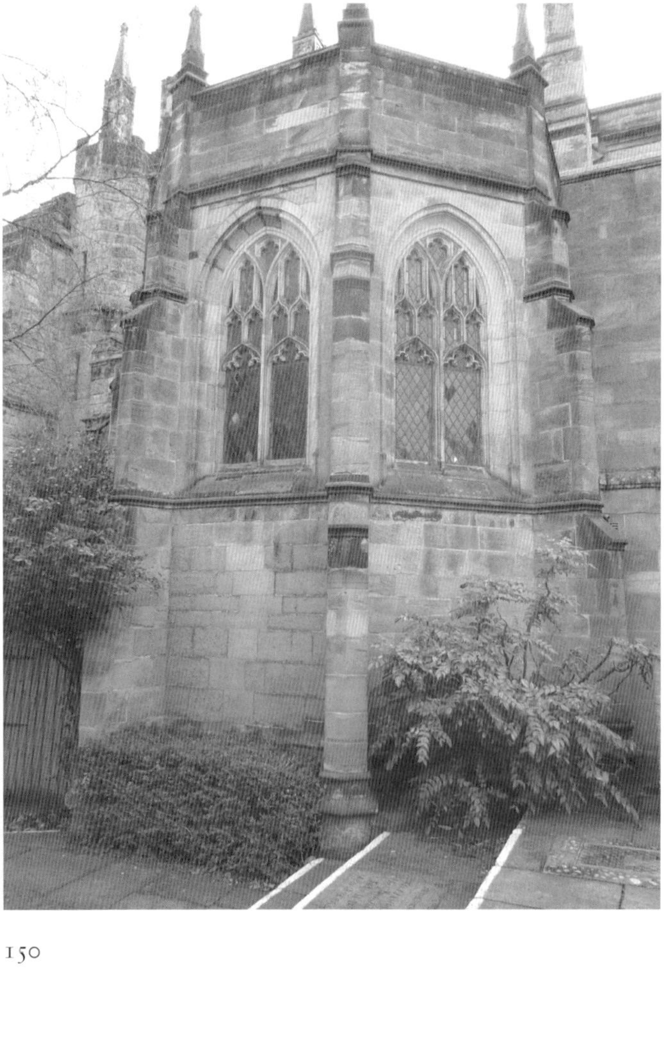

FIG. 14. Warwick, St Mary's: chapter-house
Photo, author

Warwick, under construction from 1367: they share four-centred arches with drop tracery, Y-tracery, ogee-headed lights and roundish forms in the heads (cf Figs 15, 16).[53] At St Michael's, a band of quatrefoils under the tracery lights is clearly reminiscent of works in the east end and cloister of Gloucester Cathedral, though its transition to St Michael's is seemingly via Warwick, which has a distinctive band of quatrefoils in the vault of the parclose set within the thickness of the chancel south wall. Altogether these close parallels would support a date-span for the east end of *c.* 1390–*c.* 1420. Evidence of additional patronage for the chancel is provided by Dugdale's account of the glazing. He lists a number of arms, including those of France quartered with England, the Prince of Wales and a number of dignitaries such as William Beauchamp, earl of Arundel and, notably, Richard Beauchamp, earl of Warwick (d. 1439).[54]

Sharp implies that documentary evidence confirms works were still under way in 1445, when an order of the Leet relating to prostitutes levied a fine of 10s. to the work of the church.[55] Unfortunately, like so many Leet entries, this order makes no reference to specific building works.[56] The only documentation for actual work exists in the Calendar of Papal Registers in 1450, when the drapers petitioned the pope concerning liturgical arrangements for their chapel. They stated that:

> on the north side of the choir there were two contiguous chapels, one of St Mary the Virgin, the other of All Saints, but that the parishioners, wishing to enlarge the church, have destroyed them, turned the place where they had been into the nave of the church, built another chapel of St Mary the Virgin and All Saints also on the north side of the choir, and had it dedicated by the ordinary.[57]

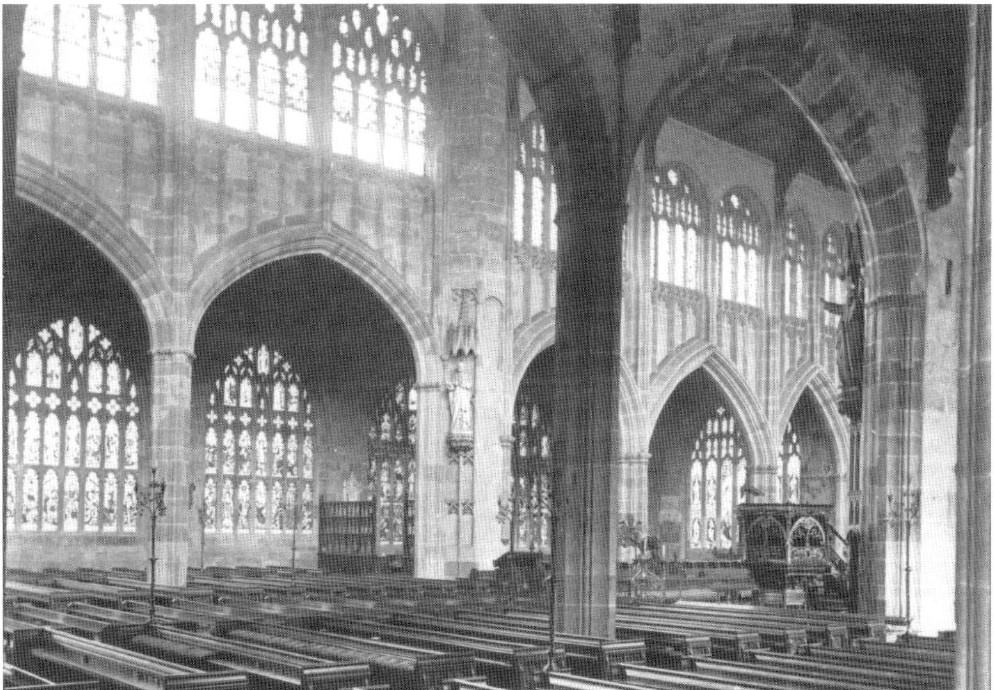

FIG. 15. Coventry, St Michael's: chancel elevation

Photo, by kind permission of Coventry History Centre

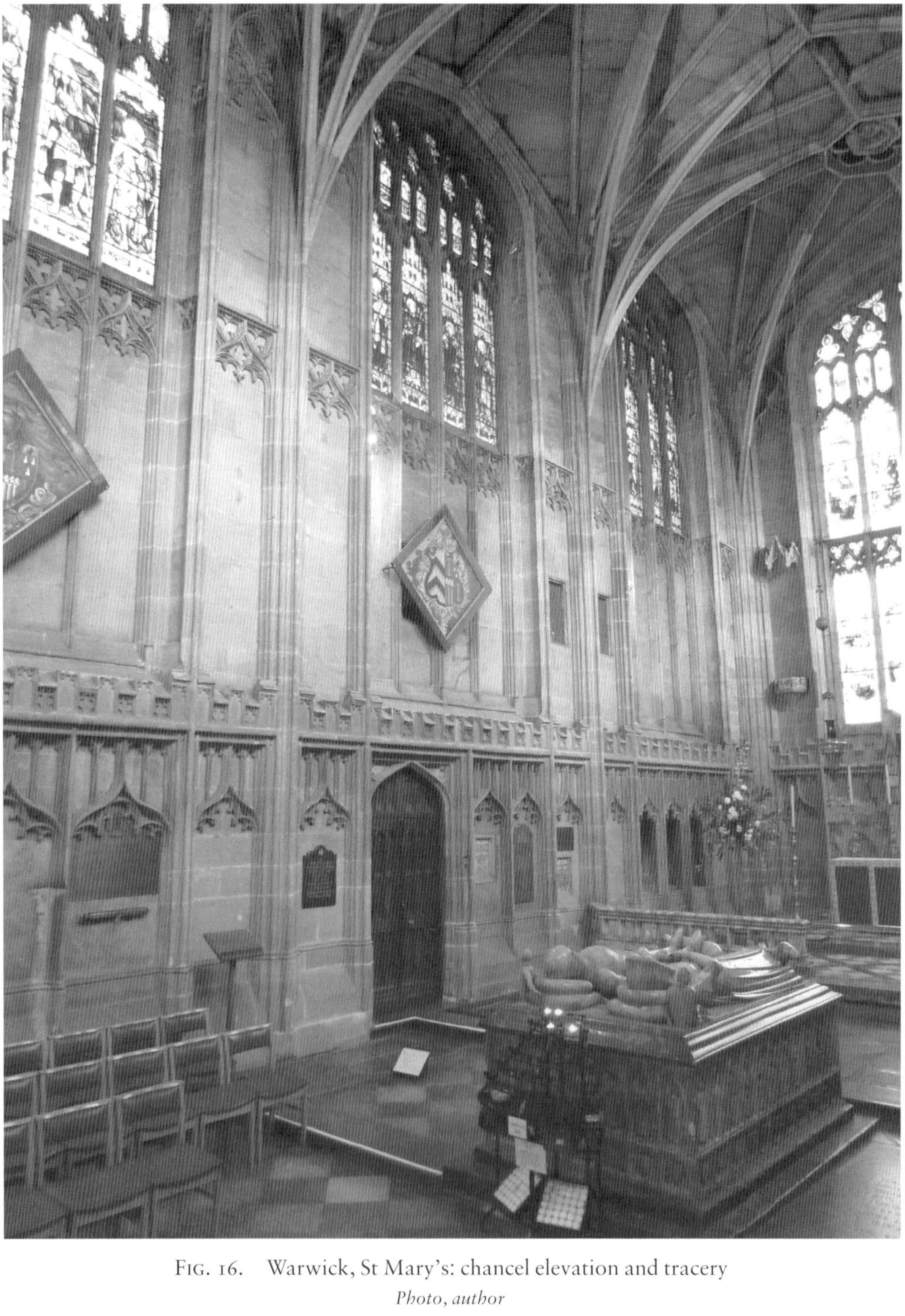

FIG. 16. Warwick, St Mary's: chancel elevation and tracery
Photo, author

This demonstrates, first, that the driving force behind the enlargement of at least this part of the church was the parishioners. Second, it confirms the continued patronage of the church by the drapers and their particular association with this chapel of St Mary; the petition includes the detailing of the three chaplaincies associated with the chapel.[58]

The design of the nave shares many general similarities with the chancel, but significant differences support an interpretation that this work followed on from those of the chancel and was perhaps under way between the 1430s and the late 1440s. Pairs of four-light windows occupy each bay, resting on a panelled wall and over a narrower nave arcade arch than the chancel (Fig. 17). The band of quatrefoils has disappeared and the heads of the lights are now two-centred without ogees. The tracery itself retains the sub-arcuated design of the apse windows, but in addition each half of the window incorporates a smaller Y-tracery feature (Fig. 18). This successful repetition of the basic unit of the tracery at different scales within the same window might be described as a leitmotif of Perpendicular architecture. All the mullions are the same size, resulting in the entire window and panelling appearing as a recessed unit suspended between the main shafts which articulate the ends and mid-points of the bays.

The presence or otherwise of ogee-headed lights cannot be taken alone as an indicator of date in a late medieval building, not least because from the time of the

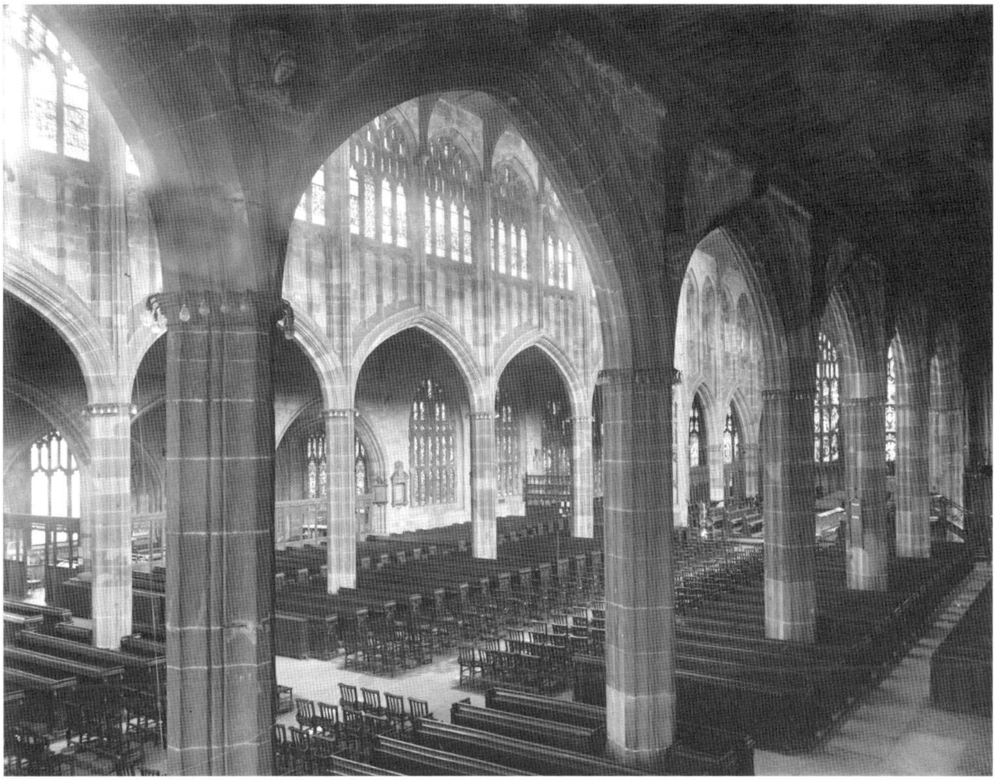

FIG. 17. Coventry, St Michael's: nave looking north, pre-1939
Photo, English Heritage, NMR

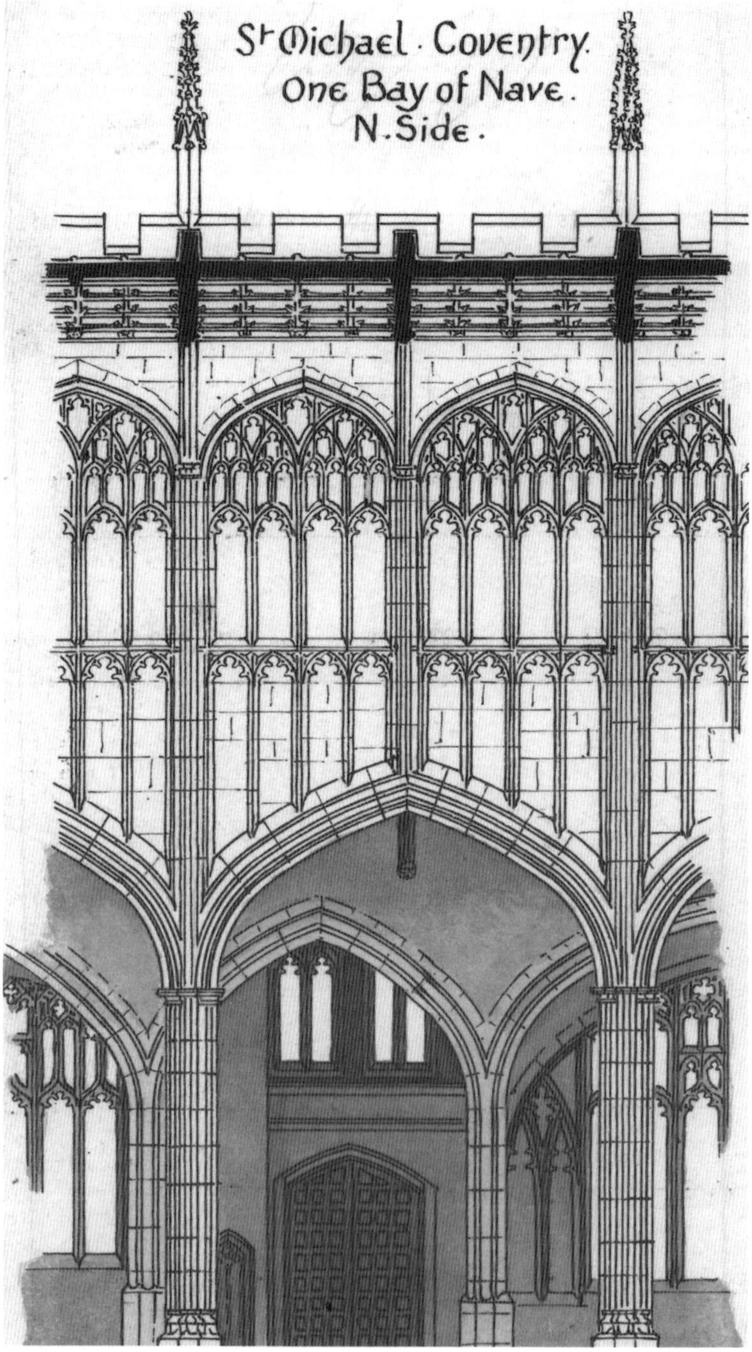

FIG. 18. Coventry, St Michael's: nave elevation
Photo, by kind permission of Coventry History Centre

construction of the south transept of Gloucester Cathedral in the 1330s, they were used in combination with other forms of arch within the same traceried design. However, there are some general trends which assist in dating in this region. The ogee as a dominant feature of traceried windows seems to have slipped out of favour by about 1440. Examples in and around Oxford at this time show a decisive shift away from multiple ogees, as, for example, at the Divinity School (1421–39), to be revived in the last quarter of the 15th century.

This does not mean an absence of architectural detail or lavish design, for St Michael's nave shares the same tracery pattern with the ornate Beauchamp Chapel at St Mary's, Warwick, designed and constructed between 1436 and about 1446 (cf Figs 18, 19).[59] The chapel's east window is a tripartite arrangement with a large central section divided from lateral sections by large mullions. It is these lateral traceries which provide a precise parallel for St Michael's nave clerestory. This suggests that the dating of St Michael's nave should be ascribed to the 1440s, following this model rather than earlier works on which the chancel was dependent. The heightening of the tower and addition of a spire must be associated with the decision to rebuild the rest of the church, and the traditional dating of these to the 1430s is feasible in this context.

Most significant for the dating is the drapers' petition of 1450, which must provide a *terminus ante quem* for the building of the main body of the church. This document is confirmatory and the north-east chancel chapels are referred to as already built. Therefore the works to the nave and the chancel aisles must have been completed at the time of the original request, of which this is confirmation.[60] This may provide the date for the insertion of a staircase in the crypt of the Drapers' Chapel. The original crypt had been extended eastwards at an unknown date, for the design of its chamfered ribs is quite distinct from those of the earlier crypt to the west, with narrow chamfers and ribs dying into the wall. They are comparable in design to ribs used in Coventry buildings in the second half of the 14th century.[61] Some form of enlargement of the chapel and its associated crypt was clearly carried out before the rebuilding of the entire church, quite possibly in the late 14th century when the 13th-century church underwent modernisation and the tower was under construction. The staircase which leads up from the southern wall of this crypt extension is clearly secondary and provides a direct link between the crypt and the west end of the relocated chapel of St Mary (see Fig. 3).

Although apparently set up by the drapers, the altar of St Mary became a focus for the emerging guilds of the city, including inevitably the St Mary's Guild. In 1392 it was amalgamated with the Guild of St John the Baptist and the Trinity Guild, and at the same time provided an additional priest, two wardens and all the necessaries and ornaments required for mass at the altar of Our Lady.[62] The Trinity Guild was the most powerful in Coventry and the close relationship with St Michael's is shown by the presence of its vicars in the list of members.[63]

The nave project provides an architectural continuity with the east end, so successfully achieved that some authors have assumed the two projects to be almost contemporary. Two factors contribute to an understanding of the relationship between the east and west ends of the building. First, and most significant, the east end is evidently the commencement of a proposed reconstruction of the entire church from the increase in both width and height which would have made a meaningful relationship with the 13th-century nave impossible. However, it is also clear that the east end and the nave were treated as separate campaigns: both in the design differences that illustrate an aesthetic shift between *c.* 1400 and *c.* 1440 and in the differences in roof heights. The proportions of the nave were largely conditioned by the existing buildings

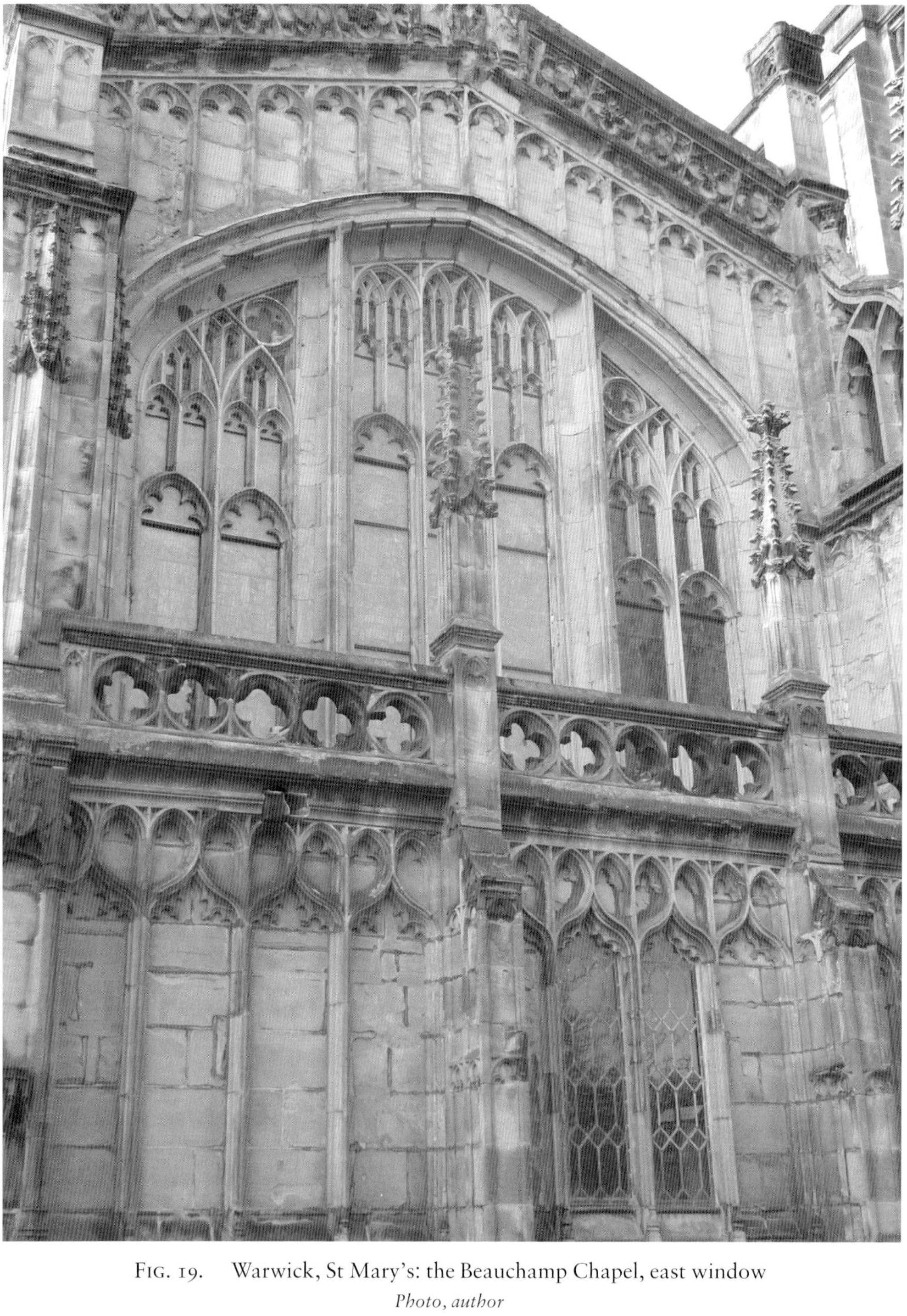

FIG. 19. Warwick, St Mary's: the Beauchamp Chapel, east window
Photo, author

to the west and east, and its new height had to relate both to the tower and to the lofty new east end. To summarise, the design confirms that works to the nave were a separate campaign but also part of a broadly conceived plan for rebuilding which was taken in the first decades of the new century. It seems most likely that the nave work was begun in the 1430s or 1440s, proceeding quickly to the north side where the 1450 reference informs us of the relocation of chapels and altars. The Smiths' Chapel, to the north of the north aisle (Fig. 3), appears in a reference of 1449, another clue that this extensive rebuilding was complete.[64]

St Michael's was probably ready for the royal visit of 1451, an event which reflected its pre-eminent position in the life of the city,[65] and which also provides a *terminus ante quem* for the main body of the church. Shortly after completion, further guild chapels were added to the south, clearly secondary and using what were the last available small plots of land between the south aisle wall and the boundary with Bayley Lane.[66] Two chapels, flanking the south porch, were constructed by the Dyers and Cappers. The former was already in use in 1463,[67] and the latter appears to have been constructed by 1458.[68] Some minor alterations may have occurred in the later part of the century,[69] but essentially the works were complete before 1480, as can be inferred from a series of references at this date in the Coventry Leet.[70] Following a complaint from the prior about tree-lopping in the churchyard and the presence of a new building against the drapery door, it was claimed that the ground upon which the said building is set is not part of the churchyard, although 'nowe of late tyme *sythen the last byldyng of Seint Michel Churche* [my italics], the parishons kepe their procession weye in the street adyoynyng to the seid byldyng' (probably Bayley Lane close to the south side of the church).[71]

St Michael's can legitimately be ranked with other great urban parish churches of the late middle ages, such as St Peter Mancroft, Norwich (*c.* 1430–55). Like St Michael's, it has no structural division between nave and chancel and has been described as a late medieval ideal in its spatial unity, contrasting with the old-fashioned cruciform plan of Holy Trinity. Coventry's greatest parish church outstripped its near neighbours both in scale and in sophistication of design. The rebuilding of St Mary's, Nottingham, between 1386 and 1401 forms an instructive comparison for the design of the interior as a whole. An analysis of St Mary's suggests many of the same models as quoted above for St Michael's. Ideas from the architecture of the earls of Warwick appear to have filtered through to Nottingham via Coventry in the 1370s. They include the use of comparable moulding profiles to St Michael's tower, in particular the use of rolls and canted fillets, an idea that stems originally from the early Perpendicular works at Gloucester Cathedral.[72] What distinguishes the elevation and pier designs of St Mary's and of the chancel and nave of St Michael's is the full-scale application of a panelled interior to a parish church. More locally, St Michael's pre-eminence is clear, for whilst the majority of churches in the surrounding area were rebuilt in the 14th century, all those reconstructed after St Michael's pay homage to it.[73]

This application of great church ideas to a parish church had been implemented at least once before at St Mary Redcliffe, Bristol, a building which may have been of some influence on Coventry. Construction of the main nave elevation was probably commenced in the last years of the 14th century and there is little doubt that, like St Michael's, it replaced a large, impressive 13th-century church.[74] Described as a church within the medieval equivalent of a millionaire's suburb,[75] it drew on the great church architecture of Wells Cathedral and Glastonbury Abbey. Awareness of Redcliffe in Coventry circles is made more likely by the special trading relationship between the two cities: Coventry merchants traded in Bristol in the late 14th and early 15th centuries and a number of Bristol merchants were members of the Coventry Trinity Guild.[76] The little that is known about the fittings of St Michael's complements the level of ambition and artistic aspiration of its architecture. In particular, the fragments of medieval glazing which survived the 1940 blitz are closely related to the works of John Thornton, one of the pre-eminent glaziers of the early 15th century.[77]

Both chancel and nave elevations of the church have two distinctive features which distinguish the design from that of St Mary Redcliffe, namely lozenge piers and paired clerestory windows.[78] In combination with the panelled elevation, these features define the most distinctive architecture of the late medieval parish church in England. The lozenge pier has a long history and in a European context is often associated with mendicant churches, which in turn influenced parish churches. It had been used in the Coventry area for the rebuilding of the alien priory at Monks Kirby (*c.* 1360–86), and a more complex version appeared at the Coventry Whitefriars after 1383.[79] It became *de rigueur* in parish churches of the late 15th and early 16th centuries.

The use of paired clerestory windows in both choir and nave is not shared by any of the models so far cited. Significant precedents are found in a series of late 13th- and early 14th-century churches in eastern England, such as Howden and Holy Trinity, Hull (both Yorks., East Riding), and Boston (Lincs.). They established a yardstick for the late medieval parish church in their scale, planning and general approach to design, having been influenced themselves by the wave of mendicant building in the 13th century. St Michael's followed this model, but with some telling differences — notably a much larger clerestory in proportion to the arcade — thereby reducing the

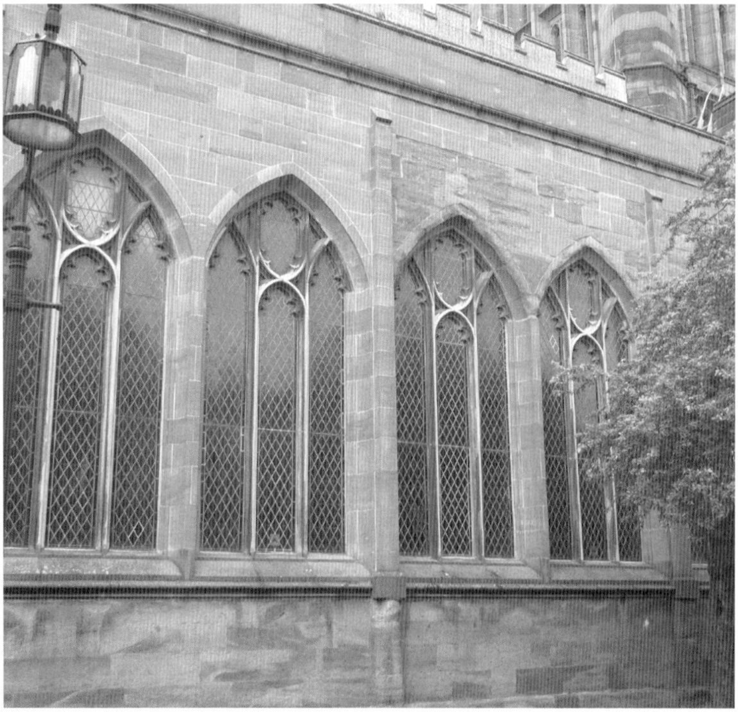

FIG. 20. Coventry, Holy Trinity: nave south aisle windows
Photo, author

dominance of the arcade as an architectural feature and replacing it with the elevation. However, it is possible that the late 14th-century clerestory at St Michael's had already used paired windows, because this feature had previously appeared in the 14th-century nave aisles at neighbouring Holy Trinity (Fig. 20). The later clerestory added to Holy Trinity's 14th-century nave also employs paired openings (Fig. 21 and Col. Pl. VIIIA in print edn). The chronological relationship of these two 15th-century works is uncertain. St Michael's clerestory is here suggested to be *c.* 1420 and that at Holy Trinity is definitely before the painting of the Doom over the crossing arch in *c.* 1435.[80] It is a moot point whether a wholesale reconstruction of St Michael's prompted new works to the late 14th-century nave of Holy Trinity, or whether Holy Trinity's attempts to modernise were taken up almost immediately by St Michael's on an altogether more impressive scale. The circumstances of the rise to pre-eminence of St Michael's strongly suggest the former.

This proposed chronology shows that the work to rebuild St Michael's was not a single campaign begun in the 1370s: the nave was constructed (and possibly designed) after the choir, but conceived alongside it. In addition, the concept of the new church and its initial design pre-dates all other complete rebuilding campaigns of comparable merchant churches in the 15th century. It may have set a standard to which patrons in Norwich and Louth, for example, could aspire in recasting their signature buildings.

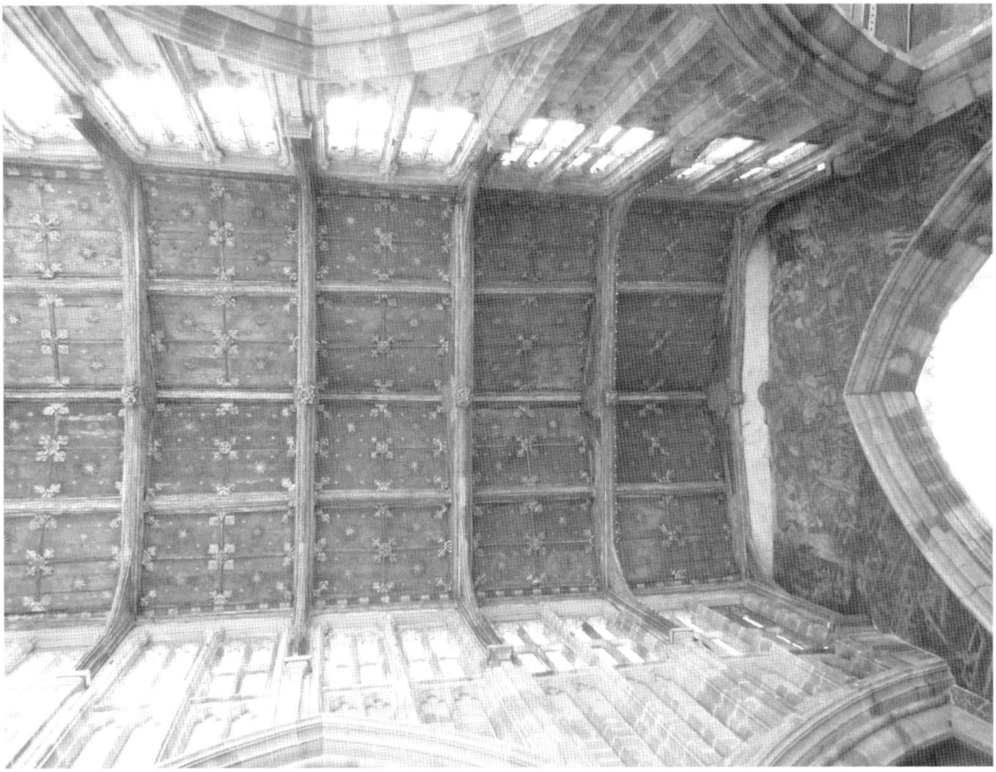

FIG. 21. Coventry, Holy Trinity: nave clerestory

Photo, author

Furthermore, it is evident that the patronage of the earls of Warwick remained a dominant force in the region, as shown by the similarity between the mouldings of the mid-15th-century guild chapels, of the dyers and cappers in particular, and the architecture of the Beauchamp chapel.[81] In form, the church draws inspiration from earlier great urban parish churches and elevation ideas from collegiate, priory and cathedral models. In these two respects St Michael's is set apart from the series of much smaller parish churches in the region and also specifically from Holy Trinity.

CONCLUSION

REASSESSING St Michael's is instructive in understanding late medieval urban churches and the broader formulation of Perpendicular architecture. It has also been shown that the concept of the mercantile, urban parish church is so associated with the late middle ages that the scale and significance of its 13th-century predecessors is often lost. Equally the influence of these earlier buildings on the proportions, form and design details can be underestimated.

The process of change for St Michael's from seigneurial chapel to the late medieval ideal of the merchants' church is a product of the post-Tripartite Indenture era in Coventry. The civic role, piety and status of Coventry's merchant class were expressed directly through the architectural magnificence of St Michael's. It overtook Holy Trinity in its modern design and in its sheer size and scale. Its new tower and spire gave it the landmark status that enabled it to rival all other ecclesiastical institutions around Hill Top and in the city as a whole. A post-medieval visitor to the city, Thomas Pennant, affirmed the success of its builders when he remarked that 'Trinity church and its spire would be spoken of as a most beautiful building, was it not eclipsed by its unfortunate vicinity to St Michael's' (Demidowicz, 'Priory', Fig. 8).[82]

ACKNOWLEDGEMENTS

Many people deserve thanks for helping this article to fruition, although inevitably any mistakes remain my own. I would like to thank Richard K. Morris and John McNeill for immeasurably improving it. Particular thanks go to Richard Goddard for being a constant source of advice and providing comment on various drafts. I am also grateful to George Demidowicz, Chris Patrick, Jeremy Ashbee and John Goodall for discussing various aspects of the text with me, and to David Stocker for assistance with Figure 11. The production of the plan of St Michael's is by kind permission of Site Vision Survey, Rugby, and I am especially grateful to Damian Taylor for carrying out amendments to the plan for the purposes of this article.

NOTES

1. J. H. Harvey, *Gothic England: a Survey of National Culture 1300–1500* (London 1947), 103.

2. Soden, in this volume, 9–10. Coss even suggests that the chapel of St Michael's sat within the castle bailey; Coss, *Early Records*, xxxii, citing the Langley Cartulary (no. 275), *in ballivo qui ducit ad ecclesiam sancti michaelis*.

3. For the topography of Coventry, especially in relation to the priory, see K. D. Lilley, 'Coventry's Topographical Development: the Impact of the Priory', in Demidowicz ed., *First Cathedral*, 72–97. Also note Goddard, *Coventry 1043–1355*.

4. Chatwin suggests a parallel with nearby Brinklow where the chapel was on the outside edge of the bailey but still used as the castle chapel; Chatwin, 'Early Coventry', 134.

5. Coss, *Early Records*, 5; 21 (no. 14) refers to the charter of Ranulf III granting tithe from his lands to the churches of St Mary, St Michael, St Chad and St Giles to Ralf his Chaplain and his successors in the chapel of St Michael.

6. For the list of disputes and the relationship with the bishop and priory, see VCH *Warwickshire* VIII, 346. See also Coss, *Early Records*, xv–xxix, for the relevant charters and his introduction to them.

7. The value of St Michael's was considerably more than nearby Holy Trinity which was £13 6s. 8d. at the same time, and aligns closely with other great urban churches of the period (e.g. St Mary Redcliffe, Bristol; Louth, Nottingham and Boston), which are all valued between £40 and £51 as compared to churches in the locality of Coventry, for example Solihull, which was valued at £20; www.hrionline.ac.uk/db/taxatio

8. See Coss, *Early Records*, xv–xxix, and Goddard, *Coventry 1043–1355*, 278.

9. References to the castle exist in 1200 and 1208, but it had apparently gone by the mid-13th century; see VCH *Warwickshire* VIII, 18.

10. For which see P. Coss ed., *The Langley Cartulary* (Stratford 1980), 119 (no. 524) — when a chantry was founded in the free chapel of Pinley by the parson of the *chapel* of St Michael's; ibid., 90 (no. 384) — grant made to Geoffrey of Langley refers to the *matricis ecclesie sancti michelis de coventr*. VCH *Warwickshire* VIII, 349 and n. 48, states incorrectly that it is first called 'church' in 1241. See Coss, *Early Records*, 186–91 (nos 360–75) for charters for the late 13th century onwards. The use of the terms 'chapel' and 'church' are unlikely to indicate a sudden change in status, as its recorded status as mother church and the presence of a burial ground make clear; ibid., 11, 13–14 (nos 2, 5, 6), 21 (no. 14) and 15 (no. 7). A late 12th-century letter of Hugh II, earl of Chester, prohibiting interference in fee or demesne of the prior and monks, contains a clear reference to the cemetery (*cimit[er]iu[m] cappelle sancti michaelis*).

11. VCH *Warwickshire* VIII, 18. The earl of Chester (Ranulf III) had died without issue in 1232 and after a brief period under his nephew, Hugh de Albany (d. 1243), the land passed to Montalt, the earl's steward, through marriage to Hugh's sister, Cecily. The priory may have used this period of rapid change to take local initiative.

12. The appropriation received papal recognition in 1399; VCH *Warwickshire* VIII, 346, n. 78. Hugh II had excluded the priory from the grant of tithes in the late 12th century.

13. Patrick, this volume, 23. He states that the earliest phases of occupation indicate a short-lived but substantial property, then there is evidence of its disappearance and an accumulation of a cultivation soil across the site, followed by developed plots in the late 13th century.

14. See Goddard, *Coventry 1043–1355*, 278–9. The burgesses challenged the prior's claim that they were not allowed to trade by presenting 12th-century charters from the earls of Chester granting them rights and liberties. Some doubt over the authenticity of the charters exists, but in any case the prior won and the burgesses were ordered to obey his rights.

15. For a fuller history of the intrigue and conflicts between the burgesses and the priory, see Goddard, *Coventry 1043–1355*, 278–89. The queen was granted Cheylesmore Manor under royal licence after the death of Robert Montalt's youngest son, Robert, without issue in 1329; see also VCH *Warwickshire* VIII, 18.

16. Goddard, *Coventry 1043–1355*, 283–96.

17. Goddard, *Coventry 1043–1355*, 247.

18. *Rolls of the Warwickshire and Coventry Sessions of the Peace 1377–97*, ed. E. Guernsey Kimball (Dugdale Society XVI, 1939), xxxvi.

19. J. Blair, 'Introduction: From Minster to Parish Church', in *Minsters and Parish Churches: the local church in transition 950–1200*, ed. J. Blair (Oxford 1988), 15.

20. Chatwin, *Early Coventry*, 133–7; also VCH *Warwickshire* VIII, 353.

21. Chatwin, *Early Coventry*, 136.

22. Its modern name is Holy Cross.

23. I am extremely grateful to John McNeill for drawing my attention to this parallel. For Winchester, see P. Draper and R. Morris, 'The development of the east end of Winchester Cathedral from the 13th to the 16th century', in *Winchester Cathedral: Nine Hundred Years*, ed. J. Crook (Chichester 1993), 178.

24. By about 1300 more than half of all parish churches had been appropriated to religious institutions; P. Draper, *The Formation of English Gothic: Architecture and Identity* (New Haven and London 2006), 40.

25. Sharp, *Papers*, 24; also VCH *Warwickshire* VIII, 348 and n. 12 which sources CRO.

26. George Demidowicz, pers. comm.

27. VCH *Warwickshire* VIII, 349; its sale was forbidden there in 1455.

28. Ibid., 348.

29. CRO PA 535/1. For references to expenditure of £100 and 21 years, see the 1647 version, CRO Acc. 37. The date varies between transcripts: CRO Acc. 48 (1703) says the tower was begun in 1374 by the Botoners and then they died, whilst CRO Acc. 28 (1588) says 1375 for the tower and spire.

30. Its marginal notes on the church and monarchs appear to be retrospective, added to a list of mayors in order to connect the names and dates with events in the city, either known or assumed.

31. For background to the annals and various versions, see F. Bliss Burbidge, *Old Coventry and Lady Godiva* (Birmingham, n.d., *c.* 1950), 208–12.

32. William was mayor for the fourth time in *c.* 1374 and Adam is listed as mayor in *c.* 1375; CRO Acc. 48 (1703). William and Adam are listed as holding the mayoral office in 1376 and 1377 respectively; CRO Acc. 28 (1588).

33. Burbidge, *Old Coventry*, 216. This is an extract from the Annals, a compilation of which is included in transcript form; whether the brass was 14th century is unclear and there are problems with using this to interpret the sequence of build.

34. Luxford, this volume, 247.

35. CRO Acc. 37 (1647) lists him as mayor in 1406; CRO Acc. 48 (1703) lists him as mayor in 1409.

36. He is stated, with Richard Luff, to have funded construction of the nave and the choir; see Luxford, this volume, 245–6. They also funded three cells between them.

37. C. Wilson, *Age of Chivalry: Art in Plantagenet England 1200–1400*, ed. J. Alexander and P. Binski (London 1987), 509, cat. no. 695.

38. The presence of an infilled pit or quarry to the north-west of the church is said to have caused settlement in the existing tower; see Woodhouse, *Coventry Churches*, 30–2, and Soden, this volume, 9.

39. Evidence of the castle ditch was found to the rear of the Drapers' Hall in Bayley Lane, which had caused subsidence to a 14th-century foundation, and which appeared to continue eastwards towards the east end of St Michael's; Patrick, this volume, 23–4.

40. A point confirmed by the work of John Oldrid Scott whilst restoring the tower, 1883–90; see VCH *Warwickshire* VIII, 354, and a series of newspaper cuttings in the Alfred Lowe Collection, Coventry History Centre. The stability of the tower had been questioned by G. G. Scott in 1851, and at his suggestion the bells were not rung, although in 1853 the practice was resumed; B. Poole, *Coventry: Its History and Antiquities* (London 1870), 169–70.

41. At Louth the tower appears to have been constructed outside the existing building with all the buttresses fully expressed, before being enclosed by extended aisles later; see N. Pevsner, J. Harris and N. Antram, *Lincolnshire*, B/E (2nd edn, 1989), 538–9.

42. A fragment of an arch for a window in the west wall of the south nave aisle is undated and contains no particularly distinguishing features. Its angle, height and proportion suggest that it survives from a 12th- or early 13th-century building, but this cannot be tested without archaeological excavation.

43. Harris, *Register of Guild of Holy Trinity*, 21, n. 2. Burbidge, *Old Coventry*, 216, includes a comparable reference from the Birmingham copy of the Annals (1709). He favours this copy as the dates relate to those used in the Coventry Leet Book; for his explanation of the differences, see ibid., 208–9.

44. VCH *Warwickshire* VIII, 353, for example, notes that '*a* great rebuilding took place between 1373 and the middle of the following century'.

45. Holy Trinity had undergone a reconstruction of the nave in the late 14th century, but without a clerestory, and it is likely that it paid architectural homage to its 13th-century predecessor.

46. J. H. Harvey, *English Mediaeval Architects: a Biographical Dictionary down to 1550* (2nd edn, Gloucester 1984), 275.

47. Sharp, *Papers*, 15.

48. This may refer to the door of the Drapers' Chapel. By 1436 the prior was ordered to stop building until it proved that he had a right to continue; *Leet Book* I, 185.

49. For terminology and nomenclature with regard tracery, see J. H. Harvey, *The Perpendicular Style 1330–1485* (London 1978), 70–1.

50. For which see Morris, 'Priory', this volume, 82.

51. That at Kenilworth has been identified as the earliest fully polygonal oriel; J. Goodall, pers. comm.

52. Morris, 'Cathedral Church', 32–4, 61.

53. R. K. Morris, 'The Architecture of the Earls of Warwick', in *England in the Fourteenth Century*, ed. W. M. Ormrod (Woodbridge 1986), 169–71.

54. Dugdale, *Warwickshire* (1730), 168.

55. Sharp, *Papers*,16; *Leet Book* I, 219–20.

56. It is a fine for the *opus ecclesie and opus ballivorum*; *Leet Book* I, 220.

57. *Cal. Papal Reg.*10, 202–3.

58. The inference that the chapel of St Mary was moving from a position now included in the east end of the nave to one in the east end of the choir aisle also confirms that the location of the early Lady Chapel must be contiguous with the surviving crypt of *c.* 1300.

59. L. Monckton, 'Fit for a King? The Architecture of the Beauchamp Chapel', *Architectural History* 47 (2004), 25–52.

60. *Cal. Papal Reg.*10, 202–3.

61. For example, the Whitefriars cloister (from 1353) and chapter-house (1370s); St Mary's Guildhall, undercroft and treasury (late 14th century); Richard K. Morris, pers. comm.

62. The guilds had informally merged between 1364 and 1369, receiving official confirmation in 1392; Harris ed., *Guild Register*, xiv. For new priests and ornaments, see VCH *Warwickshire* VIII, 348, quoting Sharp, *Papers*, 24–5.

63. Harris ed., *Guild Register*, 15, 32, 45, 58, 73, 76, 84, 102, 103, 104, 108, 109 and 110.

64. Sharp, *Papers*, 32. The earliest reference in the accounts of the Smith's Company, responsible for St Andrew's chapel is dated 1449 and refers to a table for the priest and the priest's salary.

65. *Leet Book* I, 262–6.

66. A door (now blocked) in the east wall of the south porch may indicate an earlier structure on the site of the 15th-century Cappers' chapel; Richard K. Morris, pers. comm.

67. Sharp, *Papers*, 32: a reference to the salary of their priest for a whole year is mentioned at this time.

68. See Sharp, *Papers*, 29, which refers to the accounts of the Trinity Guild (36 H 6): in 1458 there is a charge for a 'candel both for the capell'montis and s'ci Thome in St Michael's church'. St Thomas is the dedication for the Cappers' chapel to the east of the south porch; although Sharp's entry on the Cappers' chapel itself refers to the MS Annals, citing a foundation date of 1467.

69. For example, the tracery of the south-east chancel aisle is tentatively datable on stylistic grounds to the late 15th century.

70. *Leet Book* I, 446–7.

71. *Leet Book* I, 459–61.

72. Unpublished lecture on St Mary's Nottingham by the author, University of Nottingham, 24 March 2006.

73. Even on a small scale the signature features of lozenge piers, paired windows and recessed clerestories make appearances throughout the region, for example in the parish churches of Nuneaton, Southam, Brinklow and the collegiate church of Stratford-upon-Avon.

74. L. Monckton, 'The myth of William Canynges and the late medieval rebuilding of St Mary Redcliffe', in '*Almost the Richest City': Bristol in the Middle Ages*, ed. Laurence Keen, *BAA Trans.* XIX (Leeds 1997), 57–67. Redcliffe also influenced the design of the Beauchamp Chapel at St Mary's, Warwick; see Monckton, 'Fit for a King?', 25–52.

75. C. Wilson, *The Gothic Cathedral: the Architecture of the Great Church 1130–1530* (London 1990), 216–17.

76. E. Carus-Wilson, 'The overseas trade of late medieval Coventry', in *Economies et sociétés au moyen age*, ed. E. Perroy (Paris 1975), 374–6.

77. See Gilderdale Scott, this volume, 225–7.

78. A lozenge pier is longer in plan on one axis, usually the north–south one, and therefore it is symmetrical along one axis rather than both. It is believed to have been invented to create a slender elevation for the nave arcade and increase the visibility of the aisles.

79. See Woodfield, *Whitefriars*, 85–6, 134.

80. See further Gill, this volume, 209–10.

81. For the longevity of influence of these seminal buildings, see most recently L. Monckton, 'Regional Architecture or National Monument? The Architecture of Prince Arthur's Chantry Chapel', in *Arthur Tudor, Prince of Wales: Life, Death and Commemoration*, ed. S. Gunn and L. Monckton (Woodbridge 2009), 133–4.

82. Cited in D. J. H. Smith ed., *Coventry through the Ages* (Coventry 1969), 15.

The Development of St Mary's Hall, Coventry: A Short History

GEORGE DEMIDOWICZ

This paper is based upon a report submitted to the Heritage Lottery Fund for a scheme to reveal the hidden medieval kitchen within St Mary's Hall. As a result of the research which was conducted to help inform the proposals, a new interpretation of the development of hall and its associated buildings emerged. The assembly of the site on which the hall was built in the mid-14th century is presented in detail for the first time. The traditional view of two main phases of construction (mid-14th century and late 14th/early 15th century) has been upheld, but the sequence of actual building events has been radically revised and the later phase extended. It is suggested, for example, that the entrance to the main hall was moved from the west side to the east, associated with a new gateway. As a result, part of the relatively new kitchen was absorbed to provide the approach stairs and landing.

INTRODUCTION

ST MARY'S HALL is one of the most important medieval guildhalls in the country, but considering its size and status it is surprisingly little known. Anthony Emery is one of the few to give it due regard, describing it as 'the finest medieval building of its type mother church status and presence of burial ground is clearin Britain'.[1] St Mary's Hall is more accurately defined as a suite or complex of rooms, of which the hall and its undercroft below, orientated north to south, form the core (Figs 1, 2). A covered gateway and internal courtyard immediately to the east of the hall form an important part of the plan. Most of the building is constructed of local red and grey sandstone, but there are substantial timber-framed elements.

The classic medieval hall plan can be discerned in the main hall today, with an upper (dais) end at the north and a lower end at the south, separated by a screens passage (the modern screen being a steel and curtained structure). Three doors off the south side of the screen passage lead to the Old Council Chamber, kitchen and Prince's Chamber, but the origin of these doorways must lie in the buttery, kitchen and pantry of the domestic medieval hall (Figs 1–3).

Although much has been written previously on the myriad of aspects of its history, relatively little has concentrated on the physical development of St Mary's Hall in order to explain its present form.[2] Over the last fifteen years, however, it has been the subject of new research with the analysis of the surviving fabric and documentary research, particularly into medieval deeds, proving the most useful. The research was helped by the detailed and systematic listing and re-ordering of the borough archive that has been undertaken by the City Record Office (now the Coventry History Centre).

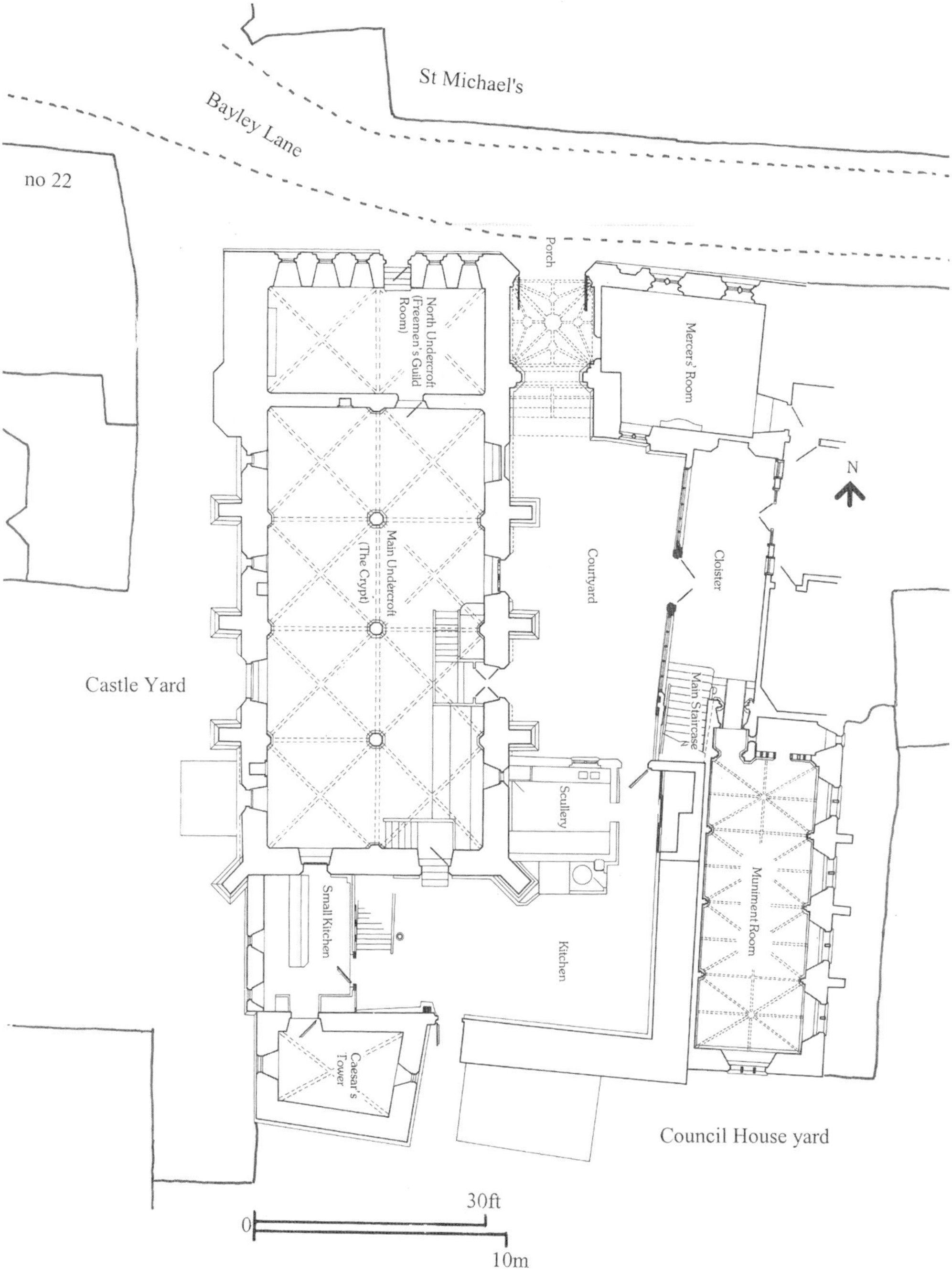

FIG. 1. Coventry, St Mary's Hall: ground-floor plan today
Coventry City Council

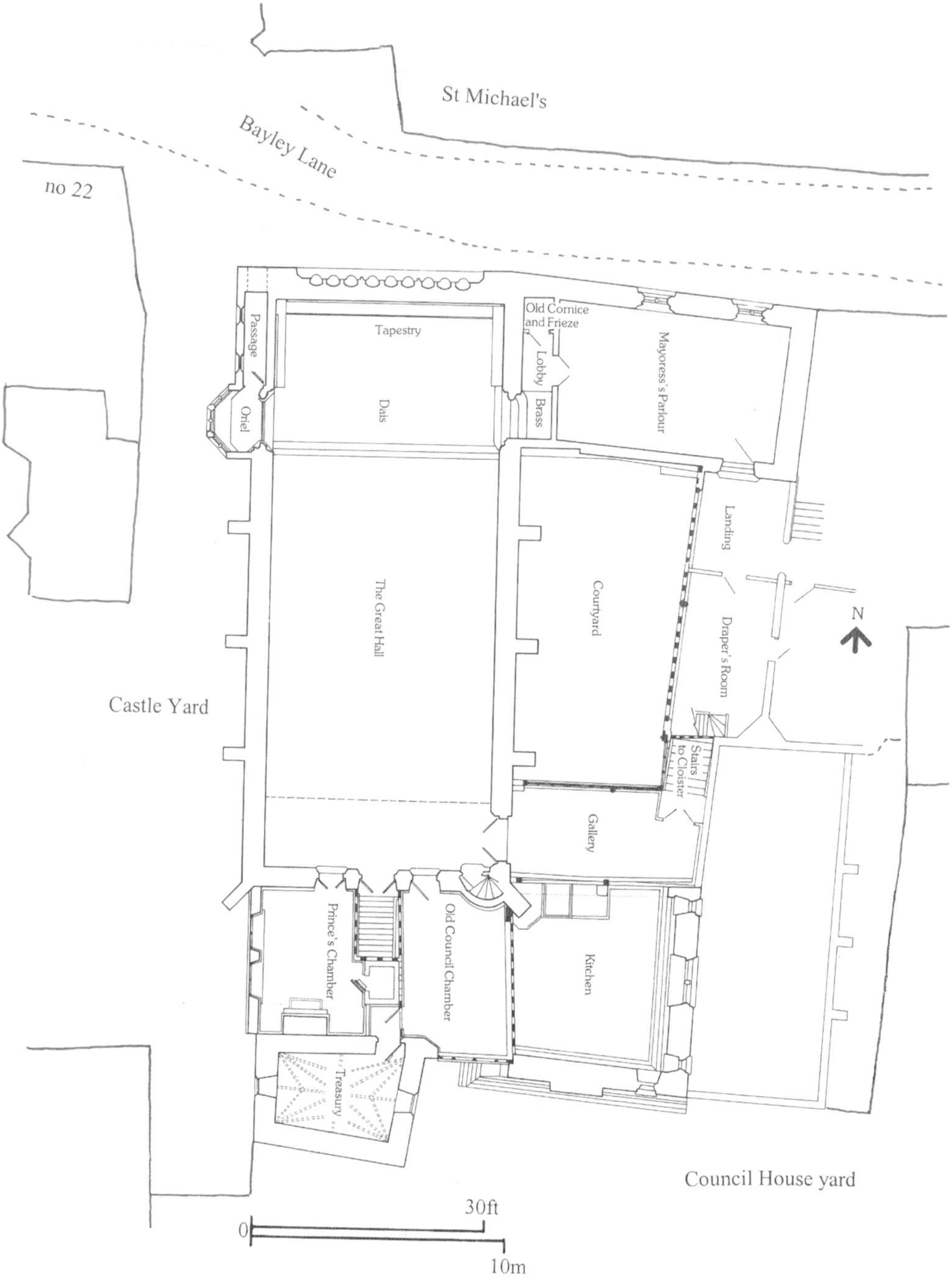

FIG. 2. Coventry, St Mary's Hall: first-floor plan today
Coventry City Council

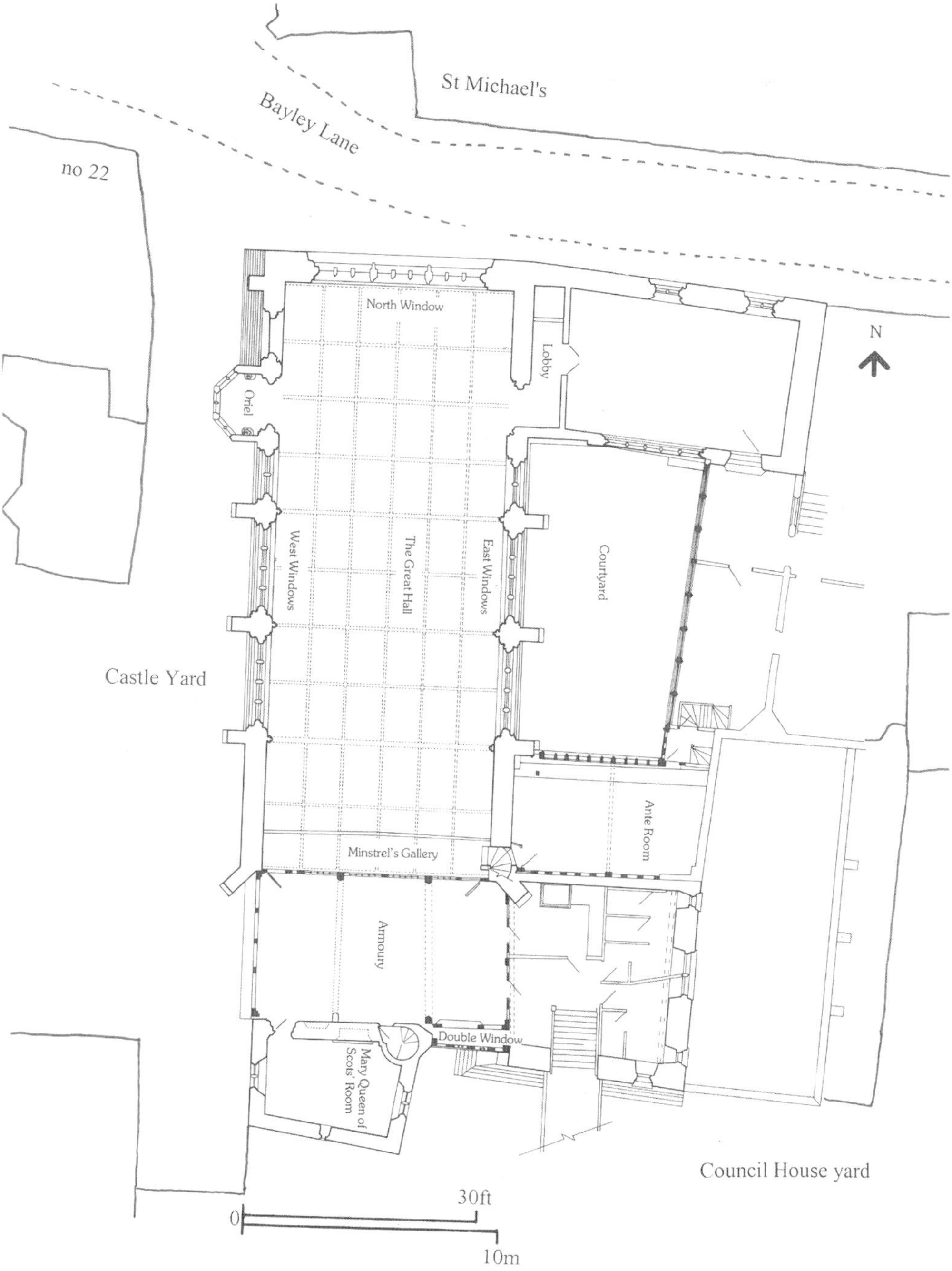

FIG. 3. Coventry, St Mary's Hall: second-floor plan today
Coventry City Council

ACQUIRING THE SITE (Fig. 4)

DEEDS and other documents have survived for the land transactions that took place before the hall was built. The earliest event, known indirectly, is the recital in an agreement of 1350 that Guy de Tylebrook, 'lately' vicar of St Michael's (1279–93), created a charge on land on the south side of Bayley Lane to support a lamp at the high altar in St Michael's.[3] This obligation passed, over half a century later, to St Mary's Guild as owners of the new hall on the site of the vicar's land. In 1350 Henry le Fleuter and his wife exonerated the guild from paying for the lamp, substituting their own land for its upkeep. According to another recital in a deed of 1341, Guy de Tillebrok sold a tenement 'towards St Michael's' to William Colle, which then passed to William's son, Henry Colle.[4] In 1336 the latter leased five cottages on the southern side of the street opposite St Michael's to John de Scarnyng.[5] The footprint of these cottages is now represented by the surviving small north undercroft that was originally reached by a door directly from Bayley Lane. In 1340 Henry Colle sold the cottages and some land at the rear, the latter presumably corresponding with the site of the first main hall, to Thomas de Keteryng, a merchant.[6] Thomas may have acquired the land on behalf of the new guild, but it is not certain. In 1341 Thomas de Keteryng granted the property to Jordan de Shepeie (Shepey) and Henry de Dodenhale, who were likely to have been prominent members of the newly founded guild of St Mary, for which letters patent had been granted on 20 May 1340.[7] Between 1342 and 1348 some additional land, a 'toft', was acquired by Shepeie and Dodenhale from Henry Ballard at the south end of the site, as it originally belonged to an Earl Street tenement.[8] This may coincide with the present Caesar's Tower or even the lower end of the hall.

For a short while Henry Colle had kept two messuages immediately to the east of the future guildhall site, but sold them in 1343.[9] On 14 April 1347 they were resold to feoffees of the guild, the west abuttal being described as 'Shepeie's and Dodenhale's tenement having become the site of St Mary's Hall'.[10] The day before, Henry de Dodenhale had conveyed to the same feoffees 'a newly-built messuage opposite St Michael's called Seynte Marie Halle', along with other property with which it had been endowed.[11] The first of many phases in the development history of the hall was complete.

Steve Bassett has suggested that a chapel known as *capella super montem* stood on or near the St Mary's Hall site. He chose this site based on topography, being 'where the highest ground in Coventry is to be found'.[12] There is no documentary evidence, however, that a chapel formed part of the guildhall complex and, since all or part of *capella super montem* was still in use in the 15th and 16th centuries, a location for it elsewhere must be sought. In view of the fact the *capella* lay within the graveyard of St Michael's, the author has proposed that it was eventually incorporated into the enlarged St Michael's church and that the surviving crypt under the north aisle originally supported it.[13]

PHASE I (Fig. 5)

THE first hall was built in the early 1340s and was likely to have been timber-framed. Deeds of the 1330s and 1340s tell us that there were five cottages on the Bayley Lane frontage facing St Michael (see above), and buildings on this frontage survived into the 1390s, hiding the hall from the street. In 1352 they were described as a tenement and shops when the guild granted a rent from them to Margaret, wife of Henry Colle,

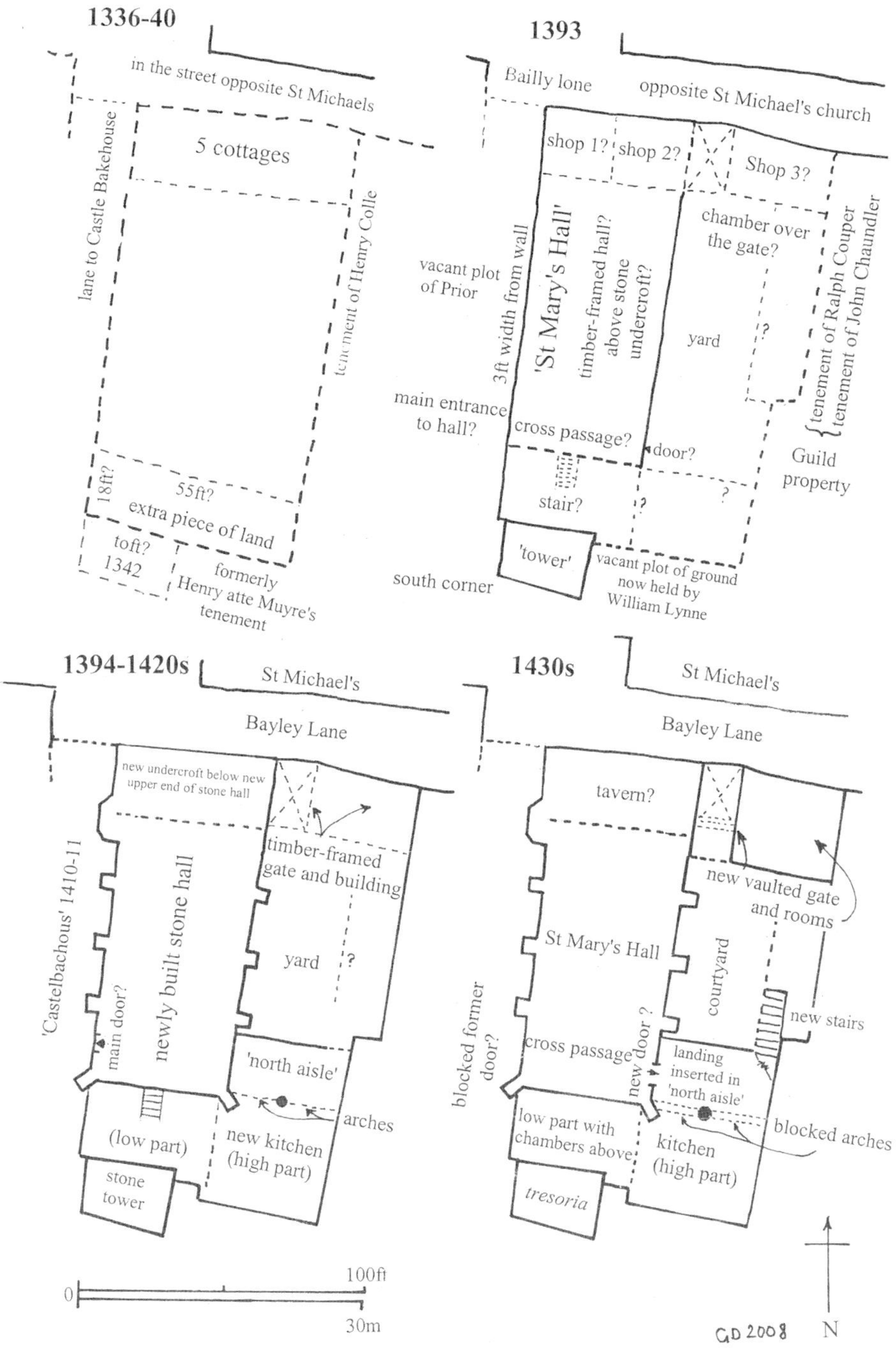

FIG. 4. Coventry, St Mary's Hall: diagrammatic plans of its development, 1336–1430s
Drawing, author

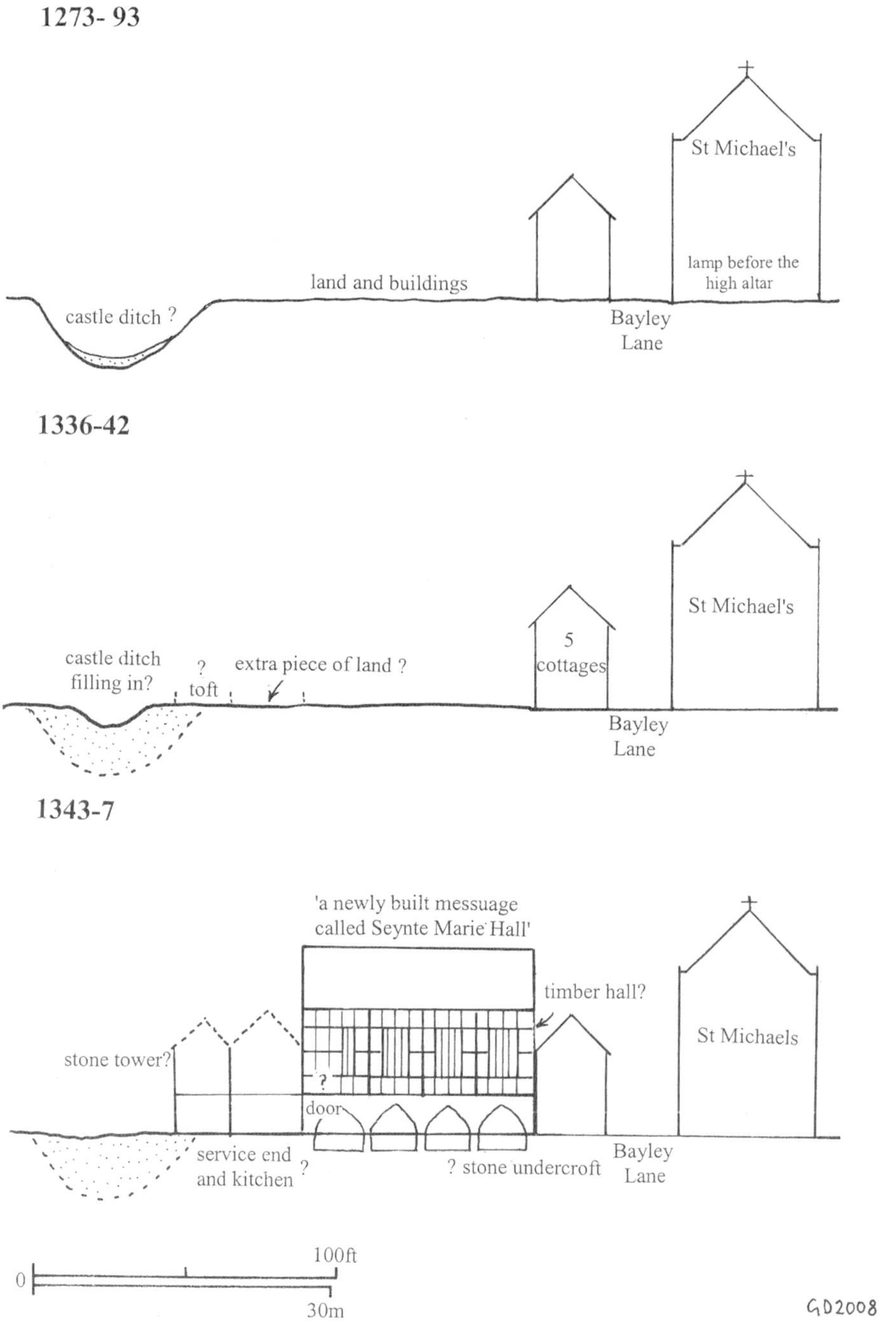

FIG. 5. Coventry, St Mary's Hall: diagrammatic sections of the development of the site, 1273–1347 (viewed from the east)

Drawing, author

perhaps in gratitude for the role her husband had played in assembling the land for the hall. Joan Lancaster has suggested that this hall was built over the present main undercroft and was contemporary with it, her main evidence being the misalignment between the responds of the undercroft vault and the later buttresses dividing the hall bays above.[14] Moreover, the buttresses themselves are not coursed into the undercroft walls. It is also worth noting that the tops of window arches (formerly access doors) in the undercroft facing the courtyard have been curiously truncated by the stone course immediately above. This truncation may have been caused by the laying of the first course of the replacement hall in stone. Alternatively, Richard Morris has proposed that all of the stone part of the main hall and the two undercrofts below represent one design and construction in the late 14th century (Phase 2 below).[15] However, though the wall dividing the undercrofts is certainly thin in relation to the outer walls, suggesting an internal partition, it may have been constructed as an external end wall against the cottages or shops that fronted the street. Moreover, the vaulting of the main undercroft springs from responds and is different to that of the smaller undercroft (that replaced the street-side buildings), which springs from corbels. It seems unlikely that two vaulting schemes would be adopted if the hall and undercrofts were constructed in a single phase.

Another complication in reconstructing this first phase is that it remains uncertain whether there was a yard on the east side of the hall, where one exists today. The two messuages immediately to the east of the new hall that were granted to the guild in the 1340s (see above) may have provided some space. Assuming that a cross-passage formed part of the hall, however, then it would have been possible to enter from either the east or west side, the latter corresponding to the 'Castle Bakehouse' plot, owned originally by St Mary's Priory (Fig. 4, top left). In 1393 a 3ft wide passageway within this plot was reserved by the guild immediately against the west side of the building (Fig. 4, top right).[16] This may have been necessary for both access and maintenance. Internal vertical joints visible today in the west wall of the cross passage may indicate the presence of a doorway in use as late as Phase 2. This could have been reached by an external staircase occupying the 3ft width of the reserved strip (the way-leave), but probably needing more space than that.

PHASE 2 (Fig. 6)

THIS was a prolonged phase beginning about 1392, rebuilding the hall completely and probably continued into the early 1430s. Later in the phase it also involved modifications to the kitchen to provide a new entrance into the reconstructed hall. The City Annals traditionally record completion in 1414, but this date may only apply to the main hall itself. In 1392 the amalgamation of the four guilds, including St Mary's, to form the Trinity Guild was accompanied by a major phase of reconstruction to reflect the power and prestige of the newly reorganised town oligarchy. In 1393 three shops still lined the street frontage, but there was also a gate with a chamber over.[17] It is not known whether this gate was in the position of the present structure, or east of it, but it possibly formed an integral part of the timber-framed shops. The first hall was demolished and replaced with the present stone structure, either erected over an existing undercroft or over an entirely new one. Integral to this major reconstruction was the removal of the street frontage shops so that the hall could also be lengthened to reach the street and create the new upper end. An undercroft (the present Coventry Freemen's Room) was built under the extension with access originally from the street

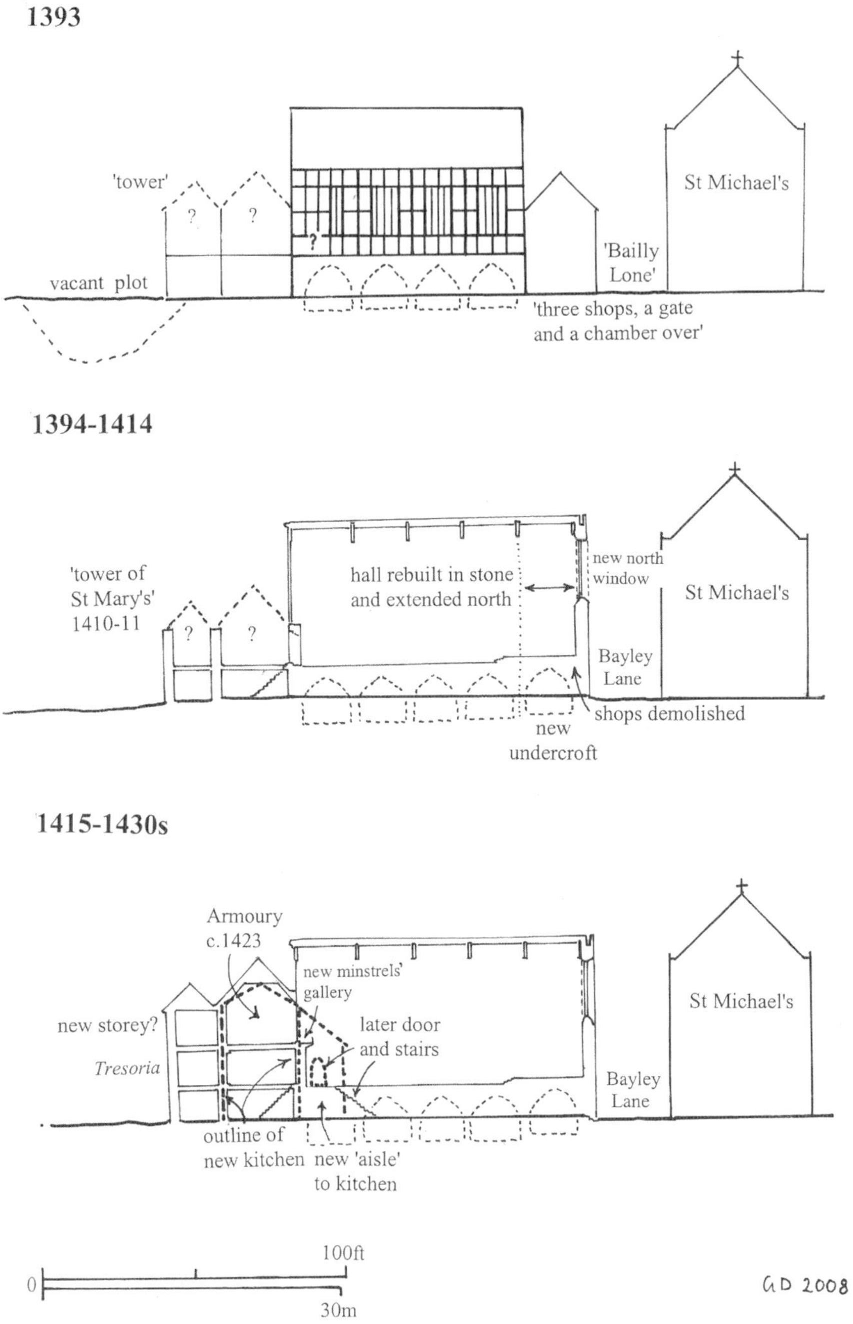

FIG. 6. Coventry, St Mary's Hall: diagrammatic sections of its development, 1393–1430s (viewed from the east)

Drawing, author

only. This undercroft was used as a tavern in the 15th century, maintaining a tradition of trading on the street frontage (Fig. 4, bottom right).[18]

At the south (lower) end of the hall three existing doors off the cross-passage have been interpreted as leading to a buttery, pantry and kitchen. The stone wall through which they are pierced is only about 3m (10ft) high and supports the minstrels' gallery. The buttery and pantry were constructed behind this wall in this phase, partly in timber-frame and partly in stone, although the general arrangement may have been earlier. The two outer doors now lead to the Old Council Chamber and Prince's Chamber respectively. The incorporation of the wall of Caesar's Tower into the Prince's Chamber strongly suggests that the tower was already in existence to this level at this time. Given that an angled external buttress supporting the south-east corner of the stone hall is visible inside the present kitchen, it follows that the latter was constructed after the new hall. Furthermore the roof of the kitchen is supported by this same buttress. Other structural evidence suggests that the kitchen may have been built as late as the 1420s (see below).

The relative tightness of the whole site, combined with a first-floor hall, meant that any kitchen needed to be reached by stairs descending to the ground floor. The buttery and pantry on the first floor prevented the main working part of the kitchen (the fireplaces) from being located immediately below them. Kitchens in manor houses were often built beyond the buttery and pantry, but here there was no space to expand further south due to the location of Caesar's Tower (see below), the surviving castle ditch and the rear of properties on Earl Street. The cooking area needed to be connected to either the east side or west side of the area below the two chambers. The west side was in the ownership of St Mary's Priory (Castle Bakehouse Yard), leaving only the area to the east to form the kitchen. It is not known whether there had been a smaller, earlier kitchen here, perhaps with a centrally placed fireplace. In the 14th century it became common to build fireplaces within the thickness of the wall, as in the present kitchen.

The full-height part of the kitchen (the 'high' kitchen), surmounted by its original coffered roof, is roughly square in shape with a pair of fireplaces in both the east and south walls (Fig. 7). A distinctive feature on the north wall is an arcade of two stone arches, now mostly blocked by a timber-framed partition that does not quite reach the floor. It is likely that these two arches originally led into a tall space with a mono-pitch roof similar to the aisle of a medieval church (Fig.4, bottom left). This would have formed a useful additional room on the north side of the kitchen. The west wall of the main kitchen consists of a suspended timber frame that forms the east wall of the Council Chamber at hall level and of the Armoury on the floor above, as well as an area of wall above the Armoury roof. It is not clear how much of this existed before the kitchen was built, but all was necessary to finish this side of the kitchen.

The north side of the 'low' kitchen aligns with the stone undercroft below the hall. Two doorways, one now blocked, connected the kitchen to the undercroft at the lower level via short flights of steps. The reason for two doors of the same size is unknown. Whatever the original arrangement, the undercroft provided convenient and spacious storage for food and drink for the kitchen and the services.

It is not known whether the buttery and pantry of this phase (later converted to the Old Council Chamber and the Prince's Chamber) supported a storey above in the position of the Armoury, as in the present arrangement. The timber-framed east wall of these two storeys forms the west wall of the 'high' kitchen. The low part of the

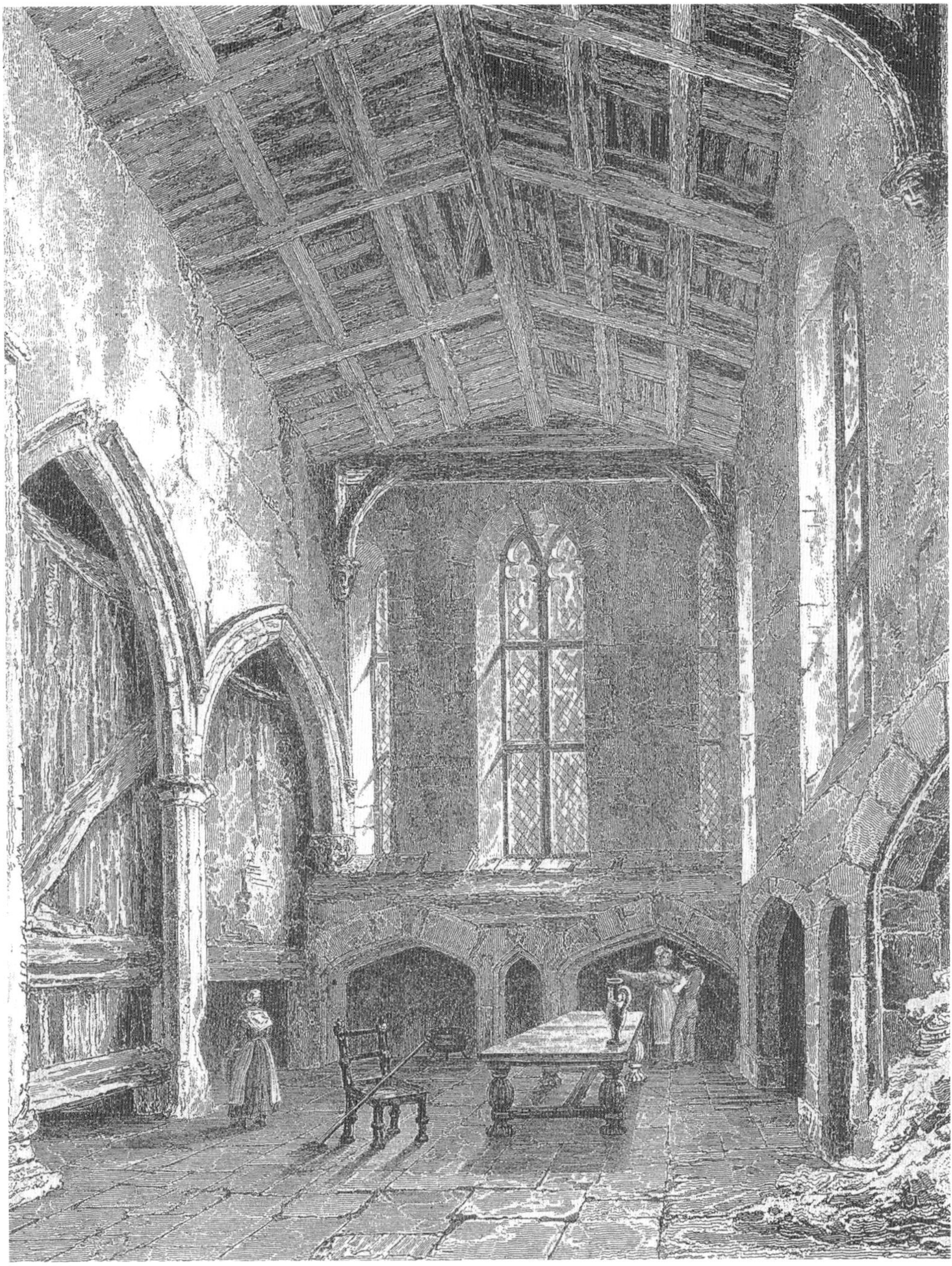

FIG. 7. Coventry, St Mary's Hall: kitchen interior looking east: engraving, Benjamin Sharp, *Coventry: Its History and Antiquities* (1870)

kitchen runs under the Old Council Chamber and Prince's Chamber, with the staircase, descending from the hall above, inserted between the chambers. The 'high' kitchen could not have been completed without the Armoury on the second floor, although an earlier kitchen may have been a lower structure. Dendrochronology has dated the Armoury to the late 1420s, which suggests that this was one of the last projects in the rebuilding of the guildhall.[19] The timber-framed north wall of the Armoury also acts as the south wall of the main hall, although the latter soars above the Armoury roof and allows light through a window into the hall (Fig. 8). It is not known how much of this timber-framed wall was constructed or 'borrowed' as part of the Armoury phase. The main timber posts and trusses of the Armoury seem to belong to a structure separate to that of the late 14th-century buttery and pantry below.

Caesar's Tower, a three-storey stone structure, is attached to the south part of the 'low' kitchen. Its original function has been the subject of much speculation.[20] Some have suggested that it formed the tower of the 12th-century castle, surviving to be

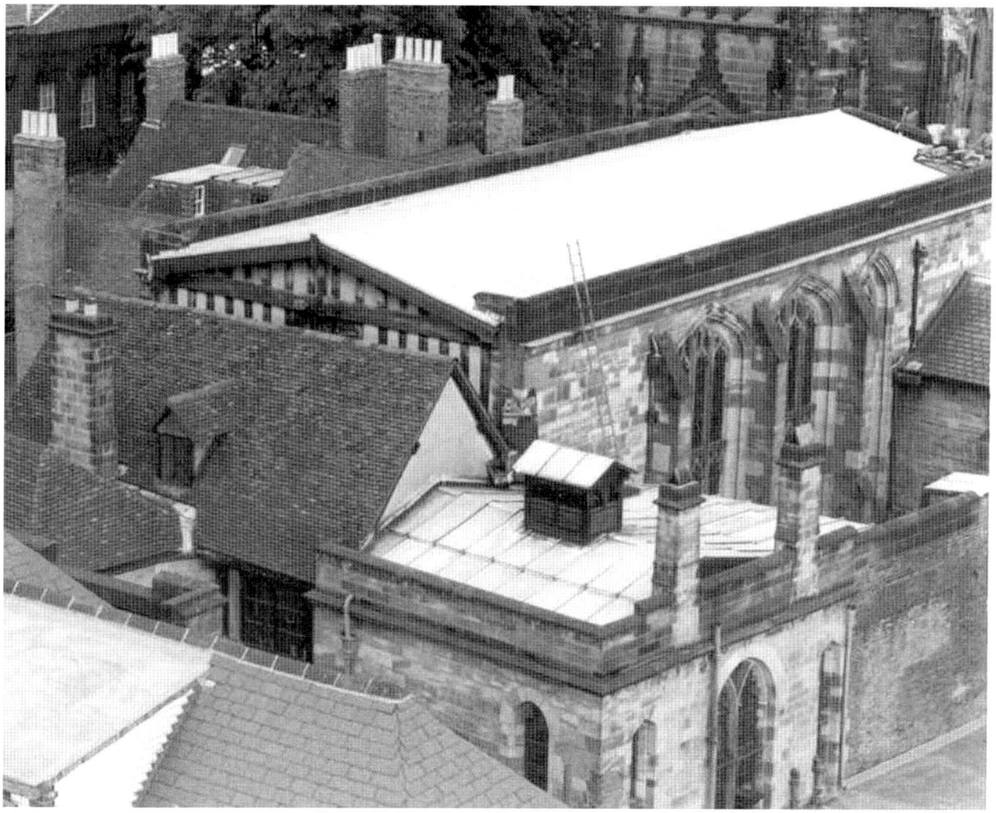

FIG. 8. Coventry, St Mary's Hall: exterior from clock tower of Council House, looking north-west. The low-pitched roof of the main hall overlooks the steeply pitched roof of the Armoury, which in turn overlooks the leaded kitchen roof with its surviving medieval roof vent (foreground); two of the kitchen chimneys are now missing

Photo, Coventry City Council

incorporated into the guildhall two centuries later. This view has been influenced by the presence of the castle bakehouse plot and castle ditch immediately to the west and south respectively. Unfortunately, there is no documentary evidence of a tower in this location before 1393, despite numerous earlier deeds.[21] The name Caesar's Tower is first recorded in the 17th century and 'Caesar' is probably a corruption or misreading of treasury (*tresoria*), for its middle storey was certainly used for this purpose in the 15th century (*tres'hows*, 1466).[22] A stone tower would certainly have been of practical use as a secure store for valuable documents, guild treasures and plate. The lowest storey connects to the 'low' kitchen, and would also form a convenient store. The middle storey is only accessible from the Old Council Chamber, although the Prince's Chamber is also built against it (Fig. 2). There is also a second-storey room (the topmost, now 'Mary Queen of Scots' Room', (Fig. 3) reached from the Armoury and, if the tower was originally of this height, then there must have been some means of access to this room before the Armoury was constructed. A third storey, reached from another door in the Armoury via a spiral staircase (now blocked), has long been demolished. Unfortunately, the tower was almost brought to the ground in the Blitz and, having been rebuilt, much evidence has been lost. Given that Caesar's Tower was already in existence in some form by 1393, it is difficult to judge whether it was constructed very early in Phase 2 (*c.* 1392) or as part of Phase 1 (early 1340s). If the latter were the case, then it would need to have been connected to the main hall in some way.

The present vaulted gate, together with the new east stair into the hall, was probably built towards the end of the Phase 2 period (*c.* 1392–early 1430s). Emery suggested that both the new hall and the stairs were inspired by John of Gaunt's great hall at Kenilworth Castle built in the 1370s.[23] If this were the case, then the construction of the kitchen and its aisle after the hall and before the stairs compromised the realisation of any master plan following the Kenilworth model. In such a tight urban site as St Mary's, such aspirations were tempered by the availability of space. It appears that the stairs were only moved from the west to the east side of the hall when the land was acquired and a new gatehouse constructed. The consequence was an awkward intrusion into the new kitchen aisle.

With regard to the new gate, Richard Morris dated it stylistically to the last decade of the 14th century,[24] but it is clear from the junction visible in the fabric on the external elevation that the hall and gate were built separately, the latter providing a fitting new entrance into a courtyard, sometime after the north end of the hall was constructed (Fig. 9, left). As late as 1410–11 it appears that the earlier gate recorded in 1393 was still standing, as a Trinity Guild tenant occupied a tenement with a 'gateway above the entrance to St Mary's Hall'. [25] The gate and adjoining rooms, now the Mayoress's Parlour (first floor) and Mercers' Room (ground floor), seem to be of one build, expensively executed in stone and unlikely to have been simply let out to tenants. The rear yard was already in existence by 1393, but its extent is not known. It would eventually provide access to the new kitchen and to the undercroft below the hall by replacing the latter's small windows with doorways (now re-formed into windows). A door, perhaps close to the present one, led into the north aisle of the kitchen.

The decision to demolish the gate and replace it with the present lierne-vaulted structure and stone-built apartments must have reflected a need to enhance the entrance into the hall, inhibited by access via the Castle Bakehouse plot, a domestic property.[26]

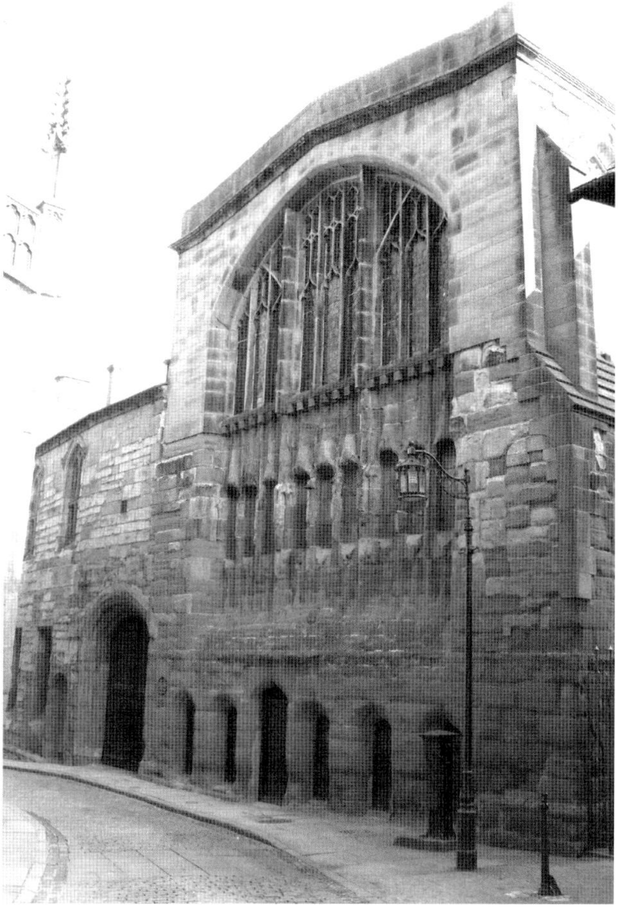

FIG. 9. Coventry, St Mary's Hall: north elevation to Bayley Lane
Photo, Coventry City Council

Therefore the construction of the new gate and the alteration of the kitchen to accommodate a new way into the hall from the east appear to be of the same phase. It is not known, however, how long the north 'aisle' of the kitchen was used for its original purpose before its upper part was appropriated for the new entrance. It is possible that the 'aisle' was given up only a few years after having been constructed perhaps in the late 1420s.

The arches into the 'high' kitchen were blocked with timber framing, a floor inserted and a staircase raised onto this 'gallery' level. An opening was broken into the hall through the stone wall on the east side of the cross-passage. The doorway here gives every impression of being secondary. The lowermost part of the 'aisle' was, however, left within the kitchen. The gallery was lit by unglazed windows overlooking the courtyard.[27] The opposite wall contains the arches into the kitchen, with infill timber-framing, and is now covered by a 17th-century tapestry. The present stair structure is medieval, but now enclosed; originally the space at the bottom of the stairs was open to the courtyard (Fig. 10).

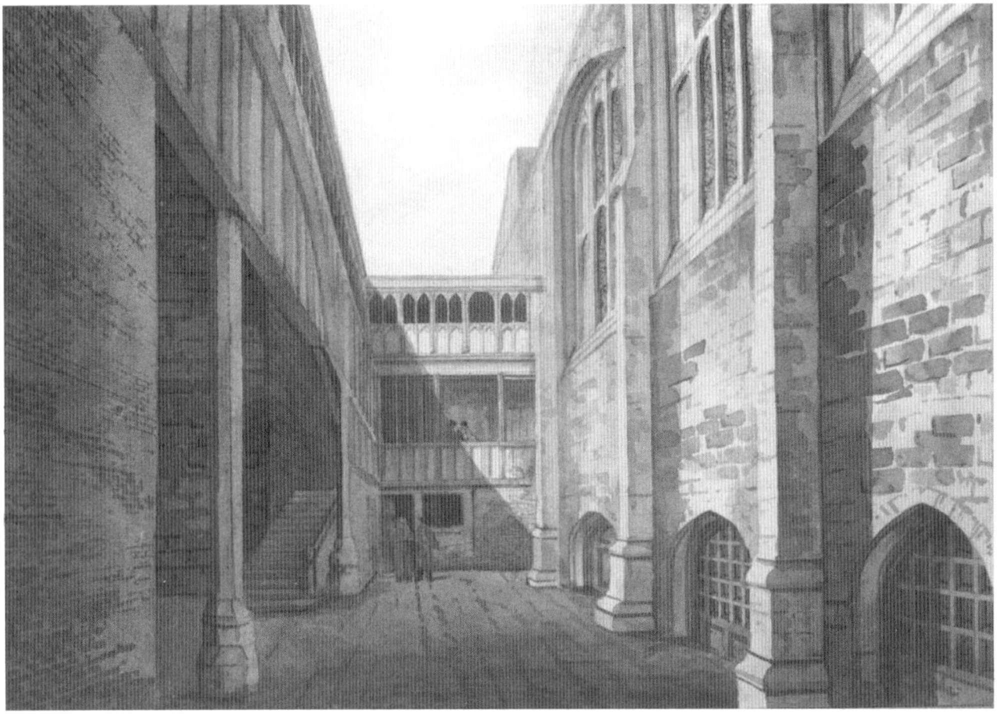

FIG. 10. Coventry, St Mary's Hall: the courtyard before alterations: watercolour, anonymous, *c.* 1800, Aylesford Collection, Birmingham Central Library

Courtesy of Birmingham Central Library

LATER MEDIEVAL PHASES AFTER 1450

THE tapestry that hangs on the north wall of the hall is a remarkable piece of work that has remained in the same place for half a millennium. Commissioned in about 1500 and made in Tournai, judging by its style, it is generally assumed to depict King Henry VI and his queen, Margaret of Anjou and their court, worshipping an image of the Virgin Mary (Fig. 11 and Col. Pl. IXB in print edn). One traditional view is that this necessitated the infilling of the lower part of the north window, but the evidence of the external fabric does not support this (Fig. 9).[28] There was, in fact, an earlier tapestry of Arras cloth hanging in 1441 and the window may have been designed to accommodate such a backdrop from the beginning.[29] Recent work on the glass of the north window has concluded that it was installed between *c.* 1420 and 1422 to celebrate the achievements of Henry V and the house of Lancaster, and was probably the work of John Thornton, the famous glass painter from Coventry and designer of the great east window at York Minster.[30]

The absorption of the kitchen 'aisle' into the new entrance also allowed the pitched roof of this structure to be removed and the space converted into a second-storey room, the original purpose of which is unknown. The ante-room, as it is now called, is reached awkwardly from the spiral staircase that connects the screens passage to the Armoury (Fig. 3). It is a timber-framed structure jettied out over the gallery entrance to

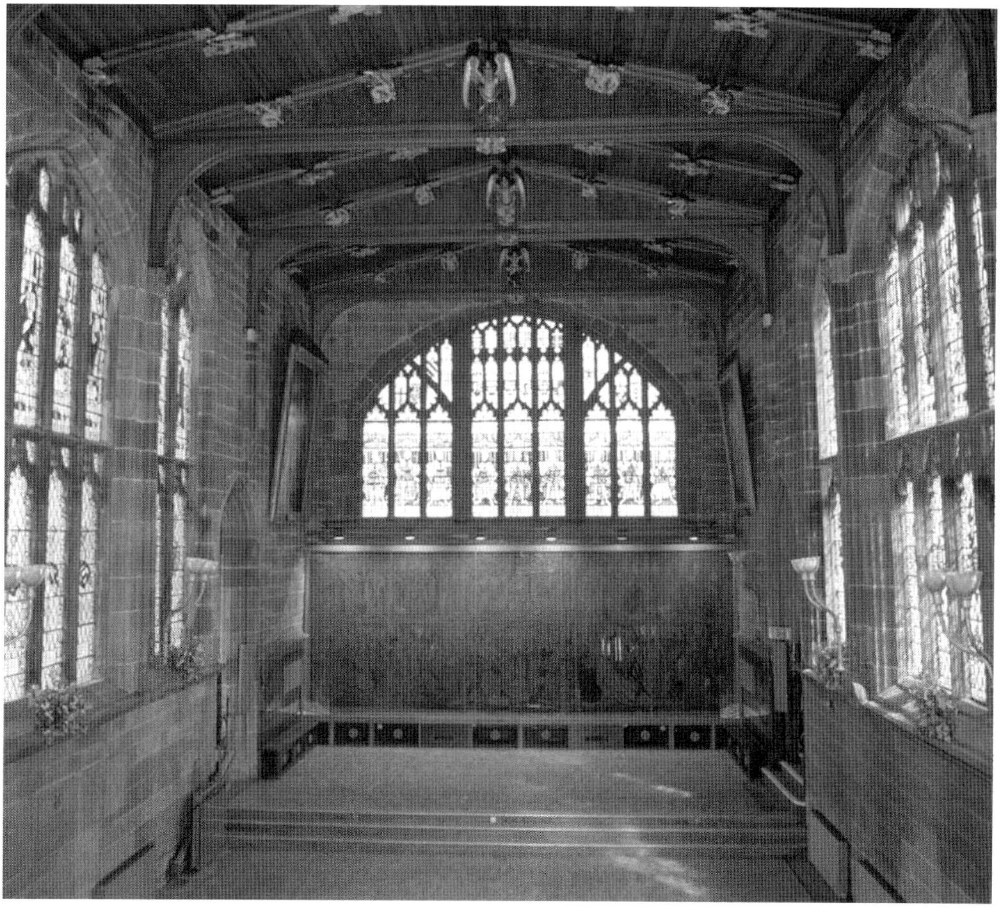

FIG. 11. Coventry, St Mary's Hall: interior of the hall looking north to the tapestry
Courtesy of Coventry City Council, St Mary's Guildhall

the hall. Its south wall is composed of the upper part of the blocking to the kitchen arches.

Therefore, by about 1500 the guildhall had reached its present form, but was only to function in this capacity for another half century.

FROM DISSOLUTION TO THE PRESENT DAY

ONLY a few of the more important changes can be mentioned that took place in the centuries that followed the dissolution of the Trinity Guild in 1547. In 1826 a major restoration took place under the direction of Stedman Whitwell. The most obvious change was to enclose the space open to the courtyard (Fig. 10) at the bottom of the main stairs. Timber frame was used in the same style found elsewhere in the building to create a vestibule, now called the Cloister (Fig. 1). In 1894 a four-bay, stone-vaulted Muniment Room was built, attached to the east wall of the kitchen to contain the city records, which had formerly been stored in Caesar's Tower and the Old Council Chamber.

The most drastic changes came as a result of the Second World War. Caesar's Tower was reduced to rubble in 1940 and incendiaries severely burnt the roof of the hall. After the war, all the surviving medieval roof structure and panelling was removed and replaced with new timber. Fortunately, the highly decorative roof bosses were stored safely away from the building during the war and were returned to their original positions.

A scheme to build a bridge from the Council House to St Mary's Hall was completed in 1956, partly funded by war damage compensation. An additional floor was inserted in the upper part of the kitchen, on which toilets and a small kitchen were located. The medieval roof close above was obscured by a new ceiling. In the late 1990s, plans were developed to reverse this scheme so that the medieval kitchen could be revealed as a single space once more, but unfortunately these have been shelved due to the drastic downturn in the economy in late 2008. This would have entailed the clearing out the modern kitchen equipment and the opening up to view the four medieval fireplaces. The inserted floor was to be removed with the ceiling above and a simple, modestly sized gallery constructed in the upper part of the kitchen to maintain the link to the bridge.[31]

SUMMARY OF PHASES 1 AND 2

THE author's research has revealed new evidence for the physical development and phasing of St Mary's Guildhall in the late medieval period. The traditional Phase 1 (early 1340s) has been confirmed, in which the hall was first built, supporting the view that a first-floor, timber-framed hall was erected on a stone undercroft. The hall did not extend to Bayley Lane, as it does today, because earlier buildings that fronted the street were preserved for a half-century more. The main entrance to the hall at this time was probably from the west side by way of the Castle Bakehouse yard. It is not clear whether there was a gate or yard on the east side until 1393. The castle origins of Caesar's Tower have been discounted, proposing that it was built as a treasury, but that its date of construction is uncertain.

Phase 2, which began in *c.* 1392 with the formation of the new Trinity Guild and prompted the rebuilding of the main hall in stone, has been extended beyond its traditional completion in 1414, with work carrying on perhaps into the early 1430s. The new hall included an extra bay northwards at its upper end, over the site of the frontage buildings which were demolished. A new undercroft was constructed below the extension with direct access from the street. At the opposite (service) end of the hall, only the lower part of the wall was constructed in stone, with three doorways. It is assumed that the two outer doors led to the buttery and pantry, suspended over a squat room (the later 'low' kitchen) which was intermediate in level between the hall and undercroft below. The central doorway led into this space but the position of an early kitchen is unknown, if it existed at all. Once the hall and its service-end rooms were finished, construction probably began in the mid- to late 1420s on the 'high' kitchen with an arcaded aisle, all in stone, and of the timber-framed room above the pantry and kitchen, now known as the Armoury. Finally, perhaps in the early 1430s, a new stone gate and apartments were constructed, which allowed the entrance to the main hall to be switched from the west side to the east, using part of the relatively new kitchen aisle.

ACKNOWLEDGEMENTS

I should like to thank Richard K. Morris for many useful discussions, all of which have helped remove inconsistencies and errors; any that remain are my responsibility.

NOTES

1. A. Emery, *Greater Medieval Houses of England and Wales 1300–1500* II (Cambridge 2000), 372.
2. Morris, 'St. Mary's Hall', 1–17; Lancaster, *St. Mary's Hall;* VCH *Warwickshire* VIII, 141–3; Emery, *Greater Medieval Houses* II, 372–4.
3. CA BA/B/16/137/12; PERSONS/20/739.
4. CA BA/B/16/14/18.
5. CA BA/H/8/350/1.
6. CA BA/H/8/350/4–5.
7. CA BA/H/350/6; Jordan de Shepeie, a wool merchant, was Coventry's second mayor in 1347, CA PERSONS/19/423. He was also a member of St Mary's Guild; Harris ed., *Guild Register*, 15. Henry de Dodenhale was a member of the first municipal council established under the 1345 charter and master of St Mary's Guild in 1351, CA PERSONS/4/482; Letters Patent, BA/B/16/2/1.
8. CA BA/B/16/15/2; BA/B/16/143/2.
9. CA BA/B/16/14/21.
10. CA BA/B/16/14/22.
11. CA BA/B/16/14/1.
12. Bassett, *Anglo-Saxon Coventry*, 12, n. 45, fig. 1.
13. See further Monckton, this volume, 139–43.
14. Lancaster, *St. Mary's Hall*, 5.
15. Morris, 'St Mary's Hall', 22.
16. CA BA/B/16/14/5.
17. Ibid.
18. Sharp, *Papers*, 213.
19. I. Tyers, 'Tree-Ring Analysis of Oak Timbers from St Mary's Guildhall, Coventry, West Midlands', Sheffield Dendrochronology Laboratory, Ancient Monuments Laboratory Report 12/95 for English Heritage (1995).
20. See e.g. Soden, this volume, 10.
21. CA BA/B/16/14/5.
22. Sharp, *Papers*, 226.
23. Emery, *Greater Medieval Houses* II, 372–4.
24. Morris, 'St Mary's Hall', 26, fig 12.
25. St Mary's Priory Cartulary, TNA 164/21, fol. 162.
26. Ibid., fol. 31; A. and E. A. Gooder, *The Register of the Cathedral Priory of St Mary, Coventry: the Pittancer's Rental 1410–11* (Birmingham 1973), 22. By the time of the cartulary, the 'castle bakehouse' tenement had been alienated to the Holy Trinity Guild.
27. A drinks' bar now occupies part of this gallery.
28. Lancaster, *St Mary's Hall*, 41.
29. Templeman ed., *Guild Records*, 143.
30. A. Rudebeck, 'John Thornton and the stained glass of St Mary's Guildhall, Coventry', *Journal of Stained Glass* 31 (2007), 14–34; half of the medieval painted glass survives. Note also Gilderdale Scott, this volume, passim.
31. G. Demidowicz, 'St Mary's Hall Kitchen, Coventry: Conservation Plan', City Development Directorate, Coventry City Council (2003); 'St Mary's Hall, Coventry: Interpretation Strategy', Stuart Davies Associates (Coventry 2006).

Made in Coventry? Seals from Coventry as Evidence of Local Craftsmanship in the Late Middle Ages

JOHN CHERRY

This finely engraved copper-alloy seal matrix of the Shearmen and Fullers of Coventry probably dates from 1439, when they were constituted as a corporate body. It shows the Adoration of the Three Kings at the Nativity of Christ. Was it made in Coventry, a notable centre of metal-working? Or was it commissioned by the fraternity from London, where there were more distinguished seal engravers? The scene of the Adoration is unusual among English seals and may have been influenced by Cologne paintings or the pageant performed by the guild. Most probably engraved by a local goldsmith, this seal reveals how such a fraternity wanted themselves represented.

AMONG seals of guilds and fraternities, the seal of the fraternity of the Shearmen and Fullers of the Guild of the Nativity of our Lord in Coventry is remarkable in three ways. Of copper alloy, it is finely engraved and shows an unusual scene. Although copper alloy is commonly used for 15th-century seals, the Coventry seal matrix appears to have been particularly well prepared for its fine engraving. This engraving was most precisely done, the figures were well proportioned, and the detail can still be read clearly. It is possible that this important guild in Coventry, a major centre of metal-working, commissioned the seal from a local metal-worker.

The copper-alloy seal matrix was acquired by the British Museum in 1989 (Figs 1, 2). It is inscribed in Gothic black-letter *Sigillu co*[mmun]*e scissor*[is] *et ffulloni ffrat*[er] *nitat*[is] *gilde nativat*[is] *d*[omi]*ni de Coventre*, indicating that it is the common seal of the fraternity of the Shearmen and Fullers of the guild of the nativity of our Lord of Coventry. The design and engraving is of high quality, and reflects the discerning patronage of an important town guild, whose legal independence it emphasises.

In the centre, the enthroned Virgin and Child is shown with the Child reaching out his right hand to receive the chalice-shaped gift presented to him by the leading Magi (Fig. 1). Behind him, two Magi bear their presents in their left hands and gesture with their right hands. The right hand of the Magi at the back points to the star which hovers beneath the clouds and sends rays of light shooting downwards. The whole design is admirably adapted to the shape of the seal. On a shield at the bottom, the heraldic bearings of the guild are shown — the shearmen's shears, handles uppermost so that the blades encompass a fuller's bat.[1]

Coventry was of considerable importance in the late middle ages. It towered over its nearest urban neighbours. Ranked amongst provincial cities as third in population to only York and Bristol in 1377, it was then more than twice the size of either Oxford or

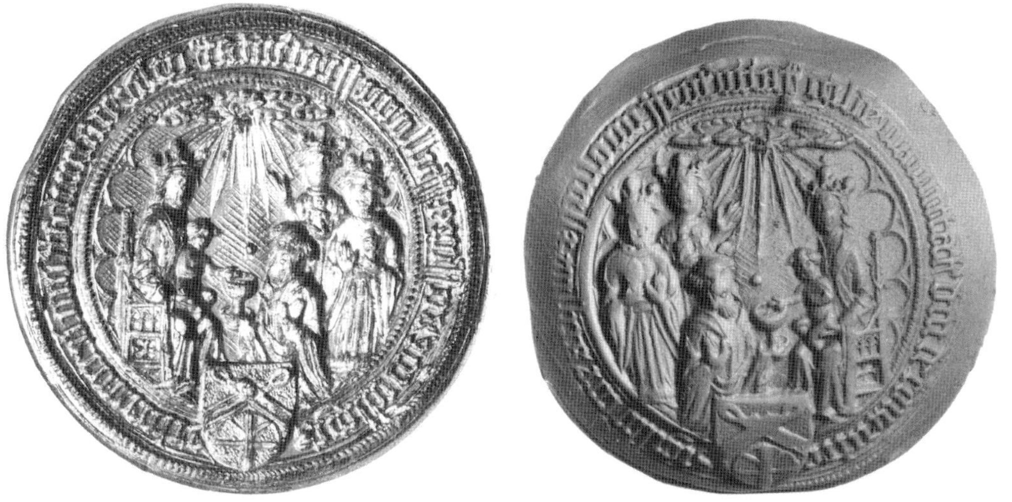

FIG. 1. Seal of the Shearmen and Fullers of Coventry: obverse of bronze seal plus impression
Reproduced with permission of the Trustees of the British Museum. Photo, British Museum

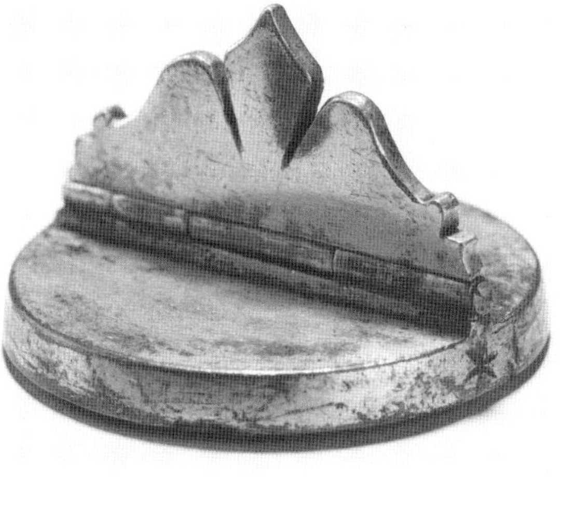

FIG. 2. Seal of the Shearmen and Fullers of Coventry: back
Reproduced with permission of the Trustees of the British Museum. Photo, British Museum

Bristol, three times the size of Nottingham or Northampton and four times the size of Derby and Lichfield.[2] There were many crafts. Apart from the shearmen and fullers, in 1449 there were drapers, dyers, girdlers, weavers, tailors, corvisers, fishmongers, whittawers, butchers, saddlers, card makers, masons, skinners, tilers, bakers, barbers, wrights, barkers and cooks. Of the metal trades, there were smiths, pinners and wiredrawers.[3]

These were a vital part of the commercial and civic life of the town. The Shearmen and Fullers were the only fraternity to have a royal licence, and this marked them out from the rest. They were constituted a corporate body in 1439 (17 Henry VI), which is the most probable date of the matrix.[4]

The scene of the Adoration of the Kings is unusual among seals. Since the fraternity was dedicated to the Nativity, one would expect a scene of the birth of Christ, as in the seal of Syon Abbey, Middlesex.[5] Traditions about the three Kings were collected and developed by the Carmelite friar, John of Hildesheim, who wrote, about 1364–75, *Historia Tria Regum*, which was widely diffused and translated into English around 1400.[6] Such translations of the History of the Three Kings were in a midland dialect. Apart from ceremonial feasting, the guild presented pageants, particularly in the miracle play at Corpus Christi. In addition, the Three Kings (or Magi) of Cologne formed part of the pageant exhibited by the guild before Prince Edward, son of Edward IV, in Cross Cheaping in 1474.[7] This is an English example of the Magi festivals that were common in Italy in the 14th and 15th centuries.[8]

Across Europe, the Adoration of the Magi was an image greatly favoured by emperors and kings. Since the Shearmen was the only Coventry fraternity to have a royal licence, this regal aspect of the story may have appealed to them, and they may have been proud that they could present this story as part of the royal entry into Coventry in 1474.[9] The iconography may have been an example of that influence of ceremony on the citizen and communal year at Coventry, as observed by Charles Phythian-Adams.[10] The iconography of the Three Kings in northern Europe was centred on the devotion to the relics that were transferred from Milan to Cologne in 1164 and enshrined in the Three Kings' shrine in Cologne Cathedral. The great shrine, which still exists, was finished in the early 13th century and the cult still commands great loyalty in Cologne. Coventry Priory had a relic of the Three Kings of Cologne at the time of the dissolution.[11]

Cologne provides examples of comparable scenes of the Adoration on seals. Although the Dominicans of Cologne of 1351 were the earliest community to use this image on their seals, the closest comparison is with the seal of Cologne University of 1392. This fine seal shows the Three Kings with the shield of the university beneath.[12] English pilgrims went to Cologne and brought back pilgrim badges of the Three Kings. One was found in London near Angel Passage on the Thames foreshore in 1983, but none have been found in Coventry. Most of them differ from the scene on the Coventry seal, since they show the kings travelling rather than adoring, perhaps appropriate for pilgrims.[13] It is possible that the iconography may have been derived from a painting, such as the Painting of the Three Kings, attributed to the Cologne master of *c.* 1400, in the Wallraf Richartz Museum in Cologne.[14] The scene of the Adoration also occurs on the small plaque of gold metal-work with black enamel found in the churchyard of Hemel Hempstead church, Hertfordshire, and now in the Victoria and Albert Museum (Fig. 3).[15]

The guild may have requested a goldsmith in Coventry to engrave the seal. Of the 108 metal-workers recorded in deeds in the late 14th and early 15th centuries, twelve were goldsmiths.[16] There is also considerable evidence for metal-working in Coventry, for high-quality metal-work being found, or at any rate lost, and other seals that may have been made in Coventry. The early topography of crafts in Coventry was elucidated by P. R. Coss who noted that the goldsmiths were concentrated in Broadgate.[17]

Archaeological evidence of metal-working consists of the finds of many moulds for use in bronze working, though none were for seal matrices. There was also discovered in Pool Meadow, between the Cox Street and Gosford Street bridges, a collection of scrap brass, pewter, and other unfinished objects which came from a medieval brass foundry.[18] Although renowned for the lesser metal-working trades, Coventry also has a claim to importance among midland towns for precious metal-working. From 1465

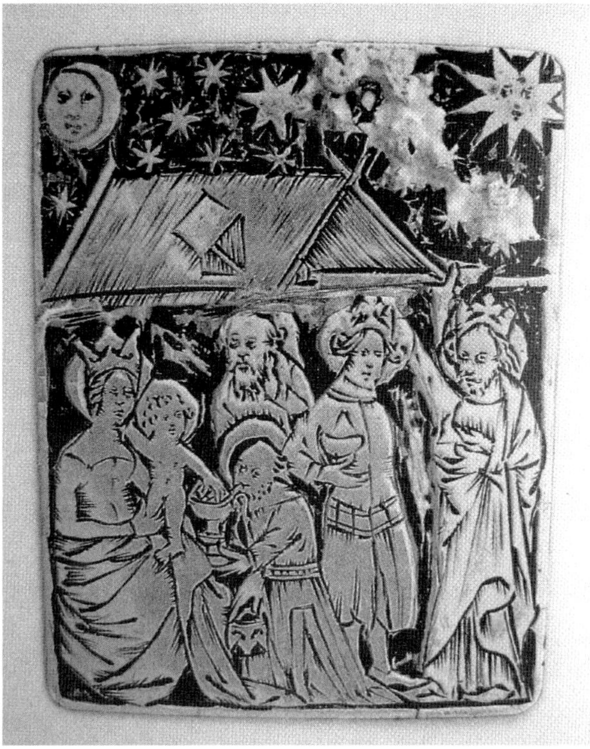

FIG. 3. Gold plaque from Hemel Hempstead showing the Adoration: Victoria and Albert Museum M.51–1975
Reproduced with permission of the Trustees of the Victoria and Albert Museum. Photo, Victoria and Albert Museum

to 1459 it was, with York, Norwich and Bristol, one of the four provincial mint towns. In 1423 it was allowed by Parliament to have a provincial silver mark, along with York, Newcastle, Lincoln, Norwich, Bristol and Salisbury. However, there was no record of any action being taken and no marked pieces of silver survive that can be attributed to Coventry. It was not until 1523 that the goldsmiths, smiths and others appear to have formed one guild.[19]

The name 'Goldsmith' appears in the Coventry Leet Book in the 15th century. Some others may also have borne the name but followed another trade. For example, the entry 'Thomas Goldsmythe', appearing from 1424 to 1471, may represent one or two people. One 'Thomas Goldsmythe' was certainly a mercer, not a goldsmith. The other, if he existed, may, or may not, have been a practising goldsmith. There are, however, at least two citizens described as goldsmiths — John Dyrham in 1424 and Reginald Bere in 1444.[20] Certainly, mayors of Coventry would occasionally commission silver gilt objects. In 1456, on the occasion of the visit of Queen Margaret of Anjou, Richard Braytoft, mayor, spent £10 10s. 1d. on 'two gilt cuppes with gilded feet'.

Metal-work of precious metal has been found in Coventry, such as the large finger ring finely engraved with the five wounds of Christ, and the gold rectangular pendant found at Coundon, with the head of Christ on one side and the other with a half-length image of Christ as the Man of Sorrows (Fig. 4).[21] An enamelled gilt bronze with silver outlined cloisons — a specifically Hungarian technique, of which the best parallel is the reliquary bust of St Ladislas, king of Hungary, now in the cathedral at Gyor — was found at the Whitefriars, Coventry.[22] Also, the cathedral priory church preserved the

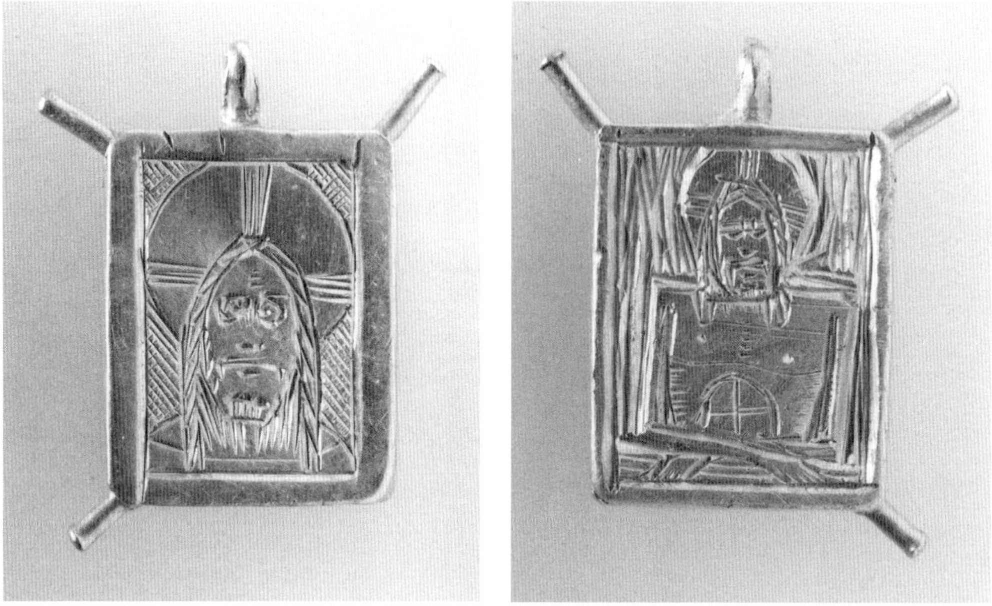

FIG. 4. Gold pendant found at Coundon, Coventry: front and back
Reproduced with permission of the Trustees of the British Museum. Photo, British Museum

head of the martyred virgin St Osburg in a case of copper and gilt. She was widely venerated in the midlands as both an object of regional pilgrimage and the subject of a brisk souvenir trade.[23]

Other guild seals which may have been produced in Coventry include those of the guild of St Mary, Trinity, and St John the Baptist (Fig. 5). This guild was founded in 1364 and amalgamated with other guilds, such as St Mary, St John the Baptist, and St Katherine in 1392. Since the seal gives prominence to St Mary and St John, it must date from after 1392, and before 1441, when it is first recorded.[24] A third Coventry guild seal is that of St Nicolas (Fig. 6), which shows a priest celebrating mass at an altar, with the hand of God descending from a cloud. It may be 14th or 15th century.[25] Of the municipal seals, the 15th-century silver mayoralty seal (the second) of Coventry was in use by 1450. It bears on the obverse an elephant supporting a triple-towered castle topped with a flag charged with three scimitars or ostrich feathers. In the background are two trees, each of two sprigs.[26] Guilds in other midland towns have fine seal matrices, such as the guild of the Holy Cross at Stratford-upon-Avon (Fig. 7). This guild was founded in the early 14th century and possessed property by 1331. It is likely that the fine seal, showing the Crucifixion under a canopy of five arches, dates from 1403 when Henry IV issued letters patent confirming the guild.[27]

An alternative view might suggest that there were strong links between Coventry and London. Richard Whittington has his arms in the stained glass windows of St Mary's Hall. John Pulteney, four times lord mayor of London, founded the Coventry Whitefriars and the arms of many London mayors are on its misericords.[28] So it is also possible that our matrix might have been engraved in London and sent to Coventry. However, in Coventry the size and wealth of the town, the metal-working tradition,

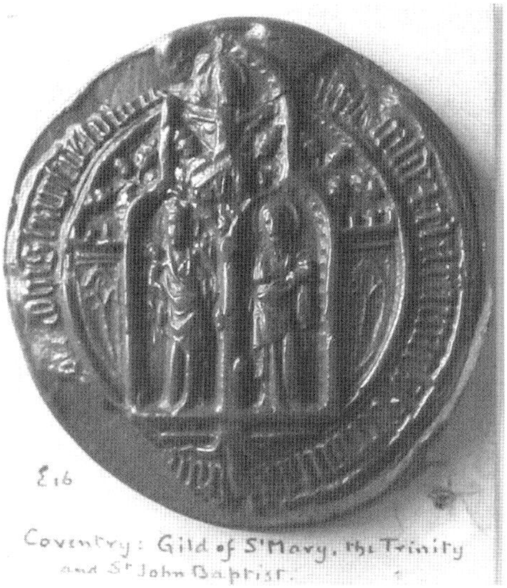

FIG. 5. Cast of seal of the Guild of the Holy Trinity, Coventry

© Society of Antiquaries of London. Photo, author

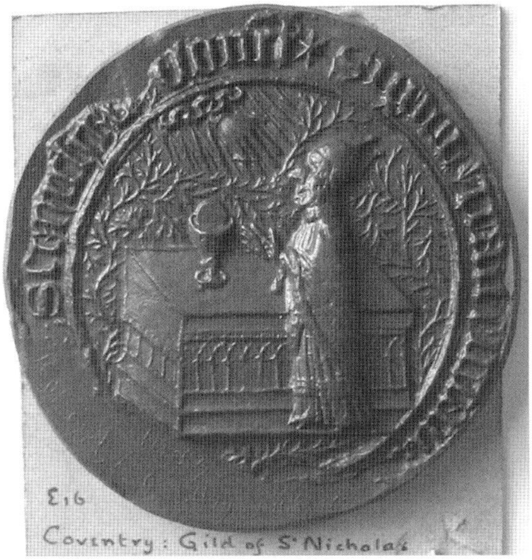

FIG. 6. Cast of seal of the Guild of St Nicolas, Coventry

© Society of Antiquaries of London. Photo, author

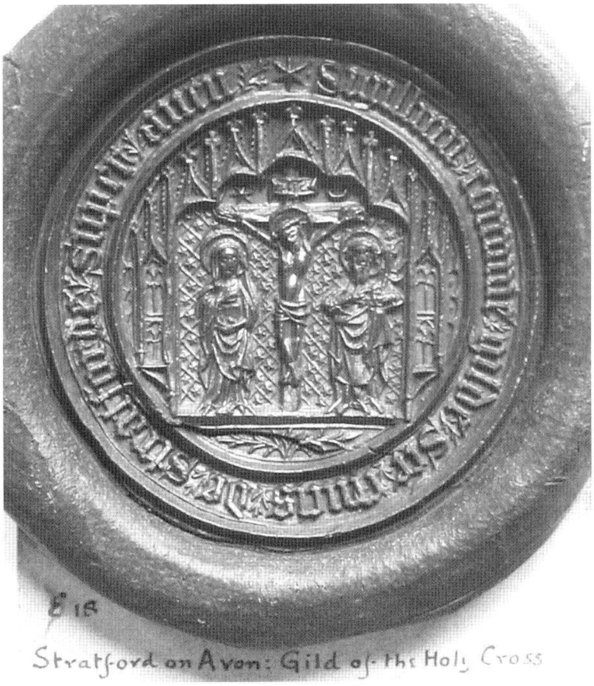

FIG. 7. Cast of seal of the Guild of the Holy Cross, Stratford-upon-Avon

© Society of Antiquaries of London. Photo, author

the importance of Coventry for hall marking in the mid-15th century, and the possession of fine metal-work within the town suggests the possibility that this seal may have been made in Coventry. The city may even have been the source of other fine seals in the midlands. If so, local seals can, in some instances, indicate the local production of metal-work, and reveal how such a fraternity wanted themselves represented by a local craftsman.

NOTES

1. British Museum (hereafter BM) P and E 1989,0604.1. The seal matrix, 48mm in diameter, has a hinged shaped handle at the back (Fig. 2). It was in the possession of the guild until the 19th century. Its history from then to 1989 is not known. See R. Marks and P. Williamson ed., *Gothic: Art for England* (London 2003), 270–1, no. 132, pl. 26.
2. C. Phythian-Adams, *Desolation of a City: Coventry and the urban crisis of the Later Middle Ages* (Cambridge 1979), 20.
3. *Leet Book* I, 247–52.
4. For guild seals in general, see E. New, 'Signs of Community or Marks of the Exclusive? Parish and guild seals in later Medieval England', in *The Parish in Late Medieval England*, ed. C. Burgess and E. Duffy, *Harlaxton Medieval Studies* XIV (Stamford 2006), 112–29; J. Cherry, 'Some Seals of English guilds and fraternities 1400–1540: iconography and patronage', in *Late Gothic England: Art and display*, ed. R. Marks (Donington and London 2007), 16–25.
5. R. Ellis, *Monastic Seals* (London 1986), M 821.
6. See the introduction to C. Horstmann's edition of both Latin and English text of John of Hildesheim's, *The Three Kings of Cologne*, EETS, Old Series no. 85 (London 1886), v–xxi, esp. pp. viii–ix.
7. For the text of the Shearman and Taylours pageant, see H. Craig, *Two Coventry Corpus Christi plays*, EETS, Extra Series, 87 (London 1902), lines 699–767, after Sharp 1825; the text was destroyed in 1879. The relationship between the seal and the play was noted by Craig on p. xvii. See also P. King and C. Davidson ed., *The Coventry Corpus Christi Plays* (Kalamazoo 2000).
8. For Italian Magi festivals, see R. C. Trexler, 'The Magi enter Florence: the Ubriachi of Florence and Venice', in *Church and Community 1200–1600: studies in the History of Florence and New Spain*, ed. R. C. Trexler (Rome 1987), 75; R. Hatfield, 'The Compagnia de' Magi', *Journal of the Warburg and Courtauld Institutes* 33 (1970), 107–61; K. Eisenblicher, 'Nativity and Magi Plays in Renaissance Florence', *Comparative Drama* 29 (1995–96), 319–33.
9. R. Trexler, *The Journey of the Magi* (Princeton 1997); W. G. Fretton, *The Fuller's Guild, Coventry* (Coventry, n.d.), 23.
10. C. Phythian-Adams, 'Ceremony and the citizen: the communal year at Coventry, 1450–1550', in *The Medieval Town: A Reader in English Urban History 1200–1540*, ed. R. Holt and G. Rosser (London 1990), 238–64.
11. *Letters and Papers Foreign and Domestic, Henry VIII* XIV (1), 69.
12. T. Diederich and M. Huiskes, 'Das Grosse Siegel der Universität Köln in neuem Licht', *Geschichte in Köln* 44 (December 1998), 139–49. I am most grateful to Dr Toni Diederich for drawing this to my attention.
13. B. Spencer, *Pilgrim souvenirs and secular badges: Medieval finds from excavations in London* (London 1998), 261–6.
14. *Late Gothic Art From Cologne*, National Gallery (London 1977), 20, no. 2.
15. Victoria and Albert Museum, M.51–1975; R. W. Lightbown, *Medieval European Jewellery* (London 1992), 533, no. 88, pl. 148.
16. VCH *Warwickshire* VIII, 331–2.
17. Coss, *Early Records*, xxxvi.
18. S. M. Wright, 'Much Park Street, Coventry', *TBWAS* 92 (1988), 1–132; P. B. Chatwin, 'Recent finds in Coventry', *TBAS* 58 (1934), 56–62.
19. Phythian Adams, *Desolation of a City* (as n. 2), 20; C. J. Jackson, *English goldsmiths and their marks* (London 1949), 269–70.
20. *Leet Book* I, 80–365 passim for Thomas, 81–301 passim for John, 214–83 passim for Reginald.
21. For Coventry ring BM P and E AF 897, see Marks and Williamson ed., *Gothic* (as n. 1), 333, no. 211. For Coundon, see *Treasure Annual Report* (1998–99), no. 174.
22. Woodfield, *Whitefriars*, 341, no. 19.

23. *Letters and Papers Foreign and Domestic, Henry VIII* XIV (I), no. 69; source Harris, *Dr Troughton's Sketches*, 7.

24. Templeman ed., *Guild Records*, plate opposite frontispiece and 32–3. This is the same as the seal of the Trinity Guild which existed in 1441–42 and is appended to documents of 1450 and 1584. In 1944 it was in the collection of Major C. Gregory Hood of Loxley Hall. This guild was the amalgamation of four separate fraternities founded in the mid-14th century. The date of unification took place sometime between 1364 and 1369, not officially confirmed until 1392; Harris ed., *Guild Register*, xiii–xiv.

25. Society of Antiquaries of London, cast D16.

26. *Proceedings of the Society of Antiquaries*, 2nd series, IV (1867–70), 156–7. This silver seal was in use by 1450 and occurs on Corporation Deed 28 Henry VI, no. 3; see VCH *Warwickshire* VIII, 415.

27. A. B. Tonnochy, *Catalogue of British Seal Dies in the British Museum* (London 1952), no. 887; W. G. de Gray Birch, *Catalogue of Seals in the Department of Manuscripts of the British Museum* I (London 1887), no. 4473; W. H. St John Hope and L. Jewitt, *The Corporation Plate of the Cities and Corporate Towns of England and Wales* (London 1895), 2, 399. For the grant of letters patent, see VCH *Warwickshire* II, 113.

28. See C. Tracy, 'The Choir-Stalls', in Woodfield, *Whitefriars*, figs 85a–b, 86a.

Coventry: A Regional Centre of Glass-Painting in the 14th Century? The Glazing of Stanford on Avon Church, Northamptonshire, and the Taxonomy of English Medieval Stained Glass Studies

RICHARD MARKS

The church of St Nicholas at Stanford on Avon, Northamptonshire, is one of the most rewarding sites for the study of medieval parish church glazing. It has attracted considerable scholarly attention over more than 150 years and thus offers insights into the historiography of English medieval glass-painting. This paper sets out the main phases and iconography of the Stanford glazing in the second half of the 14th century and examines the claim that it and other midlands glass of the period can be associated with Coventry. In the process, wider issues are raised concerning methodologies for the study of medieval glass.

THROUGH a combination of surviving (and recorded) monuments and artefacts and extensive civic records, the importance of Coventry as a centre for artistic activity in the 15th century has long been established, notably for glass-painting. Less clear, however, is its role during the preceding century. The extensive surviving glazing of this period in the parish church of St Nicholas at Stanford on Avon is one of the principal ensembles on which the claim that Coventry was a major centre of glass-painting from the early 14th century has been based. To re-visit this claim means embarking on a journey through the historiography of English medieval stained glass. In the process, methodological issues are raised which range further than whether or not the glass of one particular church can be assigned to a workshop — or workshops — in Coventry.

Stanford on Avon is a parish with a tiny community lying about five and a half miles south-east of Lutterworth and straddling the Northamptonshire and Leicestershire border; in terms of ecclesiastical jurisdiction, until the Reformation it was in the diocese of Lincoln. Outside the circle of stained glass scholarship, its church is still a relatively unknown gem. Much of a piece architecturally, it has escaped heavy-handed intrusive restoration. It houses a fine series of tombs and monuments and an historically important organ-case. Every window contains ancient glass, ranging in date from the first half of the 14th to the middle of the 16th centuries; not a great deal is *in situ*, but the quantity, date-span, iconography and quality make Stanford one of the most rewarding places for the study of medieval glass-painting in English parish churches. The various phases and changes tell us much about the community which used this church; in turn, the history of this community explains much about the contents of the windows. As a result of the conservation by Barley Studio between 1987 and 1997, it has been possible to comprehend fully the significance of the glazing.[1]

The church is a well-proportioned and spacious building entirely rebuilt in the early 14th century (Fig. 1). It comprises a chancel of three bays, a five-bay nave with north and south aisles, a south porch and a tower. The nave arcades are carried down by piers with a continuous moulding without capitals, a feature of a number of churches in the locality (e.g. Charwelton) and showing Stanford to be the work of local masons.[2] The only subsequent alterations are the 15th- or early 16th-century clerestory and the handsome timber roofs to nave and aisles. Apart from the nave clerestory windows, the fenestration is entirely original, consisting of two simple tracery patterns: intersecting throughout the chancel and in four nave windows, reticulated in the remaining nave windows. All windows are of three lights except for the five-light east window, the east windows to the aisles, both of four lights, and the two-light tower window. Four windows are now blocked: the chancel easternmost pair and the west windows of the nave aisles.

The indications are that the church was completely glazed during the second quarter of the 14th century in two phases.[3] The first comprises the canopy-work and grisaille filling the upper part of the main lights in the chancel east window, together with the seated *Maria lactans* at the apex of the centre light. Fragments suggest that a

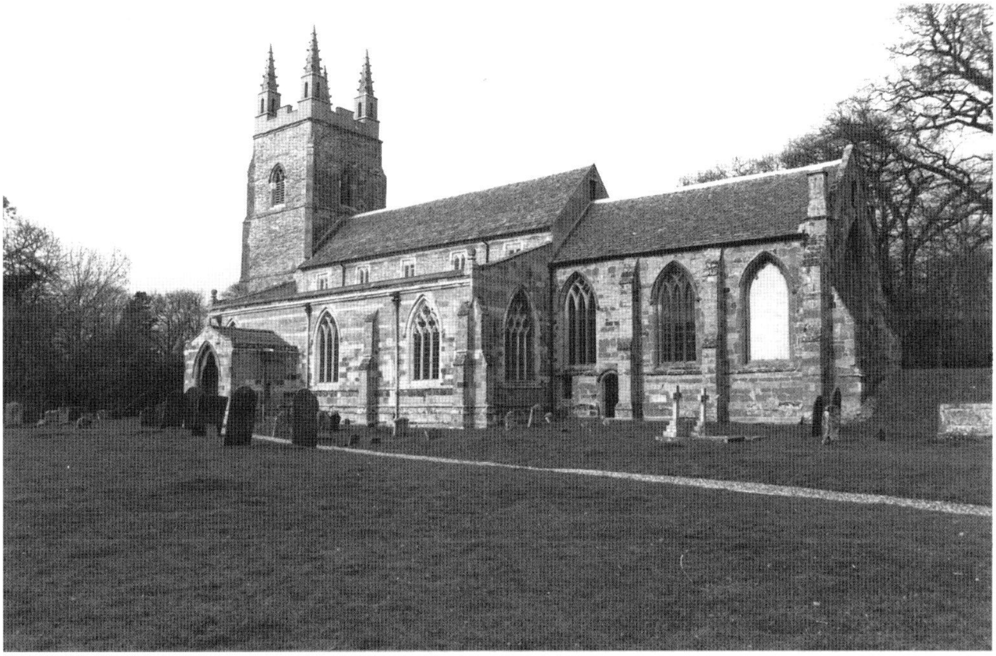

FIG. 1. Stanford on Avon: parish church of St Nicholas from the south-east
Photo, author

Christological (perhaps a Passion) cycle was placed under the band of canopies. Most of the grisaille above the heraldic glass, and the shields of arms and the crowned male bust in the tracery, are *in situ*. To the same phase belongs the band of apostles, grisaille and evangelist symbols now distributed over the four unblocked chancel windows but originally in the blocked easternmost pair and the next pair. The apostle panels are very carefully designed and executed (Fig. 2 and Col. Pl. XA in print edn; Fig. 3). In each window, a figure in pink and green garments set on a blue ground is flanked by companions in pot yellow and blue against ruby grounds. One basic canopy design is employed for the apostles and a slightly larger one in the east window. Changes are rung between covered cups, oak leaves and vine leaves in border designs, the last two counterchanged with the reserved patterns on the grounds. Yellow stain is applied sparingly and judiciously to add variety, especially on alternate covered cups and vine leaves in the borders. The grisaille which survives in some of the side window lights has oak and vine leaves springing from central stems and with yellow-stained beaded trelliswork (Fig. 9).

The shields in the east window indicate that these five windows were glazed towards the end of Edward II's reign or, more probably, shortly after the accession of Edward III. A likely *post quem* is 1324 and a *terminus ante* is provided by the use of the pre-1340 royal arms. The guiding force behind the rebuilding of the church and its glazing almost certainly was Alan of Aslackby, rector between 1308 and his death in 1337. It is very probably his body that was buried below the canopied tomb with the effigy of a priest in the nave south aisle.[4]

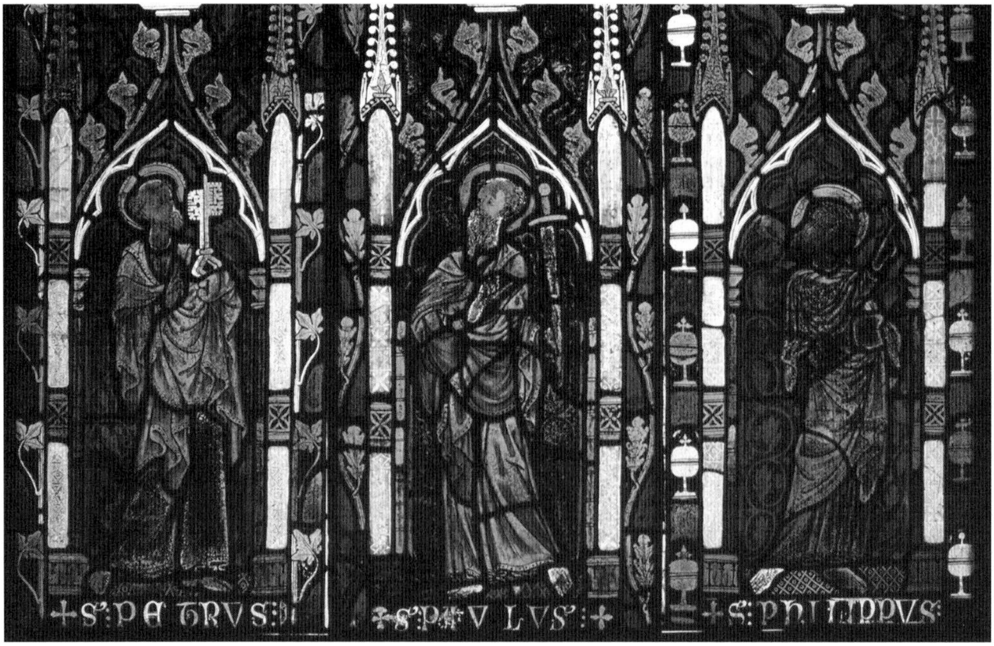

FIG. 2. Stanford on Avon: SS Peter, Paul and Philip in the chancel glazing, *c.* 1324–40
Photo, author

The second phase also seems to have conformed to a coherent iconographical programme, complementary to that in the eastern parts of the chancel. The new campaign seems to have encompassed not only the nave aisle windows, but also the westernmost pair of chancel windows. The reason why the first phase did not include the latter may have been because building work was still in progress on the eastern parts of the nave, including the chancel arch area, and it was too hazardous to risk glazing the westernmost chancel bay at this time. Of the main light glazing of Phase 2 there survive a prelate, St Margaret, St Anne teaching the Virgin to read, St Agnes and two more female saints (Fig. 4). Fragments and antiquarian sources provide evidence for a second prelate, SS Katherine of Alexandria, Elizabeth and Mary Magdalene, the last three from north aisle windows, and at least one scene — probably several — from the life of St John the Baptist. Most of the tracery glazing survives, some of it *in situ*.

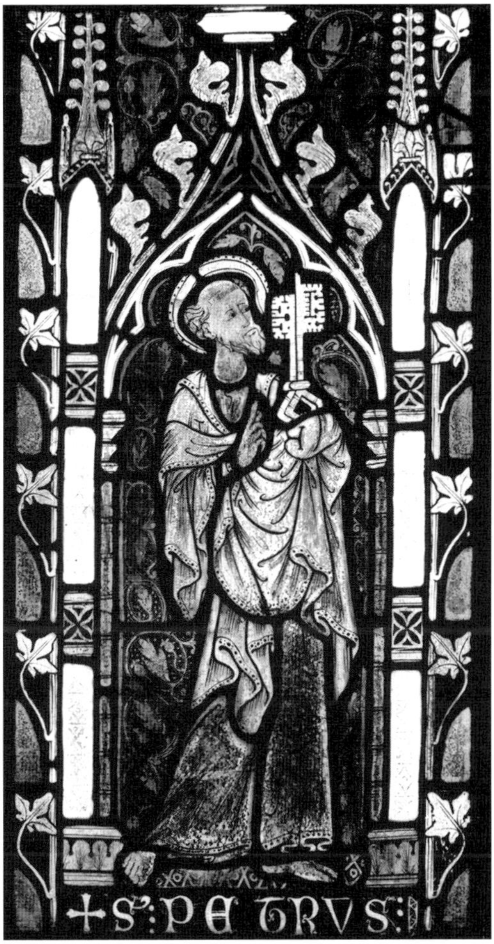

FIG. 3. Stanford on Avon: St Peter in the chancel glazing, *c*. 1324–40
Photo, National Monuments Record

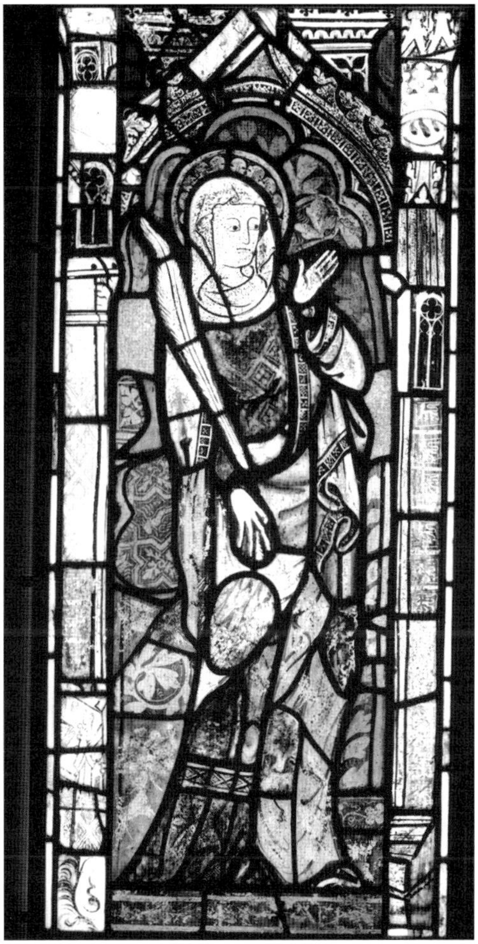

FIG. 4. Stanford on Avon: female saint in the nave south aisle east window, *c*. 1341–52
Photo, National Monuments Record

The principal remains include a Coronation of the Virgin (Fig. 5 and Col. Pl. XB in print edn), possibly St George, two abbots, two prelates and traces of two more, and a fifth prelate holding a tonsured head (Figs 6, 7). Christ in Majesty occurs twice, above angels and Christ on the Cross flanked by the Virgin and St John in both the aisle east windows. These are above former nave altars and appropriately the subject-matter emphasises the sacrament of the Mass. In the north aisle window the angels summon the dead from their graves. Angels appear in the tracery of another window and evangelist symbols in two more. There is also a Veronica and a Warning against Idle Gossip (Fig. 8), plus a fragment of the fable of the fox preaching to geese.

Neither shields of arms nor donor figures exist which might help identify the date and patron (or patrons) of the second phase, and none is recorded in the antiquarian sources. Although the Stanford parishioners themselves may have been involved, it is likely that the rector once again played a prominent role in completing the task begun by Alan of Aslackby. Of the three incumbents between the latter's death in 1337 and the middle of the century, only one occupied the position for a substantial period: John of Winwick, rector between 1341 and 1352. Like his two immediate predecessors, Winwick was a holder of high royal offices, eventually rising to be Keeper of the Privy

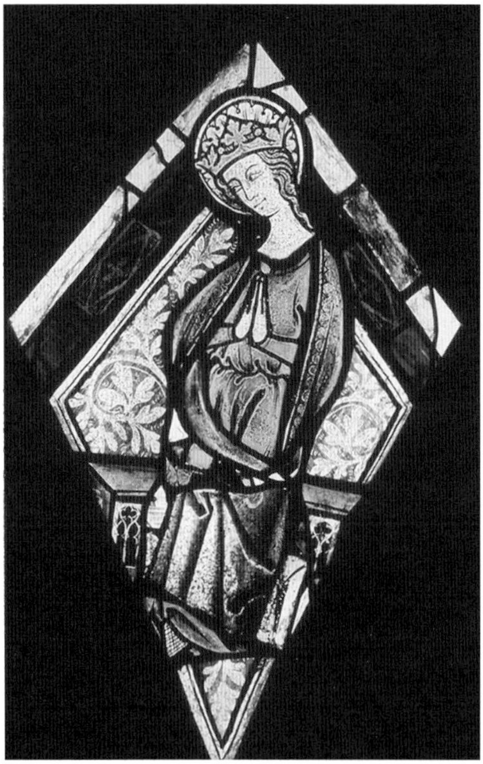

FIG. 5. Stanford on Avon: The Virgin from the Coronation of the Virgin, now in a chancel window, *c.* 1341–52

Photo, author

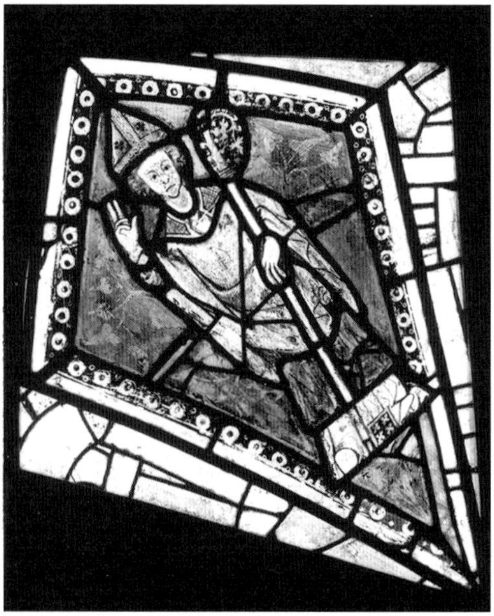

FIG. 6. Stanford on Avon: bishop or mitred abbot now in the east window, *c.* 1341–52

Photo, National Monuments Record

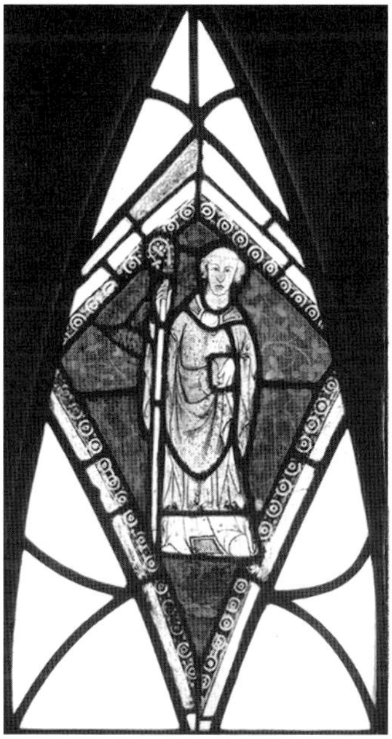

FIG. 7. Stanford on Avon: abbot now in a chancel window, *c.* 1341–52
Photo, National Monuments Record

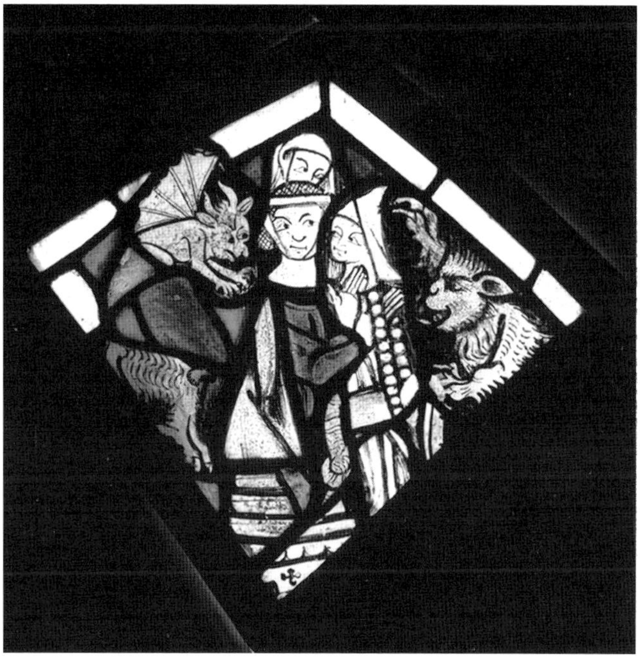

FIG. 8. Stanford on Avon: Warning against Idle Gossip, now in a chancel window, *c.* 1341–52
Photo, National Monuments Record

Seal. For him, the Stanford rectory was a sinecure and although his administrative duties meant that he can have spent little time there, he did not neglect his church. In his will of 1359, Winwick bequeathed 100s. to the fraternity of the Virgin here and a chasuble to its altar. In addition, both the will and his seal indicate his devotion to his name-saint, John the Baptist, in the light of which the evidence for the representation of this saint in the nave glazing may be significant.[5] Another relevant player, however, may well have been the Benedictine abbey of Selby in east Yorkshire, which held the advowson of Stanford; the parish was the monastery's principal estate in the south of England. *Inter alia*, its location made it a convenient stopover for the monks and their officials en route to London and Oxford and attending the triennial General Chapter of the Order in England at Northampton.[6]

The range and type of coloured glasses, the canopy and border designs and figure styles of the two phases are very different. The coloured glass in the first phase is very deep, the second phase is much more translucent (Figs 2, 5). Absent from the second phase are the triangular-shaped heads of the chancel apostles and there are fewer and less calligraphic drapery folds (Figs 1–8). The nave figures are heavily shaded with oil-based paints, which impart a much more volumetric impression and this is enhanced by the extensive use of back-painting, even in the tracery eyelets. This monumentality goes hand in hand with a three-dimensional treatment of the canopied niches. Those in the aisle east windows exhibit rudimentary perspective through the off-setting and shading of the inner faces of the sideshafts; these may be contrasted with the flatness of the niches framing the chancel apostles (Figs 2–4, 9–11). In addition, St Anne and the Virgin in the nave appear to be emerging from their niche. Two principal hands are recognisable in the second phase, both evidently working side-by-side and showing great inventiveness, no doubt determined by the designer or designers of the cartoons. There are at least eight variants of canopy design, a dozen sideshaft patterns and an attractive display of minor motifs, with fish and birds all based on natural species in the south aisle eyelets, as well as hybrids and other denizens of borders and grisaille (Figs 10, 11, 13).

The above summarises what can be deduced primarily from a study of the surviving Stanford glazing of the period. How has it been treated historiographically? The stained glass has attracted very considerable attention from the late 16th century to the present day, the differing approaches and interests placed on it reflecting the scholarly concerns

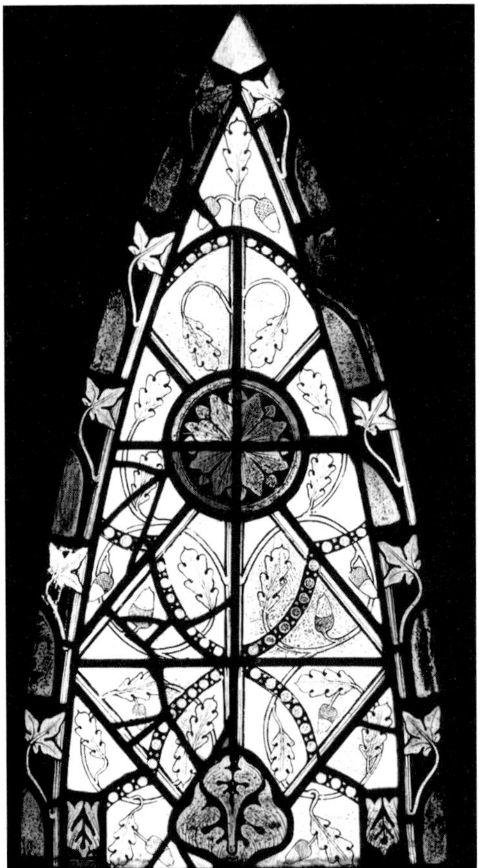

FIG. 9. Stanford on Avon: grisaille and borderwork in the chancel glazing, *c.* 1324–40
Photo, National Monuments Record

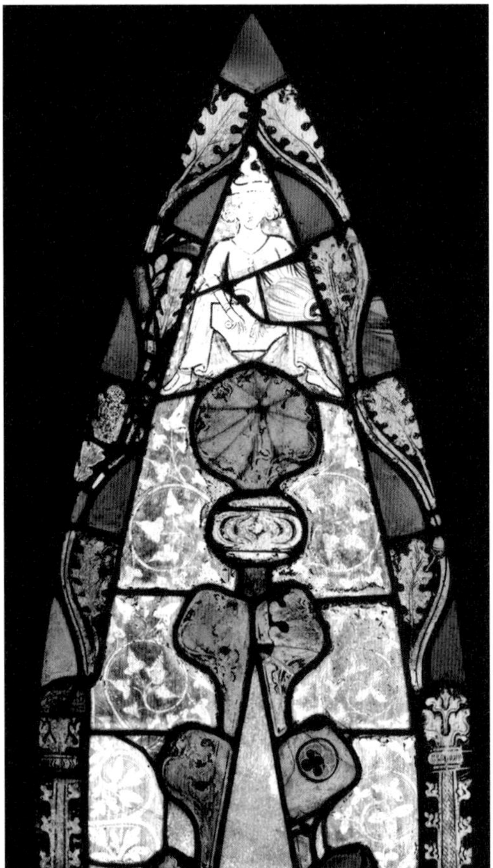

FIG. 10. Stanford on Avon: canopy top, borderwork and figure playing a dulcimer, now in a chancel window, *c.* 1341–52
Photo, National Monuments Record

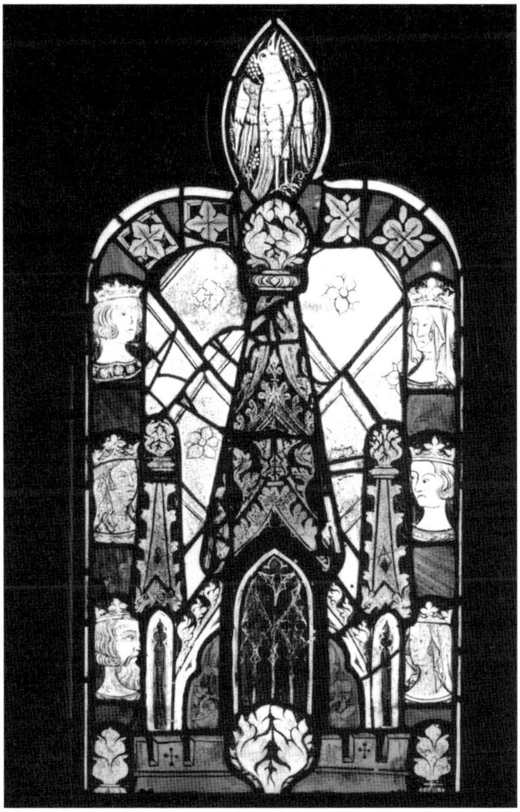

FIG. 11. Stanford on Avon: canopy top, borderwork and quarries in the nave south aisle east window *c.* 1341–52
Photo, National Monuments Record

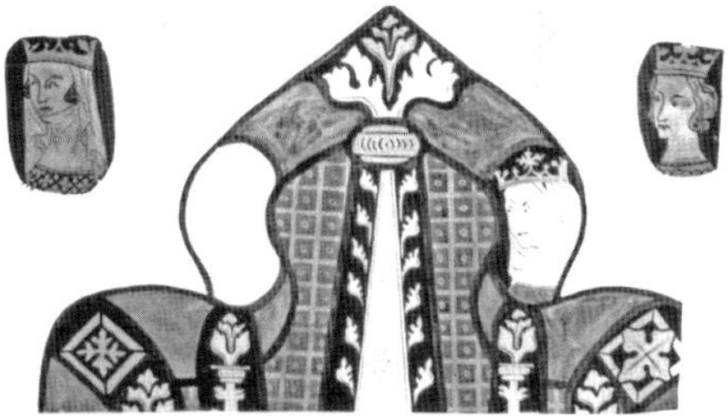

FIG. 12. Belton (Leics.): canopy top and borderwork, *c.* 1325–50
London, Victoria and Albert Museum, Dept of Prints, Drawings & Design, acc. no. B. 4.a (watercolour presented by the Revd J. H. Cardew)

of each writer's respective era. Apart from passing mention in pretty well all the standard surveys of English medieval stained glass, those who have published on it in more detail have their place in the pantheon of stained glass scholarship, notably Charles Winston, Eden, Rushforth and Peter Newton.[7] Winston was the first to take Stanford beyond the confines of antiquarianism by dating and classifying the glass and identifying the iconography.[8] The earliest published accounts of the Stanford glazing to move beyond description were those of A. H. Dyson and F. S. Eden, which appeared almost simultaneously. The former was a local historian, whose monograph on the church was published at Rugby in 1929. Eden, by contrast, was a student of English medieval glass and his article on the Stanford glazing appeared in the *Journal of the British Society of Master Glass-Painters* for 1929–30.[9] Although they do not seem to have collaborated, their methodology was basically the same: they both looked to the parish's history for its glazing affiliations and as a result Selby Abbey came into the picture, albeit in different ways. Eden suggested that the tracery prelates in the east window may have represented Selby abbots (Figs 6, 7); Dyson on the other hand

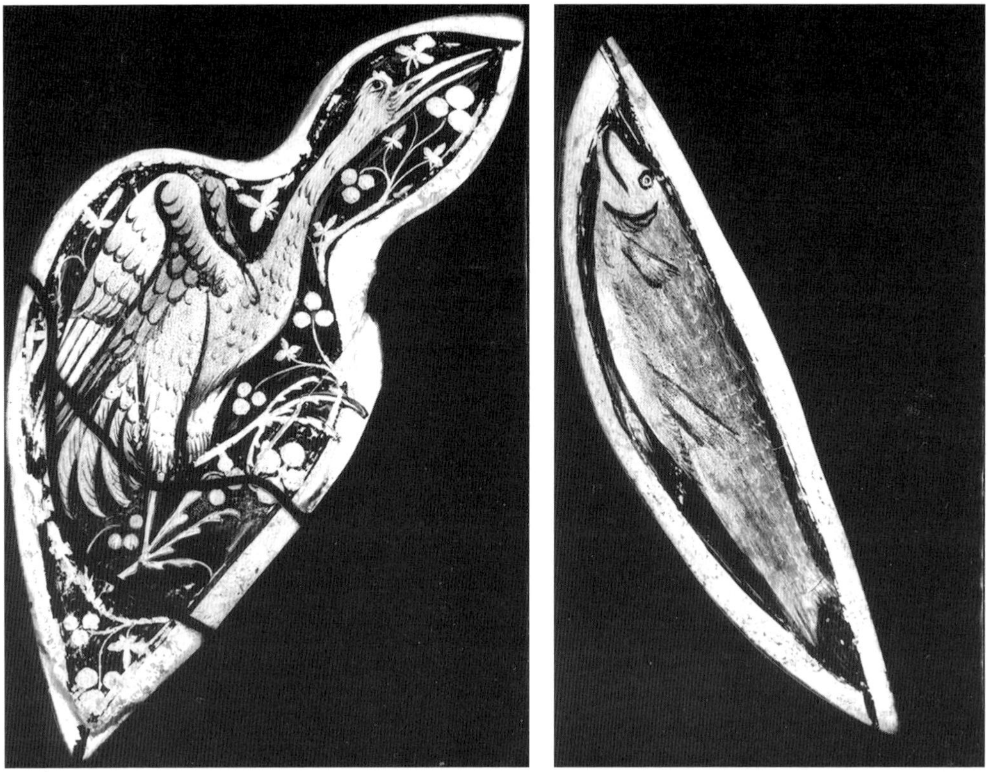

FIG. 13. Stanford on Avon: bird and fish from nave south aisle eyelets, *c*. 1341–52
Photo, National Monuments Record

considered that the east window as a whole was a memento of Edward II's visit to Selby Abbey in 1327. Neither author proposed stylistic links between Selby and Stanford, but Dyson, quoting some visitors from Yorkshire, also stated that the chancel glazing 'exactly resembles York Minster glass'. He may have invoked York because of the proximity of Selby; alternatively he might have seen the Minster as the obvious place to seek comparisons for early 14th-century glass. Next to try his hand was none other than the patrician figure of G. McNeil Rushforth, author in the 1920s and 1930s of a series of important articles and books on English medieval glass, above all *Medieval Christian Imagery*. Rushforth contributed a short section on the glass to Hamilton Thompson's article on Stanford church in the *Archaeological Journal* for 1933.[10] Evidently he was familiar with both Dyson's and Eden's publications because he repeated the former's link with York Minster, albeit specifying the nave glazing and also suggested rather vaguely that Selby Abbey may have had something to do with the Stanford glazing.

It is no criticism of these studies of the Stanford glazing that the comparisons with the Minster nave glazing do not stand up to scrutiny — neither, for that matter, does the fragment that is left of the 14th-century figural glazing in the Selby east window. At the time of writing, good photographs of the York glass were not readily available (their poor preservation still presents problems of legibility) and little attention had been paid to Selby.[11]

However, an alternative methodology was nascent at the same time as Dyson, Eden and Rushforth were publishing on Stanford. This emerged from two strands in stained glass research. The first was the discovery of documented (primarily urban-based) medieval glass-painters, notably by L. F. Salzman and Christopher Woodforde.[12] The second was an increasing awareness of parish church glazing, which manifested itself in the publication of surveys in county archaeological journals as well as studies of individual monuments. In the 1920s and 1930s these included Gloucestershire and Surrey.[13] As we shall see, the county model has its drawbacks, but has continued to flourish since the Second World War, including S. A. Jeavons' article on medieval glass in Staffordshire, which appeared in the *Transactions & Proceedings of the Birmingham Archaeological Society* for 1952.[14] In common with most of these studies, Jeavons was more of a survey than an analysis, but his noting of similarities in the glazing of several churches (outside Staffordshire as well as within it) led him to argue that they were the work of one 'school' (as he put it) which was initially peripatetic and then found a centre in Coventry. Jeavons knew the Stanford glass and considered that it was the work of this 'school' because (in his opinion) it shared certain design features with this group, including the use of the same cartoons for the tracery prelates there and in the east window main lights at Checkley (Staffs.). He was not the first to suggest that Coventry was a centre of a 'school' of glass-painting. Westlake had included the city amongst several urban-based 'schools' as early as the 1880s and in 1930–31 Bernard Rackham associated a series of 14th- and 15th-century windows in midlands churches with Coventry and also cited a reference in the city archives to a named glass-painter from the beginning of the 14th century in addition to the already-known John Thornton.[15] The 'school' label, however, is inappropriate when applied to any kind of medieval artistic production; in respect of glass-painting, it evokes an image of an Athenian academy with rows of glaziers and their apprentices sitting at their benches faithfully following the *diktats* of an *Überglasmaler*. Notwithstanding its anachronistic resonances, the 'school' terminology has enjoyed remarkable longevity amongst historians of medieval art.

While Rackham cited only some 14th-century Warwickshire glass, Jeavons looked further afield and thus implicitly rather than explicitly was thinking in regional rather than county terms in respect of centres of production. So, too, was Peter Newton when he formulated his ground-breaking and, alas, never published three-volume doctoral thesis entitled 'Schools of glass-painting in the Midlands 1275–1430', examined in 1961.[16] With Peter Newton, stained-glass studies in England entered the European methodological mainstream of art history. Supervised by Francis Wormald, he broadened approaches to the medium through his knowledge of manuscript illumination and iconography, interpretations of heraldic meaning and use of hagiographical texts as well as systematic exploration and analysis of antiquarian sources. Newton's midlands comprised the counties of Derbyshire, Leicestershire, Northamptonshire, Nottinghamshire, Rutland, Shropshire, Staffordshire and Warwickshire, and he was the first to draw attention to the riches of parish church glazing within their boundaries. He identified several different workshops, locating one in Derbyshire and also argued for the existence of a 'school' based in Coventry in the early 15th century, of which he singled out John Thornton as the leading light. Stanford features prominently in the thesis. Newton recognised that there were two phases to the 14th century, although he and I differ slightly in their dating and precise content. He compared the diaper patterns behind the chancel apostles (Figs 2, 3) with those at Noseley (Leics., before 1306); as they are now more or less completely opaque this is impossible to verify. He also followed Jeavons in relating the tracery prelates (Figs 6, 7), which he assigned to the first phase, to Checkley, although he noted that they could not be from the same cartoons as the Checkley figures are twice the size of those at Stanford; indeed, a recent side-by-side comparison of the two schemes in a conservation workshop has confirmed that they are not by the same workshop. Newton also cautiously suggested that the glazing of the south aisle east window at Thornton (Leics.) may have been by the same workshop as the Stanford Phase I glass. Thornton is less than twenty miles north of Stanford and the restoration of its medieval glass has validated his judgement. In addition, he identified glass in another Leicestershire church, at Broughton Astley, as by the workshop responsible for the Stanford Phase II glazing; this church is less than ten miles distant. Notwithstanding the fact that both Stanford and Broughton Astley are within fifteen miles of Coventry, and thus within a day's ride, Newton did not attempt to associate any of the 14th-century workshops with this city or any other urban centre in the midlands.

Two questions arise from these studies. Firstly, what are the criteria by which individual workshops are identified? Secondly, what factors might affect the establishment and location of such workshops? Regarding the first it has been traditional to focus on figure style, particularly delineation of heads and drapery folds. Also relevant are the kinds of ornamental patterns used on backgrounds, garments, haloes, crowns, border and other motifs and canopy variants; also the epigraphy of inscriptions could be instructive (although less attention has been paid to glass than to other media — notably monumental brasses). Another — and one which has been rather overlooked — is the extent to which the range and kind of coloured glass used might be the distinguishing trait of a workshop. The last is indeed perhaps the most obvious hallmark of the Stanford Phase II and Broughton Astley workshop. But the whole question remains fraught with difficulties, even leaving aside the obvious one created by massive losses, accident of survival and the poor condition and fragmentary nature of so much that has come down to us. Perhaps as a result there has been a tendency to pick and mix in this exercise. Other complicatory factors include the degree of exchange and interaction between workshops and the extent to which motifs like border designs were copied when they entered the public domain by being placed in church windows. This may apply to recorded glass in the adjacent Leicestershire churches of Osgathorpe and Belton, which in aspects of design is closely comparable with the Stanford Phase II borders (Fig. 12).[17] Again, the widespread use of stock tracery patterns like Y-tracery and cusped quatrefoils in midlands parish church architecture should inject a note of caution into attempts to identify specific cartoon designs as a mark of a workshop.

The introduction of architectural features brings us to the second question regarding the setting up and location of stained glass workshops. A key requisite must have been demand. There can be little doubt that fenestration, in both size and complexity, became a primary architectural focus from the late 13th century; with it stained glass became the principal medium for monumental painting. Which was the chicken and which the egg is impossible to answer, but it is at least certain that the midland counties witnessed a massive programme of parish church building (or rather rebuilding) during the first half of the 14th century.

Glass-painting by its nature lends itself to an urban manufacturing environment, although we need to be aware that evidence may be distorted by the comparative abundance of relevant civic archives compared with village and manorial records. It requires easy accessibility, both to potential patrons and for importing of materials, and for that a centre with good road and/or river communications is highly desirable. As for materials, while white glass could be obtained locally from the glass-making workshops of Staffordshire, the much more expensive coloured glass was imported from the Continent via ports like London, Hull, and King's Lynn — and probably Boston and Bristol.[18] In addition, it was advantageous for glass-painters to be in proximity to related crafts like stonemasons and blacksmiths.

Does 14th-century Coventry fit these criteria? During the previous century the city developed as an important regional centre, initially with a large and diverse manufacturing base which in the 14th century shifted towards trade; in the third decade Coventry's economy expanded noticeably and for one hundred years or so it was one of the most prosperous cities in the kingdom and by far the most important urban centre in the midlands. While none of the conduits by which glass was imported was close to Coventry, the same applies to other urban centres in the region. Besides, it was a centre of communications with a network of roads connecting it with other major cities and towns and it lay within a triangle formed by the ancient Fosse Way, Watling Street and Rychnield Street. Its prosperity was reflected in the large amount and scale of church building undertaken by monastic, mendicant, clerical and lay patrons within its boundaries from the late 13th century, although much seems to have been done from the 1340s.[19] Its hinterland, too, which extended into Northamptonshire and Leicestershire as well as Warwickshire, experienced much church-building activity in the 14th century. The names of no fewer than thirteen masons and nine carpenters are documented as resident in Coventry in the 14th and early 15th centuries.[20] Glaziers are recorded in the city from the early 14th century, albeit only two names are known, both from property transactions: William le Glasewryrthe/Glaswrughte (1310 and 1316) and John Glasewryghte (1340, 1349). The latter possibly is identical with John Coventre who in 1351–52 was one of the glass-painters employed by the crown on the windows of the royal chapels of St Stephen's, Westminster, and Windsor.[21] However, this dearth may reflect the selective and incomplete nature of the records. There has also been a tendency to underestimate the capacities of medieval glass-painting workshops, even when the indications are that for the most part they comprised no more than one or two master glaziers plus an assistant and an apprentice.[22]

While it remains plausible that one or both the Stanford workshops operated from Coventry, the evidence (if that is what the above amounts to) remains no more than circumstantial. Essentially, the problem lies in the dearth of glass of the period that has survived from Coventry itself. Apart from some fragments in Holy Trinity church, some of whose decorative features have affinities with the Stanford Phase II glazing, recourse has to be had to excavated scraps. The most extensive of these are from the Whitefriars church, especially its east window, but the finds date from the end of the 14th century and therefore are irrelevant to the present context.[23] As far as I am aware, the only excavated glass so far studied of the same period as the Stanford glazing are the 1,500 recognisable fragments from the Benedictine cathedral priory chapter-house published by Peter Newton.[24] He cautiously dated them to *c.* 1310–30 and found general parallels with glazing in Oxford and the midlands, including Stanford. The facial features (undulating eyebrows and curving nose profile) of the one relatively complete head are not so close to either of the Stanford phases to justify assigning them to their respective workshops and the rest of the finds are too fragmentary for any conclusive comparisons to be made.

It is equally important to bear in mind that claims could be made for the smaller and less significant county towns of Leicester and Northampton. Stanford is more or less equidistant from all three. Thornton (by the Stanford Phase I workshop) lies just north-west of Leicester and Broughton Astley, and Osgathorpe and Belton (if they are by the Stanford Phase II workshop) are also in closer proximity to Leicester than to Coventry. Through the historical connections of Stanford, it would be legitimate also to look to Northampton, through the holding of the chapters of the Benedictine Order there, or even London, because of the employment in royal service of several rectors of Stanford, especially John de Winwick. But Leicester and Northampton suffer even more than Coventry from a dearth of extant 14th-century glass and also their civic records of the period are less copious. Then there are places like Lichfield, with which two of the St Stephen's Chapel craftsmen are associated through their names; one of them (Hugh) being designated as one of the master glass-painters, responsible for designing the windows, whereas John Coventre was an executant.[25] Regrettably no relevant glass survives from Lichfield Cathedral, the east end of which was rebuilt and extended in the first half of the 14th century.

Ultimately, therefore, pending the discovery of glass closely comparable with that at Stanford on Avon, attempts to locate either or both the workshops responsible for the two early 14th-century phases in Coventry (or any other midlands urban centre) are no more than hypothetical. Nevertheless, Stanford and the glazing of other churches have much to tell us about glass-painting in the first half of the 14th century. Firstly, notwithstanding the absence of quantities of extant glass from Coventry and other urban centres, there was an enormous demand for glazing at this time in the region. Secondly, in richness, quality of design and execution (or 'artifice', to use the medieval terminology), the only distinction between the glazing of a parish church and a monastic, collegiate or even a cathedral church might be one of scale. In this respect, the band window chancel glazing scheme of Stanford is comparable with the glazing of Merton College Chapel, Oxford (*c.* 1294). Thirdly, in Stanford's case, the relatively high proportion of surviving glazing of the period, together with evidence of what has been lost, demonstrates the kinds of imagery (devotional, liturgical and moralistic) considered appropriate for a parish community which at the time was both populous (it included two hamlets as well as the village proper) and not as remote as it might appear, lying just off the Watling Street, still a major road in the middle ages.[26]

Stanford also raises wider methodological issues. Peter Newton eschewed any attempt to define a distinctive 'midlands' regional mode of glass-painting. It may well be that within Coventry and other centres workshops existed side by side, producing windows of different style, as was the case with the York Minster nave aisle glazing in the early 14th century. Viewed in this way, Coventry *et al.* may be seen as centres of glazing activity rather than purveyors of a distinctive style which spread into their respective hinterlands. Individual workshops may have dominated glazing in their locality, but the physical and social boundaries of their commissions could be more fully tested and explored by broadening the lines of enquiry beyond strictly art-historical methodologies of stylistic analysis to include the kinds of human and natural considerations (and complexities) identified in Derek Keene's recent brilliant essay on 'National and Regional Identities': geography, topography, communications, demography, occupational and familial networks, prosperity (or its absence), trade, manufacture, markets, ecclesiastical institutions and jurisdictions and local administrative structures and patronage.[27] The last, as Tim Ayers has suggested for Wells

Cathedral, can transcend regional parameters.[28] In this respect, too, Dyson's and Eden's interest in the links between Stanford and Selby was prescient and might explain the inclusion of abbots in the Stanford glazing (Figs 6, 7); nor should the involvement of successive rectors in royal administration be overlooked. In the process there is a need to define more precisely terms like 'local' and 'regional'. The county is a convenient, common organisational unit for the study of medieval stained glass (and other media), as it has been since the 1920s, but the kinds of headings just outlined do not fit neatly within county boundaries. Nor does there seem to have been a distinct awareness of county identity in the later middle ages, as is evident from William of Worcester's peregrinations in the 1470s.[29]

The subject-headings suggested by Derek Keene give rise to reflections regarding the principal centres of glass-painting in 14th-century England. The period witnessed major building projects at the great churches of Bristol, Chester, Ely, Exeter, Gloucester, Hereford, Lichfield, St Paul's London, Tewkesbury, Wells, Worcester and York; the reconstruction of their fabric brought in its train extensive painted glass. Of these buildings, only Gloucester, Tewkesbury, Wells and, above all, York have preserved substantial quantities of their glazing; at Chester, Lichfield and St Paul's none has survived. Their ambitious and individual programmes demanded careful management in execution, in some cases extending over several decades. The extent to which the workforces charged with these projects also undertook other commissions awaits further research. Tim Ayers has detected little sign that the Wells glaziers worked anywhere but the cathedral, whereas at York, some of the minster nave craftsmen were active in parish churches in and beyond the city.[30] A west midlands workshop contemporary with the Stanford Phase II workshop, and which seems to have been particularly peripatetic, was responsible for glass not only at Worcester Cathedral and Hadzor and Kempsey in the same county, but also roamed further afield to execute windows for the Cistercian abbey at Merevale at the north-east edge of Warwickshire and the Latin Chapel in the Augustinian priory of St Frideswide, Oxford.[31]

The existence of so many great church and parochial glazing projects distributed across central England from Exeter to East Anglia and Yorkshire during the first half of the 14th century renders redundant any equation of labels like 'local' or 'regional' with 'provincial' or 'inferior'. It also suggests that in this period there was no single dominant centre. The unknown quantity, of course, is the capital. Although the London Glaziers' Company existed from at least 1328 and the east end of St Paul's Cathedral was remodelled and the Greyfriars church constructed in this period, it is questionable whether London generated the level of continuous demand which could support glazing as a major activity.[32] Seen in this light, it may be significant that for the glazing of the royal chapel of St Stephen's, Westminster (1349–*c.* 1352), it was necessary to recruit glaziers from all over the country. While Black Death mortality has to be taken into account, St Stephen's may also have reflected a dearth of sufficiently skilled glass-painters available in the capital. Is it coincidental that one of the leading lights at St Stephen's was Simon of Lenne (King's Lynn), who was probably brought fresh from glazing the windows of the Lady Chapel of Ely Cathedral? The few recorded fragments of the St Stephen's windows are remarkably similar to the Ely glazing, which suggests that Ely was at least as rich and lavish as St Stephen's and may indeed have provided the model for the royal chapel.[33] Simon's fellow master glaziers numbered men whose toponyms included Chester, Lincoln, Lichfield and Lenton (Notts.).[34] This non-metropolitan diversity might serve to explain why it was two glass-painters from central England, Thomas Glazier of Oxford and John Thornton of Coventry, and not London craftsmen, who are associated with leading developments in glazing at the end of the 14th and early 15th centuries.

ACKNOWLEDGEMENTS

The author is grateful to the National Monuments Record and the Trustees of the Victoria and Albert Museum for permission to reproduce material in their collections.

NOTES

1. The most detailed accounts of the Stanford glazing are: P. A. Newton, 'Schools of glass-painting in the Midlands 1275–1430' (unpublished Ph.D. thesis, University of London, 1961), vol. 1, 2–3, 29–45; 2, 358–91. R. Marks, *The Medieval Stained Glass of the County of Northamptonshire*, *Corpus Vitrearum Medii Aevi*, Great Britain Summary Catalogue 4 (Oxford 1998), 177–271.
2. This motif was noted by N. Pevsner, *Northamptonshire* B/E (2nd edn 1973), 407.
3. Newton, 'Schools', and Marks, *Northamptonshire*, differ slightly in the dating and precise content of the two phases.
4. For Aslackby, see Marks, *Northamptonshire*, 180–1.
5. For John of Winwick, see ibid., 182; A. B. Emden, *A Biographical Register of the University of Oxford to A.D. 1500* 3 (Oxford 1959), 2063–4.
6. See J. H. Tillotson ed. and trans., *Monastery and Society in the Late Middle Ages: selected account rolls from Selby Abbey, Yorkshire, 1398–1537* (Woodbridge 1988), 16, 68, 69, 70.
7. See Marks, *Northamptonshire*, 177–9, for a complete bibliography on Stanford; a critical survey of the Northamptonshire glass historiography is on xliii–xlix.
8. Winston's account of the glass is in G. A. Poole, *Architectural Notices of the Churches of the Archdeaconry of Northampton* (London 1849), 218–28. This was based on his extensive notes and exquisite watercolours made in 1834, 1835 and 1848 (BL Add. MS 35211, iii, pp.10–33; MS 33846, ff. 7–8r; 33847, ff. 27r–35r, 36r–39r, 40r; 33851, fol. 72).
9. A. H. Dyson, *The Story of S. Nicholas Church Stanford-on-Avon and its Associations* (Rugby 1929); F. S. Eden, 'Ancient Painted Glass at Stanford-on-Avon and its Associations', *Journal of the British Society of Master Glass-Painters* 3 (1929–30), 156–65.
10. G. McN. Rushforth in A. Hamilton Thompson, 'Stanford-on-Avon', *Archaeol. J.* 90 (1933), 378–9.
11. For Selby, see D. O'Connor and H. R. Harris, 'The East Window of Selby Abbey, Yorkshire', in L. R. Hoey ed., *Yorkshire Monasticism: Archaeology, Art and Architecture from the 7th to the 16th Centuries*, *BAA Trans.* XVI (1995), 117–44.
12. L. F. Salzman, 'Medieval glazing accounts', *Journal of the British Society of Master Glass-Painters* 2 (1927–28), 116–20, 188–92; 3 (1929–30), 25–30; C. Woodforde, 'Glass-painters in England before the Reformation', idem, 6 (1935–37), 62–7, 121–8.
13. S. Pitcher, 'Ancient stained glass in Gloucestershire churches', *Transactions of the Bristol and Gloucestershire Archaeological Society* 47 (1925), 287–345; F. C. Eeles and A. V. Peatling, *Ancient Stained and Painted Glass in the Churches of Surrey*, Surrey Archaeological Collections (1930).
14. S. A. Jeavons, 'Medieval Painted Glass in Staffordshire Churches', *TBAS* 68 (1952), 25–73 (the term 'school' is used on p. 26).
15. N. H. J. Westlake, *A History of Design in Painted Glass* 2 (London and Oxford 1882), 41; B. Rackham, 'The Glass-Paintings of Coventry and its Neighbourhood', *Walpole Society* XIX (1930–31), 89–110.
16. Newton, 'Schools'. For an assessment of his contribution, see R. Marks, 'Medieval stained glass: recent and future trends in scholarship', *Journal of Stained Glass* 24 (2000), 62–79 (64).
17. London, Victoria and Albert Museum, Dept of Prints, Drawings and Design, acc. no. B. 4.a (watercolours presented by the Revd J. H. Cardew).
18. R. Marks, *Stained Glass in England during the Middle Ages* (London 1993), 30–1.
19. For medieval Coventry, see R. Goddard, *Communal Contraction and Urban Decline in Fifteenth-Century Coventry*, Dugdale Society Occasional Papers, 46 (2006); and Goddard, this volume, 36–9.
20. VCH *Warwickshire* VIII (1969), 154, table 2.

21. I am indebted to Dr Nat Alcock for providing me with transcripts of the relevant references. For the chapels at Westminster and Windsor, see Salzman, 'Accounts', 2 (1927–28), 120, 188; idem, 'The glazing of St. Stephen's Chapel Westminster, 1351–2', *Journal of the British Society of Master Glass-Painters* 1 (1924–26), 35; 2 (1927–28), 38–41.

22. Marks, *Stained Glass* (1993), 44.

23. Woodfield, *Whitefriars*, 185–244.

24. P. Newton, 'Window Glass', in Hobley, 'Cathedral Excavations', 102–11, figs 9–12.

25. Salzman, 'St Stephen's', *Journal of the British Society of Master Glass-Painters* 1 (1924–v26), 14–16, 31, 32, 35; 2 (1927–28), 39.

26. Marks, *Northamptonshire*, 179–82; idem, 'Medieval stained glass' (2000), 73–4. Evidence for the 14th-century population of Stanford can be found in manorial records and traces of the deserted village and its hamlets; for the latter see RCHME, *County of Northampton*: III, *Archaeological Sites in North-West Northamptonshire* (London 1981), 175–8, esp. figs 133, 134.

27. D. Keene, 'National and Regional Identities', in *Gothic Art for England 1400–1547*, ed. R. Marks and P. Williamson, Victoria and Albert Museum exhibition catalogue (London 2003), 46–55. A pioneering study along these lines was T. D. Atkinson, *Local Style in English Architecture: an enquiry into its origins and development* (London 1947).

28. T. Ayers, *The Medieval Stained Glass of Wells Cathedral, Corpus Vitrearum Medii Aevi*, Great Britain Volume IV (Oxford 2004), esp. 35, 454, 500; for Stanford, see above. Patronal networks in the late 15th and early 16th centuries link some of glazing of Tattershall College (Lincs.) with Great and Little Malvern priories and Westminster Abbey; R. Marks, *The Stained Glass of the Collegiate Church of the Holy Trinity, Tattershall (Lincs.)* (London and New York 1984).

29. For William of Worcester, see Keene, 'National and Regional Identities', 52. Similar limitations apply to the study of stained glass within modern national boundaries; see B. Kurmann-Schwarz, 'La recherche suisse sur le vitrail et son cadre international: avantages, handicaps et contraintes', *Zeitschrift für Schweizerische Archäologie und Kunstgeschichte* 53 (1996), 345–54 (349).

30. Ayers, *Wells*, ci; Marks, *Stained Glass* (1993), 153, 159.

31. Marks, *Stained Glass* (1993), 161–2.

32. Ibid., 41; Ayers, *Wells*, 35, 454, 500. For St Paul's in this period, see C. Davidson, 'Fabric, Tombs and Precincts, 1087–1540', in *St Paul's: The Cathedral Church of London 604–2004*, ed. D. Keene, A. Burns and A. Saint (New Haven and London 2004), 127–42 (esp. 136–9). For the building and glazing of the very important London Greyfriars church, see C. L. Kingsford, 'The Grey Friars of London', *British Society of Franciscan Studies* 6 (1915), 18, 35–42 (a list of donors of the stained glass windows is transcribed on 165–9); also E. B. S. Shepherd, 'The Church of the Friars Minor in London', *Archaeol. J.* 59 (1902), 238–87.

33. Marks, *Stained Glass* (1993), 159–61.

34. Salzman, 'St Stephen's', *Journal of the British Society of Master Glass-Painters* 1 (1924–26), 15–16, 31–5; 2 (1927–28), 38–41; idem, 'Medieval Glazing Accounts', 2 (1927–28), 120.

The Doom in Holy Trinity Church and Wall-Painting in Medieval Coventry

MIRIAM GILL

The artistic standing of medieval Coventry has received little consideration, in spite of the presence of the striking scheme of 15th-century paintings in the Charterhouse. However, the programme of conservation, which has made the Doom in Holy Trinity church accessible again, and the discovery of fragments of a later 14th-century Apocalypse cycle from the chapter-house of Coventry Priory present an opportunity for reassessment. Both schemes suggest a considerable level of artistic sophistication in the city. The Holy Trinity Doom demonstrates the persistence in Coventry of a robust form of the International Gothic Style associated with its most famous artistic son, the glazier John Thornton. The chapter-house fragments suggest a technically and iconographically complex rendering of the Book of Revelation, pre-dating the comparable cycle at Westminster and surpassing it in quality. These paintings of c. *1360–70 are witness to a desire to emulate continental models in the generation before John Thornton. Both schemes suggest the context in which the Last Judgement, the climactic scene in the famous Coventry cycle plays, may have been presented and understood. Above all, they confirm the status of late medieval Coventry as a centre of artistic ambition and stylistic innovation.*

THE artistic reputation of late medieval Coventry has long rested on its identification with a significant school of glass-painting, and particularly the figure of John Thornton, the creator of the great east window in York Minster (1405–08).[1] By contrast, until very recently wall-painting in medieval Coventry has received little attention. Urban records indicate that by the 15th century there was an identifiable community of painters in Coventry, for in 1435 they were required to contribute to the cardmakers' pageant.[2] However, almost none of their work was believed to survive: witness, for example, Davidson and Alexander's subject list, produced under the auspices of the Early Drama Art and Music Project in 1985.[3]

This absence of painting or knowledge about local painting was perhaps always more apparent than real. Polychromed wooden statues, most notably a St George from the Gosford Gate Chapel, survive from medieval Coventry.[4] In the 19th century the local antiquarian, Nathaniel Troughton, had recorded three areas of historic mural painting in Holy Trinity.[5] Paintings in St Michael's church of a head of Christ and the Virgin and Child, appearing to date from the early 14th century, were exposed by bombing in the Second World War.[6] Post-war excavation in Bayley Lane brought to light the finely painted head of a demon now preserved in the Herbert Art Gallery and Museum. The excavations of the priory site in 1965–67 uncovered fragments of painted plaster.[7] Above all, the strikingly beautiful and highly unusual remains of a refectory painting uncovered in 1917 in the city's Charterhouse has suffered an undeserved obscurity which is now addressed in this volume.[8] Even in the light of recent revelations, the artistic quality and unusual content of the Charterhouse paintings give them a strong claim to be considered as the most important scheme surviving in the city.

However, two significant developments have transformed our understanding of the artistic ambition of late medieval Coventry. The first, the focus of this paper, is the wall-painting of the Doom or Last Judgement in the parish church of Holy Trinity, a painting which was effectively 'rediscovered' from the 1980s onwards.[9] The second, a very rare instance of the archaeological discovery of masonry with figurative painting, has demonstrated the presence of an elaborate Apocalypse cycle of *c.* 1360–70 in the former chapter-house of St Mary's Cathedral Priory. These fragments were the most striking of a range of examples of masonry with painted decoration, including polychromed statuary, found during the excavations of the priory site.[10] The Apocalypse fragments discovered between 2000–02 have already been extensively presented in print and these findings will be reviewed during the discussion of the Doom's context.[11] Both of these artistically skilled and iconographically complex schemes represent a significant addition to the national corpus of surviving wall-paintings.

These painted buildings fortuitously present a very fertile pairing. Their locations are geographically close and institutionally connected: St Mary's Priory held the advowson of Holy Trinity. Both paintings depict the end of the world and the judgement of humanity. However, the visual expression of this common theme is tailored to the specific groups of viewers and the function of the respective buildings. While the elaborate apocalypse imagery at St Mary's addresses a self-consciously learned and literate audience, the painting at Holy Trinity is an example of a frequently depicted, even archetypal, parochial subject.

The Doom at Holy Trinity is now one of the most legible and complete examples of this subject to survive and its high level of artistry and detail make it one of the most significant late medieval parochial wall-paintings.[12] However, it has had a complex conservation history. It was initially uncovered in 1831 (Fig. 1 and Col. Pl. XI in print edn), found under layers of whitewash, with which it had been covered from the mid-16th century onward.[13] An area on the upper left-hand side has been severely abraded in a manner consistent with scrubbing with a hard brush, possibly with the intention of 'cleaning' the painting off the wall.[14] However, this attempt seems to have been halted and the decision that same year to employ local artist, David Gee, to restore the painting, suggests that it was rapidly coming to be regarded sympathetically.[15]

Contemporary documents give little information about the nature and extent of Gee's work, but recent analysis suggests that he strengthened the outlines around the figures, in some cases adding black outline, and that he renewed or re-coloured some areas.[16] These additions are primarily revealed by close visual analysis and the technical identification of post-medieval pigments.[17] There are also areas, such as the teeth around the mouth of Hell, where his repainting can be seen. The mural owes its current appearance, indeed some of its legibility, to Gee's interventions, but it must be admitted that they have made it more difficult to assess the artistry of the original. However, there is no evidence that his work altered the composition of the painting or substantially falsified the stylistic and iconographic details. Interestingly, in 1825 Gee had produced an illustration of the Doom painting in the Guild Chapel at Stratford-upon-Avon (post-1496) for Sharp's publication on the Coventry mystery cycle, a task which would have made him familiar with medieval iconography of the Last Judgement.[18]

The other significant intervention attributed to Gee is the application of a coating or coatings to the painting. The principal coating has been identified as 'megilp',[19] a

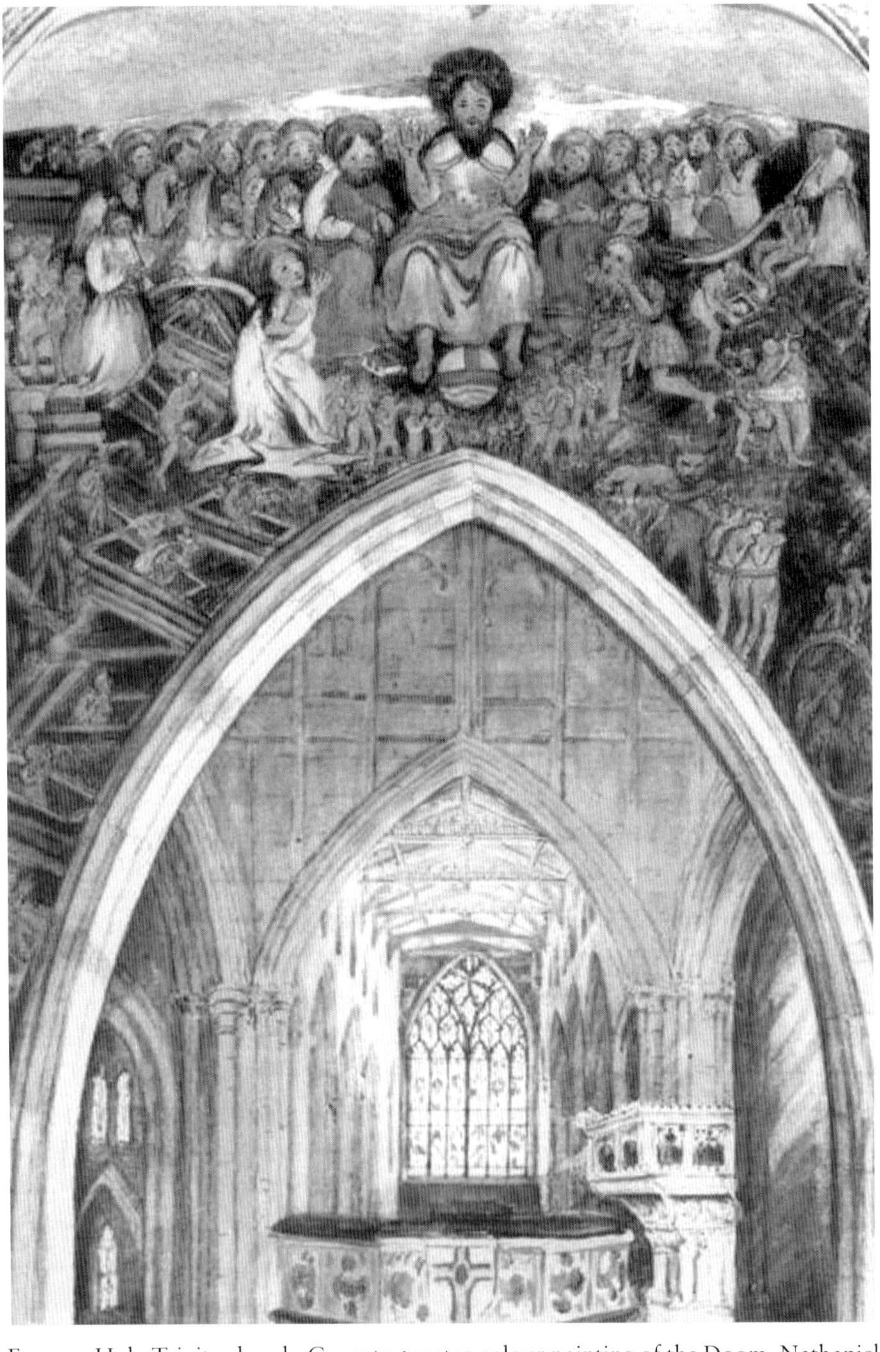

FIG. 1. Holy Trinity church, Coventry: water-colour painting of the Doom, Nathaniel Troughton, after 1855 (Troughton VIII/21)
Photo, History of Art Department, University of Warwick

bituminous mixture commonly applied to easel paintings in the earlier 19th century to give them an 'antique' appearance.[20] In 1831 Gee received five guineas for his work on the Doom, a modest sum compared to the twenty-five pounds he was paid two years later for an altarpiece at Holy Trinity.[21] The relatively small sum of money may imply that the application of the coating was his major, and for some areas of the painting, his only intervention. Technical analysis revealed areas of dirt trapped between as many as four layers of coatings, suggesting that some applications of coating date from later in the 19th century.[22] A likely context for some of these interventions is the 1855 restoration by Scott when a coating was applied to the windows of the clerestory.[23]

Reproductions and descriptions of the Doom painting in the 19th century suggest that it rapidly became hard to decipher, probably as a direct consequence of the coatings described above. In James Cherry's engraving of *c.* 1831–37 the figure of St John the Baptist is shown as a devil with a pitchfork. In 1855 Scharf described the Doom as a 'curious old brown painting' and published a sketchy engraving of it from which the interceding figure of the Virgin was omitted.[24] By 1873 the painting was described as 'almost invisible'.[25]

The main piece of antiquarian evidence which conflicts with this picture of a rapid descent into brown obscurity is Troughton's watercolour (Fig. 1). This is the only coloured representation of the mural to survive from the 19th century and it is accompanied by a detailed written description.[26] Although there are a few strange errors and omissions,[27] the watercolour is substantially accurate and includes more detail than the engravings discussed above. Troughton's drawings also record two other paintings found in Holy Trinity in 1831, a fragmentary scene of the Crucifixion with a clerical donor on the north wall of the chancel (apparently post-1460), which was subsequently destroyed, and a heraldic painting on the south-west pier of the crossing, which is now very badly damaged.[28] Although the watercolour of the Doom has been traditionally dated to the 1860s (the form of the east window and the polychromy of the font record the appearance of the interior after Scott's restoration of 1855), the detail in the watercolour and description may suggest that this was based on records made at the time this painting and that in the chancel were first uncovered.

By the middle of the 20th century the Doom was considered 'lost': indeed in the post-war period, plans were drawn up to execute a modern mural of Christ and the workers in its place.[29] Interest in the medieval painting was rekindled when a patch cleaning test undertaken by Anna Hulbert in 1986 revealed beautiful details of the right foot of Christ and adjacent figures, demonstrating that at least some of the Doom had survived.[30] More thorough investigations showed that a very extensive composition of the Last Judgement survived on the nave east wall. An infrared survey begun in 1995 and close visual inspection confirmed that the surviving painting was essentially that recorded by Troughton over a hundred years before.[31] The eventual conservation campaign aimed to reduce the coatings which over time disfigured and harmed the painting. However, it was decided to try to retain Gee's other interventions, as these now represented part of the painting's history and contributed to its legibility.

No documentary evidence for the creation of the painting survives, so its dating relies on an examination of its architectural context and especially its artistic style. The Doom painting completely covers the east wall of the nave of Holy Trinity and extends onto the soffit at the junction to the roof (Fig. 2 and Col. Pl. XII in print edn). Architectural details, such as the bust figure which bridges the junction between the nave east wall and the tower staircase low on the right-hand side, appear to be covered

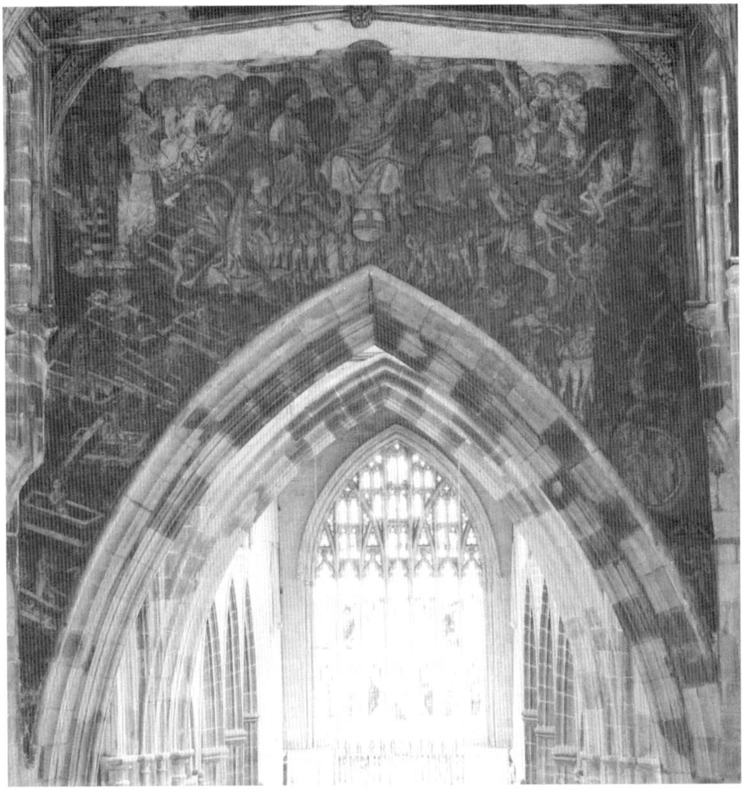

FIG. 2. Holy Trinity: the Doom painting after recent cleaning and conservation

Photo 2004, J. Burbidge

with the same layer of painted decoration.[32] It is thus clear that the painting must post-date both the remodelling of the central tower and the insertion of the nave clerestory with its associated wooden roof, implying a date no earlier than *c.* 1430.

With the exception of the small bust figure at the base of the tower staircase, a continuous flat surface had been prepared to receive the painting. This required hacking back the weathering strip for the steeply pitched, 14th-century nave roof and building up the level of the previously external areas above it: the line of the previous roof is still visible in places today (Fig. 2). The packing on the right-hand side was dislodged by aerial bombardment in the Second World War. The original support of earth, lath and plaster could be seen in the cavity prior to conservation.[33]

The nave east wall is the most common position for a painting of the Last Judgement; fifty-two of the sixty-five 15th- and 16th-century Doom paintings studied by Ashby occupy this position.[34] The scale, clear outlines and bold colouring of the Holy Trinity Doom seem to have been designed to make this image of the Last Judgement as impressive as possible to those entering the church or facing east during worship. By the late middle ages the Doom probably constituted the largest painted subject and possibly the largest area of painting in Holy Trinity, a parish church with a complex interior adorned with elaborate stone panelling and containing individual chantries and chapels, presumably defined by wooden parclose screens.

However, it is important to note that, in contrast to most churches, this location at Holy Trinity did not represent the division between the nave and the chancel. In *c.* 1391 the chancel had been extended 24ft east.[35] Indeed, the late medieval position of the rood-screen, one bay east of the crossing, is clearly indicated in the 15th-century chancel arcade. The survival of the carved stone pulpit on the south-east pier of the crossing tower confirms that this arrangement dates back at least to the 15th century and thus may pre-date the Doom painting.

Most 20th-century accounts of the painting dated it to the end of the 15th century.[36] However, the pre-conservation investigations of the painting moved this date forward with Anna Hulbert proposing a date some time in the reign of Henry VI, based on the form of the haircut of the male figure in her largest cleaning test patch (Fig. 3).[37] The pre-conservation infrared surveys revealed the detail of the horned headdresses of the alewives, previously sketchily apparent in Troughton's drawing (Fig. 4 and Col. Pl. XIIIA in print edn). The 'heart-shaped' arrangement of these horns suggests a date in the 1430s or 1440s: similar headdresses are shown on the memorial brass of 1435 to the wife and mother of Sir John Dyve at Bromham (Beds.).[38] Although it must be treated with caution, evidence from costume and armour is recognised as important in the dating of 15th-century English wall-painting.[39] Moreover, medieval polemic against alewives made reference to fashionable and alluring dress particularly in the context of

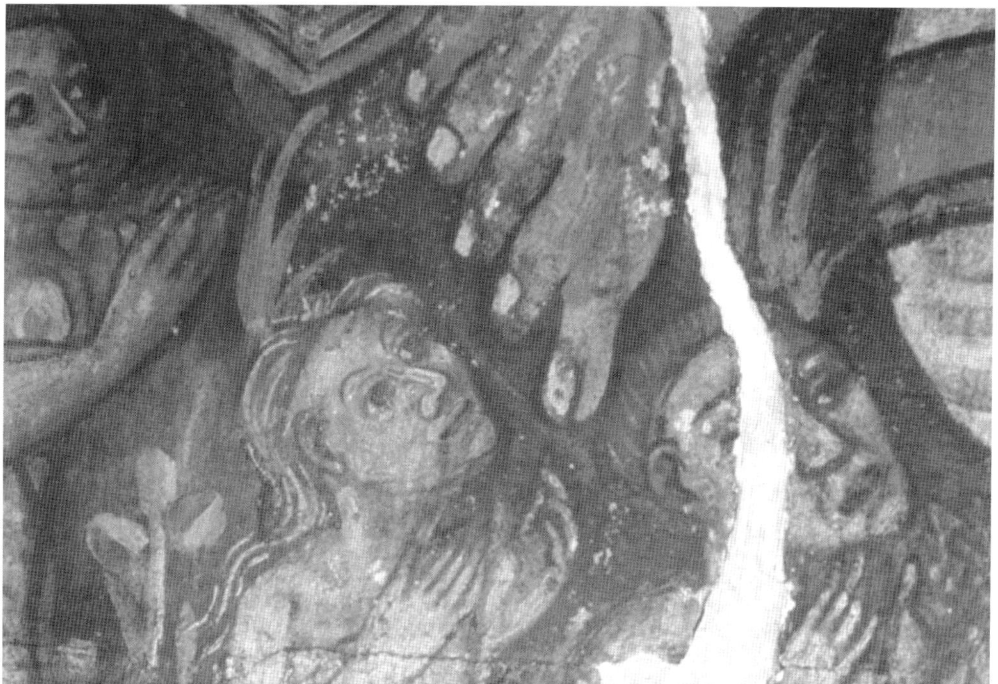

FIG. 3. Holy Trinity: the Doom, figures by the right foot of Christ

Photo, R. Stevenson

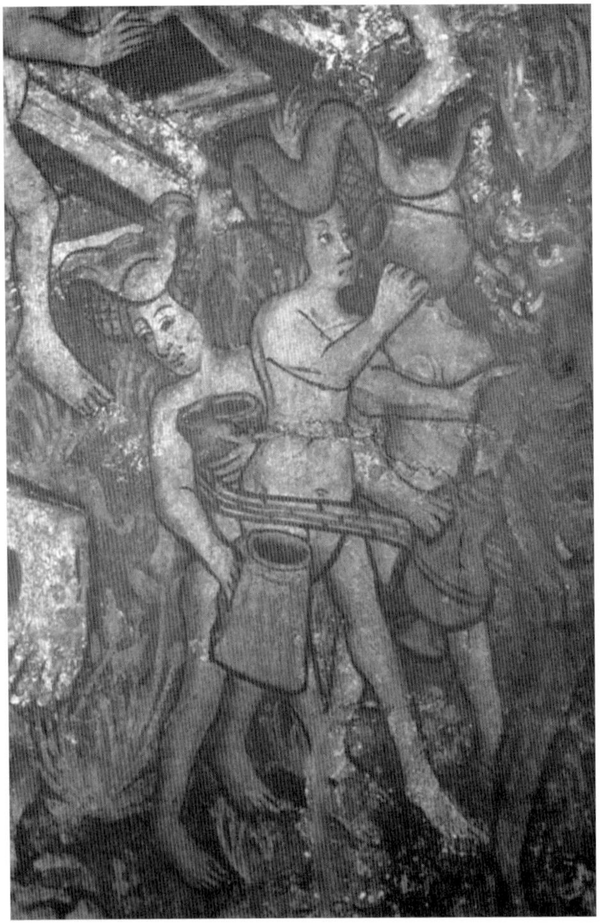

FIG. 4. Holy Trinity: the Doom, three alewives led by a demon
Photo, J. Burbidge

sexual temptation.[40] It thus seems likely that these headdresses, the only distinctive element of medieval dress in the whole painting, were intended to represent contemporary fashion.

The facial features and figure style of the Doom appear to confirm the costume evidence. The style of the painting with its substantial figures, large and prominent handling of features, illusionistic architecture and warm colours can be compared with manuscripts, such as the so-called 'Hours Elizabeth the Queen' dated to *c.* 1420–30 and probably produced in London.[41] Given the Coventry provenance of John Thornton, it is interesting to compare the treatment of figures, particularly the facial modelling, pronounced features and 'soft' hair, with the great east window at York Minster. Details in the Doom also bear comparison with glass painting from St Michael's, Coventry, from the early decades of the 15th century.[42] It appears that the St Michael's glass also included a scene of the Last Judgement, now in the Bishop Haigh Memorial Chapel (former south porch), elements of which resemble the area of the Holy Trinity Doom next to Christ's right foot (Fig. 3; Fig. 5 and Col. Pl. XIIIB in print edn).[43] While the individuals responsible for the Doom's creation cannot be identified, these stylistic

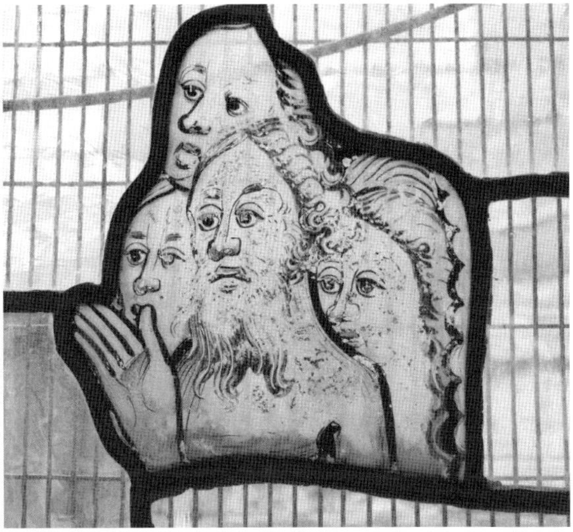

FIG. 5. Coventry Cathedral: Haigh Memorial Chapel, reset glass from St Michael's church, souls rising from the grave, detail
Photo, R. K. Morris

and iconographic similarities suggest that the painters were probably local. The lost crucifixion mural recorded by Troughton in the chancel apparently included the head of a clerical donor, but the Doom painting, like the majority of English parochial murals, does not contain any visual indication of patronage.[44] It may well have been funded by collective parochial patronage or one of the guilds which had their chapels in the church.

The Doom preserves a wealth of iconographic detail. The composition centres on the monumental figure of Christ whose hands are raised in judgement and whose cloak is open to reveal his wounded body and side (Fig. 2). A globe divided into three portions lies between his feet. He is flanked by the twelve apostles, among whom the figures of St Peter (left of Christ), St Paul (right of Christ) and St John the Divine (third from left) can be clearly identified. Beyond these to the left and right are angels blowing the last trump. Below kneel the interceding figures — on Christ's right hand, the Virgin bearing her breast, and on his left, St John the Baptist (Fig. 6). At Christ's feet, between the intercessors, are two groups of resurrected figures identified by their headgear. The even-handed treatment of the saved and the damned is emphasised by the presence of the same 'cast' of king, queen, cardinal and cleric. Two small but beautifully painted figures of a man and woman at kneel Christ's right foot (Fig. 4). Local pride has sought to associate these with Coventry's heroine, Godiva, and her husband Leofric, but it seems more likely that these figures represent Adam and Eve.

Beyond this central group, the general resurrection is shown by figures, some still wrapped in shrouds, emerging from graves and tombs (Fig. 2). The entrances to Heaven and Hell are shown diagonally opposite. In the upper left-hand portion of the painting steps lead to a doorway into Heaven where St Peter and an angel stand to welcome a figure in a papal tiara. Angels stand on the parapet above. The entrance to Hell is a monstrous mouth and souls licked by flames are visible within. Chained groups of figures are dragged towards it, while other unfortunates, including an alewife, are carried there by demons (Fig. 7).

While this Doom painting is in many ways typical of the depiction of the Last Judgement at this date, several significant aspects of its artistry and iconography were

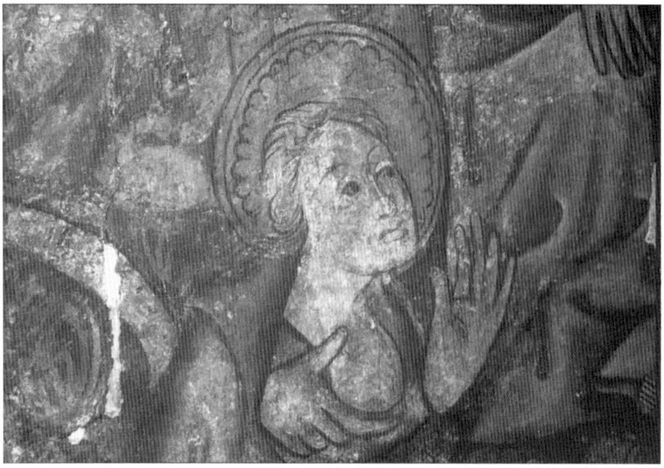

FIG. 6. Holy Trinity: the Doom, the Virgin Mary baring her breast
Photo, R. Stevenson

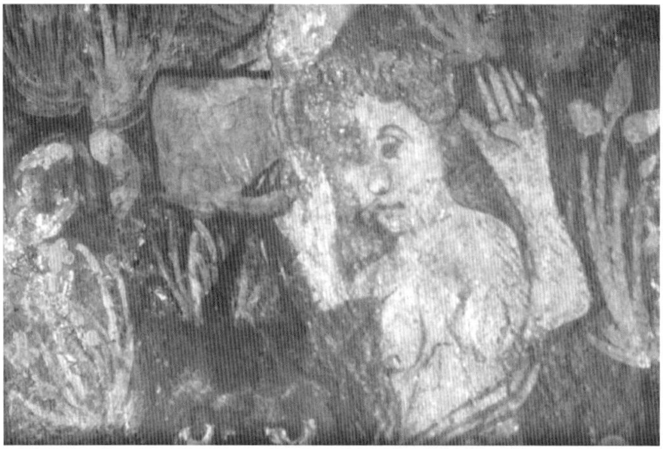

FIG. 7. Holy Trinity: the Doom, demon giving a piggyback to an alewife
Photo, R. Stevenson

only revealed by the recent technical examination. These investigations demonstrated the care which went into the design and creation of the mural. The painting was built up in layers using a broad but typical range of pigments, some of which were applied in an oil medium.[45] The main elements of the complex composition were initially outlined in red.[46] A layer of black under-painting with a pigment apparently derived from coal was used to block out the areas of background, and this served to strengthen the intensity of the green verdigris.[47] This green colour was the predominant element in a background design which imitated the fashionable *millefleurs* form of tapestry with its scatter of foliage; the setting of the Coventry Charterhouse painting is treated in a similar way.[48] Instances where minor figures were added on top of this dark under-painting, as well as elements of poor draughtsmanship and hastily executed flowers, suggest the presence of a workshop of variable skill and, in some cases, may also represent rapidly executed running repairs made later in the 15th century.[49]

Analysis has also drawn attention to a number of sophisticated artistic techniques employed on the central figure of Christ in Judgement. For example, Christ's halo not only retained gilding, but it would originally have glowed with a crimson glaze applied over gold leaf.[50] On Christ's feet two different red pigments were deliberately applied to distinguish between the appearance of fresh and dried blood, with the former being rendered with a combination of vermillion, red lead and red lake on a thin layer of carbon black (Fig. 3).[51] While these techniques contributed to the clarity and vivid colour of the painting, the emphasis on the lurid colour of fresh blood had a theological aspect, stressing Christ's suffering for human sin.[52]

Further iconographic details were revealed by the programme of conservation. Above Christ's right hand, traces of painting found on the soffit revealed a bust of an angel holding one of the instruments of the Passion, probably a spear (Fig. 7). Presentation of angels in this format can be paralleled in the later Doom at Penn (Bucks., *c.* 1500).[53] The soffit angel would be complementary to the angels blowing the last trump.

Conservation has also clarified iconographic details previously not fully understood by the author.[54] The tonsured figure on Christ's right is clearly St Peter, with his attribute, the key, at his feet. A sword pointing towards Christ's left leg seems to be a balancing attribute and identifies the figure on Christ's left as St Paul. Although St Paul was not technically numbered among the twelve disciples, he was commonly included in late medieval visual schemes in preference to the more historical figure of St Matthias. Christ thus sits between the Apostles to the Jews and the Gentiles. Interestingly, this motif with the attributes of key and sword is evoked and moralised by the vernacular preacher, John Mirk, in his book of model sermons, *Festial* (*c.* 1382–90).[55]

The iconographic detail attracting the greatest interest is the unprecedentedly large number of alewives included in the painting: a group of three chained together and led to the mouth of Hell by a demon, and a fourth on the shoulders of a large black demon (Figs 4, 7). The alewives are identified by the attribute of vessels — a jug, a bowl and ale pots — and the group chained together are also distinguished by their fashionable headdresses already discussed. Fears about short measures may be indicated by their vessels.[56] The figure of an alewife being carried piggyback into Hell (Fig. 7) seems to have enjoyed considerable currency in late medieval England. Indeed, the earliest recorded image of a dishonest alewife in the Holkham Picture Bible (*c.* 1325) is presented in this form.[57] It forms one of the incidents on the misericords of the alewife

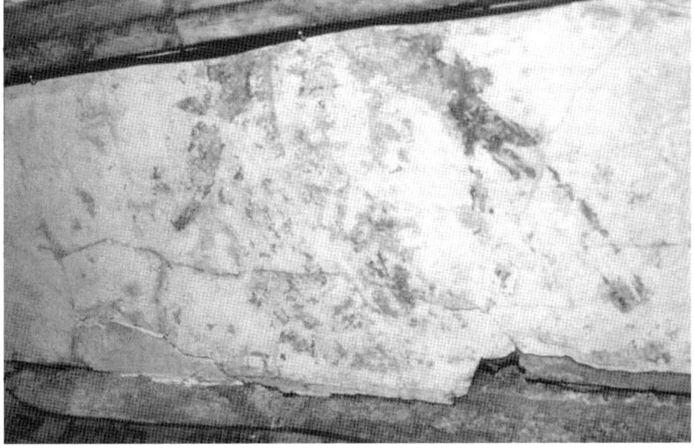

FIG. 8. Holy Trinity: the Doom, traces of an angel on the soffit
Photo, R. Stevenson

at St Laurence's church, Ludlow (*c.* 1430), as well as being found on a 15th-century roof-boss in the nave of Norwich Cathedral and in Doom paintings at St Michael's church, St Albans (lost) and St Thomas' church, Salisbury (*c.* 1470).[58] At Salisbury, the rather endearing couple recall the romantic interlude between demon and alewife in the *Chester Play of the Harrowing of Hell*.[59] Civic concern about the local trade in ale is indicated by regulations recorded in the Coventry Leet Book for 1434 and 1439.[60] Given the presence of an alewife in the Chester cycle, it is possible that alewives also featured in the Coventry plays, but inventory evidence is of little help here because the alewives' costumes and properties may well have been supplied by the cast.

Given the popularity of images of the Last Judgement in late medieval monumental art, the Holy Trinity Doom does not need to be 'explained' in any way. The 1426 reference to local fears that an earthquake presaged the end of the world tells us about medieval preoccupations, but does not have to be seen as the 'reason' for the painting.[61] However, it is relevant to examine how this theme was depicted in medieval Coventry. Before the Second World War, St Michael's contained two significant medieval representations of the Last Judgement in 15th-century glass and on a misericord of *c.* 1465 in the Drapers' Chapel, and it is probably no coincidence that the Drapers' Guild was responsible for the Doomsday play at Coventry.[62] In the light of the discovery of the Apocalypse cycle at the priory, it is interesting to note that St Michael's also contained a late 15th-century misericord of the binding of Satan (*Revelation* 20: 1–2),[63] a relatively unusual depiction of a theme from *Revelation* in parochial art.

The text of the play of the Last Judgement which concluded the famous Coventry cycle has not survived. Detailed records of the players and their properties date back only to 1562, by which time the play may already have been revised to make it more acceptable to Protestant sensibilities.[64] The play of 1562 sounds spectacular, with payments for 'kepyng of hell mowthe and the fyer', but where 'iconographic' details are discernible, such as references to 'black souls' and 'white souls', these seem to come from a stage-based tradition separate from that used in the medieval Doom. While the Holy Trinity Doom would have shaped the context in which this play was viewed we can only speculate about the extent to which the painting may have inspired or reflected Coventry's dramatic tradition.

The chapter-house Apocalypse paintings present an instructive contrast to the Holy Trinity mural. The Doom is dramatic but distant, the excavated fragments from the Priory are exquisitely detailed and intimate. Painted within the arches of the blind arcade of the monks' sedilia around the walls, they were created to invite repeated and informed study. Both paintings are technically and stylistically sophisticated, although the priory paintings have the artistic edge, uncompromised by later interventions and created for close inspection.

The excavated masonry from the priory preserves fragments of at least three scenes from what must originally have been a very long and elaborate cycle. Three pieces of masonry with significant figurative painting were found, although other fragments from the chapter-house also retained polychromy.[65] The smallest piece (T698/2) preserves the remains of a delicately painted head with a golden crown.[66] A piece with a much larger area of painting (T698/1, approximately 300 × 200mm) is now displayed in the Priory Visitor Centre.[67] It can be confidently identified as coming from an illustration of chapter four of *Revelation*. The details of the door opened in Heaven, the figures of St John the visionary and rows of venerable figures with gold crowns representing some of the twenty-four elders, are all clearly visible. The orange background is decorated with a diaper of what would have been silver stars. Above is a wing full of eyes from one of the apocalyptic beasts, possibly the lion. This would have formed the lower left part of the focal image of Christ in Majesty. The fragment suggests that the original image, probably broadly symmetrical in composition, may have extended across the bay (including the first fragment).[68] This may give us the standard size of the painted scenes at Coventry, although it is possible that this pivotal scene was accorded a larger space, as in the Apocalypse Retable attributed to Master Bertram of Hamburg (*c.* 1400) in the Victoria and Albert Museum.[69]

The third piece (T698/5) retains two significant areas of painting separated by a niche (Fig. 9), but it is less easy to identify the two scenes. To the left of the niche, faces look up into the sky (Fig. 10 and Col. Pl. XIIIc in print edn). A band of stylised cloud

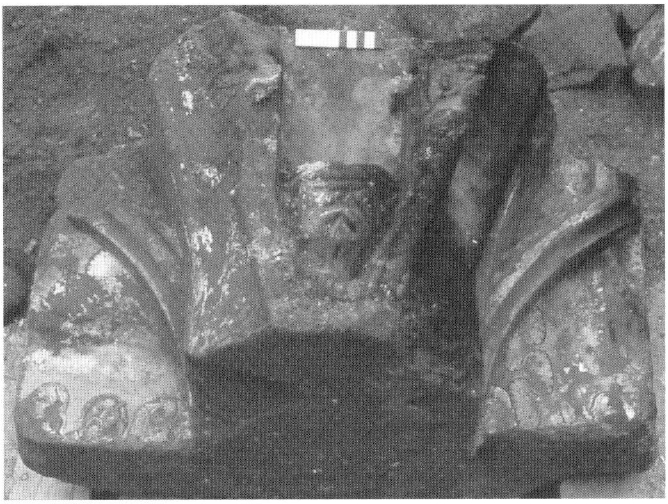

FIG. 9. Coventry Priory, chapter-house sedilia: piece T698/5, a central springer with two adjoining areas of wall-plate, scale 10cm
Photo, R. K. Morris

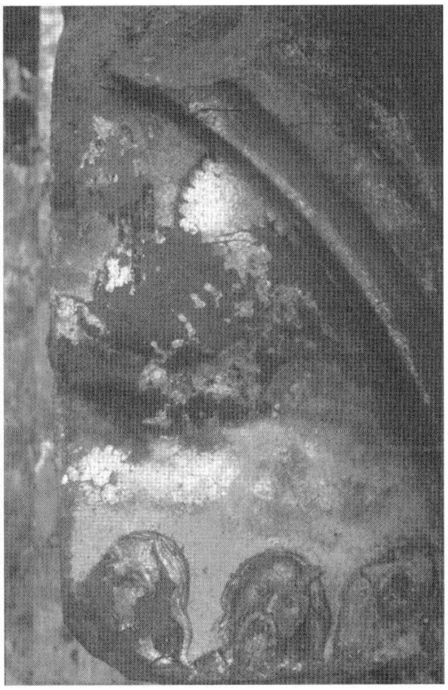

FIG. 10. Coventry Priory, chapter-house: piece T698/5, detail showing figures looking up
Photo, R. K. Morris

separates these from a wing full of eyes. It appears likely that this scene follows the convention found in English and French Apocalypse cycles of including one of the Apocalyptic beasts alongside each of the Four Horsemen of the Apocalypse.[70] The presence of human figures gazing heavenward may suggest that this scene showed Death, the final horseman.[71]

To the right of the niche is the head of the visionary St John in the left hand corner, divided from the rest of the scene by a band of stylised cloud. Beyond this are four faces (of varying ages) and a wing with eyes set against what was probably a diaper of silver stars like that on the second stone. The most likely reading is that St John is looking into Heaven and seeing a group of worshippers in adoration, probably the Adoration of the Lamb by those sealed by the angels of God (*Revelation* 7: 9–17).[72] If correct, these identifications, together with the iconography of the individual scenes, confirm the impression that the cycle 'read' from left to right. The location of the stones suggests that they came from the north wall of the chapter-house, implying a cycle organised clockwise around the building.[73]

The lavish palette at the priory includes gold for crowns and haloes and silver stars applied to the background. Analysis of the second fragment has revealed the complex technique deployed. This scene was executed on an ochre ground with pure yellow used as under-painting for the areas of gilding, while the tower was painted in a flat vermillion and then in grisaille tones before achieving its final colour and appearance.[74] This suggests a painstaking approach and one which allowed the artist considerable freedom to adjust and develop the detail of the composition.

The style of the paintings suggests that they are later than the remodelling of the chapter-house between *c.* 1310–30, although they are the first layer of complex polychromy applied to these stones.[75] The emphasis on warm colours, particularly the pink of the tower and the orange background of the heavenly scenes, suggests Italian influence. The illusionistic treatment of space and architecture and the very delicate modelling of faces and figures, including foreshortening (Fig. 10), resemble those mid-14th-century English works which emulate early Renaissance models.[76] In the corpus of English wall-paintings, it is only the murals from St Stephen's, Westminster (1350–63), which display the same stylistic and technical ambition and are also heavily dependent on Italian, specifically Sienese, models.[77] The proposed date of *c.* 1360–70 would mean that the scheme preceded the Apocalypse cycle of ninety-six scenes in the Benedictine chapter-house at Westminster Abbey, now dated to the years around 1400, as well as being artistically superior to it.[78]

Prior to the discovery of the Coventry fragments, the presence of this subject in the chapter-house at Westminster was regarded as somewhat idiosyncratic.[79] However, the choice of subject matter can be related both to the function of the chapter-house as a place of communal discipline, and to the requirement in the twelfth chapter of *The Rule of St Benedict* that monks include a recitation of one chapter of the *Book of Revelation* from memory in their celebration of the Office of Lauds every Sunday.[80] In contrast to the unified image of the Last Judgement offered by the Doom, Apocalypse cycles addressed self-consciously literate and learned viewers and expressed the centrality of the reading of Scripture within monastic life.[81]

Monumental Apocalypse schemes were almost always based on illustrations developed to accompany texts. The fashion for lavish Apocalypse books seems to have developed in England in the mid-13th century.[82] In many instances it is possible to link a monumental cycle to an identifiable tradition or 'family' of Apocalypse manuscripts. At Norwich Cathedral Priory, the communar's roll for 1346–47 records the purchase of an Apocalypse Book to serve as a model for the cloister roof bosses.[83] In the case of Westminster Abbey chapter-house it is probable that the specific manuscript exemplum survives, a later 14th-century copy (Cambridge, Trinity College, MS B. 10. 2) of a 13th-century model known as the 'expanded Metz' cycle.[84] At York Minster, in the great east window (1405–08) created by John Thornton of Coventry, it appears that two distinct visual traditions were blended to create a cycle of eighty scenes.[85] The iconographic detail of the Coventry fragments differs from the models used at Westminster and York. Indeed, details such as the illusionistic grouping of the adoring elders suggest that the as yet unidentified model may have been used with considerable freedom.

The presence of both these complex schemes in major churches in the centre of Coventry prompts a re-evaluation of the lost artistic wealth of a city so rich in religious institutions. The Apocalypse painting shows that visual sophistication and innovation in Coventry can be traced back into the later 14th century, a time of significant building schemes in the city, and decades before the now famous John Thornton departed for York. The Holy Trinity Doom demonstrates that monumental murals as well as glass painting retained a robust form of International Gothic well into the 15th century. The Apocalypse paintings predate those in the chapter-house at Westminster and surpass them in quality and possibly scale, suggesting that Coventry was an artistic centre, perhaps even an inspiration for Westminster. Their ambitious emulation of Italian forms in a period of stylistic diversity suggests a sophisticated artistic culture.[86] Although the climactic play of the Last Judgement performed by the Drapers Guild of Coventry is witnessed only by secondary documents, these paintings add significantly to our understanding of how the end of the world was pictured in the late medieval city, possibly suggesting lost details such as the presence of alewives. When these sites are added to the Charterhouse murals, and our knowledge of glass painting and polychromed sculpture, Coventry emerges as a very artistically significant city in which images of the highest quality were created and striking schemes of painting could have been viewed.

ACKNOWLEDGEMENTS

I gratefully acknowledge my debt to my Ph.D. supervisor, David Park, and to Sharon Cather and all the team from the Courtauld Institute of Art and beyond with whom I worked on the Coventry Doom in the 1990s; in particular, Robyn Pender, Helen Howard, Robert Gowing and John Burbidge, who was also generous with access to his images and research. Many times I was helped and encouraged by the incumbents and congregation at Holy Trinity, and Margaret Rylatt and the staff at the Herbert Museum and Art Gallery. I would also like thank Linda Monckton and Richard K. Morris for their support and encouragement.

NOTES

1. B. Rackham, 'The glass-paintings of Coventry and its neighbourhood', *The Walpole Society* XIX (1930–31), 89–110; T. French, *York Minster: the great east window*, Corpus Vitrearum Medii Aevi, Summary Catalogue, 2 (Oxford 1995).
2. R. W.Ingram ed., *Coventry*, Records of Early English Drama (Manchester 1981), 11.
3. C. Davidson and J. Alexander, *The Early Art of Coventry, Stratford-upon-Avon, Warwick and Lesser Sites in Warwickshire*, EDAM Reference Series 4 (Kalamazoo 1985).

4. S. Riches, 'St George and the Dragon', in *Gothic. Art for England 1400–1547*, ed. R. Marks and P. Williamson (London 2003), 397.
5. Troughton VIII/18, 20–2.
6. E. W. Tristram, *English Wall Painting of the Fourteenth Century* (London 1955), 159.
7. Hobley, 'Cathedral Excavations', 102.
8. See M. Naydenova-Slade, this volume. Note also P. Turpin, 'Ancient wall-paintings in the Charterhouse, Coventry', *Burlington Magazine*, 35 (1919), 246–56; M. Gill, 'The role of images in monastic education: the evidence from wall paintings in late medieval England', in *Medieval Monastic Education*, ed. G. Ferzoco and C. Muessig (London and New York 1999), 127–9.
9. Post-war authorities assumed the painting was 'lost': VCH *Warwickshire* VIII, 327; J. E. Ashby, 'English Medieval murals of the Doom: a descriptive catalogue and introduction' (unpublished M.Phil. thesis, University of York, 1980), 247; A. Hulbert, 'New Discoveries: Holy Trinity, Coventry: the doom awaiting rediscovery', in *The Conservator as Art Historian*, ed. A. Hulbert, J. Marsden and V. Todd (London 1993), 34.
10. R. K. Morris, 'The Worked Stones and Architectural Stonework', in Rylatt and Mason, *Cathedral Priory*, 63–82.
11. Gill and Morris, 'Apocalypse', 467–73; M. Gill, 'Appendix on wall paintings', in Rylatt and Mason, *Cathedral Priory*, 83–9; M. Gill, 'Monastic Murals and *Lectio* in the later Middle Ages', in *Medieval Monastic Culture*, ed. J. Clark and J. Greatrex (Woodbridge 2007), 63–71.
12. M. Gill, 'Significance of the site and historical setting for the "Doom" painting', in *Conservation of the 'Doom' Wall Painting, Holy Trinity Coventry: Abstract of papers presented at the Symposium in memory of Anna C. Hulbert* (2005), 11–13; M. Gill, 'Medieval Wall Painting of The Doom, Holy Trinity Church, Coventry', in *The History of British Art, 600–1600*, ed. T. Ayers (London 2008), 200–2; R. Rosewell, *Medieval Wall Paintings* (Woodbridge 2008), 74, 76.
13. Sharp, *Papers*, 96, 100; churchwardens' accounts record the removal of images during the second half of the 16th-century but do not specifically mention whitewash.
14. John Burbidge, pers. comm.
15. R. A. Clarke, *David Gee (1793–1872): An Introduction to his Life and Works*, Catalogue of an Exhibition at the Herbert Art Gallery (Coventry 1978), 1st section, 2.
16. John Burbidge, pers. comm.
17. H. Howard, 'Scientific Examination of the Doom wall painting in Holy Trinity Church, Coventry' (unpublished report, Courtauld Institute of Art, 1996), 1, 10.
18. T. Sharp, *A Dissertation on the Pageants or Dramatic Mysteries anciently performed at Coventry by the trading companies of that City chiefly with reference to the vehicle, characters, and dresses of the actors* (Coventry 1825), pl. 6.
19. Howard, 'Scientific Examination', 11–12; N. Eastlaugh, 'Development of the cleaning methodology and scientific support', in *Conservation of the 'Doom': Abstract of papers*, 23.
20. Howard, 'Scientific Examination', 11–12, pls 37–9; the surface of some of Gee's own works display the 'alligatoring' associated with this coating.
21. Clarke, *David Gee*, 1st section, 2; Sharp, *Papers*, 98.
22. J. Burbidge, 'Conservation history and treatment of the "Doom" painting', in *Conservation of the 'Doom': Abstract of papers*, 18.
23. J. R. Holliday, 'Notes on St Martin's Church [Birmingham] and the discoveries made during its restoration', *Birmingham and Midland Institute. Archaeological Section Transactions, Excursions and Reports* 4 (1873), 56; 'Worcester Diocesan Architectural Report', *Associated Architectural Societies Reports and Papers* 4, part I (1857), 320.
24. G. Scharf, 'Observations on a picture in Gloucester Cathedral, and some other representations of the Last Judgment', *Archaeologia* 36 (1855), 385, pl. XXXII, fig. 1.
25. Holliday, 'Notes', 56.
26. Troughton VIII/21–2.
27. Angels looking over the parapet of Heaven are misrepresented as figures in hats (although described by Troughton as angels) and the devil with the group of alewives shown as a male figure.
28. Troughton VIII/18, 20. For the unusual presence of yellow lead monoxide in this painting, see H. Howard, *Pigments of English Medieval Wall Painting* (London 2003), 160 n. 20.
29. WCRO, DR 801, 29.
30. Hulbert, 'New Discoveries', 34.
31. Burbidge, 'Conservation history', in *Conservation of the 'Doom': Abstract of papers*, 19.
32. John Burbidge, pers. comm.
33. Technical analysis has shown that the surface of these areas and the soffit board were prepared with calcium sulphate, for which see Howard, *Pigments*, 175.

34. Ashby, 'English Medieval murals of the Doom', 166.

35. The masonry joint for this extension can be seen high up on the sanctuary walls about 24ft from the east; VCH *Warwickshire* VIII, 327.

36. Ashby, 'English Medieval murals of the Doom', 247.

37. Hulbert, 'New Discoveries', 34.

38. M. Scott, *A Visual History of Costume: the Fourteenth and Fifteenth Centuries* (London 1986), 17, 71, 74, 77; M. Clayton, *Catalogue of Rubbings of Brasses and Incised Slabs* (London 1915), pl. 18.

39. D. Park, 'English medieval wall painting in an international context', in *Conserving the Painted Past: Developing Approaches to Wall Painting Conservation*, post-prints of a conference organised by English Heritage, London, 2–4 December 1999, ed. R. Gowing and A. Heritage (London 2003), 6.

40. H. N. MacCracken ed., *Lydgate's Minor Poems: Part II Secular Poems*, Early English Text Society, o. s., 192 (London 1934), II, 429–32; J. M. Bennett, *Ale, Beer and Brewsters in England: Women's Work in a Changing World, 1300–1600* (Oxford 1996), 133.

41. J. Backhouse, '"Hours of Elizabeth the Queen"', in Marks and Williamson, *Gothic*, 229.

42. R. Marks, *Stained glass in England during the Middle Ages* (London 1993), 182, fig. 147.

43. Rackham, 'The glass-paintings of Coventry', pl. XVI.

44. Troughton VIII/18.

45. Eastlaugh, 'Development of methodology', in *Conservation of the 'Doom': Abstract of papers*, 22.

46. Howard, *Pigments*, 146.

47. Howard, *Pigments*, 193.

48. See M. Naydenova-Slade, this volume, 275.

49. Burbidge, 'Conservation history', in *Conservation of the 'Doom': Abstract of papers*, 18; also John Burbidge, pers. comm.

50. Howard, 'Scientific Examination', 12, pls 11–14.

51. Howard, *Pigments*, 105; Rosewell, *Medieval Wall Paintings*, 137–8.

52. This aspect of the Last Judgement was explored in contemporary devotional writing and drama; see E. Duffy, *The Stripping of the Altars: Traditional Religion in England* (New Haven and London 1992), 246–8.

53. D. Park, 'Last Judgement', in Marks and Williamson, *Gothic*, 386.

54. The significance of these attributes was correctly identified by the local historians David McGrory and Tanya Fagan.

55. T. Erbe ed., *Mirk's Festial: A Collection of Homilies*, Early English Text Society, e. s., 96 (London 1905), 187; M. Gill, 'Preaching and images in late medieval England', in *Preacher, Sermon and Audience in the Middle Ages*, ed. C. Muessig (Leiden 2002), 155–80.

56. J. Goldberg, *Women, Work and Life Cycle in a Medieval Economy* (Oxford 1992), 116.

57. W. O. Hassall ed., *The Holkham Picture Book* (London, 1954), fol. 42v.

58. M. Jones, *The Secret Middle Ages* (Stroud 2002), 91–2. This scene may be the consequence of 19th-century repainting.

59. R. M. Lumiansky and D. Mills ed., *The Chester Mystery Cycle, Volume I, Text*, Early English Text Society, s. s., 3 (Oxford 1974), 337–9.

60. *Leet Book*, 169, 191–2.

61. F. B. Burbidge, *Old Coventry and Lady Godiva: Being some flowers of Coventry history gathered and arranged* (Birmingham 1952), 208.

62. Rackham, 'The glass-paintings of Coventry', 96–100; C. Davidson, 'The Lost Coventry Drapers Play of Doomsday and its Iconographic Context', *Leeds Studies in English* 17 (1986), 143. For the misericord from St Michael's, see Davidson and Alexander, *Early Art of Coventry*, fig. 12.

63. M. D. Harris, 'Misericords in Coventry', *TBAS* 52 (1927), 246–66.

64. Ingram, *Coventry*, 220–1.

65. Morris, 'The Worked Stones', 77–8.

66. See Gill and Morris, 'Apocalypse', fig. 3.

67. Gill and Morris, 'Apocalypse', 467, fig. 2.

68. Gill and Morris, 'Apocalypse', fig. 6.

69. C. M. Kauffman, *An Altarpiece of the Apocalypse* (London 1968), pl. 4.

70. S. Lewis, *Reading Images: Narrative Discourse and Reception in the Thirteenth-century Illuminated Apocalypse* (Cambridge 1995), 78–85.

71. Gill, 'Appendix on wall paintings', 84–6.

72. See further, Gill, 'Appendix on wall paintings', 84–7.

73. Gill and Morris, 'Apocalypse', 470.

74. Technical analysis undertaken by C. Hassall for Mark Perry (wrongly attributed to H. Howard in Gill 'Appendix on wall paintings', 87).

75. Gill and Morris, 'Apocalypse', 470; see Morris, 'Priory', this volume, 82–8, for the chapter-house fabric.

76. For a recent survey of this period, see M. Coker Joslin and C. Coker Joslin Watson, *The Egerton Genesis*, British Library Studies in Medieval Culture (London 2001).

77. E. Howe, 'Divine kingship and dynastic display: the altar murals of St Stephen's Chapel, Westminster', *Antiq. J.* 81 (2001), 259–303.

78. For the revised date for Westminster, see H. Howard, 'Technology of the painted past: recent scientific examination of the medieval wall paintings of the Chapter House of Westminster Abbey', in Gowing and Heritage, *Conserving the Painted Past*, 17–26; B. Turner, 'The patronage of John of Northampton: further studies of the wall-paintings in Westminster Chapter House', *JBAA* 138 (1985), 89–92.

79. P. Binski, *Westminster Abbey and the Plantagenets: Kingship and the representation of power, 1200–1400* (New Haven and London 1995), 192.

80. Binski, *Westminster*, 188; M. Gill, 'Monastic Murals and *Lectio*', 66–71.

81. M. Gill, 'Monastic Murals and *Lectio*', 69–71.

82. N. Morgan, *The Lambeth Apocalypse Manuscript 209 in the Lambeth Palace Library* (London 1990), 42.

83. M. Rose, 'The Vault Bosses', in *Norwich Cathedral: Church, City and Diocese, 1096–1996*, ed. I. Atherton, E. Fernie, C. Harper-Bill and H. Smith (London and Rio Grande 1996), 366.

84. J. G. Noppen, 'The Westminster Apocalypse and its source', *Burlington Magazine* 41 (1932), 154; Binski, *Westminster*, 192.

85. An Apocalypse of *c.* 1270 like the Douce Apocalypse and one of *c.* 1325–50 like the Lincoln College Oxford Apocalypse; N. Morgan, pers. comm.

86. For artistic patronage in later medieval Coventry, see this volume Goddard, 39–42 and Monckton, 143–60.

John Thornton of Coventry: A Reassessment of the Role of a Late Medieval Glazier

HEATHER GILDERDALE SCOTT

The survival of the terms of the 1405 contract naming John Thornton of Coventry as the glazier responsible for the great east window of York Minster, together with the spectacular achievement of the window itself, has made Thornton one of the best-known names in medieval English art. Research to date has centred on Thornton's style of glass-painting; on mapping the extensive survival of glass painted in his style, suggesting Thornton's enormous success as a glazier throughout much of the first half of the 15th century. Here, the evidence for Thornton and these patterns of glass survival are reassessed in conjunction with new research on glass in Thornton's style to consider what they reveal about his working practices, and about the organisation of his business and of the master glazier's role within it. Although evidently a glass-painter of outstanding ability, it is concluded that Thornton's success may have been due equally to other factors: a gift for innovative design; an ability to establish and manage a large, geographically diverse workshop; and to the security Thornton offered that a contract made with him would be completed successfully. As such, Thornton contributes to a more general reassessment of the late medieval glazier, in which, for the most successful practitioners, traditional perceptions of the simple craftsman are refined by emerging evidence of figures more complex in both their social identities and working practices.

PAST RESEARCH ON JOHN THORNTON OF COVENTRY

IN 1920 John Alder Knowles, son of the York stained glass conservator, John Ward Knowles, published his first thoughts on John Thornton. Over the next thirty years, assisted by the written and photographic records made by his father in the course of restoring the Minster's medieval choir glazing, Knowles would write extensively on the medieval glaziers of the city of York, and on Thornton in particular.[1] Central to Knowles' thinking was the characterisation of Thornton as a York glazier. He believed that, after coming to the city as an experienced glass-painter in 1405, to undertake the commission to fill the Minster's east window with a sophisticated narrative combining episodes from the Old Testament with an account of the Revelation of St John, Thornton remained in York for the rest of his life; and, furthermore, that his painting style formed the basis of a distinctive York 'school' of glass-painting that dominated and defined the city's stained glass output in the first decades of the 15th century.[2]

As evidence, Knowles presented documents showing that Thornton was elected a freeman of York in 1410, two years after the date stipulated in Thornton's contract for the completion of the Minster's east window.[3] He also highlighted an entry in the York

Minster fabric rolls for 1433 detailing the purchase of what appears to have been canvases and rope for repairs to a house in Stonegate, belonging to the Minster but then in John Thornton's tenure.[4]

In addition, Knowles drew on the plentiful 15th-century glass surviving in the city, highlighting its parallels with the window for which Thornton was contracted (Fig. 1 and Col. Pl. XIVA, B in print edn). Particularly striking are the distinctive heads, characterised by long bulbous-tipped noses, large round eyes and small but full pursed mouths. Common, too, is the characteristic use of predominantly white glass, its details highlighted with yellow stain, and set against blue or ruby backgrounds decorated with a 'seaweed' pattern (or, perhaps more properly, scrolling acanthus). More precisely, design and compositional parallels were found between Thornton's east window, telling the history of the world from its beginning to end, and some of the other Minster windows. The north façade window of the Minster's north choir transept, for example, was filled in *c.* 1415 with a pictorial account of the life and miracles of St William, York's 'resident' saint. It shares with the east window not only an ambitious narrative form, but also traits such as, in panels depicting emotions of grief or shame, the afflicted individuals turning their backs dramatically on the offending action, and covering their

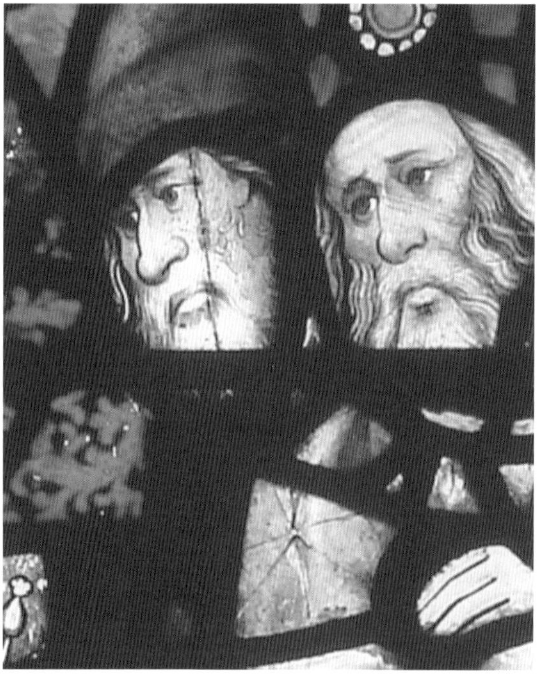

A

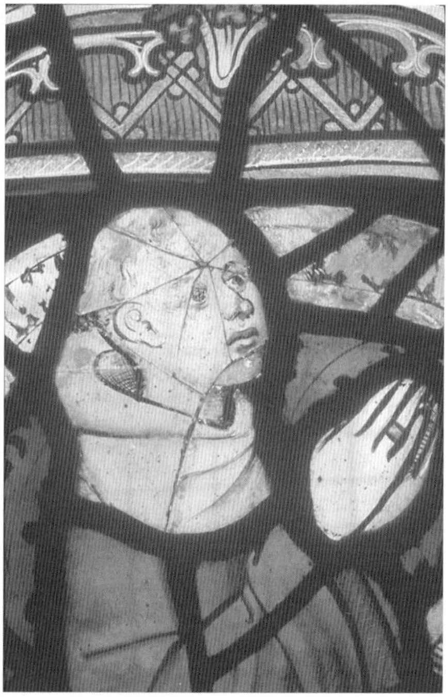

B

FIG. 1. Thornton's painting style in York

A. York Minster: the Great East window (I), for which Thornton was contracted 1405–08; detail

Photo, The York Glaziers Trust, reproduced by kind permission of the Dean and Chapter of York

B. York, All Saints, North Street: window nIV, early 15th century; detail

Photo, author

faces with their hands, whilst a companion looks on in concern (Fig. 2 and Col. Pl. XIVc, d in print edn).

One challenge to the York-centric interpretation of Thornton-style glass was, as Knowles recognised, the great east window of Great Malvern Priory (Worcs.).[5] Painted in a style directly comparable to much of the St William window (Fig. 3 and Col. Pl. XVa, b in print edn), it also shared with this work distinctive design details. Knowles suggested, for example, that the figure of Joseph of Arimathea in the scene of the Deposition at Malvern and an image of a young man hanging tapestries in the St William window were derived from a common source. In both instances, the postures of the figures are similar and, more distinctively, the rungs of the ladders fail to line up properly with the holes on the ladders' sides. Similarly, the same square-segmental belt, ending in an elaborate spoked pendant, can be found around the waist of the figure of Nicodemus, at the centre of the Malvern Deposition panel, and in a scene at York.

Within a few years of Knowles' first publications on the York 'school', Bernard Rackham, head of the Victoria and Albert Museum's ceramics and stained glass department, suggested that material painted in the Thornton style was as much a feature of the glazing in and around Coventry, Thornton's home town. He drew attention, for example, to angels in the tracery openings of the side windows of St Mary's Guildhall, and to the numerous heads from among the fragments then collected in the windows of the church of St Michael (Fig. 4).[6]

As neither the guildhall nor the St Michael's glass could be precisely dated, Rackham left open the question of whether the surviving Coventry glass predated Thornton's departure for the north, or provided evidence of the glazier's presence in the city after the completion of the York east window commission. The current guildhall complex is

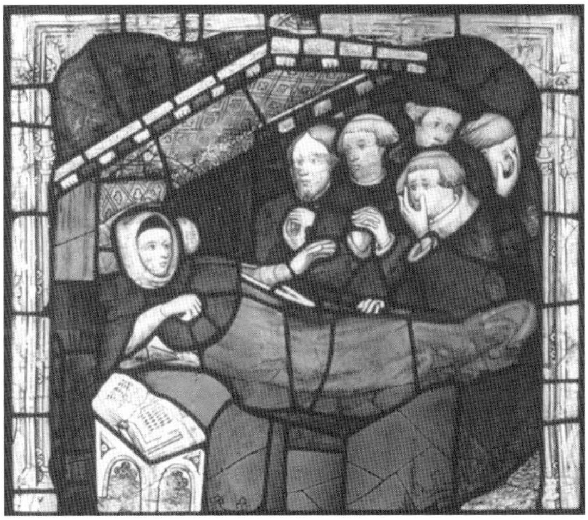

A

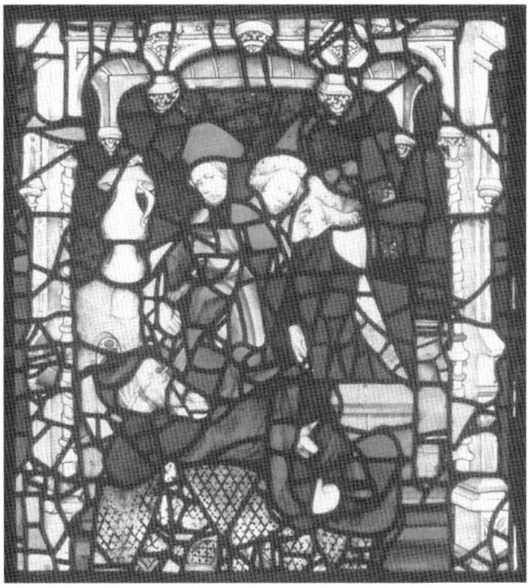

B

Fig. 2. Common design traits within York windows painted in the Thornton style

A. York Minster: St William window (nVII), St William retires from the feast, *c.* 1415

Photo, The York Glaziers Trust, reproduced by kind permission of the Dean and Chapter of York

B. York Minster: the Great East window (I), the Shame of Noah, 1405–08

Photo, The York Glaziers Trust, reproduced by kind permission of the Dean and Chapter of York

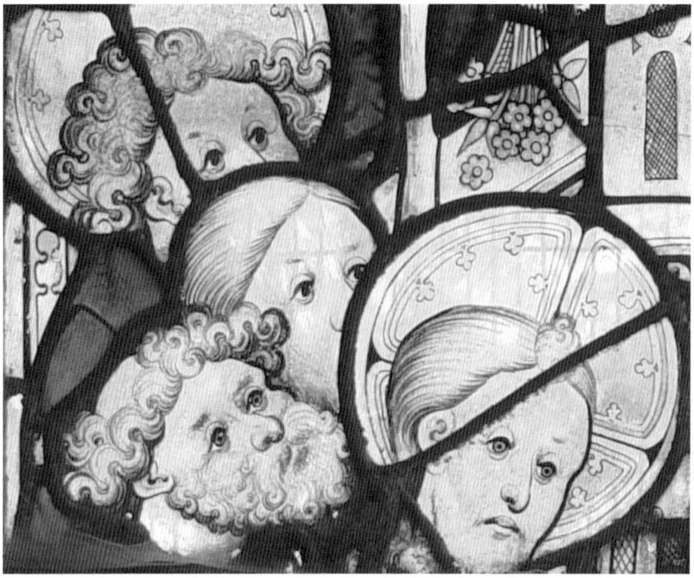

A. Great Malvern Priory: the Great East window (I), detail

Photo, John Jones

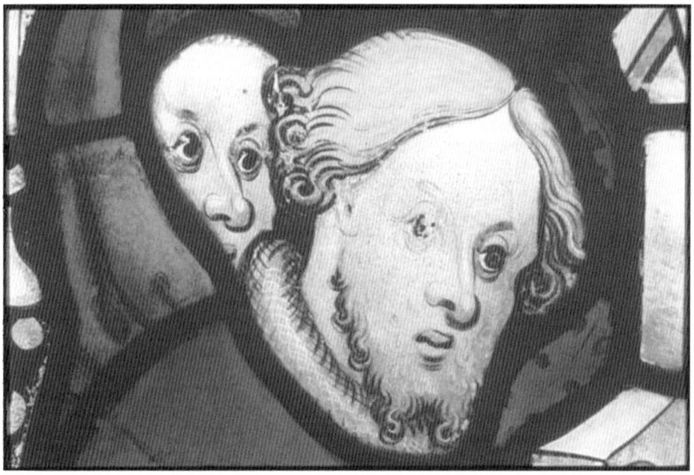

B. York Minster: the St William window (nVII), detail

Photo, The York Glaziers Trust, reproduced by kind permission of the Dean and Chapter of York

FIG. 3. The Thornton style beyond York

now thought to have been begun in the early 1390s, but work probably continued for at least the next forty years.[7] Similarly, construction on the tower at St Michael's began in *c.* 1371, but works to the main body of the church continued until the middle of the 15th century.[8]

In the late 1950s, however, entries were found by the local historian, Joan Lancaster, in the cartulary of St Mary's Priory, Coventry, demonstrating Thornton's continued association with the city. In 1411, *Johannes Thorneton' Glasier* was recorded as '*nunc manet*' in '*unum tenementum inter pontes sancti Johannis*', in the north-west of the city, whilst two years later he acquired a lease for the same residence for the next sixty

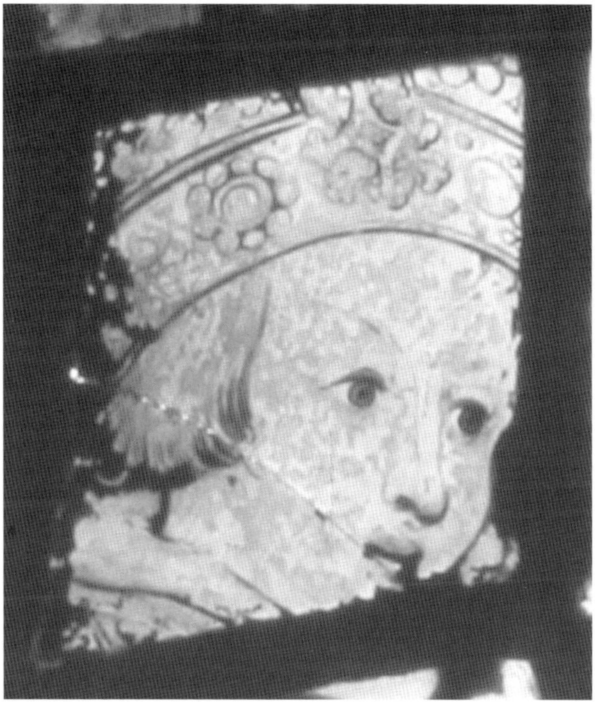

FIG. 4. Coventry, St Michael's: stray head, now in storage at Coventry Cathedral
Photo, Mike Stansbie

years.[9] These references suggest that, far from having left his native city permanently when he travelled to York in 1405, Thornton had returned to Coventry shortly afterwards. Furthermore, the length of the 1413 lease has been interpreted as evidence of his securing a long-term residence for himself and his family in the city.[10]

Subsequent research by Peter Newton on stained glass in the midlands identified work in Thornton's style throughout the region, at sites in Warwickshire, Derbyshire, Shropshire, Leicestershire and Nottinghamshire into the 1430s.[11] Ongoing research has extended the picture of Thornton's activities further. Glass at sites such as Bolton Percy (Yorkshire West Riding), Beverley Minster, Cartmel Priory (Cumbria) and Durham Cathedral has been used to demonstrate the dominance of work in Thornton's style throughout the north of England.[12] The identification of glass in the same style in parts of the midlands not covered by Newton's work, such as that from Hampton Court (Heref.) and in various minor parish churches, makes a similar point in relation to Coventry and its surroundings.[13] Indeed, glass very comparable to that associated with Thornton has also been found at sites far distant from York or Coventry, for example, at Tremeirchion and Llanrhychwyn in north Wales.[14] The evident displacement of these fragments from their original setting, however, means they need to be treated with caution as firm evidence of the painting style's spread to the region.

Nonetheless, the evidence suggests not only that Thornton most likely ran workshops out of both York and Coventry in the decades after 1405, but also that the collective reach of glaziers painting in his style was more than just regional. This conclusion prompts a range of questions, relating in particular to the potential role of a master glazier in late medieval England. Why was Thornton apparently so successful? What did he have to offer patrons of stained glass that distinguished him from his peers? To what extent was he simply a glass-painter?

THE MASTER GLAZIER IN LATE MEDIEVAL ENGLAND

SUCH questions take on a particular relevance in the context of recent findings about leading English glaziers in the late middle ages. Tim Ayers has drawn attention to the considerable social and probably economic success of John Godwin, a 15th-century west country glazier, who established himself as an important figure in the political infrastructure of the city of Wells.[15] Similar observations have also been made in relation to the York glazier, John Petty, who at the same time as securing glazing commissions in the city, rose through the ranks of civic office before being elected mayor in 1508 — the same year he made a will which indicates that he was a very wealthy individual who used his riches to secure the trappings of a luxurious lifestyle.[16] In Coventry, John Halus, glazier, and William Glasier feature among the 14th- and 15th-century members of the prestigious Trinity Guild.[17]

Recent monographs on the glass at Wells Cathedral, and at the parish church of St Peter Mancroft in Norwich, have addressed the role of the master glazier in the context of his glass-painting work, rather than his social networks. Both studies use the extant glass at their churches to throw light on the details of medieval glaziers' working practices, and emphasise the complex patterns of collaboration and cooperation evident from the glass: practices that testify to the managerial role of some medieval glaziers.[18] More generally, the work of Richard Marks has highlighted the willingness of the most highly regarded late medieval glaziers to travel considerable distances to undertake their commissions.[19]

NEW THOUGHTS ON JOHN THORNTON, GLAZIER, OF COVENTRY

LITTLE of detail is known about Thornton's own social connections or economic position; but there is evidence that he was a figure of some standing. A legacy of '*vj*s. *viij*d' was left to '*Johanni Thornton*' in the will of Stephen, second Lord Scrope of Masham (d. 1406).[20] Stephen was the brother of Richard Scrope, archbishop of York (*c.* 1350–1405), who was almost certainly instrumental in bringing Thornton to York, suggesting the glazier was a protégé of the great Scrope family.[21] His election to Freeman of York made Thornton a member of the body responsible for the governing of the city, as well as allowing him to vote, hold office and practice his trade there. His ability to maintain residences in both Coventry and York probably indicates the financial rewards his success brought.

In terms of his business practices, Thornton clearly operated like other leading glaziers, travelling across England to undertake commissions. His continued association with York and Coventry suggests an individual attuned to recognising the opportunities offered by circumstances around him. It has been argued that 'John Thornton's introduction to York was very probably the direct result of the shortage of glass-painters in the city, due to the Black Death of 1391'.[22] The same circumstances may have prompted the establishment of a workshop of some kind in the city, particularly as rising mercantile fortunes and ambitions were finding expression in the reconstruction or embellishment of many of York's parish churches.[23] Similar activity and opportunities in Coventry may explain Thornton's unwillingness to sever his ties with his home city. Of the architectural commissions in which Thornton seems certainly to have been involved, the rebuilt guildhall represented the ambition and status of the guild of St Mary, and St Michael's embodied the aspirations and success of its merchant patrons.

To understand Thornton's role as a master medieval glazier in practice, the contract for the glazing of the east window of York Minster provides a useful starting point. The document itself has long been lost, but its terms survive in the form of notes made in the late 17th century, recording the contents of the Minster's Chapter Act book for the years 1390–1410, which contained a transcription of the document.[24] They make clear that Thornton, as the glazier responsible for the window, was expected to function in at least three capacities: as glass-painter, as the window's designer, and as project manager. The extant glass in Thornton's style provides further evidence for his approaches to each of these roles.

His intended direct involvement in the painting of the York east window is clear. It was set down in his contract that he would 'paynt [the window] where need required according to the Ordination of the Dean & Chapter'. The evident skill with which the east window is painted, attesting to Thornton's great ability as an artist, no doubt goes some way to explain why the Minster authorities would make such a demand.

Significantly, however, Thornton's painting duties are the last to be described in the contract. Furthermore, the phrasing of the instruction makes it clear that he was not expected to paint the window single-handedly. In fact, that the chapter felt it necessary to include the instruction at all could indicate that contracting Thornton as a glazier did not automatically involve him picking up a paint brush. The obvious variation within the painting of the window itself reinforces the suggestion that Thornton was only one of a number of painters at work (Fig. 5 and Col. Pl. XVc, D, E in print edn).

A collective approach to painting is also evident in other projects executed in Thornton's style. In the Minster's St William window, Knowles identified at least four different painters responsible for the figural aspects of the work.[25] The glass at Great Malvern provides a model for the division of painting labour across a larger scheme,

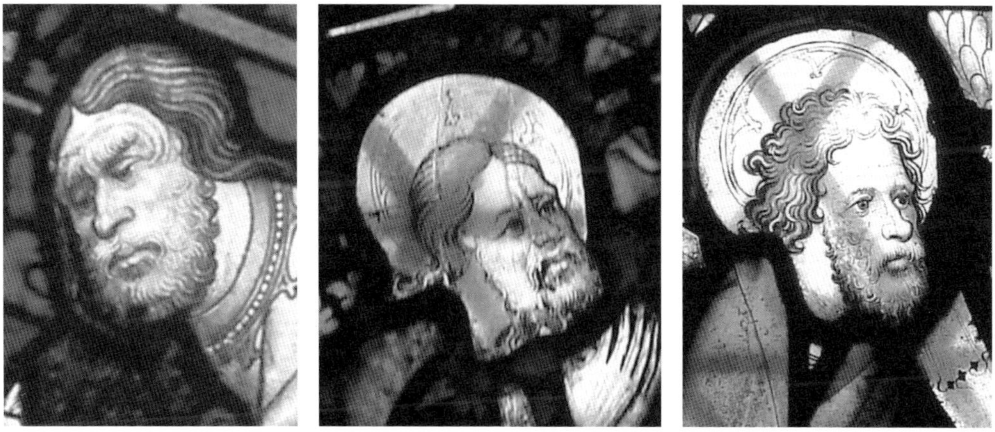

A B C

Fig. 5. A, B, C. York Minster: the Great East window (I), faces of St John from scenes from the Apocalypse, highlighting the variations within the window's painting

Photo, The York Glaziers Trust, reproduced by kind permission of the Dean and Chapter of York

rather than a single window. The majority of the priory's choir glazing belongs to the same Thornton-esque stylistic tradition, but some parts are particularly fine and closely comparable with the work associated with Thornton at York Minster. The parallels between the priory's great east window and the St William window, in particular, have already been noted. Although quite damaged in parts, the figures in the main lights of the priory's east window are, on the whole, strikingly coherent, and very plausibly the work of a single painter.[26] Many of the window's tracery lights, however, seem to have been executed by a different hand, producing figures far more linear in style, and lacking the careful modelling of the main panels. In other parts of the choir, an occasional figure strongly resembling those in the east window's main lights survives amongst glass that has some very obvious differences. For example, the figure of Simeon the priest seems to have been painted by a different hand from the more linear and less sophisticated figures of the Virgin and her attendants in the scene of the Presentation at the Temple, and of St Anne at the Birth of the Virgin, in the same window (Fig. 6).

If Thornton was primarily responsible for the main lights of the priory's east window, as well as for figures such as Simeon, it suggests that at Malvern the monastic community required Thornton personally to put his hand only to the most important glass. The significance of the east window is obvious, and the assignment of the tracery painting to a different glazier is understandable, given its distance from the viewer. The window containing the head of Simeon was also clearly important: from its position at the east end of the choir clerestory, it illuminated the church's high altar. It was also the gift of a Malvern prior, who was depicted kneeling in prayer towards the foot of the window, and whose upper body and head can be seen intruding into the scene of the

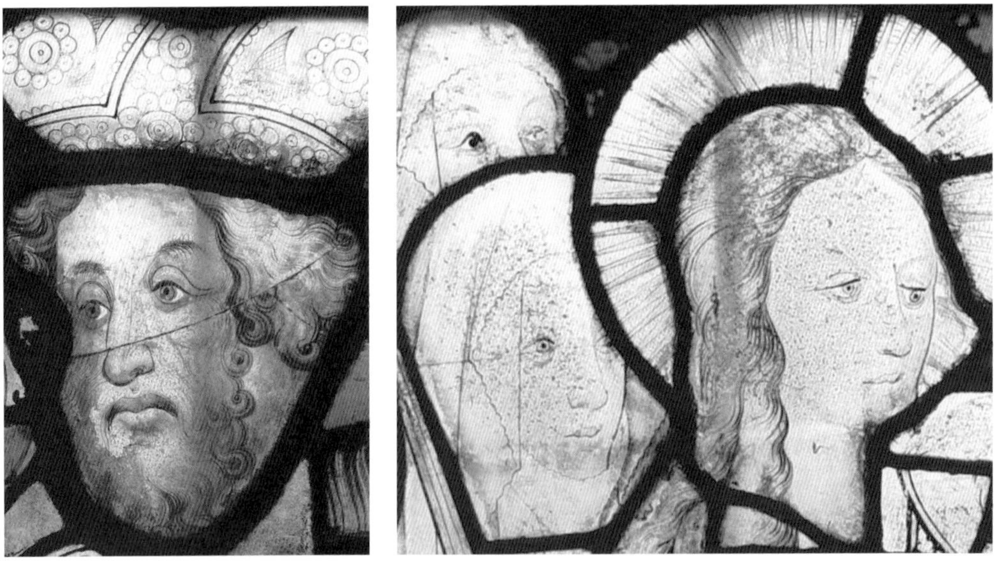

A B

FIG. 6. Variations in painting in the Thornton style: the choir glazing at Great Malvern Priory
A. Window NII, detail of Simeon the Priest
B. Window NII, detail of the Virgin and her attendants
Photos, John Jones

Virgin's birth (Fig. 7), distinguishing him from other figures of donors and benefactors, who were shown in a panel at the bottom of the window, clearly separated from the sacred subjects above.

There is evidence for this kind of separating out of a scheme's most important parts for a specific glazier at other projects, under other glaziers. At Wells Cathedral in the 14th century, the most visible parts of the east window, and its central axis, were painted by one particularly accomplished painter.[27] A greater understanding of the ways in which Thornton was involved in the painting of extended glazing programmes would almost certainly have been permitted by the glass in medieval Coventry, had more survived. The remains from St Michael's, for example, are painted in a variety of interpretations of his style, but they are now too fragmentary and decontextualised for any conclusions to be drawn.

The second of Thornton's roles, that of window designer, is given greater emphasis than that of painter in the York contract, which records the obligation that he 'with his own hands ... portrature the said Window ... in the best manner and form that he possibly could'. This determination by the Minster to ensure his commitment to the

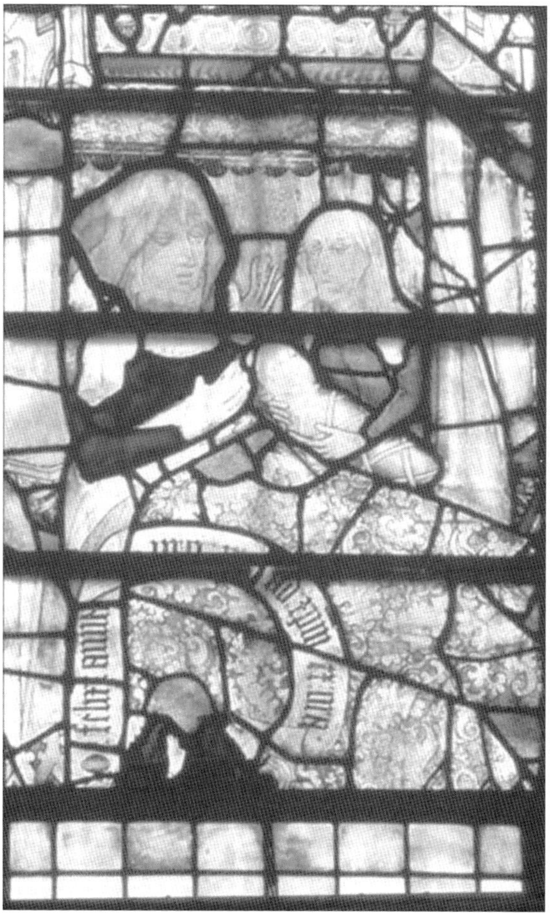

FIG. 7. Great Malvern Priory: window NII; Prior John Malvern at the scene of the Birth of the Virgin
Photo, David O'Connor

window's design is understandable, as it seems to have been an area in which Thornton both excelled and was an important innovator.

At York, Thornton was required on a number of occasions to integrate multiple sources into a successful whole. The great east window combined episodes from the Creation with those from the Apocalypse, and others from the Minster's own history; and they were organised in such a way that the central light was used to emphasise particularly important subjects, such as facing images of God the Father.[28] Similarly, Christopher Norton has recently demonstrated that in creating the St William window, Thornton wove together events described in two separate accounts of the saint's life.[29]

At Malvern, the east window was devoted to a narrative of Christ's Passion from the Entry to Jerusalem to the Descent of the Holy Ghost. This iconography not only drew on all four Gospel accounts, and edited them skilfully to condense the story into twenty-four panels, but was also organised so that each phase of the Passion occupied a separate row. The uppermost was filled with depictions of the events leading up to Christ's physical suffering, from his Entry to Jerusalem to his Condemnation by Pilate; the middle row contained imagery of the Passion itself, from his Mocking and Flagellation to his Death and Entombment; scenes relating to the Resurrection filled the lowest row of panels, concluding with Pentecost. Furthermore, the story was managed so that the Nailing to the Cross and the Crucifixion, the dramatic climax of events, were at the very centre of the window.

This skilful organisation of the material by subject matter was underscored by the use of colour. Christ, for example, was shown clothed in red or purple tones up to the point of Crucifixion; but, from the Resurrection onwards, he seems to have been represented in blue (with the exception of his wearing a tawny-coloured pilgrim's slavyn in the scene of the Journey to Emmaus).

If the management of the source material in these windows suggests Thornton's skill as a designer, their narrative form may indicate his innovations. Windows containing extended narrative cycles became enormously popular in the 15th century, but when Thornton designed the east window at York, it differed dramatically from other recent top-quality commissions. Projects by Thomas of Oxford in the 1380s and 1390s at New College, Oxford, and Winchester College, for example, were characterised by series of large standing figures within fictive niches, or by depictions of the Tree of Jesse. Work begun in the last years of the 14th century at York's great ecclesiastical rival, Canterbury Cathedral, followed a similar path when the church's west window was filled with a series of English monarchs, enclosed in architectural niches against rich, lattice-work backgrounds.

It is arguable that the narrative form of the York window was a response to specific circumstances at the Minster. York had long been disadvantaged as a great cathedral by its lack of a 'resident' saint to attract pilgrims, and it certainly could not compete with Canterbury and Becket's shrine. Christopher Norton argues that Archbishop Scrope was particularly concerned with the promotion of the northern church, and was involved in planning the glazing scheme of the entire east end of York to include the prominent windows dedicated to the great northern saints, William and Cuthbert.[30] It is worth speculating that the narrative form of these great choir windows was intended to reflect the 13th-century narrative windows that were such a spectacular and well-known feature at Canterbury.

Whilst the idea of narrative at York may have been inspired by Canterbury, the form it took was very different. The complex organisation of panels of various shapes into intricate compositions within slender lancets was replaced with uniform, rectangular panels, each comprising a scene set below an architectural canopy, arranged into neat rows that read in sequence across large multi-light openings. Narrative glass of this form was already a feature of continental glazing, apparently associated most prominently with the Germanic territories of the Holy Roman Empire. The east window of Tiefenbronn, near Strasbourg, for example, was filled with a narrative of Christ's Infancy around 1370, and in the last quarter of the 14th century, the east window of Maria am Gestade in Vienna was given over to an account of the Passion.[31] Indeed, in Nuremberg, the empire's unofficial capital, the choir of the church of St Sebald had been glazed by 1380 with a series of Christological narratives and episodes from the book of Genesis.[32]

There is no firm evidence that Thornton was directly inspired by glass of this kind, but he does seem to have had a particular interest in adopting fashionable European forms. At Malvern, the east window Passion narrative was flanked at clerestory level by images of episodes from the early lives of the Virgin and Christ. This combination was a standard iconography of tripartite carved altar-pieces of the same date, which were produced in great numbers in the Netherlands for the domestic and export markets since the late 14th century.[33]

More precisely, it has been suggested that the scene of the Last Supper at Malvern was based on a narrative altar-piece of the Infancy and Passion by the Westphalian artist, Conrad von Soest (Fig. 8).[34] Whilst not identical, the two scenes share some unusual features, such as the presence of the elderly St Paul at Christ's side, and the gesture by Judas, hiding a fish under the tablecloth. There are also compositional parallels: the apostle on the far left of each panel holds a goblet to his mouth, through which his lips can be seen, and in the foreground of each scene a long-haired apostle, intently cutting a loaf of bread, faces another in profile.

Thornton's use of European models has also been suggested in connection with other kinds of iconography. Recent work on representations of the Holy Kinship in England has highlighted a group of windows illustrating the subject and based on designs first used in Thornton-style glass in the choir of York Minster. In contrast with the apparent form of earlier English manifestations of the subject, or those with no stylistic relation to Thornton, which focus largely on the children of the Virgin and her sisters, these windows are distinctive for sharing the continental trait of prominently including the husbands of St Anne and her daughters.[35]

The last of the roles assigned to Thornton by the York Minster contract is that of project manager, where it is described in terms of his obligation to provide the materials for the window — the glass, lead, solder and so on — and also to find all sufficient workmen to complete the job. No details are given about his potential sources for either the men or materials, nor has the York east window yet been subject to the kind of detailed stylistic analysis that might reveal how he went about dividing the glazing task amongst his men.

However, some of the other windows attributed to Thornton have been looked at in this way. Collectively they are characterised by complex patterns of collaboration that might best be explained by a desire to take advantage of the piecemeal nature of the stained glass craft, and to employ simultaneously as many of the available workforce as possible. For the St William window, Knowles suggested that three different draughtsmen produced cartoons for the panels; four glass-painters painted the main figural compositions; and at least two painters worked on the backgrounds of the panels. These craftsmen worked together in a variety of combinations throughout the window, suggesting that cartoons were drawn as they were required, and that painters

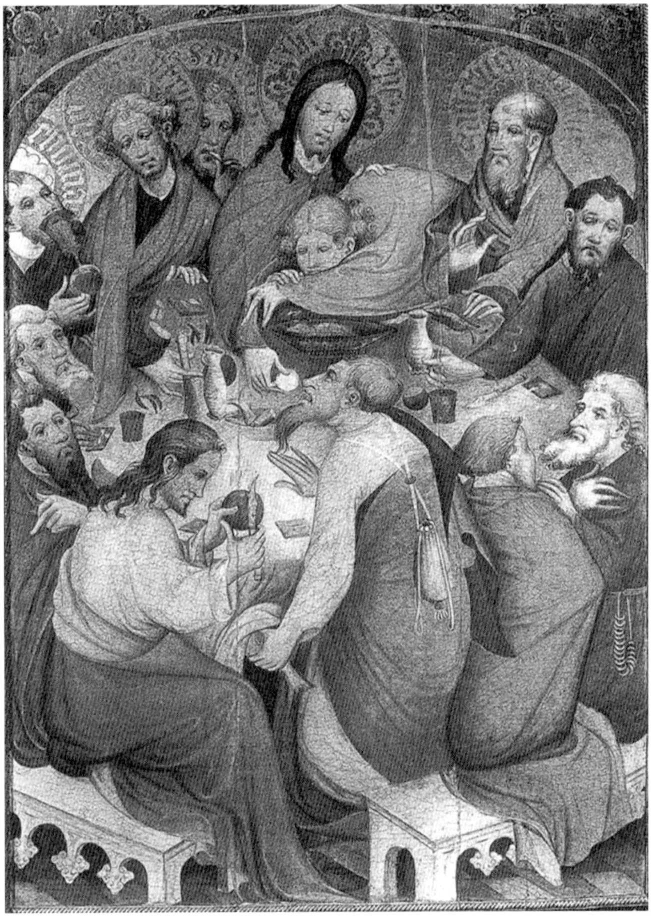

FIG. 8. Evidence of European models?
A. The Niederwildungen altar-piece by Conrad von Soest, 1403; panel of the Last Supper
Photo, Westfälisches Amt für Denkmalpflege, Münster

were given tasks as they became free, rather than the window being divided among the workforce before work began. In essence, the aim seems to have been to maximise the speed and efficiency with which the job could be completed.[36]

Elsewhere, in Thornton-style glass thought to have originally been at Hereford Cathedral, it has been suggested that different glass-painters worked together on individual figures. Some of the surviving figures incorporate large, crudely painted hands that contrast with the refinement and sophistication of the figures' faces, raising questions about what was perceived as a composition's 'marginal' aspects.[37]

At Malvern, the question of glaziers' working practice is complicated by the fact that, although all of the choir glass is of a generically 'Thornton' style, some of it might have been painted close to the middle of the century. It is not known when Thornton died — the 1433 fabric rolls reference is the latest known date — but, even if he was a young glazier when he was called to York 1405, there is a limit to how far into the century he could still have been active. As such, the choir glass at Malvern may have been managed in part by a successor, rather than by Thornton alone. Nonetheless, the glazing provides a model for how an important multi-window project might be

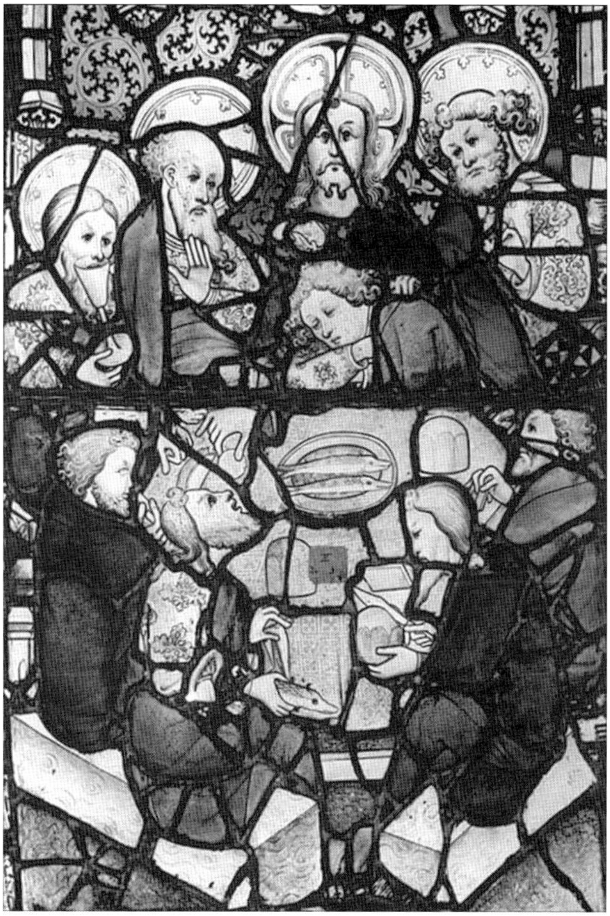

Fig. 8. Evidence of European models?
B. Great Malvern Priory: the Great East window, before 1440; panel of the Last Supper
Photo, National Monuments Record

approached. Although a number of glass-painters were clearly employed in the priory's choir, there are signs that the glass was planned collectively or centrally to at least some degree. The same designs for architectural canopies occur throughout the choir, and the same cartoons are used for multiple figures of bishops and kings in a number of the clerestory windows, as well as for sequences of donor figures at clerestory and aisle levels.

In terms of painting, the windows seem to have been divided between individuals in a manner as complex as that identified by Knowles at York. For example, the canopies of the north choir clerestory appear to have been executed by window. Those in the easternmost window (NII) are characterised by golden, fleur-de-lis shaped finials, and curly-looking crockets on stems. Those in the central opening (NIII) were painted with more solid-looking, semicircular crockets and plain finials encircled with golden balls. In the final window of the clerestory (NIV), the canopies' details are different again: the crockets are thin and weedy like those in the easternmost window, but their finials are decorated with simple gold balls, rather than fleurs-de-lis.

In contrast with this window-by-window management of the canopies, the main figures in each of the north choir clerestory windows appear to have been painted by a variety of glass-painters. In window NIII, for example, six episcopal and archiepiscopal figures were created from two cartoons, one each for figures facing left and right, but with clear differences between them (Fig. 9). A variety of motifs was used to decorate the inside edge of the figures' haloes; their fur almuces were also painted in a range of ways, some appearing uniformly soft and fluffy, others painted as if to suggest they were made up of numerous individual pieces of fur, whilst the collars of a third group were left white inside, perhaps intended to represent the animal's skin. The way in which the bishops' facial features were delineated also varies noticeably. For example, the unnamed bishop in NIII (Fig. 9A) has particularly prominent, large round eyes and a small crooked, very faintly drawn mouth. Washes of paint were used in a very limited way, mostly to create a highlight at the tip of his nose. St Dunstan was painted in an equally linear style, but his features were managed quite differently. The eyes are smaller and more elongated, whilst the mouth is broader and more firmly drawn (Fig. 9B). St Edmund, in contrast, has nicely proportioned features, well positioned on his face, and there are more signs of modelling around the eyes and mouth (Fig. 9C).

Organising these various glass-painters clearly suggests that the glazier responsible for the successful completion of the commission was a master of on-site man management. The priory's choir glazing also raises the possibility that this co-ordinating glazier had contacts with glass-painters who worked according to slightly different traditions, and who were not necessarily regular parts of his 'workshop', but on whom he might call if required.

At the west end of the priory's north clerestory is a highly unusual window (NIV) depicting the early history of the monastery's site, and the subsequent foundation of a Benedictine house (Fig. 10). This later part of the story, shown in the window's lower half, was composed of relatively conventional forms, and the usual variety of glass-painters seems to have been at work. However, in the upper part of the window, the subject matter was more unusual. Depicted here were the visions of a monk or hermit labelled Werstan, directing him to found a small chapel in a hilly landscape, perhaps intended for Malvern itself, subsequently consecrated by angels. The sequence ends in a two-stage scene showing Werstan's martyrdom within his chapel, and the destruction of his religious community. The style of the glass-painting is also distinctive. Belonging

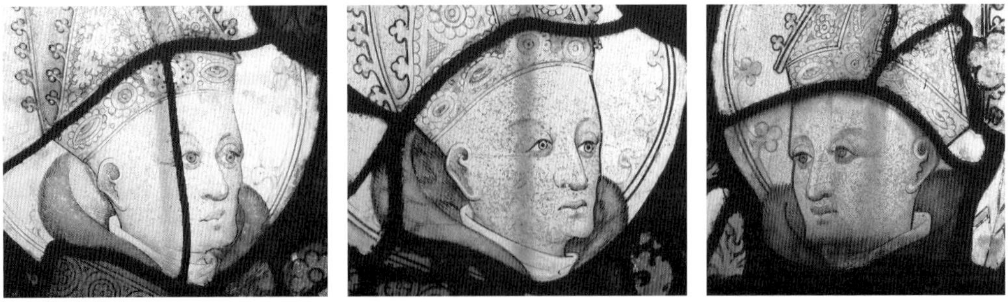

A B C

FIG. 9. Common cartoons but different hands? Great Malvern Priory: window NIII. A. An unnamed bishop; B. St Dunstan; C. St Edmund of Canterbury

Photos, John Jones

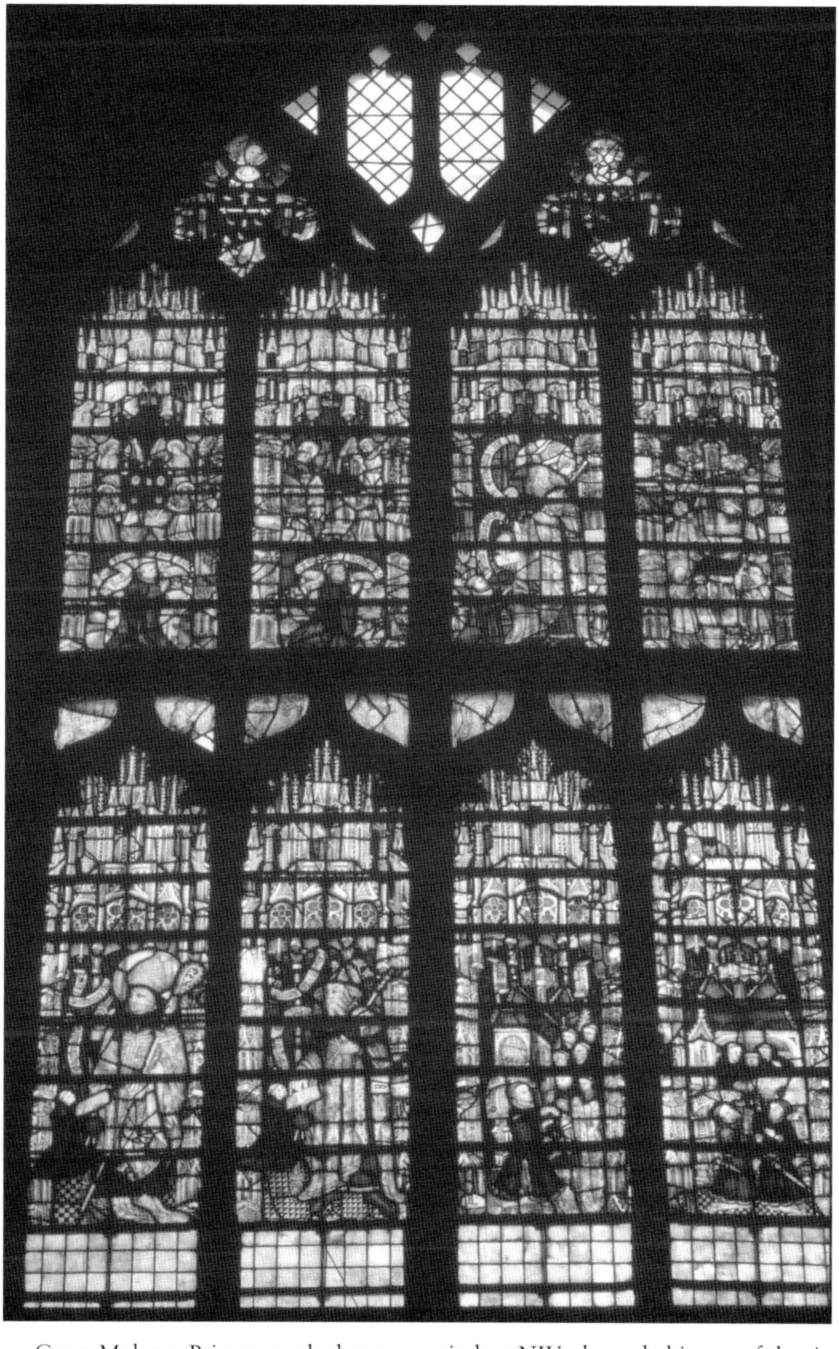

FIG. 10. Great Malvern Priory: north clerestory window NIV; the early history of the site of the monastery and the foundation of the Benedictine house
Photo, David O'Connor

generally, like Thornton's work, to the International Gothic style, the figures differ from glass elsewhere in the church in details such as the relative smallness of their eyes, the shortness and form of their noses, ending in a square, rather than bulbous tip, and their wider, less pouting mouths.

The backgrounds to the scenes in this part of the Werstan window are also distinctive, and unlike any yet found associated with glass in the Thornton style. Indeed, the backgrounds decorated uniformly with a pattern of large roses closely parallel mid-15th-century glass with Oxford associations, such as that in the ante-chapel of All Souls College, and behind figures at Newton Bromswold (Northants.).[38] Collectively, therefore, the Werstan window suggests that, when it came to glazing a window of unusual subject matter, the coordinating glazier called upon a glazier or team of glass-painters he knew to be particularly skilled at meeting such demands.

Assessing Thornton in terms of his project management and even design skills does not, perhaps, have the same obvious appeal as approaching him as a great artistic personality, as has traditionally been the case. But it is arguable that a glazier who could really be depended upon to translate a patron's wishes into a successful window design, and to get the job finished in an efficient manner, was exactly the kind of glazier that a medieval patron would value most. Whilst not wanting to take glass-painting out of glazing entirely, there is the question of where it ranked when trying to understand why leading glaziers such as Thornton were employed. Outstanding glass-painter though he evidently was, Thornton may primarily have been a brilliant businessman, who trained and managed other glass-painters; who was a master at liaising with other glaziers and at translating into glass the wishes of his clients, wherever they might be based; but who had a relatively limited involvement with the painting itself. If this was indeed the case, then the collective implication of much of the research on Thornton to date — that glass painted in his style dominated enormous areas of the north and midlands well into the 15th century — becomes much easier to understand.

ACKNOWLEDGEMENTS

I am grateful to Tim Ayers for his helpful comments on an early draft of this paper, and also to the many attendees at the conference in Coventry for their enthusiastic and constructive feedback. My thanks also go to York Glaziers' Trust, the Dean and Chapter of York Minster, John Jones, Mike Stansbie at Coventry Cathedral, and David O'Connor for their generosity in allowing the use of their images, or of images of stained glass belonging to them. Without them, this paper would be a much greyer contribution.

NOTES

1. J. A. Knowles, 'John Thornton of Coventry and the Great East Window of York Minster', *Notes and Queries*, series 12, 7 (1920), 481–3; followed by further notes, in reply to J. D. LeCouteur, in *Notes and Queries*, series 12, 8 (1921), 171–3. Id., *Essays in the History of the York School of Glass-Painting* (London 1936); id., 'Technical Notes on the St William Window in York Minster', *Yorkshire Archaeological Journal* 37 (1948–51), 148–61; id., 'John Thornton of Coventry and the East Window of Great Malvern Priory', *Antiq. J.* 39 (1959), 274–82.
2. Summarised in Knowles, 'John Thornton and Great Malvern Priory', 274–9.
3. Knowles, *York School*, 217, citing F. Collins ed., *Register of the Freemen of the City of York* I (Durham 1897), 115; T. French, *York Minster: The Great East Window* (Oxford 2003, paperback edn), 153–4.

4. '*ij lodiis empties . . . cum i fune canabi*'; Knowles, *York School*, 217, citing J. Raine ed., *The Fabric Rolls of York Minster* (Durham 1859), 54.

5. Knowles, 'St William Window', 161; 'John Thornton and Great Malvern Priory', 274.

6. B. Rackham, 'The Glass-Paintings of Coventry and its Neighbourhood', *Walpole Society* XIX (1930–31), 89–110.

7. See Demidowicz, 'Hall', in this volume, 171–7, for the guildhall architecture. R. Marks, *Stained Glass in England during the Middle Ages* (Toronto 1993), 191, suggests a date as late as the mid-15th century for the glass of the hall's north window. Note most recently A. Rudebeck, 'John Thornton and the stained glass of St Mary's Guildhall, Coventry', *Journal of Stained Glass* XXI (2007), 14–34.

8. See Monckton in this volume, 143–4, 148–57.

9. J. C. Lancaster, 'John Thornton of Coventry, Glazier', *Journal of the British Society of Master Glass Painters (JBSMGP)* 12 (1958–59), 262, citing TNA PRO E164/21, fol. 153d.

10. Ibid., 263.

11. P. Newton, 'Schools of Glass Painting in the Midlands, 1275–1430', (unpublished doctoral thesis, University of London, 1962), ch. VI: 'A "Coventry School" of Glaziers, *c.* 1398–1430'.

12. Summarised in Marks, *Stained Glass in England*, 182.

13. For Hampton Court, see M. Caviness, 'The Stained Glass from the Chapel of Hampton Court, Herefordshire', *Walpole Society* XLII (1968–70), 35–60; for other sites in the west midlands, see H. Gilderdale Scott, 'The Painted Glass of Great Malvern Priory (Worcs.), *c.* 1430–1500' (unpublished doctoral thesis, University of London, 2008), ch. IV.

14. M. Lewis, *Stained Glass in North Wales up to 1850* (Altrincham 1970), 4–5.

15. T. Ayers, 'A West Country Glazier in the Fifteenth Century: John Godwin of Wells, MP', *JBSMGP* 26 (2002), 10–16.

16. D. O'Connor, 'John Petty, Glazier and Mayor of York: an Early 16th-Century Memorial Window formerly in the South Transept of York Minster', *JBSMGP* 29 (2005), 30–44.

17. Lancaster, 'John Thornton', 261.

18. T. Ayers, *The Medieval Stained Glass of Wells Cathedral* (Oxford 2004); D. King, *The Medieval Stained Glass of St Peter Mancroft, Norwich* (Oxford 2006).

19. Marks, *Stained Glass in England*, 41.

20. Knowles, *York School*, 214.

21. French, *The Great East Window*, 5.

22. Knowles, *York School*, 212.

23. 15th-century work features in the churches of All Saints, North Street; All Saints, Pavement; Holy Trinity, Micklegate; St Helen, Stonegate; St Martin-le-Grand, Coney Street; and St Martin-cum-Gregory, Micklegate.

24. French, *The Great East Window*, 2, 5, 153–4.

25. Knowles, 'St William Window', 154–5.

26. There are, however, variations in the execution of the backgrounds and fictive architectural niches in the main light panels, suggesting that the figure painter was assisted with the arguably more marginal aspects of the window.

27. Ayers, *Stained Glass of Wells*, 290–1.

28. J. Rickers, 'Glazier and Illuminator: the Apocalypse Cycle in the East Window of York Minster and its Sources', *JBSMGP* 19 (1994–95), 270, 272.

29. Norton's research was presented at a *Corpus Vitrearum Medii Aevi* authors' meeting in Cambridge, 13 Oct. 2001; it has not been published.

30. Ultimately put up after Scrope's death; C. Norton, 'Richard Scrope and York Minster', in P. J. P. Goldberg ed., *Richard Scrope: Archbishop, Rebel, Martyr* (Donington 2007), 145–56.

31. R. Becksmann, *Die Mittelalterlichen Glasmalereien in Baden und in der Pfalz* (Berlin 1979), 232–9; E. Frodl-Kraft, *Die Mittelalterlichen Glasgemälde in Wien* (Graz, Vienna, Cologne 1962), 75–107.

32. H. Scholz, *St Sebald in Nürnberg* (Regensburg 2007), 5–12 (date), 42–59, 62–3, 66–71 (description of the windows).

33. L. F. Jacobs, *Early Netherlandish Carved Altarpieces, 1380–1550* (Cambridge 1998), 54.

34. B. Corley, 'Historical Links and Artistic Reflections: England and Northern Germany in the Late Middle Ages', in J. Mitchell ed., *England and the Continent* (Stamford 2000), 189.

35. See M. Naydenova-Slade, 'Images of the Holy Kinship in England, *c.* 1170 to *c.* 1525' (unpublished doctoral thesis, University of London, 2008), ch. 7.

36. Knowles, 'St William Window', 152–7.

37. Caviness, 'Chapel of Hampton Court', 44.

38. R. Marks, *The Medieval Stained Glass of Northamptonshire* (Oxford 1998), 148.

The Charterhouse of St Anne, Coventry

JULIAN M. LUXFORD

In addition to its cathedral priory, Carmelite and Franciscan houses, and secular ecclesiastical institutions, late medieval Coventry boasted a Carthusian monastery, located to the south of the city just outside the walls. Initiated between 1381 and 1385, and dedicated to St Anne, the priory was a standard Carthusian foundation for a prior and twelve monks, plus lay brethren. This survey of the Charterhouse is straightforward in method and aims. After brief exposition of some historical matters, the site and principal buildings of St Anne's are discussed, then aspects of its institutional life illuminated by surviving evidence for art and texts. This provides a supplement, and in some cases a corrective, to previous studies of the Charterhouse. The overarching aim is to impart a sense of the form, vitality and integrity of St Anne's, and to demonstrate that it had a significant place in the material and institutional topography of Coventry in the century and a half leading up to the Reformation.

INTRODUCTION: HISTORICAL PERSPECTIVES

LESS than half a mile south-east of Coventry's 'darkeshe depe redde' walls, on a natural terrace above the River Sherbourne, stood the Charterhouse dedicated to St Anne.[1] Begun in 1381, and thus sixth in order of foundation among England's nine Carthusian priories, it was structurally complete by the third or fourth decade of the 15th century. While textual and material evidence for its history, architecture and embellishment is limited, what exists is collectively susceptible to more informative and sympathetic interpretation than it has received to date. A general historical and environmental analysis is much to be desired, which supplements and updates the work of Carol Rowntree, Joseph Gribbin, Iain Soden, the Coventry antiquaries, and the official chroniclers of the Carthusian order.[2] It is, however, beyond the scope of this essay. In the following survey, discussion is confined primarily to aspects of the Charterhouse and its culture which relate to architecture, art and text. While the most important surviving works of art, the mutilated wall-paintings in the refectory, are discussed in detail by Mellie Naydenova-Slade elsewhere in this volume, some complementary remarks about their architectural and devotional contexts are offered below.

Three matters which provide context for the material to be discussed, and which to date have been insufficiently emphasised, require some consideration. First, like many medieval monasteries, St Anne's was subject to a threefold foundation process: symbolic, official and practical. Thus, it was first promoted by a noble who did little for it (William, Lord Zouche, of Haringworth in Northamptonshire), officially begun and endowed by a king, and built piecemeal by wealthy benefactors and the convent itself. By reputation, however, it was a royal rather than a lay foundation, which maintained edifying links with the crown throughout its existence. King Richard II's documented involvement began in March 1382, and he laid the first stone at the east end of the church (*in capite ejusdem chori orientali*) in 1385.[3] He was the Charterhouse's most generous benefactor, officially granting the fourteen-acre foundational site, plus licences to amortise spiritualities and the lordships of ten defunct alien priories (four of which were redistributed under Henry IV). Like his father, who had allied himself with Beauvale Charterhouse forty years earlier 'because of his special affection for the order', Richard and his advisers understood that supporting monks who 'abound[ed] in fervour of devotion and religious sincerity among the rest of the orders' could only enhance his personal and political reputation; he was even more generous to Mount Grace.[4] Furthermore, a tradition familiar to John Leland and encouraged to some extent by the Carthusians themselves, credited Anne of Bohemia with a leading role in the foundation.[5] The monastery also had a special relationship with Henry VI, who supported it when its possessions were 'wasted by decay and the suit of enemies' (1457). Henry was granted 'spiritual brotherhood' (*fraternacionis spiritualis*) in 1459 for (in the words of the letter of confraternity) 'your pious merits and the special devotion you have shown to us and our order ... and bearing in mind the magnificent royal gifts you have bestowed on us so abundantly'.[6] Henry VII, too, was a significant benefactor, augmenting the monastery's income with two rectorships in return for spiritual intercession.[7]

Secondly, the monks took their institutional history seriously enough to compose and apparently disseminate a detailed narrative of their house's foundation. This corresponds to a widespread concern among late medieval Carthusians, on the continent as well as within the *Provincia Angliæ*, with advertising and celebrating the foundational history of both individual charterhouses and the order generally. Coventry's narrative was partially printed by Dugdale from a fragmentary manuscript since lost.[8] As well as naming lay benefactors and recording the extent of their contributions, it acknowledged Carthusian agency in the setting up of St Anne's: Richard II is called the *principalis fundator*, but a monk of the London Charterhouse, Robert Palmer, who subsequently became prior at Coventry, is styled the 'initiator and agent' (*primus motor et causa*) of the foundation. A second Carthusian account of the priory's origins, surviving in a mid-15th-century manuscript from the charterhouse of St Margaret at Basel, also ascribes foundation to Palmer (Fig. 1).[9] It goes further, attributing to him the completion as well as initiation of the house (*incepit unum monasterium ... in honore sancte anne & laudibiliter perfecit*). This account is brief, and reads more like a hagiography of Palmer than a straightforward historical narrative: he is called 'a most devout hermit and priest' (*hermita [et] sacerdos deuotissimus*), and is credited with miracles, including the resuscitation of a dead man. There is a fairly obvious concern here with demonstrating a level of Carthusian self-sufficiency impossible in England at the turn of the 15th century. Although unlikely to have been composed at Coventry, the Basel account contains enough local detail to suggest that the monks of St Anne's circulated their foundation history, and thus indicates this history's importance for their institutional identity in general.

Thirdly, the last years of St Anne's were not as ignominious as has been supposed. If the priory was not wealthy — indeed, its net income of around £131 in 1535 made it the poorest English charterhouse — it appears to have maintained its foundational principles to the end, at least to the extent that its urban setting allowed. A growth in testamentary bequests and the absence of the Charterhouse in local records of dispute suggest that St Anne's was comfortably, if not highly, esteemed during the early 16th century.[10] In 1536, the monks were reported to Henry VIII as 'in vertue, contemplacion and religion excellent'.[11] However, two letters written early in 1539 by Cromwell's

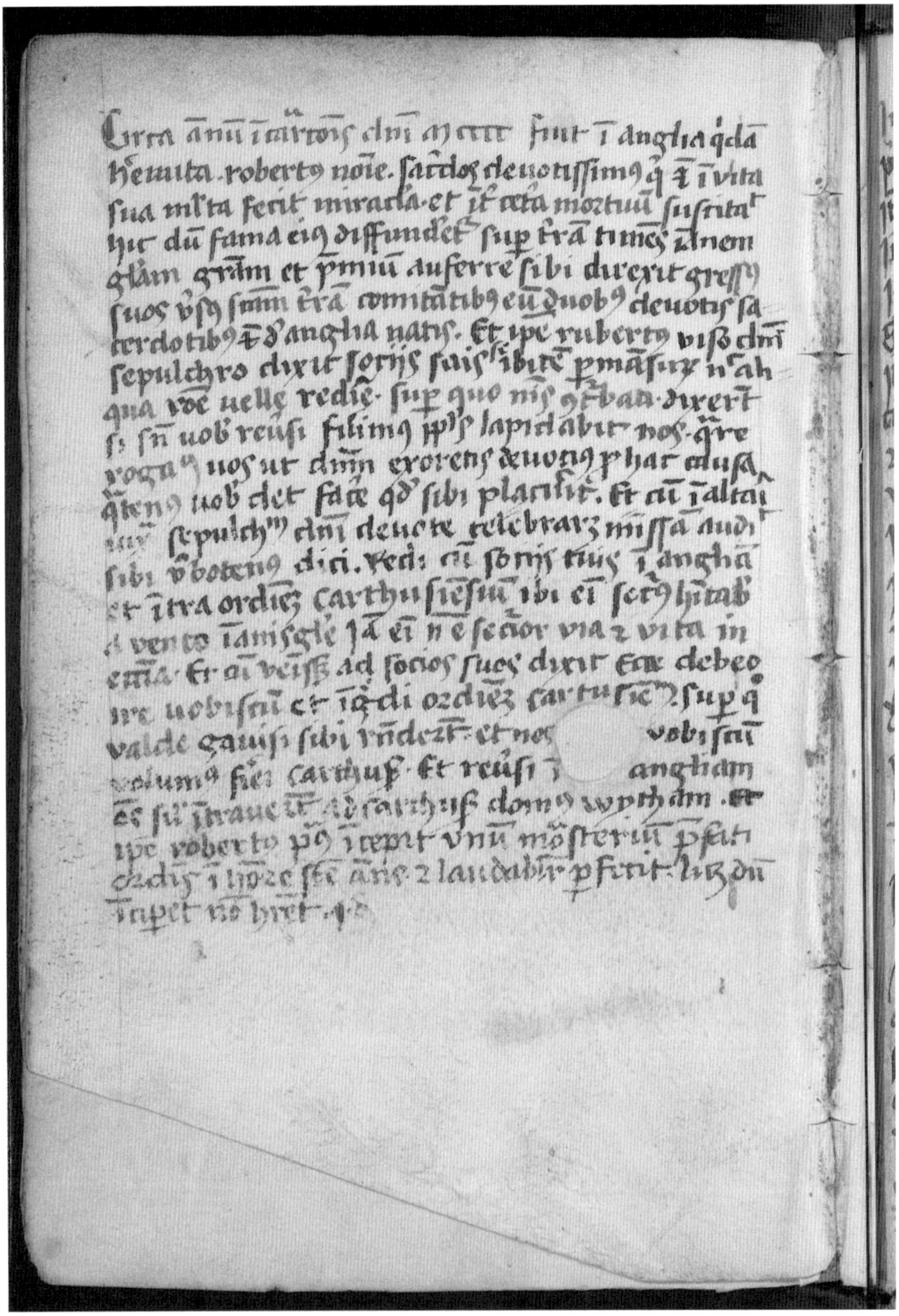

FIG. 1. Mid-15th-century account of the foundation of Coventry Charterhouse, from the Charterhouse of St Margaret, Basel; Basel, Universitätsbibliothek MS B X 30, fol. 92v

Reproduced by permission of the Öffentliche Bibliothek der Universität Basel

visitor, John London, have been misinterpreted to the disadvantage of the house's reputation. These reveal an attempt by John Brochard, prior from 1535 to 1539, to defraud the crown of Charterhouse property, some of which was long-leased, some 'hid in the earth'.[12] Brochard has consequently been characterised as immoral, self-seeking and no true Carthusian, aspersions which do him and the institution he represented no justice.[13] The monks were not sufficiently brave to die for their principles: indeed, in line with the royal proclamation of 1535, 'Papa' has been erased throughout Coventry's surviving psalter. Nevertheless, they certainly considered the property donated for their sustenance and the condition of the souls in their care sacrosanct, and not to be passively surrendered to the commissioners of a cupidous, schismatic king. Brochard and his convent, already under suspicion of sympathy with the Carthusians martyrs and the Lincolnshire and Yorkshire rebellions, were courageous rather than unscrupulous, and the fact that they avoided dissolution longer than any other religious house in Coventry is a fitting tribute to their strength of conscience.[14]

SITE AND BUILDINGS

THE prior and procurator of St Anne's were often involved in Coventry affairs, with priors even belonging to the city's eminent Trinity Guild, but most inmates of the Charterhouse must rarely have left the tapering wedge of land within their precinct's walls.[15] If the monks enjoyed a weekly extra-mural walk (*spatiamentum*), as Carthusians did elsewhere, then we know nothing about it. About half of their fourteen-acre world, probably at the southern end, was wooded at the time of the Dissolution, and the site also accommodated fish-ponds: according to Carthusian legend, a 16th-century monk named Richard Crotes tried to drown himself in one of these.[16] Towards the north stood a complex of buildings comprising inner and outer courts, whose plan has been partially recovered by excavation. This can be augmented by the description of cell location in the foundation narrative (Fig. 2).[17] Together, the buildings and their fittings were in 'verie good repaire and . . . well mayntened and kept' when valued at £89 7s. 6d. *ob. quart.* in 1535.[18] Seven years later they yielded fifty-five tons of lead, suggesting that all of the main claustral buildings were lead-roofed.[19] A bridge of two arches over the Sherbourne, destroyed in 1955, gave access to the outer court from the London Road, and a meadow on the river's west bank contained the moated chapel of St Anne and its appurtenances, in which the founding monks spent the seven years needed to make their monastery habitable. This outlying complex must have had historical and devotional significance for the convent, perhaps reflected in their lease of it for ninety-nine years in 1526.[20]

The principal standing remains are part of the western range of the inner court, which was converted into a private dwelling after the Dissolution, part of the north wall of the church, and much of the precinct wall, which reached a maximum height of approximately 3.5m (11ft 6in.). With the exception of some repair work in grey stone, perhaps from Whitley nearby, all that survives is of red Coventry sandstone. The precinct wall, an object of particular symbolic importance to Carthusians, survives to a greater extent than that of any other English charterhouse besides Mount Grace. It appears to have been repaired or partially heightened during the early 16th century and formerly supported at least one double garderobe, presumably for lay brethren and non-monastic servants, corbelled out over the Sherborne.[21] There is a postern gate at the north end of the precinct, but the main gate, located immediately east of the bridge,

Basic plan of the claustral complex. Based upon *Advances in Monastic Archaeology*, ed. R. Gilchrist and H. Mytum, BAR British Series CCXXVII (Oxford 1993), 131, C. B. Rowntree, 'Studies in Carthusian History in Later Medieval England' (unpublished D.Phil. thesis, University of York, 1981), 82, and the foundation narrative *Monasticon Anglicanum*, ed. W. Dugdale, rev. J. Caley, H. Ellis and B. Bandinel, 6 vols (London 1817-30), VI, 16-17, nos 2-4. The plan is intended to convey only a general impression of the charterhouse's layout, and does not claim strict accuracy.

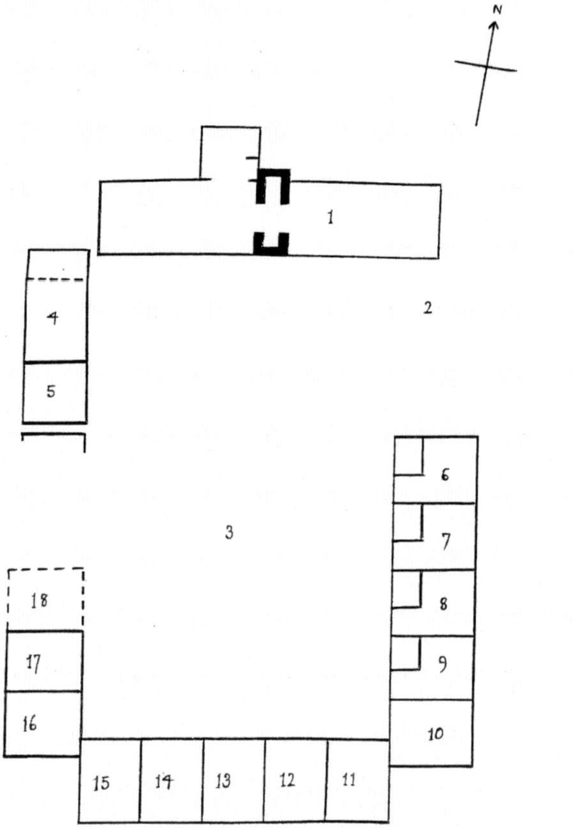

Key: 1 = church; 2 = approximate site of chapter-house; 3 = cloister garth; 4 = refectory (N. extension of post-Dissolution date); 5 = prior's cell (reception room over); 6-8 = cells (with enclosures) funded by Richard Luff and John Botoner; 9 = cell funded by Margaret Byri; 10 = cell funded by Margaret Tilney; 11 = cell funded by John Buckingham; 12 = cell funded by Thomas Beauchamp; 13 = cell funded by Adam Botoner; 14 = cell funded by Nigel Loryng; 15 = cell funded by William Tilney ('prima in parte occidentali', and thus perhaps more squarely in the angle of the cloister than shown here); 16 = cell funded by John Morton; 17 = presumed site of 12th regular cell; 18 = conjectural site of ancillary cell.

FIG. 2. Coventry Charterhouse: plan of the monastic cloister and conventual buildings, partially conjectural

Drawing, author

has vanished, and its site is unexcavated. A watercolour painted *c.* 1800 shows a gateway with lodge to the north-east of the bridge, which probably replaced or incorporated the medieval structure (Fig. 3), and a sketch of 1852 by Nathaniel Troughton apparently represents the same building.[22]

The first stone laid in 1385 belonged to the church, expressing the symbolic and functional importance of this building for the fledgling community. Relative to the claustral complex as a whole, Carthusian churches were usually small, reflecting the modesty of the order's common liturgy. Coventry's was no exception, although its maximum length of approximately 50m (164ft) made it comfortably the largest building on the site. In all, five phases of construction up to the early 16th century have been proposed. To an early presbytery and choir some 17m (56ft) long, a nave approximately 11m (36ft) long with a temporary west wall was added, followed by a tower extending 2m (6ft 6in.) north of the choir wall. Some idea of the tower's appearance may be preserved in that at Mount Grace, which has a similar rectangular plan (Fig. 4). Subsequently, the nave and presbytery each received one-and-a-half bay extensions, assumed to be a single campaign, and, finally, a two-bay chapel was annexed to the north side of the nave.[23] In fact, without doubting the accretive nature of the project, the suggested phasing is neater than the evidence can demonstrate. Except for the initial campaign of building, the work is undocumented and its chronology indistinct. In

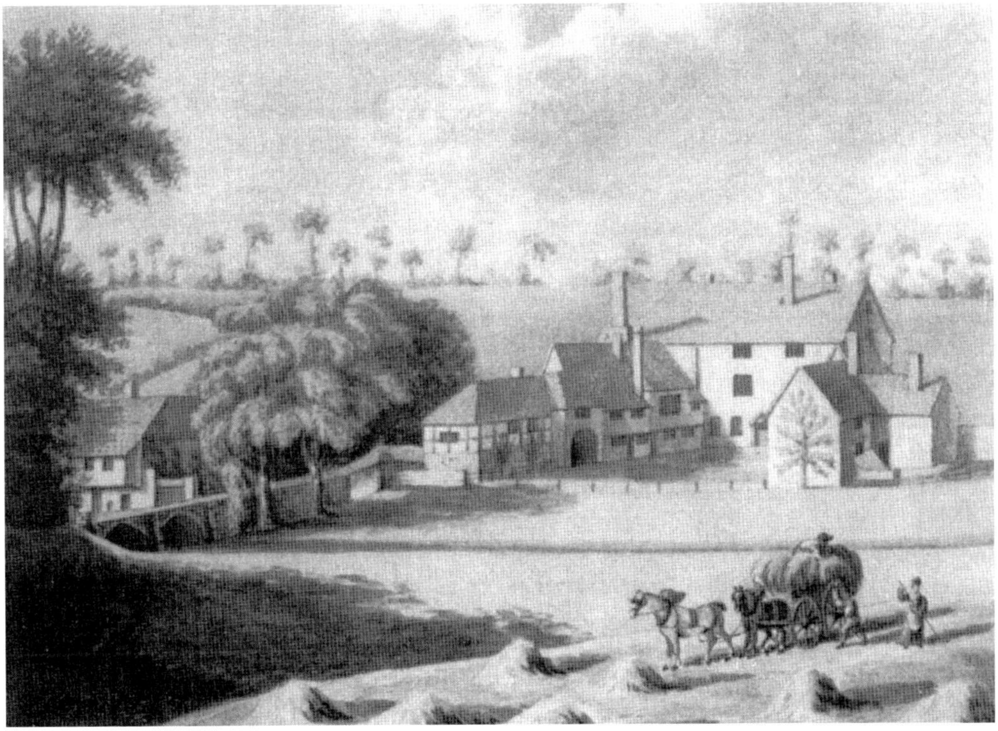

FIG. 3. The site of Coventry Charterhouse looking north-east: watercolour, anonymous, Birmingham Central Library, Aylesford Collection, Misc. Vol. 5, no. 6

Reproduced by permission of the Birmingham Central Library

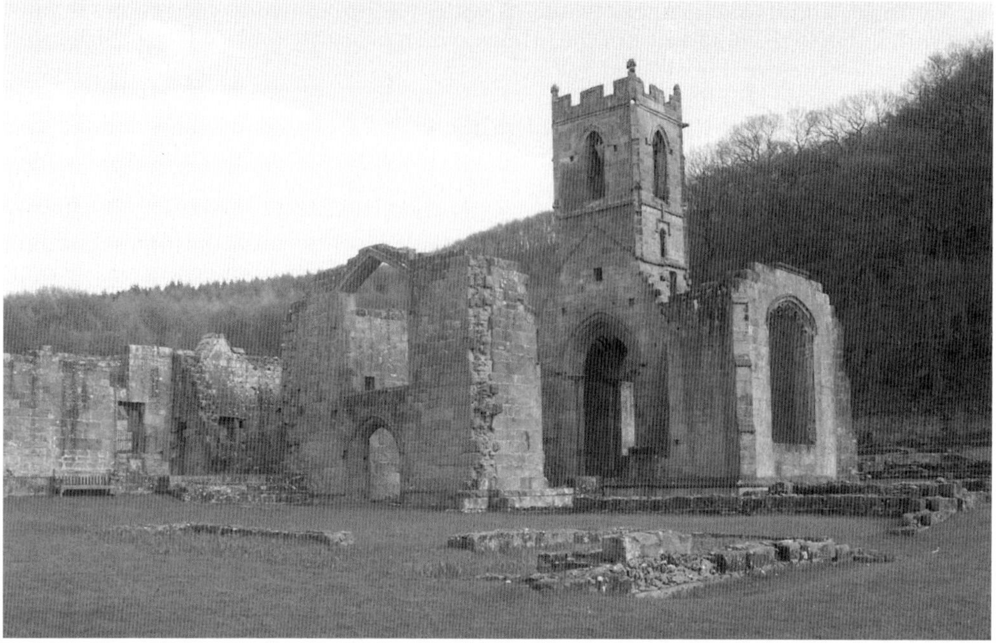

FIG. 4. Mount Grace Charterhouse: church from the south-east, showing central tower
Photo, author

particular, it may be noted that two benefactors of the 1380s, Richard Luff and John Botener, are stated in the foundation narrative to have funded construction of a nave as well as a choir (*chori et ecclesiæ*). If the funds were applied accordingly, then the first and second phases identified were probably one extended build. Some provision for the lay brethren is likely to have been made from the outset. Additionally, some of the extensions may have been necessary to accommodate the worship of twelve boys and their schoolmaster, resident at the Charterhouse from *c.* 1421.[24] A 16th-century date is convincingly posited for the two-bay chapel because, in a burial-rich church, it contained no graves.[25]

Of the chapter-house, in which the monks met each Sunday after Lauds, nothing has been excavated, but it is reasonable to suppose that, as at most charterhouses, it was a rectangular structure standing immediately south of the presbytery. The foundation narrative speaks of three cells on the east side of the cloister 'closest to the chapter house'. The cloister itself was probably little more than a pentice, and has left no visible trace, unless the string-course marking a medieval roof-line on the east side of the surviving block belonged to a northerly extension of the west walk (Fig. 5 and Col. Pl. XVIB in print edn). We can say much more about the eremitic cells, of such great practical and symbolic importance to Carthusians.[26] Four in the east range have been excavated, and the foundation narrative, which names nine cell-donors, allows us to plot the locations of eleven in total (Fig. 2). St Anne's was a standard foundation for a prior and twelve monks, and as the prior's cell is incorporated into the surviving block, this leaves two cells unaccounted for in the west range, one for permanent habitation, the other for the reception of monk-visitors or brethren sent from other

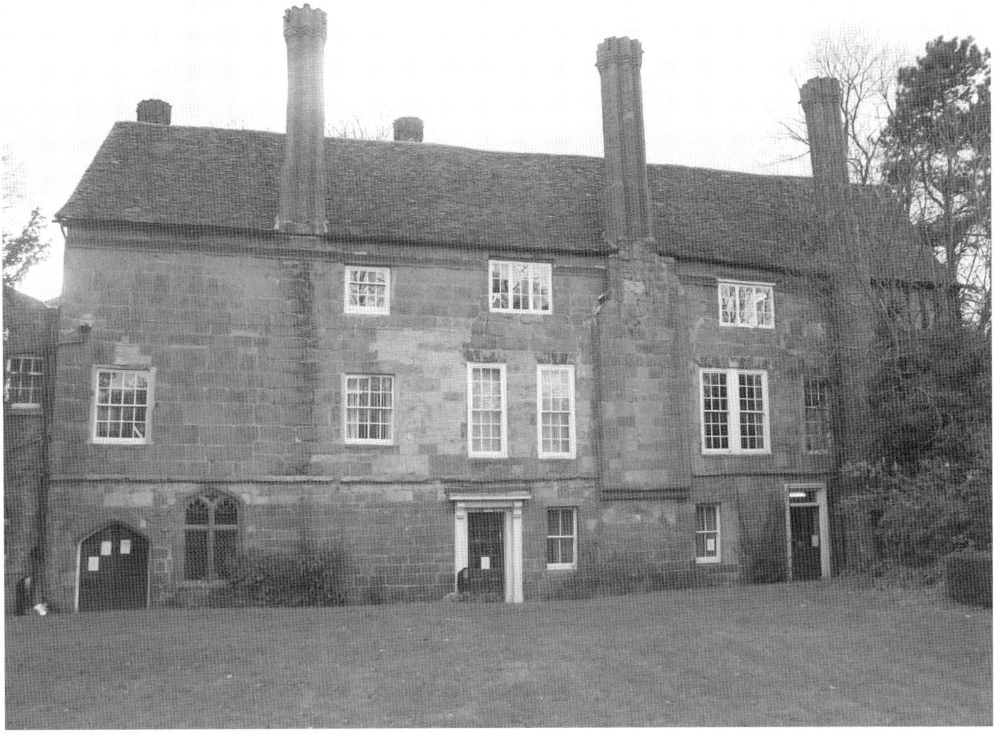

FIG. 5. Coventry Charterhouse: surviving block from the east
Photo, author

houses for convenience or correction, a duty no charterhouse could refuse.[27] A trench dug in 1987 to the south of the surviving block revealed stone foundations which may belong to one of these.[28]

Carthusian cells were two-storeyed, with discrete spaces for worship, study, sleeping, eating, and manual work separated by partitions, usually of timber. They were set in the inner corners of walled plots containing gardens. According to the foundation narrative, Coventry's early benefactors provided only £20 for each cell. This suggests buildings constructed substantially of timber, unlike those of London Charterhouse (which cost upwards of £130 each) and Mount Grace. Stone was used for foundations and the inner ground-floor walls: the lower courses of ashlar door-jambs have been excavated along the east range.[29] As at charterhouses elsewhere, the cells (and perhaps their inhabitants) appear to have been identified by letter.[30] A timber frame for a shallow-arched door, with the letter 'l' (or perhaps 'i') carved at its apex, survives reused in the western block (Fig. 6). Its width is approximately that of the surviving claustral doorways (710mm, 28in.).[31]

Like all English conventual buildings converted into private residences, the surviving block on the north-west side of the monastic cloister is imperfectly preserved. A building of two storeys, lower than the existing structure, was given a third storey, new roof, and half-timbered northern extension by post-Dissolution owners. The earliest

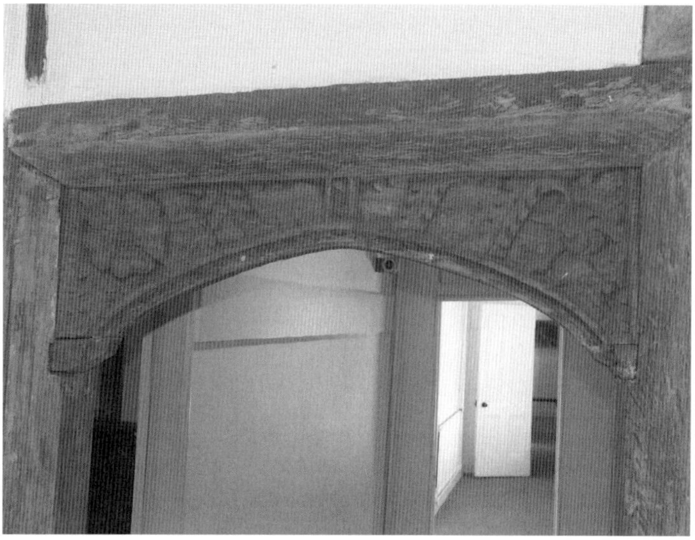

FIG. 6. Coventry Charterhouse: head of door-frame with the letter 'I' (or 'i')
Photo, author

alterations are of mid-16th-century date, the latest of the 1960s. At an early stage the internal spaces were altered by insertion of partition-walls, and corridors were driven through the main transverse wall at first- and second-floor levels. Originally the block was divided vertically by a wall, and was open to the roof-timbers on the first floor. At ground-floor level it contains a vaulted passage between the outer court and monastic cloister, whose occasional use by non-Carthusians is suggested by the existence of a sculpted corbel of a demi-angel, with a cross on its forehead and holding a shield which was probably once blazoned (Fig. 7). A sketch by Troughton shows the remains of another, lower, structure, with a medieval doorway (possibly re-set) in its east wall, on the south side of this passage (Fig. 8).

The medieval disposition and function of this building has never been fully established, largely because to date it has been thought that the current first floor is medieval along its entire length.[32] This was certainly the case at the south end, where a ground-floor room, accessible from the aforementioned vaulted passage, communicated with a first-floor chamber by a still-extant vice in the east wall. To the north, however, there was a larger room approximately 12m long by 7m wide (39 × 23ft), which stood open probably from pavement to roof. Thus what survives of this block contained three main rooms, with that at ground-floor level at the south end divided up by partitions. These assumptions rest on fairly straightforward evidence, beginning with the large room to the north. While St John Hope's argument, that the upper level of this space was the guest-hall, has been corroborated by James Hogg, Joseph Gribbin and Carol Rowntree, among others, this cannot have been the case. It is architecturally too significant within the context of the monastery as whole, and too close to the eremitic cloister, to have accommodated seculars.[33] The monumental Crucifixion on its south wall tells the story: this, as Mary Dormer Harris seems first to have realised, was the monastic refectory.[34] The painting, originally about 4m (13ft) high, dominated the room, much as did the refectory Crucifixions known or surviving at Horsham St Faith Priory (Norf.) and Cleeve Abbey (Som.). At Horsham and Cleeve, as in a number of continental examples, the base of the cross is set at least 3m (10ft) above the floor.[35]

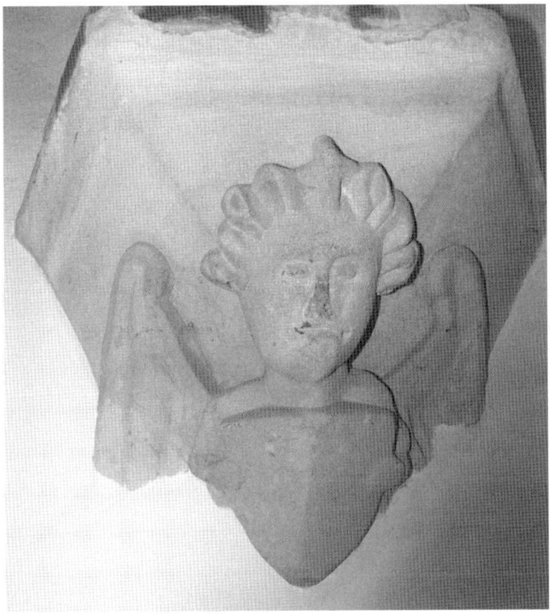

FIG. 7. Coventry Charterhouse: sculpted angel corbel west end of the vaulted passage from the presumed outer court to the monastic cloister
Photo, author

This must also have been the case at Coventry. Such a tall painting could not have been seen in correct perspective or have generated the optimum psychological effect from a floor set at the present level, or even a metre or so lower. Moreover, the medieval monumental Crucifix, whether in church, refectory, marketplace or elsewhere, was skied above the viewer as a matter of decorum. The base of the Coventry painting is set about 4.5m (14ft 9in.) above the current pavement level. This is comparatively high, but not sufficiently so to suggest the existence of a low ground floor or undercroft. Indeed, the only visible architectural evidence in either direction is the blocked doorway which led from the west cloister range into the refectory, and stood immediately north of the lavatorium (also now blocked). The sill of this doorway may have been set upon one or two low steps, but seemingly no more than that.

As in the refectory at Cleeve Abbey, the base of the Coventry Crucifixion is roughly contiguous with the sills of large traceried windows on the east side, the blocked arches of which are visible on the exterior of the wall (Fig. 5). Thus the painting and its attendant images would have been well-lit when, on Sundays and feast days, the monks entered, each bowing his tonsured pate before the crucified Christ.[36] There were no windows in the west wall, in deliberate respect, perhaps, of Carthusian immurement from the world. A post-medieval fireplace incorporated into the first-floor room probably stands on the vertical axis of a pulpit from which the order's cycle of refectory readings was delivered. Elevated pulpits remain in a number of continental charterhouses, and are also illustrated in at least one late-medieval Carthusian manuscript (Fig. 9).

The south end of the surviving block contained the prior's cell and a first-floor parlour, in which the prior is likely to have received non-Carthusian visitors.[37] While the cell was of only one storey, it was set apart by its position, the absence of an enclosing wall and garden, and its stone construction. This environmental and architectural distinction is in line with the priors' cells excavated at London, Beauvale and

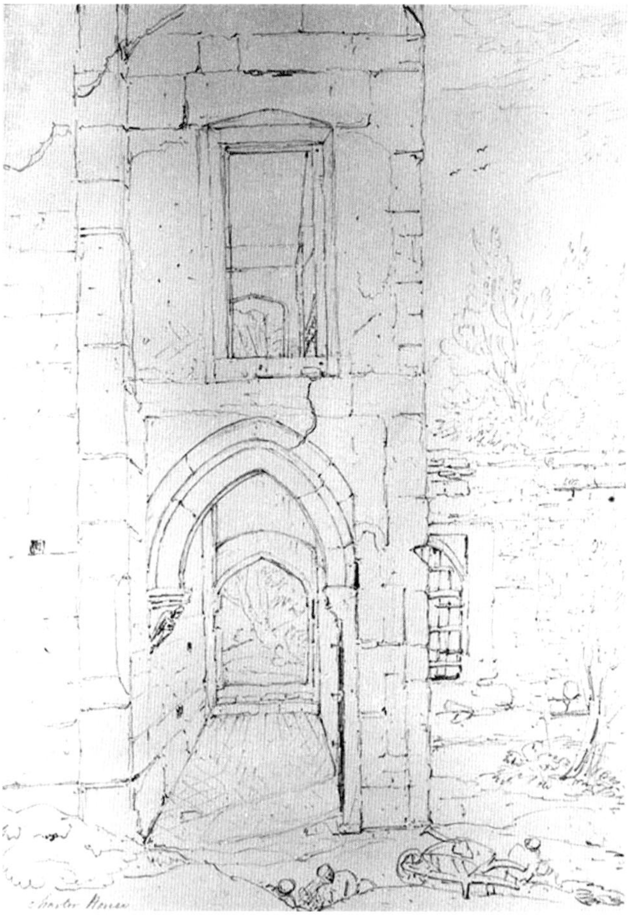

FIG. 8. Coventry Charterhouse: sketch of the south-west end of the surviving range, showing small doorway to the south of the vaulted passage, Nathaniel Troughton X/34A

Reproduced by permission of the History of Art Department, University of Warwick

Mount Grace charterhouses.[38] It must originally have been divided up by partitions, and a sacred trigram (IHS) found painted behind post-medieval panelling suggests that its walls were not wainscoted.[39] The parlour above was lit on the west side by a large window with moulded jambs, apparently square-headed (Fig. 10). What survives of this seems rather late in date — perhaps *c.* 1500 — suggesting the existence of an earlier, probably smaller, window. Mount Grace also had a first-floor reception room above the prior's cell, which was lit to east and west by oriel windows.[40] At Coventry there was no large window in the east wall, again suggesting that secular guests were denied even sight of the inner court. There were, however, smaller windows in both east and west walls at the south end of the chamber (Fig. 8). This part of the room may have been reserved for the prior's private use. Instead of a window, the centre of the east wall boasts a fireplace with shouldered lintel, while the roof-timbers above, which may have been painted, were embellished with vine-scroll and devotional carving. Some of these timbers are partially visible below the ceiling plaster, including one carrying what seems to be a Passion shield displaying the seamless robe and a dice (Fig. 11). Another such shield, also of later 15th-century date, survives at the Grande

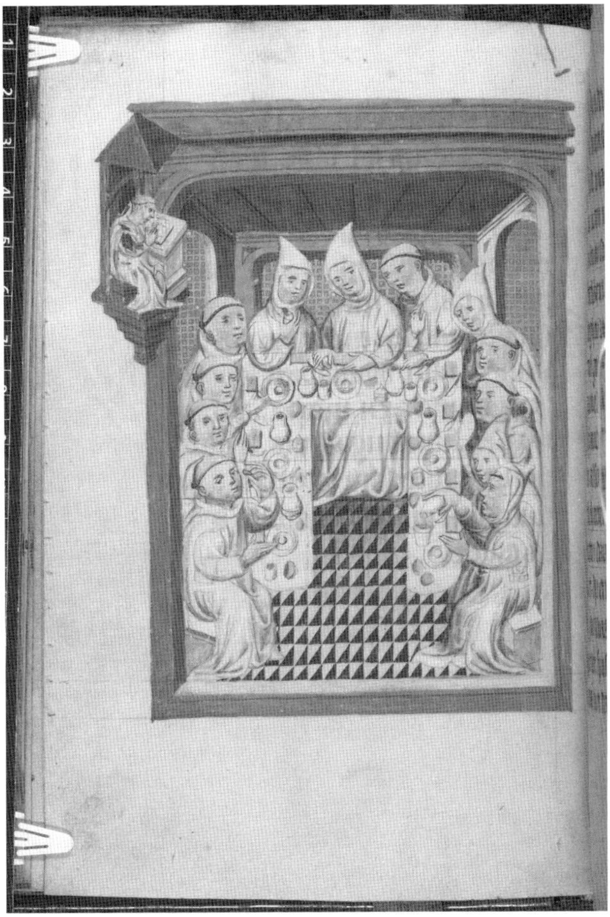

FIG. 9. Illustration of a lector reading to a Carthusian convent from an elevated refectory pulpit; incongruously, the prior and four of the monks wear their hoods at table. Dutch, late 15th- or early 16th-century; London, BL, MS Add. 25042, fol. 22v
Reproduced by permission of the British Library Board

Chartreuse, and at the London Charterhouse there is a series of Passion shields, each with an individual emblem, on the vault bosses of the church tower, built in 1519. These examples in influential and prestigious locations suggest that such iconography was once conventional in the order's houses.[41] In terms of size, comfort and embellishment, the room was thus appropriate to the reception of those important associates whose support and generosity were needed for maintenance of the Charterhouse's eremitical integrity. The prior alone would not have had licence, motive or indeed desire for such ostentation.

For the monks, completion of this building marked the end of the long process of foundation. The matter was evidently important to them, because they celebrated it in verse beneath the Crucifixion painting, appropriately rendered in Stabat-Mater strophe.[42] It informs us that 'This house has been finished' (*Fuit domus hec completa*), implying the monastery as a whole rather than the refectory by itself. It further explains that 'certainly Prior Soland toiled', literally 'sweated' (*Prior Solonde nam sudauit*), presumably in support of the work, and that 'Thomas Lambard attended to [or oversaw] it' (*Thomas Lambard procurauit*). There is an allusion here to the fact that

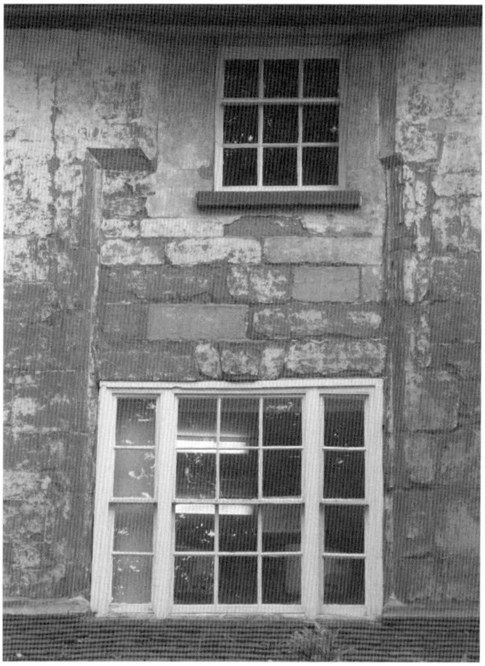

FIG. 10. Coventry Charterhouse: remains of large window in the west wall of the surviving range
Photo, author

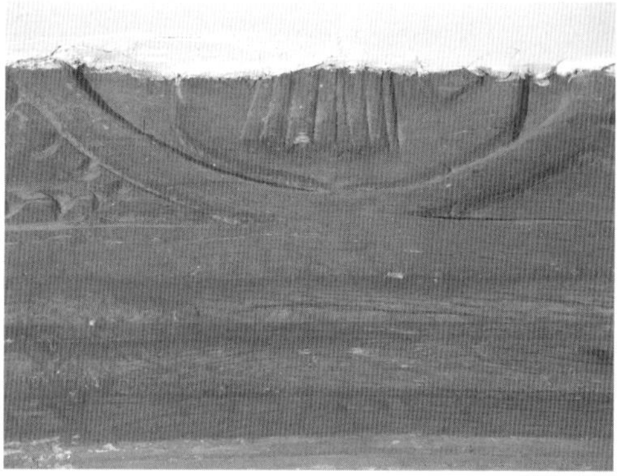

FIG. 11. Coventry Charterhouse: Passion shield, partially visible in the prior's reception room
Photo, author

Lambard also served as procurator, usually the only Carthusian obedientiary besides the prior to involve himself in external affairs.[43] The last verse is incomplete, breaking off with 'after which ...' (*post quem* ...), and thus implying that the painting was executed after Lambard's involvement had ceased. William Soland, originally of the London Charterhouse, is documented as prior from 1409 until March 1437. He may have continued in the office for some time after this: we have no obit date for him, and his successor, John Walweyn, is not documented until 1446. Thomas Lambard (or Lambert) died in 1440, after an unspecified period as procurator.[44] While the poem may have been composed after both left office, it implies that the work was completed while Soland was prior, giving a fairly secure dating envelope of 1409–37. As the building was evidently a conventual initiative rather than a product of benefaction, a date early in the period, when the monks were shackled by indigence, is unlikely. Around 1430–35 is a more cogent suggestion, and agrees better with the costume evidence of the Crucifixion painting.

We can say much less concerning the outer court on the west side of the surviving block, for no recorded excavation has been done and there are no germane documentary sources. In this court the buildings staffed by lay brethren and non-monastic servants are likely to have stood: the kitchen, bakehouse, brewery, storehouses, and other such utilitarian structures essential to monastic self-sufficiency. The watercolour cited above (Fig. 3), and a number of careful on-site drawings done in 1852 by Nathaniel Troughton

(Figs 8, 12), show extensions built at right-angles to the surviving block, at least some of which were half-timbered. All have now been demolished, and that they form a court to the west of the surviving block does no more than suggest that they preserved an original plan. Glyn Coppack states that the northern extension housed the monastic kitchen, though without citing evidence.[45] This a fair guess, as the watercolour shows a broad, high chimney, indicating a large fireplace or fireplaces, rising above the bay closest to the refectory. However, Troughton, whose accuracy is clearly to be preferred to that of the watercolour, represents the same bay of the extension, and in particular the chimney-base (the chimney-shaft may of course have been dismantled between *c.* 1800 and 1852), quite differently. Moreover, as most monastic meals were taken in the cells, a site next to the refectory was by no means necessary for a Carthusian kitchen. Provision of doles in kind, and meals for lay brethren, servants and visitors also had to be taken into account. While there are other indications in Troughton's drawing to suggest that the extension occupied the site of a medieval structure, what he shows cannot be confidently dated on either side of the Dissolution. The most that can safely be said is that the extension could have incorporated monastic fabric, or at least made use of medieval foundations.

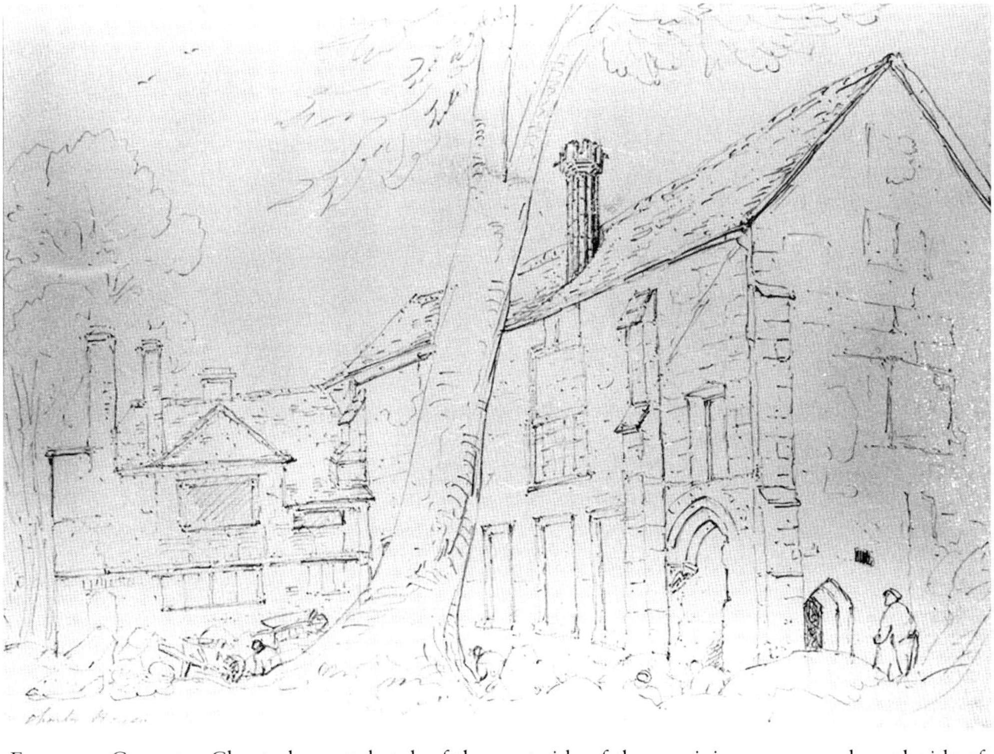

FIG. 12. Coventry Charterhouse: sketch of the west side of the surviving range, and south side of the now demolished north-west extension, Nathaniel Troughton X/34C

Reproduced by permission of the History of Art Department, University of Warwick

INSTITUTIONAL LIFE

HAVING surveyed the site and surviving architecture of St Anne's, we turn now to matters of institutional culture. We might begin by asking who lived here. If monastic convents were practical and symbolic collectives, their unity was the sum of independently significant parts. Even Carthusians believed this, to the extent, for example, that priors had their own seals, that men such as William Soland and Thomas Lambard could be individually commemorated in verse, and that cloister monks were routinely recorded by name in documentation generated by the order. In 1536, thirty-three individuals 'havyng their lyvyng of', though not necessarily all resident at, the Charterhouse were recorded, not counting the prior. These included twelve monks, all of them priests, three lay brothers, and the twelve scholars the house was bound to support.[46] From obit-lists compiled at the Grande Chartreuse we know the names of at least seventy of Coventry's monks.[47] Priors' careers can often be traced to other houses, typically London, but in only a handful of additional cases can we add anything to these *nominæ nudæ*. Verifiable toponyms were apparently rare among Coventry monks.[48] Exceptions include the famous Wycliffite, Nicholas Hereford (d. 1419), who entered St Anne's in 1417; one John Romondby (d. 1500), purportedly of noble birth, who petitioned the pope for a licence to hold an external benefice; and Robert Raby and George Rogers, monks whose illness — whether mental or physical is not stated — caused their prior to petition London for their removal in the 1520s or early 1530s.[49] Another is John Cray, a 'restless, inconstant monk' of Rochester Cathedral Priory, who took on the Carthusian vocation at London, but abandoned it almost immediately *probam me dicti ordinis non posse sufferre rigorem* ('because I cannot bear the discipline of the order'). In August 1393 he was ready to try again, and Robert Palmer, then prior of Coventry, agreed to admit him.[50] That he had found a new home with the Franciscans of Cambridge by December of the same year suggests that life at St Anne's proved no easier than what he had experienced at London.

Liturgical and devotional life at St Anne's elided to a degree unknown in Coventry's other religious houses. There is no reason to suspect that the monks were particularly unconventional, though they were not always in step with official Carthusian liturgy — they were threatened with abstinence on bread and water by the Grande Chartreuse in 1423 for attempting to embellish their observance with special offices of the Virgin Mary.[51] They will have entered church only thrice daily: during the night for matins, in the morning for conventual mass, and in the afternoon for vespers. Conventual mass was celebrated at the high altar, and a large mensa measuring 800 × 630mm which still exists, reused as an over-mantel in the surviving block, may have belonged to this (Fig. 13). The canonical hours not performed in church were recited privately by each monk in the *oratorium* of his cell. On feast-days all offices were performed in the church, and each monk must have gone to the church daily to celebrate at one of its altars. Many of these masses were presumably commensurate with intercessory obligations. While Richard II's vision of a double charterhouse staffed by monk-chaplains perpetually augmenting divine service and praying for his soul came to naught, the convent was obligated to pray for its royal founders, lay benefactors, and all departed to whom its order had granted spiritual confraternity.[52]

Evidence for five fixed altars and one portable altar has been excavated. Two of the fixed altars were in the early 16th-century chapel, perhaps suggesting increased intercession at this time.[53] A portable altar slab of Purbeck marble, inscribed with five consecration crosses, was excavated outside a small doorway in the north of the nave

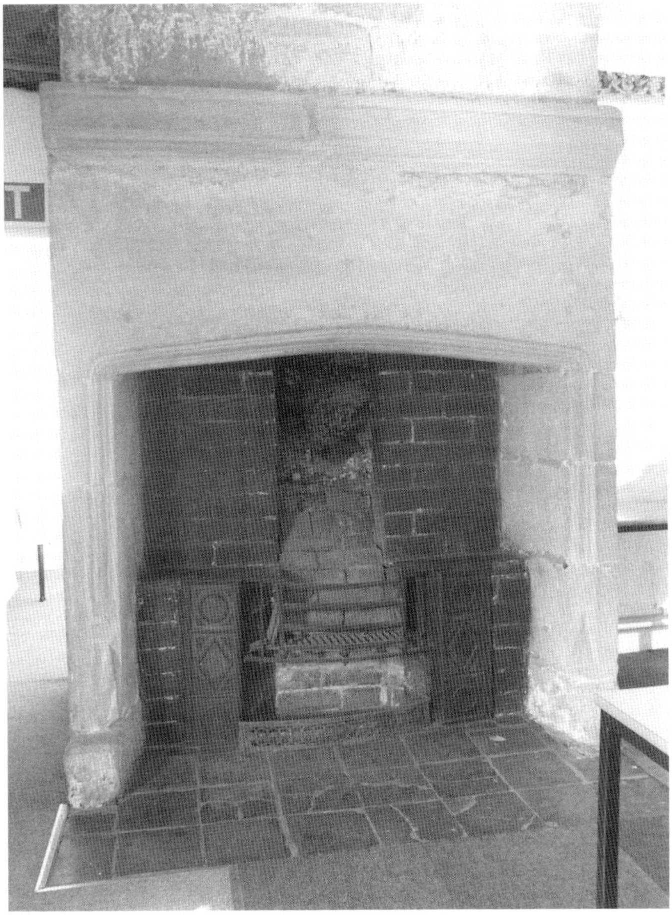

Fig. 13. Coventry Charterhouse: altar mensa reused as an over-mantel
Photo, author

(Fig. 14).[54] This location implies use within the church, while the crosses suggest a 15th-century date, because such marks are unusual on portable altars before this century. No papal licence granting St Anne's use of a portable altar has been printed, and it is possible that the object was given to the priory by a benefactor. More than 750 such altars were licensed for use in England under Pope Martin V (1417–31) alone.[55]

On surviving indications, the monks and lay brethren worshipped in a church embellished to conventional standards for its period. While later medieval Carthusians are not known as prolific patrons of art, neither did they eschew it.[56] Excavations have produced fragments of Perpendicular window tracery and the stone screens which divided the interior into its hierarchical and liturgical units.[57] The tracery is rebated, and numerous small fragments of the glass it held, some painted with foliate patterns and letters, have also been found.[58] Two panels carrying blank shields, apparently from a tomb-chest, indicate the presence of at least one raised 15th-century monument, although we have no idea whom it commemorated.[59] Better represented by survivals are the medieval pavements. Over 100 glazed tiles of single, four- and nine-unit designs from the site have been catalogued by Iain Soden, most of them in

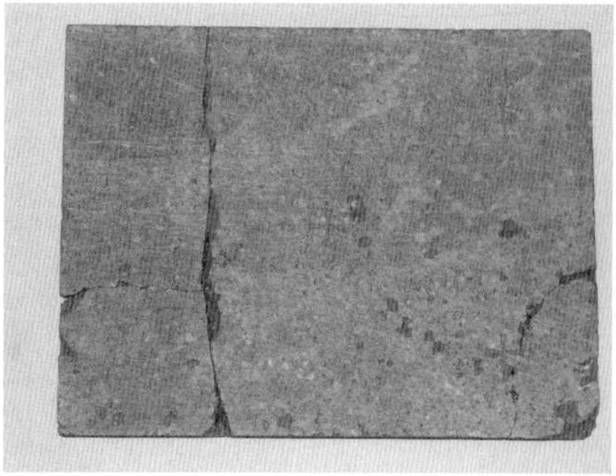

FIG. 14. Portable altar slab (360 × 270mm, 14 × 10¾in.) from the Coventry Charterhouse
Herbert Art Gallery and Museum, Coventry. Photo, author

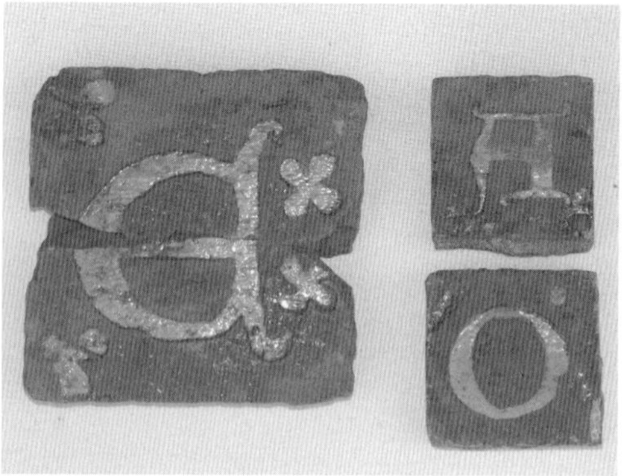

FIG. 15. Letter tiles from the Coventry Charterhouse
Herbert Art Gallery and Museum, Coventry. Photo, author

fragmentary condition. The iconographic range is considerable, but the imagery itself mainly conventional. Some are armorial, displaying the arms of Edward the Confessor (a patron saint of Axholme Charterhouse, Lincs.), Clare, Clinton of Maxstoke, Astley, Botler of Sudeley, Thomas Mowbray (the founder of Axholme), Thomas Beauchamp, and others. Locality, but not necessarily financial patronage, must help to account for some of these, while others can be understood as concessions to contemporary fashion.[60] There were no copyrights on coats of arms, and in general tile-makers and patrons could use them as they wished.[61] There are also two sizes of tile carrying Lombardic letters, which point to the presence of scriptural, votive or commemorative pavement inscriptions (Fig. 15).

The survival of alabaster figures representing Saints Denis and Lawrence suggests that at least one of the church altars had a sculpted reredos (Fig. 16).[62] They were dug up about 1750 in the garden east of the surviving block, where they were presumably secreted before they could fall into secular hands, a familiar method of image-preservation.[63] Each of these very popular saints occurs in both the Carthusian calendar and the litany of the Charterhouse's surviving psalter.[64] Stylistically, the figures are uniform and mundane: they look very much like Nottingham work of the mid- to late 15th century, although the fact that Coventry had alabaster workers of its own during the period raises the possibility of local manufacture.[65] Neither is mentioned in Francis Cheetham's summary catalogue of English medieval alabasters, which lists thirteen surviving figures of St Lawrence but only two of St Denis.[66] Each has a flat back with two lead fixing plugs, strongly suggesting incorporation into an altarpiece, although it is theoretically possible that they were mounted singly, as some alabasters were, or kept as unmounted devotional images.[67] That they were apparently singled out for preservation implies particular allegiance to these saints on the part of at least one monk.

A special devotion to the conventual patron saint is variously reflected in the surviving record. In 1526, the monks petitioned the General Chapter for permission to celebrate the feast of St Anne (26 July) in a manner commensurate with her local importance. St Anne was on the Carthusian calendar, of course, but never of special significance to the order in general. The Chapter left it to the local Carthusian visitors

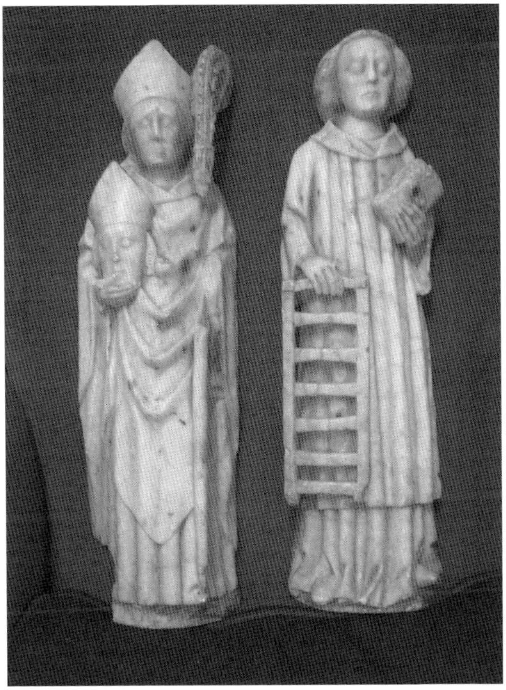

FIG. 16. Alabaster figures of Saints Denis, left (height 430mm, 17in.) and Lawrence (height 425mm, 16¾in.) from Coventry Charterhouse; Parish of The Most Holy Sacrament and St Osburg, Coventry
Photo, author

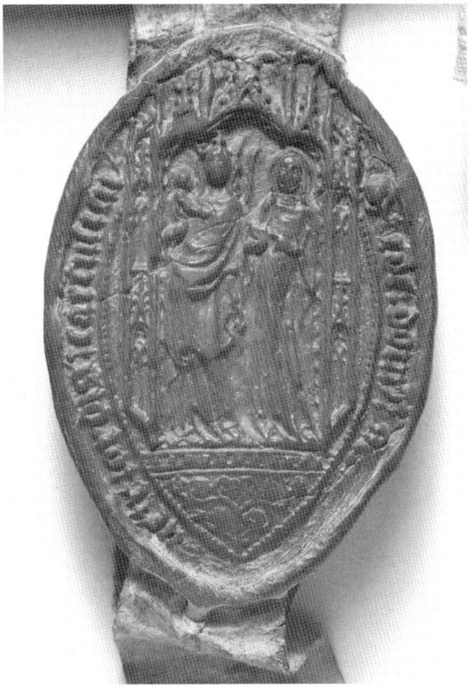

FIG. 17. Impression of the obverse of the conventual seal of Coventry Charterhouse, dated 1436; the matrix for this seal, probably of late 14th-century manufacture, was still in use at the Dissolution. London, BL, Additional Charter 7385
Reproduced by permission of the British Library Board

to decide: their decision is unrecorded, but was probably favourable to the monks.[68] Additionally, in the litany of the monastery's surviving, mid-15th-century psalter, now Cambridge, Peterhouse, MS 276, a double invocation of St Anne is specified, an honorific otherwise extended only to that great pioneering Carthusian, St Hugh of Lincoln (fol. 120r). The double invocation of these saints in the hand of the main text is sufficient to indicate that the manuscript was made specifically for (and perhaps at) the Charterhouse. The same manuscript contains a prefatory prayer invoking St Anne at the head of the female saints, corresponding to her normal position in the litany (fol. 9v). Three images of St Anne have also come down to us. The first is an incomplete wall-painting of her teaching the Virgin to read, discussed in detail elsewhere in this volume.[69] The other two are seal impressions, from the conventual seal (engraved before 1436, probably in the late 14th century), where she is shown as a matriarch standing to the left of the Virgin and Child (Fig. 17), and from Prior Thomas Tarleton's personal seal (*c.* 1521), where she again instructs her daughter.[70] There must have been further images of her in the church, and it is possible that the letter-tiles of the church pavement also reminded the monks of her role as the Virgin's *magistra* (Fig. 15).

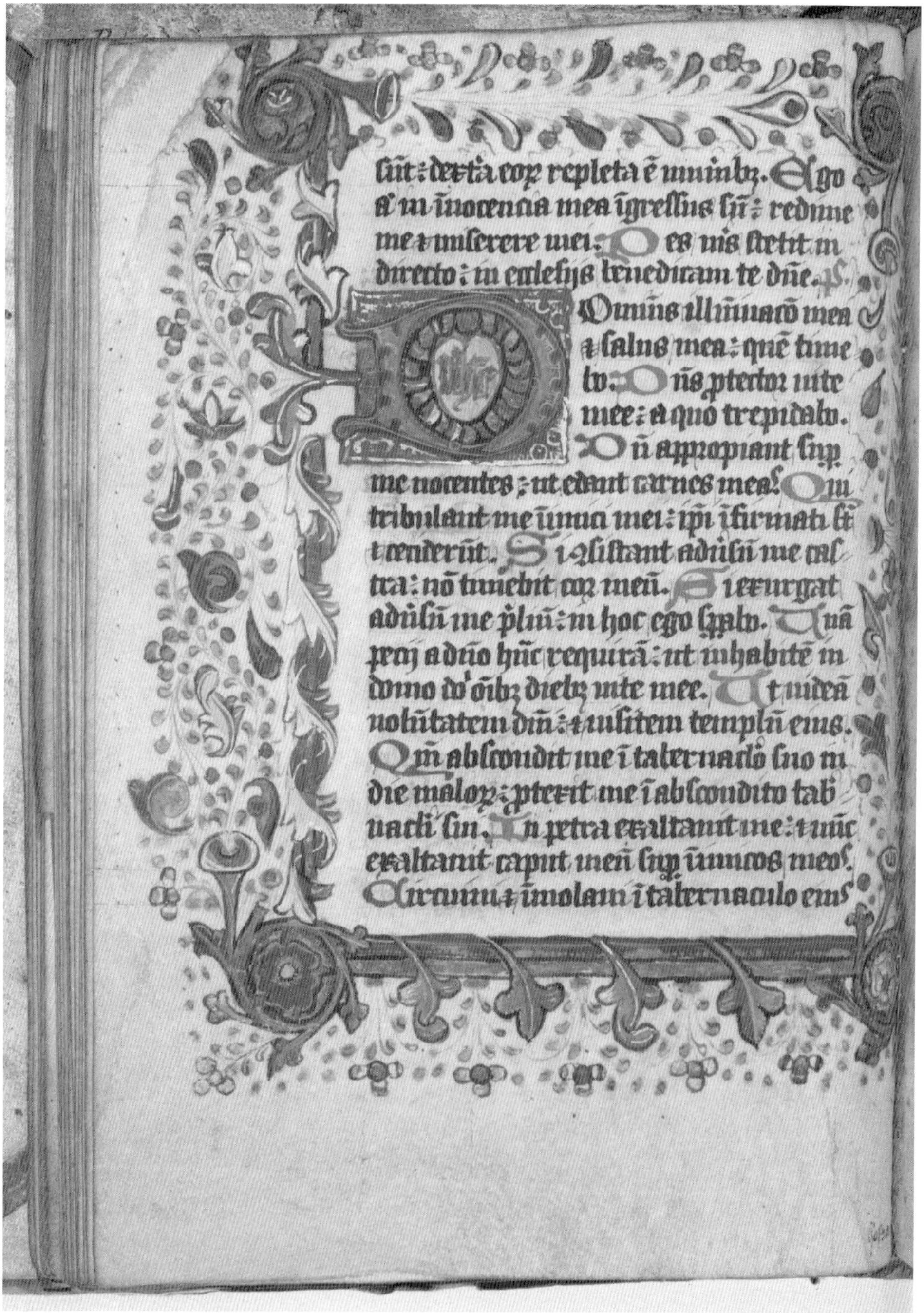

FIG. 18. Cambridge, Peterhouse MS 276, fol. 32r, probably second quarter of the 15th century
Reproduced by permission of the Master and Fellows of Peterhouse, Cambridge

For all St Anne's importance at Coventry, Christ preserved His traditional Carthusian pre-eminence. The best indications of Christocentric devotion exist in the wall-painting, the psalter, and surviving indications of pious reading and writing. In spite of all that is lost, these provide a refreshingly direct sense of the monks' spiritual pre-occupations. The only illustration in the psalter is a small heart inscribed with the sacred trigram 'IHC', which occurs on fol. 32r at Psalm 26, *Dominus illuminatio mea* (Fig. 18 and Col. Pl. XVII in print edn). This reflects Carthusian sympathy for late medieval mystical traditions which dwelt upon the sacred heart as a symbol of Christ's love, sacrifice, and protection.[71] We have already encountered a sacred trigram in the prior's cell, and it is found inscribed on a heart in other 15th-century English Carthusian manuscripts.[72] Prefacing and following the psalter text is a series of Christocentric prayers, seven of which carry promises of indulgence. These range from an offer of 5,640 days of remission for saying a specified prayer to the wounds of Christ, to 300,000 years'

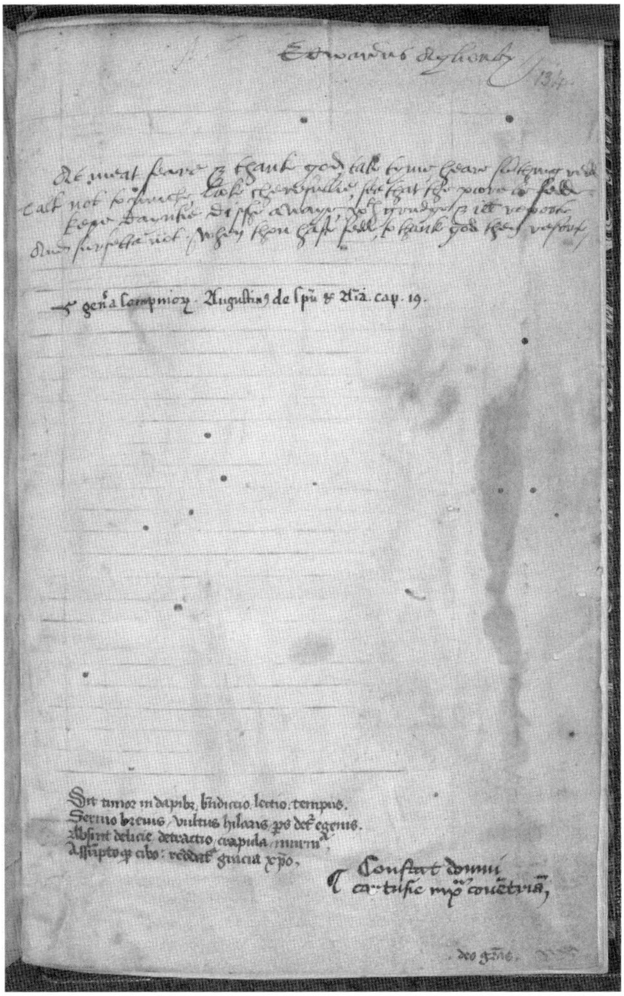

FIG. 19. End-leaf inscription taken from the didactic poem *Stans puer ad mensam*, early to mid-15th-century; the cursive inscription at the top of the page is post-medieval. London, BL, MS Royal 5 A V, fol. 134r
Reproduced by permission of the British Library Board

grace for reciting the *Stabat Mater*, the text of which follows (fols 7v, 10r). The latter calls to mind the inscription beneath the refectory wall-painting in Stabat-Mater strophe. There is St Mechtild's prayer to the 'health-bringing' wounds of Christ, Bede's prayer on the seven last words from the cross (fols 6v, 10v), and numerous others relating to Christ's body and sacrifice (e.g. fols 6r, 7r, 12r (*bis*), 16r). An indulgenced prayer ascribed to Pope John XXII begins as follows: 'Christ's soul sanctifies me; Christ's body saves me; Jesus Christ's blood intoxicates me; the water from Jesus Christ's side washes me; Jesus Christ's Passion consoles me; Jesus Christ's death gives me life' (fol. 8r). This is the 'tumbl[ing] forth [of] verbs of drinking, washing and drowning' recently analysed in the context of Holy Blood devotion by Caroline Walker Bynum.[73] No more immediate or poignant perspective for considering the Coventry monks' responses to the Crucifixion imagery in their church, refectory and oratories could be desired.

Peterhouse 276 is one of only three books from St Anne's known to survive, all of them of 15th-century date. A second, now Cambridge, Jesus College, MS 11, also relates to the psalter, being the unique surviving copy of the Franciscan Henry Cossey's rather formidable commentary on the Psalms. The third, now British Library, Royal MS 5 A V, contains works by Saints Augustine and Hugh of St Victor, and two eremitical texts — one the 14th-century *Speculum inclusorum* ('Mirror of recluses') — which would have particularly appealed to Carthusians. The *Speculum* was annotated by James Greenhalgh (d. 1530), a prolific Middle English textual critic who was briefly a monk of Coventry.[74] Folio 134r of Royal 5 A V, an endleaf, also contains a four-line addition excerpted from the didactic poem *Stans puer ad mensam*, popularised contemporaneously by John Lydgate, which reads in translation: 'Let there be fear at meals, benediction, reading, time / Let thy speech be short, thy countenance cheerful; let part be given to the poor / Let luxury be put away, detraction, drunkenness, growling / And when the food is taken, let thanks be paid to Christ'. The ruminant writer of these lines may well have had the decorum of the Charterhouse refectory in mind as he wrote (Fig. 19).[75] That the monks provided copious poor relief, and also the sort of elementary education with which the poem is usually associated, adds to the range of associations this passage elicits.[76]

James Greenhalgh was not the only Coventry monk notable for his literary work. John Norton, who was twice prior before his death in 1489, authored an important surviving spiritual treatise, *De Vita solitaria*. This survives in Oxford, Bodleian Library, MS Lat. Th. d. 27, a miscellany of texts on monasticism which was probably also a Coventry book, but which lacks the *ex libris* by which the others can be provenanced.[77] Such works as Norton's were written to help cell-bound men better understand the solitary and gruelling discipline to which they were committed. That they were read alongside commoner and indeed universal texts is seen in a surviving memorandum of books sent to St Anne's from the London Charterhouse in 1500 in the care of Brother Roger Montgomery.[78] In addition to St Brigit's *Revelationes* and Richard Rolle's *Incendium armoris*, this includes a Bible, patristic commentaries, a dictionary, a *Legenda aurea*, Peter Comestor's *Historia scolastica*, Peter Lombard's *Sententiæ*, and a copy of the *Statuta Cartusianorum*. Loan of such standard works reflects a relative rather than total lack of fundamental literature at Coventry. As the copying of holy texts was an important aspect of Carthusian devotion, one supposes that at least some of the books were intended to function as scribal exemplars.[79] It is possible, too, that the monks occasionally turned their hands to illumination as well as writing. The decorated borders (nine) and initials (thirty-five) of their surviving psalter are sufficiently idiosyncratic in ornament and quality to suggest that they could be the work

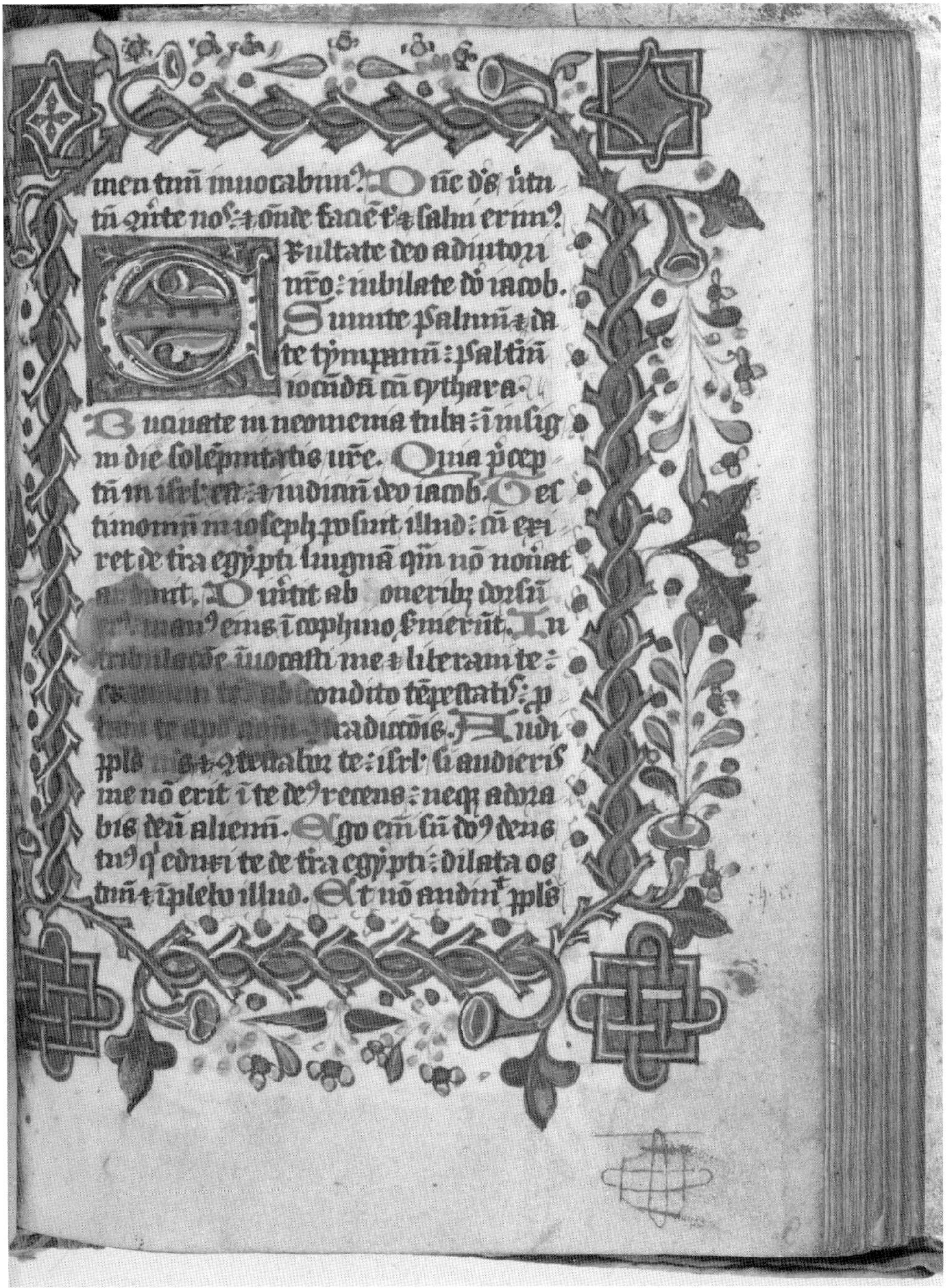

FIG. 20. Cambridge, Peterhouse MS 276, fol. 73r, probably second quarter of the 15th century
Reproduced by permission of the Master and Fellows of Peterhouse, Cambridge

of a conscientious but untrained copyist rather than a professional limner (Fig. 18; Fig. 20 and Col. Pl. XVIII in print edn). The apparatus for small-scale painting excavated at Mount Grace Charterhouse suggests an involvement in illumination which may have extended to Coventry.[80]

CONCLUSION

THE discussion to this point has focused on the internal culture of St Anne's, and this, along with the obvious importance of physical and intellectual seclusion for Carthusians, may give the impression that its monks had no involvement with material culture beyond their walls. This would be a false impression: the Charterhouse's income came mostly from properties it owned, and all of these required appropriate infrastructural maintenance and embellishment. As a concession to the fact that this topic must, for the moment, be left unexplored, we will conclude by glancing at a remarkable representation of conventual unity and purpose which formerly occupied the east window of the church of St Mary at Ecclesfield, north of Sheffield (Fig. 21). The manor and rectorship of Ecclesfield, with nearby Bradfield, a wealthy chapel of ease, was the Charterhouse's first and most lucrative endowment. The *Valor Ecclesiasticus* of 1535 assessed the combined value of these properties at £60 13s. 4d., almost half of the monastery's clear annual income.[81] Ecclesfield's status, both financial and foundational, seems to have invested it with particular significance for the monks.

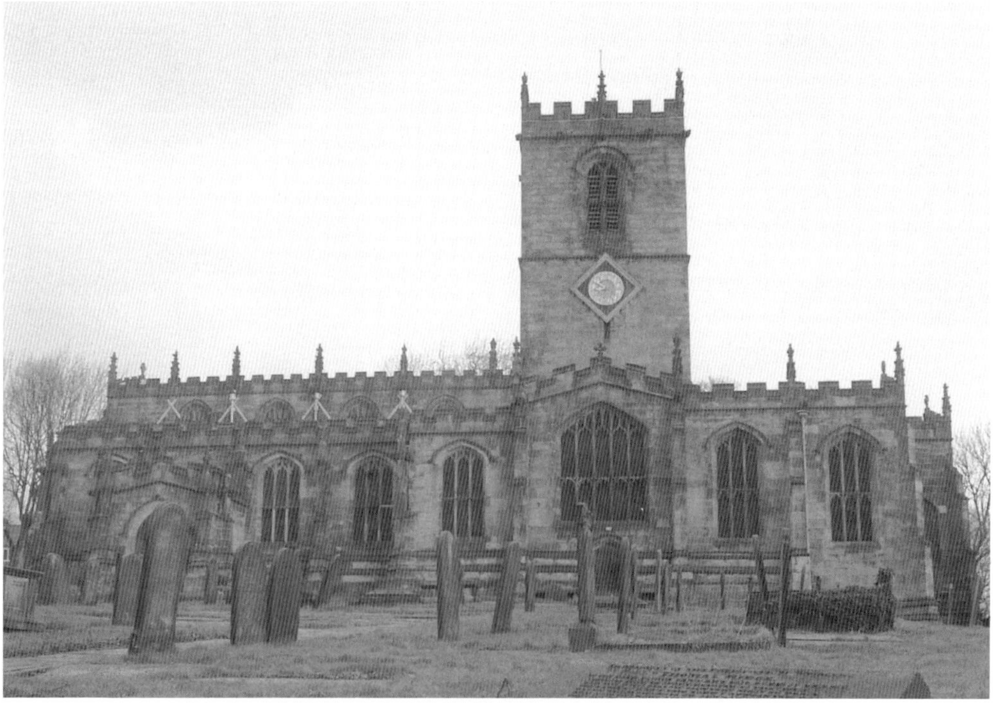

FIG. 21. Ecclesfield (Yorks W. Riding): parish church of St Mary from the south
Photo, author

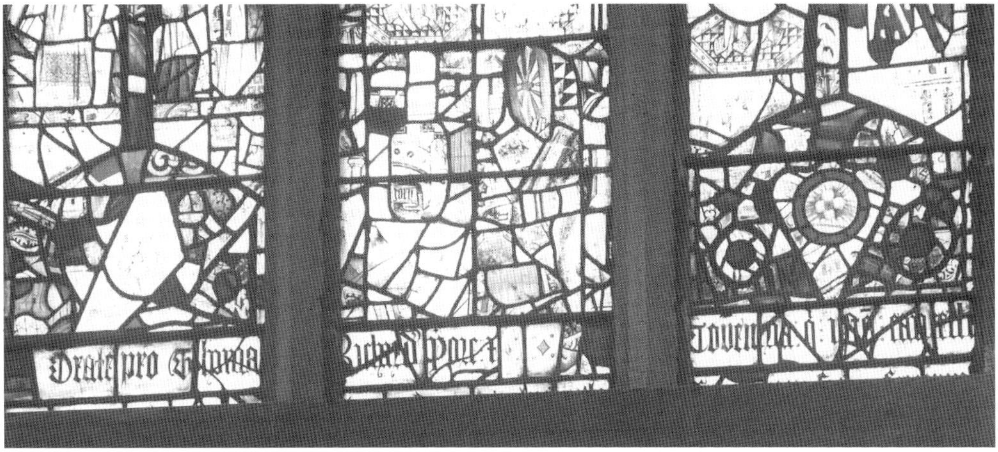

FIG. 22. Ecclesfield: parish church of St Mary, detail of inscription in window in nave north aisle
Photo, author

When the large and sumptuous parish church was remodelled and glazed around 1500, the parishioners received the full support of their corporate rector.[82] An inscription in the east chancel window recorded by the 17th-century antiquary, Roger Dodsworth, read 'Pray for Prior Thomas Richard and his convent, the house of St Anne of the Carthusian order by Coventry, who caused this chancel and window to be made.[83] Most of this inscription survives in a collection of fragments in a north nave aisle window (Fig. 22).[84] Thomas Richard is first documented as prior in 1493, and died in 1515, though whether in office or not is unknown.[85] In the glass above, Dodsworth recorded images of 'a man with twelve others with shaven crownes and white gownes kneeling'. Here was the prior with his convent around him, presiding over the chancel in generous, benevolent spirit. This colourful, luminous image of the prior and his convent kneeling together above congregation, parish priest and high altar, is an apt metaphor for the vocation of Coventry's monks in the minds of their contemporaries — to maintain, in the interests of effective intercession, an integrity which placed them above the normal run of life, and which ultimately lifted them closer to God.

ACKNOWLEDGEMENTS

I thank Garry Byrne, George Demidowicz, Dominik Hunger, Tricia Impey, David King, Scott Mandlebrote, Linda Monckton, Richard K. Morris, Mellie Naydenova-Slade, Iain Soden, Paul Thompson, and Ali Wells for help and advice.

NOTES

1. *The Itinerary of John Leland*, ed. L. T. Smith, 5 vols (London, 1964), II, 106 (quotation).
2. The best account to date is C. B. Rowntree, 'Studies in Carthusian History in Later Medieval England with Special Reference to the Order's Relations with Secular Society' (unpublished D.Phil. thesis, University of York, 1981), 76–93, 346–7, 449–52. See also J. A. Gribbin, 'Coventry', in *Monasticon Cartusiense Volume III*,

ed. J. Hogg and G. Schlegel (Salzburg 2005), 410–15; Soden, *Charterhouse*, 5–33; *Monasticon Anglicanum*, ed. W. Dugdale, rev. J. Caley, H. Ellis and B. Bandinel, 6 vols (London 1817–30), VI, 15–19; Poole, *Antiquities*, 25–9; W. G. Fretton, 'Memorials of the Charter House, Coventry', *TBWAS* 5 (1874), 26–45; M. D. Harris, 'The Charterhouse' (Old Coventry Houses, articles 3–6), *Coventry Herald*, 17–18 Nov., 1–2 and 29–30 Dec. 1916, 12–13 Jan. 1917 (all articles printed on p. 5). For references to Carthusian accounts, see Gribbin, 'Coventry', 414.

3. *Monasticon Anglicanum* VI, 17, no. 4.

4. Cf. R. G. Davies, *Richard II: the Art of Kingship* (Oxford 1999), 87; Rowntree, 'Carthusian History', 43 (quotations).

5. *Itinerary of John Leland* II, 108; *Monasticon Anglicanum* VI, 16, no. 1 (Richard's involvement 'ad instantiam specialem Annæ reginæ').

6. *Pijs vestris meritis specialique devocione quam ad nos & ordinem nostrum ... [et] pluribus eciam magnificencia regia muneribus nobis amplissime collatis prouocati*: Westminster Abbey Muniments, 650, l. 4. For a translation of this letter (but not the Latin text), see J. D. Lee, *Carthusians: an Historical and Spiritual Study* (London 1981), 2.

7. *Calendar of Patent Rolls, Henry VII (1494–1509)*, 25.

8. *Monasticon Anglicanum* VI, 16–17, nos 1–4. Subsequent references to the foundation narrative derive from this source.

9. Basel, Universitätsbibliothek MS B X 30, at fol. 92v. See *Die mittelalterlichen Handschriften der Universitätsbibliothek Basel*, ed. G. Meyer and M. Burckhardt, 3 vols (Basel 1960–75), II, 739; G. Morin, 'A travers les manuscrits de Bâle: notices et extraits des plus anciens manuscrits Latins', *Basler Zeitschrift für Geschichte und Altertumskunde* 26 (1926), 203–04.

10. Rowntree, 'Carthusian History', 347.

11. Fretton, 'Memorials', 38.

12. *Letters and Papers, Foreign and Domestic, of the Reign of Henry VIII*, ed. J. Gardiner *et al.*, 21 vols (London 1862–1910), XIV pt 1, 47, 65.

13. Soden, *Charterhouse*, 14–18; idem, 'The Carthusians of Coventry: Exploding Myths', in *Medieval Europe 1992: Religion and Belief* (York 1992), 77–81. See also G. Coppack and M. Aston, *Christ's Poor Men: the Carthusians in England* (Stroud 2002), 132.

14. Gribbin, 'Coventry', 411 (suspicion of sympathy).

15. Harris ed., *Guild Register* I, xiii, 106, 110.

16. Fretton, 'Memorials', 38 (woods); *Monasticon Anglicanum* VI, 16, no. 2 (*stagna*); D. L. Le Vasseur, *Ephemerides Ordinis Cartusiensis*, 5 vols (Montreuil-sur-Mer 1890–93), I, 578–9 (Crotes).

17. Rowntree, 'Carthusian History', 82 (useful basic plan). Regrettably, the published plans of both church and site in general differ substantially. Cf. Soden, *Charterhouse*, 34; idem, 'The Planning and Development of a Carthusian Church — the Example of St Anne's Charterhouse, Coventry', in *Monastic Archaeology: Papers on the Study of Medieval Monasteries*, ed. G. Keevill *et al.* (Oxford 2001), 162; Coppack and Aston, *Christ's Poor Men*, 39; *Advances in Monastic Archaeology*, ed. R. Gilchrist and H. Mytum, BAR British Series CCXXVII (Oxford 1993), 131. As the plan presented in this paper (Fig. 2) is based on these, it comes with a *caveat videor*.

18. Fretton, 'Memorials', 38.

19. Coppack and Aston, *Christ's Poor Men*, 142.

20. VCH *Warwickshire* VIII, 331. I thank George Demidowicz for information about the site of St Anne's chapel.

21. Work on the wall attracted a bequest of £20 in 1506. See Fretton, 'Memorials', 36 (bequest); J. Carter, *The Ancient Architecture of England* (London 1845), 38 and pl. XLIII, fig. E2 (engraving of garderobe, with fastidious description).

22. Birmingham Central Library, Aylesford Collection, Misc. Vol. 5, no. 6; Troughton X/33; Fretton, 'Memorials', 41–2.

23. Soden, *Charterhouse*, 37–52; idem, 'Planning and Development', 161–4. However, while a 16th-century date for the north chapel seems very likely (as noted below), the benefaction of 1525 cited by I. Soden, *Coventry: the Hidden History* (Stroud 2005), 92, is not secure evidence for work on it.

24. See Soden, 'Planning and Development', 161. The school, funded from the income of Swavesey Priory (Cambridgeshire), was decreed in 1399 *infra bundas Cartusiæ*. Swavesey's rents, etc., finally came to St Anne's in 1421. It is possible that the school was conducted outside the claustral complex: see A. F. Leach, *The Schools of Medieval England* (London 1915), 222.

25. Soden, *Hidden History*, 92; idem, 'Planning and Development', 164.

26. *Coutumes de Chartreuse (Consuetudines Cartusiæ)*, ed. M. Laporte, Sources Chrétiennes CCCXIII (Paris 1984), 286–95 (Guigo I's 'eulogy of the cell').

27. For an example of this at Coventry, see E. M. Thompson, *The Carthusian Order in England* (London 1930), 289–96.
28. Soden, *Charterhouse*, 62.
29. I am grateful to Iain Soden for pointing these out to me.
30. See *La Grande Chartreuse par un chartreux*, 8th edn (Paris and Grenoble 1950), 191, and, for an English example, W. H. St J. Hope, *The History of the London Charterhouse* (London 1925), 80.
31. Soden, *Hidden History*, 93.
32. Margaret Tomlinson (VCH *Warwickshire* VIII, 130) recognised that the northern part of the block may have had only one storey, although she offered no supporting arguments. Her suggestion has been ignored by all subsequent writers.
33. Harris, 'The Charterhouse' (Old Coventry Houses VI), 12–13 Jan. 1917, 5 (Hope's arguments, quoted from personal correspondence); J. Hogg, 'Royal and Aristocratic Founders of English Charterhouses', *Analecta Cartusiana* 173 (2000), 87; Gribbin, 'Coventry', 413; Rowntree, 'Carthusian History', 447.
34. Harris, 'The Charterhouse' (Old Coventry Houses VI), 12–13 Jan. 1917, 5.
35. E. W. Tristram, *English Medieval Wall Painting: the Thirteenth Century*, 2 vols (Oxford 1950), I, 360–1; II, pls 205–7 (Horsham); M. R. James, *Abbeys* (London 1926), 125 and pl. facing 127 (Cleeve); E. Borsook, *The Mural Painters of Tuscany from Cimabue to Andrea del Sarto*, 2nd edn (Oxford 1980), 42–3, 87–90 and pls 50, 106 (Florentine examples); C. E. Gilbert, 'Last Suppers and their Refectories', in *The Pursuit of Holiness in Late Medieval and Renaissance Religion*, ed. C. Trinkaus (Leiden 1974), 371–402 passim for Italian refectory Crucifixions.
36. For this practice, see *Monasticon Anglicanum* VI, ix.
37. VCH *Warwickshire* VIII, 130. W. Wyley, *The Coventry Charterhouse* (Coventry 1939), 13–14, seems first to have suggested that this was the prior's residence.
38. D. Knowles and W. F. Grimes, *Charterhouse: the Medieval Foundation in the Light of Recent Discoveries* (London 1954), 79.
39. Harris, 'The Charterhouse' (Old Coventry Houses V), 29–30 Dec. 1916, 5.
40. Coppack and Aston, *Christ's Poor Men*, 103.
41. Lee, *Carthusians*, 34 (Grande Chartreuse shield). On the work of 1519 at London (not, however, mentioning the shields), see Hope, *London Charterhouse*, 165.
42. I.e. a common strophe used in medieval Latin verse, with an aabccb rhyme-form. See, for example, C. Strong, 'History and Relations of the Tailrhyme Strophe in Latin, French and English', *Proceedings of the Modern Language Association* 22 (1907), 378–87.
43. The last two letters of *sudauit* are damaged, but, anomalously, the word must have been suspended. In any case, *sudauit*, as agreeing with *procurauit*, is required by the metre.
44. *The Heads of Religious Houses: England & Wales, III. 1377–1540*, ed. D. M. Smith (Cambridge, 2008), 356 (Soland); Rowntree, 'Carthusian History', 517 (Lambard).
45. Coppack and Aston, *Christ's Poor Men*, 106.
46. Fretton, 'Memorials', 38.
47. Rowntree, 'Carthusian History', appendix VI, 485–546.
48. Ibid., 156; cf. Soden, *Hidden History*, 96–7.
49. Rowntree, 'Carthusian History', 512; *Cal. Papal Reg.* XV (1978), 78; Thompson, *Carthusian Order*, 297.
50. J. Greatrex ed., *Biographical Register of the English Cathedral Priories of the Province of Canterbury c.1066–1540* (Oxford 1997), 598.
51. *MS. Grande Chartreuse 1. Cart. 15: Chartae Capituli Generalis 1411–1436, 2 (1418–27)*, ed. J. Hogg, *Analecta Cartusiana* 100, pt 8 (1986), 69.
52. *Calendar of Patent Rolls, Richard II (1396–1399)*, 579.
53. Soden, 'Planning and Development', 164.
54. Soden, *Charterhouse*, 126. Slab dated 'late 15th Century', but without providing any evidence.
55. J. Braun, *Der christliche Altar in seiner geschichtlichen Entwicklung*, 2 vols (Munich 1924), I, 77 (grant of portable altars a papal privilege in later middle ages), 80 (Martin V's grants), 443 (crosses only common from 15th century).
56. See, for example, D. Le Blévec and A. Girard ed., *Les Chartreux et l'art* (Paris 1989); J. Hamburger, 'The Writing on the Wall: Inscriptions and Descriptions of Carthusian Crucifixions in a Fifteenth-Century Passion Miscellany', in *Tributes in Honour of James H. Marrow: Studies in Painting and Manuscript Illumination of the Late Middle Ages and Northern Renaissance*, ed. J. Hamburger and A.-M. Bouché (Turnhout 2006), 231–52; J. Brantley, *Reading in the Wilderness: Private Devotion and Public Performance in Late Medieval England* (Chicago 2007).
57. Soden, *Charterhouse*, 122–5.

58. Ibid., 118–20; Coventry, Herbert Museum and Art Gallery, inventory number CH87/NIS/F1103 (indications of *littera textualis*).

59. Soden, *Charterhouse*, 122–3. The suggestion in idem, *Hidden History*, 132, that this distinguished Nicholas Fitzherbert's grave is improbable, as Fitzherbert left only a half-mark for a gravestone; Rowntree, 'Carthusian History', 346–7.

60. Soden, *Charterhouse*, 100–16; cf. idem, 'The Propaganda of Monastic Benefaction: Statement and Implication in the Art of St Anne's Charterhouse, Coventry', in *Meaningful Architecture: Social Interpretations of Buildings*, ed. M. Locock (Aldershot 1994), 156–9.

61. E. S. Eames, *Catalogue of Medieval Lead-Glazed Earthenware Tiles in the Department of Medieval and Later Antiquities, British Museum*, 2 vols (London 1980), I, 282–3.

62. Compare Hope, *London Charterhouse*, 185–7. The figures now belong to the Parish of The Most Holy Sacrament and St Osburg, Coventry. I am extremely grateful to the Very Revd Canon Garry Byrne for letting me inspect and photograph them.

63. Fretton, 'Memorials', 43 ('dug up ... about fifty years ago', quoting Thomas Sharp, who wrote *c.* 1807). See F. W. Cheetham, *Unearthed: Nottingham's Medieval Alabasters* (Nottingham 2004), 15–16, 21; and idem, 'A Medieval English Alabaster Figure of St. Paul', *Norfolk Archaeology* 35 (1970), 143–4 for other concealed alabasters.

64. Cambridge, Peterhouse MS 276, fol. 120r; J. Hourlier and B. Moustier, 'Le Calendrier Cartusien', *Etudes Gregoriennes* 2 (1957), 158, 160.

65. For alabaster image manufacture in Coventry, see F. W. Cheetham, *English Medieval Alabasters, with a Catalogue of the Collection in the Victoria and Albert Museum* (Woodbridge 2005), 14–15.

66. F. W. Cheetham, *Alabaster Images of Medieval England* (Woodbridge 2003), 38, 53–4.

67. Cheetham, *Unearthed*, 11.

68. Gribbin, 'Coventry', 411.

69. See Naydenova-Slade, this volume.

70. G. Vallier, *Sigillographie de l'ordre des Chartreux et numismatique de Saint-Bruno* (Montreuil-sur-Mer 1891), 219–20 (conventual); R. H. Ellis, *Catalogue of Seals in the Public Record Office*, 2 vols (London 1981–86), I, 28 (Tarleton).

71. On Mount Grace in the context of such traditions, see R. Gilchrist, *Contemplation and Action: the Other Monasticism* (London and New York 1995), 207.

72. For example Cambridge, Gonville and Caius College, MS 433/432, fol. 38r; Oxford, Bodleian Library, MS Bodley 117, fol. 9v; see also London, British Library, MS Additional 37049, fols 36v, 37r.

73. *Anima xpi sanctifica me. Corpus xpi salua me. Sanguis ihu xpi inebria me. Aqua lateris ihu xpi laua me. Passio ihu xpi conforta me. Mors ihu xpi uiuifica me.* Compare C. W. Bynum, *Wonderful Blood* (Philadelpia 2007), 12.

74. M. G. Sargent, 'James Grenehalgh: the Biographical Record', *Analecta Cartusiana* 55, pt 4 (1982), 20, 25; M. Cré, *Vernacular Mysticism in the Charterhouse: a Study of London, British Library, MS Additional 37790* (Turnhout 2006), 32 and n. 59.

75. *Sit timor in dapibus, benediccio, lectio, tempus./ Sermo breuis, vultus hilaris, pars detur egenis./ Absint delicie, detractio, crapula, murmura./ Assumptoque cibo, reddatur gracia xpo.*

76. St Anne's was prolific in its poor relief: see Rowntree, 'Carthusian History', 92–3; Thompson, *Carthusian Order*, 216–17.

77. Printed in J. P. H. Clark, 'Extracts from Writings on the Solitary Life in Ms. Bodleian Library Lat. Th. d. 27, ff. 196v–200v', *Analecta Cartusiana* 35, pt 10 (1990), 5–25.

78. Printed in *Syon Abbey with the Libraries of the Carthusians*, ed. V. Gillespie and A. I. Doyle, Corpus of British Medieval Library Catalogues IX (London 2001), 620–2.

79. *Coutumes de Chartreuse*, 178, 224 ('dei verbum manibus predicemus'); Brantley, *Reading in the Wilderness*, 54–7.

80. Coppack and Aston, *Christ's Poor Men*, 96.

81. *Monasticon Anglicanum* VI, 19, no. 17.

82. N. Pevsner and E. Radcliffe, *Yorkshire: The West Riding* B/E (Harmondsworth, 2nd edn 1967), 189–91.

83. *Orate pro Thoma Richardus Priore et eius Conventu domus Sancte Anne ordinis Cartusiani iuxta Coventriam, qui istam cancellum et fenestram fieri fecerunt*; see *Yorkshire Church Notes 1619–1631, by Roger Dodsworth*, ed. J. W. Clay, Yorkshire Archaeological Society Record Series XXXIV (Leeds 1904), 6.

84. B. Sprakes, *The Medieval Stained Glass of South Yorkshire*, Corpus Vitrearum Medii Aevi Summary Catalogue VII (Oxford 2003), 28–38.

85. *Heads of Religious Houses III*, 357. Richard's successor is not documented until March 1515, suggesting that Richard was prior until shortly before, if not the time of, his death.

A ‘bodi ful of woundis’: The 15th-Century Mural at St Anne’s Charterhouse, Coventry

MELLIE NAYDENOVA-SLADE

The medieval mural scheme in the former refectory of St Anne’s Charterhouse, Coventry, is among the finest and most important wall-paintings of the first half of the 15th century in England. It is also the only surviving monumental painting from an English Carthusian priory and is therefore of great significance for the understanding of the artistic and devotional concerns of the order. However, despite its importance and impressive nature, the mural has not been the subject of a detailed modern study. This paper offers a reconstruction of the original painting and reconsiders its date, which has been assumed to be c. *1411–17. A discussion follows of the probable reasons behind the choice of the mural’s subject matter, as well as an analysis of some of its more unusual iconographic features and their visual and textual sources. The place of the work within the context of the devotional concerns and artistic tastes of the Carthusian order is considered, and a reassessment is made of suggestions that a local family may have been commemorated in the painting.*

THE surviving range of St Anne’s Charterhouse, Coventry, contains one of the most remarkable examples of English mural painting from the first half of the 15th century.[1] It is part of a scheme which originally comprised an enormous Crucifixion flanked by two seated saints on the same scale, with several smaller figures beside the cross (Fig. 1). The largest remaining portion of this composition is found on the south wall of a room on what is now the first floor of the building, which will henceforth be referred to as the main painted room (Fig. 2 and Col. Pl. XIX in print edn). Much of the lower part of the Crucifixion scene survives, as well as the bottom half of the ermine garment of the seated figure to the east, and parts of the original inscription beneath the painting. Post-medieval alterations have subdivided the building, inserting a first-floor passage through the western side of the original space; previously the painting occupied its entire south wall, approximately 7m (23ft) wide. The large seated figure to the west has been partly obscured by the inserted passage wall and only fragments of it are now visible. These include the edge of its stone seat beside the west wall in the main painted room (Fig. 6 and Col. Pl. XXIa in print edn), as well as parts of its ermine garment, flowing blond hair and plant attribute, which survive on the continuation of the south wall in the passage, above a later doorway (Fig. 3; Fig. 4 and Col. Pl. XXa in print edn). An extra floor was added in the late 16th century during the conversion of the surviving range into a private house.[2] The top part of the mural has therefore been lost, except for a few fragments found on blocks of masonry which were reused in the construction of the new upper storey. Its full height is likely to have been around 4m (13ft), estimated on the basis of the new reconstruction drawing (Fig. 1).[3] The fine state of preservation of much of the surviving painting, which has never been subject to any restoration, can

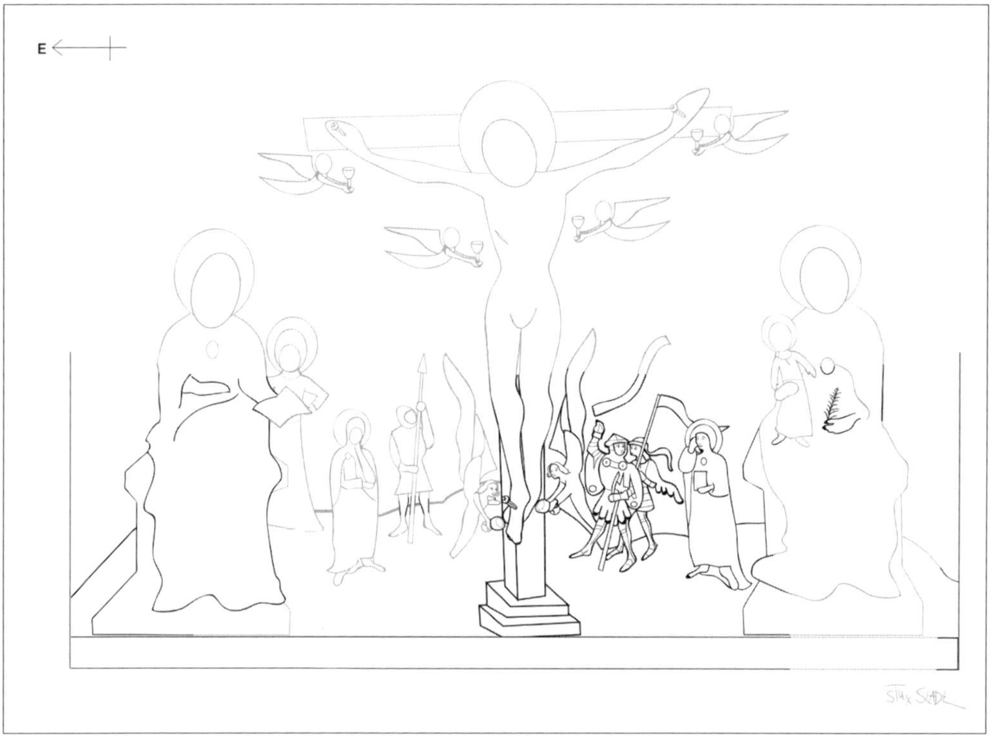

FIG. 1. Coventry, St Anne's Charterhouse: 15th-century mural, reconstruction
Drawing: Stuart Slade

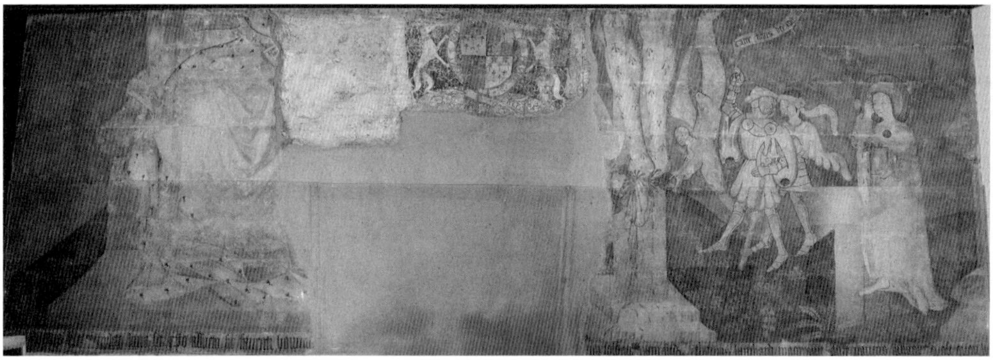

FIG. 2. Coventry, St Anne's Charterhouse: 15th-century mural
Photo, author

be attributed to the fact that the south wall was covered by wooden panelling at the time of the building's restructuring. This hid and protected the painting until the removal of the panelling in the early 20th century, and the only area of damage occurs in the middle of the wall, where a door (now blocked) was inserted. It is surmounted

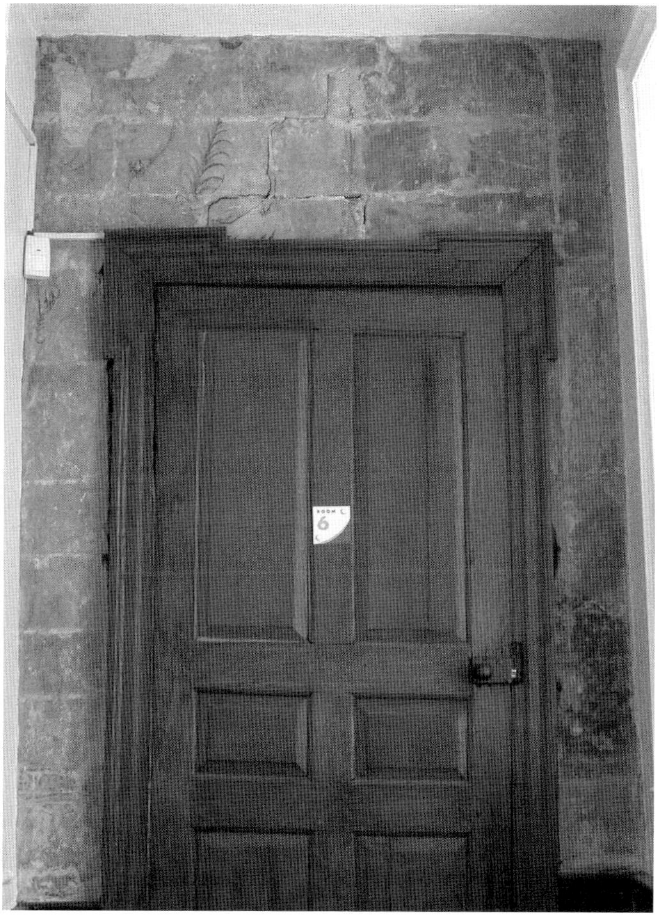

FIG. 3. Coventry, St Anne's Charterhouse: 15th-century mural, fragments in passage
Photo, author

by a painted coat-of-arms, which corresponds in style to the surviving fragments of a 16th-century mural scheme found elsewhere in the building.[4]

Julian Luxford has convincingly argued that originally the floor of the room which houses the painting would have been at pavement level and that the mural would thus have been positioned some 4.5m (14ft 9in.) above the ground.[5] Since all of the vertical partitions inside the north part of the surviving building are also later additions, the original room would have extended about 12m (39ft) in length,[6] allowing sufficient space for such a large painting positioned high above the floor to be viewed from a suitable vantage point. The room with the mural, which would thus have occupied the whole of the north part of the surviving range, was almost certainly the priory's refectory.[7]

The exceptional quality of the 15th-century painting is immediately apparent from the surviving fragments (Figs 2, 5 and 6 (Col. Pls XIX, XXB and XXIA in print edn)), which include exquisite figures rendered with soft, delicate draperies, and carefully observed naturalistic details. Only a handful of murals of such high quality survive from the period *c.* 1350–1450. They include, from before 1400, the Apocalypse murals

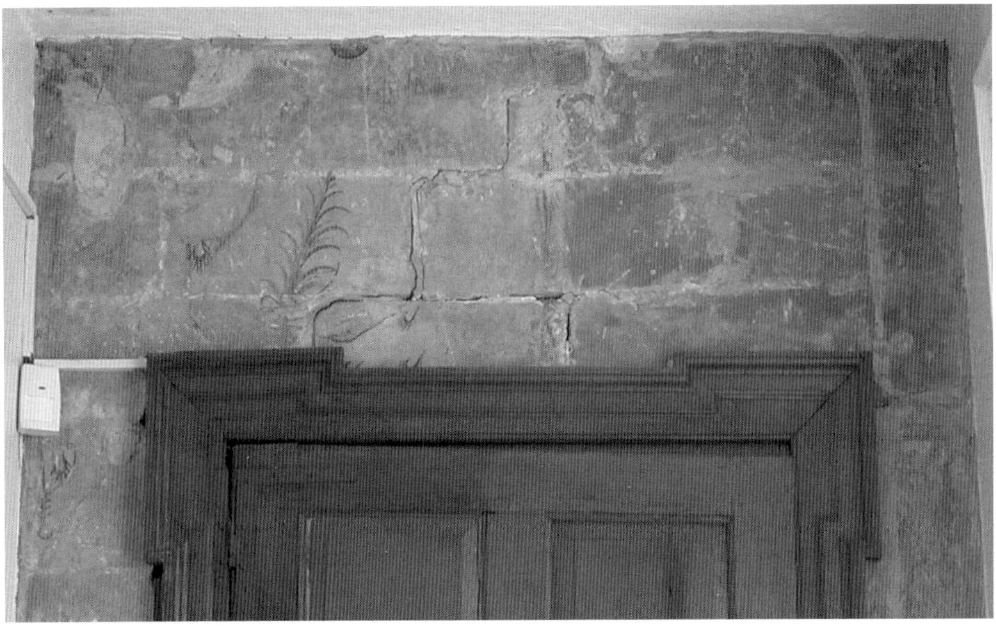

FIG. 4. Coventry, St Anne's Charterhouse: 15th-century mural, fragments in passage, detail
Photo, author

at Westminster Abbey chapter-house, the painted figures at the Byward Tower in the Tower of London, and the recently discovered fragments of an Apocalypse from the chapter-house of St Mary's Priory, Coventry.[8] The only comparable examples from the first half of the 15th century, in terms of scale and quality, are the Doom at Holy Trinity Church, Coventry and the chapel murals at Haddon Hall Chapel (Derbys.).[9] The little-known Charterhouse mural is therefore a highly significant example of wall-painting from this period. It is also the only monumental work of art to survive from any of the nine English Carthusian priories, which adds to its importance. In light of this, the lack of a detailed contextual study of the painting is surprising. Turpin published a useful account of the mural in 1919,[10] but he left much room for further research. Since then, aspects of the painting have been discussed by Iain Soden, who has argued that it probably commemorated a local landlord,[11] and by Miriam Gill, who has discussed it in the context of monastic education and in relation to other Coventry murals.[12] It has also recently received brief mention in Roger Rosewell's survey of English and Welsh wall-paintings.[13]

The surviving parts of the Crucifixion scene can serve as a guide to the whole original composition. At the bottom of the painting two angels collect blood from the wounds in Christ's feet (Fig. 5), suggesting that there would have been other angels gathering the blood from the side and hand wounds (Fig. 1). The standing haloed figure nearest to the west wall of the main painted room can be identified as St John the Evangelist (Fig. 6, right), who was frequently depicted in Crucifixion scenes to the right of the cross, holding a book and sometimes clutching his head in grief. When he is shown in this position he is always mirrored by the Virgin on the other side of the cross (Fig. 7),[14] which must have been the case in the Coventry painting. Between St John and the cross

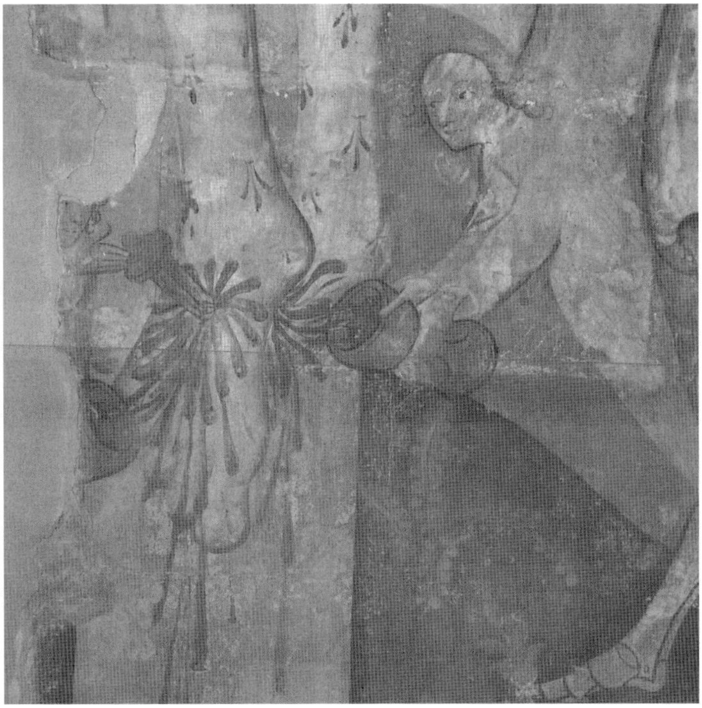

FIG. 5. Coventry, St Anne's Charterhouse: 15th-century mural, detail: angels gathering blood
Photo, author

two soldiers are depicted on a slightly smaller scale (Fig. 6, left). One holds an axe and points to the cross with his other hand. He is accompanied by a scroll inscribed *Vere filius dei erat iste*,[15] which identifies him as the centurion who was converted at the moment of Christ's death.[16] Beside him is his standard-bearer holding a flowing banner. Unlike the obvious counterpart to St John, it is more difficult to know who would have mirrored this pair to the left of the cross. However, a hypothesis can be proposed with the help of a fragment of the painting preserved on a piece of masonry reused in the east wall of the top storey of the building (Fig. 8). It depicts two armour-clad legs on green grass against a red background,[17] suggesting that it probably came from the area east of the cross, destroyed when the doorway there was inserted (Fig. 2). The most likely military figure to be found on the left side of a Crucifixion is Longinus,[18] who according to apocryphal texts pierced Christ's side. In the early middle ages, he was sometimes conflated with the centurion, but later they were depicted as distinct figures, usually on opposite sides of the cross.[19] The object which appears between the two legs on the fragment could therefore be the end of Longinus's lance. Although the overall symmetry of the painting invites speculation that Longinus, like the centurion, would have been depicted with a companion, that seems unlikely given that no trace of another figure's legs can be seen on the surviving fragment.

Of the large seated figures, that to the east was identified by Turpin as St Anne — the dedicatee of the Charterhouse — teaching the Virgin to read.[20] Although no trace of Mary survives, her original presence is signalled by the small book in the lap of the large figure, on which the fragmentary words *Domi*... and *labia* appear (Fig. 9). These are portions of the opening versicle of Matins in the Hours of the Virgin *Domine labia*

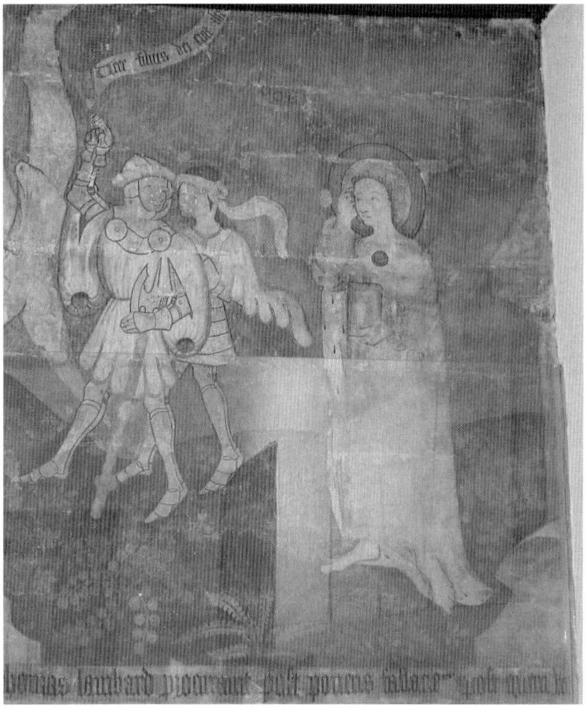

FIG. 6. Coventry, St Anne's Charterhouse: 15th-century mural, detail: the centurion and his standard bearer (left), St John the Evangelist (right)
Photo, author

mea aperies, which was a phrase frequently inscribed in the book from which St Anne teaches her daughter in representations of the Virgin's education.[21] Although in the 14th century depictions of this subject usually featured St Anne standing beside Mary, in the 15th century compositions showing her seated became more common.[22]

The large figure on the west side is much more fragmentary and harder to identify. It appears to hold another small figure whose foot is visible to the left of the upper part of the doorway in the passage (Fig. 4). Recent scholars agree that this is most likely to be the foot of Christ in a depiction of the Virgin and Child,[23] which is supported by the fact that part of the main figure's garment was blue, the colour associated with the Virgin: a portion of it survives beside the west wall of the main painted room (Fig. 6, right). In addition, the long blond hair flowing down the figure's side, visible above the doorway (Fig. 4), is typical of representations of the Virgin and Child where Mary's hair is often shown flowing freely, as befitting a maiden. Turpin had a different view, based on the spiky plant held by the figure, which he interpreted as a palm. He argued that the painting therefore depicted a martyr, possibly St Catherine, presenting a diminutive layman to the crucified Christ.[24] However, the plant is surely a lily, a flower with similar leaves which was not infrequently included in Virgin and Child images.[25] In fact, there appears to have been a tradition for depicting the Virgin with such an attribute at the Coventry Charterhouse, as indicated by a surviving impression of the priory's seal attached to a charter of 1436, which shows St Anne and the Virgin standing next to each other, with Mary holding a pointed object (Fig. 10). Although this has previously been interpreted as a sceptre,[26] its rugged edges and slight curvature suggest a plant with spiky leaves similar to the one in the mural. Moreover, as the seal gives

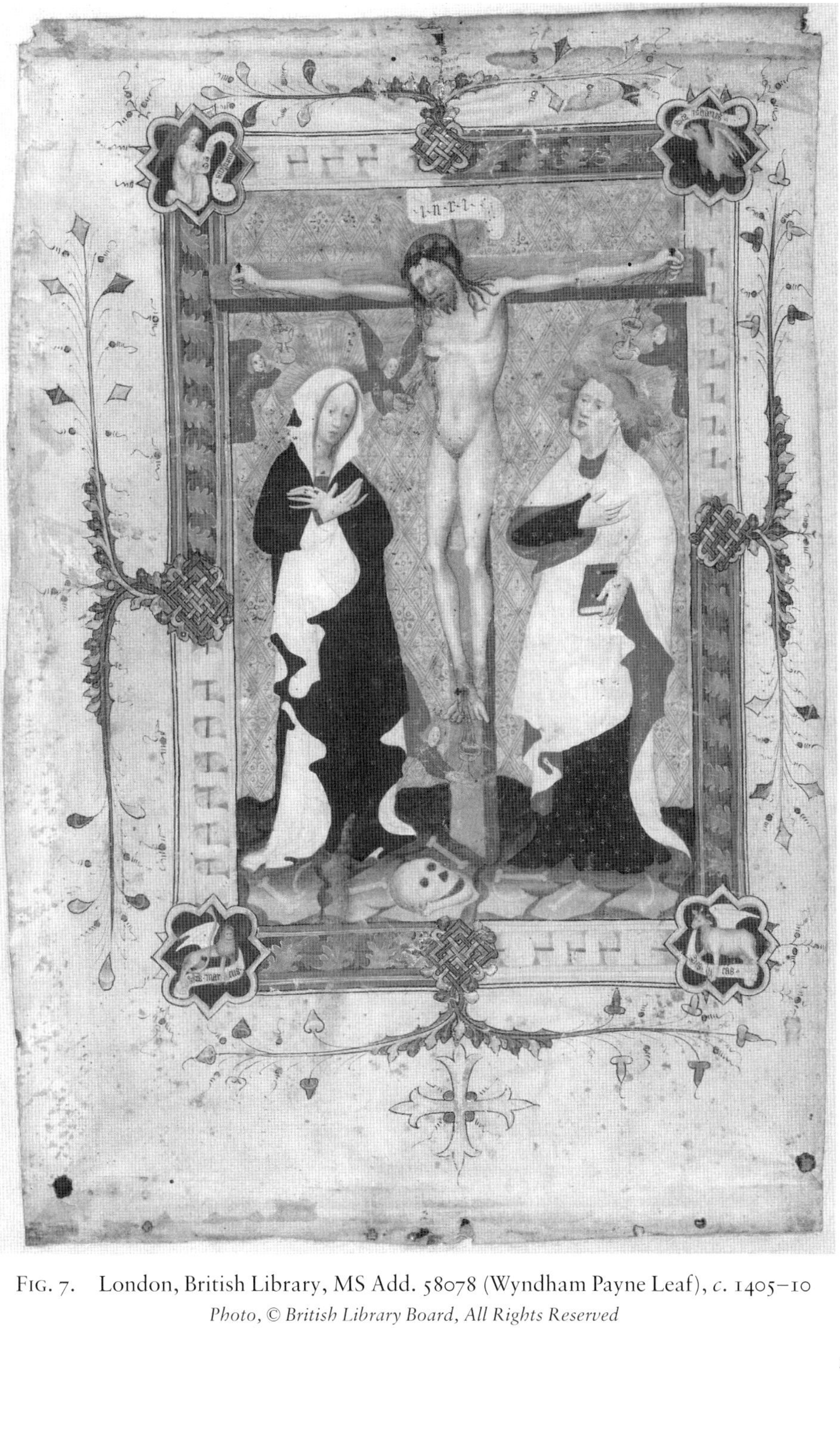

FIG. 7. London, British Library, MS Add. 58078 (Wyndham Payne Leaf), *c.* 1405–10
Photo, © British Library Board, All Rights Reserved

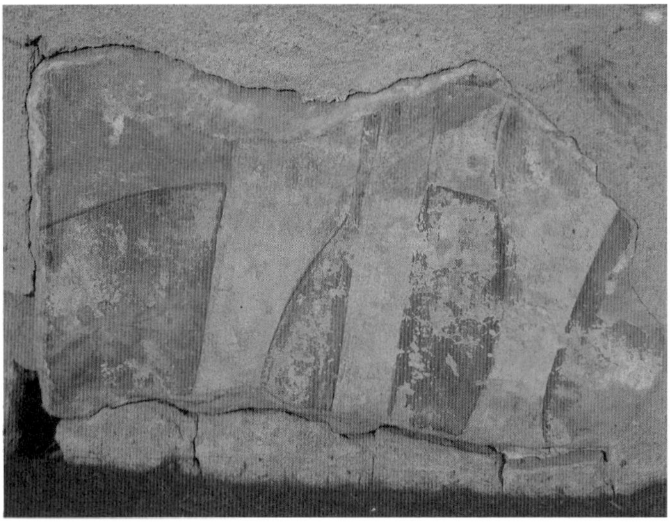

FIG. 8. Coventry, St Anne's Charterhouse: fragment of 15th-century mural reused in the top storey
Photo, author

equal prominence to St Anne and the Virgin, their depiction as counterparts in the priory's wall-painting is unsurprising.

The mural has been dated by previous scholars on the basis of the inscription found at its base, of which the following fragments still survive: *Fuit domus hec completa — laus sit Christo assueta — sic faventi homini*[*bus*] [... ...] [*P*]*rior Solonde nam sudau*[*i*]*t — Thomas Lambard procurau*[*it*] *— postponens fallacias — post quem li*[*c/e*] [...].[27] The prior named is William Soland, who is mentioned in documents from 1411 and 1417,[28] which is the date range commonly given for the painting's production.[29] Thomas Lambert's name is also linked to the Coventry Charterhouse by documentary sources and his death was recorded in 1440.[30] The 1411–17 dating for the mural seems initially sound, but a number of references to a Prior William of St Anne's Coventry, which do not give a surname, appear in later documents, including the Exchequer Accounts for 1421, 1430 and 1436, and the charter of 1436 bearing the surviving seal impression. As Carol Rowntree has suggested, this Prior William may have been William Soland, especially as no other priors of the Charterhouse are recorded in the 1420s and 30s.[31] Indeed, Smith cites a reference to Prior Soland from the Calendar of Close Rolls, apparently unknown to Rowntree, dating to March 1437.[32] In light of this, and given that Thomas Lambert did not die until 1440, a reassessment of the mural's date seems necessary.

The extant parts of the painting display some of the typical features of the International Style, such as the expressive, soft draperies in the depiction of St Anne and the careful modelling of the elegant, slender figures beside the cross (Figs 2, 6). Compared to the only other surviving 15th-century Coventry mural, the Doom at Holy Trinity of *c.* 1435,[33] the style of the painting seems more delicate and refined, which could be indicative of an earlier date. However, detailed stylistic comparison between the two paintings is problematic because of the extensive 19th-century repainting of the Doom. The work of the Coventry glaziers of this period is also in the International Style, but none of the surviving examples are similar enough to the Charterhouse mural to be used as direct stylistic parallels for the purpose of dating. Nevertheless, the evidence of

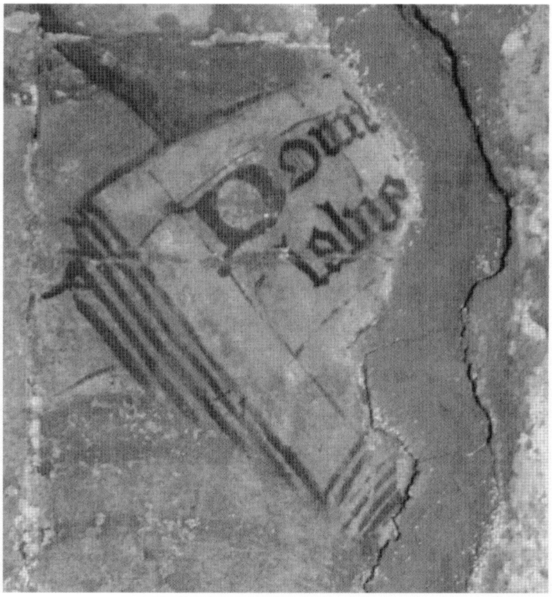

FIG. 9. Coventry, St Anne's Charterhouse: 15th-century mural, detail: book in St Anne's lap
Photo, author

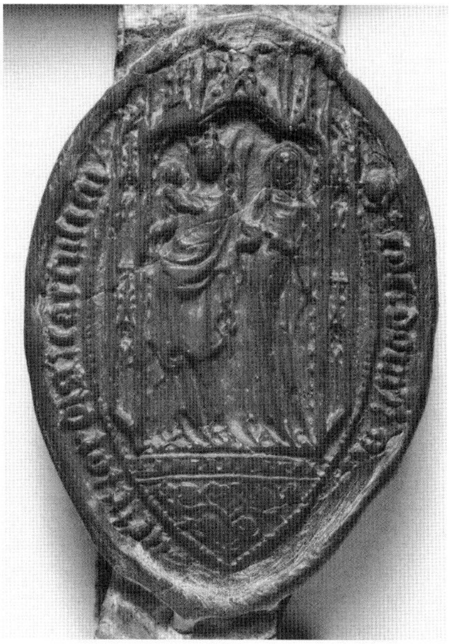

FIG. 10. London, British Library, Add. Charter 7385, seal impression
Photo, © British Library Board, All Rights Reserved

glass painting is important, because it demonstrates that high quality work in the International Style was being produced in Coventry until at least the late 1420s and early 1430s,[34] which is a trend unlikely to have been confined to the medium of stained glass. This is significant because certain details in the Charterhouse mural closely resemble works from these decades in other parts of the country. For instance, the foliage in the painting finds its closest match in the Devonshire Hunting Tapestries, executed in the second quarter of the 15th century,[35] where almost identical plant shapes can be seen (Fig. 11; Fig. 12 and Col. Pl. XXIB in print edn). Another useful indicator of date is the armour worn by the centurion and his companion, for which the best parallels can be found in the 1420s, for example in the brass of Sir Henry Parys of 1427 at Hildersham (Cambs., Fig. 13).[36] On this basis, it seems likely that the mural postdates 1411–17, and in light of the documents referring to Prior William up to 1437, a date for the painting of *c.* 1420–37 can reasonably be proposed.[37]

The Crucifixion was a common theme for medieval monastic refectories from at least the 11th century onwards.[38] In England, examples include the mid-13th-century Crucifixion at the Benedictine priory of Horsham St Faith (Norf.) and the lost late 15th-century image of Christ on the cross at the refectory of the Cistercian abbey of Cleeve (Som.).[39] Continental examples are numerous and include well known paintings such as Taddeo Gaddi's Crucifixion of *c.* 1335–40 in the convent of S. Croce, Florence, forming part of an image of the Tree of Life above a representation of the Last Supper, and Andrea de Castagno's Crucifixion of *c.* 1447–50 in the refectory of S. Apollonia, Florence, similarly above the Last Supper.[40] This Italian tendency to combine Crucifixion and Last Supper scenes speaks eloquently of the reasons behind the frequent

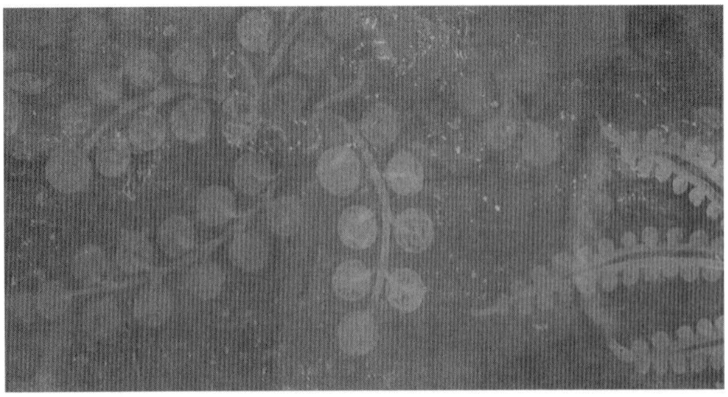

FIG. 11. Coventry, St Anne's Charterhouse: 15th-century mural, foliage detail
Photo, author

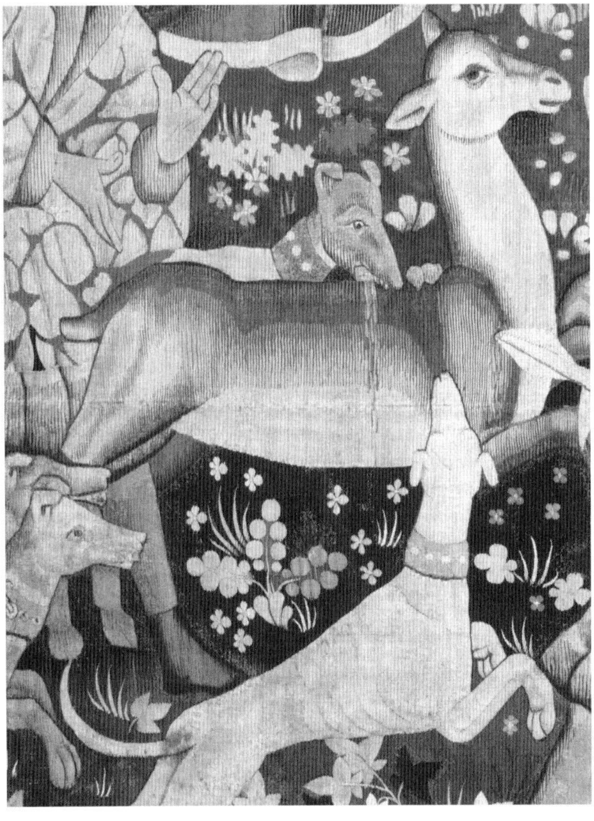

FIG. 12. Devonshire Hunting Tapestries, Deer Hunt, foliage detail
Photo, © V&A Images/Victoria and Albert Museum, London

inclusion of images of the crucified Christ on the walls of monastic refectories. The communal meal of the monks would have been seen as a parallel for the Last Supper of Christ's apostles at which the Eucharist was instituted, thus linking that meal to the flesh and blood of the suffering Christ. For a Carthusian community in particular, the Eucharistic overtones of the image may have been especially pertinent, because a Charterhouse typically consisted of twelve monks and a prior,[41] and thus the community at dinner was a living representation of the Last Supper.

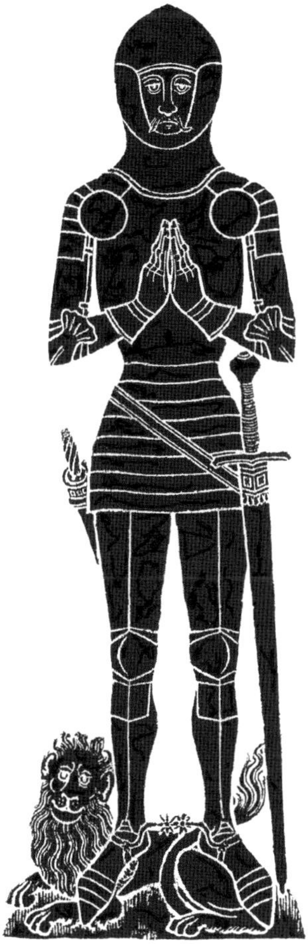

FIG. 13. Hildersham (Cambs.): Brass of Henry Parys, 1427 (rubbing)
Reproduced by courtesy of H. Martin Stuchfield

The inclusion of St Anne no doubt reflected the dedication of the priory. The representation of a monastery's dedicatee in a refectory mural is not without precedent and occurs at Horsham St Faith, where the Crucifixion is flanked by a pair of saints including St Faith. Moreover, for the community at Coventry, commemorating their patron saint may also have been a way of commemorating their chief benefactors Richard II and his wife, Anne of Bohemia, who is said to have petitioned her husband to patronise the monastery, presumably because of her devotion to her namesake St Anne.[42] The depiction of the Virgin as a counterpart to St Anne is not surprising in view of their joint representation on the priory's seal.

In addition to the overall choice of subjects for the mural, it is also necessary to examine some of its more unusual features. One is the presence of two angels with chalices at the foot of the cross (Fig. 5), rather than just one, as in other English examples of a similar date (see Fig. 7).[43] Although this can be attributed to artistic elaboration, it may have been specifically linked to devotions focusing on the five wounds of Christ, because the number of wounds would have been emphasized by having a separate angel attending to each one. Prayers addressed to the five wounds were common in 15th-century England and many depictions of the wounds survive, including several examples from Coventry churches.[44] Altars commonly bore five consecration crosses in honour of Christ's wounds, and an example can be seen at the Charterhouse itself on an altar table reused as an over-mantel on the top floor of the present building (Luxford, Fig. 13).[45] Interest in Christ's wounds among English Carthusians in particular is exemplified by some of the images found in a religious miscellany believed to be of Carthusian provenance (London, British Library, MS Add. 37049),[46] such as a drawing of the five wounds which claims to represent them in their exact real-life size (fol. 20r).[47] Although the manuscript postdates the Coventry mural by several decades,[48] it is nonetheless a good indicator of Carthusian tastes. It may also be significant that in the late middle ages devotion to the five wounds appears to have had a link with eating, as suggested by the practice of the German 14th-century mystic, Henry Suso, who drank five times during each meal in honour of the five wounds of Christ.[49] The five angels with chalices in the Charterhouse painting, therefore, could have been linked to devotions to Christ's wounds, which may have been seen — rather oddly — as particularly appropriate for a refectory.

The angels with chalices are just one aspect of the overall focus on Christ's blood in the Coventry painting, which has a decidedly gory appearance untypical of English Crucifixions from the first half of the 15th century. In part this can be attributed to artistic influences from the continent, where Eucharistic devotions and images of Christ's blood associated with them were more popular than in England.[50] More specifically, detailed representations of Christ's bleeding wounds were popular in art commissioned by or for continental charterhouses. Perhaps the best examples come from the Burgundian priory of Champmol, such as the Crucifixion panels by Jean de Beaumetz and his workshop of *c.* 1390–95, one of which is illustrated in Figure 14.[51] The profusion of blood flowing from Christ's wounds in this image is striking, and it is a motif repeated both in another of the Beaumetz panels and in a painting known as the *Retable of St Denis*, also made for Champmol.[52] English charterhouses are known to have had contact with their continental counterparts through monks moving to English priories from abroad, which would have allowed for the transmission of artistic ideas.[53]

In addition to these visual sources, devotion to Christ's blood amongst English Carthusians, which persisted in the later 15th century,[54] may have had its roots in the hagiography of St Hugh of Lincoln, who helped found the first English charterhouse.[55] In the *Magna Vita Sancti Hugonis* great prominence is given to his devotion to the Eucharist and to a number of Eucharistic miracles.[56] Douie and Farmer, who edited the text, speculated that most English charterhouses had a copy of it, or of the so-called 'Long Abbreviation' of the *Magna Vita*.[57] In fact, a copy of the Long Abbreviation is known to have been owned by the London Charterhouse,[58] from where Prior Soland came to Coventry.[59] Furthermore, in the early 15th century, the episodes from the *Magna Vita* concerning St Hugh's Eucharistic devotions appear to have been especially popular, because they were included in a work of *c.* 1408–10 by Nicholas Love, a Carthusian monk at Mount Grace Priory (Yorks.), entitled *The Mirror of the Blessed Life of Jesus Christ*. This was a loose translation of an earlier Latin text,[60] to which Love added a long Eucharistic treatise,[61] in which two Eucharistic miracles from the *Magna Vita* are recounted, one even before the famous story of the Mass of St Gregory.[62] The repetition of these episodes in this immensely popular 15th-century work, which was owned by a number of English charterhouses,[63] demonstrates the importance of St Hugh and his Eucharistic devotions for the English Carthusians,

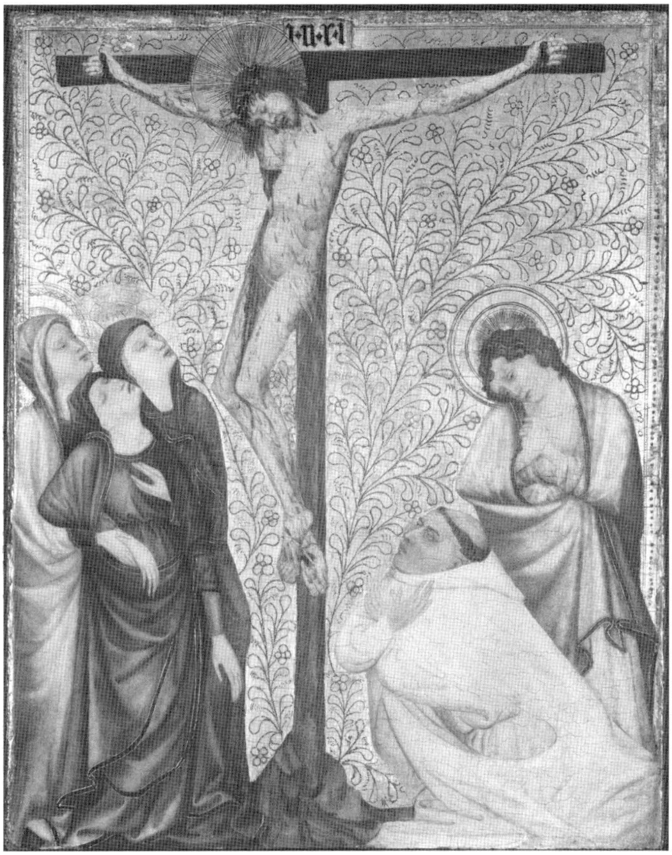

FIG. 14. Jean de Beaumetz, *The Crucifixion with a Carthusian Monk*, *c.* 1390–95
Photo, © The Cleveland Museum of Art, Leonard C. Hanna, Jr. Fund 1964.454

which may in turn supply a further explanation for the strong Eucharistic overtones of the painting at Coventry.

Whilst the overall focus on the Holy Blood can thus be explained, the patterning of Christ's skin in fleur-de-lis shapes made of droplets of blood is more difficult to account for. Turpin argued that it was typical of English mural painting, but produced only one rather unconvincing parallel, based on a drawing of an image of Christ at Breage Church (Cornw.),[64] which in reality is not very similar to that in the Coventry mural. However, the depiction of Christ's body densely covered in individual droplets of blood was not uncommon and goes back to at least the 14th century.[65] The fleur-de-lis motif seen at Coventry may therefore have been inspired by such images, perhaps coupled with relevant textual sources, which prompted the particular arrangement of the droplets. For example, the patterning of the skin, which makes it resemble printed fabric, may relate to devotional texts expressing a yearning to wear Christ's flesh as a garment.[66] Also of relevance is the literary trope of comparing Christ's wounds to plants, as expressed in one 14th-century version of Richard Rolle's *Meditations on the Passion*: 'Swete Ihesu, ȝit þi bodi is lijk to a mede ful of swete flouris & holsum herbis: / so is þi bodi ful of woundis, swete saueringe to a deuout soule, & holsum as eerbis to ech sinful man'.[67] This passage evokes an image not dissimilar to that of the body covered

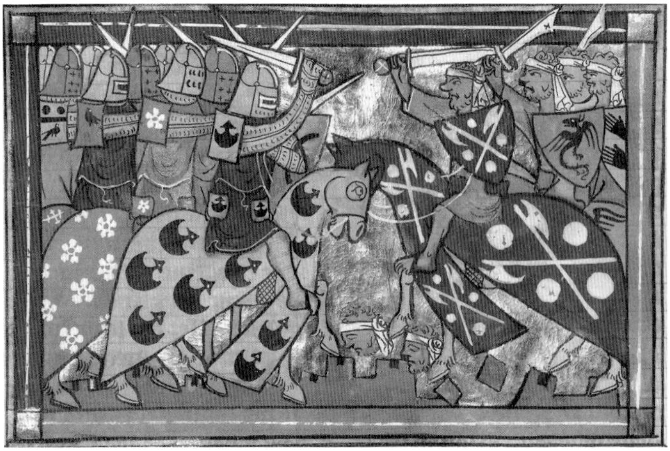

FIG. 15. Paris, Bibliothèque Nationale, MS Fr. 22495, fol. 154v: battle between the French and the Saracens, 14th century
Photo, © Bibliothèque Nationale de France, Paris

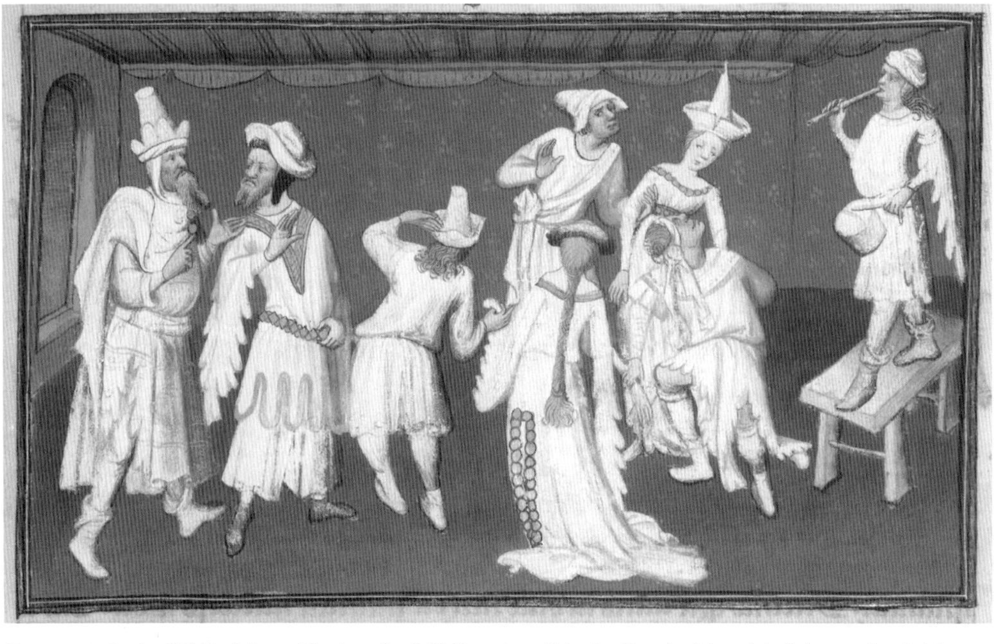

FIG. 16. Paris, Bibliothèque Nationale, MS Fr. 2810 (*Merivalles du Monde)*, fol. 44r: festivities at the court of the Grand Khan, *c.* 1413
Photo, © Bibliothèque Nationale de France, Paris

in plant-like shapes depicted on the cross at the Coventry Charterhouse. It may therefore be significant that Rolle's *Meditations*, like many of his other writings, were popular among English Carthusians, with verses attributed to him featuring in BL, MS Add. 37049 (see above),[68] and copies of his works having been owned by several English Charterhouses.[69]

Although the iconography of the mural thus represents typical Carthusian devotional concerns and artistic tastes, consideration must also be given to the issue of secular influences. Soden has proposed that the banner held by the centurion's companion may have been intended as an allusion to a local family. He noted that the three annulets on this pennant are the main elements of the arms of John Langley, who in 1417 acquired the manor of Shortly on which St Anne's Priory stood, after years of dispute.[70] While it is tempting to accept this theory, as several scholars have done,[71] it is important to note that some aspects of the visual evidence are problematic.[72] First, the headband worn by the standard-bearer, as well as his elaborate dagged sleeve, mark him out as an unsavoury character, which was a common visual ploy in this period: the headband is reminiscent of headgear worn by enemy Muslim warriors in images of battle (Fig. 15),[73] and the sleeve suggests moral degradation expressed through sartorial flamboyance (Fig. 16).[74] It therefore seems unlikely that a banner intended to honour a local family would have been placed in the hands of a man whose attire makes his moral and religious status ambiguous. Secondly, it is possible that the three circles on the banner may simply have been a detail of slightly oriental appearance used to denote the centurion's pagan status. Indeed, similar banners are often shown in contemporary

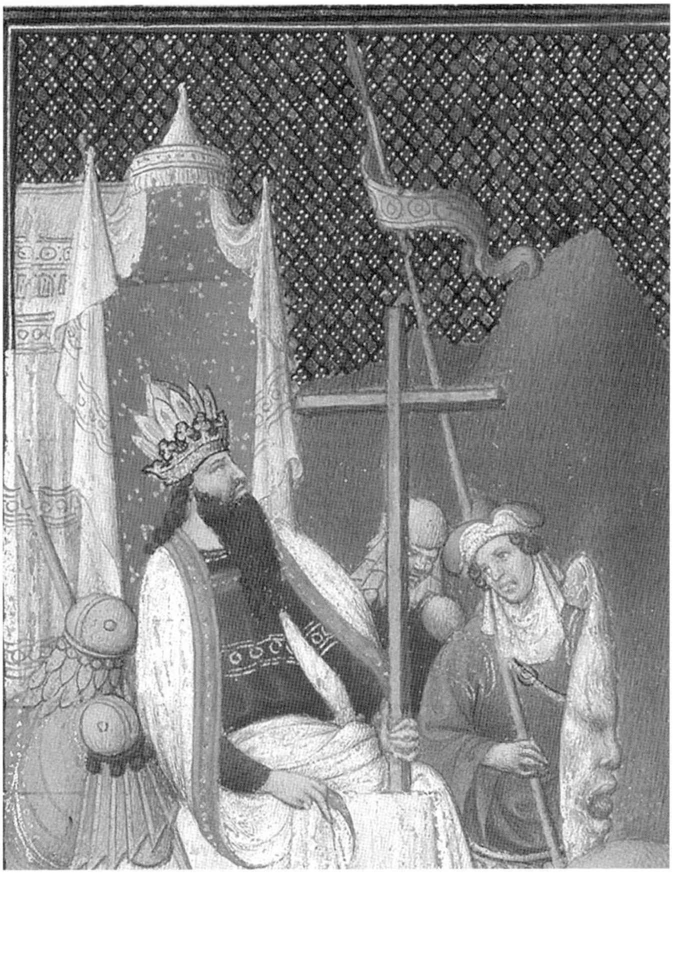

FIG. 17. The Metropolitan Museum of Art, The Cloisters Collection, 54.1.1 (*The Belles Heures of Jean Duc de Berry*), fol. 156r, detail: Emperor Heraclius and attendants

Photo, © The Metropolitan Museum of Art

French manuscripts, especially in the hands of characters from distant lands (see Fig. 17). It is therefore possible that the three annulets on the pennant at Coventry may be merely a common oriental motif, rather than a deliberate reference to the arms of the local landlord.

Rather than reflecting secular concerns, the iconography of the mural is therefore entirely in keeping with Carthusian devotional practices. Its importance lies in this and in its originality, which is reflected both in the unusual composition featuring the large flanking figures of St Anne and the Virgin, and in some of the unique smaller details. An understanding of this originality and the wide underlying frame of reference serves to emphasize the quality of the painting, which thus ranks among the English mural masterpieces of the period, not only in terms of visual splendour, but also for its iconographic interest.

ACKNOWLEDGEMENTS

I am most grateful to David Park for first bringing the Coventry Charterhouse mural to my attention and for his invaluable help throughout the research and writing of this paper, and for his many indispensable ideas. Many thanks are also due to Julian Luxford, who has been most generous in sharing both his knowledge of English Carthusian art in general and his work in progress on the Coventry Charterhouse in particular. I am also indebted to Paul Crossley for his insightful comments on an earlier draft of the paper; Stuart Slade for his reconstruction drawing of the mural and his many helpful suggestions arising from it; Miriam Gill for sharing her work on the other Coventry paintings at an early stage; Martin Stuchfield for the image of the Hildersham brass; and Linda Monckton and Richard K. Morris for their valuable ideas during our joint visit to the Charterhouse.

NOTES

1. For the building itself, see Luxford, this volume, 247–53.

2. P. Turpin, 'Ancient Wall-Paintings in the Charterhouse, Coventry', *Burlington Magazine* 35 (1919), 246–52 and pls A–C; see 249 for details of remodelling of the building.

3. The earlier reconstruction published by Turpin, 'Ancient Wall-Paintings', 252, fig. 1, shows the legs of the figure on the cross as far too short, leading him to estimate the height of the whole room as 14ft (4.27m).

4. P. Turpin, 'Ancient Wall-Paintings in the Charterhouse, Coventry II – Post-Reformation Decorative Panel in Black and White', *Burlington Magazine* 36 (1920), 84–7.

5. Luxford, this volume, 248–9.

6. Turpin, 'Ancient Wall-Paintings', 249, estimated the length of the room as 40ft (12.2m).

7. This interpretation has been accepted by, among others, Soden, *Charterhouse*, 6; G. Coppack and M. Aston, *Christ's Poor Men: the Carthusians in England* (Stroud 2002), 40, 104; and Luxford, this volume, 248–9, where he presents clear evidence to support it.

8. For the Westminster murals, see P. Binski, *Westminster Abbey and the Plantagenets: Kingship and the Representation of Power 1200–1400* (New Haven and London 1995), 187–95; H. Howard, 'Technology of the painted past: recent scientific examination of the medieval wall paintings of the Chapter House of Westminster Abbey', in *Conserving the Painted Past: Developing Approaches to Wall Painting Conservation*, post-prints of an English Heritage conference, 1999, ed. R. Gowing and A. Heritage (London 2003), 17–26. For the Byward Tower mural, see D. Park in *Age of Chivalry: Art in Plantagenet England 1200–1400*, ed. J. Alexander and P. Binski (London 1987), 509–10, cat. no. 696. For the St Mary's Apocalypse, see Gill and Morris, 'Apocalypse'; and Gill, this volume, 216–19.

9. For the Holy Trinity Doom, see Gill, this volume, 207–16. For the Haddon Hall murals, see M. Naydenova, 'Public and Private: The Late Medieval Wall Paintings of Haddon Hall Chapel, Derbyshire', *Antiq. J.* 86 (2006), 179–205.

10. Turpin, 'Ancient Wall-Paintings'.
11. I. Soden, 'The Carthusians of Coventry: Exploding Myths', *Medieval Europe 1992* York Conference, 'Religion and Belief', pre-printed Papers, VI (1994), 77–82, esp. 78–9; I. Soden, 'The Propaganda of Monastic Benefaction: Statement and Implication in the Art of St Anne's Charterhouse, Coventry', in *Meaningful Architecture: Social Interactions of Buildings*, ed. M. Locock (Aldershot 1994), 147–66, esp. 152–4, 162; Soden, *Charterhouse*, 6; Soden, *Hidden History*, 89–90.
12. M. Gill, 'The role of images in monastic education: the evidence from wall painting in late medieval England', in *Medieval Monastic Education*, ed. G. Frezoco and C. Muessig (London 2000), 117–35, esp. 127–9.
13. R. Rosewell, *Medieval Wall Paintings in English and Welsh Churches* (Woodbridge 2008), 26–8, 109, fig. 32.
14. For details of the Wyndham Payne Leaf (London, British Library, MS Add. 58078), see K. L. Scott, *Later Gothic Manuscripts 1390–1490*, A Survey of Manuscripts Illuminated in the British Isles, 6, 2 vols (London 1996), 98–100, cat. no. 25.
15. Turpin, 'Ancient Wall-Paintings', 250, inaccurately transcribed the inscription as *Ecce filus dei erat is*[*te*].
16. The inscription is a common abridgement of the words of the centurion in Mark 16:39, *Vere hic homo Filius Dei erat.*
17. I am indebted to Julian Luxford for suggesting that the legs are probably armour-clad rather than bare.
18. Turpin, 'Ancient Wall-Paintings', 250, who did not know the leg fragment but nevertheless suggested that Longinus would have been a likely counterpart to the centurion.
19. G. Schiller, *Iconography of Christian Art*, trans. J. Seligman, 2 vols (London 1971–72), II, 13, 89, 156.
20. Turpin, 'Ancient Wall-Paintings', 250.
21. P. Sheingorn, '"The Wise Mother": the Image of St Anne Teaching the Virgin', *Gesta* 32 (1993), 76. For a recent discussion of the significance of these lines, see M. Orr, 'The Fitzherbert Hours (Dunedin Public Libraries, Reed MS 5) and the Iconography of St. Anne Teaching the Virgin to Read in Early Fifteenth-Century England', in *Migrations: Medieval Manuscripts in New Zealand*, ed. S. Hollis and A. Barratt (Newcastle 2007), 228–9.
22. Orr, 'Fitzherbert Hours', 221, notes this trend in manuscript illumination.
23. Soden, 'Monastic Benefaction', 152; Gill, 'Monastic education', 129 and n. 15.
24. Turpin, 'Ancient Wall-Paintings', 250–1.
25. Orr, 'Fitzherbert Hours', 226 and n. 67, lists several manuscript examples. The motif also features in English alabasters of the Virgin and Child, as in L. Flavigny and C. Jablonski-Chauveau, *Sculptures d'albatre du Moyen Age: d'Angleterre en Normandie* (Rouen 1997), 64, 110, cat. no. 19. I am indebted to Nigel Ramsay for this reference.
26. London, British Library, Add Charter 7385; W. de G. Birch, *Catalogue of Seals in the Department of Manuscripts in the British Museum*, 6 vols (London 1887–1900), I, 523–4.
27. Based on Turpin, 'Ancient Wall-Paintings', 251, with some corrections.
28. W. G. Fretton, 'Memorials of the Charter House, Coventry', *TBWAS* 5 (1874), 40; Turpin, 'Ancient Wall-Paintings', 251, n. 8.
29. M. D. Harris, *Some Manors, Churches and Villages of Warwickshire, With an account of certain Old Buildings of Coventry* (Coventry 1937), 48; Soden, *Charterhouse*, 6; Gill, 'Monastic education', 128, caption to fig. 10.5; Rosewell, *Medieval Wall Paintings*, 27–8.
30. C. B. Rowntree, 'Studies in Carthusian History in Later Medieval England with Special Reference to the Order's Relations with Secular Society' (unpublished Ph.D. thesis, University of York, 1981), 448, 517.
31. Ibid., 551–2.
32. *The Heads of Religious Houses: England and Wales, III. 1377–1540*, ed. D. M. Smith (Cambridge 2008), 356.
33. Gill, this volume, 212–15 and Col. Pl. XII.
34. R. Marks, *Stained Glass in England during the Middle Ages* (London 1993), 182–3; Gilderdale Scott, this volume, 225–7.
35. L. Woolley, *Medieval Life and Leisure in the Devonshire Hunting Tapestries* (London 2002), 13.
36. See also the brass of Thomas, Baron Camoys of *c.* 1421 in *Gothic: Art for England 1400–1547*, ed. R. Marks and P. Williamson (London 2003), 194, cat. no. 53, pl. 100.
37. Luxford, this volume, 251–2, has also suggested a date of *c.* 1430–35.
38. Gill, 'Monastic education', 127. For details of an 11th-century Crucifixion at Desiderius's monastery refectory at Montecassino, see I. Kabala, 'Medieval decorated refectories in France, Italy and England until 1250' (unpublished Ph.D. thesis, University of Baltimore, Maryland, 2001), 329–31.
39. For Horsham, see D. Purcell, 'The Priory of Horsham St Faith and its Wall Paintings', *Norfolk Archaeology* 35 (1973), 469–73; D. Park in Alexander and Binski ed., *Age of Chivalry*, 313, cat. no. 263; D. Park and H. Howard, 'The Medieval Polychromy', in *Norwich Cathedral: Church, City and Diocese, 1096–1996*,

ed. I. Atherton, E. Fernie, C. Harper-Bill and H. Smith (London 1996), 388. For Cleeve, see M. R. James, *Abbeys* (London 1925), 125 and pl. opp. 127; R. Gilyard-Beer, *Cleeve Abbey, Somerset* English Heritage guidebook 2nd edn (London 1992), 32–6.

40. E. Borsook, *The Mural Painters of Tuscany: from Cimabue to Andrea del Sarto*, 2nd edn (Oxford 1980), 42, 87.

41. W. Braunfels, *Monasteries of Western Europe: the Architecture of the Orders* (London 1972, repr. 1980), 111.

42. E. M. Thompson, *The Carthusian Order in England* (London 1930), 210.

43. The motif of angels gathering the Holy Blood in chalices originated in Italy. The iconography is discussed in C. M. Kauffmann, *Biblical Imagery in Medieval England 700–1550* (London 2003), 252–3. Other examples of Crucifixions featuring angels with chalices in English manuscripts include: Vatican City, Biblioteca Apostolica MS Pal. Lat. 501, fol. 122v, and Vatican City, Biblioteca Apostolica MS Rossiana 275, fol. 101v, both illustrated in Scott, *Later Gothic Manuscripts*, illus. 16, 129, cat. nos 3, 129. Also London, Westminster Abbey, 37 (Litlyngton Missal), fol. 157v, illustrated in L. F. Sandler, *Gothic Manuscripts 1285–1385*, A Survey of Manuscripts Illuminated in the British Isles, 5, 2 vols (London 1986), illus. 402, cat. no. 150. For examples in alabaster, see F. Cheetham, *English Medieval Alabasters* (Oxford 1984), 245, 251–8, cat. nos 172, 178–85.

44. For discussion of texts relating to the five wounds, see L. Gougaud, *Devotional and Ascetic Practices in the Middle Ages* (London 1927), 85; D. Gray, 'The Five Wounds of Our Lord', *Notes and Queries* 208 (1963), 50–1, 82–9, 127–34, 163–8. For Coventry images, see C. Davidson and J. Alexander, *The Early Art of Coventry, Stratford-upon-Avon, Warwick and Lesser Sites in Warwickshire* (Kalamazoo 1985), 28–9, who list two 15th-century depictions of shields featuring the five wounds: on the painted nave ceiling at Holy Trinity church and on a stained glass panel from St Michael's church.

45. I. Soden, 'Coventry Monastic Conversions', in *The Archaeology of Reformation, 1480–1580*, ed. D. Gaimster and R. Gilchrist (Leeds 2003), 285; Soden, *Hidden History*, 95.

46. The manuscript is assumed to be of Carthusian provenance, because it features a text concerning the foundation of the order, several images of Carthusian monks and texts known to have been popular among Carthusians. For details, see, among others, H. E. Allen, *Writings Ascribed to Richard Rolle Hermit of Hampole and Materials for his Biography* (London 1927), 306–10; B. L. Doty, 'An Edition of BM MS Add 37049: a Religious Miscellany' (unpublished Ph.D. thesis, Michigan State University, 1969), 138; R. H. Bowers, 'Middle English Verses on the Founding of the Carthusian Order', *Speculum* 42 (1967), 710–13; J. Hogg, 'Unpublished texts in the Carthusian northern Middle English religious miscellany, British Library MS Add. 37049', in *Essays in Honour of Erwin Stürzl on his Sixtieth Birthday*, ed. J. Hogg (Salsburg 1980), 241–84, esp. 243; A. I. Doyle, 'English Carthusian books not yet linked with a Charterhouse', in *'A Miracle of Learning': Studies in manuscripts and Irish learning. Essays in honour of William O'Sullivan*, ed. T. Barnard, D. O'Crónín and K. Simms (Aldershot 1998), 122–36, esp. 128.

47. C. Bertelli, 'The *Image of Pity* in Santa Croce in Gerusalemme', in *Essays in the History of Art Presented to Rudolph Wittkower*, ed. D. Fraser, H. Hibbard and M. J. Lewine (London 1967), 40–55, esp. 48; Doty, 'An Edition of Add 37049', 123–4. For illustration, see J. Hogg ed., *An Illustrated Yorkshire Carthusian Miscellany, British Library, London, Additional MS 37049, Volume 3: The Illustrations, Analecta Cartusiana* 95 (1981), 22.

48. Doty, 'An Edition of Add 37049', 2, dates it to late in the first half of the 15th century; Scott, *Later Gothic Manuscripts*, 193, dates it to *c.* 1460–70.

49. Gray, 'Five Wounds', 83.

50. M. Rubin, *Corpus Christi: the Eucharist in Late Medieval Culture* (Cambridge 1991), 314.

51. M. Meiss, *French Painting in the time of Jean de Berry: the Limbourgs and their contemporaries*, 2 vols (London 1974), 279.

52. For the other Beaumetz panel, see ibid., fig. 360. For the *Retable of St Denis* by Jean Malouel and his follower, Henry Bellechose, see G. Le Bras, *Les Ordres Religieux: la vie et l'art*, 2 vols (Flammarion 1979), I, 619, fig. 122.

53. J. A. Large, 'The libraries of the Carthusian Order in medieval England', *Library History* 6, no. 3 (1975), 201; M. Cré, *Vernacular Mysticism in the Charterhouse: a Study of London, British Library, MS Additional 37790*, Medieval Translator, 9 (Turnhout 2006), 24–7.

54. The emphasis on Christ's blood in BL Add. 37049 is particularly pronounced. See M. V. Hennessy, 'Aspects of Blood Piety in a Late Medieval English Manuscript: London, British Library Additional 37049', in *History in the Comic Mode: Medieval Communities and the Matter of the Person*, ed. R. Fulton and B. W. Holsinger (New York 2007), 182–91.

55. For St Hugh and the first English Charterhouse at Witham, see Thompson, *Carthusian Order*, 54–68.

56. Adam of Eynsham, *The Life of St Hugh of Lincoln* (*Magna vita sancti Hugonis*), ed. D. L. Douie and H. Farmer, 2 vols (London 1961), I, 35–6; II, 86, 95.

57. Douie and Farmer in ibid., I, liv.

58. Doyle, 'English Carthusian books', 130.
59. Rowntree, 'Carthusian History', 164.
60. The *Meditationes Vita Christi* erroneously attributed to St Bonaventure; see M. G. Sargent, 'The Transmission by the English Carthusians of Some Late Medieval Spiritual Writings', *Journal of Ecclesiastical History* 27 (1976), 225–40, esp. 230. For Love's career and 1410 presentation of the text, see Rowntree, 'Carthusian History', 201. For further details of dating, see Sargent in *Nicholas Love's Mirror of the Blessed Life of Jesus Christ*, ed. M. G. Sargent (New York and London 1992), xxiv.
61. Sargent in *Love's Mirror*, xxxviii.
62. Sargent ed., *Love's Mirror*, 232–5.
63. Sargent, 'Transmission of Spiritual Writings', 231, notes that copies of the *Mirror* are known to have existed at London and Sheen charterhouses; Sargent in *Love's Mirror*, lxxii–lxxxv, records a total of 56 complete extant copies of the work.
64. Turpin, 'Ancient Wall-Paintings', 251.
65. For example, it can be seen in the Crucifixion in the Litlyngton Missal (London, Westminster Abbey, MS 37, fol. 157v) of *c.* 1383–84; see Sandler, *Gothic Manuscripts*, illus. 402, cat. no. 150.
66. A 14th-century lyric expressing this concept from the commonplace book of John of Grimestone is cited in: Hennessy, 'Blood Piety', 187.
67. C. Horstmann ed., *Yorkshire Writers: Richard Rolle of Hampole and his Followers* (Cambridge 1999), 97.
68. Doty, 'An Edition of Add 37049', 153.
69. Rowntree, 'Carthusian History', 195–6; Cré, *Vernacular Mysticism*, 24 and n. 27.
70. Soden, 'The Carthusians of Coventry', 78–9; Soden, 'Monastic Benefaction', 153–4; Soden, *Charterhouse*, 6; Soden, *Hidden History*, 89–90.
71. Coppack and Aston, *Christ's Poor Men*, 105; Rosewell, *Medieval Wall Paintings*, 109.
72. I am particularly indebted to David Park for drawing my attention to the problems associated with this interpretation.
73. D. H. Strickland, *Saracens, Demons, & Jews: Making Monsters in Medieval Art* (Princeton and Oxford 2003), 180–1.
74. R. Mellinkoff, *Outcasts: Signs of Otherness in Northern European Art of the Late Middle Ages*, 2 vols (Oxford 1993), I, 20. For discussion of the costumes in the miniature in the Belles Heures, fol. 156r, see J. Kubiski, 'Orientalizing Costume in Early Fifteenth-Century French Manuscript Painting (*Cité des Dames* Master, Limbourg Brothers, Boucicant Master, and Bedford Master)', *Gesta* 40 (2001), 172–3.

Combe Abbey: From Cistercian Abbey to Country House

WARWICK RODWELL

Combe was founded as a Cistercian abbey in 1150, rapidly attracting endowments and becoming the richest monastic house in Warwickshire. Its footprint was middle-ranking in size, and the claustral buildings lay to the north of the church. Elements of the late 12th-century east range survive, along with the 15th-century west cloister walk, part of the north walk and other structural fragments. All were incorporated in the fabric of an early Tudor courtyard mansion which was developed after the abbey was suppressed in 1539, in the shell of three of the claustral ranges; the church was demolished. Where possible, existing masonry walls were used for the ground-floor rooms, but much of the first floor comprised new timber-framed construction, the dating of which is uncertain but is not later than c. *1580. The southern aspect of the house was quickly aggrandised by constructing stone Dutch-style gables, and a remarkable porch was added to the east wing soon after 1600, associated with the brief residence of Princess Elizabeth, daughter of James I. The south-west wing was remodelled in 1667, followed by a major re-building campaign in the 1680s, when William Winde designed a monumental west range in a restrained classical style. Further alterations occurred in the Georgian era, and the Tudor east range was demolished and rebuilt in a French château style by W. E. Nesfield in 1863–64. The long occupation by the earls of Craven ended in 1923, when the estate was broken up and a large part of the house was demolished by the developer to whom it was sold. Following acquisition by Coventry City Council and several further decades of decline, Combe Abbey was finally developed as a country house hotel in the 1990s.*

COMBE Abbey lies four miles (6km) to the east of Coventry, in the modern parish of Combe Fields. Today, the house is the focus of a large new hotel complex, located in the middle of Coombe Abbey Country Park (Fig. 1 and Col. Pl. XVIA in print edn).[1] Since 1991, the house and grounds have been the subject of considerable research and archaeological recording, in conjunction with the hotel development and the creation of a visitors' centre in the park. It is hoped in due course to publish a monograph on the history, archaeology and architecture of Combe, down to the present day. Meanwhile, this paper aims to provide a résumé of the architectural development of the abbey, as it has now been revealed through archaeological research, from the 12th century to the close of the 17th.

OUTLINE HISTORY

COMBE was originally in the parish of Smite, which takes its name from the brook that flows through the area, and is a tributary of the river Sowe. The settlement of

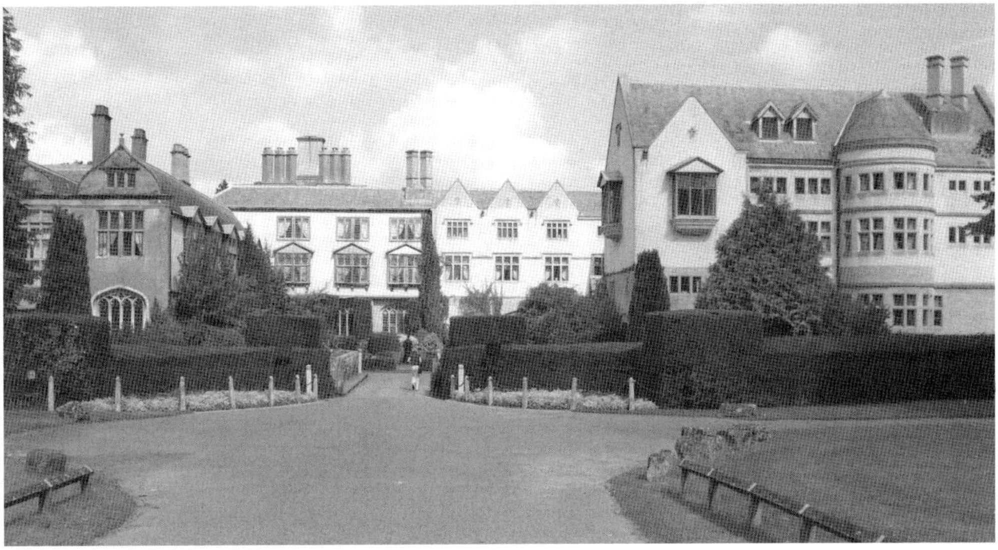

FIG. 1. Combe Abbey from the south, after the recent hotel conversion. The bridge over the moat is in the foreground; the superstructures of the east range (right foreground) and of the gabled section of the north range are new

Photo, 2010, R. K. Morris

Smite is recorded in the Domesday Survey,[2] but became depopulated before the end of the middle ages and the remains of its church of St Peter are incorporated in the farmhouse known as 'Peter Hall'. Writing in the mid-17th century, William Dugdale observed that the monks of Combe had created 'pasture ground where antiently two villages stood, the depopulation wherof hath been antient, for the vestiges are scarce to be discerned'.[3]

In 1150, Richard de Camvill founded the abbey of St Mary, Combe (*Cumba*), in the valley of the Smite Brook, on a site where no substantial occupation seems previously to have existed. He endowed it with the entire manor and sundry other lands in the Coventry area. Combe was colonised by Cistercian monks from Waverley Abbey (Surrey). The abbey's endowments increased steadily throughout the middle ages, and Combe's proximity to Coventry enabled it to benefit from the city's prosperity; consequently, by the later 13th century it was the richest monastic house in Warwickshire. The history of the abbey in the middle ages has been published elsewhere, and need not be repeated here.[4] Combe has also been the subject of several local history studies,[5] but a detailed description and analysis of the medieval buildings and landscape is still lacking. A preliminary study towards this end was carried out in 1991.[6] Although the abbey church was demolished soon after the suppression, the claustral ranges survived and were transformed into a Tudor courtyard house, which itself had a complex architectural history.

The abbey was surrendered to Dr London, the king's commissioner, on 21 January 1539, two months after he wrote to Thomas Cromwell urging him to 'go through' with the seizure of Combe while the house was still at its best, commending it as 'very commodious'. No record has survived of the dismantling of the buildings, and it is likely that they remained substantially intact, apart from the church. The king granted Combe Abbey, together with the manor of Smite, to Mary, duchess of Richmond and Somerset, for life. Thereafter, it passed into the hands of the earl of Warwick, and ultimately reverted to the crown in 1557. Robert Kelway was the next lessee of the estate, but the abbey itself was sub-let to Sir William Raynesford and sub-tenanted by Sir William Wigston. This strongly suggests that the abbey was not a mere ruin lying amidst grazing land, but had already been at least partially adapted for use as a residence of substance. Investigating the post-dissolution history of the house has been tackled on several occasions, when opportunities have arisen, and a fuller understanding of its complex architectural development is now beginning to emerge.[7] However, large sections of the medieval and Tudor fabric were progressively replaced by new ranges in the Jacobean, Stuart, Georgian and Victorian periods.

In 1581, Kelway's daughter, Elizabeth, married John Harington of Exton (Rutland), who was created Baron Harington in 1602. It is not recorded when the Haringtons moved to Combe, but it is likely to have coincided with their marriage, since the previous lease of the buildings had fallen in three years earlier. Thus, when Lord Harington died in 1613 he had probably lived at Combe for about thirty-two years, and the major building campaigns of the late 16th century must have been his work. It was during Harington's time that Combe Abbey came to national prominence, on account of his wardship of Princess Elizabeth, daughter of King James I. She lived at Combe between 1603 and 1608, and an attempt was made by the Gunpowder Plotters in November 1605 to kidnap her, but was foiled by Harington. In 1613, Elizabeth married Prince Frederick, Elector of the Palatinate on the Rhine, and eventually ascended the throne of Bohemia. The reign was short-lived, giving rise to Elizabeth's popular title, the 'Winter Queen of Bohemia'.

The abbey descended through the Harington female line to the countess of Bedford, and in 1622 was sold for £36,000 to Elizabeth, widow of Sir William Craven, late lord mayor of London. Combe passed to their son, William, who became Baron Craven in 1627. He does not appear to have been resident, although in 1634 he obtained a licence from Charles I to enclose 650 acres of demesne land to make a park. This marks the beginning of Combe Park. Craven was almost continuously away from Combe, supporting the exiled queen of Bohemia, whom he may have secretly married.

In consequence of his support for the Royalists in the Civil War, Craven's properties were confiscated by the crown in 1652. A parliamentary survey of Combe was carried out at the time of confiscation, when the property was deemed capable of making 'a convenient dwelling house for some Person of Worth, and therefore not fit to be demolished'. The earliest depiction of the house dates from 1656 (Fig. 2).[8] Craven and the exiled queen returned to England in 1660 and their confiscated property was recovered. However, it is clear that neither lived at Combe in the 1660s, since Craven leased the property to his godson, Sir Isaac Gibson, who was responsible for a fresh spate of building work, specifically the south-west wing.

Gibson departed from Combe in 1680 and Lord Craven's nephew, Sir William Craven, took up residence, immediately embarking on a major rebuilding of the west and north ranges. William Winde, a Dutch architect, was appointed to design and carry out improvements, and a large volume of architecturally informative correspondence between him and Craven has survived.[9] Winde worked mainly on the west range (1682–84), but did not complete his ambitious scheme. Combe Abbey, with its formal gardens and park, as they appeared towards the close of the 17th century, was captured in a bird's-eye view by Knyff and Kip (Fig. 3).

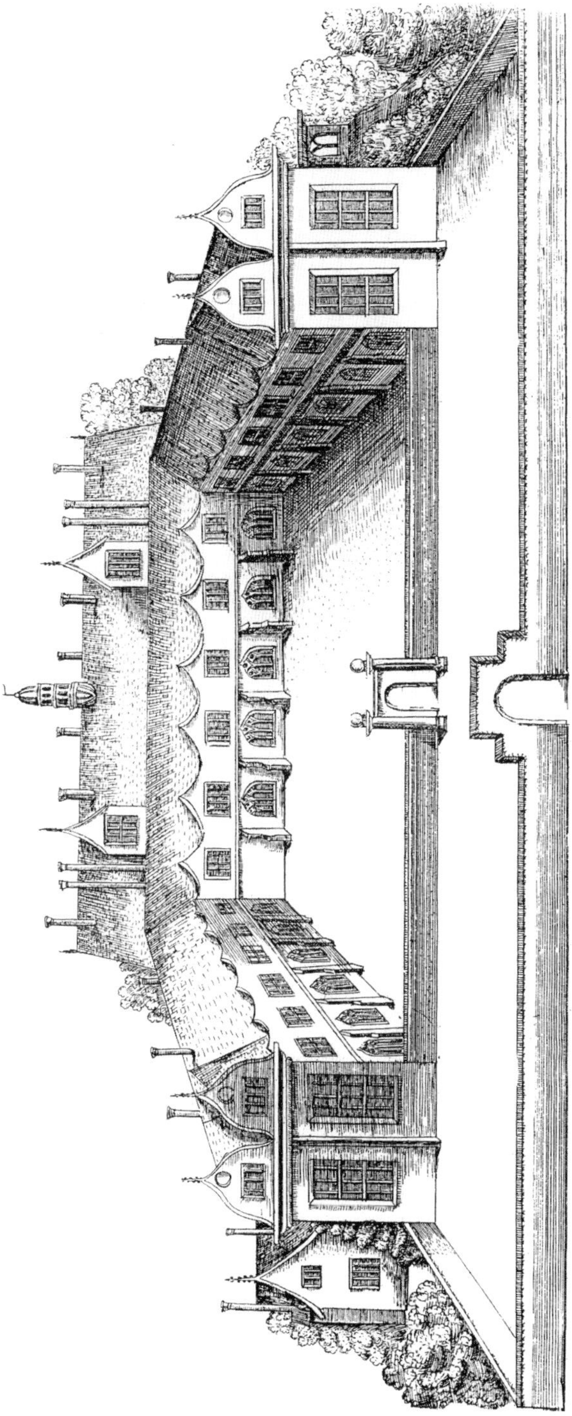

Fig. 2. Combe Abbey from the south in 1656

From D. King, The Cathedrall and Conventuall Churches of England and Wales Orthographically Delineated *(1672), pl. 60*

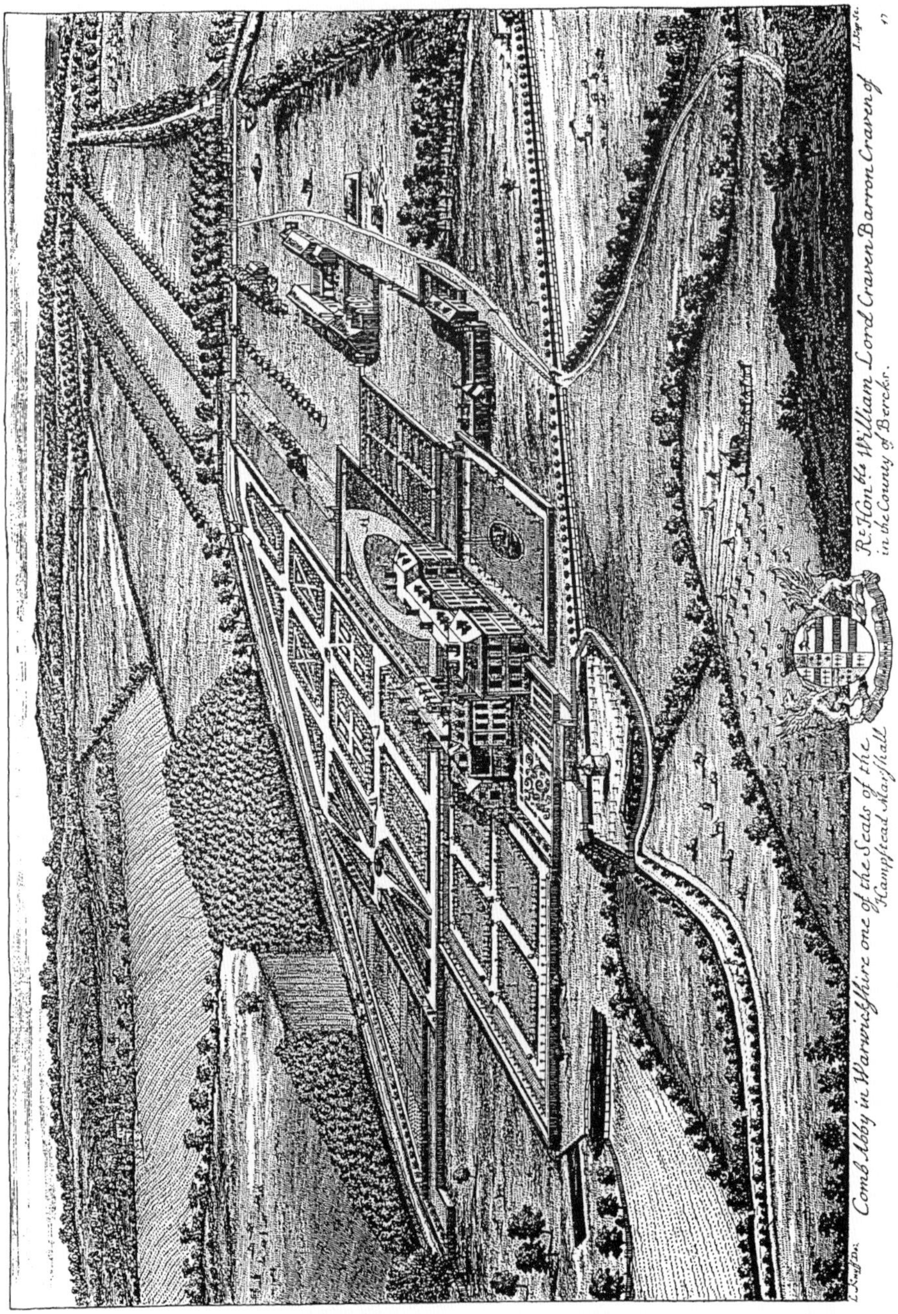

FIG. 3. Combe Abbey, birds-eye view from the north-west in 1707
From L. Knyff and J. Kip, Britannia Illustrata *(London 1707), pl. 47*

The Cravens now had a fine mansion with extensive gardens and parkland, and they progressively filled the house with exquisite furnishings, pictures and antiquities. They also built the new parish church at Binley in 1771–73, and constructed a family burial vault within it.[10] The park was remodelled by Lancelot ('Capability') Brown in 1771–76, when the formal gardens were swept away and a huge lake (known as Combe Pool) created by damming the Smite Brook.[11] Brown also carried out work on the house. An indoor tennis court was erected in *c.* 1810, and improvements were made to the great hall and other parts of the house in the 1820s. L. N. Cottingham was certainly involved at Combe and may have been the architect. However, by 1842 Edward Blore was surveying the property, but does not seem to have been commissioned to carry out any work.

It was not until the 1860s that Combe witnessed a fresh wave of change, when the eastern half of the house was entirely demolished and a new, eccentric block erected to the design of William Eden Nesfield (Fig. 4, right). Not appreciated in its day, the east wing has been described by Pevsner as 'one of the major works of that rare and highly talented architect Eden Nesfield'.[12] At the same time, his father, William Andrews Nesfield, landscaped the gardens around the abbey, constructing the canal and re-introducing the formal element that had been swept away by Brown.

The Cravens continued to live comfortably at Combe until the First World War, after which decline rapidly set in. In 1923, the contents of the house were auctioned and the estate was sold off in numerous parcels. The abbey itself was bought by J. G. Gray, a speculating builder from Coventry: he proceeded to gut the house, and demolished two-thirds of it in 1925. He remodelled the interior of the remaining part and lived

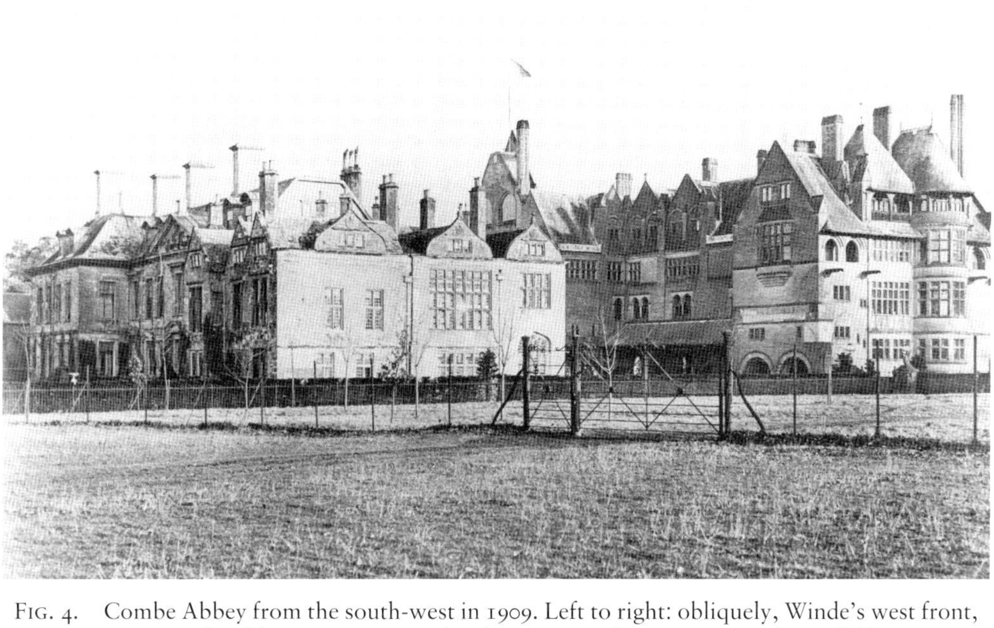

FIG. 4. Combe Abbey from the south-west in 1909. Left to right: obliquely, Winde's west front, 1682–84; Dutch gable, 1667; two Dutch gables, 1580s; cloister courtyard; Nesfield's east wing, 1863–64

Photo, Cornelia Craven, courtesy of Maxwell Craven

there until his death in 1963. The house and part of the park were then bought by Coventry Corporation, which had already acquired Combe Pool in 1958. Thus was born 'Coombe Abbey Country Park'. From 1992 onwards, the abbey buildings were commercially developed by Coventry City Council, and greatly extended to create the present country house hotel. As a precursor to that development, an archaeological assessment of the entire estate was carried out in 1991,[13] followed by limited excavations[14] and detailed structural recording in 1993–94.[15]

THE CISTERCIAN ABBEY

IT is convenient to begin with the cloister, since the post-dissolution house completely preserved its plan, incorporating the medieval fabric of three of the walks, and parts of the ranges alongside them (Figs 5, 6).[16] As subsequent rebuilding took place, the amount

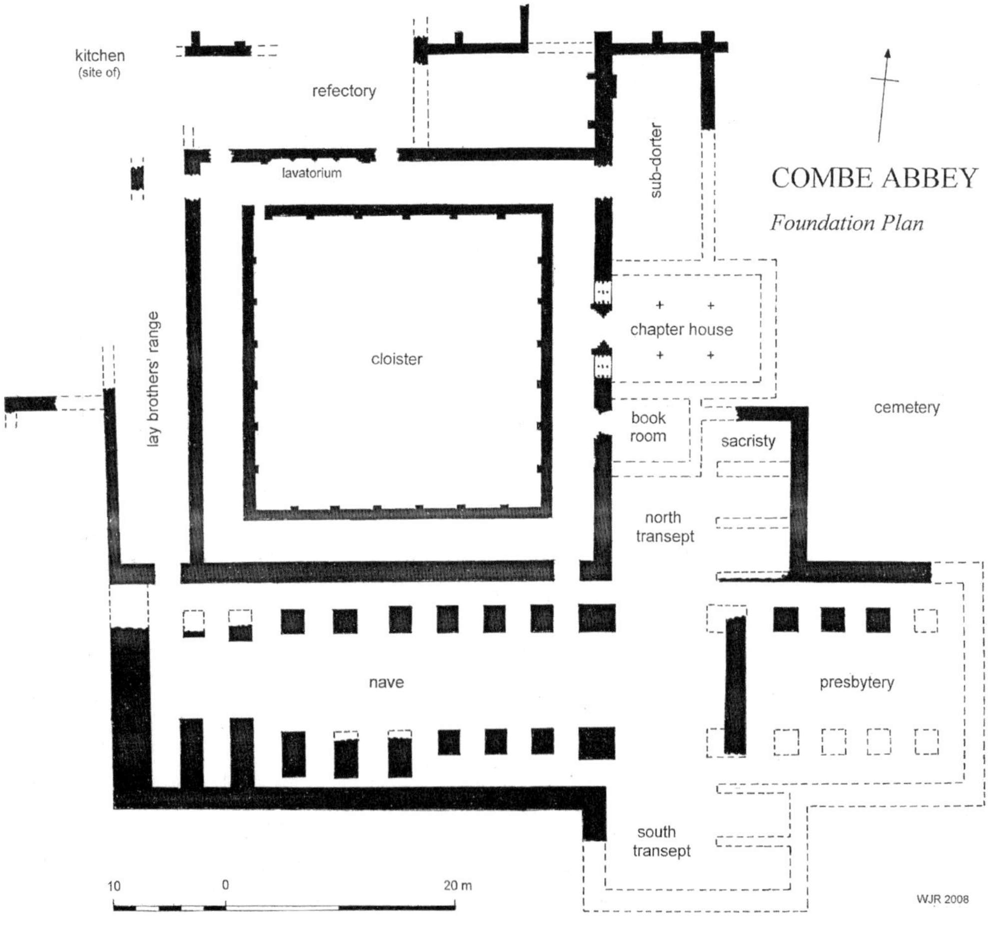

FIG. 5. Combe, the Cistercian abbey: foundation plan, compiled from various sources
Drawing, author

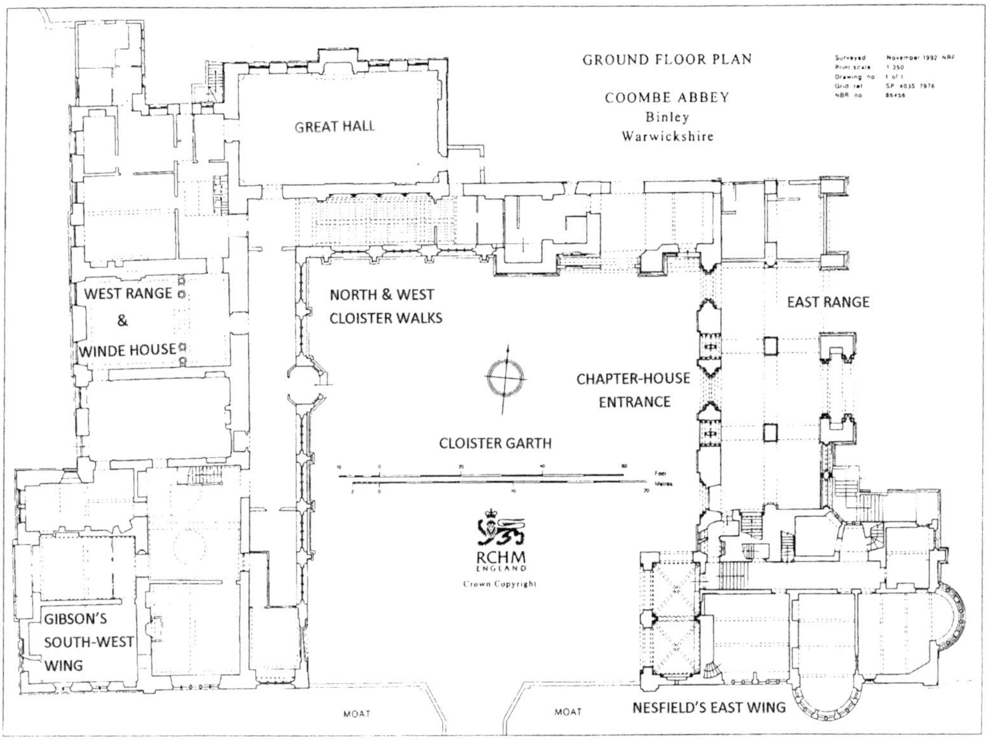

FIG. 6. Combe Abbey: ground-floor plan, RCHME 1992, with annotations
© Crown copyright, NMR

of surviving medieval structure was progressively diminished. It has long been acknowledged that the entrance façade of the chapter-house survived inside the Tudor east range, and was retained by Nesfield and incorporated in his new east wing, although the extent to which the masonry was restored, or even partially rebuilt, has been a matter for dispute (Fig. 7).[17] Some refacing and piecing-in has certainly occurred, especially on the east face of the cloister wall, where the conjunction scars of the former internal cross-walls have been obliterated, but the major elements are not antiquarian creations. The earliest known illustration of the chapter-house doorway dates from 1844,[18] confirming that it was not fabricated by Nesfield in the 1860s (Fig. 8).

The primary fabric dates from the late 12th century and is constructed from the local red sandstone ashlar, with a rubble core. The solid back wall of the east cloister walk contains a series of semicircular-headed openings with moulded arches and angle-shafts. At the centre is the ornate doorway to the chapter-house, flanked by a pair of two-light windows. The arch is of four orders with sunken rolls, imposts, decorated capitals and shafts; the hood moulding carries a broad face-cut chevron. The entire composition is repeated on both faces of the wall, showing that the arch was open and that there were no doors. The paired windows are similarly symmetrical in both directions, and share the same imposts with the doorway. Each window embodies fourteen small shafts and capitals, carved with a variety of late Romanesque detail. The

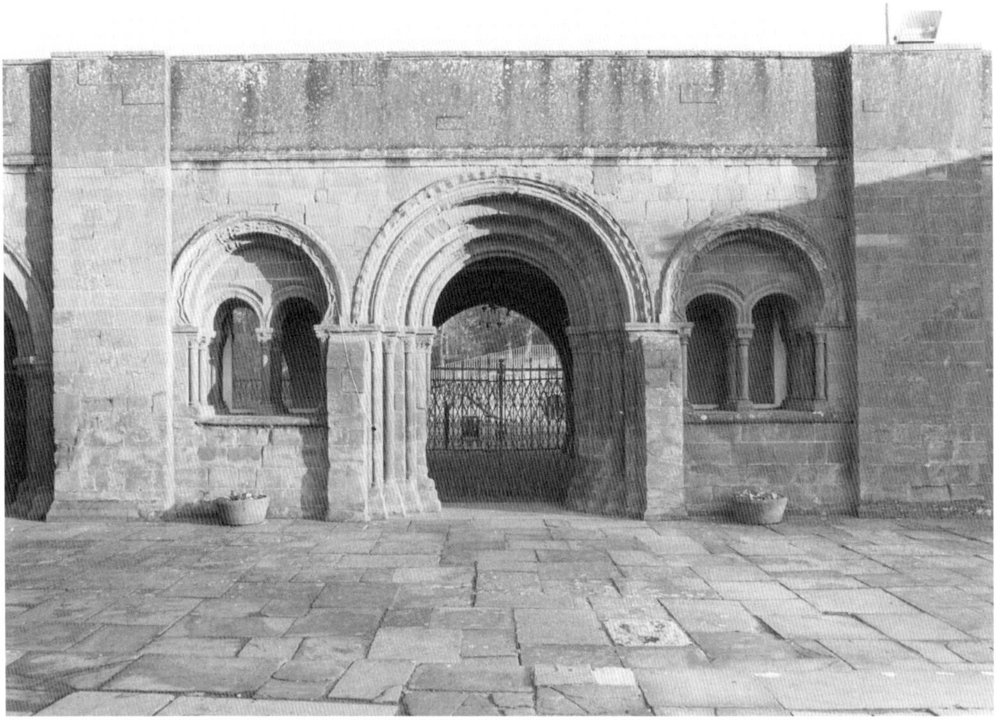

FIG. 7. Combe Abbey: Chapter-house entrance, late 12th-century, surviving in the ruins of Nesfield's east wing
Photo, 1991, author

outer arches are decorated with a face-cut chevron and have a double-chamfered hood-moulding. The horseshoe-shaped form of these arches is unusual but there is no reason to believe that it is not original; the southern window, however, had been converted into a doorway and its sub-arches have been rebuilt in segmental form. The plan of the chapter-house itself has not been recovered and it is unknown whether there was a separate vestibule, causing the structure to project well beyond the line of the east range, or whether it was a more compact rectangular structure with a quartet of internal piers, as at Buildwas (Salop.) and as conjectured here (Fig. 5). Within the area once occupied by the chapter-house (now inside the hotel foyer) and axially aligned with its doorway stands a pair of Victorian arches, side-by-side; these incorporate some genuine medieval masonry in their plinths, although it is uncertain whether any of this work is *in situ*.[19]

To the south of the chapter-house entrance is a slightly smaller but nevertheless ornate doorway which opened into the book-room and sacristy; the masonry is rebated on the east to receive a door. The arch is of three moulded orders, two of which have rolls and the middle one is square; the hood-moulding is billeted. Two of the orders of the jambs are shafted (one circular, the other polygonal in section) and have scalloped capitals on the south and leaf designs on the north. To the north of the chapter-house entrance is another doorway that gave access to the parlour in the sub-dorter (Fig. 9).

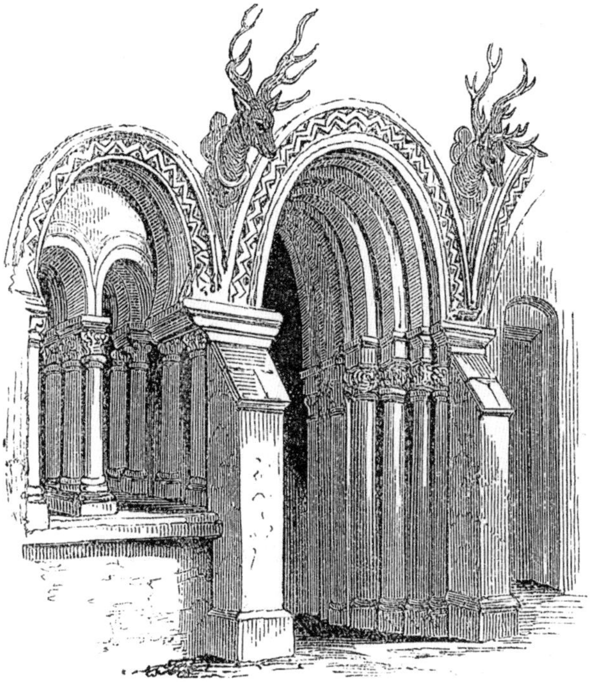

FIG. 8. Combe Abbey: Chapter-house doorway in 1846, still encapsulated within the Tudor east range

From S. C. Hall, The Baronial Halls and Picturesque Edifices of England *(1848)*

This doorway, which is plainer and has a two-centred head, was dismantled and moved southwards in 1864, but is still close to its original position.[20] As reconstructed, the feature is an open arch, not a rebated doorway. The arch is of three orders: the outermost is square, the second has an angle-roll and the third has a triplet of keel mouldings. Each order is carried by a scalloped capital: under the first is an unattached nook-shaft, the second has a small angle-roll, and the innermost has an engaged semicircular shaft. The moulded bases appear to have been spurred, but are now heavily eroded.

In the north cloister walk, part of the back wall survives, incorporating four bays of blind, trefoil-headed arcading which were uncovered during building work in *c.* 1905. The capitals are decorated with Romanesque leaf detail and chevron, and rest on triple shafts. Although heavily restored, the arcading is late 12th century and probably part of the *lavatorium*, which would have been close to the entrance to the refectory. Other fragments of upstanding early masonry are embedded in the west range, and foundations of structures in the north and east ranges, including the sub-dorter, have been recorded in excavation. The west range for the lay brothers range was narrow, and a substantial section of its outer wall survives, embedded in the later house. The overall dimension of the cloister was 34m (111ft 6in.) square, which is the same as Dore Abbey (Heref.).[21] It had been assumed that the present great hall, alongside the north cloister walk (Fig. 6), occupied the site of the refectory, but observations made during building works in the 1990s led to this being questioned. Rather, the refectory perhaps projected northwards from the centre of the range, as was commonly the case in Cistercian houses (Fig. 5).

Nothing survives of the church, which was demolished but not entirely eradicated in the mid-16th century. The site of the nave became a rectangular outer entrance court,

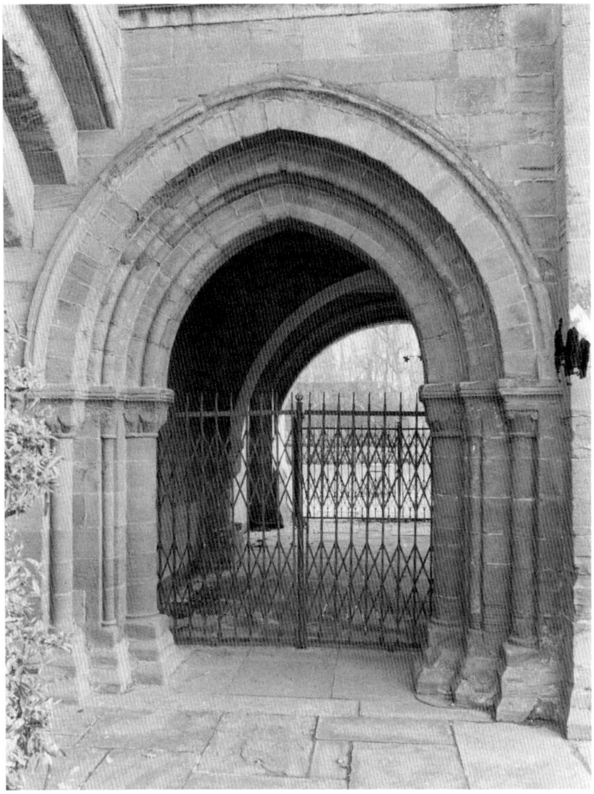

FIG. 9. Combe Abbey: late 12th-century doorway to the dorter sub-croft, repositioned by Nesfield when he rebuilt the east range in 1863–64
Photo, author

the walls of which may have reused the medieval fabric. When Nesfield created a moat on the site of the court in 1863, he dug away the entire presbytery, crossing and nave, leaving only the foundations of the transepts marooned to either side. A rough plan of the nave and presbytery was made at the time of their destruction.[22] The nine-bay nave was aisled and the piers were circular with square bases; the extra-thick foundation at the west end potentially suggests a Galilee porch (Fig. 5). A door at the last bay of the north aisle communicated with the west cloister range. When Nesfield demolished the east range, he discovered a small, late 12th-century doorway that led from the north aisle of the nave into the east cloister walk; he dismantled and reused the feature in his new north range.

The presbytery was also aisled and was of at least four — probably five — bays, but the position of the east wall was not recorded, even though Nesfield's moat passed through it. The foundation for a screen on the east side of the crossing was noted, and several small areas of mosaic floor tiling were also reported. The overall length of the church must have been at least 76m (250ft), possibly more, depending upon the nature of the eastern ambulatory. The footprint was thus closely similar to that at Dore Abbey and Margam (Glam.), both of which were just over 80m in length.[23] Foundations of the north transept were encountered during building work in 1993, and nothing is known of the south transept, except the return of its west wall. The plan suggests that the transepts were of squat proportions, with two chapels in each.

The cloister walks were reconstructed in the 15th century, retaining their original width.[24] The buttressed garth wall was fitted with a series of four-light openings with cinquefoiled heads, under a four-centred arch (Fig. 10). The east and west walks each comprised seven bays of fenestration, but the north walk had only six and there was a blank half-bay at the west end containing a small doorway. The cloister was not vaulted, but seems always to have had a pentice roof, and two-and-a-half bays of the late medieval panelled oak ceiling still survive over the north walk. The south walk was entirely removed in the 16th century, but its junction with the east and west walks was perpetuated by doorways. The arrangement is depicted in the Bucks' engraving (1729), which erroneously shows a half-bay also at the east end of the north walk (Fig. 11).[25]

Burials were encountered to the east of the cloister in the 1960s,[26] but no details are recorded, and a row of stone coffins was uncovered immediately south of the church in 1965.[27] The coffins had evidently been exhumed by Nesfield when he dug the moat, and re-interred.

POST-DISSOLUTION CONVERSION: THE FIRST PHASE

THE Tudor architecture of Combe presents two styles which are assignable to successive phases on secure stratigraphic evidence. The first is represented by timber-framed additions to at least one of the claustral ranges, and in the second phase stone-built façades were added. The sequence is preserved now only in the west cloister range,

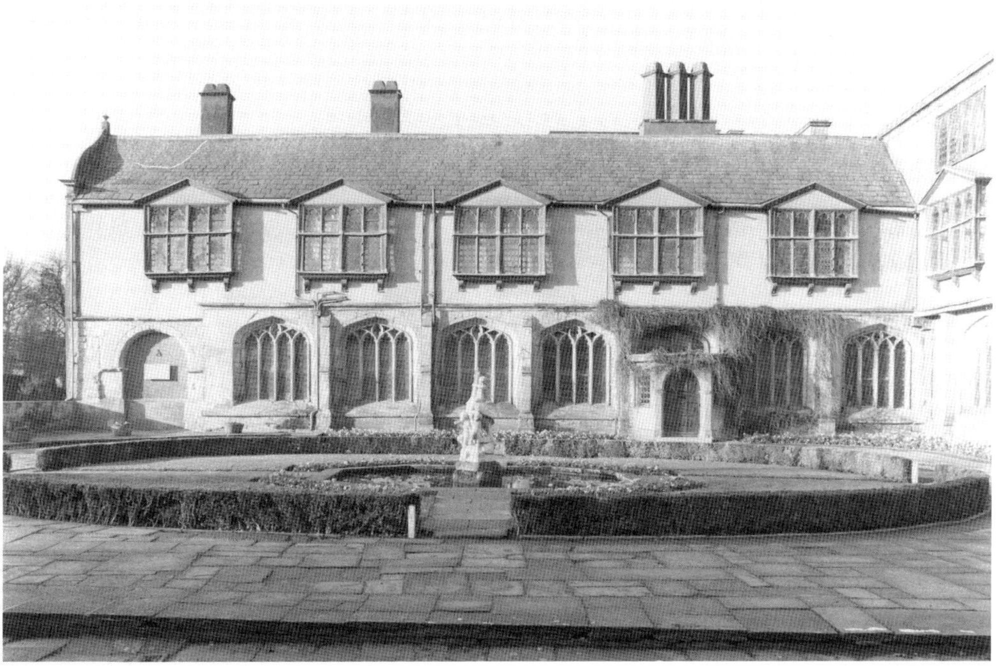

FIG. 10. Combe Abbey: west cloister viewed from the courtyard. The 15th-century arcade of seven bays survives intact; the Tudor oriel windows are in the added upper range

Photo, 1991, author

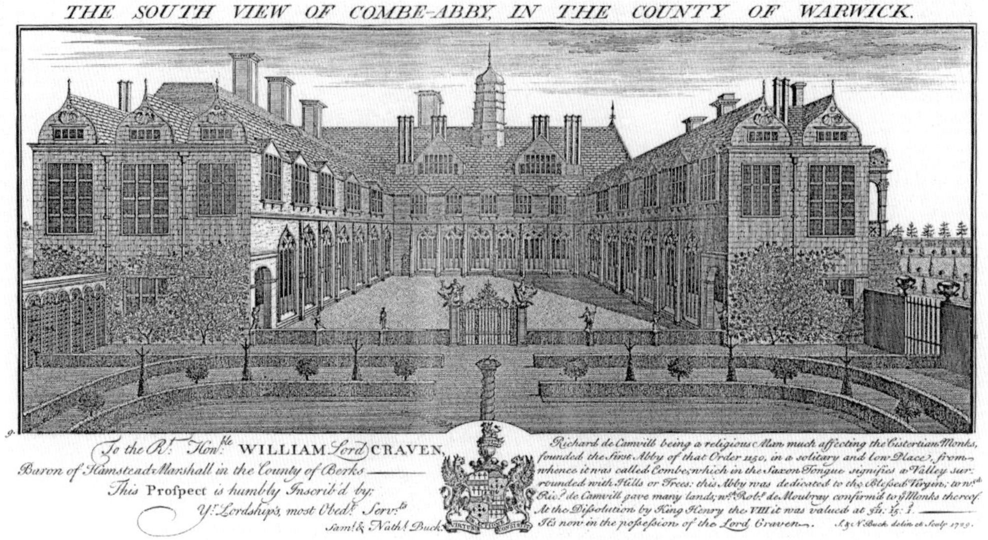

FIG. 11. Combe Abbey: view from the south in 1729, showing the conversion of three of the claustral ranges into a Tudor courtyard house

Engraving by S. and N. Buck, 1729

where the archaeology is complex and has been studied in detail by Iain Soden.[28] On the ground floor, the masonry walls of the lay brothers' range were probably retained and adapted, but at first-floor level a timber-framed unit of two bays was erected, with closely spaced studding and a fan-truss in the south gable.[29] North of this block was a small internal courtyard, the function of which was probably to light the principal stair which, according to a plan of 1678, lay at the mid-point in this range.[30] Beyond that, there were presumably further timber-framed additions which were lost during re-building in the late 17th century. At the northern end of the west range lay the medieval kitchen, which is likely to have been retained: indeed, the kitchen remained on this site until the early 20th century. It cannot now be established to what extent the north and east ranges were converted to domestic use, but the cloister walks certainly remained intact and their late medieval arcades became a notable feature of the later Tudor house.

No specific date can be assigned to the primary work, and the application of dendro-chronology is required to clarify this issue. The likelihood is that the initial conversion was restricted to the west range and occurred sometime during the period *c.* 1540–80. Weathering of the external faces of the timbers in the gable shows that they were exposed for several decades.

JOHN HARINGTON AND THE TUDOR HOUSE

ALTHOUGH the former abbey was apparently being used as a residence, at least from the 1550s, the major task of converting it into a fashionable courtyard house can hardly have been instigated by tenants whose occupancy was short-lived. Circumstantial evidence points to John Harington as the initiator of the major Tudor rebuild, probably beginning *c.* 1580. The earliest expressly dated feature was one of the first-floor chimneypieces in the south-west wing, bearing Harington's arms and the date 1590.[31] The three remaining cloister walks were retained as a corridor giving access to the ground floor rooms: they were entered from the courtyard at the south-east and south-west corners. There was no axial entrance. The monastic north range was demolished and rebuilt, with two large rooms lying parallel to the walk. Towards the west was the great hall with a lateral fireplace and north-facing windows, and to the east was a slightly smaller room which was probably the great chamber, although on the plan of 1678 it is labelled 'chapel'. No fireplace is shown in this room, but it had a large east-facing mullioned and transomed window of twenty-eight lights. Demolished in 1863, the rich interior of what is thought to be this room was captured in an engraving published in the 1840s.[32] At the junction between the two components of the range was a timber-framed staircase wing, which projected on the north side, with another large mullioned and transomed window (of thirty-two lights). There were unspecified rooms above the hall and great chamber, and a timber-framed range of five near-identical chambers — each with a fireplace and oriel window — was constructed above the cloister walk.

Similarly, a range of five rooms with oriel windows and a row of low gables was erected above the west cloister walk.[33] The style of timber framing employed is markedly different from that in the adjoining west wing: instead of heavy studding, there were large square panels infilled with wattle and daub. This framing was not intended to be visible, but to be concealed by lime-rendering which would have been decorated to represent ashlar masonry. Contemporary with the raising of the cloisters was the construction of two pairs of Dutch-style stone gables, incorporating large mullioned and transomed windows, at the southern ends of the east and west ranges (Figs 2, 4 centre). They represented an attempt to introduce symmetry and to aggrandise the approach to the house. The new windows, some of them of very considerable size, imply that the rooms were being upgraded internally, and it was the southernmost chamber on the first floor in the west wing which contained the chimneypiece dated 1590. The window of this chamber has twenty-eight lights.

The east range was also heightened and rebuilt, and provided with five oriel windows facing the courtyard, to complement those in the north and west ranges. In this case, however, the windows did not light individual rooms, but the long gallery, which we know from later references lay here. The rooms behind comprised lodgings for guests, and there was evidently a grand chamber at the southern end, since this had another mullioned and transomed window with twenty-eight lights.

It is the east range which has traditionally been associated with the occupancy of Princess Elizabeth and had its own entrance from the Renaissance great garden to the east. Leading up to that entrance was a flight of stone steps with a balustrade of pierced strapwork, and a small but highly ornate porch embodying a mixture of architectural styles. It was loosely based on a classical pillared portico with arches on the three open sides, surmounted by a frieze and moulded cornice (Fig. 12).[34] By contrast, however, the ceiling inside the porch comprised a Gothic fan-vault with a central pendentive, which was almost certainly recycled from one of the monastic buildings.[35] In place of a pediment, the arms of Princess Elizabeth were prominently displayed, carved in stone. The porch, which has often been mentioned in the literature, was dismantled by Nesfield in 1863, when the east range was demolished. He intended to reconstruct the porch as part of the rebuilding, but that did not come to pass and the fragments were dispersed around the grounds, eventually becoming incorporated into various walls.

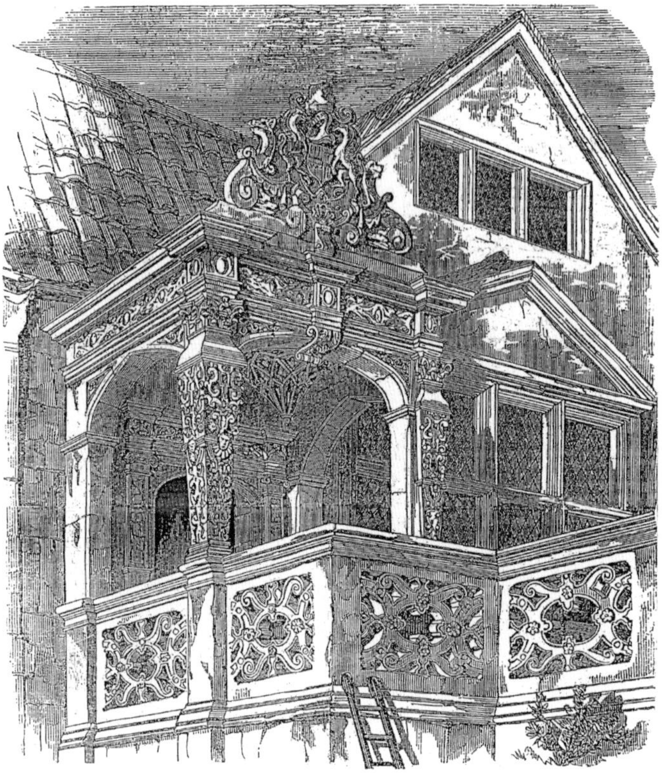

FIG. 12. Combe Abbey: Elizabethan porch on the east wing, giving access to the Renaissance great garden
From The Builder *4 (1846), 6*

The porch must have been built by Harington shortly after 1600, and was clearly an addition to what was previously a timber-framed first-floor range with east-facing gablets and oriel windows.

Soden has demonstrated that the console brackets supporting the oriel windows above the cloister walks are integral with the framing, and he made the assumption that the oriels were later than the addition of the upper ranges above the cloister walks, arguing that there had been a complete reconstruction of the timber framing in order to install the windows. That would have been a major undertaking and there is no express evidence for it. He seems to have been influenced by the apparent non-representation of oriels in King's drawing of 1656, and by their undoubted appearance in the Bucks' view of 1729 (cf. Figs 2, 11).[36] The oriels have only a very slight projection and King's view is naively drawn, without attention to detail.[37] The fact that he omits to show the tiny console brackets is not surprising. Critically, however, he includes the rows of gablets surmounting all three ranges. Since those gablets were an integral part of the design of the oriels, there can be no doubt that the present arrangement was in place before 1656.

The major part of Harington's remodelling of Combe is likely to date from the 1580s, with additional works being carried out for the accommodation of Princess Elizabeth in the early 1600s. Dutch-style ogival gables were locally fashionable at the time Harington acquired Combe, and were found, for example, on New House near Coventry, built in 1586.[38]

THE CRAVEN ERA

KING'S perspective view shows the house as it was left by Harington (Fig. 2). Although the Craven family purchased Combe in 1622, there is nothing to indicate that any substantial work was carried out until 1667, when [Sir] Isaac Gibson set about remodelling part of the west range, creating the south-west wing. He added a third south-facing gable to match the two earlier ones, with a large mullioned and transomed window at first-floor level (Fig. 4). On the west side, the wing was of three gabled bays, the central one recessed. The accommodation was on two floors and attics, and the fenestration indicates that the principal rooms again lay on the first floor (Fig. 13). A fragment of a two-storeyed medieval structure was incorporated in the north-west corner of the wing.[39] A drawing of *c.* 1684 shows not only Gibson's new west elevation, but also provides glimpses of relict features of earlier date in the north wall of his wing.[40] Further evidence for the encapsulated remains was recorded in 1993.[41]

In *c.* 1680 Lord Craven engaged William Winde to build a new suite of state and private rooms on the west and north sides of the house: drawings showing the existing and proposed arrangements have survived, along with extensive correspondence and specifications.[42] It was a grandiose scheme which envisaged the total rebuilding of both ranges, including the removal of Gibson's work of a dozen years earlier. There was to be an impressive classical west front of seven bays, flanked by projecting wings each of four bays. Accommodation was on four levels, including the basement and attic floors. It is interesting to note that the bird's-eye view of Combe by Knyff and Kip shows the house with the proposed new, but unbuilt, south-west wing (Fig. 3). This strongly suggests that their drawing, although published in 1707, dates from the mid-1680s.

Winde's plan indicates a new great hall, chapel and north-east wing, but his north elevation drawing shows only the first of these, and that was all he actually built. Construction took place in 1682–84, when three major elements were completed, two

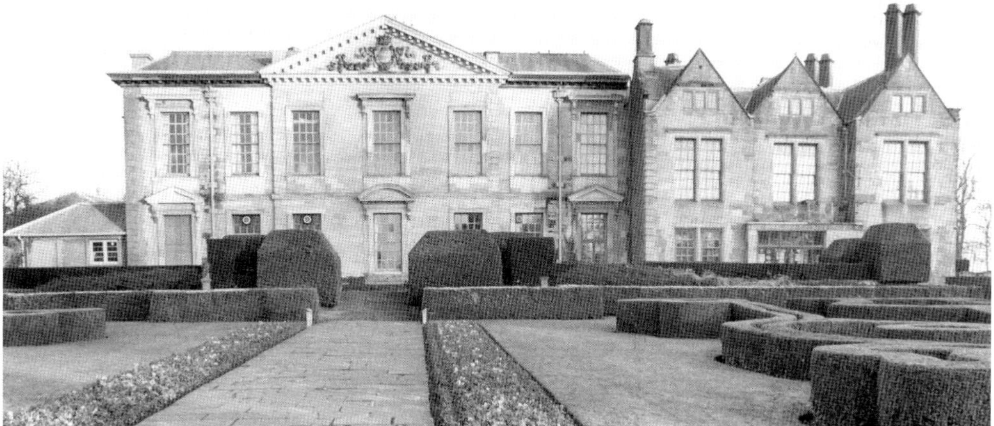

FIG. 13. Combe Abbey: west front by William Winde, 1682–84, including the triple gabled south-west wing of 1667

Photo, author

of which remain today (Fig. 13). The pedimented central west range contained the grand stair with principal reception rooms on the ground floor, the state bedchamber and other fine chambers on the first floor, servants' quarters on the second floor, and storage in the basement (which was probably modified from earlier cellarage). Gibson's south-west wing was retained, and a new north-west wing added, which had the kitchen and service rooms on the ground floor, a basement, more fine chambers on the first floor, and accommodation for servants on the second. The rebuilding of the great hall — or north parlour, as it was later called – came last, and adjoining it at the east end was another great staircase on the site of a Tudor predecessor. The stair has gone, but the parlour remains (Fig. 6) and archaeological investigation has demonstrated that it incorporates a good deal of fabric from the previous great hall, suggesting that by this stage in the building programme Winde was required to effect economies.[43]

The interiors of Winde's principal rooms were sumptuously finished, with full-height panelling, richly adorned chimneypieces and ornate plaster ceilings. For the last, he employed Edward Gouge, a leading London plasterer. Most of the 1680s work survived unscathed until 1925, and a partial photographic record exists.[44] The fixtures were largely stripped out by Gray, who sold as much architectural salvage as he could. He then demolished the north-west wing and remodelled all the rooms in the west range and south-west wing, recycling panelling and other materials that he had failed to sell at auction. As a result of Gray's savage remodelling, the interiors that survive today are but a shadow of what they were when the Cravens left Combe.

ACKNOWLEDGEMENTS

I am grateful to English Heritage and Coventry City Council for inviting me to embark on a detailed study of Combe Abbey and its setting in 1991. Since then, many colleagues and other scholars have contributed to the research and investigation of this large and complex site, and upon whose work I have drawn. I am particularly indebted to George Demidowicz for sharing the fruits of his extensive researches with me, and to Iain Soden for the benefit of discussion of his findings made during the conversion of the Abbey into a hotel.

NOTES

1 Historically, the name was usually spelled 'Combe', but 'Coombe' has become the popular modern form.

2. VCH *Warwickshire* I, 309a.

3. Dugdale, *Warwickshire* (1656).

4. VCH *Warwickshire* II, 73–5; VI, 72–4.

5. E.g. D. L. Motkin, *The Story of Combe Abbey* (Coventry 1961); R. Moore, *A History of Combe Abbey* (Coventry 1983).

6. W. Rodwell, 'Combe Abbey, Coventry, Warwickshire: an Archaeological Assessment of the Buildings, Gardens and Park' (1991), desktop study commissioned by the City of Coventry and English Heritage. See also C. Latham and H. A. Tipping, *In English Homes* (Country Life, London 1904); H. A. Tipping, 'Combe Abbey, Warwickshire', *Country Life* 26 (1909), 794–805, 840–9.

7. The principal accounts are Rodwell, *Combe Abbey*; and I. Soden, 'Buildings Analysis at Coombe Abbey, Warwickshire, 1993–94', *Post-Medieval Archaeology* 40 (2006), 129–59. See also Soden, *Hidden History*, 59–62.

8. D. King, *The Cathedrall and Conventuall Churches of England and Wales Orthographically Delineated* (London 1672, repr. 1969).

9. H. Colvin, 'Letters and Papers relating to the Rebuilding of Combe Abbey, Warwickshire, 1681–1688', *Walpole Society* L (1984), 248–309.

10. The church has been attributed to Lancelot Brown and Henry Couchman; see T. Friedman, *The Georgian Parish Church: Monuments to Posterity* (Reading 2004), 111–21.
11. D. Stroud, *Capability Brown* (London 1950), 72–4, 143–4, 219.
12. N. Pevsner and A. Wedgwood, *Warwickshire* B/E (Harmondsworth 1966), 237.
13. Rodwell, 'Combe Abbey'.
14. Unpublished archive reports in Coventry City Museum: M. Rylatt, I. Soden and J. E. Dickinson, 'Coombe Abbey, Warwickshire: An Archaeological Evaluation' (1991); J. E. Dickinson, 'Evaluation of Coombe Abbey Kennels Site, 1992' (1992); J. E. Dickinson, 'A Report on the Archaeological Works carried out in the area of the Stables, Coombe Abbey, 1993' (1993); I. Soden and J. E. Dickinson, 'Coombe Abbey, 1993: Continuing Evaluation of the Archaeology' (1993); I. Soden, 'Archaeological Evaluation of Heating and Drainage Trenches, Coombe Abbey, Warwickshire' (1994).
15. Soden, *Buildings Analysis*.
16. The ground plan of the abbey church and claustral layout has been reconstructed as a 'best fit' from various sources; the accuracy of some details cannot now be checked. Also, more than one phase of medieval construction is likely to be represented.
17. Soden, *Analysis*, 134, assigned nearly all the visible fabric to 1863–64, but, during a further examination by the present writer in 2007, the differences between late Norman and weathered Victorian masonry could clearly be discerned in many places. Variations in block size, stone colour, tooling, surface decay and mortars have all contributed to establishing the overall picture.
18. S. C. Hall, *The Baronial Halls and Picturesque Edifices of England*, 2nd edn (London 1848); the view is dated 1846.
19. In view of the uncertainty, these plinths have not been included on the plan in the text.
20. A note on Nesfield's elevation drawing reads, 'This arch to be shifted in the rebuilding'; London, Victoria and Albert Museum, Prints and Drawings Coll.
21. D. Robinson, *The Cistercians in Wales: Architecture and Archaeology, 1130–1540* (London 2006), fig. 169.
22. V&A Museum, Prints and Drawings. Variations in wall thicknesses and the plans of pier-bases are likely to be the result of the different levels to which masonry survived in the ground.
23. Robinson, *Cistercians in Wales*, figs 169 and 172.
24. Soden, *Buildings Analysis*, 134.
25. S. and N. Buck, *The South View of Combe-Abby in the County of Warwick* (1729).
26. Soden, *Buildings Analysis*, 158, n. 19.
27. D. M. Wilson and G. Hurst ed., 'Medieval Britain in 1965', *Med. Archaeol.* 10 (1966), 182.
28. Soden, *Buildings Analysis*, 136–49.
29. Ibid., fig. 6.
30. Oxford, Bodleian Library, MS Gough Drawings, a.2, fols 70v–71.
31. This was lot 228 in the sale of architectural fittings in 1925; *Coombe Abbey, Warwickshire: A Catalogue of the Remaining Valuable Contents of the Mansion*. George Loveitt and Sons (Coventry 1925).
32. Hall, *Baronial Halls*; C. J. Richardson, *Architectural Remains of the Reigns of Elizabeth and James I* (London 1840), pt 2, pl. 14.
33. It had previously been suggested by Rodwell ('Combe Abbey', 22), followed by Soden (*Buildings Analysis*, 139), that the upper floor over the west and north cloisters was originally undivided, and formed a wide corridor. While we know from later references that the long gallery lay in the east range, it would seem a profligate use of space for there to have been continuous galleries above all three walks. On balance, it is more likely that there was a series of interconnecting chambers in the north and west ranges.
34. Richardson, *Architectural Remains*, pl. 14; *The Builder* 4 (1846), 6.
35. For a view of the vault *in situ*, see J. Nash, *The Mansions of England in the Olden Time*, 2nd ser. (London 1840), title-page. Nash shows quatrefoils in the webs, which are not present on the surviving fragments.
36. Soden, *Buildings Analysis*, 142.
37. Errors and omissions in King's view are legion, including the numbers of windows shown in the cloister walks.
38. The house was demolished in 1778, but is illustrated in J. Britton, *The Architectural Antiquities of Great Britain* II (London 1835), 109.
39. Glimpsed on the far left in King's view of 1656.
40. Bodl., MS Gough Drawings a.2, fol. 81.
41. Soden, *Buildings Analysis*, 136.
42. Colvin, *Letters and Papers*.
43. Soden, *Buildings Analysis*, 142.
44. The most significant photographs are held in the archives of *Country Life*, and were taken to accompany the articles by Tipping (op. cit.).

The Chantry Chapel at Guy's Cliffe, Warwick

JOHN A. A. GOODALL

This paper discusses the history and architecture of the chantry chapel at Guy's Cliffe outside Warwick. Following a short introduction, the first section presents a brief account of the site and its development to the present day. In the second, the medieval buildings at Guy's Cliffe, and the gigantic mid-14th century sculpture of Guy that survives in the chapel there, are discussed and contextualised. The ways in which this literary fantasy found a home in the living world are explored, as well as the manner in which Guy was promoted by a noble family and assumed as an ancestor.

GUY'S CLIFFE, two miles north of Warwick, takes its name from one of the outstanding chivalric heroes of the late middle ages. The legend of Guy of Warwick, set notionally in the period of the Danish invasions, appears to have become popular from the late 12th century onwards and exists in several versions.[1] In broad outline the tale might be summarised as follows. Guy was a young man who fell in love with Felicia, the only daughter of the earl of Warwick, a companion in arms to King Arthur. She refused to marry him, however, until he demonstrated his prowess as a knight. Following years of successful foreign adventure, Guy returned home to collect his now-willing bride. On the couple's nuptial night, Guy climbed to the top of the tallest tower of Warwick Castle. Looking out from this vantage point, he was suddenly struck by the vanity of performing great deeds for a woman's hand when the service of God was the true object of life. That night he left his wife and engaged in more years of adventure as a knight of Christ.

While Guy was away on his second tour of duty, the pagan Danes challenged the English king, Athelstan, to fight for his kingdom against a giant called Colbrond. At divine direction, Guy returned anonymously from his wandering just in time to act as the English champion in the combat. Guy defeated Colbrond and England was saved from the pagans. Nevertheless, after the combat he refused to reveal his identity and travelled back to Warwick. There he lived in a cave outside the city as a hermit. After more than two years of prayer and isolation he sensed death approaching and sent to his long-abandoned wife to say that, if she came to the cave, she would be able to bury his corpse. At the same time he also passed on a warning that she would die herself only a few days later. His wife came to the cave, lamented over Guy's body, which she buried, and was soon afterwards laid to rest beside him. By the early 14th century it appears that the cave in this legend had become a physical reality.

THE HISTORY OF GUY'S CLIFFE

THE scholar and historian of the earls of Warwick, John Rous (d. 1491), served as a priest at the chantry that was established at Guy's Cliffe in the 15th century.[2] His writings contain many references to the history of the site and the foundation there.

They offer a completely different kind of information from that provided by the legal or financial documents commonly invoked to inform our understanding of medieval institutions. In addition, they have considerable authority, drawing on lost documents and Rous's personal knowledge. Where his testimony is demonstrably inaccurate, moreover, at least it records medieval tradition. Such is the case with the supposed circumstances of the foundation of a hermitage at Guy's Cliffe.

Rous attributes the establishment of a cathedral in Warwick to a bishop saint called Dubritius or Dubricius, who later moved to Wales.[3] While the activities of St Dubricius in Wales have some historical grounding, his connection with Warwick seems to be a fabrication.[4] The tradition, therefore, that Guy's Cliffe was in origin the site of a hermitage built by the bishop is certainly fictional. [5] In other words, Dubricius is one in a host of fictional heroes, like Guy himself, or like Kenelf and Kenelm, the supposed founders of nearby Kenilworth Castle,[6] commonly conjured up by medieval and Tudor historians to lend antiquity to the early narratives about important monuments.

The first historical reference to a place called Gybeclyve or Guy's Cliffe occurs many centuries later, in a royal writ of Edward III dated 26 April 1334. This granted protection to a resident hermit called Thomas de Lewes.[7] As will become apparent, there is a strong circumstantial case for supposing that this document was issued at a crucial moment in the history of Guy's Cliffe, when this hero was first appropriated by the earls of Warwick as an ancestor.[8] Despite the relative lateness of this first documentary reference, there is nothing inherently implausible about the assertion made by John Rous that a hermitage had existed on the spot since the 12th century. Writing the biography of Roger, earl of Warwick (d. 1153), Rous states that:

> ... he also gave the heremytage of Gybclyf un to the priory of Sepulcres of Warrewyk and his son earl Wallerane confermyd his gyftes and then was hit a sel [cell] to hem and oder wyle there were chanons and after secular prestys lyveng by salaryes where they might gete hem and with hem lyves armytys [hermits] and lyved un [one] party by lyverey [livery] fro the priori for then hyt was a worshipfull place and by almys from the castel and of the burges of the town and of devout peple of the cuntrey and so hit continued to the later days of Kyng Edward the third ...[9]

There is no independent confirmation of this gift, yet hermitages of this kind did exist in the 12th century, as for example that established by the popular saint, Robert, at Knaresborough, Yorkshire.[10]

After this initial mention of the hermitage in 1334, there follows more than sixty years of documentary silence. During this period, Rous records that Thomas Beauchamp (d. 1401) took control of Guy's Cliffe and compensated St Sepulchre's accordingly.

> Thys lord wher his ancetre had gevyn Guclif un to the priori of Warrwik he gate hit by change of lyvolode to hym and his Eyris fore ever more and new bylt hit the mansion undre the chapel and namyd hit Gyclif in remembrance of sir Guy.[11]

This is the first mention of a residence of any scale on the site. It is possible that previously hermits lived as troglodytes in caves carved within the cliff. In 1408 another hermit, John Burry, received a grant of 100s. per annum to pray for the good estate of Richard Beauchamp, 13th earl of Warwick (1382–1439), and his parents.[12] The new earl was an enthusiast for his literary ancestor and used the legend of Guy to bolster his image.[13] He substantially expanded the foundation in circumstances that are beguilingly described by Rous.

According to Rous, Guy's Cliffe was visited by Henry V — otherwise a noted enthusiast for chivalric romances — who planned to found a college here but was prevented by his early death. Instead, Richard Beauchamp, earl of Warwick, established:

> ... at Gybclif a chauntre of ij prystis that God wold send hym Eyre male. he did hyt by the styrryng of a holy anchoras namyd dam Em Rawghtone dwellyng at all halows in the northestrete of york and for hyt to her apperyd our lady vii tymes in on yer and seyd that in tyme to cum hyt shuld be a regal collage of the Trinyte of a kinges fundacone and hyt shuld be a gracious place to seke to for eny dises or gref and on of Seynt Gyes Eyris shuld bring hys Reliks a geyn to the same place.[14]

The establishment of the chantry for two priests is independently documented in a royal licence of 1423. This permitted the earl to found a chantry dedicated to God and St Mary Magdalene[15] in an existing chapel at Guy's Cliffe and to endow two priests to perform divine service there with up to £16 in land and rent.[16] The sum is a relatively modest one, considering that a chantry priest might then expect a salary of £10 per annum.[17] Possibly the income of the priests was paid separately by the earl of Warwick.

Seven years after the royal licence was issued a modest landed endowment worth £12 17s. 8d. ob was bequeathed to the two priests then named as serving the chantry, William Berkeswell and John Bevington.[18] The former was later appointed the dean of the collegiate church at Warwick.[19] In his will, the earl directed that the residue of his estate be bequeathed to the chantry for rebuilding the church and house there. Between 1449 and 1456 the executors accounts (now lost) record the cost of the work as £184 5d. ob.[20] The bulk of this was evidently completed by 1454–55, when two new altars were consecrated in the chapel.[21] As it presently survives, the medieval fabric of the chapel largely belongs to this period of construction, though it seems to incorporate some fragments of an earlier building.

Even before the new chapel was finished, the male line of the Beauchamp earls of Warwick failed. The heiress of the estates, Anne, was sufficiently interested in the legend of Guy to commission a new life of the hero from the monk poet, John Lydgate.[22] Her enthusiasm encouraged her husband Richard Neville, familiarly known as Warwick the Kingmaker (d. 1471), to consider further works to Guy's Cliffe. According to Rous:

> Thys noble lord [Richard Neville] was purpsid to have endowed his place of Gybclyf with more lyvolede for mo prestys and poer Gentilmen and to have woltyd and butracyd [vaulted and buttressed] sir Guys cave for fallyng downe of the hangyng rok by the avys of oder lordys sturryng hym so to doo and to let peynt Sir Gyes Image and in remembrance of seynt Gy he wold have had a certen of pore genylmen found ther as were at seynt Cros of Wynchetre by the fundacon of maister herre beauford [Henry Beaufort] cardinal and bishop of Wynchestre brodur to kyng here the foruth [Henry IV] wich place was endowed with forfet lyvelode of the Eorl of Salisbury slayn at Cissetter [Cirencester (1400)] with the Duke of Surrey. And thys lord had by auctorite of parlement recovered hit a geyn.[23]

The emphasis by Rous on the status of the poor being gentlemen is remarkable. Along with St Cross at Winchester, the only other almsmen of gentle status in the kingdom were the Poor Knights of the Royal College of St George at Windsor. The implication is that Guy's Cliffe was to be refounded on the very grandest scale. Its proposed endowment through a reclaimed estate is intriguing, too, implying some particular devotional or political concern. However, Richard Neville's plans came to nothing. According to Rous, George, duke of Clarence, also intended to fulfil the works at Guy's Cliffe proposed by his father-in-law, but died before anything could be done.[24]

Rous makes it clear that Guy's Cliffe was not a shrine: the body of the hero and his wife had been removed long before:

... at Gibclif were they both biried for ther cowd no man from thens remise hym tyl hys sworn broder sir Tyrry with home he was translate with owt let and un to thys day God for hys sake to tho that devoutly seke hym for her sekens with other grevis ar by miracle soen remedied ...[25]

He also distinguishes between Guy's martial and religious life. In the *Rous Roll* itself, Guy is portrayed in two large-scale drawings as a knight overcoming monsters, and dressed as a pilgrim with a halo and a rosary at his side. Rous, it seems, was most preoccupied by Guy as a religious figure and the last quotation goes on to read:

... and in remenbrans of hys habit [as a pilgrim] hyt were ful convenient, youe that hit plesyd, sum good lord or lady to fynd in the same place ij pore men that cowd help a prest to syng on of them to be ther continually present werying hys pilgrim habit and to show folk the place and theyr habitacion might be ful wel set over hys cave in the roke.

In other words, had a patron provided for two poor men to be attached to the chantry, a visitor would have been presented by two vivid images of this hero. On the wall would have stood a large, sculpted effigy of Guy as a knight, and attending divine service would have been a living man in the clothing of Guy as a prayerful recluse and a pilgrim. There is in this presentation of Guy more than an echo of St Christopher, who was also often represented on a large scale.

During the Reformation the chantry at Guy's Cliffe was twice valued by the king's commissioners, once in 1535 at £19 4s. 4d., and ten years later at £19 10s. 6d. In about the same period, the site was described by Leland:

There is a right goodly chapel of St Mary Magdalene upon Avon river, ripa dextra, scant a myle above Warwike. This place of some is caulyd Gibclif, of some Guy-clif; and old fame remaynethe with the people there, that Guydo Erle of Warwike in K. Athelstan's days had a great devotion to this place, and made an oratory there. Some adde unto [it,] that aftar he had done great victories in outward partes, and had bene so long absent that he was thought to have bene deade, he came and lyved in this place lyke an hermite, onknowne to his wife Felicia ontyll at the article of his deathe he shewyd what he was. Men shew a cave there in a rok hard on Avon ripe, where they say that he usyd to slepe. Men also yet showe fayr springs in a faire medow thereby, wher they say that Erle Guido was wont to drinke. This place had fore the tyme of Richard E. of Warwike only a smaule chappelle and a cottage wherin an heremite dwellyd.

Erle Richard beringe a greate devotion to the place made there a goodly chapel, dedicate to St Mary Magdalen, and founded 2. cantuars prists there [to serve God.] He set up there an ymage of E. Guido great lyke a giant, and enclosyd the silver welles in the medow with pure whit slike stone like marble, and ther set up a praty wood, antra in Saxo, the river rollynge with a praty noyse over the stones, nemusculum [ibidem opacum,] fonts liquidi [et jemnei] prate florida, [antra muscosa, rivi levis et per saxa discursus, necnon solitude et quies musis amicissima.][26]

As will become apparent, in his attribution of the sculpture of Guy to Richard Beauchamp, Leland is certainly mistaken. Following the dissolution of the chantry, Guy's Cliffe was granted in 1547 to Sir Andrew Flammock. The two last priests were Thomas Moore and Roger Higham.[27] What happened to the chantry buildings at this date is not clear, though they were evidently converted to domestic use.

Following the Reformation the earldom of Warwick passed to a succession of staunchly Protestant figures, who possibly targeted Guy's cult. Nevertheless, his reputation persisted to confront Celia Fiennes on a visit to Warwick Castle in 1697:

At ye Entrance of ye first Court ye porter diverts you wth a history of Guy Earle of Warwick, there is his walking staff 9 foote long and ye staff of a Gyant wch he kill'd thats 12 ffoote long; his sword,

Helmet and shield and breast and back all of a prodigious size, as is his wives jron slippers and also his horses armour and the pottage-pott for his supper-it was a yard over the top; there is also the bones of severall Beasts he kill'd, the Rib of ye Dun-Cow as bigg as halfe a great Cart Wheele: 2 miles from the town is his Cave dugg out by his own hands just ye dimention of his body as the Common people say, there is also his will Cut out on stone, but ye letters are much defaced; these are the storyes and meer ffiction, for the true history of Guy was that he was but a Little man in stature tho' great in mind and valour, which tradition describes to posterity by being a Gyant. Such will the account be of our Hero King William the third tho' Little in stature yet Great in atchievements and valour.[28]

Guy's memorabilia still greets modern visitors to the castle. It was first described in detail by Grose in *A Treatise on Ancient Arms and Armour* (London 1786), since when some pieces from it have been lost. It included at least two 14th-century heirlooms — Guy's coat of mail and his sword.[29]

There are parallels for this displaying the arms of fictional heroes in castles. At Arundel, the two-and-a-half-yard-long sword supposedly used by Bevis to vanquish the giant Ascupart was on display in 1634.[30] This 14th-century English sword still survives.[31] At Dover, King Arthur's association with the castle was celebrated both in the name of the great hall and by a set of bones of one of Mordred's victims.[32] Another Arthurian relic of this kind is the Round Table at Winchester. Quite as much as saints, England's chivalric heroes were provided with relics. The subject of secular pilgrimage remains to be properly explored.

Celia Fiennes also provides an intriguing reference to Guy's will. The illegible inscription to which she refers was possibly carved on a sunken panel in the roof of the cave where Guy reputedly slept. A rubbing of the inscription was published in 1876 and an enthusiastic epigrapher deciphered what has been claimed as a Saxon inscription reading (in translation), 'Cast out, thou Christ, from thy servant this burden, Guhthi'.[33] This reading seems implausible and the Saxon inscription is in fact a romantic invention, though it is possible that this panel once bore a medieval inscription.[34]

In 1751 Guy's Cliffe was sold to Samuel Greatheed, who redeveloped it as a Neo-classical house. As part of this work, he possibly added the tower to the chapel in 1764.[35] The house was further extended between 1813 and 1824 by Samuel's son, Bertie, who acted as his own architect. As part of this operation, or perhaps preceding it in 1802,[36] he restored the chapel, inserting plaster vaults and new windows into the building.[37] His work reflects an impressive understanding of the 14th-century buildings in Warwick. Further Gothic alterations were made in 1898 by the then owner, Lord Algernon Percy. In 1946 the house was sold as a hotel and six years later the interior was stripped of fittings. By 1966 it was becoming ruinous and in 1989 it was further damaged by fire during the filming of a Sherlock Holmes drama.[38] The extant buildings are currently the home to several Masonic Lodges, who maintain and repair them.

THE MEDIEVAL BUILDINGS

OUR best introduction to the early buildings at Guy's Cliffe is Dugdale's mid-17th-century topographical view (Fig. 1).[39] From right to left there are labelled the Still House [I], the House [L] and the Chapel [K]. Both of the former may have been substantially medieval structures created in the 1450s for the priests who served the chapel. Their fabric may also have incorporated the remains of the 'mansion' built by Thomas Beauchamp before his death in 1401. Unfortunately, nothing obviously remains of either in the confusing ruins, which are only partially accessible.

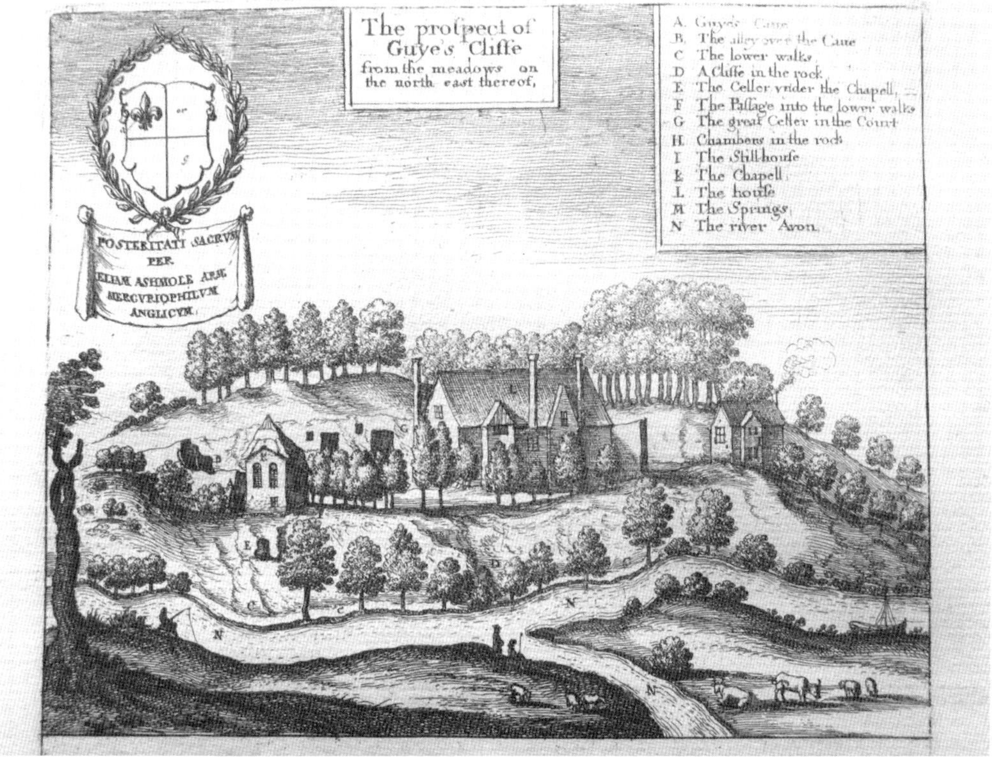

FIG. 1. Guy's Cliffe, engraving

Dugdale, Warwickshire *(1730)*

To the left of the house are two pairs of rectangular openings cut into the rock. One [G] is identified as the great cellar. Numerous tunnels and openings cut into this cliff still remain and none can be accurately dated on the basis of architectural details. The tunnels could be medieval in origin and one of them preserves a door of *c.* 1500 from Wellesbourne church.[40] Shown in the engraving below the house, on the edge of the river, is the spring.

Immediately to the bottom left of the chapel is 'Guy's Cave' [A], where the hero slept. This survives, though restored and reinforced, as does the cellar [E] under the chapel. The chapel itself is depicted as a freestanding building. Its timber-frame roof structure was replaced in the 19th century and there is now an upper chamber contrived within the building. There are two windows in the east gable end, both of which still survive but with restored tracery. The undercroft window below, and the chapel side window shown in the engraving, have also been replaced in the 19th century.

In its present form the chapel reflects the rebuilding of the 1450s. The interior is divided by an arcade of two broad arches with partially mutilated mouldings to create space for two altars (Fig. 2 and Col. Pl. XXIIA in print edn). There is no evidence for a medieval vault and the interior was almost certainly ceiled in timber. Two medieval doors survive in the building. The larger in the north wall probably served as the original entrance, though it does not appear on Dugdale's engraving. That to the south

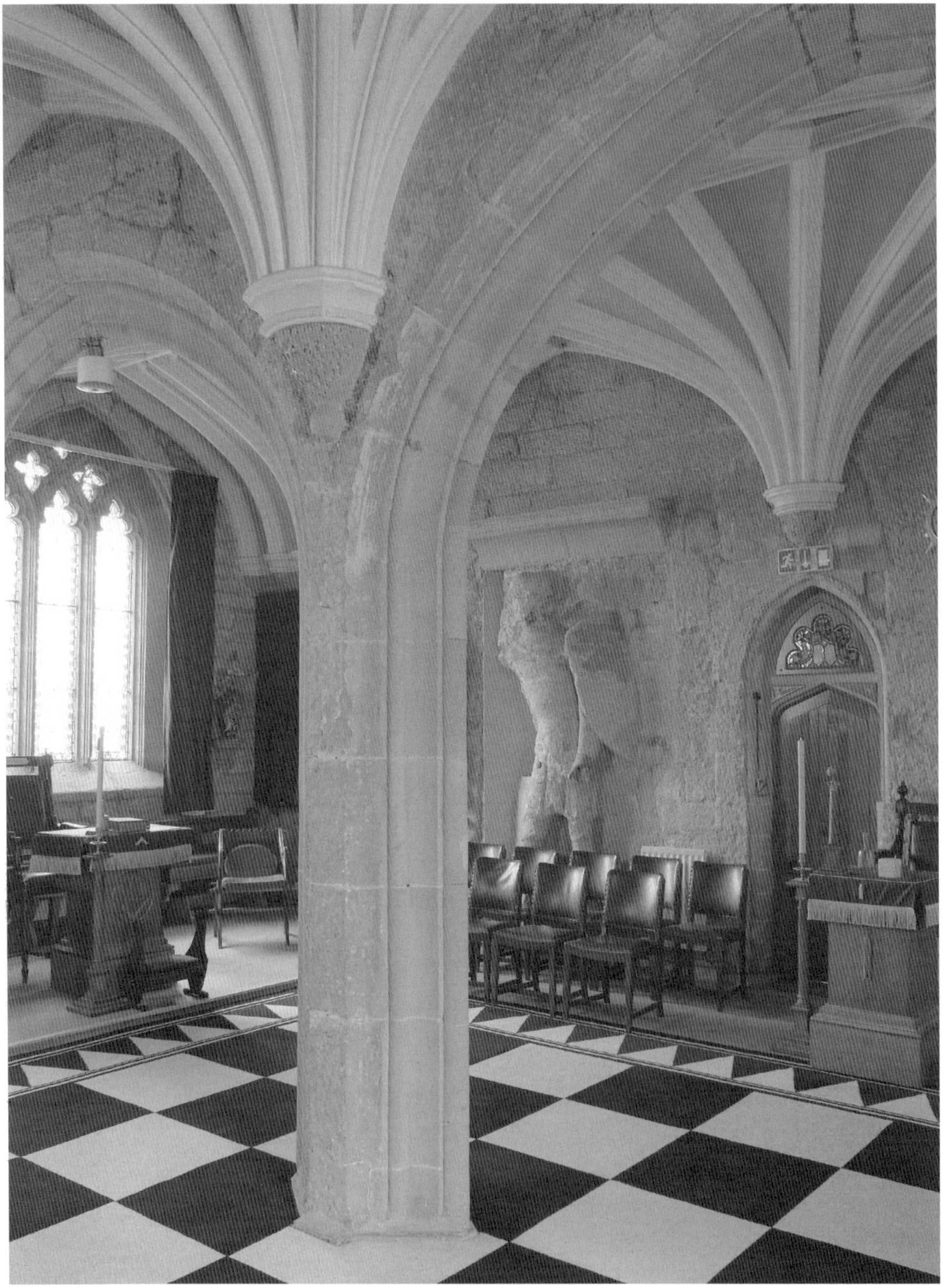

Fig. 2. Guy's Cliffe: chapel interior
Photo, Paul Barker/Country Life

may have led to a sacristy, a structure now entirely rebuilt and enlarged. This door cuts through an earlier window, possibly evidence that the 1450s chapel incorporated the remains of an earlier building. There are also two single-light windows, both probably part of the 1450s fabric. In all their technical details, the features of the 1450s work closely resemble those found at St Mary's church, Warwick, both in the church of 1367–97 and in the Beauchamp Chapel begun in the 1440s.[41]

The most remarkable internal survival within the chapel is the statue of Guy of Warwick, which stands under a broad canopy (Fig. 3 and Col. Pl. XXIIB in print edn). This larger-than-life figure is cut onto an outcrop of living rock within the south wall. Today the sculpture is badly damaged, but it was evidently of high quality. Figures on this scale cut from the living rock are very rare in England. The most obvious parallels for it are the sculpture of 1408 of St George at the Chapel of Our Lady of the Crag at Knaresborough (Yorks.; Fig. 4)[42] and the Nativity group in the so-called Hermitage at Warkworth (Northumb.).[43]

Rous records that the Duke of Clarence had proposed to paint the effigy of Guy but that his death intervened before the work was undertaken (see above). Considering

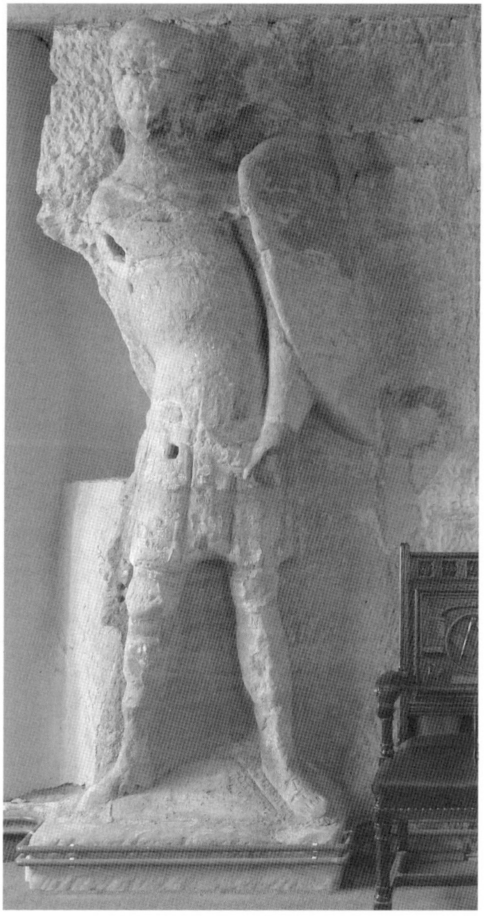

FIG. 3. Guy's Cliffe: chapel, statue of Guy of Warwick, 1340s
Photo, Paul Barker/Country Life

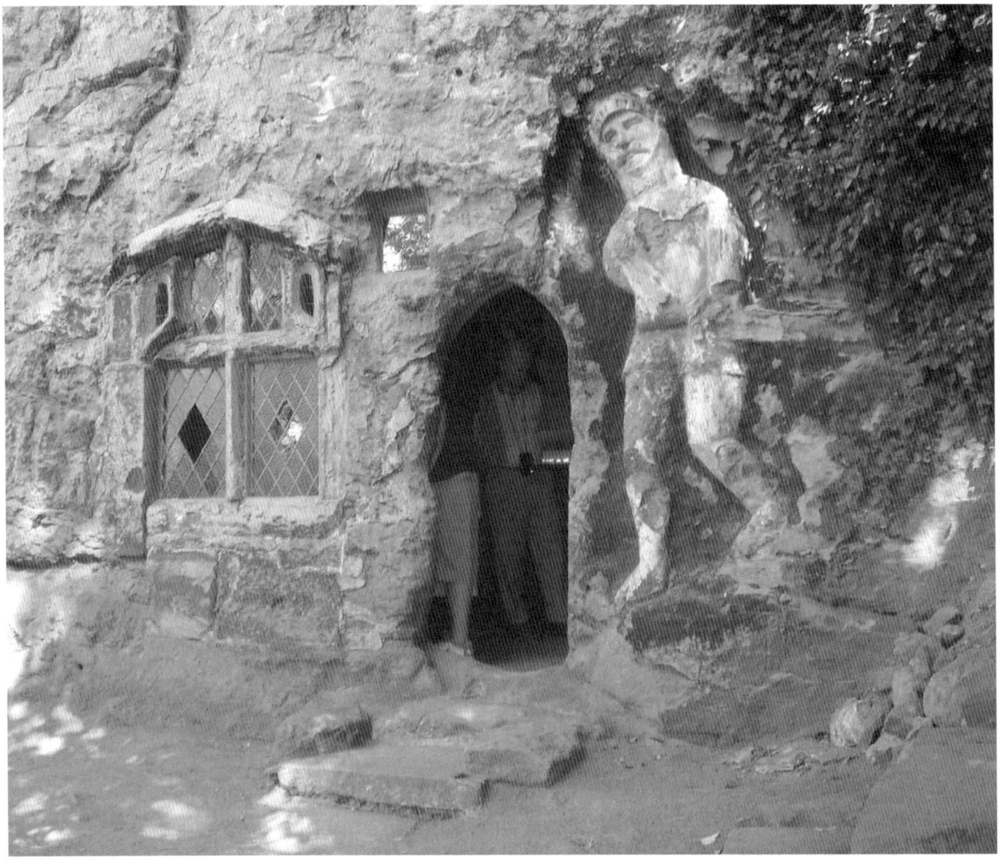

FIG. 4. Knaresborough: the chapel of Our Lady of Crag at Knaresborough
Photo, author

how widespread the practice of painting sculpture was in the middle ages, it is likely that Rous was referring to the votive redecoration of this figure rather than its first colouration. In fact, fragments of colour do survive on the sculpture, particularly around the head. They are now impossible to date, but it is likely that they at least replace a medieval scheme. Early engravings show that considerably more paint survived on the figure up until the mid-19th century. They also indicate that the shield was decorated with the ancient arms of the earls of Warwick.[44] From the late 14th century, many noble families made use of so-called ancient arms as a means of illustrating in heraldry the depth of their dynastic history.[45] Guy's arms were in fact borrowed from the Newburgh earls of Warwick, the dynasty from whom the Beauchamps inherited the title. In giving the effigy these arms, Guy was being explicitly tied into their dynastic past.

The essential details of the statue's dress and posture can still be discerned (Fig. 3). Guy is shown standing in a coat of mail, covered by a short surcoat that drops to the thighs. There is no visible evidence for cuisses but the outlines of poleyns protecting the knees are legible. The sword belt is slung below the waist and the shield on the right arm is supported by a strap over the left shoulder. A detachable coif is secured around the face and throat and there is an arming cap on the top of the head. The figure is animated, twisting round in a sinuous pose. One arm is entirely broken off at the shoulder, but the posture suggests that Guy was shown in the act of drawing his sword. This action is commonplace in English funeral effigies from the late 13th century onwards, such as the knight at Dorchester (Oxon.). It is also the posture of the much restored figure of St George at Knaresborough (Fig. 4).

Confusingly, Dugdale's engraving shows the figure of Guy with the left hand held out and the right hand clasping a drawn sword (Fig. 5). It is extremely difficult to reconcile this with the surviving sculpture or offer convincing parallels for it. The likelihood is that the artist saw the image much in its present form and inaccurately reconstructed its missing elements.

The form of the armour — combining mail and knee plates — as well as the sinuous pose suggest an early 14th-century date. In both points, the figure departs from the stiff, plate-armoured images of knights that became common from the 1360s onwards. The representation of the body helps further to narrow this dating. Particularly distinctive

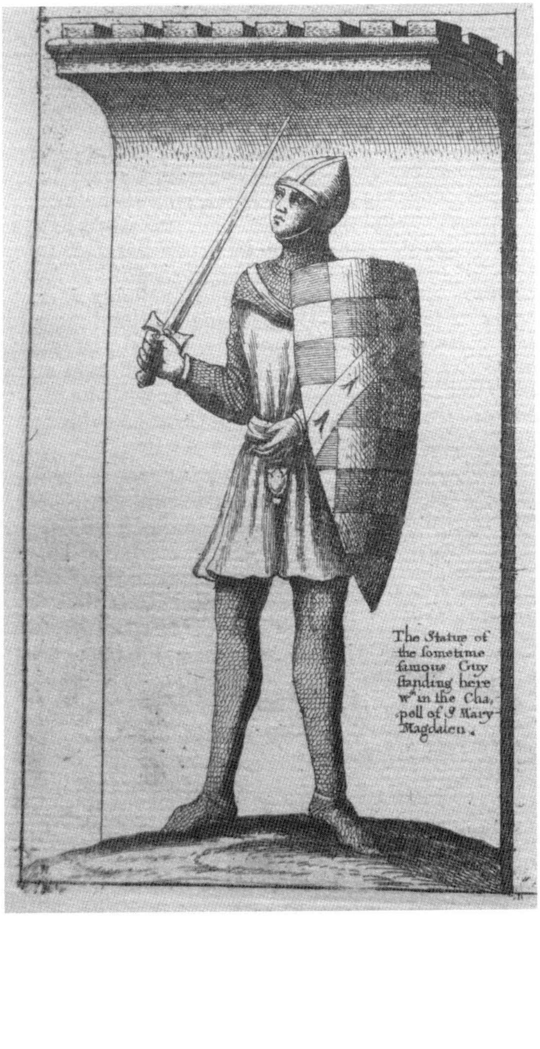

FIG. 5. Guy's Cliffe: the statue of Guy of Warwick, engraving
Dugdale, Warwickshire *(1730)*

is the carefully modelled torso with a bulging chest and flat stomach, which can be paralleled in sculpture of the 1330s and 1340s, as for example at Aldworth (Berks., Fig. 6). The Aldworth figure also shares with Guy an unusual monumentality, and because Guy did not have a reputation in the middle ages for great stature, this treatment is also arguably a point of stylistic comparison between the two. Incidentally, the chapel sculpture appears to have informed the later tradition that Guy was a giant, as noted and dismissed, for example, by Celia Fiennes.

It seems reasonable to infer from this evidence that figure of Guy was carved when the hermitage was first founded around 1330, and that it was preserved when the chapel was rebuilt in the 1450s. This earlier dating of the sculpture makes good sense from a historical perspective. There is evidence of a perceived connection between the earls of Warwick and Guy from the late 13th century onwards. The first figure, however, to show an intense interest in this was Thomas Beauchamp I (d.1369). He was involved in a very successful military career and became a founder member of the Order of the Garter. The first hint of his particular interest in this ancestral hero comes with the naming of his first son as 'Guy', probably born around 1330. Then, more explicitly, he called his third son 'Reinbrun', the name of the child supposedly conceived by Guy on his nuptial night.[46] His will of 1369 makes mention of '. . . the coat of mail sometime

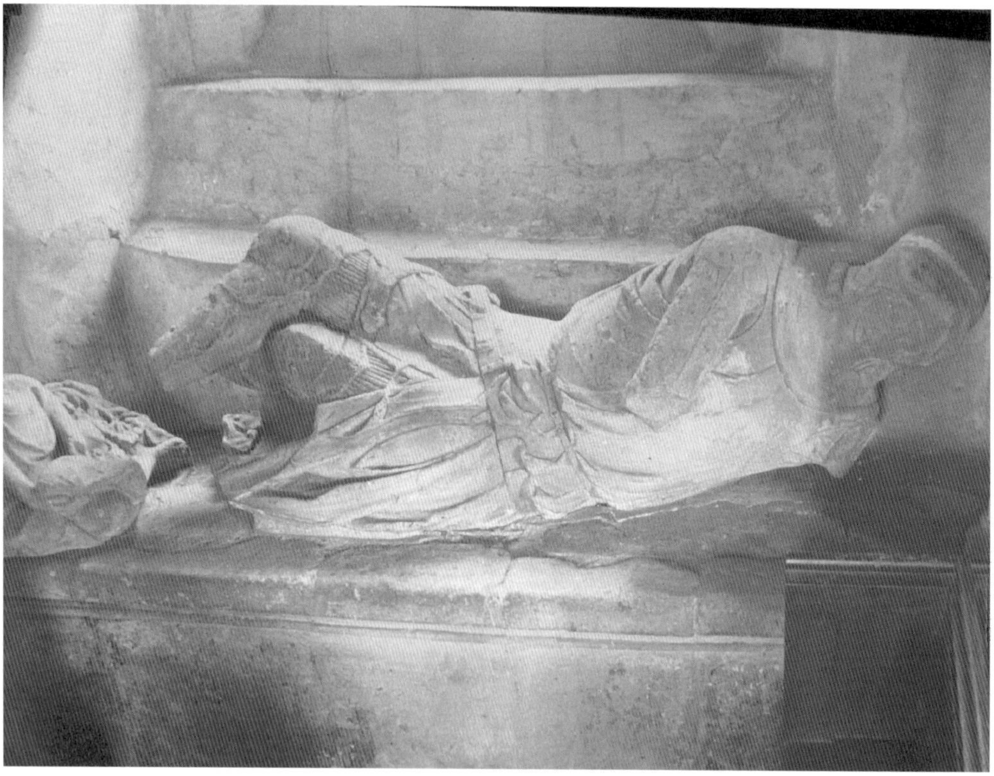

FIG. 6. St Mary's church, Aldworth (Berks.), one of the de la Beche effigies
Photo, Society of Antiquaries of London

belonging to that famous Guy of Warwick', which he bequeathed to his son and heir, Thomas II.[47] This is the first documented reference to any relic of Guy. It is very likely that this enthusiasm for Guy was fired by Edward III's parallel interest in the mythical ancestor of the English royal line, King Arthur.[48]

Over the lifetime of Thomas II (d. 1401), the family association with Guy was further developed. In 1397 Thomas brought to completion the east facade of Warwick Castle, begun in the 1340s by his father. [49] Its final element was the north-east tower, long known as Guy's Tower.[50] It is uncertain when this name first came into currency, but it is just possible that this immensely tall tower was intended from the first to be understood as the one climbed by the hero on his nuptial night. Other families made similar associations: at Raby (Co. Durham), for example, the Neville family celebrated their ancestor called Bulmer[51] by adding two panels carved with the letter 'b' to a late 14th-century tower in their castle.[52] John, Lord Neville (d. 1388), also used Bulmer's initial on his signet seal.[53]

In 1397, Thomas also finished the nave of St Mary's, Warwick, the burial church of his dynasty.[54] This operation was the final stage in a rebuilding programme that had probably been begun by his father in 1367, when all the parishes of Warwick were integrated under the control of the college.[55] As part of his work to the church some time before this, Thomas furnished the interior of the chancel, where the project of reconstruction had begun, and he probably commissioned his parents' tomb (see Monckton, Fig. 16). In the chancel and the adjacent transepts, stained glass images were installed of all his siblings. The glass has been lost, but its details are engraved in Dugdale.[56] It can be dated on the basis of the double representation of his sister Isabel (d. 1416), once as the wife of John, Lord Strange of Blakemere (d. 1375), and again as the wife of William Ufford, earl of Suffolk, whom she married on or before 12 June 1376.[57] It was presumably created, therefore, between 1376 and 1397.

This unusually large collection of familial imagery was complemented by a sculpture of Guy of Warwick. The existence of this figure is known through a reference in 1395 to 'one John Sutton, a carver, who did cut the arms of the Ancient Earl's of Warwick upon it'. [58] It is an intriguing subject of speculation as to where this figure stood or the form it took. Whatever the case, it explicitly linked the Beauchamp family with their mythical ancestor in this mausoleum church.

Meanwhile, it is in Thomas' lifetime that the first references occur to a suit of hangings depicting the life and arms of Guy of Warwick. This set of tapestries is known to have hung in Warwick Castle in 1399.[59] It was, moreover, of such perceived value that it received a specific mention in the earl's will of 1400 as '... wrought with the arms and story of Guy of Warwick ...'.[60] The set was bequeathed to the earl's son, along with the coat of mail belonging to Guy that Thomas had received from his own father. To this heirloom was then added Guy's sword, harness and 'ragged staves', the heraldic emblem of the earls of Warwick.[61]

The spirit in which such relics and representations of Guy were received by contemporaries in the 14th century is not easy to reconstruct. It is tempting to assume that a medieval audience understood the earls of Warwick literally to be the descendants of this hero, and his exploits as fact. However, it is more likely that they saw the links between the earls of Warwick and Guy as constructed but meaningful, just as idealised images of the world in *mappa mundi* coexisted from the 14th century with charts that aimed at topographical accuracy. In an age where ancestry was one of the crucial credentials for political power, the idea of a noble line extending back in time out of mind was hugely prestigious. Identifying an ancestral hermitage not far from the inherited castle and seat of the earls made that depth of history tangible. It allowed Guy and his fantastical feats to flirt engagingly with reality.

ACKNOWLEDGEMENTS

I am very grateful to Terry Roberts, Alixe Bovey and Philip Lankester in the preparation of this paper, a shorter version of which appeared in *Country Life*, 21 July 2010, 63–6.

NOTES

1. Useful critical editions include M. Mills and D. Huws ed., *Fragments of an Early Fourteenth-Century Guy of Warwick* (Oxford 1974); J. Zupitza ed., *The Romance of Guy of Warwick*, EETS, early series, 25/26 (London 1875–76). A stanzaic version of the text edited by A. Wiggins can be found on http://www.lib.rochester.edu/camelot/teams/guywint.htm. The most important recent study of Guy is V. B. Richmond, *The Legend of Guy of Warwick* (New York 1996).
2. N. Orme, 'Rous, John (*c*.1420–1492)', *Oxford Dictionary of National Biography* (Oxford 2004) [http://www.oxforddnb.com/view/article/24173, accessed 15 May 2008].
3. *The Rous Rol*, ed. W. Courthope (London 1845), no. 6.
4. D. E. Thornton, 'Dyfrig (supp. fl. *c*.475–*c*.525)', *ODNB* [http://www.oxforddnb.com/view/article/8124, accessed 15 May 2008].
5. Dugdale, *Warwickshire* (1730), 373.
6. J. Nichols ed., *The Progresses and Public Processions of Queen Elizabeth* (London 1823), 1, 428.
7. *Calendar of Patent Rolls*, 1330–34 (London 1893), 543.
8. There is evidence for a wider growth in the popularity of Guy at exactly this period, including several impressive illuminated manuscript cycles depicting his exploits; see A. Bovey, 'A Pictorial Ex Libris in the Smithfield Decretals: John Batayle, Canon of St Bartholomew's, and his Illuminated Law Book', in *Decoration and Illustration in Medieval English Manuscripts: English Manuscript Studies* 10 (2002), 60–82.
9. *Rous Rol*, no. 32.
10. B. Golding, 'Robert of Knaresborough (d. 1218?)', *ODNB* [http://www.oxforddnb.com/view/article/23733, accessed 12 June 2008].
11. *Rous Rol*, no. 48.
12. Dugdale, *Warwickshire* (1730), 273.
13. Y. Liu, 'Richard Beauchamp and the Uses of Romance', *Medium Aevum* 74 (2005), 271–87; C. Fewster, *Traditionality and Genre in Middle English Romance* (Cambridge 1987); E. Mason, 'Legends of the Beauchamps' ancestors: the use of baronial propaganda in Medieval England', *Journal of Medieval History* 10 (1984), 25–40.
14. *Rous Rol*, no. 50.
15. An Elizabethan charter makes it clear that the Mary of the dedication was Mary Magdalene not the Virgin; Dugdale, *Warwickshire* (1730), 275. She was a saint commonly associated with hermitages as a result of her own supposed retirement to the wilderness; Jacobus de Voragine, *The Golden Legend*, trans. W. G. Ryan, 1 (Princeton 1993), 380.
16. *Calendar of Patent Rolls*, 1422–29 (London 1901), 136.
17. J. A. A. Goodall, *God's House at Ewelme* (Aldershot 2001), 110, 310.
18. *Calendar of Patent Rolls*, 1429–36 (London 1907), 100.
19. VCH *Warwickshire* II, 124–9.
20. Dugdale, *Warwickshire* (1730), 273.
21. P. B. Chatwin, 'Documents of Warwick the Kingmaker, in possession of St Mary's Church, Warwick', *TBAS* 59 (1935), 8.
22. For a short discussion of this dynastic patronage with references to further reading, see A. Payne, 'The Beauchamps and the Nevilles', in *Gothic Art for England 1400–1547*, ed. R. Marks and P. Williamson (London 2003), 219–21.
23. *Rous Rol*, no. 57.
24. *Rous Rol*, no. 59.
25. *Rous Rol*, no. 22.

26. L. T. Smith ed., *The Itinerary of John Leland in or about the Years 1535–1543* 2 (London 1907–10), 45–6.
27. Dugdale, *Warwickshire* (1730), 498.
28. C. Fiennes, *Through England on a Side Saddle in the Time of William and Mary*, ed. Mrs Griffiths (London 1888), 95.
29. I. Eaves and T. Richardson, 'The Warwick Shaffron', *Journal of the Arms & Armour Society* 12, pt 4 (Sept 1987), 217–22 and pls LXXII–LXXVII. I am grateful to Philip Lankester for this reference.
30. Lieutenant Hammond, 'A Relation of a short Survey of the Western Counties', ed. L. G. Wickham-Legg, *Camden Miscellany* 16 (1936), 31.
31. I am grateful to John Martin Robinson for the details of this sword.
32. *Leland's Itinerary*, 4, 55.
33. J. T. Burgess, *Historic Warwickshire* (London 1876), 102.
34. N. Pevsner and A. Wedgwood, *Warwickshire* B/E (1966), 302.
35. According to an 1895 memorial brass in the chapel. Transcribed in A. F. Porter, *A Short History of St Mary Magdalene Chapel Guy's Cliffe Warwick*, 4th edn (Warwick 2005), 18; VCH *Warwickshire* VIII, 535.
36. The 1895 memorial brass dates the work to 1802.
37. VCH *Warwickshire* VIII, 535, dates the vaults to 1819 and 1824. I have not pursued these contradictory datings.
38. VCH *Warwickshire* VIII, 442.
39. Dugdale, *Warwickshire* (1730), 274.
40. VCH *Warwickshire* VIII, 535.
41. Though, confusingly, so do the details of later restorations.
42. Abbot Cummins, 'The Cave Chapels of Knaresborough', *Yorkshire Archaeological Journal* 28 (1926), 80–8.
43. J. A. A. Goodall, *Warkworth Castle and Hermitage*, English Heritage guidebook (London 2006), 28–31.
44. The fragmentary painting is very clear in the frontispiece of *The Noble and Renowned History of Guy, Earl of Warwick* (Chiswick 1821).
45. See J. A. A. Goodall, *The English Castle* (New Haven and London 2011), ch. 10.
46. Dugdale, *Warwickshire* (1730), 399.
47. N. H. Nicholas, *Testamenta Vetusta* 1 (London 1826), 79.
48. Recent contributions to the literature on this interest are to be found in J. Munby, R. Barber and R. Brown ed., *Edward III's Round Table at Windsor* (Stroud 2007).
49. R. K. Morris, 'The Architecture of the Earls of Warwick in the 14th Century', in *England in the Fourteenth Century*, ed. W. M. Ormrod (Woodbridge 1986), 170–3.
50. Dugdale, *Warwickshire* (1730), 401 note a, 427.
51. Or Berthram Bulmer according to Leland; *Leland's Itinerary*, 1, 75.
52. M. Hislop, 'The Castle of Ralph 4th Baron Neville at Raby', *Archaeologia Aeliana*, 5th Series, 20 (1992), 93–4.
53. J. F. Hodgson, 'Raby. In three Chapters', *Transactions of the Architectural and Archaeological Society of Durham and Northumberland* 3 (1880–85), 171.
54. Dugdale, *Warwickshire* (1730), 401.
55. VCH *Warwickshire* II, 124–9.
56. Dugdale, *Warwickshire* (1730), 398 and 400.
57. G. E. Cokayne, *Complete Peerage*, 12, pt 1 (London 1953), 433.
58. W. Dugdale, *The Antiquities of Warwickshire Illustrated* (Coventry 1765), 312b, cited in Anon., 'Report of the Summer Meetings 1924, Guy's Cliffe', *TBAS* 50 (1924), 64–6.
59. Dugdale, *Warwickshire* (1730), 402; *Cal. Pat.*, 1399–1401, 202.
60. Nicolas, *Testamenta Vetusta*, 1, 154; *Calendar of Inquisitions Miscellaneous (Chancery)* (London 1963), VI, 1392–99, item 307.
61. Nicolas, *Testamenta Vetusta*, 1, 154; Dugdale, *Warwickshire* (1730), 399.

The College of St Mary in the Newarke, Leicester

JOHN A. A. GOODALL

No consideration of early Perpendicular architecture in the midlands would be complete without reference to the lost College of St Mary in the Newarke at Leicester. This short architectural analysis aims to highlight the potential significance of the church and college as formative works in the Perpendicular style. It speculates on their relationship to the 14th-century remodelling of St Mary's, Warwick, and the great hall of Kenilworth Castle.

THE College of the Annunciation of St Mary in the Newarke was founded in 1354 by Henry of Grosmont and incorporated a hospital established by his father in 1330. It stood in a specially created bailey of Leicester Castle called the 'new work' just outside the town walls (Fig. 1). By the circumstances and terms of its foundation, the new college was a religious institution of the first importance in the English realm.[1] It was established three years after Henry of Grosmont was created duke of Lancaster, a title that recognised his position as the premier nobleman in England.

At the time, the Black Prince, Edward III's son and the heir to the throne, was the only other figure ever to have enjoyed the high dignity of a dukedom in England. The college expressed by its constitution the exceptional status of its founder: besides the hospital with an unusually large community of one hundred paupers and ten nurses, the foundation was served by a dean, twelve canons, thirteen vicars, three other clerks and a verger.[2] This composition must have been inspired by the collegiate foundations established by Edward III at Windsor and Westminster in 1348, as well as their immediate model, the Sainte Chapelle in Paris.

The latter association with the chapel of the kings of France in their palace on the Ile de la Cité was made explicit, moreover, by the gift to the Leicester college of a relic from the Crown of Thorns. This was a fragment of the chief relic of the Sainte Chapelle, which had been chosen at the invitation of the French king by the duke of Lancaster as a gift.[3] In only one detail did the foundation materially differ from the palace colleges of the English and French kings that it imitated: it was intended from the first as a dynastic mausoleum. The duke was himself laid to rest in the church, which continued to attract Lancastrian and other notable burials throughout the later middle ages. The college enjoyed a sequence of outstandingly powerful patrons and in 1545 its annual income was assessed as £842 2s. 6d. This income put the college on the same financial level as some of the greatest of the recently suppressed abbeys.[4]

Frustratingly little is known of the buildings created to house this college. Work may have begun in October 1351, when the duke was authorised to press masons and carpenters for the repair of the hospital buildings.[5] More probably, however, the comprehensive reconstruction of the entire collegiate and hospital complex was organised

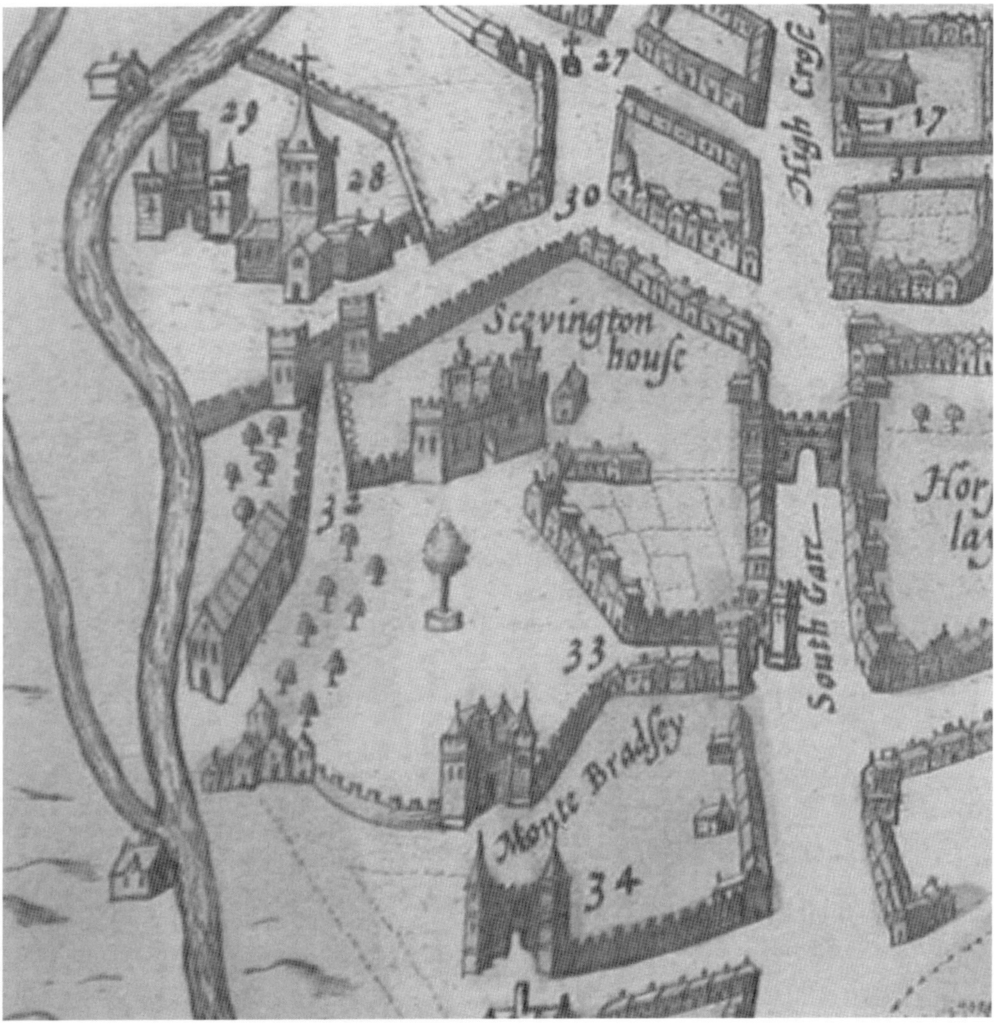

FIG. 1. The site of the Newarke, from John Speed's map of Leicester, published 1612. Top left is the castle (29) and St Mary de Castro; lower left, the surviving hospital range (32); lower right, at South Gate, the gatehouse which survives today (right of 33)

Courtesy of the Society of Antiquaries of London

in close conjunction with the foundation of the new institution in 1354. Whatever the case, certain details of the plan must have been established by the date the statutes were promulgated on 24 March 1356 because these makes certain specific topographical references. For example, the Lady Chapel is described in them as standing to the south of the church, a detail corroborated by other sources. In addition, there is mention of certain specific buildings including the chapter house.[6]

Nevertheless, construction was slow and work was evidently far from complete at the time of the duke's death in 1361. His heir, John of Gaunt, gave a yearly grant of

100 marks from his honour of Tutbury to meet the building costs. These funds were evidently insufficient, because on 16 February 1397 the master mason of the duchy of Lancaster, Robert Skillington, received a licence to gather twenty-four masons, carpenters and workmen and materials to complete the 'work begun by Henry, late duke, of erecting a church at Leycestre in honour of the Annunciation of St Mary, and diverse houses and buildings for the habitation of canons, chaplains and infirm persons living there'.[7]

However, progress must have faltered again, because on 8 November 1414, Henry V also took up the task, issuing a writ for the hire of twenty-four masons, carpenters and workmen along with materials for the project. His writ rehearses that

> the king's great grandfather founded it [the college] and began to construct certain houses, walls and buildings for the enclosure of the church and college and the habitation of the canons, clerks and infirm; and John, late duke of Lancaster, the king's grandfather, desired to complete the works and the king wishes to accelerate them.[8]

There is no documentary reference to further substantial adaptation of the collegiate buildings.

Following the suppression of the college in 1548 the church seems to have been immediately demolished, probably along with the principal collegiate buildings; it had certainly disappeared by 1590.[9] The plan of the church was briefly brought to light in about 1690 but no record of what was exposed now survives.[10] Meanwhile, the precinct was intensively developed as a prosperous enclave of the city. Curiously, the popularity of the Newarke amongst the rich burgesses of Leicester was connected to the history of the site: the extra parochial status enjoyed by the college exempted later occupants of the precinct from such responsibilities as contributions to the Poor Rates. Only the hospital, which survived the Reformation as a functioning institution, preserved its medieval buildings, though these have been heavily adapted and repaired over time.

The college precinct was further subject to intrusive 20th-century development. As late as 1902, 100ft of the hospital were demolished to make way for a new road. The site of the collegiate church, meanwhile, has been entirely overbuilt. Part of it was exposed to view in 1935, but again no architectural fragments from it or detailed records of the foundations appear to survive.[11] As a result, only four significant elements of the college exist today: the curtailed hospital range with an ancillary building (Fig. 2); a pair of re-erected arches that now stand in the basement of the Hawthorn Building of De Montfort University on the site, of uncertain provenance (Fig. 3);[12] sections of the precinct wall; and the gatehouse, now depressingly marooned in the centre of an arterial road (Fig. 4).

This last survival, the gatehouse, is a building of considerable interest with several very unusual architectural details. These include arches with straight-sided heads; ring bosses in the entrance passage vault and circular corner turrets that project at parapet level (Figs 4–6). There is no documentary evidence to date the gatehouse, but it could date to the 1350s;[13] ring bosses first appear at this time in royal building projects.[14] Likewise, corner turrets are found for the first time in English buildings from the 1330s, as for example, the great tower at Edlington (Northumb., *c.* 1340) or the barbican gate at Lewes (Sussex, *c.* 1334).[15] Finally, the distinctive arch outline is found in the Perpendicular work undertaken by John of Gaunt at Kenilworth Castle from September 1373.

In the absence of sufficient physical evidence, the best description of the collegiate buildings is provided by the antiquarian, John Leland, around 1540. He wrote:

The collegiate chirch of Newarke and the area of it yoinith to another peace of castelle ground. The college chirch is not very great, but it is exeding fair. There lyith on the north side of the high altare Henry Erle of Lancaster, withowt crounet, and 2. men childern under the arche nexte on to his hedde. On the southe side lyith Henry the first Duke of Lancaster; and in the next arche to his hedde lyith a lady, by likelihood his wife. Constance, doughtter to Peter, King of Castelle, and wife to John of Gaunt, liith afore the high altare in a tumbe of marble with an image of brasse like a queen on it. There is a tumbe of marble in the body of the quire. They told me that a countes of Darby lay biried in it . . . In the chapelle of S. Mary on the southe side of the quire ly buried t[w]o of the Shirleys, knights, with their wives; and one Brokesby an esquire. Under a piller in a chapelle of the south crosse isle lyith the Lady Hungreford, and Sacheverel her second husbande. In the southe side of the body of the chirch lyith one of the Bluntes, a knight, with his wife. And on the north side of the chirch ly 3 Wigestons, great benefactors to the college. One of them was a prebendarie there and made the fre Grammar Schole. The cloister on the south weste side of the church is large and faire: and the houses in the cumpace of the area of the college for the prebendaries be al very praty. The waulles and gates of the college be stately. The riche Cardinal of Winchester gildid al the floures and knottes in the voulte of the chirch. The large almose house stondith also withyn the quadrante of the area of the college.[16]

From this description, the following can be said about the form of the lost buildings. The college church was small, but unusually sumptuous. It was cruciform in plan and constructed with a high vault of stone, both features that allied it with the tradition of great church building. Leland's description of monuments suggests that there were aisles flanking the east end, of which the southern served as the Lady Chapel. Also, the transepts had at least one aisle. The description of the cloister to the south-west of

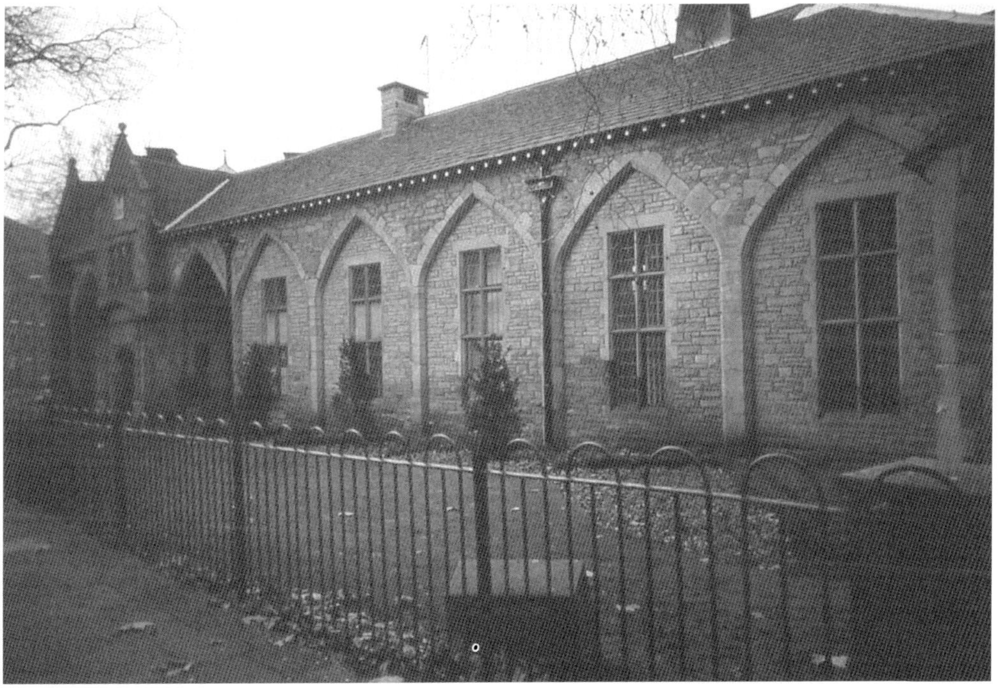

FIG. 2. Leicester, the Newarke: the remains of the hospital range, from the south-east
Photo, R. K. Morris

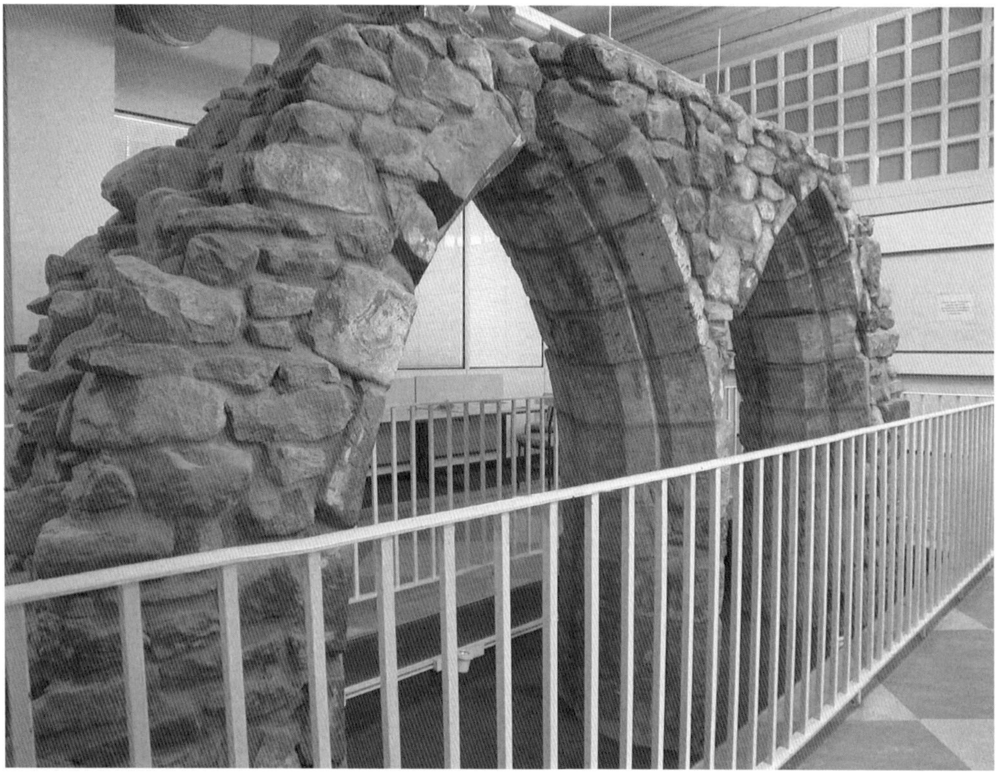

FIG. 3. Leicester, De Montfort University: re-erected arcades from the Newarke in the basement of the Hawthorn Building
Photo, author

the church is curious in one point: by implication it was not the architectural hub of the whole complex (as in a conventional monastic plan) because the houses of the canons were not all arranged immediately around it, but spread across the precinct.[17]

To Leland's description a few additional details may be added. It is known from records of excavation that the church stood to the south-east of the hospital range. Also, it can be inferred from a survey of 1546 that there was a freestanding steeple. This is clear because there was a house described as standing between the 'great steeple' and the church.[18]

In the absence of satisfactory evidence, the architectural character of the collegiate buildings must remain a matter for speculation. It is an attractive possibility, however, that they followed the artistic lead of their institutional models — the English royal chapels at Windsor and Westminster — as early works in the Perpendicular style. Certainly, the Lancastrian Works were demonstrably connected to the King's Works in the early 14th century, as evidenced, for example, by the early 14th-century use of rectangular towers respectively at Dunstanburgh Castle (from 1313) and Pickering Castle (from 1323). There is good reason to suppose, therefore, that its leading craftsmen would have been receptive to the ideas developed by Edward III's masons.[19]

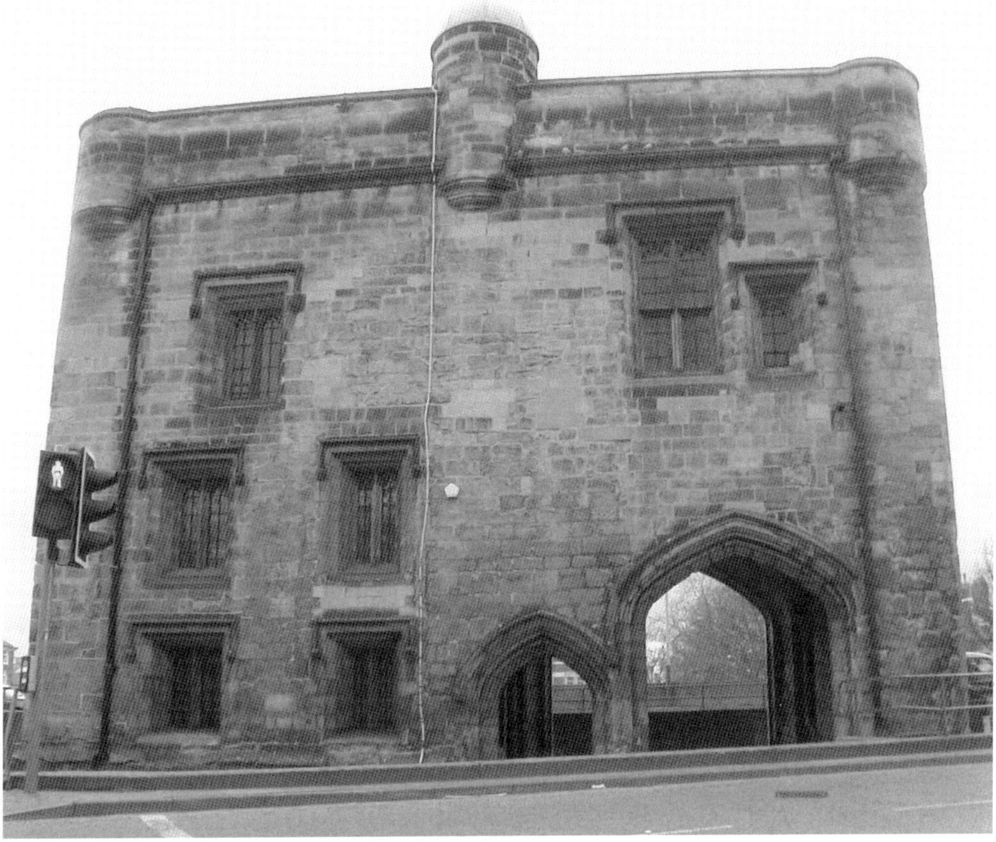

FIG. 4. Leicester, the Newarke gatehouse: entrance façade
Photo, author

A few features of the college may substantiate this suggestion. The independent design of the canon's lodgings and the cloister, for example, and the existence of a freestanding steeple echo arrangements at the college of St Stephen at Westminster (after 1354) and New College, Oxford (begun 1379), modelled on Edward III's works at Windsor. Similarly, as has been mentioned, the details of the surviving gate (though undated) point to a possible connection with the King's Works.

Further clues as to the appearance of the lost church, however, may be provided by another collegiate foundation that Our Lady of Newarke almost certainly influenced. Thomas Beauchamp, earl of Warwick, was a founder member of the Order of the Garter. It was very probably as a result of his membership to this exclusive group that he determined to create his own reformed college of St Mary beside his castle and seat at Warwick. In 1367 the earl integrated all the parishes of Warwick under the umbrella of St Mary's and, probably at the same time, began the work of reconstructing the church.[20] As at Leicester, the church was cruciform in plan[21] and the surviving chancel, one of the most inventive works of the early Perpendicular style, is vaulted in stone (Monckton, Fig. 16).[22]

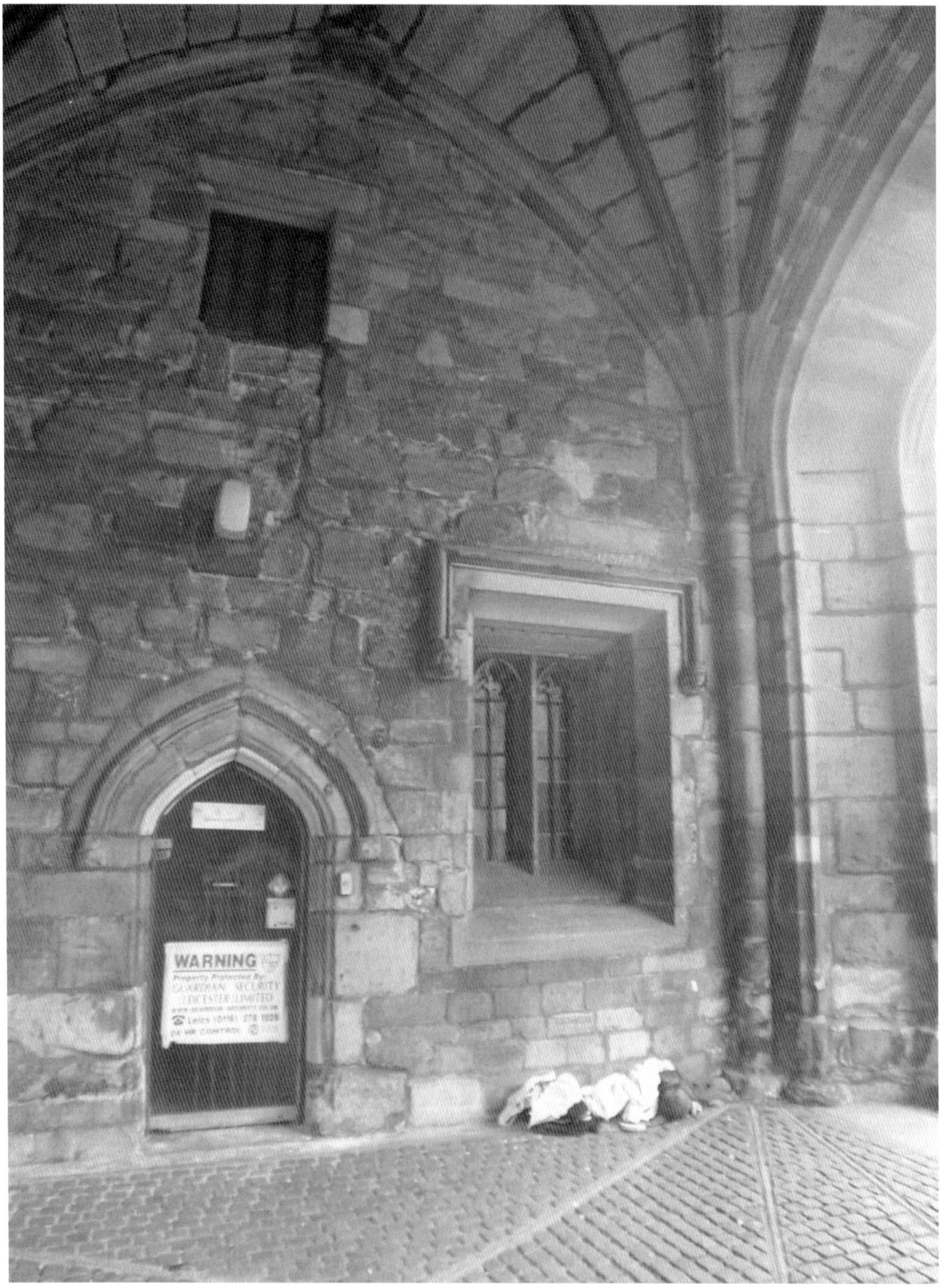

FIG. 5. Leicester, the Newarke gatehouse: the passage, detail
Photo, author

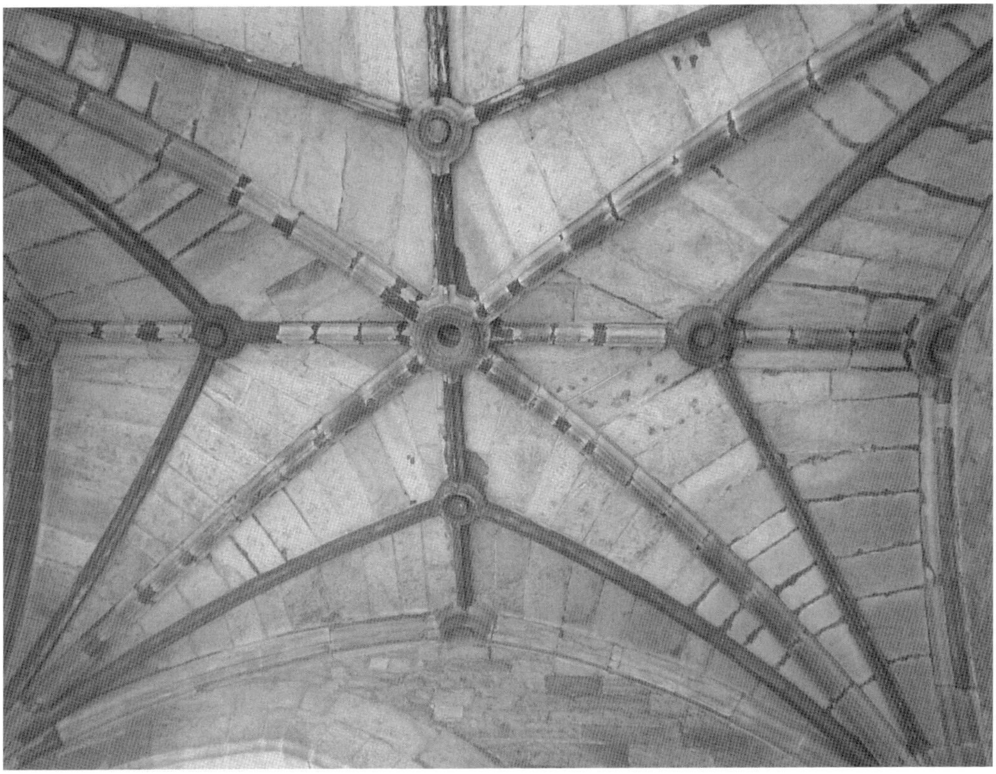

FIG. 6. Leicester, the Newarke gatehouse: the vault
Photo, author

Some details of this building, along with those of the Warwick chancel and its associated chapter-house, were to be incorporated into John of Gaunt's works at nearby Kenilworth in the 1370s.[23] One possible reason why they might have been chosen as the source for works to this great Lancastrian castle is that the designs for both buildings were actually rooted in the earlier works at Leicester. Put another way, that St Mary's Newarke introduced the Perpendicular style to the midlands, and that it was from the Lancastrian works that the designs of both the chancel of St Mary's, Warwick, and the great hall at Kenilworth Castle derived.

NOTES

1. The standard history is A. H. Thompson, *The History of the Hospital and the New College of the Annunciation of St Mary in the Newarke, Leicester* (Leicester 1937); see also J. Nichols, *The History and Antiquities of the County of Leicester* 1, pt 2 (London 1815), 329–52, and VCH *Leicestershire* II (London 1954), 48–51.
2. Thompson, *History of the Hospital*, 11–40.
3. W. M. Ormrod, 'Henry of Lancaster, first duke of Lancaster (*c.* 1310–1361)', *ODNB*, Oxford University Press, Sept. 2004; online edn, Jan. 2008 [http://www.oxforddnb.com/view/article/12960, accessed 16 June 2009].

4. Thompson, *The History of the Hospital*, 207–8.
5. *Calendar of Patent Rolls, 1350–4* (London 1907), 170.
6. Thompson, *The History of the Hospital*, 54, 57.
7. *Calendar of Patent Rolls, 1396–9* (London 1909), 74.
8. *Calendar of Patent Rolls, 1413–16* (London 1910), 265.
9. Nichols, *Leicester* I, pt 2, 339.
10. J. Nichols, *Additional Collections Towards the History and Antiquities of the Town and County of Leicester* (London 1790), 758.
11. *Leicestershire Mercury*, 4 and 5 Sept. 1935. The Leicester museum staff kindly searched their store records for me, but were unable to identify any architectural fragments in their possession.
12. Presumably not from the church, as is sometimes asserted.
13. N. Pevsner and E. Williamson, *Leicestershire and Rutland* B/E (2nd edn, 1984), 221, state it was 'built in *c.* 1410', but without any authority or explanation.
14. J. Goodall, 'The Aerary Porch and its influence on late medieval English vaulting', in *St George's Chapel Windsor in the Fourteenth Century*, ed. N. Saul (Woodbridge 2005), 171–2.
15. J. Goodall, *The English Castle, 1066–1650* (New Haven and London 2011), ch. 9.
16. *The Itinerary of John Leland in or about the Years 1535–1543*, ed. L. T. Smith (London 1907–10), I, 15–16.
17. Thompson, *The History of the Hospital*, 154.
18. Ibid., 209; Nichols, *Leicester* I, pt 2, 337.
19. See Goodall, *English Castle*, chs 8 and 10, for further discussion of these points.
20. For the chronology of the rebuilding of St Mary's, Warwick, see Goodall, 'Guy's Cliffe', this volume, 315.
21. Though arguably this form is inherited from the Romanesque church.
22. R. K. Morris, 'The Architecture of the Earls of Warwick in the 14th Century', in *England in the 14th Century*, ed. W. M. Ormrod (Woodbridge 1986), 170–3.
23. See further Morris, 'Kenilworth', this volume, 349–60.

Kenilworth Abbey Barn: Its Construction and Uses

JENNIFER S. ALEXANDER AND HARRY SUNLEY

The Barn in Kenilworth Abbey Fields has been an agricultural building in the recent past, but in the middle ages it stood in the outer court of Kenilworth Priory, later Abbey. This paper analyses for the first time the construction history of this interesting building, and demonstrates through a combination of documentary evidence and the study of masons' marks that it dates to the 14th century. The original function of the Barn is shown to be connected with the prior's guest-hall, but the presence of various scribings on the walls and floor suggest that it also had a later use as a tracing-house and workshop for stonemasons.

INTRODUCTION

KENILWORTH ABBEY was demolished at the Dissolution and little remains above ground to indicate its size or appearance apart from the gatehouse and an enigmatic building to the south of it known as the 'Barn', sited in Abbey Fields park (Fig. 1 and Col. Pl. XXIIIA in print edn). It was founded as a priory by Geoffrey de Clinton, the builder of Kenilworth Castle, and raised to abbey status in 1448. The foundation date is usually cited as being between 1123 and 1135, although one source claims that it was in existence in 1119.[1] Excavation has revealed that the church and some claustral buildings were built around the middle of the 12th century with further phases between the 13th and 15th centuries.[2] The gatehouse is dated to the 14th century (see below), but there is no agreed date or function for the Barn. It has been described as a possible guest house or infirmary, on the basis of its position in the outer court, but there is little evidence in either the structure itself or in the published documentary record to identify its original purpose more precisely. There was a stone-built barn listed in an inventory of 1650, the dimensions of which are sufficiently close to identify it as the current building, indicating that it had passed into agricultural use by then, and it continued to serve that purpose during the 19th century.[3]

DESCRIPTION AND FABRIC ANALYSIS

THE Barn is a two-storeyed building, constructed out of ashlar blocks of local red sandstone (Fig. 1). It measures about 12.60m by 7.75m (about 41 × 25ft) externally and has walls of about one metre in thickness, measured at ground level.[4] It sits approximately in line with the south range of the cloister on a sloping site. Build-up of soil has obscured the base of the walls, particularly on the north, but traces of a stepped plinth can still be seen on the north-west corner. For an ostensibly simple building it has a complex building history. Both gables have been rebuilt in brick (or brick and

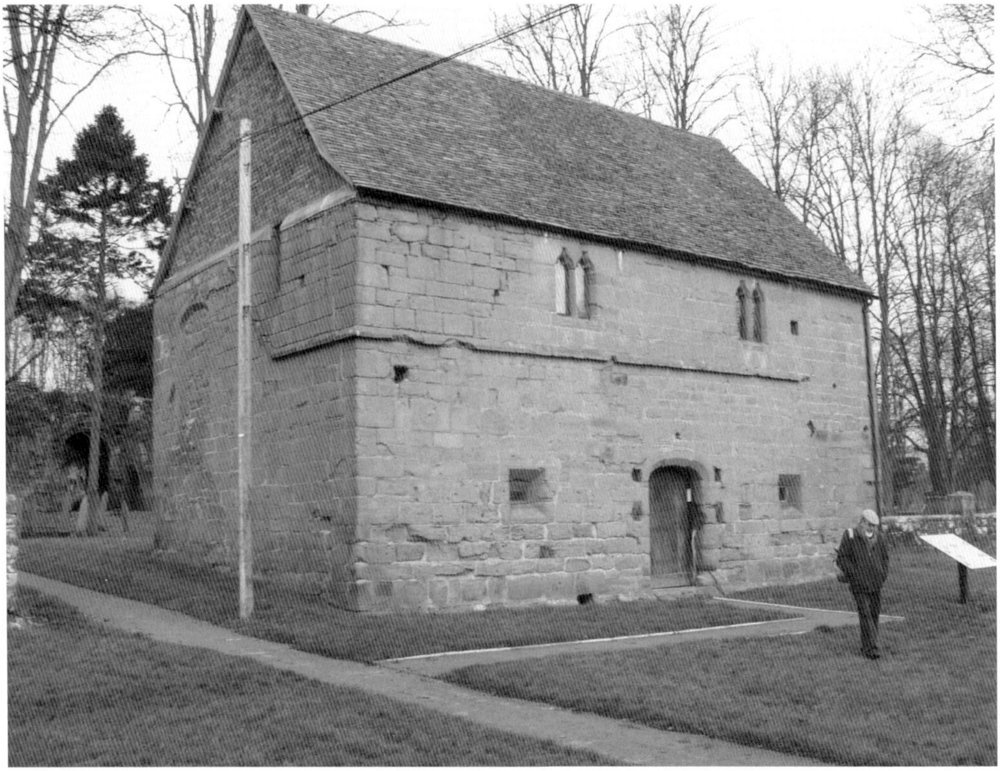

FIG. 1. Kenilworth Abbey: the Barn, from the south-west, with Harry Sunley
Photo, J. S. Alexander

timber), openings have been blocked, features such as a pentice and an external stair to the upper floor removed, and certain architectural features are badly fitted. In the recent past the upstairs floor has been reinstated, although at a slightly higher level than its predecessor, and the building now serves as a museum for Kenilworth and for the abbey site.

The ground floor has a wide doorway approximately in the centre of the south wall with a three-centred arched head on a chamfer moulding. A porch was attached in a later phase, after the removal of the pentice roof (Fig. 1). To the right of the door there are slots for the roof timbers of a single-storey building running south, and an open-sided cart-shed can be seen here in a 19th-century photograph. It probably replaced a similarly constructed earlier structure, perhaps the continuation of the pentice to the south to join the Barn to further buildings.

Lighting for the ground floor is provided by pairs of small square windows with deep reveals and shouldered lintels in the north, south and east walls, but none is now visible in the west wall. However, on the interior, there is an unusable chute and window, blocked by the stair on the exterior. The window head must have been repositioned since it is an external one, and it seems to be part of a reworking of the interior which also affected the north wall, where there is now a potentially usable chute between two windows. These are situated directly opposite the south door, each under a rere-arch over square-cut jambs. On the exterior (Fig. 2) there is an area of disturbed masonry here, suggesting that these features represent a remodelling of this area. The small size of the windows on the ground floor implies that security was of some importance for the building.

The ground-floor room is a single space without any evidence for substantial masonry walls to subdivide it, and it does not seem to have been vaulted. The new upper floor is supported on beams that are of deeper section than any medieval joists, and these sit on the off-set of the lower walls caused by the upper walls being thinner. Parts of the floor are still stone-flagged and there are slight indications that there were light partitions at some stage.

The upper room was of higher-status than the lower one and seems also to have been a single space (Fig. 3). Its windows are larger, and, although none has survived in its original form, their design and quality suggests the relative importance of this chamber. The south wall has a pair of windows, each of two lights with cusped ogee heads which finish, unusually, as squares rather than as points, and resemble the broad nib of a pen (Fig. 1). The north windows (Fig. 2) lack their original heads, and it is noticeable that there are no hood-moulds to any of the openings in the Barn, and that all the arches and rere-arches are of the less common three-centred type. On the interior it is evident that the top two or three courses of walling have been lost and the rere-arches of the

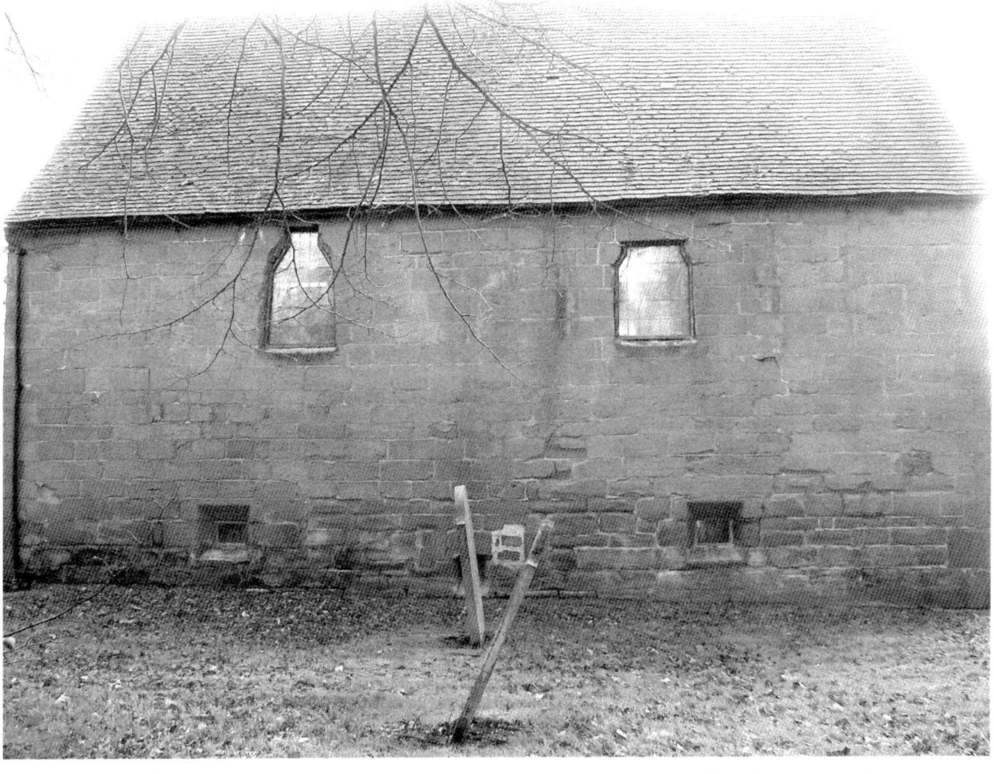

FIG. 2. Kenilworth Abbey: the Barn, north elevation; the chute is behind the left-hand headstone

Photo, J. S. Alexander

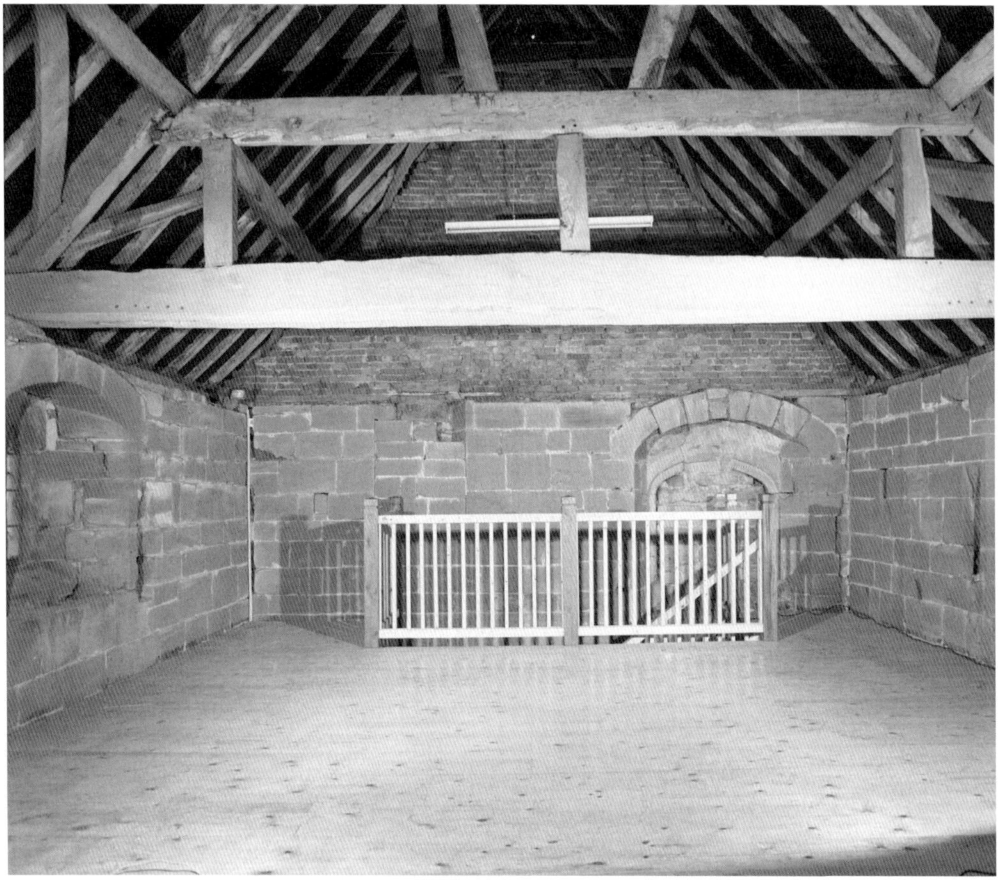

FIG. 3. Kenilworth Abbey: the Barn, upper floor looking west
Photo, History of Art Department, University of Warwick

windows are now level with the tops of the walls and are much disturbed. The window inserted in the east wall has lost its head and sill, but chamfer stops are still present on the exterior jambs and the remains of the window seats can be seen on the interior (Fig. 4). There is also a large scar on the exterior, now filled with brick, which looks as if it might have been part of a narrow chimney, but there is no trace of one on the interior face of the wall. The scar is clearly visible in the 1729 Bucks' engraving, although its purpose is not evident (Fig. 5).

Access to the upper floor was through a door in the west wall reached by an external staircase and protected by the roof of the pentice. As a result there was little room for a window and a small opening higher up lights the south-west corner (Fig. 6). The window head extended into the gable and has been lost in the rebuilding of that area. The upper door has the same shaped head as the south door and is of similar size. It is rebated on the inside and there is no evidence for a draw-bar (Fig. 3).

The roof consists of two irregularly spaced trusses made up of a tie-beam and upper and lower collars with queen posts, with two levels of purlins supported on wind

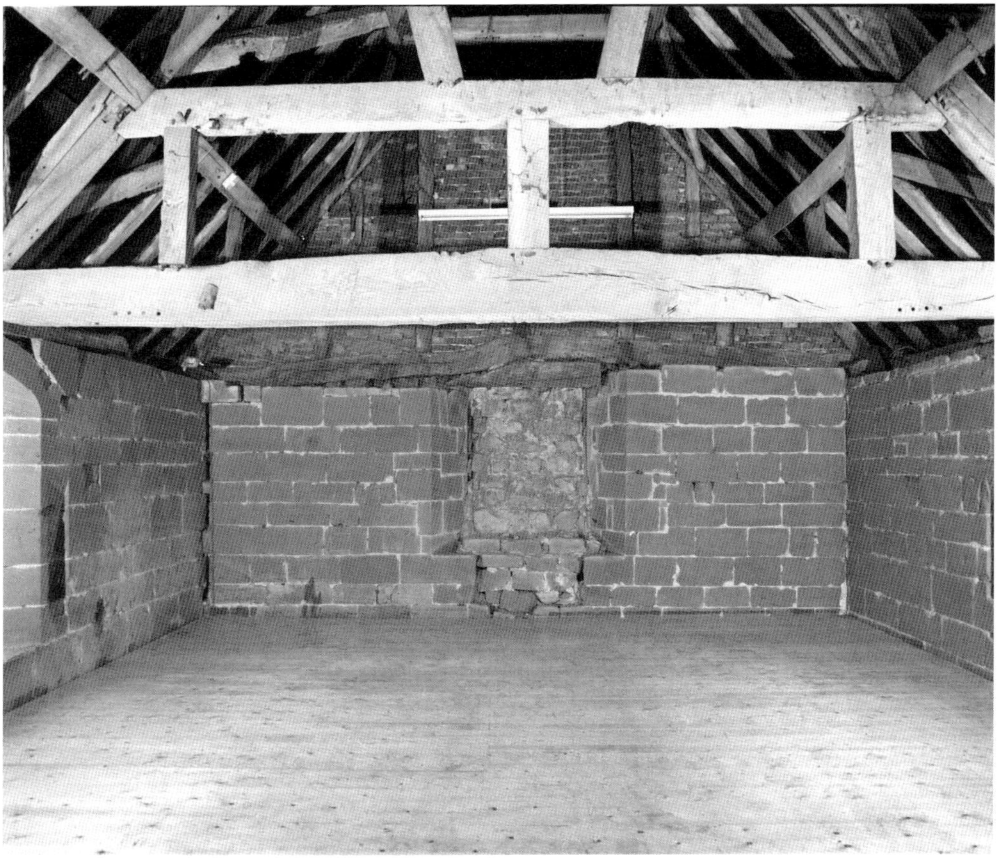

FIG. 4. Kenilworth Abbey: the Barn, upper floor looking east
Photo, History of Art Department, University of Warwick

braces. The trusses were not made specifically for this building but must have been brought here and re-erected, because the tie-beams are positioned directly on top of the windows, and the struts intended for the empty mortices on their undersides would have been sited in front of the windows (Fig. 3). The timbers have a scientific felling date of *c.* 1600,[5] and the roof was evidently in place by 1650 when the Barn was described as being of three bays.[6] The source of the roof-frames is not clear, although they are most unlikely to have come from the abbey site itself, and may possibly have been moved from a building in the castle, perhaps becoming available as a result of post-Civil War dismantling.[7] The current brick gables belong to the rebuilt roof and are of light construction.

THE EVIDENCE OF THE MASONS' MARKS AND SCRIBINGS

MASONS' marks are to be seen on all surfaces of the building, predominantly on the interior, but some survive on the exterior as well. The marks were put on the ashlar blocks by the masons responsible for cutting the stone to shape, ready for use by the

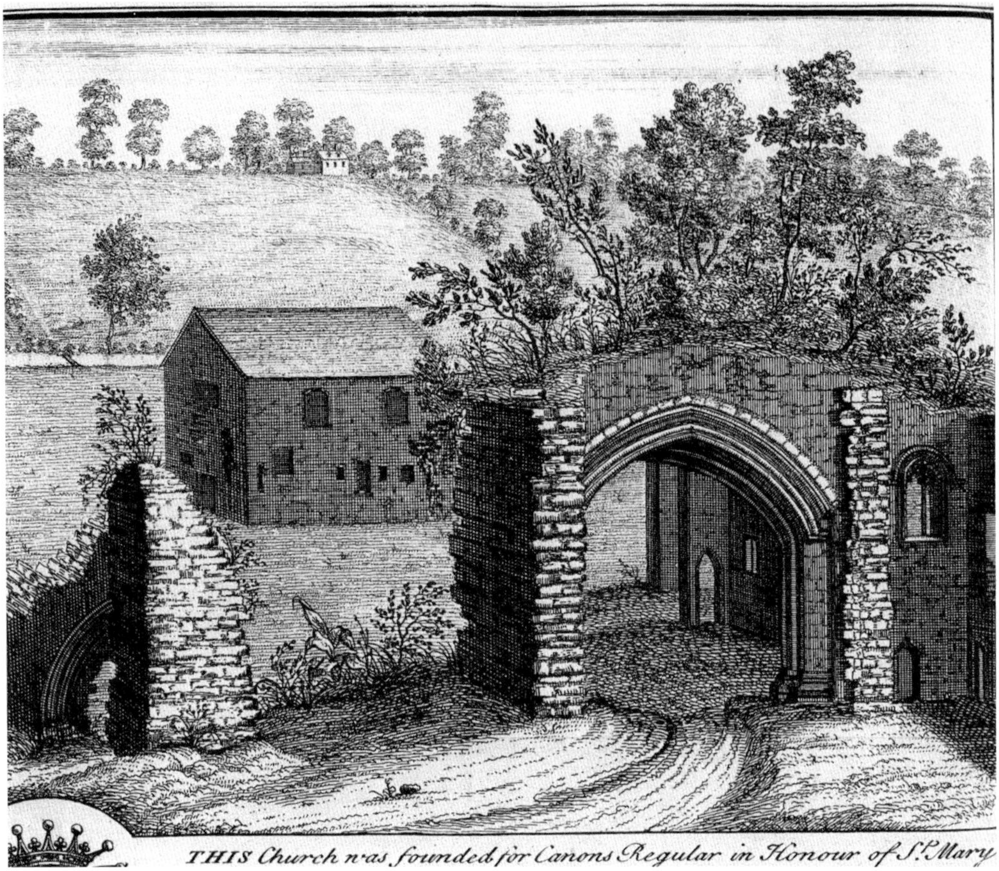

FIG. 5. 'The East View of Kenilworth Priory', S. and N. Buck, engraving, 1729: detail, the Barn and the gatehouse (actually from the north-east)

walling masons who erected the building. They enabled the paymaster to assess each mason's output when they were on piecework.[8] The marks are of the type commonly found on medieval buildings, consisting of a series of lines crossing at angles, without any compass-drawn examples (Fig. 7), although there is also a large collection of compass scribings on the building. Most of the walling has been available to the authors for examination, with the exception of the areas on the east and west walls hidden behind the floor joists. Weathering of the exterior surfaces and damage to the lower courses of the east wall have doubtless removed some marks. Nevertheless, over 430 marks have been recorded externally and internally and the proportion of marked to unmarked stone is about 1:4, rising to between 1:3 and 1:2 in certain areas. The marks are found on ashlar, on the shaped stones of window embrasures, on shouldered lintels and also on the voussoirs of the arches over the north recess and the south door, proving that all these features are original to the building. The maximum number of different masons' marks is thirty-nine, of which nineteen only appear once, and while it might be possible to regard four such marks as damaged, or as poorly executed versions

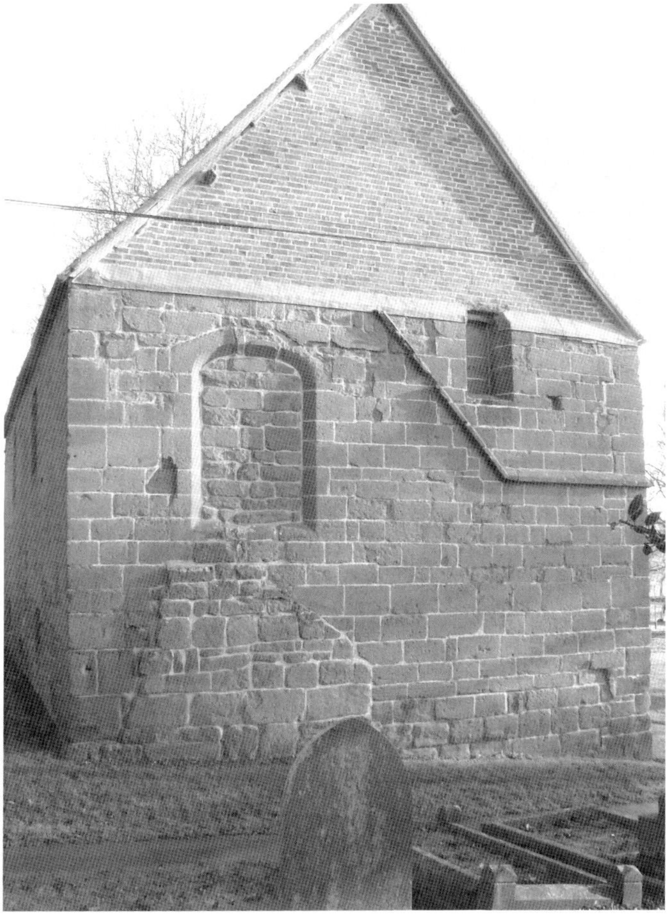

FIG. 6. Kenilworth Abbey: the Barn, west elevation
Photo, J. S. Alexander

of others, there is less certainty about the other fifteen (Fig. 8).[9] There seems to be a core of four or five masons who produced a considerable number of blocks each, ranging from 3z1 who cut fifteen ashlars to 11x1, responsible for 77 blocks including voussoirs for rere-arches, and 4b1 who achieved a recorded total of 102 blocks. A second group of five masons cut between five and twelve blocks and a further group of twenty-seven only produced between one and four blocks each. This is consistent with the working practices of medieval building sites in which some masons worked for short periods while others were retained for longer stretches of time.[10]

The quantity of masons' marks on the interior surfaces of the two floors is similar, but the number of masons at work is quite different. While twenty-nine masons cut the 178 marked ashlars for the ground floor walls, only twelve masons worked the 201 marked blocks for the upper floor. It is clear that certain masons were only introduced once the interior walling had reached a certain stage. Mark 11x1, which can be found 77 times in the building, only occurs after the north and south walls had been started. The west wall had risen higher than the two longer walls by this stage and most of the ground floor of the east wall was standing. 11x1's work included several voussoirs for

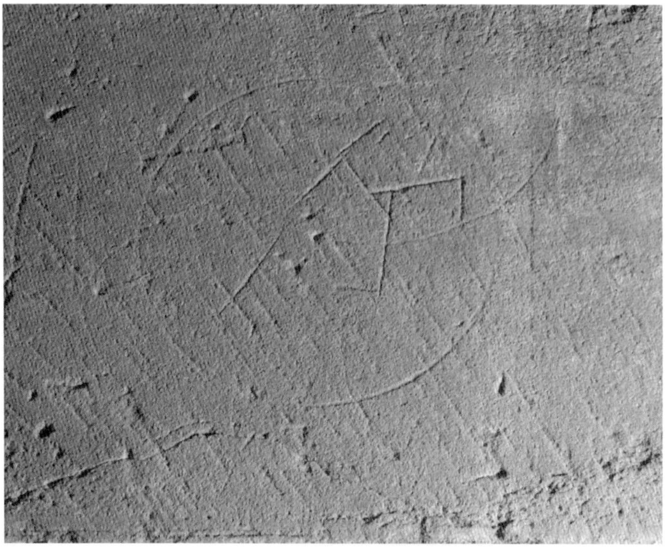

FIG. 7. Kenilworth Abbey: the Barn, mason's mark 6a15
Photo, J. S. Alexander

the south door and the north recess, and blocks with his mark are otherwise found predominantly on the upper level. In total there are eleven examples of his work on the ground floor, apart from the voussoirs, which account for another seven, whereas there are 59 examples upstairs. There are twice as many blocks with the mark 4b1 on the upper floor as on the lower; 68 out of a total of 102, spread over all four walls, with fewest on the west wall at either level. His work occurs on window and door embrasures as well as on ashlar. 5x15 was cutting stone that was used for the middle courses of the ground floor and for the lower courses of the upper walls, but his work is not found at a higher level. He also cut stone for window embrasures at both levels of the building. Other masons worked mostly on the ground floor. Work of a mason such as 3s1, who marked 54 ashlars, is only found at first-floor level up to course two, while the majority of his blocks are distributed evenly between the walls of the ground floor. Similarly 3z1's work can be found on the upper interior surfaces of the ground floor, but is only seen once on the first floor. These very specific sitings of marks suggest that work was progressing rapidly and that the building campaign was not protracted.

In addition to the masons' marks, scribings drawn with compasses can be found on both interior and exterior surfaces. They comprise a variety of designs, ranging from simple circles and six-petal rosette types through to more complex examples based on cross shapes (Fig. 9). In some cases the drawing was done before the block was cut to shape, but others were clearly cut *in situ*. Compass-drawn designs, in particular six-petal rosettes, are very common and have been recorded on stone ossuaries from Roman Palestine as well as on English post-medieval timber-framed buildings.[11] A particularly fine 14th-century set can be seen on the stonework of the tithe barn at Bradford-on-Avon (Wilts.). Their purpose on buildings is not clear. It has sometimes been assumed that their presence around openings indicates an apotropaeic function,[12] but it might equally be suggested that the marks were cut there because the light made it easier for the scribe to see what he was doing. Where there are large collections of marks, as at Kenilworth, the simplest explanation is that masons were practising their skills with compasses on the blocks of stone close to hand.

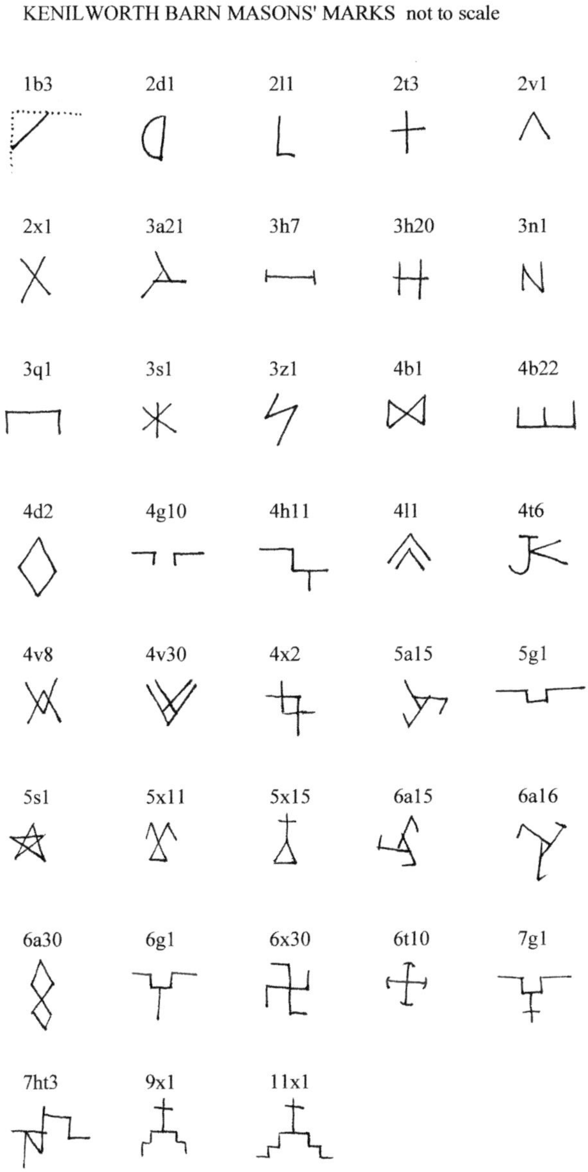

FIG. 8. Kenilworth Abbey: the Barn, coding sheet of masons' marks
Drawing, J. S. Alexander

INTERPRETATION OF THE BUILDING SEQUENCE

THE anomalies in the building, and the evidence of the masons' marks, suggest that the construction of the Barn was carried out in four unequal phases that followed closely upon each other. In the first phase, a single-storey structure with thin walls was built, with a south door that was narrower than the current one, and off-set. In the second phase this building was made stronger by the thickening of its walls on the interior, probably in preparation for the third phase in which the whole building was given an

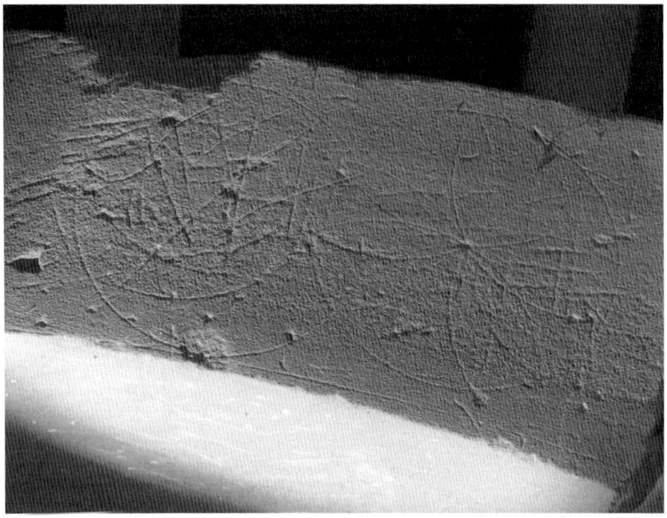

FIG. 9. Kenilworth Abbey: the Barn, compass scribings
Photo, J. S. Alexander

upper floor. The present south door was added at the second stage, and the ground-floor windows were given shouldered lintels with new embrasures. A pentice covered the new door and continued around onto the west wall to provide protection for the door that accessed the new upper storey in the third phase. A recess was left in the centre of the north wall, the purpose of which seems to have been to provide a chute flanked by two small windows, since it proved impossible to fit a chute and its lighting in the west wall once the outside stair was in place. The last phase involved finishing the interior of the first floor by building its inner skin of masonry, but this construction seems to have been rushed, with little attention paid to aligning the courses across corners. The north wall was already finished before the east wall received its inner skin, as the north-east corner shows. Settlement there has pulled the joint apart and the somewhat *ad hoc* construction of the corner is very clear. At a later date the east wall was breached to insert a large window with window seats (Fig. 4).

THE FUNCTION OF THE BARN

THE question remains as to the original use and date of the building. A recently identified source for the history of the abbey is the Strecche Chronicle, a collection of papers written around 1422, which includes references to events at Kenilworth Priory.[13] It was written by John Strecche, a canon of Kenilworth, and the section on the priory is the subject of current study.[14] Certain buildings, but not the Barn, can be directly identified from the Chronicle. However, Strecche describes the gatehouse as being the work of Henry Bradway (1361–75), constructed with a vault and battlemented walls, and there are connections between the gatehouse and the Barn through the masons' marks (Fig. 10 and Col. Pl. XXIIIB in print edn; Fig. 11).[15] It is not usually the case that buildings can be linked by masons' marks since coincidences are many and these can result in spurious links being proposed, but within one site where the materials are the same and the marks are distinctive it is sometimes possible to suggest a connection. In this case, the two buildings are in close proximity and made of the same stone, and so it is reasonable to link them, especially as the three shared marks, 6a15, 6a16 and 6x30,

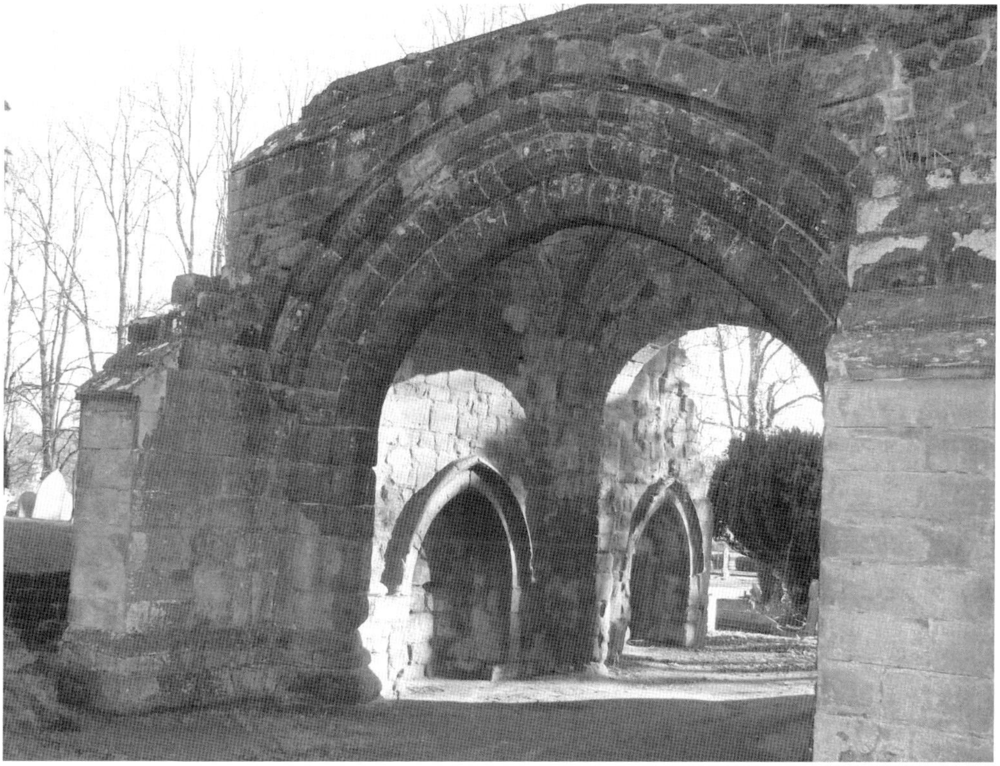

FIG. 10. Kenilworth Abbey: the gatehouse, from the north
Photo, J. S. Alexander

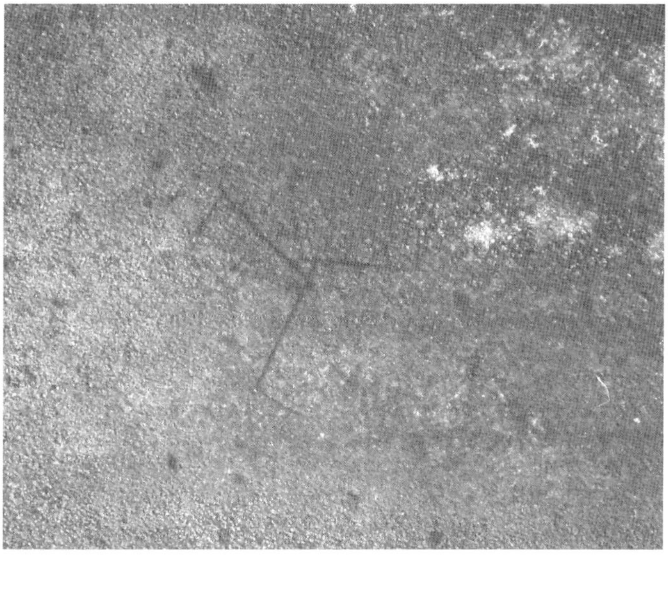

FIG. 11. Kenilworth Abbey: the gatehouse, soffit of the north arch, masons' mark 6a16
Photo, J. S. Alexander

are particularly distinctive (cf. Figs 7, 11). Both buildings have other marks which are not shared, so the building works are probably not contemporary, but they are likely to be close in date.

In an entry in the Strecche Chronicle describing the work of Prior Warmington (1311–43),[16] references to work on the nave of the church, the cloister, and to various buildings in the outer court show that the priory had an active works department during the first half of the 14th century, for which the appropriation of the churches of 'Colynton' (presumably Colyton, Devon) and Churchover (Warks.) in the early 1330s will have provided a useful source of revenue.[17] The outer court buildings are a hall for the prior with a portico and an exterior kitchen; a large chamber 'in which malt is collected'; a granary with a lead roof in the middle of the court; and a workroom 'built new from the ground'.[18] If the Barn can be identified from this list, it might relate to the prior's hall. The ogee-headed windows would be appropriate for a hall. The small size of the Barn does not suggest a use for the collection of malt. The malt-house at the home grange of Bridlington Priory, for example, was much bigger, 'containing in length North and South XLIIII yerds and in breddith XVII yards'.[19] It seems unlikely to have been a granary, either, since most buildings of this type were wooden structures raised up on piers or staddle-stones.[20]

While the description of a workroom (*sarteria*) might relate better to the later use of the Barn, the reference to a portico (*porticu*) on the prior's hall and an exterior kitchen does fit quite well with our building. However, the single-space interiors and lack of facilities such as garderobes and fireplaces, with no possibility of an open hearth for either floor, might mitigate against the Barn having a domestic function. Comparison with other priors' halls is instructive here. Michael Thompson has commented on a general trend for abbots and priors to move out of the cloister into separate dwellings during the 13th century.[21] In the case of the Augustinians, new buildings were often constructed either in the west range of the cloister, or in the adjacent area of the outer court, but there seems to have been little uniformity in either the size or the form of the abbot's or prior's house. Not all would have been as grand and elaborate as the 14th-century abbot's hall and private chamber at Haughmond (Salop.), and even the earlier structures for the abbot there are larger than the Barn.

The arrangements for the prior at Ely Cathedral Priory offer us an alternative possibility. He had a suite of buildings constructed over a period of time and linked by passageways, some at first-floor level. As well as providing the prior's hall, and Prior Crauden's 14th-century chapel, these buildings also included the guest houses.[22] If the Barn at Kenilworth was built with the prior's hall in the first half of the 14th century, then it may well have been an addition to an existing range of buildings and been linked to them, and to other parts of the complex, by the pentice on its south side. If its construction was towards the end of Prior Warmington's period, in the late 1330s to the mid-1340s, then its date would be close enough to the completion of the gatehouse (1361–75)[23] for some of the same masons to be able to work on both buildings. Archaeological investigation of the ground around the Barn is required to provide further evidence.

THE LATER USE OF THE BARN

AT a later date the building may have been used as a workshop by the masons, with a tracing-house (or *trasura*)[24] for the master mason on the upper floor in which architectural designs were worked out. Tracing houses, both within buildings and freestanding, are mentioned in documents, and examples survive of ecclesiastical ones at York Minster and Wells Cathedral.[25] The upper walls in the Barn have several incised drawings in the north-east corner, and one window splay has the remains of several curves drawn from templates. The lines are incomplete but extend over several stones and must have been cut *in situ*; while they may have served no more complex purpose than to sharpen an iron point, they have been cut decisively and are not merely graffiti.

A more interesting drawing in the north-east corner shows the outline of the head of an arch as a pair of parallel arcs (Fig. 12). It extends over four courses, includes a base-line and a centre-line, and measures 1.52m (5ft) in width and 0.86m (2ft 10in.) in height. The lower left side has been destroyed by a hole cut into the wall but it is otherwise undamaged. On the right side the outline of the arch extends a little below the base-line, crossing two vertical lines dropped below the base-line here, but no part of the design is continued onto the courses beneath. The drawing was done *in situ*, but its close proximity to the east wall means that it cannot have been drawn with a pair of compasses since the estimated radii of the arcs are 2.60m (8ft 6in.) and 2.65m (8ft 8in.), and it must have been drawn from a template. When the drawing was measured it was found that the two sides of the arch are a mirror-image of each other, and so the template will have been made for one side of the arch and reversed to complete the drawing, with the centre- and base-lines allowing for a precise alignment. The arch

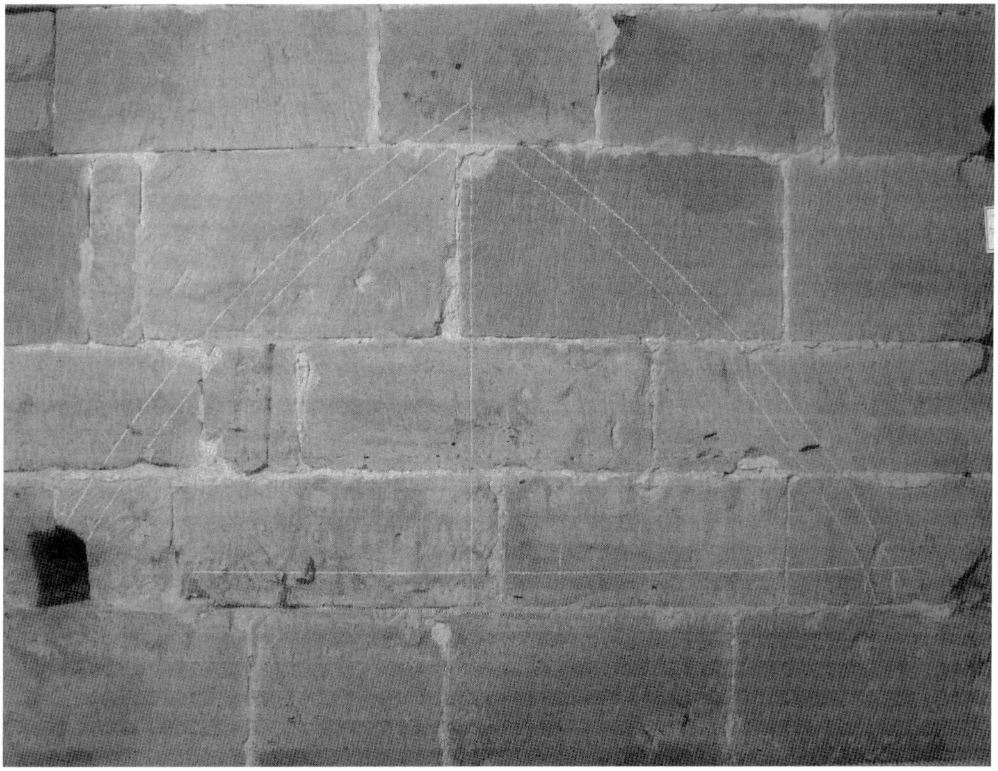

FIG. 12. Kenilworth Abbey: the Barn, upper floor, north wall: incised outline of an arch
Photo, J. S. Alexander

template does not fit any extant feature in the Barn,[26] and though there are two instances of segmental arches of similar form at Kenilworth Castle, in Mortimer's Tower and the western curtain wall (Fig. 13), their radii are considerably smaller.[27] These parts of the castle are generally dated to the early 13th century.

The large single space of the upper floor, with its good lighting, would have provided an excellent site for a *trasura*, with a plaster floor on which to lay out large-scale designs, or resolve geometric problems (Fig. 4). The access to the upper floor from the exterior would have allowed for full use of the floor, giving an uninterrupted space of over 60 sq. m (about 645 sq. ft),[28] and would also have enabled the work of the two levels of the building to have been kept separate. Unfortunately, the loss of the original floor makes it impossible to establish whether the upper room had a plaster floor.

There is still evidence of masons' use of the ground floor for geometrical laying-out where some flagstones remain, despite later reworking. The central section of the floor is probably original, made up of rectangular slabs of blue lias that are 70mm (2¾in.) thick, and there are numerous lines cut into the surface of these slabs. The group of stones with lines is concentrated in the well-lit area near the south door and to the west

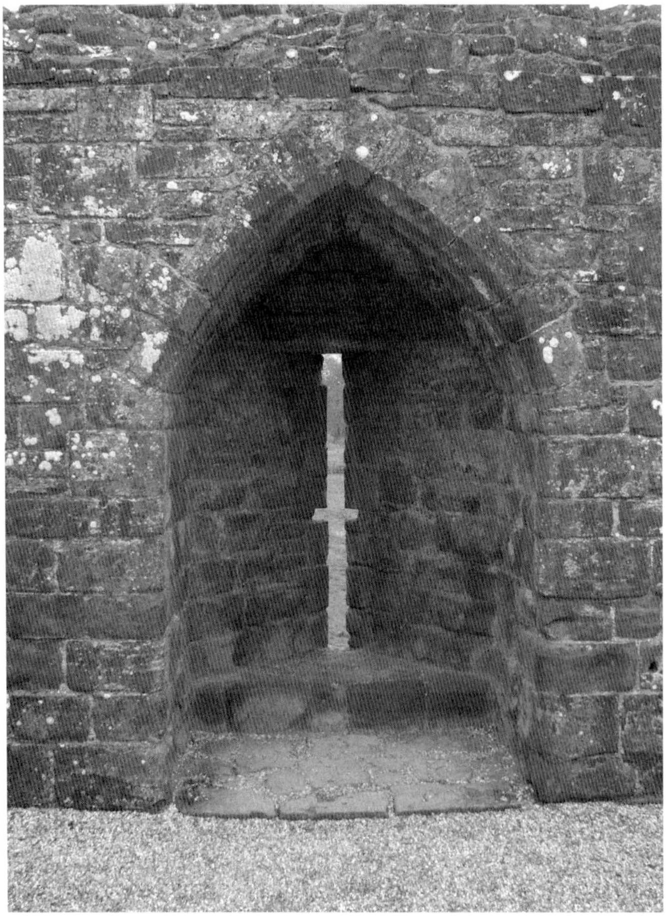

FIG. 13. Kenilworth Castle: Mortimer's Tower, an arrow-loop
Photo, J. S. Alexander

of it. Single deeply cut lines remain from drawings on four or five slabs, but one drawing survives more fully and its lines can be traced (Fig. 14). They are part of a grid, with lines crossing and creating trapezoidal shapes; there are no curves or compass-drawn elements. A similar grid can be seen scribed on the plaster floor of the York *trasura* where it evidently served as a reference since compass points have been driven repeatedly through its intersections (Fig. 15). It is the type of standard matrix that would be a useful tool, either for teaching apprentices, or for establishing standard elements and lengths.[29] The dates of the inscribed lines are impossible to define precisely but it is unlikely that they would have been made after the working life of the abbey or castle had ended. The Strecche Chronicle describes building work by abbots Henry Bradway (1361–75), on the gatehouse and enclosing walls, and his successor Walter Charleton (1375–85), who continued the work on the precinct walls and restored the chapter-house.[30] Work on the castle was in progress at intervals through the 14th to early 16th centuries, and saw a substantial series of campaigns in the Elizabethan period for Robert Dudley (*c.* 1569–75).

The evidence of the arch drawing on the upper floor and the scribed grid on the lower floor, together with the open space and size of the building, support the idea that the Barn functioned at some stage as a masons' workshop. The lower floor, with its stone flags, would have been a very useful space in which stonemasons could have

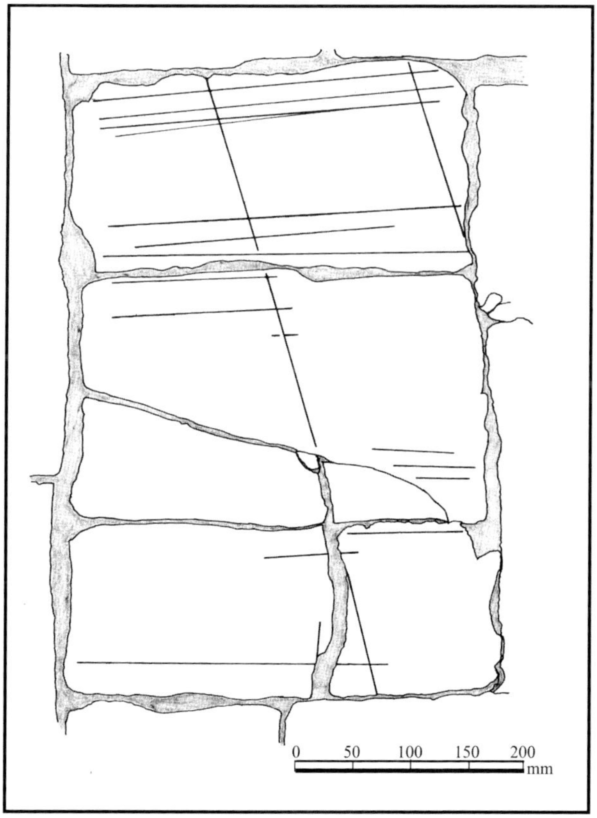

FIG. 14. Kenilworth Abbey: the Barn, ground floor: a grid incised on the floor slabs, detail
Drawing, J. S. Alexander

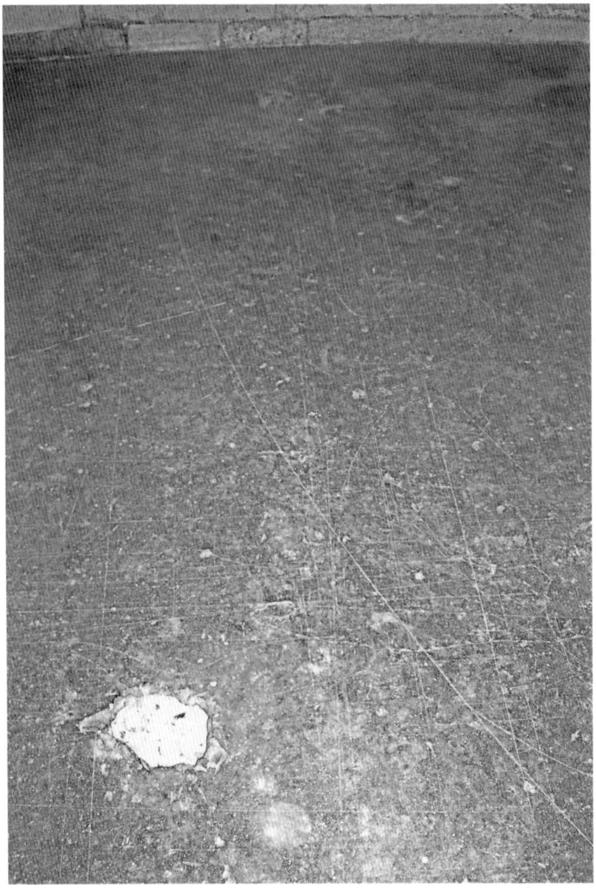

FIG. 15. York Minster: chapter-house vestibule, upper floor: the masons' tracing-house floor
Photo, J. S. Alexander

worked, and the fracturing of the heavy flags would be consistent with stone-handling in this area. Additionally, the small windows afforded security, and its clear space was suitable for setting up bankers for masons. The chute in the north wall could have allowed dust and debris to have been disposed of easily and the floor kept clean for use as a working space. The upper floor, which was accessed separately, would have been a clean space in which the master mason would have been able to carry out design work away from the noise and dust of the working masons on the ground floor.

NOTES

1. For 1119, see the Chronicle of John Strecche (early 15th century), London, British Library, Add. MS 35295; G. M. Hilton, 'The chronicle of John Strecche and its place in medieval historical records of England and Kenilworth Priory', *Bull. John Rylands Library* 85 (2007, for 2003), 23–36, which describes the chronicle and identifies the passages relating to the priory, but does not discuss them in detail. The main modern accounts of the abbey's history are VCH *Warwickshire* II, 86–9; and H. Sunley and N. Stevens, *Kenilworth: the story of the abbey* (London 1995).

2. E. Carey-Hill, 'Kenilworth Abbey: a record of the ruins excavated in 1890 and 1922–3', *TBWAS* 52 (1928), 184–227.
3. The National Archive E317/15; Carey-Hill, 'Kenilworth', 197.
4. Actually the north wall is 12.60m, the south wall 12.62m; the west wall is 7.73m, the east wall 7.79m.
5. R. E. Howard, 'Tree Ring Analysis of Timber from the Barn, Abbey Fields, Kenilworth', Nottingham University Tree-Ring Dating Laboratory Report (2002).
6. CA, M1245. There are also three crudely cut slots between the windows located low down in the north and south walls: they look as if they were intended to support roof timbers, but do not relate to the current roof and may never have been used.
7. The slighting of the castle seems to have commenced late in 1649 or early in 1650. See E. Carey-Hill, 'The Hawkesworth Papers, 1601–60', *TBWAS* 54 (1929–30), 50; H. Sunley, 'Colonel Hawkesworth and the slighting of the castle', *Kenilworth History* (2007–08), 8–10.
8. For the uses of masons' marks in buildings archaeology, see J. S. Alexander, 'Masons' marks and the working practices of medieval stone masons', in *Who built Beverley Minster?*, ed. P. S. Barnwell and A. Pacey (Reading 2008), 21–40.
9. Marks 6g1, 7g1 and 9x1 are probably rubbed examples of mark 11x1, and 5a15 may be a damaged form of 6a15.
10. For example, see A. Erskine ed. 'The accounts of the fabric of Exeter Cathedral, part 1, 1279–1326, part 2, 1328–1353', *Devon and Cornwall Record Society*, ns 24 (1981), 26 (1983).
11. For compass-drawn rosettes on early ossuaries, see R. Houston Smith, 'Decorative geometric designs in stone; the rediscovery of a technique of Roman-Byzantine craftsmen', *The Biblical Archaeologist* 46 (1983), 175–86.
12. B. Meeson, 'Ritual marks and graffiti: curiosities or meaningful symbols?', *Vernacular Architecture* 36 (2005), 41–8.
13. BL, Add. MS 35295; see further note 1.
14. C. Hodgetts, 'Progress Report', *Kenilworth History 2000–2001*, 5, brief extracts drawing attention to the value of the document. Full transcription of the relevant passages by Brian Jackson is in progress; he has kindly made his work available to us in advance of publication, and we are grateful to him for discussion of the chronicle.
15. Richard Morris has proposed three phases of work at the gatehouse on the basis of the moulding profiles, with Bradway's work representing the final phase. The masons' marks shared with the Barn are all on the latest phase of the work; see also Morris, 'Kenilworth', this volume, 351–2. We are grateful to Dr Morris for sharing his unpublished work with us.
16. BL, Add. MS 35295, fol. 255v.
17. VCH *Warwickshire* II, 86.
18. *Aulam etiam prioris cum porticu et coquina exteriori his duobus conversis operantibus a solo exerunt et edificavit praeteria magnam cameram in quam bracium colocatur edificavit. Et granarium in medio curis fecit et cum plumbo cooperit. Domo* [?] *etiam de sartaria de novo a terra edificavit*; BL, Add. MS 35295, fols 255v–56.
19. Although it did have 'a prety Howse with a Chamber where the Hervest men dyd alwayes dine' nearby, which may have been smaller; cited in J. C. Dickinson, *Monastic Life in Medieval England* (London 1961), 14–15.
20. The Bridlington granary also had a lead roof, but measured 26 by 10 yards (23.8 × 9m); Dickinson, *Monastic Life*, 14.
21. M. Thompson, *Cloister, Abbot and Precinct in Medieval Monasteries* (Stroud 2001), 69–78.
22. A. Holton-Krayenbuhl, 'The prior's lodgings at Ely', *Archaeol. J.* 56 (1999), 294–342.
23. BL, Add. MS 35295, fol. 257; see also Morris, 'Kenilworth', this volume, 351–2.
24. See L. F. Salzman, *Building in England down to 1540: a Documentary History* (Oxford 1952), 21.
25. For an excellent re-evaluation of tracing houses, see A. Holton, 'The working space of the medieval master mason: the tracing houses of York Minster and Wells Cathedral', *Proceedings of the Second International Congress on Construction History* (2006), 1579–97.
26. Except that adjacent windows have a similar span.
27. The widths and heights of the castle arches are relatively close in size to the Barn template, but the radius of the arc of the latter is about twice as large.
28. For comparison, York's *trasura* floor has a useable space of almost 70 sq. m (753 sq. ft), and it may also have extended into the eastern arm of the roof space; Holton, 'Working space', 1581.
29. This aspect of the York tracing floor has yet to be investigated, but it would be logical to suggest that one part of the floor had a standard set of lengths and angles laid out for masons' reference.
30. BL, Add. MS 35295, fols 257, 259v.

Sidelights on the 14th-Century Architecture at Kenilworth Castle

RICHARD K. MORRIS

In 1944 John Harvey published 'Sidelights on Kenilworth Castle', an invaluable article setting out much of the documentary evidence for the medieval works at the castle. The sidelights in my paper focus more specifically on the 14th-century works of the earls and dukes of Lancaster, and the potential evidence for their buildings from the fabric. It examines the provenance and stylistic affiliations of the carved stones associated with the collegiate chapel planned by Thomas, earl of Lancaster (1298–1322), demonstrating that they are by the same masons whose best known works are in the north-east midlands, such as Hawton church (Notts.). The fine residential tower, the Water Tower, is also attributed to Thomas' patronage. Turning to the later buildings, an evaluation of the moulding profiles of the hall and apartment ranges is used to re-examine the modern attribution of these works to John of Gaunt in the 1370s. Enough evidence of variations and inconsistencies is assembled to float the idea that substantial remains survive from the times of his predecessors, especially Henry of Grosmont (1345–60), who thus may possibly have introduced the first-floor hall.

STUDIES of the later medieval fabric of Kenilworth Castle have concentrated almost entirely on the fine buildings attributed to John of Gaunt, duke of Lancaster (1362–99): the great hall with the Strong and Saintlowe towers, the apartments and Gaunt's Tower — traditionally called 'Lancaster's Buildings' (Fig. 1 and Col. Pl. XXIVA in print edn; Fig. 10).[1] However, the earls (later dukes) of Lancaster had held the castle since 1266 and were the leading magnates of the 14th century, so that we should expect significant works also to be undertaken for them during this period.[2] This paper aims to identify the evidence for such works, paying particular attention to surviving fabric at the castle and priory, and including some previously unidentified worked stones in the English Heritage store at Atcham (Shrops).

WORKS FOR THOMAS OF LANCASTER (1298–1322)[3]

THOMAS was a great builder and has been compared with Ralph Lord Cromwell or William Lord Hastings in the next century.[4] Kenilworth Castle was just one of his numerous residences on which he lavished expenditure. He visited the castle frequently up to 1318 and based his exchequer there, and, in addition to buildings, he added 800 acres to the park.[5] The account-roll for 1313–14 records work on a new hall and chapel, as well as the rebuilding of a stable, granary, and mill.[6] Today only the foundations of the chapel remain from these recorded works, but the Water Tower is also likely to have been built in his time (Fig. 2).

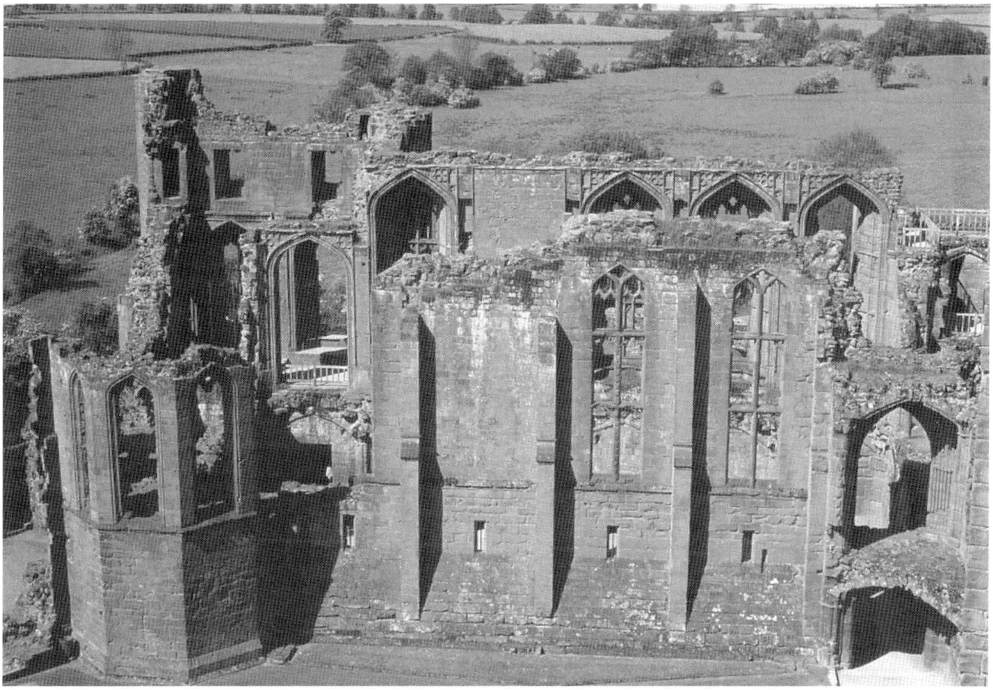

FIG. 1. Kenilworth Castle: the great hall, viewed from the great tower
Photo, 1985, author

The new chapel was commissioned in 1313 and intended to have been a collegiate establishment dedicated to St Mary and served by thirteen canons.[7] Such foundations were exceptional acts of aristocratic patronage, for example the cruciform chapel at Warkworth Castle for Henry Percy, 2nd earl of Northumberland (early 15th century),[8] and most notably St George's Chapel at Windsor for King Edward III (1348). In this context, Kenilworth is an unusually early example. In the event, the college was never established, probably because of Thomas' early death after the battle of Boroughbridge (1322), and possibly also because of considerable antipathy on the part of the Augustinian canons at Kenilworth Priory, originally set up about 1120 to serve the religious requirements of the lords of the castle. However, the building can be identified with the foundations in the base court of a large freestanding chapel with part-octagonal apse (Figs 2, 3). The fact that the master mason, Richard de Thwaites, is documented in charge of its works between 1313 and 1322,[9] and that worked stones apparently belonging to it survive in storage at Atcham, suggest that the chapel was at least partially built — perhaps even completed structurally. What happened to it thereafter is not recorded, but in 1524 its foundations seem to have been reused for one of the timber-framed buildings brought from the 15th-century Pleasance.[10] The earl of Leicester cleared this area of the base court probably about 1570, burying the foundations, which were apparently not to be fully exposed again until the 1930s.

The worked stones which are attributed here to the chapel derive from two features — window tracery and liturgical fittings. All the pieces of tracery, which appear to be mainly cusped heads of lights, are now in store at Atcham and share a

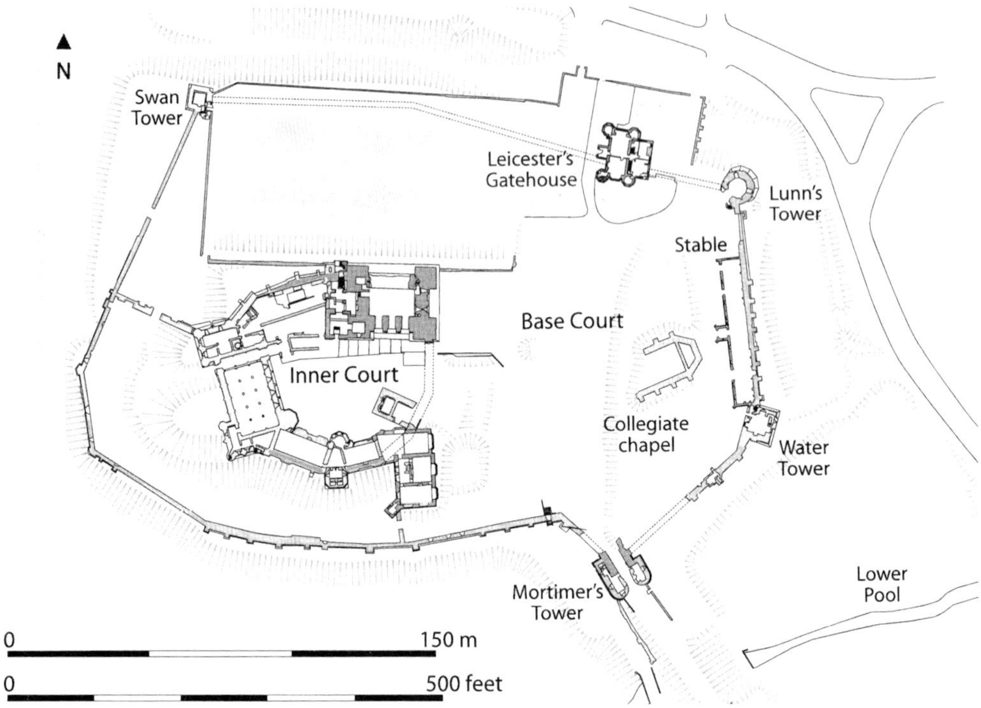

FIG. 2. Kenilworth Castle: site plan
Drawing, R. Lea, © English Heritage

mullion profile of an axial roll-and-fillet with lateral hollow chamfers (Fig. 4C).[11] They are different to any other mullions surviving in the castle buildings, but they are similar to mullions from works elsewhere of comparable date to the chapel, for example the chapter-house of Coventry Benedictine Priory (*c.* 1310–30) and the refenestration of Kenilworth Priory church (*c.* 1320s).[12] On the other hand, they are not the same size as the Kenilworth Priory examples and so unlikely to be from monastic spoil reused at the castle after the priory's dissolution. Therefore it is proposed that this collection of tracery stones was uncovered on the chapel site shortly after the Ministry of Works took over the care of the castle in 1937, perhaps having been reused as hard-core for the floor or foundations of the 1524 timber-framed building. With regard to the liturgical fittings, the key piece of evidence is the jamb of a sedilia[13] still extant in a raised section of wall on the south side of the chapel (Fig. 3). Almost certainly this section was rebuilt by the Ministry of Works,[14] but it is very probable that these stones, along with almost all the fittings' stones now at Atcham, were recovered on this site in the 1930s; and evidently some were already known in the later 19th century, when the base court was still a farmyard.[15] In 1884 G. T. Clark noted 'parts of the sedilia which have been dug up' on the chapel site.[16] Several of the Atcham stones are from the same template as the jamb, and others undoubtedly belong with them, notably ones carved with diaper ornament (Fig. 5).[17]

Moreover, this group of chapel stones is given coherence by parallels for its mouldings and decorative repertoire in churches in the north-east midlands well known for

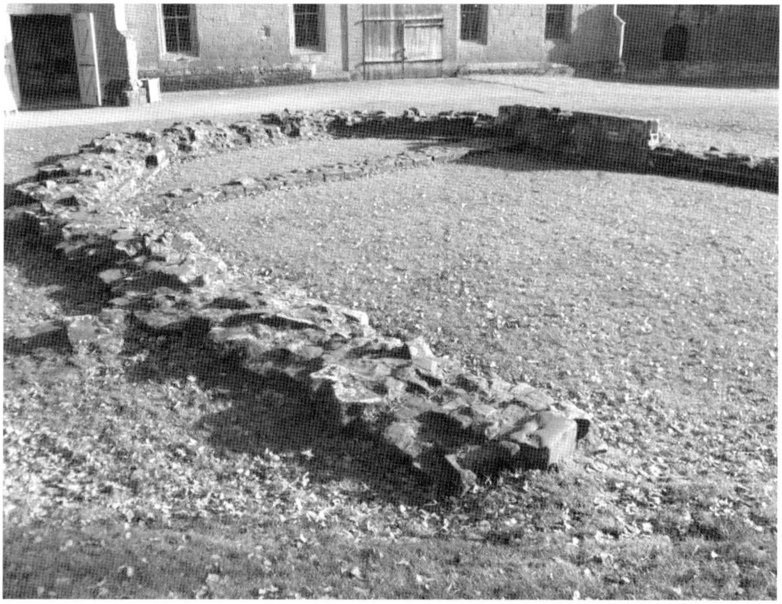

FIG. 3. Kenilworth Castle: base court, foundations of the chapel, looking towards the stable
Photo, author

their elaborate fittings — at Lincoln Cathedral and Southwell Minster (the pulpitum screen), and notably in the chancels at Hawton (Notts.) and Heckington (Lincs.). Particularly distinctive is the pentagonal profile of the sideshaft with bead mouldings at all the angles (Fig. 4E), seen also, for example, at Hawton (Fig. 6),[18] and the profile of the jamb itself (Fig. 4D) is repeated in the sedilia on the east side of the Southwell screen. Many of the Atcham stones are carved with fine, minuscule mouldings, which are characteristic of the group as a whole, especially for canopy work (Figs 5 right, 6), and floral diaper set in squares, as found, for instance, in the screens at Southwell and Lincoln, and looser foliate diaper, as at Hawton (see Fig. 5 left).[19] The stylistic affiliation of the Kenilworth stones is further substantiated by the master mason's name, 'Thwaites', to be associated with Lincolnshire and Yorkshire. It should be no surprise that Thomas of Lancaster, with major land-holdings in the north-east, should have craftsmen from this area in his employ.[20] Work influenced from this area has also been identified by the author at Coventry Cathedral (nave windows) and Priory (chapter-house) in this period, and continuing to the 1340s (refectory pulpit).[21] However, the remarkable thing about the Kenilworth chapel stones is that, if they belong with the documented dates for the commission (1313–22), they pre-date virtually all the other works in this north-east midland style, hinting at the potential importance of the earl of Lancaster's patronage for perhaps initiating and certainly popularising this elaborate strand of Decorated style.

The Water Tower sits at the south-east corner of the base court, overlooking the former lower pool, from which presumably it derives its name (Fig. 2). Externally its martial attributes include cruciform loops with oillets and pyramidal spurs at its angles

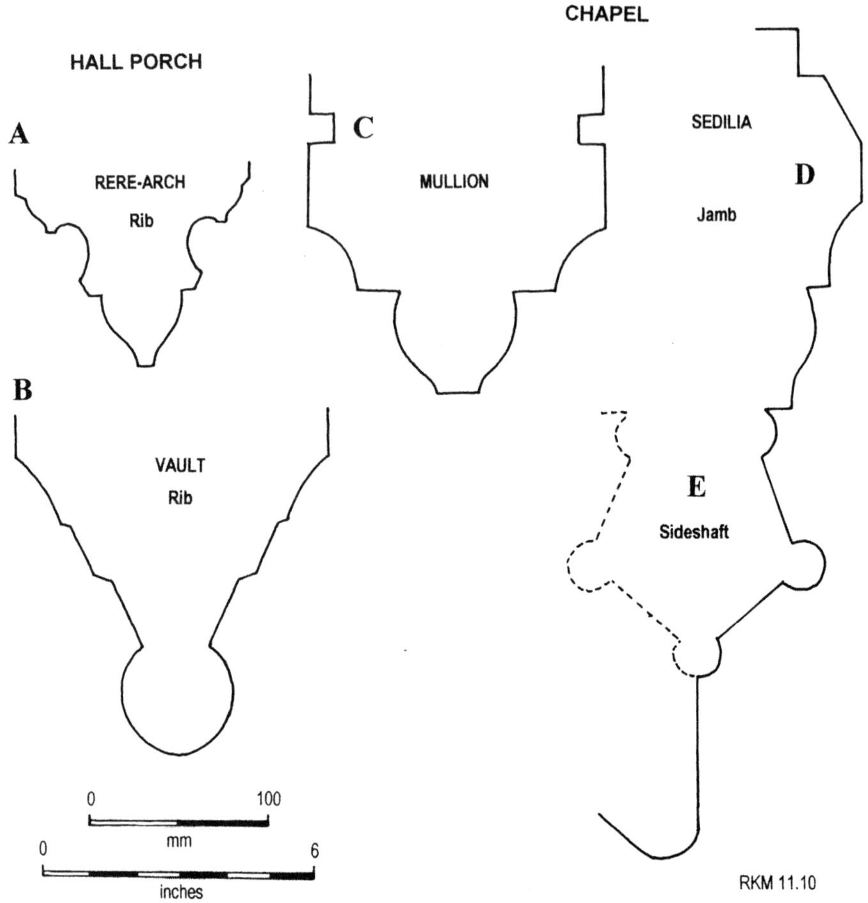

FIG. 4. Kenilworth Castle: moulding profiles, chapel stones and hall porch ribs
Drawing, author

(Fig. 7 and Col. Pl. XXIVB in print edn),[22] both paralleled in the works of *c.* 1270–96 at Goodrich Castle (Herefs.) for Thomas' royal relative, William de Valence.[23] The prominent two-light windows of the first-floor chamber have plate tracery in their heads,[24] and this feature has led previous commentators to place the tower earlier, in the mid-13th century (Fig. 8).[25] However, the bold statement made by the windows may be more indicative of their real date, two lights with central mullion having replaced the single lancets usual in wall-towers of the 13th-century. They may be compared with the two-light windows in the gatehouse and wall-towers at Thomas of Lancaster's great new work of 1313–22 at Dunstanburgh Castle (Northumb., Fig. 9).[26] The Dunstanburgh examples are more severe externally, which is probably to be explained by the much greater strategic significance of the castle, but their interior effect with window seats is not dissimilar to the Water Tower. The accommodation in the latter consisted of two large chambers, both furnished with fireplaces and latrines, and probably intended to be independent lodgings. An internal spiral stair, rising next

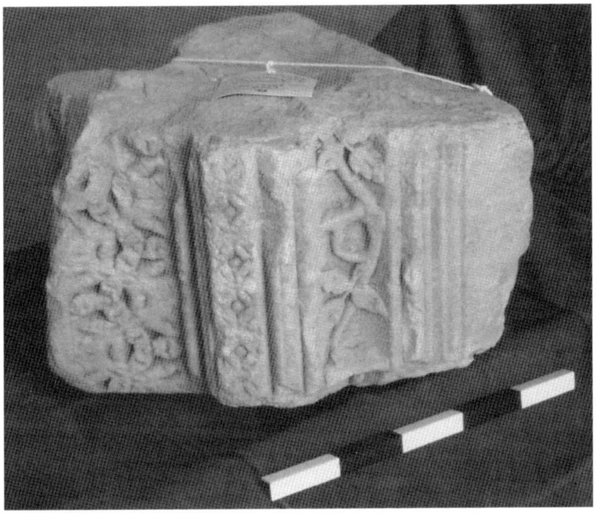

FIG. 5. Kenilworth Castle: carved stone attributed to the chapel sedilia, scale 25cm; English Heritage store, Atcham 88112681
Photo, author

to the entrance to the ground-floor chamber, gave access to the upper chamber by way of a smart rib-vaulted lobby: a feature which suggests that the tower is no earlier than Thomas of Lancaster's time, and which is reminiscent of the treatment of the lobbies in the later Caesar and Guy Towers at Warwick Castle.[27] The superior chamber probably housed one of Thomas' leading retainers, or possibly a household officer such as the marshall — the stables are adjacent.[28] The Water Tower belongs with the fashion at this period for erecting well-appointed residential towers, of which Marten's Tower at Chepstow Castle (Monm.) and the great tower at Knaresborough (Yorks.) are grander exemplars.[29]

HENRY OF GROSMONT AND JOHN OF GAUNT (1345–99)

IN 1327 Kenilworth Castle was restored to Henry, younger brother of the disgraced Thomas of Lancaster. At Henry's death in 1345, he was succeeded by his son, Henry of Grosmont, earl (and from 1351, duke) of Lancaster, and a founder member of the Order of the Garter. On his death in 1361, the castle passed to his son-in-law, John of Gaunt, fourth son of King Edward III, and the greatest nobleman in later 14th-century England. In terms of surviving fabric, Gaunt was the most ambitious builder at Kenilworth since King John, but we should not underestimate the patronage of Henry of Grosmont.[30] Therefore this section of the paper attempts to disentangle the physical evidence for their works in the hall and apartment ranges (Fig. 10).

Three dates for documented major building works there should be borne in mind. First, a contract of 1347 to construct a new roof for a hall, of the same dimensions as the present one, has been interpreted as indicating a drastic remodelling of an existing hall to produce an aisle-less ground-floor hall as fashionable as contemporary Penshurst (Kent).[31] Thus there is clear evidence that substantial works were undertaken in the inner court during Henry of Grosmont's tenure. Second, between *c.* 1373 and 1380, major expenditure is recorded which is now generally accepted as producing the present first-floor great hall with its services (the Strong Tower), retiring rooms (Saintlowe Tower), and probably its remodelled apartments in the south range (Figs 1, 10).[32]

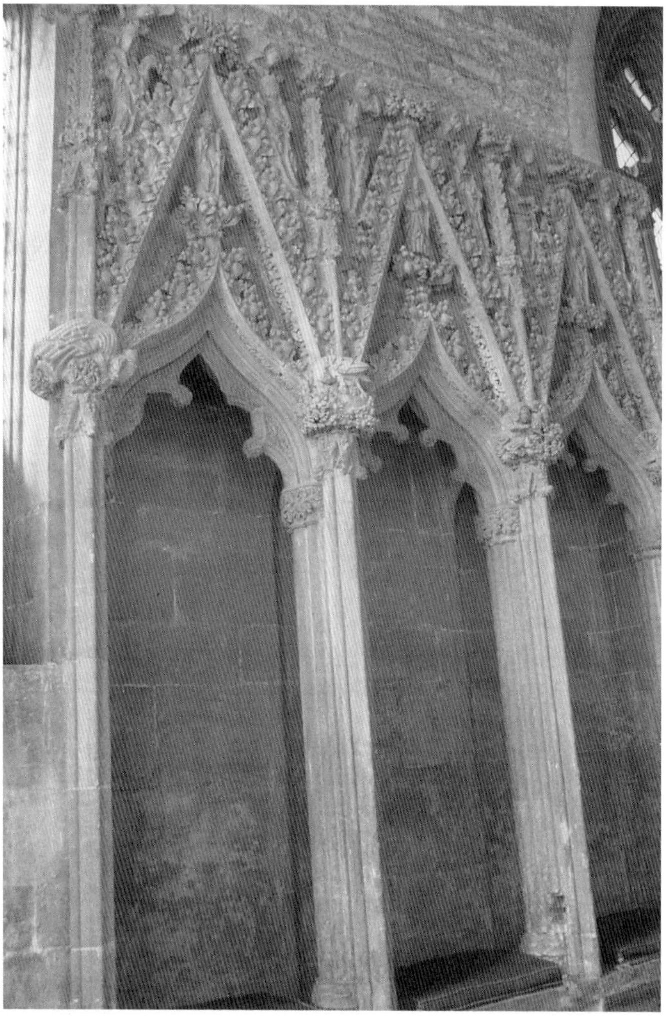

FIG. 6. Hawton (Notts.), All Saints church, sedilia
Photo, author

Third, further substantial expenditure *c.* 1390–93 under the master mason, Robert Skillington, persuaded earlier commentators — notably John Harvey — that this was the time when the present great hall and services were actually constructed.[33]

The mouldings of various features extant in the surviving fabric reveal a number of inconsistencies, from which in theory three styles may be identified: termed here 'A', 'B' and 'C' for simplicity. Style A is restricted to the entrance archway in the hall porch, carved in the arch with bands of foliate decoration in hollow mouldings (Fig. 15B), and the tierceron vault in the rere-arch of the porch (Fig. 11 top). Their mouldings, especially the fussy profile of the vault-rib (Fig. 4A), have links to the north-east midlands style of the chapel. On the other hand, style B relates very closely to the local output of a group of masons from what I have termed elsewhere 'the Ludlow workshop', after the area where much of their activity is to be identified.[34] One of its characteristic mouldings is the sunk chamfer, which appears at the castle in the service

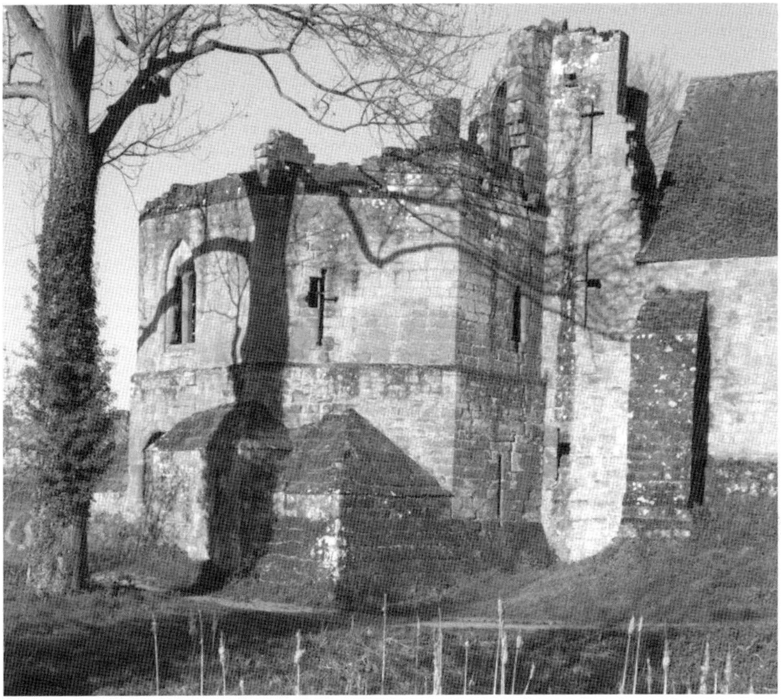

FIG. 7. Kenilworth Castle: Water Tower, from the north-east
Photo, author

doors to the hall (Fig. 12 right),[35] in windows and doors in the great chamber (Figs 13C, 14 top right) and in the ground-floor windows of the centre oriel (Figs 13D, 14).[36] Also the stepped chamfer was used for mullions, and at Kenilworth it occurs in the main windows of the centre oriel and the hall bay window (Fig. 13B) and the ribs of the panelled vault of the hall porch (Figs 4B, 11 bottom). Then the cladding of the great hall constitutes style C, distinguished by a simple architectural vocabulary of monumental roll and hollow mouldings applied to wall-panelling, window traceries and fireplaces (Figs 15A, 16). It is in the spirit of Lethaby's 'big and bare style' of the age of the great master masons, Henry Yeveley and William Wynford (*c.* 1360–1400).[37] In addition, it should be noted that another distinctive moulding, the double ogee, appears in the corner responds of the great hall (Figs 12, 15C).[38] This moulding was employed occasionally by the Ludlow group, but it was also increasingly found in Perpendicular works in the second half of the 14th century and, in fact, at Kenilworth it must belong in execution with style C.[39] The mouldings of the north-west and south-west responds are clearly carved from the same blocks as the style C wall-panelling (Fig. 12 centre-left).

On the basis of these three styles, a theoretical sequence can be attempted for the periods of work represented in the hall and apartment ranges. The entrance arch and vaulted rere-arch of the hall porch relate to a style in vogue between *c.* 1320 and 1350, as seen in works of this period at St Mary's Cathedral Priory, Coventry. The former Hospital of St John in Coventry also appears to be a work of *c.* 1330–40

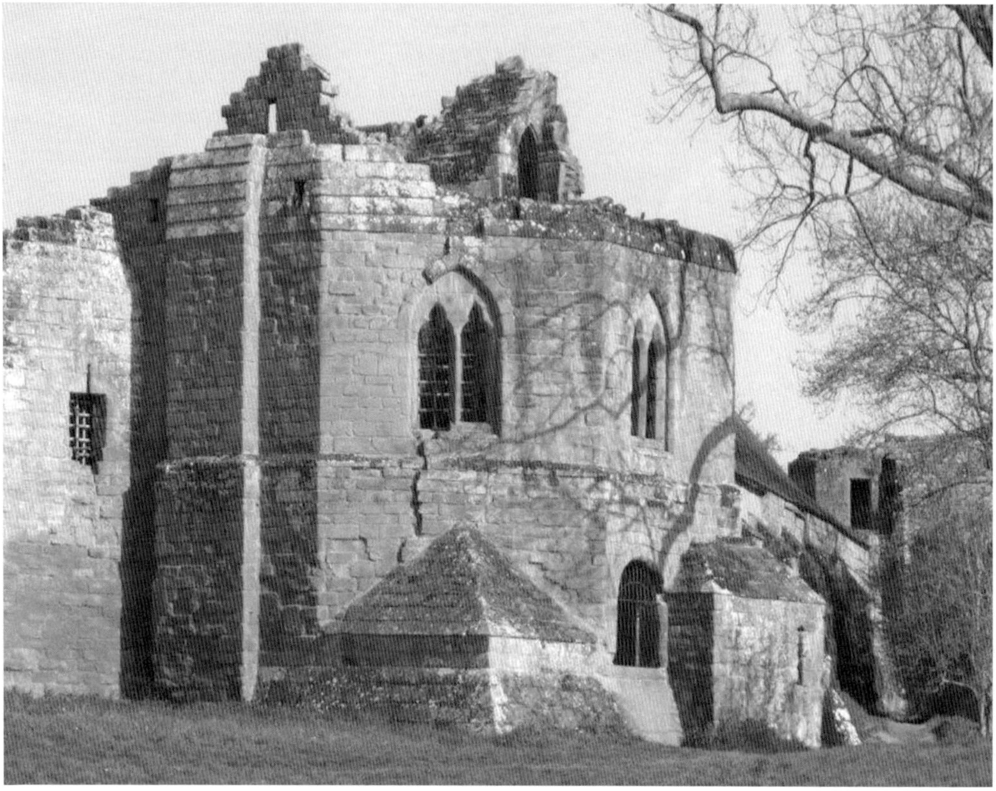

FIG. 8. Kenilworth Castle: Water Tower, from the south-east
Photo, author

in this style (Morris, 'Priory', Fig. 17), and the first stage in the 14th-century rebuilding of Kenilworth Priory Gatehouse as well: the hoodmoulds of the recesses in its passage are virtually identical to ones used in the chancel at Hawton (Notts., *c.* 1330–40) (Figs 15D, 17). In the light of these comparisons, the arch and rere-arch at the castle are quite likely to have been executed for Henry of Grosmont — if not even for his father, Henry (1327–45); subsequently to be dismantled and reused in a later rebuilding of the hall.

Next would come style B of the Ludlow workshop, whose masons followed up a generation of activity at churches in north Herefordshire (*c.* 1340–70) by taking a major role in the construction of the new chancel at St Mary's collegiate church, Warwick (1370s, Monckton, Fig. 16).[40] They were apparently also responsible for executing the main phase of work at Kenilworth Priory gatehouse documented under Prior Bradway (1361–75).[41] Double ogee mouldings are the most prominent feature of the gatehouse, employed for the main arches (Figs 15E, 17 top), and sunk chamfers appear in the one surviving window (Fig. 13E),[42] and at the neighbouring parish church of St Nicholas, in the former north-west porch of presumably about the same date. For style C, specific parallels are harder to come by, but comparisons have been drawn by John Harvey with works of William Wynford, such as the remodelling of Winchester Cathedral nave

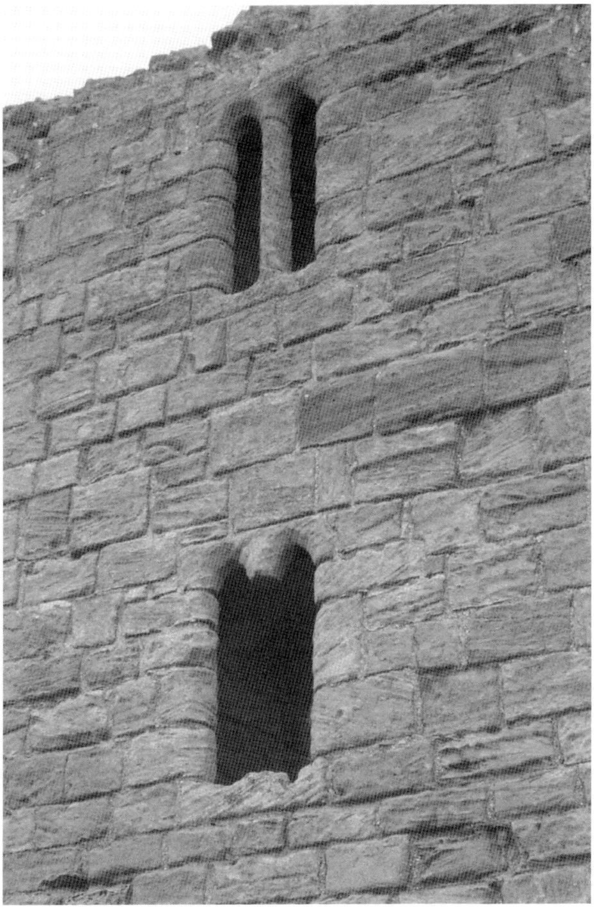

FIG. 9. Dunstanburgh Castle (Northumb.): Constable's Tower, windows
Photo, author

(mainly after 1394), and also with the new tower of St Michael's church, Coventry (*c.* 1373–95).[43]

So the revamping of the great hall in style C could be as late as the works documented in 1390–93, in which case style B could represent the earlier phase of John of Gaunt's works, 1373–80, or even date from Henry of Grosmont's time. In support of an attribution to Grosmont, the use of the sunk chamfer for window mullions is found in several areas of England in the high Decorated period *c.* 1320–50,[44] but is virtually unknown in Perpendicular-style buildings from the second half of the 14th century and later. In the case of the service door with sunk chamfers at the north end of the great hall, it is in bond with the end-wall of the hall (Fig. 12 right) and a vertical masonry break separates the wall from the respond and style C wall-panelling (Fig. 12 centre). Thus we may have identified an earlier end-wall to the hall associated with sunk chamfer work. In the case of the sunk chamfer window jamb at the north-east corner of the great chamber, it is harder to interpret the relationship of its stonework to that of the adjacent centre oriel, because of the mutilation and refacing in Leicester's time (Fig. 14). However, it would appear that the return of the masonry towards the oriel is

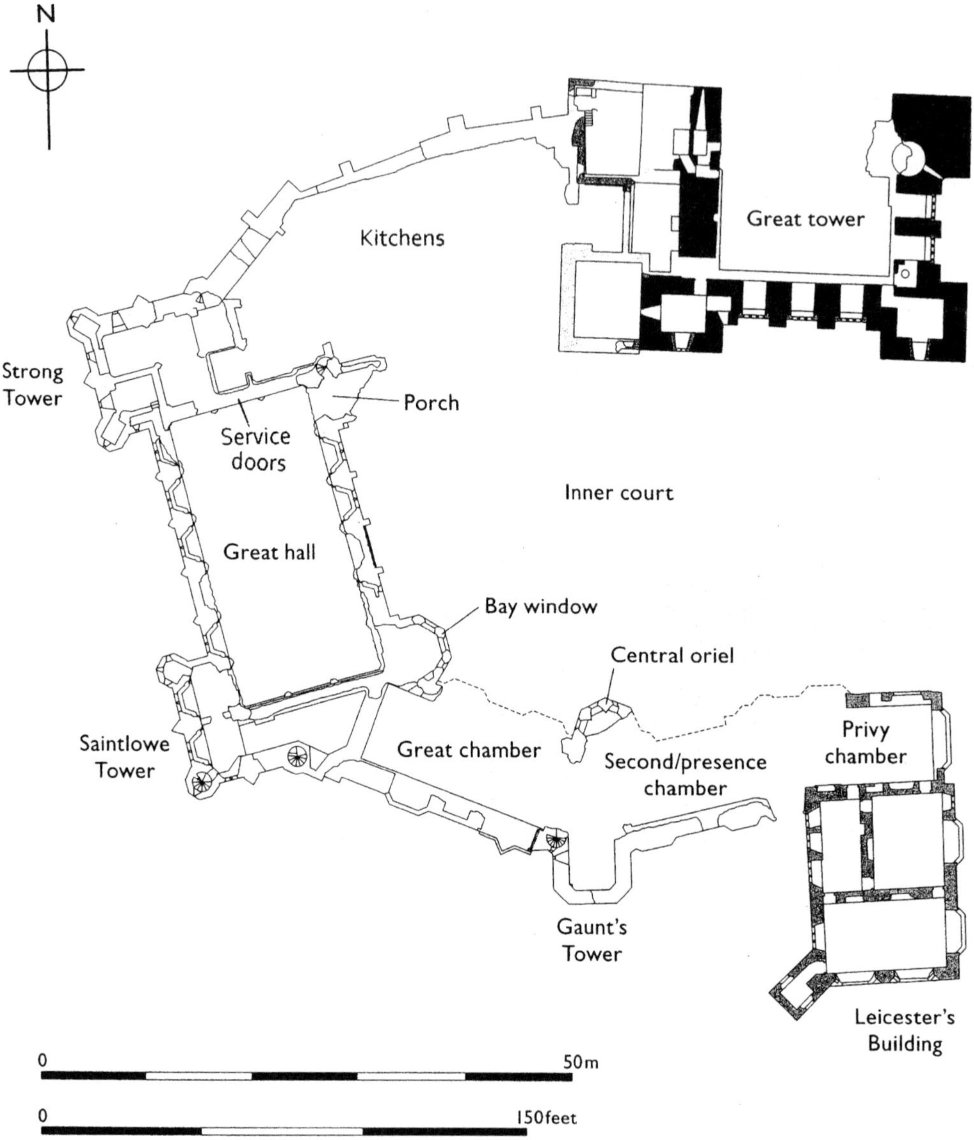

FIG. 10. Kenilworth Castle: inner court, the hall and medieval apartments, plan at first-floor level; the Great Tower is 12th century and Leicester's Building 16th century

Drawing R. Lea, © English Heritage

mainly in course with the stones of the window jamb, so that a projecting feature at this point was planned with the chamber windows.

To summarise the above discussions, it is quite possible that the archway and rere-arch of the hall porch are reused from the hall of Henry of Grosmont (*c.* 1347–49) or from that of his father, Henry. They may not be *in situ* and may originally have

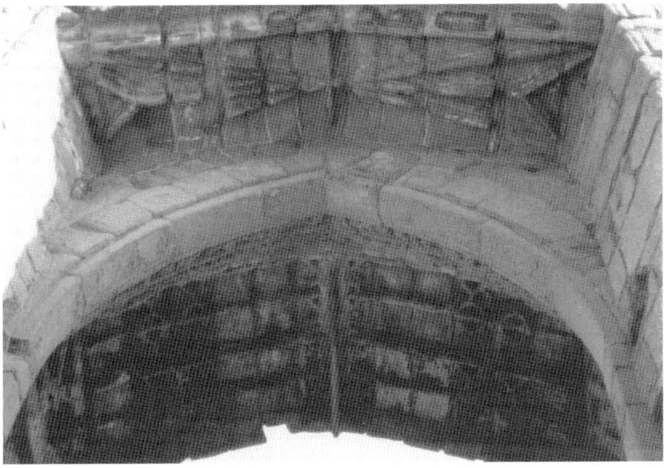

FIG. 11. Kenilworth Castle: the great hall, porch vaults
Photo, author

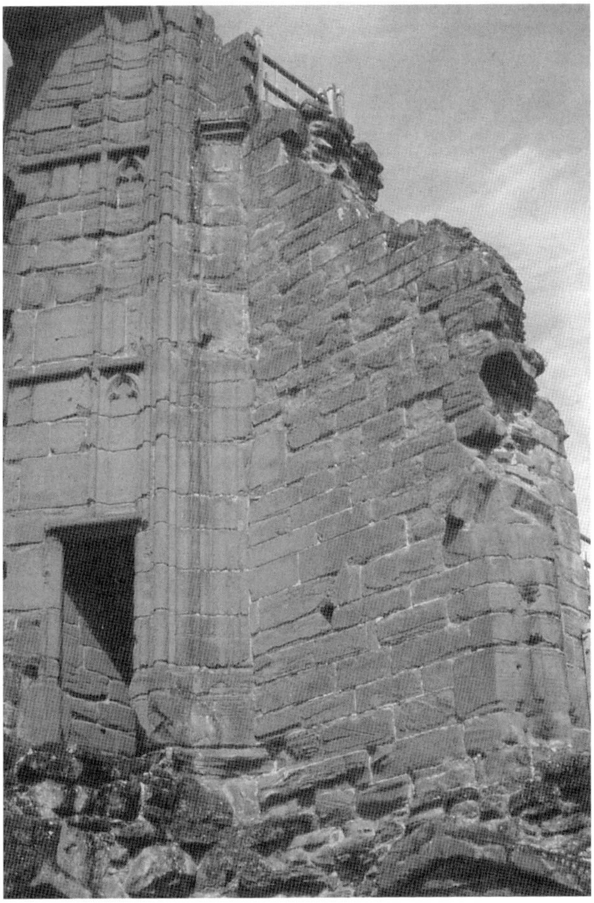

FIG. 12. Kenilworth Castle: the great hall, north-west respond (left) and former door to the services (right)
Photo, author

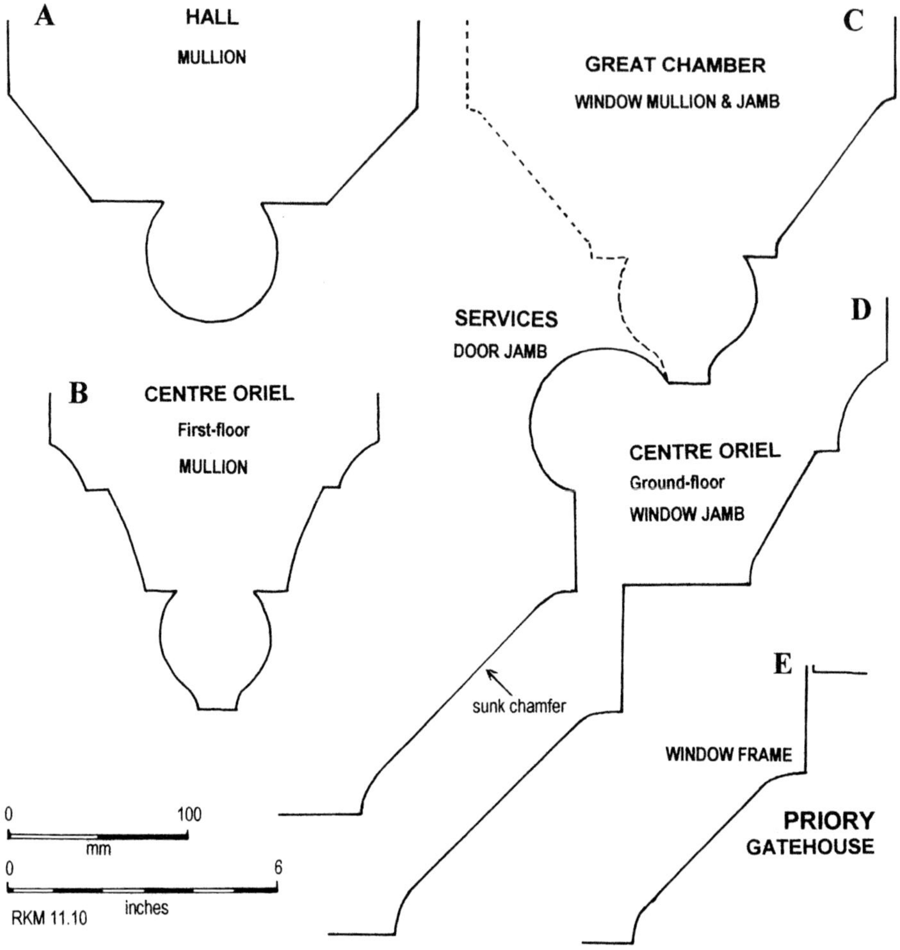

FIG. 13. Kenilworth Castle and Priory: moulding profiles, sunk chamfer, etc.
Drawing, author

belonged with a ground-floor hall; the rere-arch vault looks as if it might have been reassembled (Fig. 11). If we separate the sunk chamfer features from the other output of style B, a case can also be made that they could belong with Grosmont's works. The great chamber windows are so different to the style C mouldings of the great hall (cf. Fig. 13A, C), and sunk chamfer mullions are much more likely to pre-date *c.* 1360. The implication would be that the centre oriel was also planned, and probably built, in Grosmont's time, which would make it contemporary with the Rose Tower at Edward III's new royal lodgings in the upper ward at Windsor Castle (1357–65). The Rose Tower has been seen as the model for the Kenilworth oriel, though the primary function which they share — a private stair from the courtyard to the great chamber — had precedents in the earlier 14th century.[45] Turning to the sunk chamfer service doors in the great hall, if the end wall with the surviving door jamb pre-dates the style C

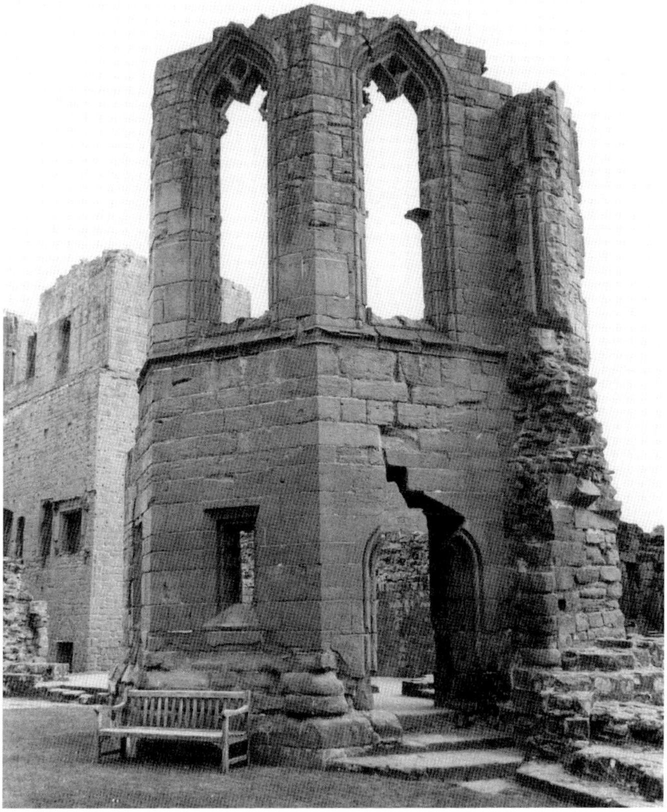

FIG. 14. Kenilworth Castle: apartments, the central oriel; the great chamber window jamb is top right

Photo c. 1980, A. Watson, History of Art Department, University of Warwick

cladding of the hall, then there must surely have been a first-floor hall on the site by then. The jamb stones are integral with the wall, and unlikely to have been dismantled from a ground-floor hall and reassembled in their present position. So the creation of a first-floor hall might be part of the works for Grosmont alluded to in the 1347 contract, rather than later for John of Gaunt, as proposed by all previous writers.[46] Aristocratic great halls over undercrofts are found earlier in the 14th century, as at Ludlow and Warwick castles, so a dependence on a Windsor model is again unnecessary.[47] One implication of this hypothesis is that the vaulted undercrofts of the hall (Fig. 16) and the porch, and the vaulted rooms of the Strong Tower, would surely have to have been built in Grosmont's time as well. They have always been placed in John of Gaunt's time because of their four-centred arches and apparently excellent correspondence with the bays of the hall above (Fig. 16), but in fact their distinctive style of details, with minimal 'swallow's nest' capitals and chunky polygonal ribs, finds no known parallel either locally or nationally and so they could as well be mid-14th century as later.

This is as far as one can push an argument for the survival in the fabric of features from the time of Henry de Grosmont, and perhaps of that of his father. If a date for these works before 1360 is thought to be untenable, then presumably the sunk chamfer features must belong with the rest of the output of style B in John of Gaunt's major works of *c.* 1373–80.[48] As a result, if one wished to locate styles B and C in

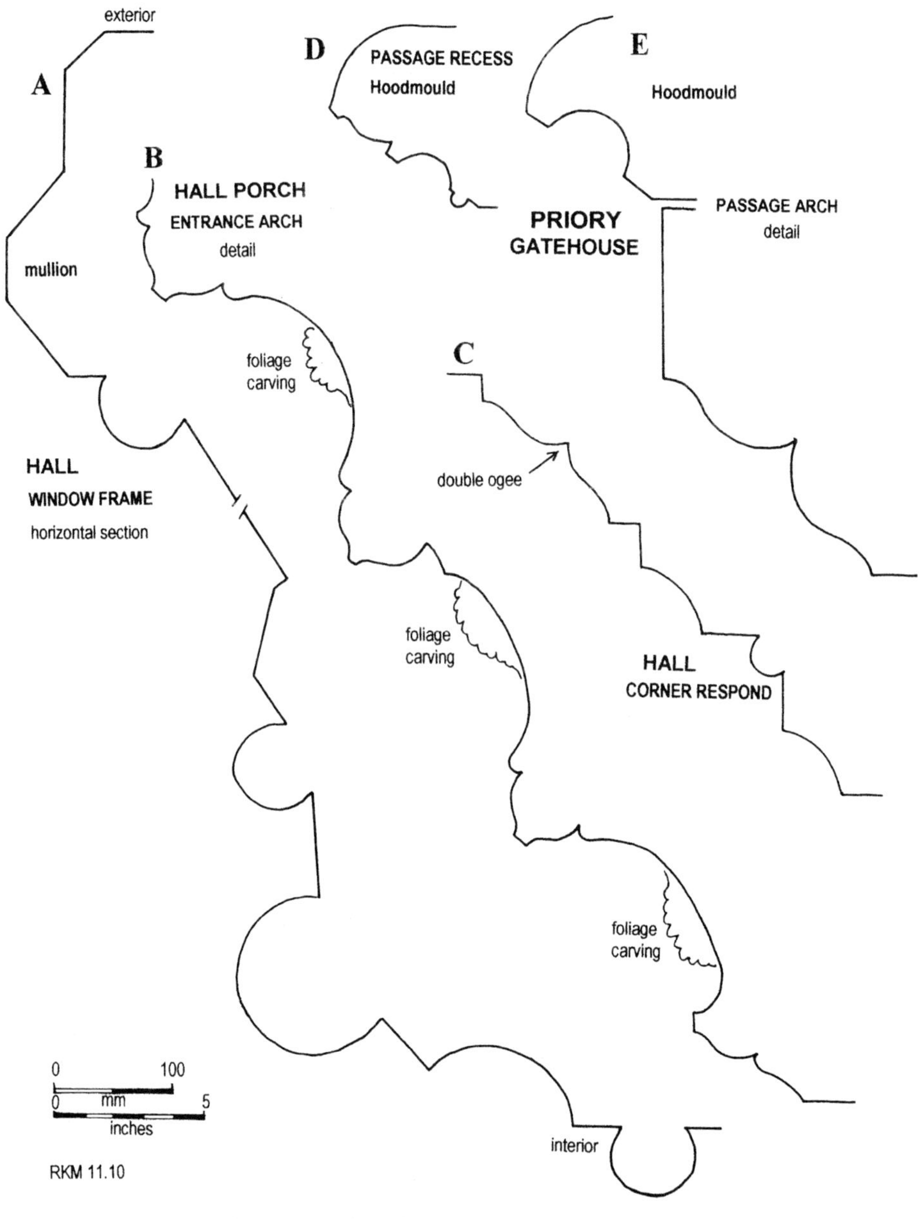

FIG. 15. Kenilworth Castle and Priory: moulding profiles, double ogee etc.
Drawing, author

different periods, then the final cladding of the great hall, together with the stylistically similar upper part of the Saintlowe Tower, might be relocated at its traditional date of 1390–93. However, other explanations are possible, which may sometimes be complementary to the above ideas rather than exclusive. The execution of residential

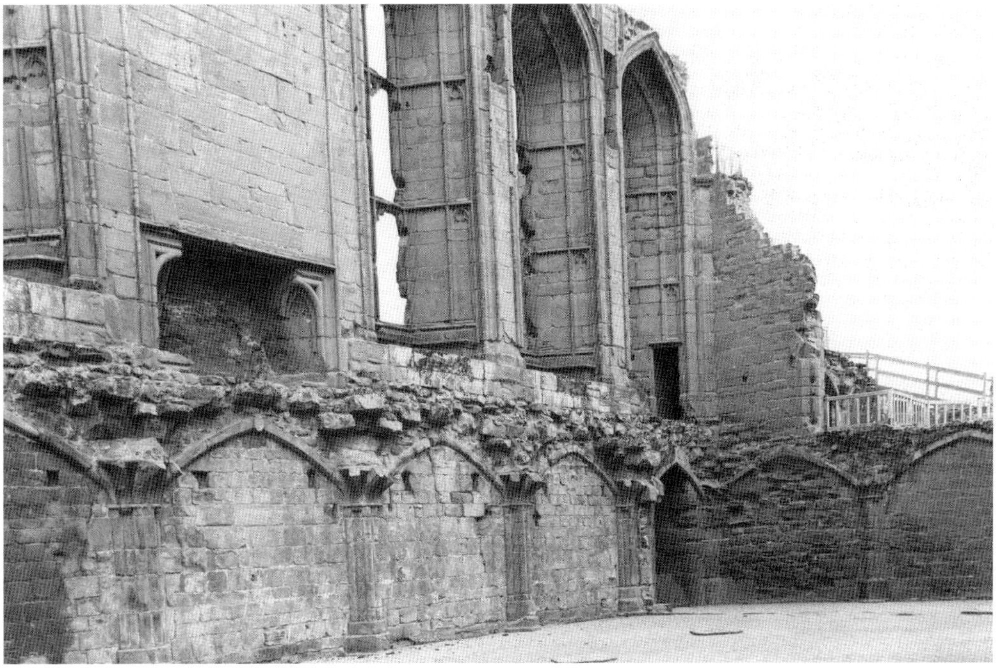

FIG. 16. Kenilworth Castle: the great hall and undercroft, looking north-west to the former services

Photo c. 1980, A. Watson, History of Art Department, University of Warwick

commissions for great aristocratic patrons tend to be required urgently, so sizeable workforces were employed and piece-work was common. Thus at Kenilworth in the 1370s it is possible that masons of the Ludlow group, carving mouldings in the local style B, were engaged alongside (or within the same time-span as) masons cutting detail in the more London-oriented style C: a procedure not dissimilar to work on the new east end of St Mary's, Warwick, in the same decade. There, details of the Ludlow group are found in combination with (and subordinate to) a framework of forms derived from the new Perpendicular east end at Gloucester (then abbey, now cathedral).[49] Another factor influencing the differences of detail at Kenilworth is an apparently conscious intention to create a hierarchy of window designs, which incorporates not only tracery but also their mouldings. Thus, the hall windows are almost devoid of mouldings to the exterior, in contrast to the moulded frames and fussier tracery of the hall bay window, denoting the dais end of the hall, and of the centre oriel, marking the private entrance to the lord's apartments (cf. Figs 1, 14). Judging from the surviving jamb at its north-east corner (Fig. 14 right), the great chamber windows were different again, but unfortunately their tracery has not survived.

Michael Thompson, writing in 1977, opined that 'it is unlikely that we shall learn more about the earlier stages of the hall *from the visible masonry*' (my italics).[50] I trust that I have demonstrated above that considerable inconsistencies and variety are present in the fabric of 'Lancaster's buildings', which suggest a more complicated building history than most accounts imply. This brief paper has tried to create a

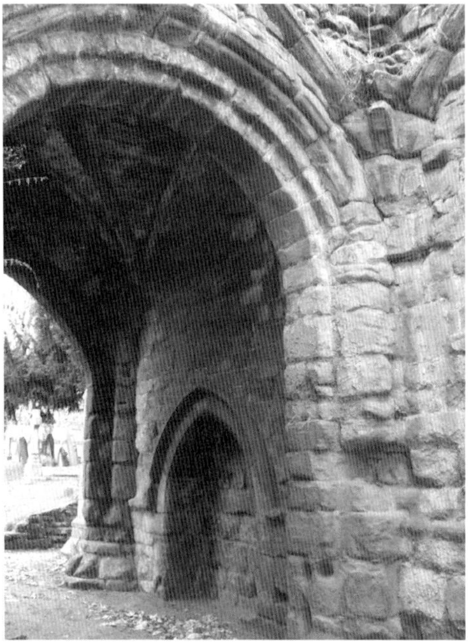

FIG. 17. Kenilworth Priory: gatehouse passage
Photo, author

possible narrative from these stones, but I am painfully aware that the range of evidence has had to be restricted. Only with archaeological excavation and a stone-by-stone survey, including evidence like masons' marks, will a more convincing story be told.[51] In the meantime, perhaps Thompson was right.

ACKNOWLEDGEMENTS

I owe a longstanding debt to the late John Harvey, for his encouragement to re-examine the 14th-century work at Kenilworth Castle, a monument which he first surveyed back in 1938. I have benefited from more recent discussions with Jennifer Alexander, John Goodall, Michael Thompson and Christopher Woolgar. At English Heritage, Gill Chitty (in *c.* 1990) and David Robinson have been most helpful in facilitating my research; and at Atcham I am indebted to Sara Lunt, Cameron Moffett and Heather Bird. Nonetheless, the views expressed in this paper are mine, as also any mistakes.

NOTES

1. First called 'Lancaster's Buildings' in Dugdale, *Warwickshire* (1656), 'Prospect of Kenilworth Castle from the old parke' (caption). John of Gaunt styled himself earl of Lancaster in 1361, and was created duke in 1362.
2. For the various earls and dukes, see R. K. Morris, *Kenilworth Castle*, English Heritage guidebook (2nd edn, London 2010), 41–5.
3. Thomas received grant of his father's lands, including Kenilworth, in 1298.
4. J. R. Maddicott, *Thomas of Lancaster 1307–1322: a Study in the Reign of Edward II* (Oxford 1970), 26.
5. Maddicott, *Lancaster*, 32.
6. Ibid., 25–6.

7. VCH *Warwickshire* VI, 135. The chapel used to be popularly called 'John of Gaunt's Chapel': see T. Oakley, *Ye Castell of Kyllingworth: The Visitors' 'Handy Guide'* (Kenilworth 1886), plan; Anon., *Kenilworth Castle: An Illustrated Guide* (Ministry of Public Building and Works guidebook, 1958), 10.

8. H. Summerson, *Warkworth Castle* (English Heritage guidebook, London 1995), 7, 20; the church was probably never finished and, like Kenilworth, the college was never established.

9. J. H. Harvey, *English Mediaeval Architects: a Biographical Dictionary down to 1550* (2nd edn Gloucester 1984), 299 (Thwaites, Richard de).

10. N. A. D. Molyneux, 'Kenilworth Castle in 1563', *English Heritage Historical Review* 3 (2008), 51–3.

11. Warwick Mouldings Archive (WMA) drawing reference KEC1120; examples of the larger pieces on the open shelves at Atcham are 88112627, 2638, 2645, 2660, 2662, 2668, 2669, 2672, 2679, 2826, 2887; and there are more smaller pieces in the mezzanine boxes (as recorded by the author in 2006–07). For mouldings terminology, see R. K. Morris, 'An English Glossary of Medieval Mouldings', *Architectural History* 35 (1992), 11–15.

12. For Coventry, see Morris, 'Priory', this volume, 83, Fig. 14A.

13. It is now in approximately the position of the sedilia, but other types of liturgical fitting are a possibility.

14. The wall bears a plaque of 1966 commemorating De Montfort's parliament (1265) and the 700th anniversary of the siege of Kenilworth (1266).

15. See E. H. Knowles, *The Castle of Kenilworth: a Handbook for Visitors* (Warwick 1872), pl. 11 (this stone is Atcham 88112681, and currently on display in the exhibition in the castle stable). Though the chapel does not appear in Knowles' plans of the castle, it is shown in outline in Oakley, 'Handy Guide', 1886, and was known to exist in 1884; see G. T. Clark, *Mediaeval Military Architecture in England* II (London 1884), 141.

16. Clark, *Military Architecture*, 141.

17. For example, Atcham 88112814 (probably from the springing of a sedilia arch) incorporates the pentagonal sideshaft shape of the sedilia jamb and the delicate mouldings of diaper pieces such as 88112685; WMA drawings KEC1111 and 1118 respectively.

18. The exact shape varies between examples at Kenilworth, Hawton, Heckington and Southwell — pentagon, lozenge, hexagon — but all share the angle facing forward and the bead mouldings.

19. Also 88112682 (WMA KEC1119), perhaps from a window rere-arch, has an axial roll-and-fillet with canted lateral fillets, a profile popular at Southwell. It was provisionally catalogued as a vault springer, but in fact there is no evidence that the chapel was stone-vaulted.

20. Hugh de Tichmers (Titchmarsh) was another master mason linked with Coventry (1312) and with work experience in the north-east (Knaresborough Castle), though not known to have worked for Lancaster. See Morris, 'Priory', this volume, 70; J. Goodall, 'A Royal Gift', *Country Life* (17 Jan. 2008), 72–5.

21. See Morris, 'Priory', this volume, 84, 86, 92. For another stone with mouldings in this style, found unstratified on a tenement site in the city centre, see R. K. Morris, 'Coventry, land off Priory Street, Archaeological Excavations 2006: Birmingham Archaeology Project No. 1417: Worked Stone, Ref.4057⟨173⟩' (unpublished report for Birmingham Archaeology, Nov. 2007).

22. The spurs appear rather clumsy and they have been partly restored (cf. Knowles, *Kenilworth Castle*, pl. 1, *c.* 1870). Perhaps they were after-thoughts, to counter possible subsidence, but the right-hand one appears to be essential for the passage to the garderobe, which may help explain their shape.

23. See J. Ashbee, *Goodrich Castle* (English Heritage guidebook, 2005), 32–3, for dating evidence and parallels for Goodrich.

24. The windows were illustrated in their present form in 1872 in Knowles, *Kenilworth Castle*, pls 1, 14, and have been restored in parts since. The large ground-floor aperture (and a similar one facing the base court) has been opened since the middle ages (ibid., pl. 1), and was originally a small window, of unknown form.

25. For example, M. W. Thompson, *Kenilworth Castle, Warwickshire* (Department of the Environment guidebook, London 1977), 22.

26. See J. Ashbee, 'Thomas, Earl of Lancaster, and the Great Gatehouse of Dunstanburgh Castle', *English Heritage Historical Review* 1 (2006), 28–35.

27. See R. K. Morris, 'The Architecture of the Earls of Warwick in the Fourteenth Century', in *England in the Fourteenth Century*, ed. W. M. Ormrod (Woodbridge 1986), 166–9.

28. The present stables date to 1553, but it is quite likely that stables existed in this location since at least the 13th century.

29. See Goodall, 'A Royal Gift', 74.

30. See Goodall, 'Newarke', this volume, for Henry of Grosmont's foundation of a college at Leicester Castle.

31. M. W. Thompson, 'Three Stages in the Construction of the Hall at Kenilworth Castle', in *Ancient Monuments and their Interpretation: Essays presented to A. J. Taylor*, ed. M. R. Apted, R. Gilyard-Beer and A. D. Saunders (Chichester 1977), 211–18.

32. A. Goodman, *John of Gaunt: The Exercise of Princely Power in Fourteenth-Century Europe* (London 1992), 305–06; C. Wilson, 'The Royal Lodgings of Edward III at Windsor Castle', in *Windsor: Medieval Archaeology, Art and Architecture of the Thames Valley*, ed. L. Keen and E. Scarff, *BAA Trans.* XXV (Leeds 2002), 66–8; R. K. Morris, *Kenilworth Castle* (English Heritage Guide 2006), 20.

33. J. H. Harvey, 'Sidelights on Kenilworth Castle', *Archaeological Journal* CI (1944), 95–6.

34. R. K. Morris, 'Late Decorated Architecture in Northern Herefordshire', *Woolhope Naturalists' Field Club Transactions* XLVI, pt 1 (1982), 36–53, where all the comparative profiles are illustrated.

35. Only the west jamb of the westernmost door survives from what must have been a standard three-door arrangement.

36. Only a jamb of the easternmost window in the north wall of the great chamber survives, partly mutilated in the 16th century by Leicester's refacing and refenestration of this elevation. No other worked stones from medieval windows survive in the great chamber or second chamber.

37. W. R. Lethaby, *Westminster Abbey and the King's Craftsmen* (London 1906), 220, cited in J. H. Harvey, *The Perpendicular Style 1330–1485* (London 1978), 99.

38. Only three responds survive: the south-east corner of the hall is lost.

39. For the double ogee, see R. K. Morris, 'The development of later Gothic Mouldings in England *c.* 1250–1400, Part I', *Architectural History* 21 (1978), 35–7.

40. Morris, 'Late Decorated', 49–52; also Morris, 'Architecture of the Earls of Warwick', 169–71, which updates some of the chronology proposed in my 'Late Decorated' paper.

41. For dating evidence, see further Alexander and Sunley, this volume, 336.

42. The upper floor of the gatehouse is lost, and thus its main windows. However, stones from sunk chamfer mullions, found in 2006 reused for the drain in the castle stable (built 1553), do not match any in the castle and may thus have a priory provenance, perhaps the gatehouse; excavation reported in B. Gethin and C. Rann, 'Archaeological recording of the conversion of Leicester's stables and associated service trenches at Kenilworth Castle' (Warwickshire Museum Field Services, unpublished report 0859, 2008).

43. Harvey, 'Sidelights', 96; Harvey, *Perpendicular*, 112; M. Bullen *et al.*, *Hampshire: Winchester and the North* B/E (2010), 575, for the latest dating of Winchester nave by John Crook. For St Michael's tower, see Monckton, this volume, 143–7.

44. For example, south-east England and the Severn valley; Morris, 'Later Gothic Mouldings, Part I', 20–1, 29, 34.

45. Wilson, 'Royal Lodgings of Edward III', 66–7 (Windsor as model for Kenilworth), 44–5 and 68 (earlier precedents).

46. For example, Thompson, 'Three Stages of the Hall', 215–16.

47. Morris, 'Architecture of the Earls of Warwick', 173–4.

48. The great chamber window jamb is from exactly the same template as the service door jamb, so the presumption is that they belong to the same campaign, i.e. the chamber windows cannot be attributed to Grosmont and the hall service doors to Gaunt.

49. Morris, 'Architecture of the Earls of Warwick', 170; Morris, 'Late Decorated', 52.

50. Thompson, 'Three Stages of the Hall', 213.

51. English Heritage commissioned photogrammetric elevations of the interior (only) of the great hall in 1988, in advance of a plan to introduce a new floor. Elsewhere on the site, in 2008 Jennifer Alexander and the author visited the Water Tower, which is rich in masons' marks and deserving of a full survey. She noted that they are distinctly different to those of the 'Barn' (*c.* 1330) on the Kenilworth Priory site, thus confirming the earlier date for the Water Tower; for the Barn's masons' marks, see Alexander and Sunley, this volume, 331–6.

Previous Volumes in the Series

Copies of these may be obtained from Maney Publishing,
Joseph's Well, Hanover Walk, Leeds LS3 1AB, UK
www.maney.co.uk